The SANDERS Price Guide to

SPORTS AUTOGRAPHS

Third Edition

THE WORLD'S LEADING AUTOGRAPH PRICING AUTHORITY

George Sanders, Helen Sanders,
Ralph Roberts, and Chuck McKeen

ALEXANDER Books

The Leading Autograph Reference Publisher ™

Publisher: Ralph Roberts
Vice-President/Publishing: Pat Roberts
Director of Autograph References
    and Chairperson of Advisory Board: Helen Sanders

Cover Design: Gayle Graham, Ralph Roberts

Executive Editor: Susan Parker

Editors: Helen Sanders, George Sanders, Pat Roberts, Ralph Roberts, Susan Parker,
    Gayle Graham

Interior Design and Electronic Page Assembly: **WorldComm**®

Printed in the United States of America

10 9 8 7 6 5 4 3 2 1
Third Edition

ISBN 1-57090-078-7

Library of Congress Catalog Card Number: 98-88668

The authors and publisher have made every effort in the preparation of this book to ensure the
accuracy of the information including autograph pricing and facsimiles. However, the information
in this book is sold without warranty, either expressed or implied. **Be sure to read Chapter 7 in
this book for how our pricing works and how to use those prices.** Neither the authors nor
Alexandor Books will be liable for any damages caused or alleged to be caused directly, indirectly,
incidentally, or consequentially by the information in this book.

The opinions expressed in this book are solely those of the authors and are not necessarily those
of Alexander Books.

Trademarks

Names of products mentioned in this book known to be or that are suspected of being trademarks
or service marks are capitalized. Use of a product or service name in this book should not be
regarded as affecting the validity of any trademark or service mark.

Alexander Books—a division of Creativity, Inc.—is a full-service publisher located at 65
Macedonia Road, Alexander NC 28701. Phone (828) 252-9515 or (828) 255-8719 fax or
sales@abooks.com. Dealer inquiries welcome.

Internet web sites: **http://www.autograph-book.com** and **http://www.abooks.com**

Contents

About This Price Guide

by Ralph Roberts, coauthor and publisher

This is our <u>seventh</u> autograph price guide. The first two were published by the Wallace-Homestead Book Company of Radnor, Pennsylvania—owned by Capital Cities/ABC at that time and now by Krause Publications of Iola, Wisconsin. These are **The Price Guide to Autographs** 1st and 2nd editions, and were released in 1988 and 1991 respectively. Our third price guide, **The 1994 Sanders Price Guide to Sports Autographs**, was published by Scott Publishing—the famous stamp guide people—in 1994. The fourth book (and the 3rd edition of general prices) was **The 1994-95 Sanders Price Guide to Autographs**, the first published by Alexander Books of Alexander, North Carolina—our current publisher—who also published the **1995-1996 Sanders Price Guide to Sports Autographs** (2nd edition of this price guide). The sixth price guide was **The Sanders Price Guide to Autographs** (4th edition) and the seventh you now hold in your hands: **The Sanders Price Guide to Sports Autographs** (3rd edition). The next edition of the general price guide (**The Sanders Price Guide to Autographs**, 5th edition) is under way and will be released in early 1999. (See page 448 for an early bird offer!)

We have various other autograph-related books in the works and continue in our committment of bringing you the very best autograph reference library available anywhere!

The autograph field has grown dramatically in the last few years, just as our efforts in compiling the best price guides in the hobby have also expanded severalfold. This price guide reaches new heights of completeness with the most names and prices of any autograph price guide ever published. That's the goal we strive for with every new edition, and that's the good news.

The bad news is that this book—even though it has more names and more prices than you've ever had in one convenient place before—*has only sports-related names and prices.* All other names and materials are to be found in our general edition, **The Sanders Price Guide to Autographs**. We simply have too many names and prices to put everything into one volume anymore. So, yes, you'll need both books, but these two volumes together now give you over *twelve hundred* pages of the best information available in the world of autographs.

To order our general price guide, simply call or fax 1-800-472-0438, or access **www.autograph-book.com** for secure Visa/Mastercard ordering, or send a check for $28.95 (includes $4 shipping and handling in the U.S. only—overseas inquire as to shipping) to Alexander Books, 65 Macedonia Road, Alexander NC 28701 USA. Our e-mail address is **sales@abooks.com**.

Ralph Roberts
November 1998

Ralph Roberts—coauthor and publisher—sometimes doubles as a forklift operator (above) at his publishing company, Alexander Books. With over 300 titles in print and distributing for more than 50 other publishers, Ralph loves autographs and still managed to find the time (right) to personally typeset this book.

Acknowledgments

These are the splendid men and women (in alphabetical order) who have made the interesting hobby of autograph collecting one of the most rewarding experiences of our lives. They are, in varying degrees, responsible for the happiness and financial gains that make this never-ending pursuit such a truly exciting undertaking. In most cases this list includes personal friends, acquaintances, competitors, suppliers, members of the media, family members, and, most importantly, learned advisors. Not one forger or spin doctor is included.

Jon Allan
Bob Allen (*Antique Week*)
Allan Abrams (Toledo *Blade*)
Tim Anderson
Russell Atwood, *Arts & Entertainment*
Al Avalon, Hawaii
Jack L. Bacon
Edward Baig (*Business Week*)
Arbe Barais
Catherine Barnes
Robert F. Batchelder
Chris Bell, Midpoint
Mary A. Benjamin
Saimi Rote Bergmann (The Repository, Canton, OH)
Jim Berland
Barbara Bigham (*Autograph Times*, Phoenix, AZ)
Norman Boas
Warren Boroson (Hackensack *Sunday Record*)

Harvey Brandwein
Fremont Brown, Asheville
Brenda Burch (WLOS-TV, Asheville, NC)
Walter Burks
Carol Cain (Mobile Alabama *Register*)
Dr. Ronald R. Caldwell
Paul Carr
John E. Carter
Dwight Chapin (San Francisco *Examiner*)
John Crudele (New York *Post* Syndicate)
Duane Dancer (KLIF, Dallas)
Roy and Mies Deeley (England)
Suzanne Dolezal (Detroit *Free Press*)
Amy Dunkin (*BusinessWeek*)
Sophie Dupre (England)
Carla Eaton

Robert "Bob" Eaton
Tom Eisaman
Bob Erickson (Pres., UACC)
Nancy Fraser, Midpoint
	Trade Books
Clifford O. Feingold, D.D.S.
Phillip Fiorini (*USA Today*)
Cathy & Roger E. Gilchrist
Bud Glick
Anita Gold, syndicated
	columnist
Cy Gold, Ace Enterprises
Miegan & Chandler Gordon
Marilyn Greenwald (*Boys
	Life* magazine)
Gil and Karen Griggs
Jim Hagar
Diane Hamilton
Donn Harmon
Gary Hendershott
Stephen Hisler
Jeanne Hoyt
Jaime Hubbard, *Financial
	Post*, Toronto
A. Bruce Hunt III
Christopher C. Jaeckel
Betty, Susan & Greg
	Johnson
Eric Kampmann, Midpoint
	Trade Books
Eileen Keiter
Sandy Kenyon, KQNA,
	Arizona
Kristin & Michael Kern
	(Oregon)
Susan and Peter Kerville
	(Australia)
Carol King (Asheville, NC)
Stephen Koschal (Florida)
Pierce A. Koslosky, Jr.
	(Omaha, Neb.)
Gail Kump, Midpoint
John La Barber
Neale Lanigan
John Laurence (Florida)

Kenneth R. Laurence
	(Florida)
Gary & Connie Lawrence (IL)
Alan Levi
Stephen Levy
Jerry D. Litzel (Ames, Iowa)
James Lowe
David H. Lowenherz
George S. Lowry
Bill Luetge
Joe and Scott Lusk (TN)
Bill Maloney (Software
	Solutions, Asheville NC)
Cathy Marshall (CNN News)
Emma & J.L. Mashburn
Dr. Michael J. & Patrice
	Masters
Frank & Ruth Ann Matthews
Rebecca May *curiocity for
	kids*
Ann McCutchan (Gannett
	News Service)
Pam & Chuck McKeen
Beth McLeod (South Palm
	Beach *County Living*)
Harold P. Merry
C.J. Middendorf (San Diego,
	CA)
Bonni J. Miller (*Goldmine*
	magazine)
George Robert Minkoff
Michael Minor
Stuart J. Morrissey
Howard S. Mott
Matthew Mrowicki and the
	CACC
J.B. Muns
Harry Nadley, Phila.
Donn Noble
William J. Novick
Karen & James Oleson
Nancy Page
Basil "Bill" Panagopulos
Beverly Parkhurst, Dallas
Jerry E. Patterson

ACKNOWLEDGEMENTS 7

Louise Pennisi
Cordelia & Tom Platt
Robert L. Polk
Talmage Powell
Angelica Giesser & Udo
    Prager (Germany)
ProComm Studio Services
    (Arden, N.C.)
Stephen S. Raab
Larry Rafferty
Celeste & Ray Rast
Diana J. Rendell
Annette Reynolds, Baton
    Rouge *State-Times*
Tracy & John Reznikoff
Brian Riba
Stanley J. Richmond
Pat Roberts
Hinda Rose (England)
Sheila & Rhodes T. Rumsey
Bill Safka
Joseph R. Sakmyster
Rebecca & Stephen G.
    Sanders
Dana and George M.
    "Sandy" Sanders
Richard Saunders
Todd Savage, Chicago
    Tribune
Harris Schaller, UACC
David Schulson
Gemma Sica
Ann & Louis Sica, Jr.
Kaye & Merv Slotnick
James Smalldon
Pat & Jim Smith (Wells,
    Maine)
Dr. Lewis C. Sommerville
William W. Stanhope
Christophe Stickel
Jim Stingl, Milwaukee
    Journal/Sentinel
Jim Stinson
Gerard A.J. Stodolski
Georgia Terry

Bob Tollett
E.N. Treverton
Louis Trotter
Wallace Turner (New York
    Times)
Larry Vrzalik
Susan Sanders Wadopian
Joan, Erin & Lael Wadopian
Joel Sanders Wadopian
John Waggoner (*USA
    Today*)
Dewey Webb (Phoenix,
    Arizona *New Times*)
Daniel Weinberg
Bob Wieselman, UpTime
    Computers, Asheville
Michelle and Tom Williams
John Wilson (England)
Al Wittnebert (Treasurer,
    UACC)
Chris Wloszczyna (*USA
    Today*)
Jaye Wright (*Florida Today*)
Dr. Ellis "Bill" Zussman
    (Wisconsin)

The
SANDERS
Price Guide to

SPORTS
AUTOGRAPHS

Section 1:
INFORMATION

In Memoriam: George Sanders (February 11, 1924—August 26, 1998)

Chapter 1

GEORGE SANDERS 1924-1998
IN MEMORIAM

He was a nationally recognized expert on signatures and handwriting, author, movie actor, news commentator, columnist, public speaker, teacher, radio and television emcee, businessman, rancher, actor, talk show host, award-winning disc jockey and, through it all, one of the premier autograph collectors in the world but, above all, wanted to known for what he truly was, an American patriot.

To all of our great loss in the autograph hobby, George R. Sanders of Enka, North Carolina passed away suddenly August 26, 1998, in Marietta, Ohio while on vacation after turning in his portion of this book. He was 74.

Sanders—not to be confused with the other movie actor of the same name—was actually the better known celebrity during the 1950s and 60s in Hollywood. George was constantly on radio and television in Los Angeles during those years as an announcer, talk show host, major movie premiere master of ceremonies, and the star of many hundreds of commercials.

"You're the George Sanders I should have married," Zsa Zsa Gabor, ex-wife of the "other" George Sanders, once told him.

George chats with legendary director Alfred Hitchcock at a movie premiere in Hollywood.

Sanders' face was everywhere in those days, especially in the greater Los Angeles and area. While he was forced to accept billing as "Greg Sanders" in the over twenty movies he had parts in because of the "other" Sanders, he won a court case in Hollywood establishing "George Sanders" as his broadcast name because he was the more recognizable of the two.

Leaving Hollywood in the late 1960s, Sanders spent several years as a broadcast celebrity, newsman, and station owner in Portland, Oregon. He and his wife Helen and the rest of his family then moved to New Zealand.

Because of his expertise in broadcasting, Sanders was quickly pressed into service by the government of New Zealand. For five years he worked with Radio New Zealand, ending up as Acting Director General of all broadcast operations in that county.

Retiring from yet another highly successful career, Sanders and his family moved back to the United States twenty years ago, choosing the Asheville, North Carolina area as their home. Settling in the small, picturesque village of Enka, just outside of Asheville, George and Helen engaged in their lifelong hobby of autograph collecting, unwittingly starting George's final career, the one for which he is best known today–autographs!

Sanders had began his autograph collecting career early. As a youngster during the 1930s in his hometown of Detroit, he worked at the famous radio station WXYZ. There, among other shows, he provided all the child voices (both male and female) on the now classic nationally broadcast radio drama, "The Lone Ranger." This gave him access to many other celebrities of the day—some of whom he interviewed on the air—and he began collecting their autographs.

George in 1939 (age 15) interviews famous boxer Jake "Raging Bull" La Motta on the air.

In his decades as a newsman and talk show host, in fact for well over 50 years, Sanders amassed what was indisputably one of the world's leading autograph collections, consisting of many tens of thousands of signatures. Nor was this collection restricted to living luminaries–every president of the United States, Queen Elizabeth I, Robert E. Lee, Abraham Lincoln, Napoleon, Greta Garbo, Chief Sitting Bull, and thousands more came into the holdings of George and Helen.

More About George Sanders

George's demanding life led him to meet and know political and civil rights leaders, artists, statesmen, athletes, and celebrities from every walk of life—the famous and the infamous. Harry S. Truman, John F. Kennedy, Richard Nixon (a friend of 40 years standing), Martin Luther King, Robert Kennedy, Ronald and Nancy Reagan, Cecil B. DeMille, Clark Gable, Katharine Hepburn (George conducted her first exclusive interview ever recorded at that point in time and later aired on NBC's "Monitor"), and Ty Cobb, John Wayne, Ted Williams, Jack Nicklaus, Jimmy Hoffa—these are only a few of the movers and shakers who have given Sanders exclusive interviews on such talk shows as his long-running nationally syndicated radio and television program, "Sanders Meanders" (1948-1960).

One of his television shows, "Success Story," was nominated for an Emmy for two years running in the 1950s. By a nationwide poll he was selected disc jockey of the year in 1950 (a youthful Elizabeth Taylor presented George with his trophy as "King of the Disk Jockeys"). He was also coanchor of the nationally syndicated "Ted Husing Sports Show" (1958-1962) and hosted several Hollywood TV game shows. His long experience as a broadcast station executive here in the United States also resulted in Sanders being tapped to be Assistant, then Acting Director-General of Broadcasting in New Zealand, a position he held for several years.

As a newscaster, TV anchor for Richfield (now Arco) news, and an actor himself in over 20 motion pictures and on television—he has appeared on "Wild Bill Hickok" with Guy Madison and Andy Devine, and also on "December Bride" with Spring Byington and Harry Morgan—it was only natural that Sanders should start collecting the signatures of the hundreds of celebrities with whom he came in contact. This interest of George and his wife Helen in autographs was soon expanded into one of the nation's finest private collections of historical documents, letters, manuscripts, and signed photographs. He also served as a regional director of the U.A.C.C., an international autograph collectors' organization. (See Chapter 4 for about about this fine organization.)

Sanders' experience in writing was also extensive. These hundreds of credits include his regular columns (*In the Spotlight*) in the White Newspaper Syndicate (25 cities, 1939-1941), the Clarke Newspapers from 1963-69, as well as *Home Magazine* (1965-69), *College Humor*, *Country Song Roundup* and *Melodyland* (Contributing Editor), *Western Life*, *Coronet*, *Dog World*, *Terrier News*, Los Angeles *Herald-Express* , *Radio-TV Life*, Detroit *News*, *Esquire*, and many others. He also taught Communications at Portland State University, and Lewis and Clark College for several years.

After retiring from broadcasting for the final time and moving to North Carolina, the Sanders—George and Helen—became internationally famous as significant autograph collectors, buying and selling rare and valuable signatures. In 1986—in partnership with author Ralph Roberts—they began producing the undisputed "bible" of autograph collectors everywhere, the award-winning Sanders Price Guides to Autographs—widely recognized as the world's leading authority on the value of signatures.

Just before departing on his final trip, George had turned in his tenth book on autographs to his publisher, the one you are now reading.

George Sanders leaves behind his wife Helen, sons George M. "Sandy" and Stephen, daughter Susan, several granddaughters, and a legion of friends in all walks of life. He will be sorely missed but his work lives on. One of those works is the Sanders Price Guides to Autographs. Helen Sanders is editor-in-chief now of the guides. Ralph Roberts and his company, Alexander Books, remains the publisher. You'll see several books in the next few years with the Sanders name on them, all inspired by George's lifetime work and achievement in the field of autographs.

A Farewell Salute to George Sanders

George Sanders was larger than life. He had it all: looks, brains, wealth, fame, charisma, grace and a beautiful wife and family. He excelled at everything he undertook and he had several successful careers. He was a man who can only be described in superlatives. He chose to devote his considerable talents to the autograph hobby which, as a result, will never be the same. **The Sanders Price Guide to Autographs**, written by he and his wife, Helen, instantly became the Bible of autograph collecting and revolutionized the hobby.

George promoted integrity and cooperation among autograph dealers, organizations and collectors. He was loved and respected by all. We salute George Sanders, and his long and productive life. He will be missed but never forgotten. His many contributions will live on in the annals of autograph collecting.

Mike Minor
Larry Vrzalik
Lone Star Autographs

Michael Minor

Larry F. Vrzalik

Goodbye, George

It was our very great privilege to be able to call George Sanders a friend. We discovered a number of years ago that we lived only 20 minutes from the Sanders and that we shared a great passion for autographs. George and Helen very graciously welcomed us into their home on numerous occasions, and we will always treasure the memory of stimulating conversation on a wide range of subjects (yes, even on religion and politics), often into the wee hours of the morning. George was a fount of knowledge about autographs and a spellbinding teller of tales from his vast experience in Hollywood and all over the world. Not only will he be greatly missed in the international autograph world, he will be especially missed in this corner of North Carolina.

—Michael and Patrice Masters

My Remembrance of Two Great Men

by Chuck McKeen

In the incredibly short period of 18 days this summer, my life was changed forever.

On August 8, 1998, my dad died. Eighteen days later a dear friend and mentor followed him.

My dad's name was Robert Blanck. He was my stepfather, but I never knew him as anything but dad. He died three years to the date after my mother, Marion. Like mom, he was buried three days later, on the date Pam and I were married.

On August 26, my very dear friend George Sanders joined mom and dad.

Dad and George were two of the three most influential men in my life. The third of that group, Father Norman Aldred of Oregon, still lives. To the three of them I owe pretty much everything. They made me what I am, in pretty much every way. My love for all three has become ever stronger over the years.

All three were cut pretty much from the same cloth. Dad and George were WWII veterans. Both stood the test of combat, and were not found wanting. Each came out of the war with physical damage because of a willingness to stand up for the country and the people they loved.

Each of these men was very willing to do battle for what he believed. That special brand of courage and determination that was steeled in war stood both well in the 53 years that followed combat. Both were successful men, and both believed strongly in the virtues and the need for hard work.

They had so many similarities. Dad and George both absolutely loved their homes. They both had exactly what they wanted for life. They both LIVED. They had fun. They enjoyed the time they had.

Both of these guys were a joy to be with—full of stories that kept everyone laughing, entranced, amazed. They were unique men, made so by the lives they lived. They were a by-product of the Great Depression. Each was forged by the knowledge that they had lived through that horrible period of time and each believed that if it had happened once it could happen again.

Then these men stood the test of war, and again, each believed that this was not a time they cared to see again in their lives, although both knew that war is such a human quality that it is almost as great a certainty as exists in this world.

They came home, they married, they raised families, and they worked. Then they died. Both unexpectedly. Both leaving great voids in the lives of friends and family they left behind.

As a final coincidence, both died when hearts that had been tested in so many ways, finally, simply, wore out.

I lost my dad, who showed by example an unbelievable courage that I have never seen matched in my life. He had three amputations in his last years, because of the scourge of diabetes, but he never faltered in his ability to enjoy life, and to live it on his terms.

I lost my friend and mentor, who shared my love of broadcasting and my love of sports and my love of autographs. He made me a national figure in this hobby of autographs, and he never stopped promoting me. He would turn aside national publicity for himself, and have reporters of various publications call me for information on the hobby. He had the faith in me to make me a part of his many books, and in this last publication we worked on together, he made me a coauthor.

In the end, both died facing forward, like the combat soldiers they were. They didn't run from God, but embraced Him.

I am certain that mom and dad were waiting for George when he left this world. I don't know what to make of this, but the day after I found out George had died, my brother Dennis Blanck called me from Minnesota. He had been cleaning out dad's piano bench, and had found an article that either mom or dad had clipped from an early 1950s country music magazine.

The article was written by George Sanders. So I know that dad shook his hand when George entered that new life, and I know that mom gave him a hug. And I know they are sharing some laughs over me.

One other thing I know. As a first order of business in heaven, George went over and asked God for an autograph.

So, goodbye for now to these fine and honorable men. My most sincere wish is that when my time here is over, that I will be allowed to join them and mom and my grandparents and other friends and relatives in the presence of God.

They have left lives that should serve as beacons for us all. Paths that we can hope to follow, because these were good men. They weren't perfect men. They never claimed to be, but I'll stand up for either of them any time, anywhere. It was my privilege to have Bob Blanck for a father, and George Sanders for a friend.

It was always a pleasant break in my workday to hear George's voice on the other end of the line. He was a regular customer ordering items from my catalog for a good many years. With that distinctive voice of his, you always knew it was George on the other end of the line. One thing he said to me years ago that has always stuck in my mind is that when you are writing about autograph collecting never, ever say anything negative about the hobby. There's too much good to write about, and I've always followed that advice. He was a good man.

—*Jim Stinson, Jim Stinson Sports Collectibles*

That's George (above) kneeling in front of baseball legends (l to r) Ty Cobb, Fred Haney, and George Sisler. George attended many functions in Hollywood and elsewhere as a broadcast celebrity and always got autographs. Inset, a facsimile of a Ty Cobb sig. Right, George, summer 1998.

Chapter 2

SPORTS LEAD THE WAY!

by Chuck McKeen

In the midst of the incredible growth in the hobby of collecting autographs, sports, as always, is leading the way. While I can't supply documentation, it certainly appears that more people collect sports autographs than any other area of the hobby. Just the sheer number of athletes makes that understandable. Autographs don't come from just the pros, or the college stars. For every autograph signed on that level there are countless signed by the heroes in high schools, and other areas of amateur sports. Most of us have done that—gotten something signed by someone we admire who is playing in a lesser league than the majors.

Sports are everywhere and they take every imaginable form. The Olympic Games are a wonderful example. Look at Nagano, Japan. There were competitors in the so-called major sports such as figure skating, hockey, and skiing, but just look beyond those games: bobsledders, ice dancers, lugers, cross-country skiing, ski jumping, curling, speed skating, hot dog aerialists, snowboarding, and more! All are sources for autographs.

Every sport has fans. Each sport, each athlete, has people who admire them, who want their autographs. We're all different. We all have our own likes and dislikes. We all have people we admire. Most of us are more than willing to ask these performers—these celebrities—for an autograph.

You look at the big picture on athletics and for autograph seekers the past has been wonderful, the present is great and the future is incredible. There are opportunities for autographs everywhere and it is only going to get better.

You can enjoy this hobby however you wish. There are always opportunities for autographs—it means getting up and going after them. You can't sit at home anymore and just write for autographs and get them. You have to go out and be where the athlete is. Today the athlete is more places and more visible in many ways than ever before.

Or if you wish, you can purchase autographs of your heroes. There is now more opportunity in this area than ever before. The items are out there and, for the most part, the cost is very reasonable. Combine purchasing the items you can't get yourself with going out and getting what you can, and the possibilities of putting together a meaningful sports autograph collection are endless.

The demand for autographs of sports figures is up and will continue rising. Athletes at every level sign thousands of sports autographs every day. No other area of this hobby can come even close to those figures.

The fans' appetite for sports autographs is incredible. It takes every form you can imagine—photos, trading cards, programs, magazines, scorecards, caps, helmets, shoes, pucks, footballs, baseballs, basketballs, every form of equipment possible, and every item of clothing that can exist. You name it and the items are being signed.

They are signed and they are kept and they are hoarded and they are displayed just about every way they can be displayed. Sometimes the person who obtained them keeps them, often they are sold. It makes no difference really, either way the items go to a fan.

We are talking major interest here. We are talking fans that want a piece of the action—something they can call their own from someone they admire. And we are talking big business! Who knows how many people make their living from selling these autographs which come in such varied form? Thousands of people? Certainly.

What so many athletes don't realize is that they are among the people who are making their living at least partly because of these autographs that they sign. Sports is entertainment. What Babe Ruth, George Mikan, Jesse Owens, and the other greats of old knew was that every autograph they signed increased their value as a performer.

This is a complicated time for both those who collect and those who sell sports autographs. This is, in many ways, the greatest time yet for this field, and in some ways it is the worst of times. Of course that's always the case. Despite any drawbacks, the good far outweighs the bad in sports autographs today. The potential for the future is almost beyond imagination. The issues that have divided athletes from fans are going to be resolved—they have to be. It is in everyone's best interests that they are.

SO, sports autographs today: Where are we now? Where have things changed? What's going to happen?

The future is bright. Here's how we see the situation, and what is coming.

There are Good Points and Bad Points

The sheer growth of numbers of serious autograph collectors in sports, and the changes in what they collect, has been astonishing. The most dramatic aspect of this has been the change in tastes among those who collect sports autographs over the past 20 years.

The fact is that sports have always provided the most interest and the most opportunity for autograph seekers. The reasons are obvious—we all have heroes and we have them at every stage of our lives.

When we're pre-teens we idolize the kids who are just older than us—our favorite high school athletes. Everywhere, in every little town in America, kids get their young idols to sign scraps of paper, high school programs, and newspaper articles. Every small town newspaper in the country features stories and photos of the newest crop of young athletic stars. Every town has young kids out there getting slightly older kids to sign those newspaper articles.

When the kids get a little older and move into high school

Chuck McKeen and son Sean with football legend Joe Namath. "Joe Willie was great when we asked for a photo after doing the customary comparing of knee operations. Joe asked how many I had had—I said 'eight.' He was quiet, looking down at my knees, obviously thinking. He then looked up: 'Well, I guess it could have been worse,' he said. My daughter Marin took the photographs. First, the camera wasn't turned on. Joe was patient. 'It works better turned on,' he said. Our kids don't embarrass easily, and Marin asked Joe to show her how to turn it on, and then took the photo. Joe shook hands and went to tee off at the celebrity golf tournament he was in. Later the photos came back. Marin had cut our heads off!"

there are still their fellows to observe as heroes and also the athletes who have moved up the next step: to junior college or college status.

Those same newspapers still exist, and they still publish the stories about the athletic endeavors of the stars wearing the local colors. Each step up that the athlete takes, there are more admirers watching and more autographs being signed.

The fact is that sports are everywhere in this country and all around the world. We grow up with athletic stars all around us—using the next locker in high school; swimming in competition at every level at the pool just down the street; or sitting at the next table in the local restaurant. These athletes have always been a part of our lives. They've been our next-door neighbors. We admire our athletes and we want a token of their relationship to us—something to keep forever—an autograph.

Even now, until an athlete reaches the very top levels of pro sports, he or she is usually accessible to the fans. Very few athletes through college will turn down autograph requests. They are faced with it all through their lives, and they tend to regard such requests as a neat thing—an honor.

Oh, that attitude has changed somewhat now for some members of that upper echelon of college stars. These people are already so convinced of their individual greatness and that they are destined to reach hallowed ground as athletes on a national—nay, a world-level. They for the most part, of course, are fools. Only a handful reach that level. Most of these athletes who have already turned their backs on all who have supported them during their entire athletic lives won't make that absolute top name.

Athletes and autographs have always gone together, even into the top level. Up until the past few years, at least.

Replay your memories of sports and sports heroes. Talk to those who came before you and see what they remember. You are all going to come to pretty much the same conclusion—athletes were, by and large, always very accommodating when it came to autographs.

Certainly, there were exceptions. Bill Russell turned thumbs down on autographs for most of his life. He was accessible through the first few years of his pro career. Then he changed, and for whatever reason he stopped signing—at least until people started shoving ungodly amounts of money before him for the "privilege" of getting his autograph. Amazing how that changed his attitude.

Mike Marshall, who was an outstanding baseball relief

pitcher for years, turned down autograph requests. Mickey Mantle, in person at least, had the ability to be very confrontational and uncooperative with autograph seekers. Strangely enough, he honored mail requests for years. Of course The Mick was a contradiction in many ways over much of his life, so it shouldn't surprise anyone that he continued the tradition through autographs.

Still, the overwhelming fact was that athletes were accessible for autographs. Maybe they didn't always feel like signing, but usually they did it. They understood that their own status depended on having fans continue to admire them. They saw the connection between fans and their salaries. They saw that it was in their own self-interest to sign autographs.

Athletes of yore understood that the closer fans felt to them, the more appeal they had as entertainers, and thus the more value they had to their employers. And perhaps there was even the realization that, in the end, the fan *is* the employer.

Change Doesn't Mean Lack of Opportunities

Today in many ways the professional athlete has been insulated from the fan. Their parking lots are fenced off at the stadiums. The athlete doesn't stand and sign autographs for 10-20 minutes after a game. They can zip by the fans, with their windows closed and ignore requests. You can't get to them after a game, because they are protected by security guards. Owners have given in to the demands of players who in many cases don't want to have contact with fans.

The professional autograph seeker has become more and more important to satisfy the hunger for sports autographs. These same athletes who have cut themselves off from the ordinary fan, using every excuse one can imagine, are now faced with professionals among their counterparts.

The fact is that these professional autograph seekers aren't as easy to evade as ordinary fans. These are people who make their living by providing autographs for fans who can get them no other way and they are very good at their work.

No matter how much they dislike it, today's athletes are the subjects of demand as far as autographs are concerned. Because of the fact that much of their lives are run by exact schedules, their whereabouts are known to these professionals who aren't afraid to be where the athletes can't evade them.

Every day that the athletes are performing, whether travelling, or at practices, or on game days, they are in situations where they can be approached for autographs. All but a handful of the athletes end up virtually every day having photos and equipment thrust before them for signatures. They might not like it, but unless they want real confrontations every day, some items are signed each time they go through the gauntlet of pens

Chuck, Sean, and famous football place kicker Jan Stenerud. "Jan is a darn good golfer, but had just been in a sand trap when I saw him. I said, 'Jan, Jan... Vikings don't belong in the sand.' He, of course, was a great kicker for Minnesota as well as Kansas City and Green Bay in his long NFL career.

and hands and arms and bodies. Autographs are obtained every day. These autographs then make their way into the hobby, being exchanged for pay.

The number of autographs available to fans today far exceeds the number at any other time in sports history. The professional autograph seeker has seen that fans want top-notch material: color photographs—8x10s, 11x14s, 16x20s. Fans want signed jerseys and helmets and the rest—signed with uniform numbers and nicknames and honor designations such as "MVP" added. Professional collectors get this material for them. These are items that were not available until the professional took over. Incredible material is signed every day and made available to the public.

Some of the athletes don't like it, they feel they are being taken advantage of. This situation doesn't have to exist. The solution is a simple one. Athletes need to honor the fans and their requests for autographs. Not every autograph, not every situation, but at least sign autographs like athletes historically always have.

Many athletes have reached agreements with the professional collectors, and do private signings for pay. Great idea—everyone comes out ahead. There needs to be a combination of signing for pay and signing for free. No one should begrudge an athlete making some extra money by signing autographs in certain situations. There is nothing wrong with it and some great items can be added to the public collections in this method. Maybe at the same time the athletes could quit bitching and moaning about how the weight of the world is on their shoulders. If you're going to take the money, you've got to do something for it, and they're paid for more than playing the game, despite what some athletes think. They do have obligations, and they need to start living up to them.

Collectors also have great opportunities to get the stars of tomorrow while they are still in college or in minor league play. At some time, every big name was known only to the local fans and fans who saw that player on a visiting team.

They all were available for autographs. All a collector

needed was the foresight and the willingness to put in some time and use imagination to get nice material autographed.

Michael Jordan's successor is out playing basketball today in some high school. He'll go into college and play there. He will be a part of the community for some period of time. Do your work and go find him. Get him to sign neat things.

There's an up and coming Mark McGwire or John Elway or Mark Messier being prepared right now. Every sport has its stars of 10 years from now out playing somewhere. A lot of people make the top rung these days.

There are more than 1,200 NFL players and some 750 major league baseball players. Also, there are about 300 NBA guys, hockey is booming and women's basketball is hitting, and the Olympics are constantly generating new names to collect. There are athletes everywhere, and every one of them has fans. Some people collect college players, some collect minor leaguers, and some collect women stars.

Some, as we said earlier, collect lugers and snowboarders and hot dog aerialists. And a huge percentage of these people welcome the opportunity to sign. They do like the contact with fans. Go out and meet them. Get yourself up, go out, and have some fun with them.

For those athletes you can't meet, go ahead and buy some autographs. Buy the things you like and invest in autographs and have fun with the hobby of today.

Changes

The biggest change, besides having more temperamental athletes to deal with than ever before, is that today people want quality items. You rarely see 3x5 cards being signed by athletes today. The reason is obvious: who wants a signed 3x5 card when you can have a signed piece of equipment, or a great photo?

Some people still get 3x5s to mat with photos. They can look very nice and be very meaningful additions to a collection. But for the most part the 3x5 card has gone the way of the dinosaur as far as current athletes are concerned.

That is not the case for autographs of the athletes of yesterday. In many cases all you can find are index cards for the players who have left us to hopefully join that greater game always in progress on that Field of Dreams.

For those of us who were around as sports autographs moved through their infancy in the 1970s and into what they are today, we know that index cards were one of the prime items used for autographs up until that decade. That's when photos and equipment started to become popular. Before that time photos of players weren't all that common or easy to get. Teams had picture packs, and in some cases, such as the LA Dodgers, they had very nice color 8x10s that were available for collectors. But there weren't that many people out getting autographs.

Oh, there were plenty of people getting things signed, but much of that material didn't exist for too long. Along with baseball cards, mothers who felt their little boys no longer wanted those scraps of paper signed by athletes dumped autographs by the hundreds of thousands into the fire. Programs, newspaper articles, baseball cards—all signed by various athletes—were turned into soot and ashes and smoke rising into the sky. Many ended up being turned in to help the country during various war drives.

Autographs were kept, sure. But it wasn't as much of a passion as it is today. They didn't mean as much. They weren't real treasures.

Certainly there were only half as many people in the country, too. Athletes weren't as visible. The games were just getting going, just reaching into the appetites of the country. Oh, everyone who had a chance would ask Babe Ruth for an autograph or their local hero. The opportunities for meeting athletes, however, weren't what they are today. Just getting to a game was available only to a small percentage of fans. Most read the newspapers and listened to the radio and dreamed of what these athletes were like. They couldn't meet them. Money wasn't available to be spent. Even sending a letter was something only a small percentage of fans could do.

So, today, collectors who are looking back into history and time to piece together items signed by athletes of long ago are hindered by the sheer lack of numbers of items that were signed, and are hindered by the lack of variety of these particular items.

You come down to signed index cards and pieces of paper, some signed programs, maybe some newspaper articles, that sort of thing. Signed photos are tough to find for the athlete of 60 years ago and, let's face it, that means for those who performed in what some see as the real golden period of athletics in this country.

The athletes of earlier times who were still alive in the 1970s had photos sent to them to be signed; but compared to today there were so few collectors working, so few really trying to save what was almost lost to the grave. Guys who were more than willing to sign autographs in the 1970s only received a literal handful of photos to sign through the mail or in person. Dave Bancroft, for example, probably didn't sign more than a couple hundred 8x10 photos before he passed away early in the 1970s. He was more than willing to sign them, but no one had them and no one asked.

One of the sports that is really showing that today is hockey. There is a big upsurge in interest in hockey autographs. Unfortunately much of what is presenting itself is in the form of plain signatures, some letters, some signed programs, and a handful of photos.

The result is that in hockey, especially in the way of Hall of Fame members, all that is around right now is signatures. And these are going at auction for horrendous prices. Even hockey Hall of Famers who died into the 1980s will routinely bring $100-200 for a simple signature. And at auction, who knows—there are hockey HOFers who are bringing atrocious prices in this manner.

My feeling is that there are a lot of hockey autographs out there—mostly in Canada, perhaps, but that these guys signed and signed a lot. The signatures will come out, especially when word gets around that they are going for big money.

That is one of the reasons that for this book: I have not turned to auction results to determine my recommendations on prices. Auctions aren't dependable in this manner—all it takes is two collectors who desperately want an item to drive an auction result sky high. It can be unreasonable and wrong as far as true value goes.

The material that is available for autographs today, as far as the athlete of yesterday is concerned, depends on what the collectors of that day went out and got signed. In all too many cases that means plain signatures.

There are also signed trading cards around. Thankfully collectors of the 1960s and before obtained many signed trading cards. That still was hindered by access to the athlete, and it wasn't until around 1970 those collectors started mailing lots of cards to athletes for signing. For the most part the athletes of that time were very responsive to these requests.

Baseball, of course, led the way—there were lots more cards around to get signed as that was the main sport of inter-

Sean McKeen with catcher/slugger Johnny Bench. "Sean wanted the photo taken with Bench, otherwise I wouldn't have done that. John can be very difficult for fans. He can be a very unwilling autograph signer—to him, every autograph is something someone is going to sell, and he will tell you that. When I asked if he would pose for a picture with Sean, he said 'Oh, all right,' in a not very friendly tone. He was the best all-round catcher I ever saw, one of the best to ever play the game. But I wouldn't ask Johnny Bench for an autograph if he paid me."

est. Still, signed baseball cards from before 1970 were relatively uncommon, and are today.

For collectors in the other sports there are real rarities as far as signed trading cards are concerned. There weren't many of us getting the football cards of the 1950s and 1960s signed. I, personally, have about 500 from that time period—cards I had the football players sign myself. I collect very little today, but I still have those signed cards of heroes of the gridiron who I admired as I grew up.

Signed cards for basketball players are almost non-existent even into the 1970s. The cards were printed in much smaller number, and there just were not as many collectors for that sport as baseball or football.

In hockey, you will probably find a lot of signed trading cards, etc., in Canada. That still would seem to be a relatively untouched market for this material.

It is my opinion that signed trading cards are among the most underpriced autographed items available, and should be among the most highly sought. Trading cards are for the most part color photos showing athletes in their prime, in their uniforms, and at their absolute best. Many collectors are only now coming to understand just how great some of our long-deceased athletes were—guys like Alan Ameche and Eddie Price in football. Today there aren't many of their signed cards out there. It's a shame and a real tragedy because once these guys were gone, then the opportunity to produce a true piece of history went with them.

Sex in Sports

Oh, yes, the day has come. The fact is that pretty girls are now much more evident in athletics and that there are lots of people out there who collect sports autographs only of attractive women. This is not to ignore the fact that there are undoubtedly female collectors who are accumulating autographed photos of good-looking guys. Mainly, however, guys are the ones who are involved in this area, and that is seeing a real increase in demand for autographed photos of certain athletes.

Like it or not, this is a fact. Look at the demand and the prices realized for many of the gymnasts—particularly those from the USA. Shannon Miller, Dominique Moceanu, Kerri Strug, and the other members of that great USA team of gymnasts from 1996 and Atlanta are highly sought autographs. You can interpret this any way you want, but as one who is very closely involved in this hobby I can guarantee you that the reason many collectors want signed photos of these girls is the fact that they are attractive. I know what their autographs should sell for. Shannon and Dominique and Kerri should be in the area of $20-30. Years have passed since their heroics in Atlanta. Those three regularly bring prices of $50 for nice signed color 8x10s. The reason is that collectors, mainly men, want signed photos of them because these young ladies are attractive.

Some people are going to have a big problem with that. Whether they accept it or not isn't going to matter. The fact still remains that this IS A FACT. Sex appeal is a part of the game, and especially when it comes to autographed photos of female athletes.

Pretty ladies have been around sports forever. Gussie Moran was one beautiful tennis player. She used that fact, and had a lot of the tennis community upset with her. So did Karen Fageros.

Jan Stephenson and Laura Baugh had plenty of enemies on the ladies golf tour because they were gorgeous and they were not afraid to use that beauty to make themselves more attractive to sponsors and to pull in some dollars.

Katarina Witt was a great ice skater, but she also had incredible beauty off the ice and form and she knew that. She was quoted as saying that she had the "boobs and the bun" and she realized that. She knew those attributes didn't hurt any when lining up endorsements and being sought after for performances. It might not have hurt when it came to men judges either. Now, of course, she's appearing nude in *Playboy*.

Jennifer Chandler is an incredibly beautiful Olympic gold medal winning diver. She's not a common autograph and she hasn't been active for a long time, but a signed photo of her in a swimming suit will sell, whether she has a gold medal around her neck or not.

The list goes on and on.

This is going to be argued about and a lot of people aren't going to like it. But in the end, the value of autographs comes down to supply and demand. There is incredible demand for photos showing attractive athletes. Because there are more men collectors than women, or men are more willing to spend the money, there is increased demand for autographed photos of pretty ladies.

Whether it is the late, great Florence Griffith Joyner or Wendy L. Williams or any other Olympic medalist or, in some cases, not even ladies who were necessarily winners on the biggest stages of competition, men want their signed photos.

It doesn't hurt that costumes and uniforms tend to be fairly skimpy to start with. Look at figure skating in all of its aspects: costumes for these ladies show a lot, and they are wearing less and less material every time around. Hey—these people are entertainers.

I'll never forget interviewing the late Howard Cosell, who was a guest on a sports radio show hosted along with former NFL quarterback Greg Barton. Howard alluded to this a couple of times—that it was entertainment, not sport. I finally put that question to him directly whether he felt the entertainment angle was the key one now in athletics. He put it bluntly: of course it was! Athletes are entertainers first and foremost. Sports is entertainment. One of the aspects of entertainment certainly can be and is sex appeal. It isn't the entirety of sports, but it is a part.

I can remember Chris Evert when she was about sixteen saying that all of the wonderful terms people were using to describe her as a great tennis player were nice. What she wanted someone to say, though, was that she was sexy. She made that statement very bluntly, and it was obvious that Chris already knew she was sexy. She just wanted to start hearing that from other people.

Most athletes work hard and long at being in shape. They have to, obviously. They also are, obviously, going to be proud of the results of that work. No reason they shouldn't.

The opposite sex is going to take note of this attractiveness. There are many gorgeous and incredibly talented female athletes and they are in more demand among many men collectors than other athletes.

Sex appeal, beauty, and attractiveness are all factors in selling signed photos. As more women become involved in athletics, their physical beauty will become more and more involved in the interest in autographs. There's nothing bad about this at all, although some people will say there is.

Why Collect Autographs

Some people have problems with autographs. They don't understand why they are collected. They don't understand why they are meaningful. If someone enjoys getting autographs, what difference should it make why they enjoy it? Different strokes for different folks—you remember that one, don't you? Not me, I'm too young.

If you want to come up with reasons for collecting autographs, consider these examples.

An autograph is a piece of that person passed on to history. It's something that person held onto, and signed their name too—in their own individual manner, with their own individual words. It shows pride in their accomplishments and tells something about what they were by the way they sign.

In some cases there are signed typescripts which tell about that person, or give a quote, or give something of what made them special. These are pieces of history.

Can you imagine holding in your hands something signed by Jesus? Or Mohammed? Or Buddha? Nothing sacrilegious intended with that thought, but can you imagine holding something that any of them held? To see how they signed their names? Knowing what we know about them, can you imagine the thrill?

I've had the joy of owning a piece of paper signed by Sitting Bull. I held it in my hands and I thought that a truly incredible human being held that and affixed his identity to it, and I could almost hear the yells and the shots and the suffering and imagine feeling the bayonet finally putting an end to that Indian leader's life.

These are items in many cases touched by greatness, great human beings who showed something special, something that made them stand apart from everyone else. Maybe they all weren't and aren't truly wondeful people. But they were all wonderful athletes. Some were the best to do what they did.

Autographs—a mystery, yeah. A pleasure—oh boy, most certainly.

We all have to hope that they can be enjoyed both by those who give the autographs and by those who treasure them.

For collectors in the field of sports, there are more opportunities for enjoyment than in any other area. It's all there before you. It's all obtainable.

More than anything else, you have to have fun with this. Maybe if we all have enough fun, if we all enjoy it enough, maybe the athletes will enjoy it, too. Maybe not.

It is about time, however, that they lighten up and accept the fact that autographs go with the territory. That with the money and with the privilege of playing the game and entertaining millions, comes the obligation to mingle with those of us who enjoy their skills.

They are different than most of us in that they can do what virtually everyone would dearly love to do; they can play the game better than anyone else.

We admire that. All we want is a little piece of that action for ourselves. A little reminder that those who play the game understand that if it weren't for us they would be playing it with no crowds watching, and with the only money on the line being that which players tossed into a pool for the winning side.

This can be and should be a win-win game. Fun for us all.

Autographs: what a blast! It's a great day for the hobby. Tomorrow should be even greater.

Chuck McKeen is an entertainment and sports autograph dealer living in Hillsborough, Oregon. A longtime friend of George and Helen Sanders, Chuck has coauthored all three editions of **The Sanders Price Guide to Sports Autographs**. *See his ad on page 446 of this book.*

Rocky Marciano—who retired as undefeated heavyweight champion of the world—being interviewed by George Sanders. Marciano tragically died soon afterwards.

Chapter 3

COLLECTING BOXING AUTOGRAPHS

by James "Jim" Stinson

In the early part of this century, America's favorite spectator sport was boxing. *It* not baseball was our national pastime. The names of John L. Sullivan, James J. Corbett, and Jack Dempsey were known to every man, woman, and child in every household in this country (and many worldwide). In 1921, 80,183 sports fans paid to see Jack Dempsey knock out Georges Carpentier: ringside tickets cost an amazing $50.00 EACH (that is $50.00 in 1921, folks!). Even more amazing, 120,757 people paid to see the first Jack Dempsey vs. Gene Tunney bout in 1926.

Baseball gradually saw the tide of public interest begin to shift in its favor in the late 1920s with the popularity of Babe Ruth and others and eventually claimed the popular handle of "America's National Pastime."

In the early days of television, boxing made a resurgence in the popular culture. With the crude camera equipment that existed in those days, it was easier to film a boxing match in a ring containing two men and a referee than it was to film a large baseball field with the action spread out over a bigger area. As a result of this exposure, an entire generation of future autograph collectors became familiar with names like Kid Gavilan, Carmen Basilio, Gene Fullmer, Sugar Ray Robinson, Floyd Patterson, and Rocky Marciano.

Several scandals involving the fixing of matches and the alleged involvement of organized crime in the sport hurt its

Cuban legend Kid Gavilan gives Jim Stinson a quick lesson in boxing in 1989.

rising popularity and by the early 1960s many sports fans were again looking elsewhere for entertainment.

Muhammad Ali changed all that when he did to boxing what Babe Ruth had done to baseball over fifty years before. The terms "rope-a-dope" and "float like a butterfly—sting like a bee" became part of the national vernacular. The era of the 1970s in boxing saw some of the greatest combined talent in all of the various weight divisions that the sport had ever seen. Many of the sports *all time* greats held championships in the 1970s. Ruben Olivares and Carlos Zarate (bantamweight), Alexis Arguello and Eder Jofre (featherweight), Roberto Duran (lightweight), Carlos Monzon (middleweight), Bob Foster (light-heavyweight), Muhammad Ali, George Foreman, and Joe Frazier (heavyweight).

The emergence of the so-called alphabet divisions helped only to water down the importance of a single world title in each of the weight divisions. Some fighters—however—have been so good that their popularity transcended these alphabet designations names like Sugar Ray Leonard, Marvin Hagler, Tommie Hearns, Larry Holmes, Mike Tyson, and Evander Holyfield needed no introduction and no sanctioning body for the public to know they were champions.

Today's boxing picture is quite different. With the exception of the ageless George Foreman, few fighters today can claim the national spotlight and cross over into the household-name category. Boxing today has taken a back seat to more popular spectator sports such as football and basketball. However, few sporting events can generate the excitement of a heavyweight championship bout between two worthy combatants.

From a collecting perspective, until around 1988, people collecting boxing memorabilia were few and far between. The price of vintage boxing memorabilia was scandalously cheap compared with their counterparts in baseball and the other sports. Boxing was the hobby's carrot-topped stepchild. That all began to change in 1989. The so-called "explosion" of values of boxing memorabilia and autographs was nothing more than the boxing arm of the hobby correcting itself. Has the demand slowed? Possibly. Around 1995 most boxing autographs were selling for about 20% less than they were in the late 1980s and early '90s. A slow steady increase since then has seen prices of autographed items of the more popular names finally arrive back at where they were. In some cases, especially with regard to popular modern-day heavyweights like Rocky Marciano and Sonny Liston, the increase in price has been dramatic.

Boxing's popularity is fueled by the fact that it is a "world" sport. The same boxers popular in this country have achieved proportionate fame overseas. Fans in both Australia and the United Kingdom have become avid collectors of boxing autographs. Can the same thing be said about baseball or football?

Ask a sports fan in England or Germany who Joe Louis or Muhammad Ali was and they'll tell you. Ask them the same question about Mickey Mantle or Ted Williams and they might not even know who you are talking about. This means that in terms of collecting, the sports that have been the most popular with collectors in this country (baseball, football, basketball, etc.) will *never* have the same far reaching appeal that boxing does to potential collectors worldwide. That just might be an indication that when it comes to the popularity of boxing autographs and memorabilia, like the great Jimmy Durante would say, "You'se ain't seen nuthin' yet!"

Collecting the Heavyweights

Collecting autographs of all the former heavyweight champions seems to be the most popular single area of collecting. From Evander Holyfield back to John L. Sullivan, there is a linear connection that dates to before the turn of the century. To collectors attempting to accomplish this goal there are a couple of scarce autographs with the most difficult being that of Marvin Hart who many would say might not have actually been a true heavyweight champion at all. James Jeffries, when retiring undefeated in 1905, named Hart and Jack Root as the two he would like to see fight for the coveted title. Hart knocked Root out in 12 rounds. After closing out his ring career in 1910, he

Marvelous Marvin Hagler and Jim Stinson—Boston, 1994.

drifted into obscurity and died in 1931. There could very well be only two or three authentic Marvin Hart autographs in the entire hobby.

The second most difficult would be Robert Fitzsimmons. At one time he also held the middleweight and light-heavy-weight titles. Fitzsimmons bested "Gentleman" Jim Corbett in 1897. He died of tuberculosis in 1917. Although signatures do exist due to his worldwide exposure as a vaudeville enter-tainer, collectors will find the acquisition of Fitzsimmons autograph to be both a difficult and expensive proposition.

In the modern era Rocky Marciano and Sonny Liston will prove to be a challenge for collectors rounding out their collections of all of the heavyweight champs. Both are tough to find in authentic form for different reasons. Due to Rocky's immense popularity, through-the-mail requests were usu-ally signed by a secretary or a family member. Liston was basically illiterate, and rumor has it, only learned to sign his name shortly before winning the heavyweight title in 1962. Through-the-mail requests were almost always signed by his wife and in person Liston's signature was slow and labored. Add to this Liston and Marciano's untimely deaths and the reasons for the scarcity of their signatures can be fully understood.

The other weight divisions also have some signatures that are desirable and considered extremely rare. Stanley Ketchel is probably the most sought after of the non-heavyweight signatures and the rarest. The few Ketchel signatures that have surfaced in the past dozen or so years were usually signed "Young Ketchel" as opposed to his full proper name. Ketchel was only 24 years old when he was shot to death by a jealous husband in 1910. Salvador Sanchez, the great Mexican featherweight champion, who held the title from 1980 until his death in a car accident in 1982 is for obvious reasons almost impossible to find. He was only 22 years old when he died.

Add to these the hundreds of names of fighters that have held the distinction of being able to call themselves at one time of another "World Champions" and you have a large, diversified field of collecting to draw from. It all promises to offer autograph collectors challenges and the fun that goes along with it for years to come.

Jim Stinson is a sports autograph dealer specializing in baseball and boxing. His in-person private signings with legendary boxers have taken him around the world from Sydney, Australia and Buenos Aires, Argentina to Rome, Italy. He boasts the largest selection of autographed boxing photos in the world. See his ad on page 441 of this book.

George Sanders visited the International Boxing Hall of Fame in Canastota, New York in 1997.

Chapter 4

THE U.A.C.C.

(Universal Autograph Collectors Club)

by Bob Erickson, UACC President

Editors' Note: The enjoyment of your hobby is greatly enhanced when you band together with those of similiar interests. In the wonderful field of autographs, we feel the U.A.C.C. is the leading organization for autograph collectors and this fine organization is endorsed by the Sanders Price Guides to Autographs. We recommend that you consider membership.

The Universal Autograph Collectors Club (U.A.C.C.) is the world's largest organization for autograph collectors with over 2,000 members in the United States, Canada, and more than 25 other countries. Founded in New York in 1965, the U.A.C.C. is a federally recognized nonprofit educational organization whose purpose is to inform U.A.C.C. members and the public at large about all aspects of autograph collecting through its publications, shows, and seminars.

By joining the U.A.C.C., you will receive our renowned 64-page bimonthly journal, *The Pen and Quill,* which features articles and news on autographs in all areas, including U.S. presidents, authors, scientists, aviators, astronauts, royalty, entertainers, athletes, military leaders, Nobel Prize winners, and explorers, to name a few. Studies of authentic, secretarial, Autopen, rubber-stamped, facsimile, and forged signatures help collectors to make informed decisions when purchasing autographic material. Celebrity addresses are published in each issue to assist collectors who enjoy writing for autographs. The U.A.C.C. also sponsors annual literary awards in addition to paying for articles published in *The Pen and Quill*.

You may also have your name and address published as a new member in *The Pen and Quill*. By so doing, you will receive free autograph catalogues from our dealer members and auction houses. Or you can place a free classified ad in *The Pen and Quill* to list your wants, sell your extra material, or just communicate with other members about your common interests.

All members are required to abide by a strict Code of Ethics and violations of that Code are enforced by the U.A.C.C. Ethics Board. By dealing with other U.A.C.C. members, you can be assured that the Ethics Board will assist you in any dispute involving another member who has violated the Code of Ethics. Members who refuse to abide by an Ethics Board decision are subject to sanctions, including expulsion, with notice to members published in *The Pen and Quill*.

The U.A.C.C. also offers its members the opportunity to purchase uncommon autographic material and reference works at affordable prices through the "U.A.C.C. Warehouse" page in *The Pen and Quill*. The U.A.C.C. sponsors autograph shows in major U.S. cities and London, England featuring educational displays, autograph dealers who abide by the U.A.C.C. Code of Ethics, and celebrity guests. Seminars are occasionally held in conjunction with the shows to educate our members and the public on all aspects of collection and preservation, and identification of non-authentic (bogus or forged) material.

Finally, the U.A.C.C. sponsors mail auctions through *The Pen and Quill* as well as an annual live floor auction near Washington, DC. These auctions are another avenue to assist our members who buy and sell autographs.

To learn more about the U.A.C.C., send your request for a brochure and membership application to **U.A.C.C., Dept. SPG, PO Box 6181, Washington, DC 20044-6181**. You can also get membership information and an application by visiting our Internet web site at **http://www.uacc.org**. We hope you will join our universe of fellow collectors soon.

Chapter 5

A GEORGE SANDERS SPORTS PORTFOLIO

by Helen Doolittle Sanders and Ralph Roberts

To the dedicated seeker of authentic sports autographs there can be no more genuine thrill than to receive a favorite athlete's "in person" signature. As a professional sports broadcaster, interviewer, newspaper and magazine columnist, actor, master of ceremonies for countless sports banquets and long-time radio and TV broadcasting executive in the U.S. and New Zealand, author George Sanders had the good fortune of meeting, shaking hands and swapping sports yarns with the greatest names in athletics from archery to weightlifting. He hobnobbed with amateur and pro sports stars who were happy to appear with him on various programs from 1940 through 1973.

On golf courses, horse and auto racing tracks, sports arenas, baseball diamonds and dugouts, bistros and bars, wrestling mats, boxing rings, horseshoe pits, bowling alleys and football stadia, in their homes, in their agents' offices, he had microphones and pen in hand. As a lifelong collector, he saw to it that the sports celebrity of the moment could easily accommodate the oft-repeated, "May I have your autograph please?"

As his wife and partner for almost 50 years, Helen Sanders toted cameras, microphones, tape recorders and the always present leather bound autograph guest books. Having been captain of her high school basketball and softball teams, she naturally shared George's intense interest in sports. It was a lifetime of good fun kibitzing with the likes of Ted Williams, Ty Cobb, Tom Harmon, Rams running back Dick Bass, lightweight boxing champ Jimmy Carter, boxers Vince Martinez and Chuck Davey,

"Slapsy Maxie" Rosenbloom, baseball stars Andy Pafko, Roy Smalley, middleweight champ Ceferina Garcia, Heisman Trophy winner Terry Baker, Joe DiMaggio, quarterbacks John Brodie and Jim Plunkett, ends Del Shofner and "Crazy Legs" Elroy Hirsch. Thanks to George's chosen profession and his hobby, Helen mixed with the best. Before she became Mrs. Sanders, her proud father placed his precious only daughter on the lap of San Francisco Seals' player-manager Lefty O'Doul when she was only a babe. It seemed that Helen was predestined to be a part of sports autograph collecting.

On the following pages are many examples of photo opportunities that clearly illustrate how most sports celebrities are usually cooperative and generally delighted to pose and oblige polite collectors with their coveted autographs. You will find some splendid facsimiles of the signatures of these sports figures included, as well.

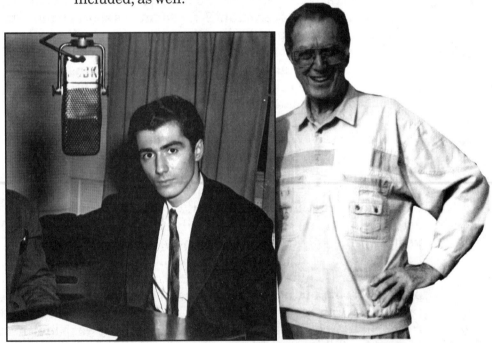

George Sanders (above) in 1939, age 15, was already a veteran broadcaster, having begun as a child actor on WXYZ in Detroit. To the right, age 74, in 1998— he still had his looks and was still doing commercials. His was an incredible life!

While this book is very much a memorial to George Sanders—who passed away just before its publication—the photographs that follow are far more than just a celebration of his life. George undisputedly—thanks to the luck and glory of his profession as broadcaster and journalist and always an autograph collector over almost 60 years of this most interesting century—amassed more *documented* in-person autographs than any other person in history. We have literally thousands of glossy 8x10 photographs of George with about every celebrity you can think of to prove this fact. They all signed for him and were glad to do it. This incredible experience and expertise of his in the collection of *authentic* signatures began these autograph price guides 10 years ago, and will continue them for many years to come. George Sanders has left behind a vast legacy of autographic information that continues to benefit the thousands of collectors and dealers using the **Sanders Price Guides to Autographs**.

Photograph Credits

We wish to thank some of the world's most talented photographers, who opened their respective lenses and expended countless old-fashioned flashbulbs so they might capture so many memorable moments in the company of a variety of sports giants.

These professional photographers include Julius "Bud" Clauss from University of Detroit days, the late Carl Vermilya (KPTV-Channel 12, Portland, Oregon), John A. Boyer (Los Angeles), Photo-Art Commercial Studios of Portland, Oregon, Irving L. Antler (Hollywood), Frank Parr (Portland, Ore.), Rothschild Photos (Los Angeles), William Fraker (R.K.O., Paramount Pictures in Hollywood), Sam J. Cole (Monrovia, Calif.), Coy Watson (Los Angeles), Alva Gregory (Paramount Pictures publicist), Davis Photos (Azusa, Calif.), Dick Farris (Portland, Ore.), O'Brien Photos (Altadena, Calif.), Helen Doolittle Sanders and our dear friend and fellow worker for 15 wonderful years, Bruce Luzader of beautiful Portland, Oregon. Without all of the above it would be difficult to document so many rare encounters.

A Sports Portfolio

Horse racing jockey Eddie Arcaro with George, and Eddie's signature. In the interest of saving some space, we are superimposing sigs on photos.

Boxer Tony Armstrong gives George Sanders some batting tips during a charity game in Hollywood. Tony's sig also appears above.

George (seated front) with the 1968 Portland Beavers minor league baseball team. Several of the players went on to play in the major leagues. Getting autographs of local minor league players can pay off big time later.

(above) N.Y. Yankees outfielder Johnny Lindell, George Sanders, and no-hit Cincinnati pitcher Ewell Blackwell fishing in California in the 1950s.

(right) Signed photograph of Cincinnati Reds pitcher Ewell Blackwell.

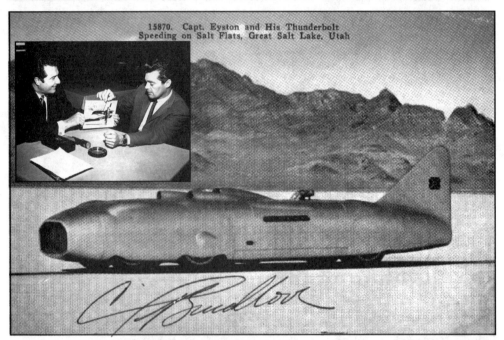

(inset) George interviews speedster Craig Breedlove who, until recently, held the world land speed record. Above, Breedlove has signed a postcard showing an earlier record attempt on the Salt Flats by Captain Eyston in 1937.

George with NFL quarterback John Brodie and (inset) Brodie's signature.

George with tennis great Louise Brough Clapp and (inset) Clapp sig.

The lightweight boxing champion of the world, Jimmy Carter, always dined at "George Sanders' Lark Restaurant" in Los Angeles when he was training in the area during the 1950s. The quiet, well-mannered, little pugilist was always a welcome guest and here he's hosted by the entire Sanders clan. From left to right: Grace R. Sanders, her son George, the champ, and George R. Sanders, Sr. The Lark was at 3624 West Third Street in Los Angeles and visited by many celebrities in the years the Sanders family ran it—a great source of autographs for George! (top left) A signed photograph of Jimmy Carter.

George at a Los Angeles charity baseball game in the 1950s with Groucho Marx and baseball legend Ty Cobb. Inset is Cobb's sig.

Before the Braves moved to Milwaukee, then to Atlanta, they were the Boston Braves! Left, George interviews Braves' catcher Del Crandell. Right, a signed photograph of Crandell.

Washington Senators baseball player and manager Joe Cronin with George. Cronin has signed the photo on his suit jacket. Inset is a Cronin baseball card.

Heisman Trophy winner Glenn Davis with George (left) at a West Point football reunion. Above, First Day Cover signed by Davis and Doc Blanchard.

Above, George goes fishing with Indy racing champion Ralph DePalma. Inset is DePalma's sig. Left, the 1908 120 horse-power Fiat that he drove for the fastest three laps in America's first Grand Prix.

Above left, George gets Baseball Hall of Fame pitcher Bob Feller's autograph.
Above right, a HOF plaque card autographed by Bob Feller.

Above, Olympic skier Jean Saubert, George, and
Gretchen Fraser, the first American woman to win
a gold medal in skiing (1948). Her sig inset. Right,
George with Olympic ice skating gold medalist
Peggy Fleming and her sig inset.

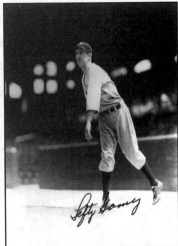

Above left, Hall of Fame pitcher Lefty Gomez on "The Eye Opener" TV show with host Sanders and St. Louis Cardinals manager Vern Benson. Above right, signed photograph of Gomez.

George with Navy football hero Otto Graham and a Graham inscription inset.

Left, inscription to George from All American Michigan halfback and pro football star Tom Harmon. Above, a youthful George poses with Harmon.

Above, Parnelli Jones signed photo. Right, George interviews Jones with Jones' STP-Paxton Turbine race car in the foreground.

RALPH McPHERRAN KINER

Outfielder
Bats: Right   Throws: Right
Ht: 6'2"   Wt: 195 lbs
Born: Santa Rita, New Mexico 10/27/22

Playing Record
1946-53 Pittsburgh Pirates
1953-1954 Chicago Cubs
1955 Cleveland Indians

Games	1472	Triples	39
At Bats	5205	Home Runs	369
Runs	971	Runs Batted In	1015
Hits	1451	Batting Average	.279
Doubles	216		

Hall of Fame

INDUCTION DAY
August 18, 1975
Cooperstown, New York

Top left, Baseball Hall of Fame member Ralph Kiner with George at a fishing event in the 1950s. Above, Kiner's signed HOF induction card. Below, George at Cooperstown points to Kiner's plaque. Kiner has signed the photograph.

Left, star right guard Jerry Kramer of the Green Bay Packers discusses his book with George. Sig inset.

Left, SP of the "Raging Bull," Jake La Motta. Above, George Sanders (r), age 15, in 1939 interviews La Motta on the radio. George had begun his radio career several years before as a child actor on WXYZ in Detroit.

Above, a signed photograph of Australian tennis champion Rod Laver as he stretches to make one of his sizzling returns. Right, Rod and George Sanders hobnob during George's days covering news and sports in Portland, Oregon.

To George Sanders = A fine gentleman and a superb performer = Frank Leahy

Above, inscription by famed Notre Dame coach Frank Leahy to George. Left, George with Leahy during a reunion at Notre Dame, one of the schools that George attended.

George arm wrestles on the air with NFL star Gene "Big Daddy" Lipscomb. George lost.

Left, George (center back) and bandleader Harry James fielded a softball team consisting of 10 of the world's greatest jockeys, including Johnny Longden. Above, a Longden SP.

Heavyweight boxing champion of the world Joe "the Brown Bomber" Louis with George and George M. "Sandy" Sanders in Los Angeles in the summer of 1958, and a Louis signature inset.

New Orleans Saints NFL quarterback Archie Manning (sig inset) with Mrs. Manning and George. The Mannings are parents of current NFL great quarterback Peyton Manning, who was an All American while playing for "Big Orange" Tennessee.

Above (left, standing) rodeo champion Larry Mahan, George Sanders, and Ken "Festus" Curtis of "Gunsmoke" fame. Seated is country and western composer Rudy Sooter. Photograph is signed by Mahan and Sooter, and was taken in the early 1970s in Portland, Oregon while George was working on KWJJ. Left, cowboy Mahan is interviewed by rancher Sanders.

George Sanders with Olympic champion, congressman, and fitness advocate Bob Mathias.

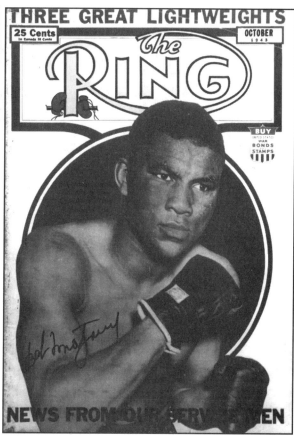

George (above) barely gets in this photo with boxing champ Bob Montgomery. Right, an autographed boxing magazine cover featuring Montogomery in October 1943.

Signed photograph of legendary pro football Hall of Famer Bronko Nagurski. Inset, photo of Nagurski with George Sanders at Nagurski's gas station in International Falls, Minnesota in 1966.

George Sanders (right center, kneeling) covers a golfing event featuring Jack Nicklaus (left center, white hat). Inset is a card signed by Nicklaus.

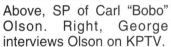

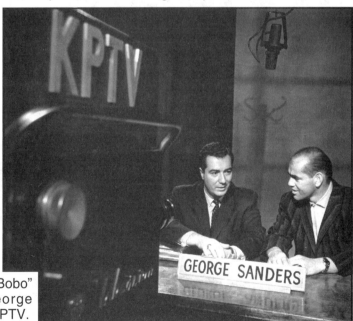

Above, SP of Carl "Bobo" Olson. Right, George interviews Olson on KPTV.

A SANDERS SPORTS PORTFOLIO   65

The great olympic sprinter Jesse Owens—the man who embarrassed Hitler at the 1936 Berlin Olympics—talks to George for KWJJ, Portland, Oregon. Inset, top, is a dollar bill signed by Owens, which is worth a whole lot more than a dollar now!

George with baseball legend Satchel Paige who said, "Don't ever look back, something might be gainin'." Inset is Satchel's signature.

Above, Heisman Trophy and Super Bowl winner Jim Plunkett & George. Right, FDC signed by Plunkett.

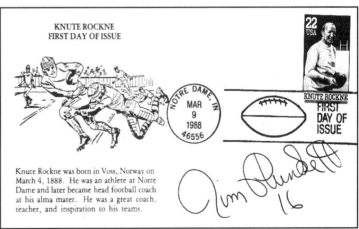

KNUTE ROCKNE
FIRST DAY OF ISSUE

Knute Rockne was born in Voss, Norway on March 4, 1888. He was an athlete at Notre Dame and later became head football coach at his alma mater. He was a great coach, teacher, and inspiration to his teams.

George with Mel Renfro of the Dallas Cowboys in George's office in Portland in the early 1970s. Note all the framed photographs of celebrities with George on the wall. They are just a few of the thousands we have from George's long and very eventful career. Inset is a signed photograph of Renfro.

Sportscaster Ted Husing, boxing great Slapsie Max Rosenbloom, and George discuss boxing during an interview. Inset is a Rosenbloom signature.

Jackie Robinson—member of the Baseball Hall of Fame and breaker of the color barrier in the major leagues—spoke with George on Portland's KWJJ radio.

Left to right, San Diego attorney Jack Crumley, immortal boxing champion Barney Ross, lightweight champion Lauro Salas, Sanders, and advertising executive Leonard Robin during a 1949 charity softball game in Hollywood. Inset is Ross' sig.

Winner of five gold medals for Olympic swimming, Don Schollander shakes hands with George Sanders in the early '70s. Above, his sig.

Left to right, George Sanders, Ty Cobb, Danny Murtaugh, and the legendary Baseball Hall of Famer George Sisler. Inset is Sisler's sig.

A young George Sanders watched elderly legend Tris Speaker (l) give batting tips.

A SANDERS SPORTS PORTFOLIO   71

The Oakland Raiders' NFL powerhouse Jack Tatum (above) signs the ever-present Sanders autograph album during a function in the early 1970s. George was never bashful in politely asking a celebrity for his or her autograph. Left, a signed photograph of Tatum.

A very young George (above) with tennis super legend Big Bill Tilden. Right, a rare signed sketch of Tilden.

George with Los Angeles Lakers star and Basketball HOF member, Jerry West.

A signed photograph of Baseball Hall of Famer Ted Williams with George.

Chapter 6

AUTOGRAPH DEALERS, YOU NEED THEM!

by George Sanders

This chapter is directed at anyone who foolishly believes that a truly fine sports collection can be acquired without drawing from the huge inventories of proven, respected, longtime dealers or reputable auction houses. Obviously, it would be great if the collector could grab especially rare signatures, signed photographs and sports memorabilia with just in-person forays into sports exhibitions, shows and games but unfortunately Babe Ruth, Ty Cobb, Lou Gehrig, Jim Thorpe, Vince Lombardi, Bobby Jones, Bill Tilden and countless other sports immortals aren't signing anymore.

Finding a Dealer

If you are sincere in your desire to collect the greatest all-time athletes it is mandatory that you eventually turn to the offerings of a professional dealer. Your choice of a dealer or a gaggle of dealers with whom you feel secure will come only when you have thoroughly investigated the various candidates who wish to receive your money.

These are some of the qualities you should look for in the dealerships of your choice. First and foremost, they must readily agree, in writing, to totally guarantee the authenticity of every signature or autographed item they sell you. If they can't or won't offer you such a warranty, pass them by as they should be peddling worthless oil leases, dubious stock tips or be employed as racetrack touts. There is no place in this hobby for such questionable, even dishonest, behavior. If the dealer is not certain of his or her material why should it be offered to a customer?

No collector in their right mind should ever agree to hand over hard-earned money for any unauthenticated material. There are no exceptions to that rule. In short, buying any autograph "as is" can most assuredly be a reckless pursuit, particularly with lazy or careless auction houses that stipulate such an irresponsible condition.

Why should you be so cautious? With the hobby growing in record leaps and sometimes startling bounds, unscrupulous forgers, fast-buck manipulators and sleazy con men and, yes, women have begun to worm their way into the marketplace with bogus autographs and highly questionable memorabilia. You obviously require the expertise of specialists who have the experience to tell a phony and absolutely bogus signature from the "write stuff."

With rare exceptions, I have found in my 50 years of collecting and over 30 years of PURCHASING autograph material that most full-time dealers are highly knowledgeable, courteous, interesting, peculiarly candid, and enormously interested in the hobby they represent. They sell with charming grace and buy with all the toughness of a river pirate. Some have become lifelong friends whose personal lives have intertwined with our own. Most are not eligible for sainthood but I trust them completely.

There are even a few blatant thieves whose light-fingered talents keep honest dealers tensely alert at public autograph shows, as well as in the privacy of their respective offices or galleries. Such felons then slither around shows offering their stolen goods to unsuspecting collectors. If you are approached at shows by "wandering" peddlers who somehow "forgot" to rent a booth, give them a wide berth and none of your cash. You can't afford their suspicious bargains unless you enjoy visits from the F.B.I. or postal authorities.

Customers of thieves are treated like the "fences" they've become and you certainly won't enjoy returning your ill-

Who's the only U.S. president ever to be inducted into a sports hall of fame? Ronald Reagan—seen here in 1957 with wife Nancy and interviewer, George Sanders—was inducted into the Sportswriters and Sportscasters National Hall of Fame in honor of his career as a play-by-play announcer and sports broadcaster. Reagan has always been generous to autograph collectors.

gotten material nor the loss of your investment. In other words, sometimes a "real bargain" is a real bummer!

You wouldn't purchase a diamond ring or a rare coin from some obscure dealer or a fast-talking stranger on the street. If an autograph dealer refuses to guarantee all material and offer to repay your investment in full should the item prove to be bogus or stolen, do not deal with that person. Good dealers make worthwhile suggestions and search out special items that will make your collection more valuable.

Dealer Catalogs

All major autograph dealers offer excellent catalogues; nearly every week I discover some signature, signed photo or document that I never dreamed would become available to me. Also, I find worthwhile bargains because I thoroughly enjoy shopping through the various catalogues offered by more than a hundred dealers in the United States, Canada and overseas. Even wise dealers make mistakes and frequently underprice an item that has little interest or value for them but has been largely unobtainable for the collector who wants or needs it.

Be extremely cautious in how you haggle or bargain with dealers. If you're too penurious or demanding in dealing, you will be punished in subtle ways. If they find you to be cheap, difficult in manner, overly critical of material, you will find that your copy of their catalogue is mailed to you on a much later date than their preferred customers. That means every other collector has pawed over the dealer's material long before you ever had an opportunity to see or buy it. In brief, you saved a few dollars earlier but now you are never going to see his rare good stuff. Asking for discounts on rarities is like asking a dealer if he or she would consider selling one of their children at any price.

Don't waste a dealer's time with tales of how you acquired some precious autograph through the mail or by outwitting some other dealer. They could care less and you have only warned them that you have a big mouth that might embarrass them someday. All dealers know each other. There are no secrets in the world of autographs and excessive collector bragging does not add to the real value of your collection. Some dealers like each other and will only warn the dealer you duped that you are a fast-talking wise guy. Just be polite, informed and keep your triumphs to yourself. A few dealers have very poor telephone manners and you will dread dealing with them, but if they've got something you need, you'll ignore their attitude problems and go for the prize. Some dealers have such bad manners and ugly dispositions that even if they have a much-needed piece, you do as we do and pray that they'll apply for Chapter 11 in your lifetime!

In-Person Autographs Are Nice, But...

Please don't delude yourself that you can ever own a truly valuable collection by only acquiring whatever autographs you can get for postage charges and by begging from sports celebrities in person. I've done both. I have collected thousands of "in-person" autographs for free because I was a professional broadcaster and journalist with easy access to sports figures and public figures from every walk of life. However, my contemporary collection of such wonderful material does not match the value of my cash investments in this fast-growing hobby.

Of course in-person collecting is wondrous fun, filled with the excitement of the hunt and the ultimate joy of personally contacting one of your favorite athletes. Alas, collectors cannot contact the dead, and it is the dead who have become the most sought-after in the autograph world. The man who paid over $23,000 for "Shoeless" Joe Jackson's signature has topped us all and if we want a signature like his, we won't find it in a bargain basement or grossly underpriced in some fool's catalogue.

Face the facts, it's not the living we really covet, it's all those super stars who've gone to the Great Autograph Album in the sky. This is where accredited dealers become skilled mediums for seances that bring the writings of Rube Foster, Babe Didrikson Zaharias, Grover Cleveland Alexander, Eddie Cicotte, Rogers Hornsby, Jim Thorpe, Suzanne Lenglen, Maureen "Little Mo" Connolly, Gertrude Ederle, Ray Ewry, John L. Sullivan, George Gipp, Wilbur Shaw, Barney Oldfield, Tris Speaker, Amos Alonzo Stagg, Walter Camp, Jackie Robinson, Knute Rockne and the Four Horsemen of Notre Dame into your appreciative hands and thus into your treasured collection of proven historically important sports luminaries.

Don't sell yourself or your collection short by failing to have the confidence of intelligent investment, and don't attempt to build a valuable collection without the learned skills of an honest dealer or auction house.

Dealers Come in All Sizes

Dealers come in all sizes and descriptions. They may have the warm drawl of the deep South, the comfortable, humorous speech of the Southwest, the prim, often cool enunciations of the Northeast, the oft harsh accents of the Bronx, Brooklyn or Manhattan, the terse twang of the Midwest or the enthusiastic, press agentry patter of Hollywood and LaLa Land not including San Francisco where sophistication is a way of life.

There are cynical curmudgeons, scholarly gentlemen, there are ever-so-pleasant and equally learned sportswomen, there are entertaining humorists, there are always good-friends-to-be. Try not to become captivated by just one dealer, even though you may feel quite secure in dealing only with that "special" one.

Catalogues of sports autographs, like their various publishers, have their own personalities, so do not dismiss a list run off from a copier because you think it may contain less desirable or more common sports material. On the other hand, do not be wary of a slick, profusely illustrated, luxuriously presented catalogue because you've assumed its autographs will be too expensive. You'll find superb buys in both.

You'll have the choice of hundreds of items every month offered for sale by over a hundred dealers and auction houses who all give you selectivity and competitive pricing. You will find whatever you seek if you simply make an earnest effort to acquire every available catalogue, via advertisements in this book plus the *Sports Collectors Digest*, *Tuff Stuff*, *Autograph Times*, The Universal Autograph Collectors Club (UACC) publication *The Pen and Quill* and want ads in the back of many sports publications.

Don't be tentative or shy about contacting and buying from autograph dealers. They are a necessary addition to your life if you sincerely intend to become a serious collector with an investment potential. In time you will discover several dealers who are just right for you and your bank account, and the union of interests that ensues will be entirely rewarding to you both.

I wish you good fortune, good hunting, and good catalogue reading.

Chapter 7

HOW TO USE THIS BOOK

by Helen Sanders

The growth of this collectible has prompted the publication of a new edition of **The Sanders Price Guide to Sports Autographs**. Little did we know when the original **Price Guide to Autographs** was published that a separate price guide for sports would be necessary. It shouldn't surprise us however when we take a look at the Dow Jones Average of 1993 and compare it to the current Dow Jones Average. Just as the stock market has shown amazing growth so, too, have the number of sports fans grown along with the media coverage.

Although this is a price guide, do not be guided down an unrealistic path. The prices herein are not, I repeat **not**, carved in stone! This is a **guide**, so use some common sense. This is a **guide**, so **negotiate**. While instant replay in football has not yet been adopted, it is still being negotiated. As regards instant replay, it was thought, and is still thought, that a closer look, an alternative judgment, might produce a fairer decision. We feel, therefore, that this book might give you an opportunity to arrive at a fairer decision when you are buying or selling autographs.

However, there is no way that the authors of this book can put a price on the fun and joy of collecting. That is a very personal thing. What you collect and the way you collect is what is important to you, and should be for your enjoyment. One cannot put a price on the priceless!

Because you cannot collect everything you want in person

and you cannot expect busy professionals to answer all your mail requests, you must ultimately acquire the autographs you need from an autograph dealer. Yes, it is wonderful that those that you collected in person did not cost you anything, but the time will come when you will want to purchase the missing autographs that you do not already own. You will definitely want these purchases to come from a **reliable** source, namely, from a **reliable** dealer! We cannot stress that word enough.

What are you going to pay for them? Well, that is the purpose of this price guide—to give you a helping hand.

Condition

The most condition-sensitive purchase you have made (or will make) is probably a used car. When you are just looking, it is generally with an open mind. But when you have narrowed your investment down to make, model, year and price, the condition of that car becomes very important—so too, with your investment in an autograph. If you are a graduate of baseball card collecting and are now collecting baseball cards **SIGNED** by the player whose image is depicted on those cards, then you already understand the meaning of condition. Those dirty, bent, torn or mutilated unsigned cards are not worth the same amount of money as a clean, bright card in mint condition. Autographed material is judged the same way.

The prices quoted in this book are for material in fine condition. If you are fortunate enough to find autographs in superb or exceptionally good condition they are worth a premium. Of course the reverse is true when a piece is damaged and it must be appraised accordingly.

Price Categories

In the autograph world we have discovered that most sports collectors specialize in either signatures (SIG) or signed photographs (SP). We have, therefore, limited our prices to these two categories adding a column with a limited number of autographed balls and/or hockey pucks. Until there is a consistent demand as well as large enough supply of signed documents and letters, we will not clutter the pages with the columns necessary to handle the data. FYI: In time, you will discover that both signed letters and documents are generally more valuable than a simple signature or inscribed photo.

Please do not limit yourself to just signatures and signed photos. There is a whole world of excitement awaiting you if you can hold in your hand a letter from Babe Ruth, Bobby Jones, Jim Thorpe, Babe Didrikson Zaharias, Knute Rockne, Jack Johnson or any contemporary golf, swimming, baseball, football or basketball hero. It doesn't have to be addressed to you. Its value lies in the fact that you possess some very personal thoughts of a sports immortal who is idolized by thousands.

We also hope that you realize the value and importance of **women** athletes. Their contribution to the whole sports picture is immeasurable. Their obvious ability in track, swimming, golf, tennis, basketball, gymnastics, ice skating, softball etc. makes them internationally recognized and highly collectible.

Prices

All available retail prices, offerings, estimates and realized reports have been used to arrive at the prices quoted in this book. We do not make them up. We have had discussions with many dealers as well as collectors in the field to discover what they have paid for rarer pieces and what they are asking for them. The prices in this guide, therefore, represent the figures we have calculated to be an average price for a fine item offered by an informed reputable dealer to an informed buyer.

If you were to buy an item from your favorite sports or autograph dealer you could expect to pay a retail price and the prices you see in this book are retail prices. On the other hand, if you were to sell to a dealer you could expect to receive less than the retail value of the current offering price. Dealers vary in their offers from 25% to 50%. As time goes by, however, and pieces become rarer or more sought after, the value could surpass its original price and would sell at a premium, therefore creating a profit for the owner. The reverse could also be true.

Please remember that the dealer has expenses you do not have, such as rent, advertising costs, catalogs, insurance, travel to sports shows, booth or table rental and those good old inevitable taxes. Keep in mind, also, that the piece he buys from you may stay in his inventory for a long time and, perhaps, never be sold. To offer you 50% or less, therefore, would be a fair markup considering the dealer's risk.

In estimating the prices that appear in this book we have taken great care. We must grant, however, that sales are frequently made in excess of these estimates as well as sales made at prices lower than those printed due to bargaining, trading or condition.

Some other factors that determine the price you may either pay or receive for an item are:

- Changes in popularity and/or lack of local interest.
- Oversupply
- Rarity (either temporary or permanent)
- Exceptional condition or importance
- Geographical differences in popularity

While there are thousands of names in this book, there is at least an equal number not represented. Why not? Well, this is neither an almanac nor an encyclopedia where you might find complete lists of all the names as well as the sports connected to them. This is not intended to be that type of book. We have given you, however, names of sports participants that have signed pieces which are, or have been, offered for sale. These items have been actually collected. An almanac or encyclopedia would have all the names in all the sports... but no prices! They are excellent reference books! Our book is a **TOOL** to be used as such! *All* names in *all* sports are not listed because their autographs are not recorded as having been bought or sold within the scope from which we gather our information. We do not, therefore, place a value on unrecorded items.

Since our last edition we have changed the format of the publication to make it easier for the collector to use. The names are now all in alphabetical order, not scattered throughout the book under a <u>specific</u> <u>sports</u> <u>category</u>. We have also included a Comment Column which may or may not include additional details. Although the pertinent Signed Ball/Puck column has a limited number of entries, we hope to enlarge it in time.

> **WARNING:** We have just been informed the signature of Mark McGwire is at this very moment being forged and sold in the city of St. Louis and elsewhere. Please be cautious and *KNOW YOUR DEALER!*

In order to upgrade our pricing and extensive database we are always grateful to receive your mail on this subject. (Mail to: Autograph House, P.O. Box 658, Enka, NC 28728)

We have made every effort to ensure the accuracy of the names, dates, prices and facsimiles contained in this book. The authors and publisher will in no event be liable for any loss of profit or any other damage, including but not limited to special, incidental, consequential, or other damages.

George and Helen Sanders during a visit to the offices of Alexander Books.

The Home Run Kings: Mark McGwire and Sammy Sosa

by Chuck McKeen

Not only baseball got turned topsy-turvy this year with the incredible home run feats of Mark McGwire and Sammy Sosa. Their exploits have also completely taken the autograph world by storm.

There is simply no precedent for what has happened in either baseball or autographs: 70 home runs by McGwire, 66 by Sosa tore apart record AND pocket books.

The question that keeps being asked is: what value do autographs of these two men have? The only logical answer is the old one that they are worth whatever someone will pay. That seems to be a lot.

Prices for signed photos of these guys apparently have reached as high as $250—maybe more. We're not talking about some special commemorative items here, just regular old signed photos.

Other signed items including bats, balls, and jerseys, are apparently selling for even greater prices.

Now, logic says that these prices will not continue. Of course, logic might be wrong. There are just so many variables at play here.

Both men have been very willing autograph signers over the years. Both seem likely to continue to sign autographs. These are good guys, who understand that their fame and their very considerable salaries come because fans like them and admire them.

However, for right now and perhaps for the foreseeable future, you can be pretty sure that any purchase of signed photos of Mark and Sammy will be in the three-figure range. So, maybe you can pick up a small signed photo of either at $100—maybe not, it might be $200 or more. During this 1998-99 off-season, with the luster still strong from the incredible showings, that $250 figure could look good.

It's all going to depend on the photo and the signature, and you can be sure a special photo is going to be in even higher demand, with higher cost.

McGwire was kind enough to sign some photos I took of him hitting HR #39 in 1987, after setting a new major league rookie home run record. The photos are only 4x6 inches in size, but he signed them both very nicely, adding the date and the home run number. It may well be that there are no others like these around ... so what is the value?

That's what we are all asking about things signed by these guys. Answers aren't coming easily, and may well be based on what the future holds for them on the playing field.

There are just so many variables, that this question might be answered every day on a case-by-case situation. And it could be a long time before that situation changes, and a norm is found.

Exciting, huh?

Above, portion of a photo signed by slugger Mark McGwire, who beat both Babe Ruth's and Roger Maris' single season home run records of 60 and 61 respectively with 70 of his own, followed closely by his friend Sammy Sosa, who turned in 66 of his own. Right, a ball autographed by the Babe himself!

George Sanders interviews Baseball Hall of Famer Ted Williams.

The
SANDERS
Price Guide to

SPORTS
AUTOGRAPHS

Section 2:

PRICES

NOTES: Read Chapter 7 for a full explanation of pricing!

NAME	Name of a person or group
CATEGORY	The sport in which the person is best known
+	Known to be deceased
SIG	Signature
SP	Signed photograph
BALL	Signed ball (or puck, etc.)
COMMENT	Additional information

Above are the headings for the sports autograph prices in this book. There are many abbreviations in the COMMENT columns. We have tried to keep these as standard as possible. Those collectors in specific sports will recognize those acronyms particular to their field of interest such as *NBA* for the National Basketball Association, *CHOF* for College Football Hall of Fame, etc. *HOF* is Hall of Fame and refers to that person's particular sport. We, alas, have neither the time nor space to define every abbreviation used but have opted instead to pack as much information as possible into these pages.

PLEASE NOTE: Where a person's name appears twice (once without prices) such as the very first entry (Hank Aaron), it is not a mistake. We are simply using this device to impart additional pricing information in the COMMENT column (i.e. we needed some extra room).

As to the "+" or "known to be deceased" column, we have added this information because it does affect pricing. However, we do not claim this column to be complete. Like life and death, it is a work in progress.

The BALL column refers to a signed "ball" in that specific sport. Obviously a baseball in Baseball, a hockey puck in Hockey, and so forth.

We know there may be omissions or mistakes in some of the entries, or additional information that could be added. We <u>encourage</u> you to inform us of such and will add that data to future editions. Please send it to us in writing via letter, fax, or e-mail. Address:

Sports Autograph Corrections
c/o Alexander Books
65 Macedonia Road
Alexander, NC 28701 USA   fax: 1-828-255-8719   e-mail: ralph@abooks.com

PRICES

NAME	CATEGORY	+	SIG	SP	BALL	Comment
Aaron, Hank	Baseball					P-S HOF $30,Grt.Mo.$35
Aaron, Hank	Baseball		10	45	50	HOF 1982. Gold Pl $25
Aaron, Tommie	Baseball		18	50		Debut 1962
Aaron, Tommy	Golf		5	25	35	
Aase, Don	Baseball		3	6		Debut 1977
Abbott, Glenn	Baseball		3	6		Debut 1973
Abbott, Jim	Baseball		8	18		Debut 1989
Abbott, Senda Berenson	Basketball	+	18	40		HOF 1984
Abdul-Aziz, Zaid	Basketball		3	6		played NBA 68-77
Abdul-Jabbar, Kareem	Basketball		12	25	165	HOF 1995. NBA 69-88
Abdul-Jabbar, Karim	Football		5	24	130	NFL
Abdul-Rahmad, Mahdi	Basketball		4	8		played NBA 64-73
Abdur-Rahim, Shareef	Basketball		6	28		
Abel, Clarence	Hockey	+	10	22		1973 US HOF
Abel, Joy	Bowling		5	10		1984 Women's IBC HOF
Abel, Sid	Hockey		5	12		1969 HOF fwd
Abell, Earl	Football	+	15	50		CHOF Colgate
Aber, Alf	Baseball		8	18		Debut 1950 Indians
Abernathie, Bill	Baseball		3	8		Debut 1952
Abernathy, Ted	Baseball		3	7		Debut 1955
Abernathy, Ted	Baseball		4	9		Debut 1942
Abernathy, Woody	Baseball		3	9		Debut 1946
Abernethy, Tom	Basketball		3	6		played NBA 76-80
Aberson, Cliff	Baseball		8	18		Debut 1947
Able, Frosty	Basketball		4	10		played NBA 55
Abner, Shawn	Baseball		3	8		Debut 1987
Abrahams, Harold	Olympic		30	75		100 Meters
Abramovic, John	Basketball		5	12		played NBA 46-47
Abramowicz, Dan	Football		3	7		NFL
Abrams, Cal	Baseball		4	8		Debut 1949 Brklyn. Dodg.
Abrams, George	Baseball		10	22		Debut 1923 Reds
Abrego, Johnny	Baseball		3	6		Debut 1985
Abreu, Joe	Baseball		4	8		Debut 1942
Accola, Paul	Skiing		5	18		Alpine. World Cup Champ
Acker, Jim	Baseball		3	6		Debut 1983
Acker, Tom	Baseball		3	7		Debut 1956
Ackerman, Buddy	Basketball		4	12		played NBA 53
Ackerman, Rosie	Track		8	16		

NAME	CATEGORY	+	SIG	SP	BALL	Comment
Ackley, Fritz	Baseball		3	5		Debut 1963
Acres, Mark	Basketball		3	6		played NBA 87-
Acton, Bud	Basketball		3	6		played NBA 67
Acton, Rick	Golf		5	20	20	
Adair, Jerry	Baseball		10	22		Debut 1958
Adair, Jimmy	Baseball		10	22		Debut 1931
Adair, Rona	Golf		75	195		
Adamle, Mike	Football		4	10		NFL
Adamle, Tony	Football		5	10		NFL
Adams, Ace	Baseball		4	10		Debut 1941
Adams, Alvan	Basketball		4	10		played NBA 75-87
Adams, Bob	Baseball		18	45		Debut 1925
Adams, Bob	Baseball		3	6		Debut 1977
Adams, Bobby	Baseball		4	8		Debut 1945
Adams, Buster	Baseball		4	12		Debut 1939
Adams, Charles "Babe"	Baseball		42	100		Debut 1906
Adams, Dick	Baseball		4	12		Debut 1947
Adams, Don	Basketball		3	6		played NBA 70-76
Adams, Doug	Baseball		4	8		Debut 1969
Adams, Dwight "Red"	Baseball		7			Debut 1946 Cubs
Adams, Earl "Sparky"	Baseball		18	45		Debut 1922 Cubs
Adams, Frank	Horse Racing		5	10		HOF 1970 jockey
Adams, George	Basketball		3	6		played NBA 72-74
Adams, Glenn	Baseball		3	6		Debut 1975
Adams, Herb	Baseball		4	8		Debut 1948
Adams, Jack	Hockey		15	35		1959 HOF fwd
Adams, Jimmy	Golf		25	65	50	
Adams, John	Golf		5	20	20	
Adams, John	Horse Racing		10	20		HOF 1965 jockey
Adams, Lynn	Golf		5	20	20	
Adams, Michael	Basketball		4	8		played NBA 85-
Adams, Mike	Baseball		3	6		Debut 1972
Adams, Ricky	Baseball		3	6		Debut 1982
Adams, Spencer	Baseball		18	35		Debut 1923
Adamson, Mike	Baseball		3	6		Debut 1967
Adcock, Joe	Baseball		5	10		Debut 1950 Reds
Adcock, Mitch	Golf		5	20	20	
Adderley, Herb	Football		8	20	95	1980 HOF DB
Addie, Bob	Sports Writer		3	8		
Addie, Pauline Betz	Tennis		20	50		HOF 1965
Addis, Bob	Baseball		5	10		Debut 1950 Braves
Addison, Rafael	Basketball		3	9		played NBA 86
Adduci, Jim	Baseball		3	9		Debut 1983
Adee, George	Tennis	+	30	55		HOF 1964
Adelman, Rick	Basketball		3	6		played NBA 68-74
Aderholt, Morrie	Baseball		35	75		Debut 1939
Adkins, Charles	Boxing		5	10		
Adkins, Derrick	Olympic		3	15		Gold Med. 400 meter H
Adkins, Dewey	Baseball		8	28		Debut 1942
Adkins, Dick	Baseball		20	55		Debut 1942
Adler, Kim	Bowling		2	8		Tourney winner
Adlesh, Dave	Baseball		3	9		Debut 1963
Afenir, Troy	Baseball		7	16		Debut 1987
Agajanian, Ben	Football		5	16		NFL Kicker
Agajanian, J. C.	Auto Racing	+	20	40		HOF 1992
Agase, Alex	Football		7	20		CHOF Purdue

NAME	CATEGORY	+	SIG	SP	BALL	Comment
Agassi, Andre	Tennis		12	55		
Agee, Tommie	Baseball		5	12		Debut 1962
Agganis, Harry	Baseball		225	500		Debut 1954
Agganis, Harry	Football	+	125	400		CHOF Boston U
Agler, Brian	Basketball		2	5		Women's ABL-Coach
Aguayo, Luis	Baseball		5	12		Debut 1980
Aguilera, Rick	Baseball		4	12		Debut 1985
Aguirre, Hank	Baseball		14	35		Debut 1955
Aguirre, Mark	Basketball		4	12		played NBA 81-
Ahern, Kathy	Golf		5	20	20	
Ahmann-Leighton, Chrissy	Olympic		3	14		Gold Med. Swimming
Aikens, Willie	Baseball		3	8		Debut 1977
Aikin, Henry	Basketball		4	10		played NBA 66-68
Aikman, Troy	Football		15	55	175	NFL
Aillet, Joe	Football		25	50		1989 CHOF coach
Ainge, Danny	Basketball		4	10	95	played NBA 81- Coach
Ainsmith, Eddie	Baseball		18	55		Debut 1913
Aitch, Matt	Basketball		4	12		played NBA 67
Aitcheson Jr, Joe	Horse Racing		12	30		HOF 1978 jockey
Aitchison, Raleigh	Baseball		20	65		Debut 1911 Brklyn.Dodg.
Aitken, Johnny	Auto Racing	+	30	60		
Aker, Jack	Baseball		3	9		Debut 1964
Akerfelds, Darrel	Baseball		3	9		Debut 1986
Akers, Bill	Baseball		25	65		Debut 1929
Aki-Bua, John	Olympic		15	35		Hurdles
Akins, Virgil	Boxing		20	40		
Alarie, Mark	Basketball		3	8		played NBA 86-
Alban, Dick	Football		6	14		NFL
Albers, Kristi	Golf		5	20	20	
Albert, Frank	Football		10	22		CHOF Stanford
Alberts, Butch	Baseball		3	9		Debut 1978
Albright, Jack	Baseball		8	20		Debut 1947
Albright, Tenley	Olympic		10	25		HOF 1983. Figure Skating
Albury, Vic	Baseball		3	10		Debut 1973
Albus, Jim	Golf		5	20	25	
Alcaraz, Luis	Baseball		8	20		Debut 1967
Alcindor, Lew (Abdul-Jabbar)	Basketball		300	750	800	HOF'95, played NBA 69-88
Alcock, John	Baseball		25	65		Debut 1914
Alcorn, Gary	Basketball		4	12		played NBA 60
Alcott, Amy	Golf		5	20	25	
Alderman, Grady	Football		4	10		NFL
Aldred, Norman	Broadcaster		3	9		Sports Broadcaster
Aldrete, Mike	Baseball		3	9		Debut 1986
Aldrich, Jay	Baseball		3	10		Debut 1987
Aldrich, Malcolm	Football	+	25	75		CHOF Yale
Aldridge, Vic	Baseball		30	68		Debut 1917
Aleksinas, Charles	Basketball		3	10		played NBA 84
Aleno, Chuck	Baseball		6	18		Debut 1941 Reds
Alesi, Jean	Auto Racing		4	8		
Alexander, Bill	Football		35	75		1951 CHOF coach
Alexander, Bob	Baseball		8	16		Debut 1955
Alexander, Buddy	Golf		5	20	20	
Alexander, Dale	Baseball		40	125		Debut 1929
Alexander, Doyle	Baseball		3	10		Debut 1971
Alexander, Fred	Tennis	+	20	70		HOF 1961
Alexander, Gary	Baseball		3	10		Debut 1975

NAME	CATEGORY	+	SIG	SP	BALL	Comment
Alexander, Grover	Baseball		650	1100	5500	HOF '38.B&W PC $1000
Alexander, Hugh	Baseball		15	65		Debut 1937 Indians
Alexander, John	Football	+	20	65		CHOF Syracuse
Alexander, Manny	Baseball		2	5		Debut 1992
Alexander, Matt	Baseball		3	10		Debut 1973
Alexander, Skip	Golf		10	30	35	
Alford, Stephen	Basketball		3	8		played NBA 87-89
Alfredsson, Helen	Golf		5	20	25	
Ali, Muhammad	Boxing		35	75		74-77/78 Hvy-Wt Champ
Alicea, Luis	Baseball		5	12		Debut 1988
Allan, Randy	Basketball		3	10		played NBA 88-
Allanson, Andy	Baseball		3	9		Debut 1986
Allard, Brian	Baseball		3	9		Debut 1979
Allem, Fulton	Golf		5	20	25	
Allen, Bernie	Baseball		7	15		Debut 1962 Twins
Allen, Bill	Basketball		6	15		played NBA 67
Allen, Bill	Bowling		7	22		1983 PBA HOF
Allen, Bob	Baseball		20	45		Debut 1937
Allen, Bob	Baseball		5	12		Debut 1961
Allen, Dick	Baseball		20	45		Debut 1963
Allen, Ethan	Baseball		20	57		Debut 1925 Reds
Allen, Forrest "Phog"	Basketball	+	30	75		HOF 1959. Coach
Allen, George	Football		20	55		NFL
Allen, H.T."Pug"	Baseball		12			1st FL-born in majors
Allen, Hank	Baseball		4	10		Debut 1966 Senators
Allen, Harold	Bowling	+	10	25		1966 ABC HOF
Allen, Jack	Golf		350	995		
Allen, Jamie	Baseball		4	10		Debut 1983
Allen, Kim	Baseball		4	10		Debut 1980
Allen, Lloyd	Baseball		4	10		Debut 1969 Angels
Allen, Lucius	Basketball		4	12		played NBA 69-78
Allen, Marcus	Football		12	50	95	Heisman Trophy USC '81
Allen, Mel	Broadcaster		12	40		1972 Ntl S&S HOF
Allen, Michael	Golf		5	20	25	
Allen, Neil	Baseball		3	9		Debut 1979
Allen, Newton	Baseball		75	175		Possible HOFer, Negro League
Allen, Paul	Basketball-NFL		7	25		2-sport owner
Allen, Richie	Baseball		4	15		Debut 1963 Phillies
Allen, Robert	Basketball		3	10		played NBA 68
Allen, Rod	Baseball		3	10		Debut 1983
Allen, Ron	Baseball		3	10		Debut 1972
Allen, Scott	Olympic		7	18		Figure skating
Allen, Terry	Boxing		8	18		
Allen, Terry	Football		5	18	75	NFL Redskin Rusher
Allen, Willie	Basketball		3	10		played NBA 71
Allenson, Gary	Baseball		3	10		Debut 1979
Alley, Gene	Baseball		3	10		Debut 1963 Pirates
Allie, Gair	Baseball		8	18		Debut 1954
Allietta, Bob	Baseball		4	12		Debut 1975
Allin, Bud	Golf		5	10	20	
Allison, Bob	Baseball		25	65		Debut 1958
Allison, Bobby	Auto Racing		8	22		HOF 1992, HOF 1993
Allison, Davey	Auto Racing		50	125		Killed in copter crash
Allison, Donnie	Auto Racing		6	15		
Allison, Glenn	Bowling		5	15		1979 ABC HOF
Allison, James A.	Auto Racing	+	22	45		

The Sanders Price Guide to Sports Autographs **3rd Edition**

NAME	CATEGORY	+	SIG	SP	BALL	Comment
Allison, Odis	Basketball		4	12		played NBA 71
Allison, Wilmer	Tennis	+	35	75		HOF 1963
Alliss, Percy	Golf		35	85		
Alliss, Peter	Golf		5	20	25	
Allred, Beau	Baseball		3	9		Debut 1989
Alluns, Darrel	Basketball		3	12		played NBA 83
Almada, Mel	Baseball		16	36		Debut 1933
Almon, Bill	Baseball		3	10		Debut 1974
Almquist, Oscar	Hockey	+	10	25		1973 US HOF coach
Alomar, Roberto	Baseball		7	45		Debut 1988
Alomar, Sandy	Baseball		8	20		Debut 1964 Braves
Alomar, Sandy Jr.	Baseball		7	25		Debut 1988
Alou, Felipe	Baseball		6	12		Debut 1958
Alou, Jesus	Baseball		6	15		Debut 1963
Alou, Matty	Baseball		5	12		Debut 1962
Alou, Moises	Baseball		5	20		Debut 1990
Alphand, Luc	Skiing		5	18		Alpine. World Cup Champ
Alston, Dell	Baseball		3	10		Debut 1977
Alston, Tom	Baseball		9	22		Debut 1954
Alston, Walter	Baseball					P-S HOF $1000.
Alston, Walter	Baseball		42	165	675	HOF 1983. Gold Pl. $100
Altman, George	Baseball		8	18		Debut 1959 Cubs
Altobelli, Joo	Baseball		6	12		Debut 1955
Alusik, George	Baseball		6	12		Debut 1958
Alvarado, Luis	Baseball		10	24		Debut 1968
Alvarez, Barry	Football		2	5		Wisconsin Coach
Alvarez, Orlando	Baseball		10	22		Debut 1973
Alvarez, Ossie	Baseball		10	22		Debut 1958
Alvis, Max	Baseball		5	12		Debut 1962 Indians
Alworth, Lance	Football		10	30	100	1978 HOF end/WB
Alyea, Brant	Baseball		3	10		Debut 1965
Alzado, Lyle	Football		50	130		NFL
Amalfitano, Joey	Baseball		3	10		Debut 1954
Amanar, Simona	Olympic		7	35		Gold Medal. Gymnastics
Amaro, Rubem	Baseball		4	12		Debut 1958
Ambers, Lou	Boxing		10	30		Lightweight Champ.
Ambler, Wayne A.	Baseball		8	25		Debut 1937
Ameche, Alan	Football	+	125	325	350	CHOF WI, Heisman '54
Amelung, Ed	Baseball		5	15		Debut 1984
Ames, Knowlton	Football	+	50	200		CHOF Princeton
Amling, Warren	Football		8	22		CHOF Ohio State
Ammaccapane, Danielle	Golf		5	20	25	
Amoros, Sandy	Baseball		40	90		Debut 1952
Anderegg, Robert	Basketball		5	15		played NBA 59
Andersen, Larry	Baseball		3	9		Debut 1975
Anderson, Alf	Baseball		15	35		Debut 1941 Pirates
Anderson, Allan	Baseball		3	9		Debut 1986
Anderson, Andrew	Basketball		3	15		played NBA 67-73
Anderson, Andy	Baseball		12	38		Debut 1948
Anderson, Bob	Baseball		5	15		Debut 1957
Anderson, Brady	Baseball		8	38		Debut 1983
Anderson, Bud	Baseball		3	10		Debut 1982
Anderson, Cadillac	Basketball		5	12		played NBA 87-
Anderson, Clifford	Basketball		3	15		played NBA 67-70
Anderson, Craig	Baseball		3	12		Debut 1961 Cards
Anderson, Dan	Basketball		3	15		played NBA 67-73

NAME	CATEGORY	+	SIG	SP	BALL	Comment
Anderson, Dave	Baseball		3	10		Debut 1983
Anderson, Dave	Writer		5	12		1990 Ntl S&S HOF
Anderson, Donny	Football		6	18		CHOF Texas Tech
Anderson, Dwain	Baseball		3	12		Debut 1971
Anderson, Dwight	Basketball		3	10		played NBA 82
Anderson, Ed	Football		30	65		1971 CHOF coach
Anderson, Ferrell "Andy"	Baseball		20	48		Debut 1947 Brklyn Dodg.
Anderson, Gary	Football		6	15		NFL
Anderson, Gil	Auto Racing	+	38	65		
Anderson, Glenn	Hockey		6	18		
Anderson, Harold "Andy"	Basketball	+	15	35		HOF 1984. Coach
Anderson, Harry	Baseball		15	50		Debut 1957
Anderson, Hunk	Football	+	35	90		CHOF Notre Dame
Anderson, J.J.	Basketball		3	12		played NBA 82-84
Anderson, Jamie	Golf		450	1200		
Anderson, Jerome	Basketball		4	12		played NBA 75-76
Anderson, Jessie	Golf		50	125		
Anderson, Jim	Baseball		3	10		Debut 1978
Anderson, Jim	Basketball		2	6		(Coach, O.S.U.)
Anderson, John	Baseball		7	18		Debut 1958
Anderson, John	Hockey		4	12		
Anderson, John G.	Golf		35	95		
Anderson, Keith	Basketball		3	15		played NBA 73
Anderson, Ken	Football		10	28		NFL
Anderson, Kenny	Basketball		4	22		NBA
Anderson, Kent	Baseball		3	10		Debut 1989
Anderson, Larry	Baseball		3	10		Debut 1974
Anderson, Michael	Basketball		3	10		played NBA 88-
Anderson, Mike	Baseball		3	10		Debut 1979
Anderson, Mike	Baseball		3	12		Debut 1971
Anderson, Miller	Olympic		4	12		Diving
Anderson, Morton	Football		5	15	85	NFL
Anderson, Neal	Football		6	15		NFL
Anderson, Ottis	Football		5	20	85	NFL
Anderson, Paul	Olympic		10	25		Weightlifting
Anderson, Peter	Golf		395	995		
Anderson, Richard	Basketball		3	12		played NBA 82-89
Anderson, Rick	Baseball		3	10		Debut 1979
Anderson, Rick	Baseball		3	10		Debut 1986
Anderson, Ron	Basketball		3	9		played NBA 84-88
Anderson, Scott	Baseball		3	10		Debut 1987
Anderson, Sparky	Baseball		7	15		Debut 1959
Anderson, Stephen	Olympic		12	25		110 meter hurdles
Anderson, Willie	Basketball		4	12		played NBA 88-
Anderson, Willie	Golf		495	950		PGA HOF 1975
Anderzunas, Walter	Basketball		7	18		played NBA 63
Andrade, Billy	Golf		5	25	25	
Andrade, Cisco	Boxing		8	16		
Andre the Giant	Wrestling		15	35		Professional Wrestler
Andreason, Larry	Olympic		3	10		Diving
Andres, Ernie	Baseball		10	24		Debut 1946
Andretti, John	Auto Racing		6	15		
Andretti, Mario	Auto Racing		12	35		HOF 1990
Andretti, Michael	Auto Racing		10	30		
Andrew, Kim	Baseball		3	12		Debut 1975
Andrews, "Nate"	Baseball		4	18		Debut 1937 Cards

NAME	CATEGORY	+	SIG	SP	BALL	Comment
Andrews, Donna	Golf		5	20	25	
Andrews, Fred	Baseball		3	10		Debut 1976
Andrews, Hub	Baseball		6	18		Debut 1947
Andrews, John	Baseball		3	10		Debut 1973
Andrews, Mike	Baseball		3	12		Debut 1966
Andrews, Rob	Baseball		3	12		Debut 1975
Andrews, Stan	Baseball		15	35		Debut 1939
Andrews, Theresa	Olympic		3	9		Swim/backstroke
Andrews, William	Football		6	14		NFL
Andreychuk, Dave	Hockey		5	15		
Andrie, George	Football		5	15		NFL
Andrus, Wm. "Bill"	Baseball		25	65		Debut 1931 Senators
Andujar, Joaquin	Baseball		3	12		Debut 1976
Ane, Charles	Football		8	22		NFL
Angelini, Norm	Baseball		3	12		Debut 1972 K.C.
Angle, Kurt	Olympic		2	5		Gold Med. Wrestling
Angott, Sammy	Boxing		20	40		Lightweight Contender
Angotti, Lou	Hockey		7	20		
Angsman, Elmer	Football		12	40		NFL
Anielak, Don	Basketball		7	22		played NBA 54
Ankenman, Pat	Baseball		20	65		Debut 1936
Anmstrong, Bruce	Football		3	7		NFL
Anschutz, Jody	Golf		5	20	20	
Anson, Cap	Baseball	+	1600	4000	17000	HOF 1939. BB S $17,000
Anthony, Bessie	Golf		75	195		
Anthony, Earl	Bowling		8	18		1986 ABC HOF, PBA
Anthony, Eric	Baseball		3	10		Debut 1989
Antolick, Joe	Baseball		10	25		Debut 1944
Antonelli, Johnny	Baseball		7	20		Debut 1948
Antonello, Bill	Baseball		8	20		Debut 1953 Dodgers
Antuofermo, Vito	Boxing		15	35		World Middle-wt.Champ.
Aoki, Isao	Golf		5	20	25	
Aouita, Saud	Track		12	28		
Aparicio, Luis	Baseball					P-S HOF $25, Grt.Mo.$25
Aparicio, Luis	Baseball		10	35	30	HOF 1984. Gold Pl $15
Aplund, Harold	Bowling	+	10	25		1978 ABC HOF
Apodaca, Bob	Baseball		3	10		Debut 1973
Apostoli, Fred	Boxing		45	95		Middle-wt. Champ.
Appier, Kevin	Baseball		3	6		Debut 1989
Appleby, Stuart	Golf		5	15	20	
Appling, Luke	Baseball			30		HOF 1964. Gold Pl $15
Appling, Luke	Baseball		15	40	80	P-S HOF $55,Grt.Mo.$70
Apps, Syl	Hockey		9	22		1961 HOF fwd
Aragon, Angel, Sr.	Baseball		40			Debut 1914 Yankees
Aragon, Art	Boxing		12	25		
Arbanas, Fred	Football		6	15		NFL
Arcaro, Eddie	Horse Racing		25	50		HOF 1958 jockey
Arcel, Ray	Boxing		20	40		Trainer 20 World Champs
Arceneaux, Stacey	Basketball		6	18		played NBA 61
Archer, George	Golf		10	25	25	
Archer, Jimmy	Baseball		45			Debut 1904 Pirates
Archibald, John	Bowling		7	15		1989 PBA HOF-Merit Serv.
Archibald, Nate	Basketball		8	25		HOF 1991
Archie, George	Baseball		25	65		Debut 1938 Tigers
Ard, Jimmie	Basketball		4	15		played NBA 70-78
Ardell, Dan	Baseball		4	12		Debut 1961

NAME	CATEGORY	+	SIG	SP	BALL	Comment
Arenas, Joe	Football		8	20		NFL
Arfons, Art	Auto Racing		12	30		HOF 1991
Arft, Hank	Baseball		7	14		Debut 1948 Browns
Arguello, Alexis	Boxing		18	38		Lightweight Champ.
Arizin, Paul	Basketball		8	22		HOF 1977
Arlauckas, Joe	Basketball		3	12		played NBA 87
Arledge, Roone	Broadcaster		7	15		
Arlin, Steve	Baseball		3	10		Debut 1969
Armas, Tony	Baseball		5	15		Debut 1976
Armbrister, Ed	Baseball		4	12		Debut 1973
Armour, Tommy	Golf		450	695		PGA HOF 1976
Armour, Tommy III	Golf		5	20	25	
Armstead, Ray	Olympic		3	12		Track relay
Armstrong, Curly	Basketball		10	45		played NBA 41-50
Armstrong, Debbie	Olympic		6	15		Alpine Skiing
Armstrong, George	Baseball		10	35		Debut 1946
Armstrong, George	Hockey		7	20		1975 HOF fwd
Armstrong, Henry	Boxing		125	225		Multi-Class Wld.Champ.
Armstrong, Mike	Football	+	22	50		1957 CHOF coach
Armstrong, Neill	Football		3	6		NFL
Armstrong, T. Robert	Basketball		5	25		played NBA 56
Armstrong, Tate	Basketball		3	15		played NBA 77-78
Armstrong, Wally	Golf		7	25		
Arnelle, H. Jesse	Basketball		5	25		played NBA 55
Arnett, Jon	Football		6	15		NFL
Arnette, Jay	Basketball		5	25		played NBA 63-65
Arnold, Chris	Baseball		3	12		Debut 1971
Arnovich, Morrie	Baseball		39	80		Debut 1936
Arnzen, Bob	Basketball		5	18		played NBA 69-73
Arrigo, Jerry	Baseball		5	20		Debut 1961
Arroyo, Luis	Baseball		6	20		Debut 1955
Arthurs, John	Basketball		3	20		played NBA 69
Asadoor, Randy	Baseball		3	10		Debut 1986
Asbell, Jim	Baseball		25	70		Debut 1938
Ashburn, Richie	Baseball				30	Gold Pl. $15
Ashburn, Richie	Baseball		10	18	25	HOF 1995. P-S $30
Ashby, Alan	Baseball		3	10		Debut 1973
Ashe, Arthur	Tennis		50	125		HOF 1985
Ashenfelter, Horace	Olympic		7	20		3,000 M Steeplechase
Asher, Barry	Bowling		3	12		1988 PBA HOF-Vet.
Ashford, Emmett	Baseball		85			1st black Maj.L. Ump.
Ashford, Evelyn	Olympic		10	30		100 M Dash
Ashford, Tucker	Baseball		3	10		Debut 1976
Ashley, Jean	Golf		5	25		
Ashton, Brent	Hockey		3	12		
Ashworth, Gerald	Olympic		4	9		400 meter relay
Askew, Vincent	Basketball		3	6		played NBA 87-
Asmonga, Don	Basketball		5	25		played NBA 53
Aspromonte, Bob	Baseball		4	12		Debut 1956
Aspromonte, Ken	Baseball		4	12		Debut 1957
Asselstine, Brian	Baseball		3	10		Debut 1976
Assenmacher, Paul	Baseball		3	10		Debut 1986
Astroth, Joe	Baseball		10	25		Debut 1945
Atchison, Ron	Football		4	10		1978 Canadian HOF
Atha, Richard	Basketball		5	25		played NBA 55-57
Atkins, Doug	Football		6	15	85	1982 HOF DL

NAME	CATEGORY	+	SIG	SP	BALL	Comment
Atkins, Jim "Buddy"	Baseball		4			Debut 1950 Red Sox
Atkins, William	Football		5	12		NFL
Atkinson, Juliette	Tennis	+	15	35		HOF 1974
Atkinson, Ted	Horse Racing		25	55		HOF 1957 jockey
Attell, Abe	Boxing		255	300		12x Fthr-Wt. Wld. Champ.
Attles, Al	Basketball		5	15		played NBA 60-70
Atwater, Steve	Football		5	15		NFL
Atwell, Toby	Baseball		8	22		Debut 1952
Atwood, Bill	Baseball		12	45		Debut 1936
Atwood, Susie	Olympic		3	8		Swim/backstroke
Aubrey, Emlyn	Golf		5	20	20	
Aubuchon, Chester	Basketball		10	45		played NBA 46
Auch, Susan	Speed Skating		4	14		Olympic Medal.
Auchterlonie, Harry	Golf		35	95		
Auchterlonie, William	Golf		375	1125		
Auer, Victor	Olympic		3	6		Rifle
Auerbach, Red	Basketball		15	35	150	HOF 1968 Coach
Auerbach, Rick	Baseball		4	10		Debut 1971
Augustile, Jerry	Baseball		6	20		Debut 1955
Augustine, Dave	Baseball		3	10		Debut 1973
Auker, Eldon	Baseball		15	45		Debut 1933 Tigers
Aulby, Mike	Bowling		2	8		PBA 1996. Player-of-Year
Aulds, Doyle	Baseball		8	20		Debut 1947
Ault, Doug	Baseball		3	12		Debut 1976
Austin, Bill	Football		12	35		NFL
Austin, Charles	Olympic		3	15		Gold Med. High Jump
Austin, Debbie	Golf		10	20	25	
Austin, H.W. "Bunny"	Tennis		18	40		
Austin, Jimmy	Baseball		65	138		Debut 1909
Austin, John	Basketball		4	18		played NBA 66-67
Austin, Ken	Basketball		4	18		played NBA 83
Austin, Mike	Olympic		4	8		Swim/relay
Austin, Tracy	Tennis		8	15		HOF 1992
Austin, Woody	Golf		5	20	20	
Autry, Darnell	Football		4	15		
Autry, Martin	Baseball		40	95		Debut 1924
Autry, W. A.	Baseball		50	150		Debut 1907
Averill, Earl	Baseball					HOF 1975. Gold Pl.$35
Averill, Earl	Baseball		25	80	475	P-S HOF $725
Averill, Earl Jr.	Baseball		4	15		Debut 1956
Averitt, Bird	Basketball		4	12		played NBA 73-77
Avery, Steve	Baseball		8	30		Debut 1990
Avila, Bobby	Baseball		8	20		Debut 1949
Awtrey, Dennis	Basketball		3	12		played NBA 70-81
Axthelm, Pete	Writer		7	16		
Aycock, Tommy	Golf		7	25	20	
Aylward, Dick	Baseball		12	25		Debut 1953
Ayton, Laurie	Golf		30	95		
Azcue, Joe	Baseball		15	40		Debut 1960
Azinger, Paul	Golf		15	25	30	
Azzi, Jennifer	Olympic		2	5		Gold Med. Basketball

NAME	CATEGORY	+	SIG	SP	BALL	Comment
Baba, Ali	Wrestling		10	20		Professional Wrestler
Babashoff, Jack	Olympic		4	10		Swim/100 free
Babashoff, Shirley	Olympic		7	20		Swimming
Babe, Loren	Baseball		20	48		Debut 1952
Babers, Alonzo	Olympic		5	15		400 Meters
Babich, Johnny	Baseball		15	55		Debut 1934 Brklyn Dodg.
Babilonia, Tai	Olympic		6	18		Figure Skating
Babitt, Shooty	Baseball		3	12		Debut 1981
Babka, Richard	Olympic		4	10		Discus
Babych,David	Hockey		3	12		
Babych,Wayne	Hockey		3	15		
Bach, John	Basketball		10	50		played NBA 48
Bach, Michael	Olympic		3	6		Rowing
Bachli, Douglas	Golf		14	40		
Bachman, Charlie	Football		20	45		1978 CHOF coach
Back, Leonard	Football	+	10	22		1971 Canadian HOF
Backhaus, Robin	Olympic		3	8		Swim/butterfly
Backman, Lester	Baseball		30			Debut 1909
Backman, Wally	Baseball		3	10		Debut 1980
Backstrom,Ralph	Hockey		7	18		
Backus, Billy	Boxing		12	25		
Bacon, Everett	Football		8	25		CHOF Wesleyan
Bacon, William	Basketball		4	15		played NBA 72
Badgro, Red	Football		10	35	110	1981 HOF end/WB
Baechtold, James	Basketball		10	40		played NBA 52-56
Baer, Gordy	Bowling		5	10		1987 ABC HOF
Baer, Max	Boxing		150	285		1934-35 H-Wt Champ
Baerga, Carlos	Baseball		8	35		Debut 1990
Baetz, Helen	Bowling		5	10		1977 Women's IBC HOF
Baeza, Braulia	Horse Racing		15	35		HOF 1976 jockey
Bagby, Jim Jr.	Baseball		12	30		Debut 1938 RedSox
Bagby, Jim Sr.	Baseball		138	325		Debut 1912. 31 wins 1920
Bagnell, Reds	Football		10	28		CHOF Pennsylvania
Bagwell, Bill	Baseball		15	35		Debut 1923
Bagwell, Jeff	Baseball		7	25		Debut 1991
Bahnsen, Stan	Baseball		3	10		Debut 1966
Bahr, Chris	Football		3	8		NFL
Bahr, Matt	Football		3	8		NFL
Bailes, Margaret	Olympic		3	10		Track relay
Bailey, Ace	Hockey		50	125		1975 HOF fwd
Bailey, Bill	Horse Racing		5	10		Jockey
Bailey, Bob	Baseball		4	10		Debut 1962
Bailey, Byron	Football		4	10		1975 Canadian HOF

NAME	CATEGORY	+	SIG	SP	BALL	Comment
Bailey, Carl	Basketball		3	15		played NBA 81
Bailey, Donovan	Olympic		8	40		Gold; 100 meters; WR
Bailey, Ed	Baseball		10	35		Debut 1953 Reds
Bailey, Gus	Basketball		4	15		played NBA 74-79
Bailey, Harold	Football	+	6	16		1965 Canadian HOF
Bailey, Harry L. "Bill"	Baseball		20	40		Debut 1911
Bailey, James	Basketball		3	12		played NBA 79-87
Bailey, Mark	Baseball		3	10		Debut 1984
Bailey, Thurl	Basketball		4	10		played NBA 83-
Bailor, Bob	Baseball		3	10		Debut 1975
Bain, Don	Hockey		85	195		1945 HOF fwd
Baines, Harold	Baseball		4	12		Debut 1980
Baird, Al	Baseball		35	95		Debut 1917
Baird, Butch	Golf		10	25	25	
Baiul, Oksana	Olympic		8	60		Olymp.Gold.Figure Skating
Baker, Bill	Baseball		10	50		Debut 1940
Baker, Buck	Auto Racing		10	50		legendary early stock cars
Baker, Buddy	Auto Racing		5	15		
Baker, Cannonball	Auto Racing	+	25	55		HOF 1989
Baker, Chuck	Baseball		3	6		Debut 1978
Baker, Del	Baseball		22	50		Debut 1914
Baker, Doug	Baseball		3	6		Debut 1984
Baker, Dusty	Baseball		4	9		Debut 1968
Baker, Floyd	Baseball		4	10		Debut 1943 Browns
Baker, Frank	Baseball		275	400	3650	HOF '55.B&W PC $1000
Baker, Frank	Baseball		3	12		Debut 1969
Baker, Frank	Baseball		3	12		Debut 1970
Baker, Frank	Bowling		5	10		1975 ABC HOF-Mer.Serv.
Baker, Gene	Baseball		8	18		Debut 1953
Baker, Helen	Bowling		5	10		1989 Women's IBC HOF
Baker, Hobey	Football	+	25	60		CHOF Princeton
Baker, Hobey	Hockey	+	60	125		1945 HOF fwd
Baker, Jack	Baseball		3	10		Debut 1976
Baker, Jesse	Baseball		35	82		Debut 1919
Baker, Jimmie	Basketball		3	10		played NBA 75
Baker, John	Football	+	30	65		CHOF Southern California
Baker, Kathy	Golf		9	20	25	
Baker, Laurie	Hockey		3	10		Women's Team USA
Baker, Lawrence, Sr.	Tennis	+	15	35		HOF 1975
Baker, Moon	Football	+	30	65		CHOF Northwestern
Baker, Norman	Basketball		10	50		played NBA 46
Baker, Sam	Football		4	12		NFL
Baker, Terry	Football		10	25		CHOF OSU. Heisman '62
Baker, Thane	Olympic		8	22		200 Meters
Baker, Tom	Bowling		2	8		Tourney winner
Baker, Vin	Basketball		5	25		Sonics
Baker-Finch, Ian	Golf		20	70	25	
Bakken, Jim	Football		4	12		NFL
Balas, Mitch "Mike"	Baseball		5			Debut 1938 Bost. Braves
Balaz, John	Baseball		3	12		Debut 1974
Balbach, Louis	Olympic		8	25		Diving
Balboni, Steve	Baseball		3	10		Debut 1981
Balcena, Bobby	Baseball		4	15		Debut 1955
Balding, Al	Golf		12	35	50	
Baldschun, Jack	Baseball		3	10		Debut 1961 Phillies
Baldwin, Billy	Baseball		3	10		Debut 1975

NAME	CATEGORY	+	SIG	SP	BALL	Comment
Baldwin, Frank	Baseball		6	18		Debut 1953
Baldwin, Reggie	Baseball		3	12		Debut 1978
Bales, Lee	Baseball		4	15		Debut 1966
Baley, John	Basketball		3	12		played NBA 82-
Balfour, Leslie	Golf		350	995		
Ball, Catie	Olympic		3	9		Swim/breaststroke
Ball, Jerry	Football		4	12		NFL
Ball, John, Jr.	Golf		450	1250		PGA HOF 1977
Ball, Neal	Baseball		40			1st unassist'd triple play
Ballard Jr, Del	Bowler		4	8		
Ballard, Greg	Basketball		4	12		played NBA 77-88
Ballard, Harold	Hockey		40	95		Hockey HOF 77
Ballard, Jimmy	Golf		5	20	20	
Ballesteros, Seve	Golf		15	60	50	
Ballin, Harold	Football	+	20	65		CHOF Princeton
Balon, Dave	Hockey		5	18		
Baltimore, Herk	Basketball		10	50		played NBA 46
Bamberger, George	Baseball		4	8		Debut 1951 Brewers
Bamberger, Hal	Baseball		4	8		Debut 1948
Banach, Ed	Olympic		3	9		Wrestling
Banach, Lou	Olympic		3	9		Wrestling
Banaszak, Pete	Football		5	12		NFL
Bancroft, Dave	Baseball		125	275	2900	HOF 1971.Gold Pl. $650
Bando, Chris	Baseball		3	10		Debut 1981
Bando, Sal	Baseball		4	12		Debut 1966 Brewers
Banducci, Bruno	Football		20	65		NFL
Banke, Paul	Boxing		15	32		Super Bantam-Wt.
Banker, Bill	Football	+	20	45		CHOF Tulane
Bankes, James	Baseball		5	15		1950, Negro League
Bankhead, Dan	Baseball		28	60		Debut 1947
Bankhead, Fred	Baseball		20	50		1936-48, Negro League
Bankhead, Garnett	Baseball		20	45		Debut 1947, Negro League
Bankhead, Joe	Baseball		15	35		Debut 1948, Negro League
Bankhead, Sam	Baseball		90	225		7x All Star, Negro League
Bankhead, Scott	Baseball		3	10		Debut 1986
Banks, Carl	Football		6	15		NFL
Banks, Ernie	Baseball					HOF 1977. Gold Pl. $12
Banks, Ernie	Baseball		15	30	40	P-S HOF $40, Grt.Mo $45
Banks, Eugene	Basketball		3	12		played NBA 81-86
Banks, George	Baseball		11	25		Debut 1962
Banks, Henry	Auto Racing		5	10		
Banks, Walter	Basketball		3	12		played NBA 70
Bankston, Bill	Baseball		45	95		Debut 1915
Bannerman, Murray	Hockey		4	15		
Bannister, Alan	Baseball		3	15		Debut 1974
Bannister, Floyd	Baseball		3	10		Debut 1977
Bannister, Kenneth	Basketball		3	12		played NBA 84-88
Banonis, Vince	Football		20	45		CHOF Univ. Detroit
Bantom, Michael	Basketball		3	8		played NBA 73-81
Baptiste, Kirk	Olympic		5	12		200 Meters
Barbary, Red	Baseball		8	25		Debut 1943
Barber, Bill	Hockey		9	18	15	1990 HOF fwd
Barber, Jerry	Golf		15	25	45	
Barber, John	Basketball		8	35		played NBA 56
Barber, Miller	Golf		5	20	30	
Barber, Steve	Baseball		3	10		Debut 1960 Orioles

NAME	CATEGORY	+	SIG	SP	BALL	Comment
Barber, Walter "Red"	Broadcaster		18	55		1973 Ntl S&S HOF
Barbieri, Jim	Baseball		3	12		Debut 1966
Barbuti, Ray	Olympic		18	50		400 meters
Barfield, Jesse	Baseball		5	12		Debut 1981
Barger-Wallach, Maud	Tennis		15	40		HOF 1958
Barker, Cliff	Basketball		8	40		played NBA 49-51
Barker, Len	Baseball		3	10		Debut 1975
Barker, Ray	Baseball		4	10		Debut 1960
Barker, Rolf	Baseball		2			
Barker, Sue	Tennis		5	15		
Barker, Thomas	Basketball		3	12		played NBA 76-78
Barkley, Charles	Basketball		10	35	150	played NBA 84-
Barkley, Iran	Boxing		10	22		
Barkley, Red	Baseball		12	45		Debut 1937
Barkman, Jane	Olympic		3	6		Swim/relay
Barksdale, Don	Basketball		8	40		played NBA 51-54
Barlick, Al	Baseball					HOF 1989. Gold Pl.$20
Barlick, Al	Baseball		10	25	42	P-S HOF $40, Grt.Mo.$25
Barlow, Thomas "Babe"	Basketball	+	20	65		HOF 1980
Barna, Babe	Baseball		20	45		Debut 1937
Barnard, Arthur	Olympic		4	10		110 M Hurdles
Barnes, Bad News	Basketball		7	18		played NBA 64-73
Barnes, Brian	Baseball		4	10		Debut 1990
Barnes, Brian	Golf		10	35	25	
Barnes, Bruce	Baseball		10	25		Debut 1953
Barnes, E.D. "Red"	Baseball		30			Senators 1927-31
Barnes, Everett "Eppie"	Baseball		40	90		Debut 1923 Pirates
Barnes, Harry	Basketball		5	15		played NBA 68
Barnes, Jesse	Baseball		142	170		Debut 1915
Barnes, Jim	Golf		165	450		PGA HOF 1989
Barnes, John F.	Baseball		35	80		Debut 1926
Barnes, Lee	Olympic		30	80		Pole Vault
Barnes, Lefty	Baseball		35			Debut 1924 ChiSox
Barnes, Lute	Baseball		3	12		Debut 1972 NY Giants
Barnes, Marvin	Basketball		5	15		played NBA 74-79
Barnes, Randy	Olympic		3	15		Gold Med; Shot Put
Barnes, Randy	Olympic		4	15		Shot Put
Barnes, Sam	Baseball		30	95		Debut 1921 Tigers
Barnes, Skeeter	Baseball		3	12		Debut 1983
Barnes, Stanley	Football	+	10	25		CHOF Southern Calif.
Barnes, Virgil	Baseball		65			Pitcher. 1923-24 Wld.Ser.
Barnett, Dick	Basketball		8	22		played NBA 59-73
Barnett, Gary	Football		2	5		College Coach of Year
Barnett, Jim	Basketball		3	10		played NBA 66-75
Barnett, Nate	Basketball		3	10		played NBA 75
Barney, Lem	Football		8	20	90	1992 HOF DB
Barney, Rex	Baseball		20	50		Debut 1943
Barnhart, Clyde	Baseball		30	90		Debut 1920 Pirates
Barnhart, Dan	Boxing		5	10		Boxing Mgr.
Barnhart, E.V. Barney	Baseball		30			Debut 1924 Browns
Barnhart, Vic	Baseball		10	35		Debut 1944
Barnhill, John	Basketball		6	30		played NBA 62-71
Barnhill, Norton	Basketball		3	15		played NBA 76
Barnhorst, Barney	Basketball		10	50		played NBA 49-53
Barnum, John	Golf		10	35	40	
Barnum, Leonard	Football		6	15		NFL

NAME	CATEGORY	+	SIG	SP	BALL	Comment
Barone, Dick	Baseball		6	20		Debut 1960
Barr, Beth	Olympic		4	8		Swim/relay
Barr, Dave	Golf		5	20	25	
Barr, John	Basketball		10	50		played NBA 46
Barr, Michael	Basketball		4	12		played NBA 72-76
Barr, Moe	Basketball		4	15		played NBA 70
Barr, Terry	Football		6	18		NFL
Barragan, Cuno	Baseball		8	25		Debut 1961
Barrasso, Tom	Hockey		5	30		
Barrera, Laz	Horse Racing		10	30		HOF 1979 trainer
Barrett, Bob	Baseball		35	95		Debut 1923
Barrett, Charles	Football	+	20	40		CHOF Cornell
Barrett, Charles "Red"	Baseball		15	55		Debut 1937
Barrett, Ernie	Basketball		10	45		played NBA 53-55
Barrett, Johnny	Baseball		25	65		Debut 1942
Barrett, Marty	Baseball		4	10		Debut 1982
Barrett, Michael	Basketball		4	15		played NBA 69-72
Barrett, Tina	Golf		5	25	25	
Barrett, Tom	Baseball		3	10		Debut 1988
Barrette, Leanne	Bowler		4	8		
Barrios, Jose	Baseball		5	15		Debut 1982
Barron, David	Baseball		40	85		Debut 1929
Barron, Herman	Golf		20	55		
Barrow, Ed	Baseball		200	460	3250	HOF '53. B&W PC $1850
Barrow, John	Football		5	10		1976 Canadian HOF
Barrowman, Mike	Olympic		3	10		Gold Medal. Swimming
Barry, Arthur	Golf		295	950		
Barry, Brent	Basketball		3	12		NBA
Barry, Jack	Baseball		150			SS for Connie Mack inf
Barry, Marty	Hockey		55	175		1965 HOF fwd
Barry, Rich	Baseball		3	12		Debut 1969
Barry, Rick	Basketball		8	26	125	HOF 1986
Barry, Sam	Basketball	+	22	45		HOF 1978 Coach
Bartell, Dick	Baseball		20	55		Debut 1927 Pirates
Bartels, Ed	Basketball		10	50		played NBA 49-50
Bartholome, Earl	Hockey		10	50		1977 US HOF
Bartirome, Tony	Baseball		6	14		Debut 1952
Bartkowski, Steve	Football		10	20		NFL
Bartley, Boyd	Baseball		6	14		Debut 1943
Bartley, William	Baseball		30	60		Debut 1903 Giants
Bartling, Irv	Baseball		35	70		Debut 1938
Bartolo, Sal	Boxing		15	35		
Bartoloile, Victor	Basketball		4	12		played NBA 71
Barton, Bob	Baseball		4	10		Debut 1965
Barton, Greg	Football		4	12		NFL
Barton, Greg	Olympic		3	12		Kayak
Barton, Pam	Golf		50	125		
Barton, Taylor	Football		5	20		Colorado QB
Barton, Vince	Baseball		35	95		Debut 1931
Bartosch, Dave	Baseball		6	18		Debut 1945
Barwegan, Dick	Football		7	17		NFL
Basgall, Monty	Baseball		8	18		Debut 1948 Pirates
Bashore, Walt	Baseball		22	65		Debut 1936
Basilio, Carmen	Boxing		15	40		Welter & Mid-Wt Champ
Basinski, Eddie	Baseball		4	12		Debut 1944 Brklyn Dodg.
Baskerville, Jerry	Basketball		3	10		played NBA 75

NAME	CATEGORY	+	SIG	SP	BALL	Comment
Basrak, Mike	Football		3	10		Duquesne
Bass, Dick	Football		6	15		NFL
Bass, Kevin	Baseball		4	10		Debut 1982
Bass, Randy	Baseball		4	10		Debut 1977
Bass, William	Baseball		55	125		Debut 1918
Bassett, Carroll	Horse Racing		15	40		HOF 1972 jockey
Bassett, Tim	Basketball		3	12		played NBA 73
Bassey, Hogan "Kid"	Boxing		18	38		
Bassham, Lanny	Olympic		5	12		Rifle
Bassler, Harry	Golf		10	36		
Bassler, Johnny	Baseball		55	125		Debut 1913
Baston, Bert	Football	+	25	65		CHOF Minnesota
Batchelder, Joseph E.	Baseball		30			Debut 1923 Braves
Bateman, John	Baseball		5	15		Debut 1963
Bates, Billy	Baseball		3	10		Debut 1989
Bates, Billy Ray	Basketball		4	12		played NBA 79-82
Bates, Charlie	Baseball		30	95		Debut 1927
Bates, Del	Baseball		3	10		Debut 1970
Bates, Hubert	Baseball		15	65		Debut 1939
Bates, Ray	Baseball		55	125		Debut 1913
Bathe, Bill	Baseball		3	12		Debut 1986
Bathgate, Andy	Hockey		8	18	15	1978 HOF fwd
Batiste, Kevin	Baseball		3	10		Debut 1989
Batstone, Harry	Football	+	12	25		1963 Canadian HOF
Battalino, Battling	Boxing		35	75		
Batten, George	Baseball		55	125		Debut 1912
Battey, Earl	Baseball		8	20		Debut 1955
Battle, John	Basketball		3	10		played NBA 85-
Battles, Cliff	Football		70	265		1968 HOF QB
Batton, David	Basketball		3	10		played NBA 82-83
Batts, Lloyd	Basketball		3	10		played NBA 74
Batts, Matt	Baseball		4	12		Debut 1947 RedSox
Bauer, Alice	Golf		5	25	35	
Bauer, Dave	Golf		5	20	25	
Bauer, Hank	Baseball		5	15		Debut 1948
Bauer, John	Skiing; Cross Country		2	6		U.S. Champion
Bauer, Marlene	Golf		10	30		
Bauer, Seth	Olympic		3	5		Rowing
Bauer, Sybil	Olympic		7	20		Swim/backstroke
Bauer, Bobby	Hockey		5	15		
Baugh, Laura	Golf		5	20	25	
Baugh, Sammy	Football		20	45	225	1963 HOF QB
Baughan, Maxie	Football		5	15		CHOF Georgia Tech
Baum, John	Basketball		3	15		played NBA 69-73
Baumann, Charles	Baseball		55	125		Debut 1911
Baumer, Jim	Baseball		5	15		Debut 1949
Baumgarten, Elmer	Bowling	+	10	20		1963 ABC HOF-Mer.Serv.
Baumgartner, Bruce	Olympic		3	6		Wrestling
Baumgartner, John	Baseball		4	8		Debut 1953
Baumholtz, Frank	Baseball		12	25		Debut 1947 Reds
Baun, Bob	Hockey		6	15		
Bausch, James	Football	+	18	40		CHOF Kansas
Bausch, Jim	Track		6	15		
Bavaro, Mark	Football		3	12	85	NFL
Bavasi, Buzzie	Baseball		10	25		Dodger Exec.
Baxes, Jim	Baseball		8	18		Debut 1959

NAME	CATEGORY	+	SIG	SP	BALL	Comment
Baxes, Mike	Baseball		6	12		Debut 1956
Baxter, Rex	Golf		5	20	25	
Bayer, George	Golf		10	30	35	
Bayless, William	Olympic		4	10		Yachting
Baylor, Don	Baseball		5	12		Debut 1970
Baylor, Elgin	Basketball		10	25	125	HOF 1976
Bayne, Howard	Basketball		3	12		played NBA 67
Beach, Bill	Bowling		5	10		1991 ABC HOF
Beach, Ed	Basketball		10	45		played NBA 53
Beagle, Ron	Football		7	15		CHOF Navy
Beall, Bob	Baseball		3	10		Debut 1975
Beamon, Bob	Olympic		20	40		Long Jump
Beamon, Charlie Jr.	Baseball		3	16		Debut 1978
Bean, Andy	Golf		5	20	25	
Bean, Billy	Baseball		3	10		Debut 1987
Beane, Billy	Baseball		3	10		Debut 1984
Beard, Albert	Basketball		3	12		played NBA 67
Beard, Amanda	Olympic		3	10		Gold Med. Swimming
Beard, Butch	Basketball		3	12		played NBA 69-73
Beard, Frank	Golf		5	25	25	
Beard, Ralph	Baseball		10			Cardinals 1954
Beard, Ralph	Basketball		15	40		played NBA 49-50
Beard, Ted	Baseball		8	22		Debut 1948 Pirates
Bearden, Gene	Baseball		8	20		Debut 1947
Bearnarth, Larry	Baseball		5			Debut 1963 Mets
Beasley, Charles	Basketball		3	15		played NBA 67-70
Beasley, John	Basketball		3	12		played NBA 67-73
Beasley, John	Football		3	12		NFL
Beasley, Lew	Baseball		3	10		Debut 1977
Beattie, Bob	Olympic		3	6		Olympic Ski Coach
Beaty, Zelmo	Basketball		7	18		played NBA 62-74
Beauchamp, Jim	Baseball		4	12		Debut 1963 Cards
Beaumont, Ginger	Baseball		72	150		Debut 1899
Beaupre, Don	Hockey		5	15		
Beaver, Joe	Rodeo		3	12		All-around cowboy
Beazley, Johnny	Baseball		3			Debut 1941 Cards
Beban, Gary	Football		6	22		CHOF UCLA.Heisman '67
Bechett, John	Football	+	15	40		CHOF Oregon
Beck, Byron	Basketball		3	12		played NBA 67-76
Beck, Chip	Golf		5	25	25	
Beck, Clyde	Baseball		20	55		Debut 1926
Beck, Ernest	Basketball		10	40		played NBA 53
Beck, Fred	Baseball		95			Home run leader 1910
Beck, Volker	Olympic		8	18		Hurdles
Beck, Walter "Boom Boom"	Baseball		28	85		Debut 1924 Browns
Beck, Zinn	Baseball		40	100		Debut 1913
Beckenbauer, Franz	Soccer		7	15		
Becker, Beck	Basketball		3	12		played NBA 67-72
Becker, Boris	Tennis		12	30		
Becker, Elizabeth	Olympic		10	24		Diving
Becker, Heinz	Baseball		8	22		Debut 1943
Becker, Joe	Baseball		16	40		Debut 1936 Indians
Becker, Moe	Basketball		10	50		played NBA 45
Beckert, Glenn	Baseball		4	15		Debut 1965
Beckley, Jacob	Baseball		2200	4200	4500	HOF 1971
Beckman, John	Basketball	+	18	38		HOF 1972

NAME	CATEGORY	+	SIG	SP	BALL	Comment
Bedell, Howie	Baseball		4	16		Debut 1962
Bedell, Robert	Basketball		3	12		played NBA 67-70
Bedford, Gene	Baseball		50	125		Debut 1925
Bedford, William	Basketball		3	15		played NBA 86-
Bednarik, Chuck	Football		6	20	100	1967 HOF OL
Bedwell, H. Guy	Horse Racing		30	65		HOF 1971 trainer
Bee, Clair F.	Basketball	+	35	75		HOF 1967-Contributor
Beecher, Jimmy	Baseball		4			
Beeler, Jodie	Baseball		10	22		Debut 1944
Beenders, Hank	Basketball		10	50		played NBA 46-48
Beggs, Joe	Baseball		30	80		Debut 1938 Yankees
Behagen, Ron	Basketball		3	15		played NBA 73-79
Behan, Lillian	Golf		5	20	25	
Behm, Donald	Olympic		3	5		Wrestling
Behm, Forrest	Football		8	22		CHOF Nebraska
Behnke, Elmer	Basketball		15	50		played NBA 51
Behr, Karl	Tennis	+	15	40		HOF 1969
Bejma, Ollie	Baseball		15	75		Debut 1934
Belanger, Frenchy	Boxing		20	45		
Belanger, Mark	Baseball		4	10		Debut 1965
Belardi, Wayne	Baseball		4	10		Debut 1950
Belinsky, Bo	Baseball		6	18		Debut 1962
Beliveau, Jean	Hockey		6	18	20	1972 HOF fwd
Bell, Art	Golf		5	20	25	
Bell, Beau	Baseball		45	100		Debut 1935
Bell, Bert	Football	+	200	450		1963 HOF contributor
Bell, Bobby	Football		6	20	85	1983 HOF LB
Bell, Brad	Golf		5	20	25	
Bell, Buddy	Baseball		4	10		Debut 1972
Bell, Dennis	Basketball		3	16		played NBA 73-75
Bell, Earl	Olympic		10	28		Pole Vault
Bell, Eddie	Football		4	15		NFL
Bell, Fern	Baseball		18	60		Debut 1939
Bell, Gary	Baseball		3	10		Debut 1958
Bell, George	Baseball		5	14	35	Debut 1981
Bell, Greg	Football		3	10		NFL
Bell, Greg	Olympic		5	14		Long Jump
Bell, Gus	Baseball		18	45		Debut 1950
Bell, James "Cool Papa"	Baseball					P-S HOF $85, Grt.Mo.$90
Bell, James "Cool Papa"	Baseball		20	65	185	HOF 1974. Gold Pl. $35
Bell, Jay	Baseball		4	10		Debut 1986
Bell, Juan	Baseball		3	10		Debut 1989
Bell, Kevin	Baseball		10	10		Debut 1976
Bell, Les	Baseball		25	75		Debut 1923 Cards
Bell, Matty	Football	+	40	100		1955 CHOF coach
Bell, Peggy Kirk	Golf		10	35	35	
Bell, Ricky	Football		40	125		NFL
Bell, Terry	Baseball		3	10		Debut 1986
Bell, Whitey	Basketball		6	20		played NBA 59-60
Bella, Zeke	Baseball		4	16		Debut 1957
Bellamy, Walt	Basketball		7	20		HOF 1993. NBA 61-74
Belle, Albert	Baseball		10	42		Debut 1989
Belliard, Rafael	Baseball		4	10		Debut 1982
Bellington, Norman	Olympic		3	6		Kayak
Bellino, Joe	Football		18	36		CHOF Navy. Heisman '60
Bellisimo, Lou	Bowling	+	8	18		1986 ABC HOF-Mer.Serv.

NAME	CATEGORY	+	SIG	SP	BALL	Comment
Belloir, Bob	Baseball		3	10		Debut 1975
Bellows,Brian	Hockey		5	16		
Belote, Melissa	Olympic		6	12		Swim/100 M Back
Belousouva, Ludmilla	Olympic		15	35		Figure Skating
Below, Marty	Football		12	35		CHOF Wisconsin
Beman, Deane	Golf		5	20	30	
Bembridge, Maurice	Golf		10	35	35	
Bemoras, Irving	Basketball		12	40		played NBA 53-56
Benbow, Leon	Basketball		6	12		played NBA 74-75
Benbrook, Al	Football	+	25	50		CHOF Michigan
Bench, Johnny	Baseball					P-S HOF $50, Grt.Mo.$45
Bench, Johnny	Baseball		15	30	35	HOF 1989. Gold Pl.$28
Bender, Chief	Baseball		362	600	2975	HOF '53. B&W PC $1250
Benedict, Bruce	Baseball		4	10		Debut 1978
Benedict, Clint	Hockey		75	195		1965 HOF goal
Benes, Joe	Baseball		30	75		Debut 1931
Benge, Ray	Baseball		40	95		Debut 1925 Phillies
Bengough, Benny	Baseball		70	140		Debut 1923
Bengston, Phil	Football		4	10		NFL Packers Coach
Benitez, Wilfredo	Boxing		15	35		Jr. Middle-Wt Champ
Benjamin, Benoit	Basketball		4	10		played NBA 85-
Benjamin, Joel	Chess		8	25		U.S. Champion
Benjamin, Mike	Baseball		3	10		Debut 1989
Benjamin, Stan	Baseball		12	45		Debut 1939
Benkovic, Frank	Bowling		6	15		1958 ABC HOF
Benneet, Melvin	Basketball		3	10		played NBA 75-81
Bennett, Brooke	Olympic		3	12		Gold Med. Swimming
Bennett, Bruce	Olympic		10	20		Track-Field. "Tarzan"
Bennett, Cornelius	Football		5	18	85	NFL
Bennett, Edgar	Football		5	15	70	NFL
Bennett, Joe	Baseball		35	75		Debut 1923
Bennett, John	Olympic		3	10		Long Jump
Bennett, Spider	Basketball		5	15		played NBA 68
Benoit, Joan	Olympic		8	16		Marathon
Bensinger, Bob	Bowling	+	12	22		1969 ABC HOF-Mer.Serv.
Benson, Kent	Basketball		3	10		played NBA 77-87
Benson, Vern	Baseball		12	55		Debut 1943 Cards
Bentley, Doug	Hockey		60	180		1964 HOF fwd
Bentley, Jack	Baseball		60	125		Debut 1913
Bentley, Max	Hockey		60	150		1966 HOF fwd
Benton, Butch	Baseball		3	10		Debut 1978
Benton, James	Football		10	35		NFL
Benton, Stan	Baseball		35	95		Debut 1922
Bentsen, William	Olympic		3	6		Yachting
Benvenuti, Nino	Boxing		30	60		Middle-wt Champ.
Benz, Amy	Golf		5	20	25	
Benzinger, Todd	Baseball		4	10		Debut 1987
Berardi, Joe	Bowling		5	12		1990 PBA HOF
Berardino, Johnny	Baseball		15	38		Debut 1939 Browns
Berasategui, Alberto	Tennis		4	15		Top 25
Berberet, Lou	Baseball		8	15		Debut 1954
Berbick, Trevor	Boxing		15	35		Hvy-Wt. Champ. 1986
Berce, Eugene	Basketball		10	50		played NBA 48-49
Berenson,Red	Hockey		7	16		
Berezhnaya,E.&Sikharulidze A	Olympic		10	38		Medalists.Pairs fig.skating
Berg, Moe	Baseball		400	950		Debut 1923

NAME	CATEGORY	+	SIG	SP	BALL	Comment
Berg, Patty	Golf		10	35	35	PGA, LPGA HOF '74,'51
Bergamo, Augie	Baseball		35	75		Debut 1944
Berganio, David, Jr	Golf		5	25	25	
Bergen, Gary	Basketball		10	35		played NBA 56
Berger, Boze	Baseball		12	25		Debut 1932
Berger, Gerhard	Auto Racing		4	10		
Berger, Johnny	Baseball		40	85		Debut 1922
Berger, Wally	Baseball		19	52		Debut 1930 Bost. Braves
Berger, Winfred	Bowling		5	12		1976 Women's IBC HOF
Bergere, Cliff	Auto Racing	+	55	115		
Bergh, Larry	Basketball		3	15		played NBA 69
Bergmann, Dave	Baseball		3	10		Debut 1975
Bergmann, Glenn	Baseball		4			
Bergoust, Eric	Skiing		3	10		Freestyle, Olympic Gold
Berkoff, David	Olympic		3	6		Swim/relay
Berland, Robert	Olympic		3	6		Judo
Berlenbach, Paul	Boxing		15	30		Lt.Hvywt Champ.
Berlinger, Barney	Track		6	14		
Berman, Bob	Baseball		50	125		Debut 1918 Senators
Berman, Chris	Broadcaster		3	6		Sports
Bernhardt, Juan	Baseball		4	15		Debut 1976
Berning, Suzie Maxwell	Golf		5	25	30	
Bero, Johnny	Baseball		10	22		Debut 1948
Berra, Dale	Baseball		4	10		Debut 1977
Berra, Yogi	Baseball					P-S HOF $35, Grt.Mo.$25
Berra, Yogi	Baseball		10	25	35	HOF 1972. Gold Pl. $20
Berres, Ray	Baseball		35	75		Debut 1934 Dodgers
Berry, Charlie	Baseball		75	150		Debut. 1925
Berry, Charlie	Football	+	35	90		CHOF Lafayette
Berry, Claude	Baseball		75	195		Debut 1904
Berry, Cornelius	Baseball		8	30		Debut 1948
Berry, Joe	Baseball		50	125		Debut 1921
Berry, Ken	Baseball		4	10		Debut 1962
Berry, Raymond	Football		10	20	90	1973 HOF end/WB
Berry, Rick	Basketball		6	12		played NBA 88
Berry, Walter	Basketball		3	10		played NBA 86-89
Berryhill, Damon	Baseball		5	12		Debut 1978
Bertell, Dick	Baseball		3	10		Debut 1960
Bertelli, Angelo	Football		10	25		CHOF ND.Heisman '43
Berteotti, Missie	Golf		5	20	25	
Bertoia, Reno	Baseball		4	12		Debut 1953
Bertrand, John	Olympic		3	6		Yachting
Berwanger, Jay	Football		15	30		CHOF, Heisman 1935
Beshore, Delmer	Basketball		3	10		played NBA 78-83
Besselink, Al	Golf		30	60	35	
Bessent, Don	Baseball		16	34		Debut 1955
Bessone, Peter	Hockey		5	15		1978 US HOF
Best, Greg	Olympic		5	10		Equestrian
Beswick, Jim	Baseball		3	10		Debut 1978
Betcher, Frank	Baseball		65	175		Debut 1910
Bethea, Bill	Baseball		4	12		Debut 1964
Bettancourt, Larry	Baseball		30	85		Debut 1928
Bettencourt, L.	Football	+	20	40		CHOF St. Mary's
Bettenhausen, Gary	Auto Racing		8	20		
Bettenhausen, Tony	Auto Racing	+	35	80		HOF 1991, HOF 1997
Bettina, Melio	Boxing		65	150		Light Hvy-Wt. Champ.

NAME	CATEGORY	+	SIG	SP	BALL	Comment
Bettis, Jerome	Football		6	20	125	NFL
Betts, Huck	Baseball		40	125		Debut 1920 Phillies
Betz (Addie), Pauline	Tennis		20	50		HOF 1965
Betz Addie, Pauline	Golf		10	35	45	
Beurlein, Steve	Football		4	10		NFL
Bevacqua, Kurt	Baseball		3	10		Debut 1971
Bevan, Hal	Baseball		15	35		Debut 1952
Bevens, Bill	Baseball		25	65		Debut 1941 Yankees
Beverly, Randy	Football		3	10		NFL
Beyer, Udo	Olympic		8	25		Shot Put
Bezdek, Hugo	Football		15	45		1954 CHOF coach
Biagetto, Leo	Golf		10	30	35	
Biakabutuka, Tim	Football		5	15	100	NFL
Bialosuknia, Wesley	Basketball		3	15		played NBA 67
Biancalana, Buddy	Baseball		3	10		Debut 1982
Bianchi, Al	Basketball		4	16		played NBA 56-65
Bianco, Tommy	Baseball		3	10		Debut 1975
Biasatti, Henry	Basketball		10	50		played NBA 46
Biasetti, Hank	Baseball		6	12		Debut 1949
Bibby, Henry	Basketball		3	10		played NBA 72-83
Bibby, Jim	Baseball		5	18		Debut 1972
Bible, Dana X.	Football	+	90	175		1951 CHOF coach
Bichette, Dante	Baseball		8	30		Debut 1988
Bickerstaff, Bernie	Basketball		5	10		NBA Coach
Bickford, Vern	Baseball		35	75		Debut 1948
Bidwill, Charles	Football	+	400	850		1967 HOF contributor
Biedenbach, Edward	Basketball		3	12		played NBA 68
Bielke, Don	Basketball		4	35		played NBA 55
Biellmann, Denise	Figure Skating		3	22		World Champion
Bielski, Dick	Football		6	18		NFL
Bierman, Bernie	Football	+	60	150		1955 CHOF coach
Bies, Don	Golf		5	20	25	
Biffle, Jerome	Olympic		4	14		Long Jump
Bigelow, Robert	Basketball		3	12		played NBA 75-78
Bigelow, Tom	Auto Racing		10	25		
Biggio, Craig	Baseball		5	30		Debut 1988
Biggs, Verlon	Football		3	12		NFL
Bignotti, George	Auto Racing		15	45		HOF 1993
Biitner, Larry	Baseball		3	12		Debut 1970
Bilardello, Dann	Baseball		3	10		Debut 1983
Bileck, Pam	Olympic		3	6		Gymnastics
Biletnikoff, Fred	Football		10	20	100	1988 HOF end/WB
Bilko, Steve	Baseball		30	90		Debut 1949
Billick, George	Bowling		5	12		1982 ABC HOF
Billingham, Robert	Olympic		3	6		Yachting
Billings, Dick	Baseball		3	12		Debut 1968 Senators
Billings, Haskell	Baseball		7	28		Debut 1927 Detroit
Billings, Josh	Baseball		50	125		Debut 1913
Billingy, Big Train	Basketball		6	18		played NBA 71
Bilozerchev, Dmitri	Olympic		7	28		Olymp.Gold.Gymnastics
Bing, Dave	Basketball		5	18		HOF 1989-90
Bingaman, Les	Football		75	225		NFL
Binion, Joe	Basketball		3	10		played NBA 86
Binks, George "Bingo"	Baseball		6	22		Debut 1944 Senators
Bionda, Jack	Lacross		5	10		
Biondi, Matt	Olympic		5	18		Swimming,Olymp. Gold

NAME	CATEGORY	+	SIG	SP	BALL	Comment
Biras, Steve	Baseball		28	65		Debut 1944
Bird, Jerry	Basketball		5	35		played NBA 58.
Bird, Larry	Basketball		15	50		HOF. NBA 79-91
Birdsong, Otis	Basketball		5	15		played NBA 77-83
Birrer, Werner J. "Babe"	Baseball		4			Debut 1955 Tigers
Bisher, Furman	Writer		5	12		1989 Ntl S&S HOF
Bishop, Bill	Football		5	10		NFL
Bishop, Don	Football		7	16		NFL
Bishop, Gale	Basketball		10	50		played NBA 48
Bishop, Georgianna M	Golf		65	175		
Bishop, Lisa	Bowling		2	8		Tourney winner
Bishop, Max	Baseball		38	90		Debut 1924
Bishop, Mike	Baseball		3	10		Debut 1983
Bishop, Ted	Golf		35	95		
Bivins, Jimmy	Boxing		5	10		Hvywt. Contender
Bjorkman, George	Baseball		3	10		Debut 1983
Bjurstedt (Mallory), Molla	Tennis		12	38		HOF 1958
Blab, Uwe	Basketball		4	10		played NBA 85-
Black, Dave	Golf		10	30	35	
Black, Hawk	Basketball		10	50		played NBA 47-51
Black, Joe	Baseball		5	14		Debut 1952
Black, John L.	Golf		15	40		
Black, Larry	Olympic		5	10		200 Meters
Black, Norman	Basketball		3	6		played NBA 80
Black, Ronnie	Golf		5	20	25	
Black, Thomas	Basketball		3	12		played NBA 70
Blackaby, Ethan	Baseball		3	12		Debut 1962
Blackbum, Woody	Golf		5	20	25	
Blackerby, George	Baseball		12	55		Debut 1928
Blackman, Bob	Football		6	15		1987 CHOF coach
Blackman, Rolando	Basketball		5	15		played NBA 81-
Blackmar, Phil	Golf		5	20	25	
Blackwelder, Myra	Golf		5	20	25	
Blackwell, Cory	Basketball		3	10		played NBA 84
Blackwell, Ewell	Baseball		15	35		Debut 1942 Reds
Blackwell, Nathaniel	Basketball		3	16		played NBA 87
Blackwell, Tim	Baseball		3	10		Debut 1974
Blackwood, Glenn	Football		5	12		NFL
Blackwood, Lyle	Football		5	12		NFL
Blades, Benny	Football		3	15		NFL
Blades, Brian	Football		4	18		NFL
Blades, Ray	Baseball		45	90		Debut 1922
Bladt, Rick	Baseball		3	12		Debut 1969
Blaik, Earl	Football	+	40	125		1965 CHOF coach
Blair, Bonnie	Olympic		10	32		Speed Skating. Gold Med.
Blair, Buddy	Baseball		4	10		Debut 1942
Blair, Paul	Baseball		4	10		Debut 1964 Orioles
Blake, Bob	Hockey		5	15		1985 US HOF
Blake, Jay Don	Golf		5	25	25	
Blake, Jeff	Football		5	15	95	NFL
Blake, Toe	Hockey		40	85		1966 HOF fwd
Blalock, Jane	Golf		5	20	25	
Blancas, Homero	Golf		12	25	25	
Blanchard, Felix "Doc"	Football		10	20		CHOF Army. Heisman '45
Blanchard, Johnny	Baseball		4	15		Debut 1955
Blanck, Dan	Hammer Throw		3	10		Midwest Record

NAME	CATEGORY	+	SIG	SP	BALL	Comment
Blanck, Dennis	Auto Sports		3	10		Demolition Derby
Blanco, Damaso	Baseball		6	15		Debut 1972
Blanco, Ossie	Baseball		5	15		Debut 1970
Bland, John	Golf		5	20	25	
Blanda, George	Football		10	25	100	1981 HOF QB
Blaney, George	Basketball		3	9		played NBA 61
Blankenship, Lance	Baseball		3	10		Debut 1988
Blankers-Koen, Fannie	Olympic		65	125		Track. Gold Med.HOF '82
Blanks, Larvell	Baseball		3	10		Debut 1972
Blasingame, Don	Baseball		4	12		Debut 1955
Blass, Steve	Baseball		6	15		Debut 1965
Blatnik, Jeff	Olympic		6	12		Wrestling
Blatnik, Johnny	Baseball		15	45		Debut 1948
Blattner, Buddy	Baseball		10	40		Debut 1942 Cards
Blauser, Jeff	Baseball		6	20		Debut 1987
Blaylock, Marv	Baseball		4	15		Debut 1950
Blears, Lord	Pro Wrestling		35	75		
Bledsoe, Drew	Football		8	48	150	NFL QB
Blefary, Curt	Baseball		4	12		Debut 1965
Bleibtrey, Ethelda	Olympic		10	25		Swim/100 M free
Bleier, Rocky	Football		5	15		NFL
Blemker, Ray	Baseball		3			Debut 1960 K.C.
Blessitt, Ike	Baseball		3	10		Debut 1972
Blevins, Leon	Basketball		10	50		played NBA 50
Blin, Jurgen	Boxing		8	20		
Block, John	Basketball		4	15		played NBA 66-75
Block, Seymour	Baseball		5	30		Debut 1942
Blocker, Chris	Golf		10	30	40	
Blocker, Terry	Baseball		3	10		Debut 1985
Blomberg, Ron	Baseball		3	10		Debut 1969
Blomquist, Ralph	Golf		10	10	40	
Blood, Ernest "Prof"	Basketball	+	30	85		HOF 1960 Coach
Bloodworth, Jimmy	Baseball		20	45		Debut 1937 Senators
Bloom, Mike	Basketball		10	50		played NBA 47-48
Bloomfield, Clyde	Baseball		3	12		Debut 1963
Blouin, Jimmy	Bowling	+	12	38		1953 ABC HOF
Blount, Mel	Football		6	18	85	1989 HOF DB
Blowers, Mike	Baseball		3	12		Debut 1989
Blozis, Al	Football	+	15	45		CHOF Georgetown
Blue, Vida	Baseball		5	15		Debut 1969
Bluege, Ossie	Baseball		30	85		Debut 1922 Senators
Bluege, Otto	Baseball		25	65		Debut 1932
Blum, Walter	Horse Racing		20	45		HOF 1987 jockey
Blume, Ray	Basketball		3	12		played NBA 81
Bluth, Ray	Bowling		7	20		1973 ABC, '75 PBA HOF
Blyleven, Bert	Baseball		4	12	22	Debut 1970
Boak, Chet	Baseball		8	20		Debut 1960
Boatwright, P.J. Jr	Golf		25	60		
Bobb, Nelson	Basketball		10	50		played NBA 49-52
Bobek, Nicole	Olympic		5	28		Figure Skater
Bobo, Hubert	Football		4	12		NFL
Boccabella, John	Baseball		4	10		Debut 1963
Bocek, Milt	Baseball		10	35		Debut 1933
Bochte, Bruce	Baseball		4	12		Debut 1974
Bochy, Bruce	Baseball		3	12		Debut 1978
Bock, Ed	Football		6	30		CHOF Iowa State

NAME	CATEGORY	+	SIG	SP	BALL	Comment
Bockhorn, Bucky	Basketball		4	22		played NBA 58-64
Bockman, Eddie	Baseball		7	18		Debut 1946
Boddicker, Mike	Baseball		12	27		Debut 1980
Bodine, Brett	Auto Racing		4	15		
Bodine, Geoff	Auto Racing		5	15		
Bodis, Joe	Bowling	+	15	30		1941 ABC HOF
Boehmer, Len	Baseball		3	12		Debut 1967 Reds
Boerwinkle, Tom	Basketball		4	12		played NBA 68-77
Boesel, Raul	Auto Racing		5	18		
Bogart, John R.	Baseball		40			Debut 1920 Tigers
Bogener, Terry	Baseball		3	15		Debut 1982
Boggs, Phil	Olympic		35	85		Diving
Boggs, Wade	Baseball		9	25		Debut1982
Boglioli, Wendy	Olympic		4	8		Swim/relay
Bogues, Muggsy	Basketball		4	15		played NBA 87-
Bohlen, Philena	Bowling	+	10	35		1955 Women's IBC HOF
Bohn, Parker III	Bowling		2	8		Tourney winner
Bohrer, Thomas	Olympic		3	6		Rowing
Boisclair, Bruce	Baseball		3	10		Debut 1974
Boitano, Brian	Olympic		10	22		Figure skating
Boivin, Leo	Hockey		7	18		1986 HOF def
Boken, Bob	Baseball		25	55		Debut 1933 Senators
Bokina, Joe	Baseball		15			Debut 1936 Senators
Bol, Manute	Basketball		4	18		played NBA 85-
Boland, Ed	Baseball		20	45		Debut 1934
Bolden, Jeanette	Olympic		5	10		Track relay
Bolden, Leroy	Football		12	28		NFL
Boles, Carl	Baseball		3	15		Debut 1962
Bolger, Jim	Baseball		4	12		Debut 1950 Reds
Bolger, William	Basketball		5	45		played NBA 53
Bolin, Bob	Baseball		3			Debut 1961 Giants
Bollegraf, Manon	Tennis		12	45		
Bolling, Frank	Baseball		4	12		Debut 1954
Bolling, Jack	Baseball		12	45		Debut 1939
Bolling, Milt	Baseball		4	12		Debut 1952
Bollweg, Don	Baseball		4	12		Debut 1950 Cards
Bolstorff, F. Douglas	Basketball		4	9		played NBA 57
Bolt, Mae	Bowling		5	10		1978 Women's IBC HOF
Bolt, Tommy	Golf		15	40	50	
Bolton, Cecil	Baseball		25	65		Debut 1928
Bolton, Cliff	Baseball		20	55		Debut 1931
Bomar, Buddy	Bowling	+	20	45		1966 ABC HOF
Bomar, Lynn	Football		10	30		CHOF Vanderbilt
Bomeisler, Bo	Football	+	20	55		CHOF Yale
Bonallack, Michael	Golf		5	20	35	
Bonalle, George	Basketball		5	20		played NBA 61
Bonavena, Oscar	Boxing		8	18		
Bond, Matthew	Olympic		3	6		Swim/relay
Bond, Phillip	Basketball		3	12		played NBA 77
Bond, Walt	Baseball		45	75		Debut 1960
Bondeson, Paul	Golf		10	35	30	
Bondra, Peter	Hockey		4	20	30	
Bonds, Barry	Baseball		10	35		Debut 1986
Bonds, Bobby	Baseball		6	20		Debut 1968 Giants
Bongiovanni, Nino	Baseball		12	35		Debut 1938
Bonham, Ron	Basketball		3	18		played NBA 64-67

NAME	CATEGORY	+	SIG	SP	BALL	Comment
Bonilla, Bobby	Baseball		5	25		Debut 1986
Bonilla, Juan	Baseball		4	10		Debut 1981
Bonioi, Chris	Football		5	15	75	NFL
Bonnell, Barry	Baseball		3	10		Debut 1977
Bonner, Bob	Baseball		3	10		Debut 1980
Bonnett, Neil	Auto Racing		50	125		
Bono, Steve	Football		5	15	75	NFL
Bonthron, Bill	Track		7	16		
Bonura, Zeke	Baseball		20	55		Debut 1934 ChiSox
Booker, Buddy	Baseball		3	10		Debut 1966
Booker, Butch	Basketball		3	15		played NBA 69
Booker, Rod	Baseball		3	10		Debut 1987
Bool, Al	Baseball		20	45		Debut 1928
Boon, Dickie	Hockey		85	160		1952 HOF def
Boone, Bob	Baseball		4	10	20	Debut 1972 Phillies
Boone, Brett	Baseball		4	18		3rd Generation MLB
Boone, Lute "Danny"	Baseball		45	125		Debut 1913 Yankees
Boone, Ray	Baseball		4	15		Debut 1948 Indians
Boone, Ron	Basketball		7	15		played NBA 68-80
Booth, Albie	Football	+	60	165		CHOF Yale
Boozer, Bullet Bob	Basketball		8	18		played NBA 60-70
Boozer, Emerson	Football		4	15		NFL
Boozer, John	Baseball		5			Debut 1962 Phillies
Borah, Dr. Charles E.	Olympic		5	15		Track
Borchelt, Earl	Olympic		3	6		Rowing
Bordagaray, Stanley	Baseball		25	75		Debut 1934
Borden, Amanda	Olympic		3	35		Gold Medal. Gymnastics
Borden, Nate	Football		6	14		NFL
Borders, Pat	Baseball		3	10		Debut 1988
Borg, Bjorn	Tennis		10	30		HOF 1987
Borgmann, Benny	Basketball	+	20	45		HOF 1961
Borgmann, Glenn	Baseball		3	10		Debut 1972 Twins
Borkowski, Bob	Baseball		8	25		Debut 1950 Cubs
Bornheimer, Jake	Basketball		25	50		played NBA 48-50
Borom, Red	Baseball		8	22		Debut 1944
Boros, Julius	Golf		5	25	50	PGA HOF 1982
Boros, Steve	Baseball		3	8		Debut 1957
Borotra, Jean	Tennis		10	35		HOF 1976
Borowy, Hank	Baseball		15			Debut 1942 Yankees
Borries, Fred	Football	+	15	45		CHOF Navy
Borsavage, Ike	Basketball		10	50		played NBA 50
Borschuk, Lo	Bowling		5	10		1988 Women's IBC HOF
Bortz, Mark	Football		3	10		NFL
Boryla, Vince	Basketball		25	65		played NBA 49-53
Borzov, Valeriy	Olympic		20	45		100 Meters
Bosch, Don	Baseball		3	10		Debut 1966
Boschman, Laurie	Hockey		3	15		
Bosely, Bruce	Football		22	55		CHOF West Virginia
Bosetti, Rick	Baseball		3	10		Debut 1976
Bosley, Thad	Baseball		3	10		Debut 1977
Bosseler, Don	Football		5	15		NFL
Bossy, Mike	Hockey		8	24	30	1991 HOF fwd
Bostic, Jim	Basketball		3	12		played NBA 77
Bostock, Lyman	Baseball		60	175		Debut 1975
Boston, Daryl	Baseball		3	10		Debut 1984
Boston, Lawrence	Basketball		3	10		played NBA 79

NAME	CATEGORY	+	SIG	SP	BALL	Comment
Boston, Ralph	Olympic		10	22		Long Jump
Bostwick, George H.	Horse Racing		15	40		HOF 1968 jockey
Boswell, Ken	Baseball		3	10		Debut 1967
Boswell, Tommy	Basketball		3	10		played NBA 75-79
Botkin, Freda	Bowling		5	10		1986 Women's IBC HOF
Botsford, Beth	Olympic		3	9		Gold Med. Swimming
Bottari, Vic	Football		5	15		CHOF California
Bottom, Joseph	Olympic		3	8		Swim/butterfly
Bottomley, Jim	Baseball		325	600	2375	HOF 1974
Bouchard, Butch	Hockey		12	25		1966 HOF def
Bouchee, Ed	Baseball		20	65		Debut 1956
Boucher, Al	Baseball		70	165		Debut 1914
Boucher, Frank	Hockey		75	150		1958 HOF fwd
Boucher, George	Hockey		75	150		1960 HOF def
Boucher, Medric	Baseball		20	40		Debut 1914
Boudreau, Lou	Baseball					P-S HOF $25, Grt.Mo.$25
Boudreau, Lou	Baseball		10	20	25	HOF 1970. Gold Pl.$10
Boudrias, Andre	Hockey		6	18		
Bouldin, Carl	Baseball		4			Debut 1961 Senators
Boulmetis, Sam	Horse Racing		10	20		HOF 1973 jockey
Boult, Elliott	Golf		5	20	25	
Bourjos, Chris	Baseball		3	10		Debut 1980
Bourque, Pat	Baseball		3	10		Debut 1971
Bourque, Phil	Hockey		10	28		
Bourque, Ray	Hockey		10	35	35	
Bousfield, Ken	Golf		5	25		
Boutiette, KC	Speedskating		2	6		US Record holder
Bouton, Jim	Baseball		6	14		Debut 1962
Boutsen, Thiery	Auto Racing		4	12		
Bouvia, Gloria	Bowling		5	12		1987 Women's IBC HOF
Bovell, Joe	Boxing		5	10		Hvy-Wt. Contender
Boven, Donald	Basketball		16	50		played NBA 49-52
Bovrell, Joe	Boxing		5	10		
Bowa, Larry	Baseball		4	10		Debut 1970
Bowden, Bobby	Football		3	10		Coach. FL State
Bowden, George	Golf		45	195		
Bowden, Terry	Football		3	7		Coach Auburn
Bowden, Tommy	Football		2	5		Tulane Coach
Bowe, Riddick	Boxing		15	60		Hvy-Wt. Champ.
Boweers, Billy	Baseball		7	22		Debut 1949
Bowen, Sam	Baseball		3	10		Debut 1977
Bowens, Tommie Jr.	Basketball		3	18		played NBA 67-69
Bower, Johnny	Hockey		9	25	30	1976 HOF goal
Bowie, Dubbie	Hockey		80	200		1945 HOF fwd
Bowie, Sam	Basketball		3	12		played NBA 84-
Bowiee, Anthony	Basketball		3	10		played NBA 88-
Bowlin, Hoss	Baseball		3	10		Debut 1967
Bowling, Orbie	Basketball		6	18		played NBA 67
Bowling, Steve	Baseball		3	10		Debut 1976
Bowman, Bob	Baseball		4	16		Debut 1955
Bowman, Christopher	Olympic		6	14		Figure skating
Bowman, El	Baseball		45	125		Debut 1920 Senators
Bowman, Ernie	Baseball		6	22		Debut 1961
Bowman, Joe	Baseball		10	45		Debut 1932 A's
Bowman, Nate	Basketball		3	15		played NBA 66-71
Bowman, Scotty	Hockey		4	20	25	1991 HOF

NAME	CATEGORY	+	SIG	SP	BALL	Comment
Box, Ab	Football		4	8		1965 Canadian HOF
Boxberger, Loa	Bowling		5	10		1984 Women's IBC HOF
Boyd, Bob	Baseball		4	15		Debut 1951 White Sox
Boyd, Bob	Football		5	10		NFL
Boyd, Bob	Football		6	16		NFL
Boyd, Dennis	Basketball		3	12		played NBA 78
Boyd, Dennis "Oil Can"	Baseball		10	25		Debut 1982
Boyd, Fred	Basketball		3	12		played NBA 72-77
Boyd, Gary	Baseball		4			Debut 1969 Indians
Boyd, Ken	Basketball		3	12		played NBA 74
Boyd, Tom	Golf		45	195		
Boydston, Max	Football		4	14		NFL
Boyer, Clete	Baseball		6	15		Debut 1955
Boyer, Cloyd	Baseball		2			Debut 1949 Cards
Boyer, Joe	Auto Racing	+	22	45		
Boyer, Ken	Baseball		70	225		Debut 1955.
Boykoff, Big Hesh	Basketball		10	50		played NBA 47-50
Boyland, Doe	Baseball		3	10		Debut 1978
Boyle, Ralph	Baseball		40	90		Debut 1929
Boyles, Harry	Baseball		12	30		Debut 1938 ChiSox
Boynes, Winford III	Basketball		3	10		played NBA 78-80
Boynton, Ben	Football	+	25	55		CHOF Williams
Boynton, Frank	Golf		5	20	25	
Brabham, Geoff	Auto Racing		4	12		
Brabham, Jack	Auto Racing		6	18		HOF 1990
Bracey, Stephen	Basketball		3	12		played NBA 72-74
Bradd, Gary	Basketball		3	15		played NBA 64-70
Braddock, James J.	Boxing		225	400		1935-37 H-Wt Champ
Bradford, Buddy	Baseball		4	12		Debut 1966
Bradford, James	Olympic		3	8		Weightlifting
Bradford, Vic	Baseball		4	10		Debut 1943
Bradley, Alex III	Basketball		3	10		played NBA 81
Bradley, Alonzo	Basketball		3	10		played NBA 77-83
Bradley, Bill	Basketball		12	30	150	HOF 1982
Bradley, Bill (Ky)	Basketball		3	10		played NBA 67
Bradley, Dudley	Basketball		3	10		played NBA 79-88
Bradley, Jack	Baseball		55	125		Debut 1916
Bradley, James	Basketball		3	10		played NBA 73-75
Bradley, Joseph	Basketball		10	50		played NBA 49
Bradley, Michael	Golf		5	25	25	
Bradley, Pat	Golf		10	25	35	LPGA HOF 1991
Bradley, Phil	Baseball		4	10		Debut 1983
Bradley, Scott	Baseball		3	10		Debut 1984
Bradley, Tom	Baseball		4			Debut 1969 Cal. Angels
Bradshaw, George	Baseball		8	22		Debut 1952
Bradshaw, Harry	Golf		20	50	75	
Bradshaw, Terry	Football		10	25	150	1989 HOF QB. Heisman
Brady, Bob	Baseball		6	18		Debut 1946
Brady, Brian	Baseball		3	10		Debut 1989
Brady, Cliff	Baseball		40	85		Debut 1920
Brady, Mike	Golf		70	225		Old PGA HOF 1960
Bragan, Bobby	Baseball		10	40		Debut 1940 Phillies
Bragg, Don	Olympic		7	20		Pole Vault
Braggs, Glenn	Baseball		3	12		Debut 1986
Braid James	Golf		345	845		PGA HOF 1976
Braitz, Michael	Basketball		3	12		played NBA 77-85

NAME	CATEGORY	+	SIG	SP	BALL	Comment
Bramble, Livingstone	Boxing		7	15		
Bramhall, Art	Baseball		12	38		Debut 1935
Bramham, William G.	Baseball		10			Executive
Branca, Ralph	Baseball		7	15		Debut 1944 Dodgers
Brancato, Al	Baseball		8	20		Debut 1939
Branch, Adrian	Basketball		3	10		played NBA 86-
Branch, Cliff	Football		10	18		NFL
Branch, Mel	Football		4	12		NFL
Brand, Daniel	Olympic		3	6		Wrestling
Brand, Glen	Olympic		3	6		Wrestling
Brand, Ron	Baseball		6	14		Debut 1963
Brandon, Steve	Writer		2	4		
Brandon, Terrell	Basketball		5	20		
Brands, Tom	Olympic		2	5		Gold Med. Wrestling
Brandt, Allie	Bowling	+	12	25		1960 ABC HOF
Brandt, Jackie	Baseball		6	15		Debut 1955
Brannan, Otis	Baseball		45	90		Debut 1928
Brannum, Robert	Basketball		10	45		played NBA 48-55
Branson, Brad	Basketball		3	10		played NBA 81-82
Branson, Herman	Basketball		3	12		played NBA 65-67
Brant, Marshall	Baseball		3	12		Debut 1980
Brantley, Mickey	Baseball		3	10		Debut 1986
Brasco, James	Basketball		10	35		played NBA 52
Bratcher, Joe	Baseball		35	85		Debut 1924 Cards
Bratkowski, Zeke	Football		4	14		NFL
Bratschi, Fritz	Baseball		40	90		Debut 1921
Bratton, Johnny	Boxing		15	32		
Braun, Carl	Basketball		8	22		played NBA 47-61
Braun, Steve	Baseball		3	10		Debut 1971
Bravo, Angel	Baseball		10	35		Debut 1969
Bray, Clarence W. "Buster"	Baseball		20	60		Debut 1941 Bost. Braves
Brayton, Scott	Auto Racing		20	45		
Brazill, Frank	Baseball		40	95		Debut 1921
Bream, Sid	Baseball		3	10		Debut 1983
Breazeale, Jim	Baseball		3	10		Debut 1969
Brecheen, Harry	Baseball		6	14		Debut 1940 Cards
Breech, Jim	Football		3	10		NFL
Breeden, Danny	Baseball		3	10		Debut 1969
Breeden, Hal	Baseball		3	10		Debut 1971
Breeding, Marv	Baseball		3	12		Debut 1960 Orioles
Breedlove, Craig	Auto Racing		20	45		HOF 1993
Breen, George	Olympic		3	7		Swim/400 free
Breen, Joseph	Football	+	10	22		1963 Canadian HOF
Bregman, James	Olympic		3	6		Judo
Breland, Mark	Boxing		8	18		Welter-Wt Champ
Bremer, Herb	Baseball		30	65		Debut 1937
Brenly, Bob	Baseball		4	10		Debut 1981
Brennan, Joe	Basketball	+	25	50		HOF 1974
Brennan, Peter	Basketball		3	35		played NBA 58
Brennan, Terry	Football		4	10		NFL
Brennan, Thomas	Basketball		4	9		played NBA 54
Brenzel, Bill	Baseball		30	75		Debut 1932
Bresnahan, Roger	Baseball		750	1750	5667	HOF 1945
Bressler, Rube	Baseball		75	180		Debut 1914
Bressoud, Ed	Baseball		4	15		Debut 1956
Breton, Jim	Baseball		50	125		Debut 1913

NAME	CATEGORY	+	SIG	SP	BALL	Comment
Brett, George	Baseball		18	45		Debut 1973
Brett, Ken	Baseball		4	10		Debut 1967 RedSox
Brettschneider, Carl	Football		5	14		NFL
Breuer, Randy	Basketball		3	10		played NBA 83-
Breunig, Bob	Football		5	12		NFL
Brewer, Charles	Football	+	25	100		CHOF Harvard
Brewer, Gay	Golf		10	25	35	
Brewer, Jim	Baseball		14	30		Debut 1960 Cubs
Brewer, Jim	Basketball		4	12		played NBA 73-81
Brewer, Mike	Baseball		3	10		Debut 1986
Brewer, Ron	Basketball		3	12		played NBA 78-85
Brewer, Tom	Baseball		7	15		Debut 1954
Brewer, Tony	Baseball		3	10		Debut 1984
Brewster, Charlie	Baseball		9	35		Debut 1943
Brewster, Darrell	Football		8	20		NFL
Brian, Frank	Basketball		10	45		played NBA 47-55
Brickell, Fred	Baseball		35	85		Debut 1926
Brickell, Fritzie	Baseball		50	125		Debut 1958
Brickhouse, Jack	Broadcaster		6	15		1983 Ntl S&S HOF
Brickowski, Frank	Basketball		3	10		played NBA 84-
Brideweser, Jim	Baseball		10	25		Debut 1951
Bridgeman, Junior	Basketball		4	12		played NBA 75-86
Bridges, Alice	Olympic		7	20		Swim/backstroke
Bridges, Rocky	Baseball		4	12		Debut 1951
Bridges, Tommy	Baseball		85	195		Debut 1930
Bridges, William	Basketball		3	18		played NBA 62-74
Bridgewater, Brad	Olympic		3	12		Gold Medal. Swimming
Bridwell, Al	Baseball		80	150		Debut '05."Merkie Boner"
Brief, Anthony "Bunny"	Baseball		70	135		Debut 1912 STL Browns
Briggs, Dan	Baseball		3	12		Debut 1975
Briggs, John	Baseball		3	12		Debut 1964 Cubs
Bright, Harry	Baseball		8	20		Debut 1958
Bright, Johnny	Football	+				CHOF Drake
Bright, Johnny	Football	+	50	125		Canadian HOF 1970
Brightman, Al	Basketball		10	50		played NBA 46
Briles-Hinton, J	Golf		5	20	25	
Briley, Greg	Baseball		3	10		Debut 1988
Brimsek, Frank	Hockey		7	18		1966 HOF goal.
Brimsek, Frank	Hockey		7	18		1973 US HOF
Brindley, Audley	Basketball		10	50		played NBA 45
Brinker, Maureen (See Connolly)	Tennis					
Brinkman, Chuck	Baseball		3	10		Debut 1969
Brinkman, Ed	Baseball		3	10		Debut 1961 Senators
Brinkopf, Leon	Baseball		4	15		Debut 1952
Brion, Cesar	Boxing		15	30		Argentine H-wt
Brisco-Hooks, Valerie	Olympic		7	22		200 M Dash
Brisker, John	Basketball		3	12		played NBA 69-74
Brisky, Mike	Golf		5	20	25	
Bristow, Allan	Basketball		3	12		played NBA 73-82
Brito, Gene	Football		100	225		NFL
Britt, Tyrone	Basketball		4	15		played NBA 67
Britt, Wayman	Basketball		4	15		played NBA 77
Brittain, Gus	Baseball		40	95		Debut. 1937
Brittain, Michael	Basketball		3	12		played NBA 85-86
Britton, Bill	Golf		5	20	25	
Britton, David	Basketball		3	10		played NBA 80

NAME	CATEGORY	+	SIG	SP	BALL	Comment
Britton, Stephen Gil	Baseball		60	145		Debut 1913 Pirates
Britz, Jerilyn	Golf		5	20	25	
Brix, Herman	Olympic		10	20		Track
Broadbent, Punch	Hockey		15	35		1962 HOF fwd
Broadhurst, Paul	Golf		5	20	25	
Brock, Greg	Baseball		3	10		Debut 1982
Brock, Lou	Baseball					P-S HOF $22.Grt.Mo.$25
Brock, Lou	Baseball		10	20	25	HOF 1985. Gold Pl. $14
Brock, Pete	Football		3	10		NFL
Brock, Stan	Football		4	10		NFL
Brockington, John	Football		7	15		NFL
Broda, Turk	Hockey		80	150		1967 HOF goal
Brodeur, Martin	Hockey		8	28	30	
Brodie, John	Football		6	18		CHOF Stanford
Brodie, John	Golf		5	20	25	
Broeg, Bob	Writer		5	12		
Brogan, James	Basketball		3	12		played NBA 81-82
Broglio, Ernie	Baseball		4			Debut 1959 Cards
Brohamer, Jack	Baseball		4	10		Debut 1972
Brokaw, Gary	Basketball		3	10		played NBA 74-77
Bromwich, John	Tennis		10	25		HOF 1984
Bronkie, Herman	Baseball		75	150		Debut 1910
Brook, Tom	Football	+	10	22		1975 Canadian HOF
Brooke, George	Football	+	25	100		CHOF Pennsylvania
Brookens, Tom	Baseball		4	10		Debut 1979
Brookes, Norman	Tennis	+	20	40		HOF 1977
Brookfield, Emery	Basketball		10	50		played NBA 46-49
Brookins, Clarence	Basketball		3	12		played NBA 70
Brooks, Albert	Football		5	22		NFL Packer Receiver
Brooks, Bobby	Baseball		3	10		Debut 1969
Brooks, Herb	Hockey		8	20		1990 US HOF coach
Brooks, Hubie	Baseball		4	12		Debut 1980
Brooks, James	Football		4	15		NFL
Brooks, Jonathan	Baseball		75	165		Debut 1925
Brooks, Mark	Golf		5	20	25	
Brooks, Michael	Basketball		3	12		played NBA 80-87
Brooks, Robert	Football		4	12	75	NFL
Brooks, Scott	Basketball		3	10		played NBA 87-
Brooks, Steve	Horse Racing		25	60		HOF 1963 jockey
Brookshier, Tom	Football		5	14		NFL
Brosch, Al	Golf		10	35		
Brosius, Eddie	Bowling	+	10	22		1976 ABC HOF
Broskie, Sig	Baseball		20	45		Debut. 1940
Brosnan, Jim	Baseball		4	12		Debut 1954
Broten, Aaron	Hockey		4	14		
Broten, Neal	Hockey		7	16		
Brough (Clapp), Louise	Tennis		10	35		HOF 1967
Brouhard, Mark	Baseball		3	12		Debut 1980
Brouillard, Lou	Boxing		15	30		Welter-Middle wt. Champ.
Brouthers, Art	Baseball		90	200		Debut 1906
Brouthers, Dan	Baseball		2000	5000	7800	HOF 1945
Brovia, Joe	Baseball		6	18		Debut 1955
Brower, Bob	Baseball		3	10		Debut 1986
Brower, Frank	Baseball		50	125		Debut 1920
Brower, Lou	Baseball		10	25		Debut 1931
Brown, Alice	Olympic		3	7		Track sprints

NAME	CATEGORY	+	SIG	SP	BALL	Comment
Brown, Anthony	Basketball		3	6		played NBA 84
Brown, Barney	Baseball		25	75		Debut 1931, Negro League
Brown, Bill "Boom Boom"	Football		5	14		NFL
Brown, Billy Ray	Golf		5	20	25	
Brown, Bobby	Baseball		6	12		Debut 1946
Brown, Bobby	Baseball		6	20		Debut 1979
Brown, C.S., Mrs.	Golf		125	295		
Brown, Charley	Football		3	15		NFL
Brown, Chris	Baseball		3	10		Debut 1984
Brown, Cindy	Olympic		2	7		Gold Medal. Basketball
Brown, Curt	Baseball		3	10		Debut 1973
Brown, D. Wes	Football	+	10	22		1953 Canadian HOF
Brown, Darrell	Baseball		3	10		Debut 1981
Brown, Darrell	Basketball		10	50		played NBA 48
Brown, Dave	Football		5	12	75	NFL
Brown, David	Golf		375	875		
Brown, Delos	Baseball		50	165		Debut 1914
Brown, Dick	Baseball		30	65		Debut 1957
Brown, Don	Baseball		25	50		Debut 1915
Brown, Ed	Football		6	16		NFL
Brown, Eddie	Baseball		54	145		Debut 1920
Brown, Eddie	Football		3	12		NFL
Brown, Edward D.	Horse Racing		25	50		HOF 1984 trainer
Brown, Eric	Golf		15	45		
Brown, Fred	Baseball		100	250		Debut 1901
Brown, Fred	Basketball		4	12		played NBA 71-83
Brown, Gates	Baseball		6	14		Debut 1963
Brown, George	Basketball		10	35		played NBA 57
Brown, George	Football		15	35		CHOF Navy/San Diego St. 5
Brown, George	Hockey	+	10	22		1973 US HOF admin
Brown, Gordon	Football	+	25	100		CHOF Yale
Brown, Hardy	Football		25	65		NFL
Brown, Harold	Basketball		10	50		played NBA 45
Brown, Ike	Baseball		4	8		Debut 1969 Tigers
Brown, J. Kevin	Baseball		10	35		Debut 1986
Brown, Jake	Baseball		8	15		Debut 1975
Brown, Jerome	Football		30	65		NFL
Brown, Jim	Football		13	35		1971 HOF RB
Brown, Jimmy	Baseball		25	65		Debut 1937 Cards
Brown, Joe	Boxing		15	35		Lt-Wt. Champ.1956-62
Brown, John	Basketball		3	12		played NBA 73-79
Brown, John Jr.	Football	+	20	60		CHOF Navy
Brown, Johnny Mack	Football	+	65	175		CHOF Alabama
Brown, Judi	Olympic		3	8		400 M Hurdles
Brown, Keith	Track		7	15		
Brown, Larry	Baseball		4	12		Debut 1963 Indians
Brown, Larry	Football		5	12		NFL
Brown, Lawrence	Basketball		3	12		played NBA 67-71.Vet Coach
Brown, Leon	Baseball		3	10		Debut 1976
Brown, Leon	Basketball		10	50		played NBA 46
Brown, Lewis	Basketball		3	12		played NBA 80
Brown, Lindsay	Baseball		45	95		Debut 1937
Brown, Lomas	Football		3	10		NFL
Brown, Marty	Baseball		3	10		Debut 1988
Brown, Michael	Basketball		3	15		played NBA 86-
Brown, Mike	Baseball		3	12		Debut 1983

NAME	CATEGORY	+	SIG	SP	BALL	Comment
Brown, Mordecai	Baseball		500	1000	5500	HOF 1949
Brown, Ollie	Baseball		3	10		Debut 1965
Brown, Oscar	Baseball		3	12		Debut 1969
Brown, Patricia "Specs"	Baseball		30			1st Fem. Cooperstown
Brown, Paul	Baseball		4			Debut 1961 Phillies
Brown, Paul	Football	+	35	85	325	1967 HOF coach
Brown, Pete	Golf		5	20	25	
Brown, Randy	Baseball		3	12		Debut 1969
Brown, Raymond	Football		7	30		CHOF Southern California
Brown, Rickey	Basketball		3	12		played NBA 80-81
Brown, Robert	Basketball		10	50		played NBA 48-49
Brown, Roger	Basketball		15	30		played NBA 67-71
Brown, Roosevelt	Football		10	20	85	1975 HOF OL
Brown, Simon	Boxing		8	18		
Brown, Stanley	Basketball		16	50		played NBA 47-51
Brown, Ted	Football		4	12		NFL
Brown, Tim	Football		12	28		NFL
Brown, Tim	Football		15	30	85	ND Heisman '87. NFL
Brown, Tim	Football		6	14		NFL
Brown, Tom	Baseball		3	12		Debut 1963
Brown, Tom	Football		6	18		1984 Canadian HOF
Brown, Tommy	Baseball		6	20		Debut 1944
Brown, W. Roger	Basketball		3	12		played NBA 72-79
Brown, Walter	Hockey	+	45	125		1973 US HOF admin
Brown, Walter A.	Basketball	+	40	85		HOF 1965
Brown, Warren	Writer		5	10		
Brown, Willie	Football		6	16	85	1984 HOF DB
Brown, Keith	Hockey		4	15		
Browne, Byron	Baseball		3	12		Debut 1965
Browne, Earl	Baseball		15	45		Debut 1935
Browne, James	Basketball		16	50		played NBA 48-49
Browne, Jerry	Baseball		3	10		Debut 1986
Browne, Mary	Tennis		18	40		HOF 1957
Browne, Olin	Golf		5	20	25	
Browne, Pidge	Baseball		8	20		Debut 1962
Browner, Clint	Auto Racing	+	20	45		
Browner, Joey	Football		5	12		NFL
Browner, Ross	Football		3	9		Notre Dame-NFL
Browning, Kurt	Figure Skating		3	15		4x World Champ.
Browning, Tom	Baseball		8	20		Debut 1984.No Hit Pitcher
Broyles, Frank	Football		6	20		1983 CHOF coach
Brubaker, Bill	Baseball		20	43		Debut 1932
Bruce, Earle	Football		2	5		College Coach of Year
Bruce, Issac	Football		5	15	75	NFL
Bruce, Lou	Baseball		85	200		Debut 1904
Bruce, Tom	Olympic		3	7		Swim/100 breast
Bruce-Brown, David	Auto Racing	+	25	60		
Brucker, Earle	Baseball		8	22		Debut 1948
Brucker, Earle Sr.	Baseball		25	55		Debut 1937
Bruckmiller, Andrew	Baseball		10			Debut 1905
Brue, Bob	Golf		5	20	25	
Bruen, James	Golf		25	70		
Bruggy, Frank	Baseball		55	130		Debut 1921
Brugnon, Jacques	Tennis	+	15	35		HOF 1976
Bruguer, Sergi	Tennis		8	18		
Brumel, Valeriy	Olympic		35	85		High Jump

NAME	CATEGORY	+	SIG	SP	BALL	Comment
Brumley, Mike	Baseball		3	10		Debut 1987
Brumley, Tony	Baseball		4	12		Debut 1964
Brummer, Glenn	Baseball		3	10		Debut 1981
Brunansky, Tom	Baseball		4	12		Debut 1981
Brundage, Avery	Olympic		65	165		President I.O.C.
Brunell, Mark	Football		6	28	85	NFL
Brunkhorst, Bronk	Basketball		3	10		played NBA 63
Brunnell, Mark	Football		4	25		
Bruno, Frank	Boxing		12	25		Hvy-Wt.
Bruns, George	Basketball		3	12		played NBA 72
Brunsberg, Arlo	Baseball		3	10		Debut 1966
Bruton, Bill	Baseball		15	45		Debut 1953
Bryan, Billy	Baseball		3	15		Debut 1961 A's
Bryan, Jimmy	Auto Racing	+	30	65		
Bryant, Bart	Golf		5	20	25	
Bryant, Bobby	Football		5	14		NFL
Bryant, Brad	Golf		5	20	25	
Bryant, Clay	Baseball		15			Debut 1935 Cubs
Bryant, Derek	Baseball		3	10		Debut 1979
Bryant, Don	Baseball		3	12		Debut 1966
Bryant, Emmette	Basketball		4	15		played NBA 64-71
Bryant, Joseph	Basketball		3	12		played NBA 75-82
Bryant, Kobe	Basketball		12	40	100	NBA Lakers
Bryant, Mark	Basketball		3	15		played NBA 88-
Bryant, Paul "Bear"	Football	+	85	200		1986 CHOF coach
Bryant, Ralph	Baseball		3	10		Debut 1985
Bryant, Rosalyn	Olympic		8	20		Track relay
Bryant, Wallace	Basketball		3	12		played NBA 83-85
Brye, Steve	Baseball		3	10		Debut 1970
Bubka, Sergei	Olympic		15	45		Pole vault
Bubser, Hal	Baseball		45	110		Debut 1922
Bucceroni, Dan	Boxing		5	10		
Bucci, George Jr.	Basketball		3	12		played NBA 75
Bucha, Johnny	Baseball		6	20		Debut 1948 Cards
Buchan, William	Olympic		3	6		Yachting
Buchanan, Buck	Football		30	80		1990 HOF DL
Buchanan, Ken	Boxing		15	35		Light-wt Champ.
Buchek, Jerry	Baseball		4	12		Debut 1961
Bucher, Jim	Baseball		20	55		Debut 1934
Buck, Jack	Broadcaster		6	15		1990 Ntl S&S HOF
Buck, Mack	Baseball		6	18		Debut 1956
Buckhalter, Joseph	Basketball		3	25		played NBA 61-62
Buckingham, Greg	Olympic		3	7		Swim/medley
Buckley, Kevin	Baseball		3	6		Debut 1984
Buckner, Bill	Baseball		5	14		Debut 1969 Dodgers
Buckner, Cleveland	Basketball		3	30		played NBA 61-62
Buckner, Pam	Bowling		5	10		1990 Women's IBC HOF
Buckner, Quinn	Basketball		3	12		played NBA 76-85
Buckwalter, Bucky	Basketball		3	8		Longtime exec.
Bucyk, John	Hockey		5	16	18	1981 HOF fwd
Budaska, Mark	Baseball		3	6		Debut 1978
Budd, David	Basketball		3	25		played NBA 60-64
Budde, Ed	Football		5	14		NFL
Buddin, Don	Baseball		4	15		Debut 1956
Budge, Don	Tennis		12	35		HOF 1954
Budke, Mary	Golf		5	10	25	

NAME	CATEGORY	+	SIG	SP	BALL	Comment
Budko, Walter	Basketball		16	50		played NBA 48-51
Buechele, Steve	Baseball		3	10		Debut 1985
Bueno, Maria	Tennis		10	28		HOF 1978
Buford, Don	Baseball		4	10		Debut 1963
Buhl, Bob	Baseball		8	16		Debut 1953
Buhner, Jay	Baseball		12	38		Debut 1987
Buirleson, Tom	Basketball		6	15		played NBA 74-80
Bujack, Fred	Bowling	+	12	35		1967 ABC HOF
Bulkeley, Morgan	Baseball		1475	4200		HOF 1937
Bulla, Johnny	Golf		40	95	75	
Bullard, George	Baseball		8	15		Debut 1954
Bulling, Terry	Baseball		3	12		Debut 1977
Bullock, Eric	Baseball		3	10		Debut 1985
Bullough, Henry	Football		5	15		NFL
Bumbry, Al	Baseball		4	10		Debut 1972
Bunce, Lawrence	Basketball		3	15		played NBA 67-73
Bunch, Greg	Basketball		3	15		played NBA 78
Buncom, Frank	Football		5	15		NFL
Bunetta, Bill	Bowling		5	22		1968 ABC HOF
Bunker, Paul	Football	+	25	75		CHOF Army
Bunkowsky, Barb	Golf		5	20	25	
Bunn, John	Basketball	+	35	95		HOF 1964
Bunning, Jim	Baseball		6	15	35	HOF 1996.P-S HOF $35
Buntin, Bill	Basketball		3	15		played NBA 65
Bunting, William	Basketball		3	15		played NBA 69-71
Buoniconti, Nick	Football		5	12		NFL
Burbrink, Nelson	Baseball		4	12		Debut 1955
Burch, Billy	Hockey		35	100		1974 HOF fwd
Burch, Elliot	Horse Racing		25	60		HOF 1980 trainer
Burch, Preston M.	Horse Racing		40	95		HOF 1963 trainer
Burch, W.P.	Horse Racing		45	95		HOF 1955 trainer
Burda, Bob	Baseball		4	15		Debut 1962 Giants
Burden, Doug	Olympic		3	6		Rowing
Burden, Ticky	Basketball		3	15		played NBA 75-77
Burdette, Lew	Baseball		6	15		Debut 1950 Braves
Bure', Pavel	Hockey		5	30	35	NHL
Burford, Chris	Football		4	15		NFL
Burgess, Smoky	Baseball		15	50		Debut 1943 Cubs
Burgess, Tom	Baseball		7	18		Debut 1954
Burghley, Lord	Track		25	75		
Burgo, Bill	Baseball		8	22		Debut 1943
Burich, Bill	Baseball		8	22		Debut 1942
Burick, Si	Writer		3	8		1985 Ntl S&S HOF
Burk, Adrian	Football		10	22		NFL
Burkam, Bob	Baseball		55	125		Debut 1915
Burke, Billy	Golf		120	250		Old PGA HOF 1966
Burke, Glenn	Baseball		12	25		Debut 1976
Burke, Jack Sr	Golf		70	195		
Burke, Jack, Jr.	Golf		15	30	35	Old PGA HOF 1975
Burke, Leo	Baseball		3	15		Debut 1958
Burke, Les	Baseball		65	140		Debut 1923
Burke, Lynn	Olympic		3	6		Swim/relay
Burke, Patrick	Golf		5	20	25	
Burkemo, Walter	Golf		90	50		
Burkett, Jessie	Baseball		850	2250	5300	HOF '46. B&W PC $1650
Burkman, Roger	Basketball		3	12		played NBA 81

NAME	CATEGORY	+	SIG	SP	BALL	Comment
Burks, Ellis	Baseball		4	18		Debut 1987
Burleson, Rick	Baseball		4	10		Debut 1974
Burlew, Fred	Horse Racing		18	35		HOF 1973 trainer
Burling, Catherine	Bowling		10	30		1958 Women's IBC HOF
Burlt, Richard	Basketball		10	45		played NBA 52
Burman, Bob	Auto Racing	+	30	75		
Burmaster, Jack	Basketball		10	50		played NBA 48-49
Burns, David	Basketball		3	15		played NBA 81
Burns, George	Golf		5	25	25	
Burns, George H.	Baseball		65	135		Debut 1914
Burns, George J.	Baseball		60	125		Debut 1911
Burns, Jack	Baseball		45	150		Debut 1930
Burns, Jack	Golf		375	1000		
Burns, James	Basketball		3	15		played NBA 67
Burns, Joe	Baseball		50	125		Debut 1924
Burns, Joe	Baseball		65	165		Debut 1910
Burns, Nina	Bowling		5	20		1977 Women's IBC HOF
Burns, Tommy	Boxing		325	600		1906-08 H-Wt Champ
Burns, Tommy	Horse Racing		12	25		HOF 1983 jockey
Burns,Charlie	Hockey		5	15		
Burnside, Carabeth	Snowboarding		2	14		World's best
Burr, Leslie	Olympic		5	10		Equestrian
Burrell, Leroy	Swimming		5	15		World Rec'd. 100-Meters
Burridge,Randy	Hockey		5	15		
Burright, Larry	Baseball		3	15		Debut 1962
Burris, Arthur	Basketball		10	50		played NBA 50-51
Burris, Paul	Baseball		3	7		Debut 1948
Burrough, Ken	Football		6	15		NFL
Burroughs, Don	Football		6	15		NFL
Burroughs, Jeff	Baseball		4	12		Debut 1970
Burrow, Robert	Basketball		10	45		played NBA 56-57
Burrus, Dick	Baseball		65	175		Debut 1919
Burton Jr., Nelson	Bowling		6	20		1981 ABC HOF
Burton Sr., Nelson	Bowling		10	35		1964 ABC HOF
Burton, Brandie	Golf		5	20	25	
Burton, Dick	Golf		65	260		
Burton, Edward	Basketball		6	20		played NBA 61-64
Burton, Ellis	Baseball		6	18		Debut 1958
Burton, Kyle	Golf		5	20	25	
Burton, Mike	Olympic		6	12		Swimming-1500 M Free
Burton, Richard	Golf		70	175		
Burtt, Steven	Basketball		3	12		played NBA 84-87
Busby, Jim	Baseball		4	15		Debut 1950 ChiSox
Busby, Paul	Baseball		15	45		Debut 1941
Busby, Steve	Baseball		4			Debut 1972 K.C.
Busch, Ed	Baseball		10	35		Debut 1943
Buse, Don	Basketball		4	12		played NBA 72-84
Bush, Bullet Joe	Baseball		56	200		Debut 1912
Bush, Donie	Baseball		50	150		Debut 1908
Bush, Guy	Baseball		50	130		Debut 1923 Cubs
Bush, Lesley	Olympic		8	22		Diving
Bush, Randy	Baseball		3	10		Debut 1982
Bush, Walter	Hockey		5	12		1980 US HOF admin
Bushnell, Asa	Olympic		30	80		Olympic Executive
Buskey, Mike	Baseball		3	10		Debut 1977
Buss, Jerry	Basketball		6	15		Owner Lakers

NAME	CATEGORY	+	SIG	SP	BALL	Comment
Busse, Ray	Baseball		3	10		Debut 1971
Bussey, Dexter	Football		3	15		NFL
Busson, Jack	Golf		60	150		
Bustion, David	Basketball		3	15		played NBA 72
Butcher, Donnie	Basketball		3	22		played NBA 61-65
Butcher, Hank	Baseball		40	110		Debut 1911
Butcher, Susan	Dog Sled Racing		6	25		Idiotard winner
Butcher, Garth	Hockey		3	15		
Butell, D.	Baseball		3			
Butera, Sal	Baseball		3	10		Debut 1980
Butka, Ed	Baseball		4	10		Debut 1943
Butkus, Dick	Football		10	28	140	1979 HOF LB
Butland, Bill	Baseball		8			Debut 1940 Boston
Butler, Al	Basketball		5	22		played NBA 61
Butler, Art	Baseball		40	90		Debut 1911
Butler, Bill	Football		5	15		NFL
Butler, Brett	Baseball		4	12		Debut 1981
Butler, Greg	Basketball		3	12		played NBA 83-
Butler, Jack	Football		8	18		NFL
Butler, Johnny	Baseball		55	125		Debut 1926
Butler, Kevin	Football		3	12		NFL
Butler, Michael	Basketball		3	15		played NBA 68-71
Butler, Robert	Football	+	25	75		CHOF Wisconsin
Butner, Bill	Golf		5	20	25	
Button, Dick	Olympic		7	25		Figure Skating
Butts, James	Olympic		3	15		Triple Jump
Butwell, Jimmy	Horse Racing		15	30		HOF 1984 jockey
Buzas, Joe	Baseball		5	15		Debut 1945
Buzhardt, John	Baseball		3	15		Debut 1958
Byars, Keith	Football		3	12		NFL
Bye, Karyn	Olympic		2	8		Olympic Hockey Pioneer
Byerly, Eldred W. "Bud"	Baseball		6			Debut 1943 STL Cards
Byers, Eben	Golf		175	450		
Byers, J.D.	Horse Racing		30	65		HOF 1967 trainer
Byers, Randell	Baseball		3	10		Debut 1987
Byers, Walter	Administrator		3	15		
Byner, Earnest	Football		4	15		NFL
Byrd, Harry	Baseball		12	12		Debut 1950 A's
Byrd, Sam	Golf		45	125		
Byrd, Walter	Basketball		3	15		played NBA 69
Byrne, Bobby	Baseball		70	125		Debut 1907
Byrne, Tommy	Baseball		4	14		Debut 1943 Yankees
Byrnes, Martin	Basketball		3	12		played NBA 78-82
Byrnes, Milt	Baseball		25	55		Debut 1943
Byrnes, Thomas	Basketball		10	50		played NBA 46-50
Byrum, Curt	Golf		5	20	25	
Byrum, Tom	Golf		5	20	25	
Bytzura, Michael	Basketball		10	50		played NBA 44-46

NAME	CATEGORY	+	SIG	SP	BALL	Comment

NAME	CATEGORY	+	SIG	SP	BALL	Comment
Caballerro, Putsy	Baseball		4	12		Debut 1944
Cabell, Enos	Baseball		4	10		Debut 1972
Cable, Barney	Basketball		8	35		played NBA 58-63
Cabrera, Francisco	Baseball		3	12		Debut 1989
Cacek, Craig	Baseball		3	12		Debut 1977
Caddel, Ernie	Football		30	65		NFL
Cadle, George	Golf		20	45		
Cadore, Leon	Baseball		150			5/20/20. Longest game
Cafego, George	Football		10	30		CHOF Tennessee
Cafego, George	Football		6	12		NFL
Cafego, Tom	Baseball		45	95		Debut 1937
Caffie, Joe	Baseball		4	15		Debut 1956
Cage, Michael	Basketball		3	15		played NBA 84-
Cage, Wayne	Baseball		3	12		Debut 1978
Cagle, Chris	Football	+	35	140		CHOF SW La. /Army
Cahill, Mabel	Tennis	+	15	45		HOF 1976
Cahill, Tom	Football		2	5		College Coach of Year
Cain, Bob	Baseball		3	10		Debut 1949
Cain, John	Football	+	20	55		CHOF Alabama
Cain, John Paul	Golf		5	25	25	
Calabrese, Gerry	Basketball		10	50		played NBA 50-51
Calcavecchia, Mark	Golf		10	25	30	
Calderon, Ivan	Baseball		4	10		Debut 1984
Calderone, Sammy	Baseball		6	15		Debut 1950
Caldwell, Charlie	Football		15	45		1961 CHOF coach
Caldwell, James Jr.	Basketball		5	35		played NBA 67-68
Caldwell, Joe	Basketball		5	25		played NBA 64-71
Caldwell, Ray	Baseball		50	125		Debut 1910
Caldwell, Rex	Golf		5	20	25	
Calhoun, Corky	Basketball		3	12		played NBA 72-79
Calhoun, Lee	Olympic		15	50		110 M Hurdles
Calhoun, William	Basketball		10	38		played NBA 47-54
Caliperi, John	Basketball		3	7		NBA Coach
Callaghan, Marty	Baseball		45	65		Debut 1922
Callahan, Dave	Baseball		45	66		Debut 1910
Callahan, Leo	Baseball		45	95		Debut 1913
Callahan, Mushy	Boxing		15	30		Welter-wt Champ.
Callahan, Thomas	Basketball		10	50		played NBA 46
Callaway, Frank	Baseball		40	90		Debut 1921
Callen, Gloria	Swimming		8	25		
Callison, Johnny	Baseball		5	14		Debut 1958
Calloway, Ely	Golf		15	40		
Calvello, Ann	Roller Derby		4	12		

NAME	CATEGORY	+	SIG	SP	BALL	Comment
Calverley, Ernest	Basketball		10	50		played NBA 46-53
Calvin, Mack	Basketball		6	25		played NBA 69-80
Camacho, Hector "Macho"	Boxing		15	35		Light-wt Champ.
Camby, Marcus	Basketball		5	22	100	
Camelli, Hank	Baseball		4	20		Debut 1943
Cameron, Ed	Football		6	30		CHOF Washington & Lee
Cameron, Fred L.	Marathon		20	65		
Cameron, Harry	Hockey		50	175		1962 HOF def
Cameron, Michelle	Olympic		3	9		Synch. Swimming
Cameron, Paul	Football		6	15		NFL
Cameron, Scotty	Golf		10	25	30	
Camilli, Dolf	Baseball		10	25		Debut 1933
Camilli, Doug	Baseball		3	10		Debut 1960
Camilli, Lou	Baseball		3	10		Debut 1969
Caminiti, Ken	Baseball		4	22		Debut 1987
Camnitz, Howie	Baseball		90			Pitt.'04-14. 25 Game wins.
Camp, Walter	Football	+	350	700		1951 CHOF coach
Campanella, Roy	Baseball					Grt.Mo.$225
Campanella, Roy	Baseball		175	275	400	HOF 1969. P-S HOF$250
Campanella, Roy	Baseball		450	800	3500	Pre-Accident
Campaneris, Bert	Baseball		4	12		Debut 1964
Campanis, Al	Baseball		4	12		Debut 1943
Campanis, Jim	Baseball		3	10		Debut 1966
Campbell, Bill	Golf		20	50		PGA HOF 1990. Contrib.
Campbell, Bruce	Baseball		10	28		Debut 1930
Campbell, Clarence	Baseball		8	25		Debut 1940
Campbell, Dave	Baseball		3	10		Debut 1967
Campbell, David	Football	+	25	100		CHOF Harvard
Campbell, Donald	Boat Racing		20	70		
Campbell, Earl	Football		8	24	125	'91 HOF RB.Heisman '77
Campbell, Gina	Boat Racing		5	10		
Campbell, Jim	Baseball		3	12		Debut 1962
Campbell, Jim	Baseball		3	12		Debut 1970
Campbell, Joe	Baseball		3	12		Debut 1967
Campbell, Joe	Golf		20	45		
Campbell, Marion	Football		5	12		NFL
Campbell, Michael	Golf		5	20	25	
Campbell, Milt	Olympic		5	15		Decathlon
Campbell, Oliver	Tennis	+	18	48		HOF 1955
Campbell, Paul	Baseball		8	25		Debut 1941
Campbell, Ron	Baseball		3	12		Debut 1964
Campbell, Sir Malcolm	Auto Racing	+	100	250		HOF 1990, HOF 1994
Campbell, Tonie	Olympic		3	9		110 meter hurdles
Campbell, Tony	Basketball		3	12		played NBA 84-
Campbell, Vin	Baseball		35	95		Debut 1908
Campbell, William	Baseball		20	60		Debut 1933
Campi, Lou	Bowling	+	12	32		1968 ABC HOF
Camporese, Omar	Tennis		4	8		
Canadeo, Tony	Football		6	18	85	1974 HOF RB
Canale, George	Baseball		3	10		Debut 1989
Candaele, Casey	Baseball		3	12		Debut 1986
Candelaria, John	Baseball					Debut 1975
Candeloro, Phillipe	Olympic		7	25		Medalist. Figure Skating
Canel, Buck	Broadcaster		5	12		
Cangelosi, John	Baseball		3	10		Debut 1985
Canipe, Paul	Golf		5	20	25	

NAME	CATEGORY	+	SIG	SP	BALL	Comment
Cann, Howard	Basketball		25	65		HOF 1967-Coach
Cannizzaro, Chris	Baseball		4	15		Debut 1960
Cannon, Billy	Football		45	90		LSU. Heisman '59. NFL
Cannon, Jack	Football	+	15	60		CHOF Notre Dame
Cannon, Jimmy	Writer	+	8	25		1986 Ntl S&S HOF
Cannon, Joe	Baseball		3	12		Debut 1977
Cannon, Lawrence	Basketball		5	15		played NBA 69-73
Canseco, Jose	Baseball		7	25		Debut 1985
Cantaline, Anita	Bowling		5	15		1979 Women's IBC HOF
Cantwell, Tom	Baseball		30	55		Debut 1909 Cin. Reds
Canzoneri, Tony	Boxing		100	165		Light-wt Champ.
Capelli, Ivan	Auto Racing		4	8		
Caponi, Donna	Golf		5	20	25	
Cappelletti, Gino	Football		20	32		Heisman '73.Penn.St.NFL
Capra, Nick	Baseball		3	10		Debut 1982
Capri, Pat	Baseball		7	22		Debut 1944
Capriati, Jennifer	Tennis		8	38		
Capron, Ralph	Baseball		40	95		Debut 1912
Caras, Jimmy	Billiards		4	15		
Caray, Harry	Broadcaster	+	8	20		1989 Ntl S&S HOF
Caray, Skip	Broadcaster		6	6		
Carbajal, Michael	Boxing		15	38		Jr.Fly-Wt Champ.
Carbo, Bernie	Baseball		3	10		Debut 1969
Carbonneau,Guy	Hockey		5	26		
Card, Frank	Basketball		3	12		played NBA 68-77
Cardenal, Jose	Baseball		4	15		Debut 1963
Cardenas, Leo	Baseball		4	15		Debut 1960
Carew, Rod	Baseball					P-S HOF $30.Grt.Mo.$30
Carew, Rod	Baseball		10	25	30	HOF 1991. Gold Pl.$25
Carey, Andy	Baseball		4	14		Debut 1952
Carey, Bob	Football		10	35		NFL
Carey, Jim	Hockey		6	25	30	
Carey, Max	Baseball					HOF 1961
Carey, Max	Baseball		32	165	762	Gold Pl.$60,B&W PC $65
Carey, Rick	Olympic		4	12		Swim/100 M Back
Carey, Tom	Baseball		15	75		Debut 1935
Carideo, Frank	Football		7	25		CHOF Notre Dame
Carisch, Fred	Baseball		80	200		Debut 1903
Carl, Harland	Football		3	15		NFL
Carl, Howard	Basketball		8	35		played NBA 61
Carlesimo, P.J.	Basketball		3	8		Controversial Coach
Carleton, James "Tex"	Baseball		25	85		Debut 1932
Carlin, Jim	Baseball		6	38		Debut 1941
Carlisle, Chester	Basketball		10	50		played NBA 46
Carlisle, Daniel	Olympic		3	7		Trap shooting
Carlisle, Rick	Basketball		3	12		played NBA 84-87
Carlos, Don	Basketball		6	30		played NBA 63
Carlos, John	Olympic		10	35		200 Meters
Carlson, Adolph	Bowling	+	15	55		1941 ABC HOF
Carlson, Al	Basketball		3	15		played NBA 75
Carlson, Henry "Doc"	Basketball	+	22	60		HOF 1959 Coach
Carlson, Swede	Basketball		12	75		played NBA 46-50
Carlton, Guy	Olympic		3	8		Weightlifting
Carlton, Steve	Baseball					P-S HOF $35
Carlton, Steve	Baseball		10	22	25	HOF 1994. Gold Pl. $30
Carlyle, Cleo	Baseball		40	90		Debut 1927

NAME	CATEGORY	+	SIG	SP	BALL	Comment
Carmel, Duke	Baseball		4	12		Debut 1959
Carmichael, Al	Football		6	20		NFL
Carmichael, Harold	Football		6	16		NFL
Carmichael, John	Writer		3	6		
Carner, JoAnne	Golf		10	25	25	PGA, LPGA HOF '85,'82
Carnera, Primo	Boxing		225	450		1933-34 H-Wt Champ
Carneseca, Lou	Basketball		5	15		HOF 1992-Coach
Carnett, Eddie	Baseball		8	45		Debut 1941
Carnevale, Ben	Basketball		20	65		HOF 1969-Coach
Carney, Charles	Football	+	15	45		CHOF Illinois
Carney, Lester	Olympic		6	16		200 Meters
Carney, Robert	Basketball		10	50		played NBA 54
Carnnibear, Hiram	Rowing		110	220		
Caroline, J. C.	Football		7	22		CHOF Illinois
Carpenter, Bill	Football		10	35		CHOF Army
Carpenter, Hunter	Football		20	75		CHOF VPI
Carpenter, Ken	Football		5	18		NFL
Carpenter, Lew	Football		3	15		NFL
Carpenter, Rob	Football		3	12		NFL
Carpenter, Robert	Basketball		10	50		played NBA 40-53
Carpenter-Phinney, Connie	Olympic		3	8		Cycling
Carpentier, Georges	Boxing		130	275		Hvy-wt Champ.
Carr, Antoine	Basketball		3	12		played NBA 84-
Carr, Austin	Basketball		4	15		played NBA 71-80
Carr, Catherine	Olympic		3	8		Swim/breaststroke
Carr, Henry	Olympic		7	18		200 Meters
Carr, Joe	Football	+	450	1250		1963 HOF contributor
Carr, Joe	Golf		25	50	50	
Carr, Kenny	Basketball		3	12		played NBA 77-86
Carr, M. L.	Basketball		4	12		played NBA 75-84
Carr, Nate	Olympic		3	6		Wrestling
Carr, William	Olympic		15	45		400 meters
Carrasquel, Chico	Baseball		8	30		Debut 1953
Carreon, Camilo	Baseball		15	35		Debut 1959
Carreon, Mark	Baseball		3	10		Debut 1987
Carrier, James	Basketball		3	18		played NBA 67-72
Carrier, Mark	Football		4	12		NFL
Carrier, Mark	Football		4	15		NFL
Carrigan, Bill	Baseball		70	145		Debut 1906
Carrington, Robert	Basketball		3	15		played NBA 77-83
Carroll, Charles	Football		6	30		CHOF Washington
Carroll, Dixie	Baseball		32	85		Debut 1919
Carroll, Joe Barry	Basketball		3	8		played NBA 80-88
Carroll, Ralph	Baseball		45	125		Debut 1916
Carroll, Tommy	Baseball		4	15		Debut 1955
Carruthers, Kitty & Peter	Olympic		5	18		Figure Skating
Carson, Carlos	Football		3	12		NFL
Carson, Walter	Baseball		25	60		Debut 1934
Carson, Jimmy	Hockey		6	24		
Carswell, Frank	Baseball		4	25		Debut 1953
Carter, Anthony	Football		6	18		NFL
Carter, Butch	Basketball		3	12		played NBA 80-85
Carter, Chris	Football		6	18	100	NFL
Carter, Don	Bowling		8	32		1970 ABC, '75 PBA HOF
Carter, Gary	Baseball		4	15	40	Debut 1974 Montr.
Carter, George	Basketball		3	18		played NBA 67-75

NAME	CATEGORY	+	SIG	SP	BALL	Comment
Carter, Howard	Baseball		40	95		Debut 1926
Carter, Howard	Basketball		3	12		played NBA 84
Carter, Hurricane	Boxing		22	48		
Carter, Jake	Basketball		10	50		played NBA 48-49
Carter, James	Basketball		3	20		played NBA 69-76
Carter, Jim	Golf		5	20	25	
Carter, Jimmy	Boxing		25	55		Light-wt Champ. 3x
Carter, Joe	Baseball		5	20		Debut 1983
Carter, Keith	Olympic		4	10		Swim/breaststroke
Carter, Ki-Jana	Football		4	12	70	Penn. St. RB
Carter, LaVerne	Bowling		5	15		1977 Women's IBC HOF
Carter, Michael	Olympic		3	8		Shot Put
Carter, Otis	Baseball		35	75		Debut 1925
Carter, Pancho	Auto Racing		7	15		
Carter, Reginald	Basketball		3	15		played NBA 80-81
Carter, Ronald Jr.	Basketball		3	8		
Carter, Ruben "Hurricane"	Boxing		15	40		
Carter, Steve	Baseball		3	10		Debut 1989
Cartwright, Alexander	Baseball		1025	3200		HOF 1938
Cartwright, Bill	Basketball		4	15		played NBA 79-
Carty, Jay	Basketball		4	15		played NBA 68
Carty, Rico	Baseball		4	15		Debut 1963
Caruana, Frank	Bowling	+	10	22		1977 ABC HOF
Caruthers, Edward	Olympic		4	12		High Jump
Casals, Rosemary	Tennis		8	18		HOF 1996
Casanova, Len	Football		8	22		1977 CHOF coach
Casanova, Paul	Baseball		4	12		Debut 1965
Casares, Rick	Football		12	38		NFL
Case, Everett	Basketball	+	18	45		HOF 1981 Coach
Case, George	Baseball		12	2530		Debut 1937
Case, John R.	Olympic		15	50		U.S.A. 1912
Casey, Bernie	Football		5	20		NFL
Casey, Edward	Football	+	25	75		CHOF Harvard
Casey, Joe	Baseball		55	125		Debut 1909
Casey, Mickey	Baseball		20	55		Debut 1930, Negro League
Casey, Tom	Football		4	8		1964 Canadian HOF
Casey, Jon	Hockey		4	10		
Cash, Cornelius Jr.	Basketball		3	15		played NBA 76
Cash, Dave	Baseball		4	12		Debut 1969
Cash, Norm	Baseball		35	85		Debut 1958
Cash, Pat	Tennis		5	12		
Cash, Ron	Baseball		3	12		Debut 1973
Cash, Sam	Basketball		4	18		played NBA 72
Cashman, Wayne	Hockey		5	18		
Casper, Billy	Golf		10	25	25	PGA HOF 1978
Casper, Dave	Football		3	10		NFL
Cassady, Harry	Baseball		75	175		Debut 1904
Cassady, Howard	Football		6	25		CHOF OSU.Heisman '55
Cassell, Ollan	Olympic		3	7		Track relay
Cassini, Jack	Baseball		7	25		Debut 1949
Cassio, Marty	Bowling	+	12	30		1972 ABC HOF
Castellani, Rocky	Boxing		10	22		
Castellano, Graz	Bowling	+	8	28		1976 ABC HOF
Castiglia, Jim	Baseball		6	25		Debut 1942
Castiglione, Pete	Baseball		6	22		Debut 1947
Castilla, Vinny	Baseball		5	20		Debut 1991

NAME	CATEGORY	+	SIG	SP	BALL	Comment
Castillo, Carmen	Baseball		4	12		Debut 1982
Castillo, Juan	Baseball		4	12		Debut 1986
Castillo, Manny	Baseball		4	12		Debut 1980
Castillo, Marty	Baseball		4	16		Debut 1981
Castillo, Tony	Baseball		3	12		Debut 1978
Castino, John	Baseball		3	10		Debut 1979
Castino, Vince	Baseball		20	45		Debut 1943
Castleman, Clyde	Baseball		3	9		Debut 1934
Castleman, Foster	Baseball		4	18		Debut 1954
Catchings, Harvey	Basketball		3	18		played NBA 74-84
Cater, Danny	Baseball		3	12		Debut 1964
Cates, Eli	Baseball		70	150		Debut 1908
Catledge, Terry	Basketball		3	15		played NBA 85-
Catlett, Sid	Basketball		3	15		played NBA 71
Cattage, Bobby	Basketball		3	12		played NBA 81-85
Caulfield, John	Baseball		12	42		Debut 1946
Caulkins, Tracy	Olympic		7	20		Swim/400 Ind. Med.
Causey, Wayne	Baseball		4	15		Debut 1955
Cauthen, Steve	Horse Racing		8	25		HOF 1994 jockey
Cavanaugh, Chris	Olympic		3	6		Swim/relay
Cavanaugh, John	Baseball		50	110		Debut 1919
Cavanaugh, Matt	Football		3	12		NFL
Cavanough, Frank	Football		15	45		1954 CHOF coach
Cavaretta, Phil	Baseball		8	22		Debut 1934
Cavenall, Ronnie	Basketball		3	15		played NBA 84-88
Cawley, Warren	Olympic		4	10		Hurdles
Cedeno, Cesar	Baseball		4	14		Debut 1970
Cejka, Alexander	Golf		5	20	25	
Cepeda, Orlando	Baseball		4	18	25	Debut 1958
Cerdan, Marcel	Boxing		200	350		
Cerone, Rick	Baseball		3	10		Debut 1975
Cerrudo, Ron	Golf		5	20	25	
Cerv, Bob	Baseball		8	18		Debut 1951
Cervi, Al	Basketball		6	22	100	HOF 1984
Cetlinski, Matt	Olympic		3	6		Swim/relay
Cey, Ron	Baseball		4	12		Debut 1971
Chace, Malcolm	Tennis	+	18	50		HOF 1961
Chacon, Bobby	Boxing		12	30		Feather&Jr.Light-wt Champ.
Chacon, Elio	Baseball		5	15		Debut 1960
Chadwick, Bill	Hockey		5	18		1974 US HOF ref
Chadwick, Elizabeth	Golf		5	20	25	
Chadwick, Florence	Swimming		10	30		Cross Channel Records
Chadwick, Henry	Baseball		1375	4250		HOF 1938
Chaffee, Jon	Golf		5	20	25	
Chaffee, Suzy	Olympic		5	15		Skiing
Chagnon, Leon	Baseball		20			Debut 1932 Pirates
Chaisson, Ray	Hockey	+	10	25		1974 US HOF
Chalk, Dave	Baseball		4	12		Debut 1973
Chamaco, Joe	Pocket Billiards		40	110		
Chamberlain, Guy	Football	+	250	550		1965 HOF player/coach
Chamberlain, Joe	Baseball		15	55		Debut 1934
Chamberlain, William	Basketball		3	18		played NBA 72-73
Chamberlain, Wilt	Basketball		35	100	250	HOF 1978
Chambers, Al	Baseball		4	12		Debut 1983
Chambers, Cliff	Baseball		3			Debut 1943 Cubs
Chambers, Doris	Golf		80	225		

NAME	CATEGORY	+	SIG	SP	BALL	Comment
Chambers, Jerry	Basketball		5	25		played NBA 65-73
Chambers, Tom	Basketball		4	18		played NBA 81-
Chamblee, Brandel	Golf		5	20	25	
Chambliss, Chris	Baseball		4	12		Debut 1971
Champion, Mike	Baseball		3	12		Debut 1976
Champion, Mike	Basketball		3	10		played NBA 88
Chance, Bob	Baseball		3	15		Debut 1963
Chance, Dean	Baseball		6	18		Debut 1961
Chance, Frank	Baseball		1050	3250	7250	HOF 1946
Chandler, A.B. "Happy"	Baseball					P-S HOF $60, Grt.Mo.$70
Chandler, A.B. "Happy"	Baseball		15	45	125	HOF 1982. Gold Pl. $22
Chandler, Bob	Football		10	40		NFL
Chandler, Don	Football		4	15		NFL
Chandler, Jeff	Boxing		15	35		Bantam-wt Champ.
Chandler, Jennifer	Olympic		6	24		Diving
Chandler, Spurgeon "Spud"	Baseball		15	48		Debut 1937
Chandler, Wes	Football		4	15		NFL
Chandnois, Lynn	Football		5	22		NFL
Chaney, Darrel	Baseball		3	16		Debut 1969
Chaney, Don	Basketball		4	15		played NBA 68-73
Chaney, John	Basketball		10	50		played NBA 46-49
Chang, Michael	Tennis		10	45		
Chankle, Joel	Olympic		3	7		110 meter hurdles
Chant, Charlie	Baseball		3	15		Debut 1975
Chaplin, Ed	Baseball		40	90		Debut 1920
Chapman, Ben	Baseball		20	45		Debut 1930
Chapman, Calvin	Baseball		15	55		Debut 1935
Chapman, Dr. Tim	Cross Country		3	6		
Chapman, Emily	Bowling	+	10	32		1957 Women's IBC HOF
Chapman, Fred	Baseball		18	60		Debut 1939
Chapman, Glenn	Baseball		15	55		Debut 1934
Chapman, Harry	Baseball		10	35		Debut 1912
Chapman, Kelvin	Baseball		3	12		Debut 1979
Chapman, Rex	Basketball		3	18		played NBA 88-
Chapman, Richard	Golf		50	125		
Chapman, Sam	Baseball		7	30		Debut 1938
Chapman, Sam	Football		5	20		CHOF California
Chapman, Wayne	Basketball		3	22		played NBA 68-71
Chapot, Frank	Olympic		5	10		Equestrian
Chappas, Harry	Baseball		3	12		Debut 1978
Chappell, Leonard	Basketball		4	22		played NBA 62-71
Chappuis, Bob	Football		4	18		CHOF Michigan
Charboneau, Joe	Baseball		4	12		Debut 1980
Charles, Bob	Golf		10	20	30	
Charles, Ed	Baseball		4	12		Debut 1962
Charles, Ezzard	Boxing		95	175		1949-51 H-Wt Champ
Charles, Kenneth	Basketball		3	20		played NBA 73-77
Charles, Lorenzo	Basketball		3	15		played NBA 85
Charleston, Oscar M.	Baseball		1350	3600	7000	HOF 1976
Charlton, Bobby	Soccer		15	30		
Charlton, Norm	Baseball		3	10	25	Debut 1968
Charron, Guy	Hockey		4	20		
Chartak, Mike	Baseball		22	95		Debut 1940
Chase, John	Hockey		5	20		1973 US HOF
Chase, LeRoy	Bowling	+	8	22		1972 ABC HOF-Mer.Serv.
Chatham, Buster	Baseball		25	60		Debut 1930

NAME	CATEGORY	+	SIG	SP	BALL	Comment
Chavez, Julio Cesar	Boxing		15	45		3x World Champion
Cheeks, Maurice	Basketball		5	18		played NBA 78-
Cheeseborough, Chandra	Olympic		3	8		400 meters
Cheever, Eddie	Auto Racing		4	8		
Cheevers, Gerry	Hockey		6	25	18	1985 HOF goal
Chelios, Chris	Hockey		4	25	25	
Chen, Tze-Chung	Golf		10	35	40	
Cheney, Larry	Baseball		15	45		Debut 1913
Cheng, Chi	Track		12	30		
Chenier, Philip	Basketball		4	18		played NBA 71-80
Chenoweth, Dean	Auto Racing	+	18	50		HOF 1991
Chenoweth, Dean	Boat Racing		25	95		
Chervinko, Paul	Baseball		22	65		Debut 1937
Chesbro, Jack	Baseball		1050	3625	10000	HOF 1946
Chester, Raymond	Football		5	18		NFL
Cheveldae, Tim	Hockey		3	15		
Chevrolet, Gaston	Auto Racing	+	275			
Chevrolet, Louis	Auto Racing	+	750			HOF 1992, HOF 1995
Chievous, Derrick	Basketball		3	15		played NBA 83-
Childress, Joe	Football		5	15		NFL
Childress, Ray	Football		3	12		NFL
Childs, Frank E.	Horse Racing		5	15		HOF 1968 trainer
Chiles, Rich	Baseball		3	12		Debut 1971
Chin, Tiffany	Figure Skating		3	18		U.S. Champion
Chiniglia, Giorgio	Soccer		7	22		
Chiozza, Dino	Baseball		25	65		Debut 1935
Chiozza, Lou	Baseball		20	55		Debut 1934
Chipman, Arthur	Football		4	12		1969 Canadian HOF
Chipple, Walt	Baseball		10	25		Debut 1945
Chism, Tom	Baseball		3	12		Debut 1979
Chitalada, Sot	Boxing		7	15		Fly-Wt. Champ.
Chiti, Harry	Baseball		8	22		Debut 1950
Chmura, Mark	Football		5	20		NFL Packer Tight End
Chollet, LeRoy	Basketball		10	50		played NBA 49-50
Chones, Jim	Basketball		4	15		played NBA 72-81
Chorkina, Svetlana	Olympic		7	35		Gold Medal. Gymnastics
Chow, Amy	Olympic		5	45		Silver Med. Gymnastics
Chozen, Harry	Baseball		10	35		Debut 1937
Chrisley, Neil	Baseball		4	15		Debut 1957
Christ, Frederick	Basketball		10	45		played NBA 54
Christ, George	Golf		40	95		
Christensen, Bruce	Baseball		3	12		Debut 1971
Christensen, Calvin	Basketball		10	50		played NBA 50-54
Christensen, John	Baseball		3	10		Debut 1984
Christensen, Todd	Football		4	15		NFL
Christensen, Walter	Baseball		35	85		Debut 1926
Christian, Bill	Hockey		5	14		1984 US HOF
Christian, Bob	Baseball		40	82		Debut 1968
Christian, Bob	Basketball		3	22		played NBA 69-73
Christian, Dave	Hockey		4	12		
Christian, Neil	Golf		70	170		
Christian, Roger	Hockey		5	15		1989 US HOF
Christiansen, Jack	Football	+	75	225		1970 HOF DB
Christie, Linford	Olympic		5	22		Olymp.Gold. 100-Meters
Christie, Michael	Golf		5	20	25	
Christie, Walter	Auto Racing	+	20	45		

NAME	CATEGORY	+	SIG	SP	BALL	Comment
Christman, Mark	Baseball		30	75		Debut 1938
Christman, Paul	Football	+	30	95		CHOF Missouri
Christmas, Steve	Baseball		3	12		Debut 1983
Christopher, Joe	Baseball		4	10		Debut 1959
Christopher, Lloyd	Baseball		4	15		Debut 1945
Christy, Dick	Football		20	75		NFL
Chubin, Chube	Basketball		5	25		played NBA 57-63
Church, Emory "Bubba"	Baseball		5			Debut 1950 Phillies
Churla, Shane	Hockey		5	20		
Churry, John	Baseball		40	90		Debut 1924
Chuvalo, George	Boxing		10	30		
Ciaffone, Larry	Baseball		7	22		Debut 1951
Cias, Darryl	Baseball		3	10		Debut 1983
Ciccarelli, Dino	Hockey		7	22		
Cicero, Joe	Baseball		40	90		Debut 1929
Cicotte, Eddie	Baseball		157	362		Debut 1905
Cieslak, Ted	Baseball		6	22		Debut 1944
Cifers, Ed	Football		8	35		NFL
Cihocki, A1	Baseball		6	22		Debut 1945
Cihocki, Ed	Baseball		15	50		Debut 1932
Cimoli, Gino	Baseball		8	19		Debut 1956
Cink, Henri	Golf		5	20	25	
Cipriani, Frank	Baseball		4	15		Debut 1961
Cisar, George	Baseball		15	42		Debut 1937
Ciuci, Henri	Golf		90	225		
Claar, Brian	Golf		5	20	25	
Clabaugh, John	Baseball		25	75		Debut 1925
Clair, Frank	Football		4	10		1981 Canadian HOF
Claire, Ebba St.	Baseball		15	38		Debut 1951
Clampett, Bobby	Golf		5	20	25	
Clancy, John	Baseball		30	95		Debut 1924
Clancy, King	Hockey		50	225		1958 HOF def
Clanton, Eucal	Baseball		49	90		Debut 1922
Clapp, Charles	Olympic		3	8		Rowing
Clapper, Dit	Hockey		60	225		1947 HOF def
Clarey, Doug	Baseball		3	12		Debut 1976
Clark, Allie	Baseball		7	24		Debut 1947 Yankees
Clark, Archie	Basketball		6	22		played NBA 66-75
Clark, Bobby	Baseball		3	12		Debut 1979
Clark, Carlos	Basketball		3	15		played NBA 83-84
Clark, Clarence	Golf		65	195		
Clark, Clarence	Tennis	+	12	50		HOF 1983
Clark, Dave	Baseball		3	10		Debut 1986
Clark, Don	Hockey		4	12		1978 US HOF admin
Clark, Dutch	Football	+	65	145		1963 HOF QB
Clark, Frank	Golf		35	95		
Clark, Gary	Football		5	15		NFL
Clark, Glen	Baseball		4	15		Debut 1967
Clark, Gordon	Golf		5	20	25	
Clark, Howard	Golf		5	20	25	
Clark, Jack	Baseball		4	12		Debut 1975
Clark, Jerald	Baseball		3	10		Debut 1988
Clark, Jim	Baseball		3	12		Debut 1971
Clark, Jim	Baseball		6	24		Debut 1948
Clark, Jimmy	Auto Racing	+	90	350		HOF 1990, HOF 1990
Clark, Jimmy	Golf		25	55		

NAME	CATEGORY	+	SIG	SP	BALL	Comment
Clark, Joseph	Tennis	+	15	45		HOF 1955
Clark, Kristen	Skiing; Alpine		2	6		U.S. Champion
Clark, Mary Ellen	Olympic		2	10		Medal Platform Diving
Clark, Mel	Baseball		6	22		Debut 1951
Clark, Richard	Basketball		4	22		played NBA 67-68
Clark, Ron	Baseball		3	15		Debut 1966
Clark, Will	Baseball		5	28		Debut 1985
Clarke, Bobby	Hockey		5	22	25	1987 HOF fwd
Clarke, Fred	Baseball		280	500	3125	HOF 1945, B&W PC $525
Clarke, Grey	Baseball		7	25		Debut 1944
Clarke, Horace	Baseball		4	14		Debut 1965
Clarke, Leon	Football		6	20		NFL
Clarke, Stu	Baseball		22	70		Debut 1929
Clarke, Tom	Baseball		60			Debut 1909 Reds Catcher
Clarkson, Buzz	Baseball		9	32		Debut 1952
Clarkson, John	Baseball		1650	3000		HOF 1963
Clary, Ellis	Baseball		5	18		Debut 1942
Clause, Frank	Bowling	+	8	28		1980 ABC HOF
Clavet, Francisco	Tennis		6	15		
Clawson, John	Basketball		3	20		played NBA 68
Clay, Cassius	Boxing		135	325		1964-68 H-Wt Champ
Clay, Dain	Baseball		6	30		Debut 1943
Clayton, Mark	Football		4	12		NFL
Cleamons, James	Basketball		3	15		played NBA 71-79
Clearwater, Keith	Golf		5	20	25	
Cleary, Bill	Hockey		5	15		1976 US HOF
Cleary, Bob	Hockey		5	15		1981 US HOF
Cleary, Paul	Football		5	20		CHOF Southern California
Cleghorn, Sprague	Hockey		50	125		1958 HOF def
Clemens, Bob	Baseball		50	125		Debut 1914
Clemens, Chet	Baseball		25	65		Debut 1939
Clemens, Clem	Baseball		50	110		Debut 1914
Clemens, Doug	Baseball		4	15		Debut 1960
Clemens, John	Basketball		3	20		played NBA 65-75
Clemens, Roger	Baseball		16	67	52	Debut 1984
Clemens, Roger "Rocket"	Baseball		15	60		
Clement, Bill	Hockey		3	15		
Clemente, Roberto	Baseball		312	400	2350	HOF 1973
Clements, Lennie	Golf		5	20	25	
Clendenon, Donn	Baseball		4	12		Debut 1961
Clevenger, Zora	Football	+	18	60		CHOF Indiana
Clift, Harland	Baseball		20	40		Debut 1934
Clifton, Herman "Flea"	Baseball		8	30		Debut 1934
Clifton, Sweetwater	Basketball		15	55		played NBA 50-57
Cline, Ty	Baseball		4	12		Debut 1960
Clines, Gene	Baseball		4	12		Debut 1970
Clinton, Lu	Baseball		4	12		Debut 1960
Closs, William	Basketball		10	50		played NBA 46-51
Clothier, William	Tennis	+	20	65		HOF 1956
Cloud, Jack	Football	+	7	30		CHOF William and Mary
Cloutier, Joe	Auto Racing	+	35	85		
Cloutier, Real	Hockey		3	15		
Cloyd, Paul	Basketball		10	50		played NBA 47-49
Cluggish, Bob	Basketball		10	50		played NBA 46
Clyde, Benjamin	Basketball		4	20		played NBA 74
Coachman, Alice	Olympic		8	25		High Jump

NAME	CATEGORY	+	SIG	SP	BALL	Comment
Coage, Allen	Olympic		3	6		Judo
Coakley, Andy	Baseball		65			Player & Gehrig Coach
Coan, Gil	Baseball		8	22		Debut 1946
Coates, Ben	Football		5	22	100	NFL
Cobb, Randall "Tex"	Boxing		10	22		
Cobb, Ty	Baseball		462	1350	2750	HOF 1936.B&W PC$1300
Cobbledick, Gordon	Writer		3	6		
Coble, Dave	Baseball		35	80		Debut 1939
Coburn, Doris	Bowling		5	20		1976 Women's IBC HOF
Cochet, Henri	Tennis	+	22	80		HOF 1976
Cochran, Barbara	Olympic		8	22		Alpine Skiing
Cochran, Gary	Football	+	25	100		CHOF Princeton
Cochran, Richard L.	Olympic		3	8		Discus
Cochran, Roy	Olympic		5	15		400 M Hurdles
Cochran, Russ	Golf		5	20	25	
Cochran, Welker	Pocket Billiards		25	75		
Cochrane, Dave	Baseball		3	10		Debut 1986
Cochrane, Mickey	Baseball		175	375	2175	HOF 1947. B&W PC $725
Cockerill, Kay	Golf		5	20	25	
Cockroft, Don	Football		3	12		NFL
Cocks, W. Burling	Horse Racing		10	25		HOF 1985 trainer
Cody, Josh	Football	+	18	60		CHOF Vanderbilt
Coe, Charles	Golf		55	115		
Coe, Dawn	Golf		5	20	25	
Coe, Sebastian	Olympic		20	40		Track 1500 Meters
Coetzee, Gerrie	Boxing		15	30		1983-84 H-Wt Champ
Coetzer, Amanda	Tennis		6	15		
Coffey, Jack	Baseball		35			Debut 1909.Inf/Reds&Det.
Coffey, Paul	Hockey		6	28	30	
Coffey, Tommy Joe	Football		4	8		1977 Canadian HOF
Cofield, Frederick	Basketball		3	6		played NBA 85-86
Cogan, Kevin	Auto Racing		7	16		
Cogdill, Gail	Football		6	18		NFL
Coggins, Frank	Baseball		4	18		Debut 1967
Coggins, Rich	Baseball		4	15		Debut 1972
Cohen, Alta	Baseball		30	95		Debut 1931
Cohen, Andy	Baseball		25	65		Debut 1926
Cohen, Tiffany	Olympic		6	18		Swim/400 M Free
Cohn, Alfred	Bowling		5	14		1985 ABC HOF
Coker, Jimmie	Baseball		4	15		Debut 1958
Coker, John	Bowling	+	8	18		1980 ABC HOF-Mer.Serv.
Cokes, Curtis	Boxing		10	22		
Col1ins, Donald	Basketball		3	12		played NBA 80-86
Colangelo, Jerry	Basketball		2	5		Suns Exec.
Colavito, Rocky	Baseball		10	25		Debut 1955
Colbern, Mike	Baseball		3	10		Debut 1978
Colbert, Jim	Golf		5	20	25	
Colbert, Nate	Baseball		4	12		Debut 1966
Cole, Bobby	Golf		5	20	25	
Cole, Dave	Baseball		6			Debut 1950 Bost. Braves
Cole, Dick	Baseball		6	22		Debut 1951
Cole, Ed	Baseball		12			Debut 1938 STL Browns
Cole, Willis	Baseball		55	125		Debut 1909 Outf Chi Sox
Colella, Lynn	Olympic		3	7		Swim/butterfly
Colella, Rick	Olympic		3	8		Swim/200 breast
Coleman, Ben	Basketball		3	12		played NBA 86-

NAME	CATEGORY	+	SIG	SP	BALL	Comment
Coleman, Clarence	Baseball		4	15		Debut 1961
Coleman, Curt	Baseball		35	100		Debut 1912
Coleman, Dave	Baseball		3	10		Debut 1977
Coleman, Don	Football		5	18		CHOF Michigan State
Coleman, E. C.	Basketball		3	15		played NBA 73-78
Coleman, Georgia	Olympic		10	45		Diving
Coleman, Gordy	Baseball		5			Debut 1959 Cleve.
Coleman, Jack	Basketball		12	50		played NBA 49-57
Coleman, Jerry	Baseball		6	14		Debut 1949
Coleman, Joe H.	Baseball		2			Debut 1965 Senators
Coleman, Joe P.	Baseball		10			Debut 1942 Phil.
Coleman, Norris	Basketball		4	12		played NBA 87
Coleman, Ray	Baseball		4			Debut 1951 Browns
Coleman, Vince	Baseball		5	10		Debut 1985
Coles, Chuck	Baseball		4	15		Debut 1958
Coles, Darnell	Baseball		5	10		Debut 1983
Coles, Neil	Golf		10	30	35	
Coletta, Chris	Baseball		4	10		Debut 1972
Collett, Wayne	Olympic		5	10		400 Meters
Collier, Blanton	Football		10	22		NFL
Collier, Chuck	Bowling	+	8	22		1963 ABC HOF-Mer.Serv.
Collier, Jeanne	Olympic		5	18		Diving
Collier, Phil	Writer		4	8		
Collingham, Janet	Golf		5	20	25	
Collins, Arthur	Basketball		4	12		played NBA 80
Collins, Bill	Golf		25	50		
Collins, Dave	Baseball		5	12		Debut 1975
Collins, Doug	Basketball		8	20	100	played NBA 73-80, Coach
Collins, Eddie	Baseball		235	425	5000	HOF 1939. B&W PC $790
Collins, Eddie Jr.	Baseball		15	55		Debut 1939
Collins, Gary	Football		4	15		NFL
Collins, James	Baseball		50	125		Debut 1931
Collins, Jennifer	Skiing; Alpine		2	6		U.S. Champion
Collins, Jimmy	Baseball		1000	1933	5775	HOF 1945
Collins, Jimmy	Basketball		4	18		played NBA 70-71
Collins, Joe	Baseball		15	35		Debut 1948
Collins, John E.	Baseball		40	90		Debut 1914
Collins, Kerry	Football		7	28	90	NFL Panthers QB
Collins, Kevin	Baseball		5	15		Debut 1965
Collins, Ray	Baseball		35	95		Red Sox 1909-15
Collins, Tony	Football		4	12		NFL
Collinsworth, Chris	Football		5	15		NFL
Collombin, Rolland	Olympic		10	28		Alpine skiing
Collum. Jackie	Baseball		7			Debut 1951STL Cards
Colman, Frank	Baseball		19	40		Debut 1942
Colo, Don	Football		8	16		NFL
Colone, Bells	Basketball		6	50		played NBA 48
Colter, Steve	Basketball		10	15		played NBA 74-83
Coltiletti, Frank	Horse Racing		15	35		HOF 1970 jockey
Coluccio, Bob	Baseball		4	12		Debut 1973
Colville, Neil	Hockey		45	110		1967 HOF fwd
Colwel, Paul	Bowling		5	12		1991 PBA HOF
Comaneci, Nadia	Olympic		15	40		Gymnastics
Combs, Earl	Baseball		65	350	2200	HOF 1970. Gold Pl.$140
Combs, Edwin	Basketball		3	12		played NBA 83
Combs, Glenn	Basketball		3	15		played NBA 68-74

NAME	CATEGORY	+	SIG	SP	BALL	Comment
Combs, Merrill	Baseball		12	45		Debut 1947
Comeaux, John	Basketball		4	18		played NBA 67
Comegys, Dallas	Basketball		3	12		played NBA 87-
Comer, Wayne	Baseball		4	10		Debut 1967
Comiskey, Charles	Baseball		608	1375	8000	HOF 1939
Comiskey, J. Louis	Baseball		75	250		Brother of Charles
Comley, Lawrence	Basketball		3	15		played NBA 63
Command, Jim	Baseball		6	22		Debut 1954
Compston, Archie	Golf		65	195		
Compton, Mike	Baseball		4	12		Debut 1970
Compton, Pete	Baseball		55	125		Debut 1911
Conacher, Charlie	Hockey		45	140		1961 HOF fwd
Conacher, Lionel	Football	+	12	22		1963 Canadian HOF
Conacher, Roy	Hockey		8	32		
Conatser, Clint	Baseball		6	22		Debut 1948
Concannon, Jack	Football		4	14		NFL
Concepcion, Dave	Baseball		5	15		Debut 1970
Concepcion, Onix	Baseball		4	12		Debut 1980
Cone, Carin	Olympic		7	22		Swim/backstroke
Cone, David	Baseball		6	28	30	Debut 1986
Cone, Fred	Football		4	18		NFL
Conerly, Charlie	Football		15	45		CHOF Mississippi
Congdon, Charles	Golf		35	80		
Congdon, Jeffrey	Basketball		5	22		played NBA 67-71
Conigliaro, Billy	Baseball		10	15		Debut 1969
Conigliaro, Tony	Baseball		55	195		Debut 1964
Conlan, Jocko	Baseball					P-S HOF $85
Conlan, Jocko	Baseball		20	45	95	HOF 1974. Gold Pl $25
Conlan, Shane	Football		3	10		NFL
Conley, Bob	Baseball		4			Debut 1958 Phillies
Conley, George	Basketball		3	20		played NBA 67
Conley, Mike	Olympic		4	25		Triple Jump
Conlin, Edward	Basketball		6	45		played NBA 55-61
Conlon, Art	Baseball		28	65		Debut 1923
Conn, Billy	Boxing		15	35		Lt. Hvy-Wt Champ.
Connally, Fritz	Baseball		3	10		Debut 1983
Connally, George "Sarge"	Baseball		40			Debut 1921 ChiSox
Connatser, Bruce	Baseball		40	95		Debut 1931
Connell, Alex	Hockey		45	155		1958 HOF goal
Connell, Joe	Baseball		35	70		Debut 1926
Connelly, Lex	Rodeo		5	12		
Connelly, Lynn	Golf		5	20	25	
Connelly, Wayne	Hockey		4	18		
Conner, Bart	Olympic		6	18		Gymnastics
Conner, Clyde	Football		5	18		NFL
Conner, Dennis	Yachting		15	45		
Conner, Frank	Golf		7	25	25	
Conner, Jimmy	Basketball		3	12		played NBA 75
Conner, Lester	Basketball		3	10		played NBA 82-
Connolly, Harold	Olympic		10	20		Hammer Throw
Connolly, James B.	Olympic		50	200		Track-1st U.S. Gold
Connolly, Maureen	Tennis	+	195	400		HOF 1968
Connolly, Olga	Olympic		8	22		Track
Connolly, Thomas	Baseball		650	1525	6875	HOF '53. B&W PC $1175
Connor, George	Football		6	18	85	1975 HOF LB
Connor, Richard	Olympic		3	7		Diving

NAME	CATEGORY	+	SIG	SP	BALL	Comment
Connor, Roger	Baseball		1875	4500	8000	HOF 1976
Connors, Chuck	Baseball		10	25		Also "The Rifleman"
Connors, Jimmy	Tennis		10	70		
Connors, Merv	Baseball		8	38		Debut 1937
Conrad, Joe	Golf		22	55		
Conrad, Mad	Aviation		45	175		
Conradt, Jody	Basketball		2	5		Women's Coach
Conroy, Bill	Baseball		15	45		Debut 1935 A's
Conroy, Pep	Baseball		30	90		Debut 1923
Conroy, Tony	Hockey	+	10	25		1975 US HOF
Considine, Bob	Writer	+	8	18		1980 Ntl S&S HOF
Consolo, Billy	Baseball		4	15		Debut 1953
Convington, Wes	Baseball		9	30		Debut 1956
Conway, Charlie	Baseball		55	140		Debut 1911
Conway, Curtis	Football		4	12	70	NFL
Conway, Hollis	Olympic		3	9		High Jump
Conway, Rip	Baseball		50	125		Debut 1918
Conzelman, Jimmy	Football	+	125	480		1964 HOF QB
Coody, Charles	Golf		10	25	35	
Coogan, Dale	Baseball		10	35		Debut 1950
Cook, Bert	Basketball		10	45		played NBA 54
Cook, Bill	Hockey		50	175		1952 HOF fwd
Cook, Cliff	Baseball		4	15		Debut 1959
Cook, Darwin	Basketball		3	15		played NBA 80-90
Cook, Jeffrey	Basketball		3	10		played NBA 79-87
Cook, John	Golf		5	25	25	
Cook, Luther	Baseball		50	125		Debut 1913
Cook, Norman	Basketball		3	12		played NBA 76-77
Cook, Robert	Basketball		10	50		played NBA 48-49
Cooke, Allen	Baseball		22	50		Debut 1930
Cooke, David	Basketball		3	10		played NBA 85
Cooke, Jack Kent	Franchise Owner		10	25		3 Sport Owner
Cooke, Joseph	Basketball		3	15		played NBA 70
Coolbaugh, Scott	Baseball		3	10		Debut 1989
Coombs, Cecil	Baseball		60	125		Debut 1914
Coombs, Jack	Baseball		150			Debut 1906. Standg.Rec'd
Cooney, Gerry	Boxing		10	20		Hvy-Wt Contender
Cooney, James E.	Baseball		45	100		Debut 1917 Bost. RedSox
Cooney, Johnny	Baseball		40	48		Debut 1921 Bost. Braves
Cooper, Ashley	Tennis		10	38		HOF 1991
Cooper, Cecil	Baseball		5	15		Debut 1971
Cooper, Charles	Basketball	+	15	55		HOF 1976 "Tarzan"
Cooper, Christin	Olympic		6	28		Alpine skiing
Cooper, Chuck	Basketball		10	50		played NBA 50-55
Cooper, Claude	Baseball		50	125		Debut 1913
Cooper, Earl	Auto Racing	+	45	160		
Cooper, Gary	Baseball		3	10		Debut 1980
Cooper, Harry "Lighthorse"	Golf		15	25	30	PGA HOF 1992
Cooper, Henry	Boxing		10	35		Brit. Hvy-Wt Champ.
Cooper, Joseph	Basketball		4	12		played NBA 81-84
Cooper, Michael	Basketball		6	20		played NBA 78-
Cooper, Pat	Baseball		6	22		Debut 1946
Cooper, Pete	Golf		25	70		
Cooper, Walker	Baseball		14	40		Debut 1940 Cards
Cooper, Wayne	Basketball		4	15		played NBA 78-
Cooper, Wilbur	Baseball		75	200		Debut 1912

NAME	CATEGORY	+	SIG	SP	BALL	Comment
Cope, Derrike	Auto Racing		5	14		
Copeland, Hollis	Basketball		3	15		played NBA 79-80
Copeland, Lillian	Olympic		20	75		Track
Copeland, Royal	Football		4	8		1988 Canadian HOF
Cora, Joey	Baseball		4	22		Debut 1987
Corbett III, Young	Boxing		18	38		
Corbett, Doug	Baseball		3			Debut 1980 Twins
Corbett, Gene	Baseball		15	40		Debut 1936
Corbett, James J.	Boxing		425	800		1892-97 H-Wt Champ
Corbin, Tyrone	Basketball		3	15		played NBA 85-
Corbin, William	Football	+	25	100		CHOF Yale
Corbitt, Claude	Baseball		22	65		Debut 1945
Corbus, William	Football		6	28		CHOF Stanford
Corcoran, Fred	Golf		50	125		PGA HOF 1975, Contrib.
Corcoran, Tim	Baseball		3	10		Debut 1977
Cordero Jr, Angel	Horse Racing		8	29		HOF 1988 jockey
Corey, Mark	Baseball		3	10		Debut 1979
Corley, Kenneth	Basketball		10	50		played NBA 46
Corley, Raymond	Basketball		10	50		played NBA 49-52
Cornelius, Kathy	Golf		15	45	30	
Corrales, Pat	Baseball		4	12		Debut 1964 Phillies
Correa, Ed	Baseball		4	10		Debut 1985
Correll, Vic	Baseball		3	12		Debut 1972 RedSox
Corriden, John Jr.	Baseball		7	22		Debut 1945
Corriden, John Sr.	Baseball		65	165		Debut 1910
Corrigall, Jim	Football		4	8		1990 Canadian HOF
Corson, Shayne	Hockey		3	18		
Coryell, Don	Football		3	6		NFL
Corzine, David	Basketball		3	12		played NBA 78-
Coscarart, Joe	Baseball		7	32		Debut 1935
Coscarart, Pete	Baseball		6	30		Debut 1938 Brklyn Dodg.
Cosell, Howard	Broadcaster		15	50		
Cosey, Ray	Baseball		3	10		Debut 1980
Costa, Alberta	Tennis		4	18		Broke to 20
Costa, Carlos	Tennis		8	18		
Costas, Bob	Broadcaster		5	10		
Costello, Larry	Basketball		7	18		played NBA 54-67
Costello, Pat	Bowling		5	10		1986 Women's IBC HOF
Costie, Candy	Olympic		5	20		Synch. Swimming
Cote, Pete	Baseball		28	60		Debut 1926
Cothren, Paige	Football		6	18		NFL
Cotter, Squire	Baseball					
Cottier, Chuck	Baseball		4	10		Debut 1959
Cotto, Henry	Baseball		4	10		Debut 1984
Cotton, Henry	Golf		75	275		
Cotton, John	Basketball		10	50		played NBA 48-53
Coughran, John	Basketball		3	12		played NBA 79
Coughtry, Marlan	Baseball		3	15		Debut 1960
Coulon, Johnny	Boxing		50	110		
Coulter, Art	Hockey		6	25		1974 HOF def
Coulter, DeWitt	Football		20	65		NFL
Coulter, Tom	Baseball		3	15		Debut 1969 Cards
Counsilman, James "Doc"	Swimming		8	28		
Counts, Mel	Basketball		6	15		played NBA 64-65
Couples, Fred	Golf		15	30	35	
Courier, Jim	Tennis		12	50		

NAME	CATEGORY	+	SIG	SP	BALL	Comment
Cournoyer, Yvan	Hockey		7	28	30	1982 HOF fwd
Court, Margaret	Tennis		10	38		
Courtin, Stephen	Basketball		4	18		played NBA 64
Courtnall, Geoff	Hockey		5	20		
Courtnall, Russ	Hockey		3	18		
Courtney, Chuck	Golf		15	40		
Courtney, Clint	Baseball		15	40		Debut 1951
Courtney, Tom	Olympic		10	20		Track
Cousins, Robin	Olympic		6	15		Figure Skating
Cousy, Bob	Basketball		10	35	150	HOF 1970
Covaleski, Stan	Baseball		25	100	325	HOF 1969. Gold Pl $35
Coveleski, Stan	Baseball					P-S HOF $575
Cowan, Billy	Baseball		5	15		Debut 1963 Cubs
Cowan, Gary	Golf		10	30	25	
Cowan, Hector	Football	+	25	100		CHOF Princeton
Cowan, John	Golf		45	195		
Cowens, Al	Baseball		4	12		Debut 1974
Cowens, Dave	Basketball		7	24	125	HOF 1991
Cowher, Bill	Football		3	12		NFL Steelers Coach
Cowley, Bill	Hockey		7	15		1968 HOF fwd
Cox, Billy	Baseball		68	142		Debut 1941
Cox, Bobby	Baseball		4	8		Debut 1968 Yankees
Cox, Bobby	Football		3	12		NFL
Cox, Ernest	Football	+	12	24		1963 Canadian HOF
Cox, Fred	Football		4	15		NFL
Cox, Jeff	Baseball		3	10		Debut 1980
Cox, Jim	Baseball		3	10		Debut 1973
Cox, John	Basketball		3	12		played NBA 82
Cox, Johnny W.	Basketball		4	20		played NBA 62
Cox, Larry	Baseball		3	10		Debut 1973
Cox, Ted	Baseball		3	10		Debut 1977
Cox, Wesley	Basketball		3	12		played NBA 77-78
Cox, Wiffy	Golf		50	165		
Cox, William J.	Golf		50	150		
Coy, Edward	Football	+	60	200		CHOF Yale
Cozart, Charlie	Baseball		12			Debut 1945 RedSox
Crabbe, Buster	Olympic		40	125		Swim/sprints
Craft, Harry	Baseball		10	32		Debut 1937 Reds
Crafter, Jane	Golf		5	20	25	
Craig, Pete	Baseball		6			Debut 1964 Senators
Craig, Rodney	Baseball		4	12		Debut 1979
Craig, Roger	Baseball		3	28		Debut 1955. '59 shutouts
Craig, Roger	Football		8	35	85	NFL
Craig, Ross	Football	+	10	22		1964 Canadian HOF
Cram, Jerry	Baseball		4			Debut 1969 K.C.
Cramer, Roger	Baseball		20	55		Debut 1929 Phillies
Crampton, Bruce	Golf		5	25	25	
Crandall, Del	Baseball		4	12		Debut 1949 Braves
Cranz, Christi	Skiing		5	10		
Cravath, Gavvy	Baseball		70	150		Debut 1908
Craven, Murray	Hockey		3	15		
Crawford, "Shag"	Baseball		4	10		Legendary Umpire
Crawford, C.R. "Pat"	Baseball		20	50		Debut 1929 NY Giants
Crawford, Fred	Basketball		3	20		played NBA 66-73
Crawford, Fred	Football	+	15	55		CHOF Duke
Crawford, Glenn	Baseball		18	45		Debut 1945

NAME	CATEGORY	+	SIG	SP	BALL	Comment
Crawford, Hasely	Olympic		8	20		100 Meters
Crawford, Jack	Tennis		6	20		HOF 1979
Crawford, Jim	Auto Racing		4	8		
Crawford, Ken	Baseball		35	75		Debut 1915
Crawford, Richard	Golf		15	40		
Crawford, Robert	Horse Racing		10	30		HOF 1973 jockey
Crawford, Rufus	Baseball		4	16		Debut 1952
Crawford, Rusty	Hockey		45	150		1962 HOF fwd
Crawford, Sam "Wahoo"	Baseball					B&W PC $400
Crawford, Sam "Wahoo"	Baseball		150	350	2200	HOF 1957. Gold Pl $400
Crawford, Willie	Baseball		4	15		Debut 1964
Cray, James	Olympic		3	15		Hockey
Craybas, Jill	Tennis		3	6		1996 NCAA Champion
Crayne, Dick	FootBall		10	20		
Creavy, Tom	Golf		45	170		
Creavy, William	Golf		25	75		
Creeden, Cornelius	Baseball		30	70		Debut1943
Creeden, Pat	Baseball		15	48		Debut 1931
Creekmur, Lou	Football		5	15	80	1975 HOF. NFL
Creger, Bernie	Baseball		5	22		Debut 1947
Creighton, Adam	Hockey		4	18		
Creighton, Jim	Basketball		4	12		played NBA 75
Cremins, Bobby	Basketball		2	5		Georgia Tech Coach
Crenshaw, Ben	Golf		15	25	35	
Crespi, Frank	Baseball		6	22		Debut 1938
Cretier, Jean-Luc	Olympic		8	22		Gold Med. Alpine Skiing
Crevier, Ronald	Basketball		3	10		played NBA 85
Crews, Tim	Baseball		4	12		Debut 1987 Dodger
Cribbs, Joe	Football		4	15		NFL
Crighton, Hec	Football	+	10	22		1986 Canadian HOF
Crimmins, John	Bowling		7	18		1962 ABC HOF
Cripe, Dave	Baseball		3	10		Debut 1978
Criscione, Dave	Baseball		3	10		Debut 1977
Criscola, Tony	Baseball		10	35		Debut 1942
Crisler, Fritz	Football		28	65		1954 CHOF coach
Crisman, Otey	Golf		30	75		
Criss, Charles	Basketball		4	15		played NBA 77-84
Critchfield, Russell	Basketball		5	18		played NBA 68
Critchley, Diana	Golf		75	235		
Crite, Winston	Basketball		4	12		played NBA 87-
Critz, Hugh	Baseball		45	100		Debut 1924 Reds
Croce, Stefania	Golf		5	20	25	
Crocker, Faye	Golf		15	40	30	
Crocker, James	Basketball		10	50		played NBA 48-52
Croft, Robert	Basketball		4	18		played NBA 70
Cromartie, Warren	Baseball		4	12		Debut 1974
Crompton, Geoff	Basketball		3	12		played NBA 78-83
Cronin, Carl	Football	+	12	25		1967 Canadian HOF
Cronin, Jim	Baseball		28	70		Debut 1929
Cronin, Joe	Baseball					HOF '56. P-S HOF $1100
Cronin, Joe	Baseball		30	102	412	Gold Pl.$35,B&W PC $40
Crosby, Bing	Golf		65	188		PGA HOF 1978, Contrib.
Crosby, Ed	Baseball		3	12		Debut 1970
Crosby, Elaine	Golf		5	20	25	
Crosby, Nathanial	Golf		5	20	25	
Crosby, Terry	Basketball		3	12		played NBA 79

NAME	CATEGORY	+	SIG	SP	BALL	Comment
Crosetti, Frankie	Baseball		6	18		Debut 1932
Cross, Jeff	Baseball		6	38		Debut 1942
Cross, Jeff	Basketball		3	10		played NBA 85
Cross, Jeff	Football		3	9		NFL
Cross, Peter	Basketball		3	12		played NBA 70-72
Cross, Russell Jr.	Basketball		3	12		played NBA 83
Crossfield, Scott	Auto Racing		5	10		Speed Records
Crossin, Francis	Basketball		10	50		played NBA 47-49
Crouch, Jack	Baseball		28	80		Debut 1930
Croucher, Frank	Baseball		25	65		Debut 1939
Crouse, Clyde	Baseball		40	90		Debut 1923
Crow, Don	Baseball		3	10		Debut 1982
Crow, John David	Football		6	20		TX A&M. Heisman '57
Crow, Lindon	Football		5	15		NFL
Crow, Mark	Basketball		4	10		played NBA 77
Crow, William	Basketball		4	14		played NBA 67
Crowder, Alvin	Baseball		55	125		Debut 1926
Crowder, Keith	Hockey		4	14		
Crowe, Alberta	Bowling	+	8	18		1982 Women's IBC HOF
Crowe, George	Baseball		10	30		Debut 1952
Crowley, Ed	Baseball		30	65		Debut 1928
Crowley, Terry	Baseball		4	10		Debut 1969
Crozier, Roger	Hockey		4	20		
Cruchon, Steve	Bowling	+	8	22		1983 ABC HOF-Mer.Serv.
Cruickshank, Bobby	Golf		178	360		Old PGA HOF 1967
Cruise, Walt	Baseball		40	95		Debut 1914
Crum, Denny	Basketball		9	18		HOF 1994 Coach
Crumling, Gene	Baseball		7	28		Debut 1945 Cards
Crump, Arthur	Baseball		30	85		Debut 1924
Cruthers, Charles	Baseball		45	100		Debut 1913
Cruyff, Johan	Soccer		6	25		3x Europe Player of Year
Cruz, Hector	Baseball		4	12		Debut 1973
Cruz, Henry	Baseball		4	12		Debut 1975
Cruz, Jose	Baseball		4	15		Debut 1970
Cruz, Julio	Baseball		4	12		Debut 1977
Cruz, Todd	Baseball		4	12		Debut 1978
Cruz, Tommy	Baseball		4	12		Debut 1973
Csonka, Larry	Football		8	35	140	1987 HOF RB
Ctvrtlik, Bob	Volleyball-Beach		4	15		
Cubbage, Mike	Baseball		3	12		Debut 1974
Cuccinello, Al	Baseball		12	35		Debut 1935 NY Giants
Cuccinello, Tony	Baseball		15	40		Debut 1930 Reds
Cuellar, Mike	Baseball		8	15		Debut 1959
Cueto, Alfonso	Basketball		4	18		played NBA 69-70
Cuevas, Pipino	Boxing		18	38		Welter-Wt Champ.
Culberson, Leon	Baseball		10	38		Debut 1943
Culbertson, Ely	Bridge		30	90		
Culbreath, Joshua	Olympic		4	9		Hurdles
Cullen, John	Hockey		3	15		
Cullen, Tim	Baseball		3	12		Debut 1966
Cullenbine, Roy	Baseball		15	55		Debut 1938
Culllen, Jack	Baseball					Debut 1962 Yankees
Cullman, Joseph F. 3rd	Tennis		8	35		HOF 1990
Cullop, Nick	Baseball		30	75		Debut 1926
Culmer, Wil	Baseball		3	10		Debut 1983
Culp, Benny	Baseball		8	35		Debut 1942

NAME	CATEGORY	+	SIG	SP	BALL	Comment
Culp, Ray	Baseball		6			Debut 1963 Phillies
Cummings, Bill	Auto Racing	+	30	75		
Cummings, Candy Wm.	Baseball		1850	4750		HOF 1939
Cummings, Edith	Golf		85	185	25	
Cummings, Napolean	Baseball		50	125		Played 14 Seasons Negro League
Cummings, Patrick	Basketball		3	12		played NBA 79-
Cummings, Terry	Basketball		6	22		played NBA 82-
Cunning, Michael	Golf		5	20	25	
Cunningham, Dick	Basketball		3	15		played NBA 68-75
Cunningham, Gary	Basketball		5	10		Coach
Cunningham, Glenn	Olympic		45	110		Track/distance
Cunningham, Joe	Baseball		5	18		Debut 1954 Cards
Cunningham, Randall	Football		8	22	100	NFL
Cunningham, Ray	Baseball		25	55		Debut 1931
Cunningham, Sam	Football		4	15		NFL
Cunningham, Wm."Billy"	Basketball		9	22	100	HOF 1986
Cuozzo, Gary	Football		3	15		NFL
Cupit, Buster	Golf		5	20	45	
Cupit, Jacky	Golf		17	42	25	
Cure, Armand	Basketball		6	50		played NBA 46
Cureton, Earl	Basketball		4	15		played NBA 80-89
Curl, Rod	Golf		5	20		
Curran, Francis	Basketball		10	50		played NBA 47-49
Curren, Kevin	Tennis		4	10		
Currie, Andrew	Football	+	10	22		1974 Canadian HOF
Currin, Perry	Baseball		6	22		Debut 1947
Curry, David	Golf		5	20	25	
Curry, Dell	Basketball		3	10		played NBA 86-
Curry, Donald	Boxing		10	22		
Curry, John	Olympic		18	45		Figure skating
Curry, Tony	Baseball		4	16		Debut 1960
Curtis, Ann	Olympic		12	38		Swim/400 M Free
Curtis, Glenn	Auto Racing	+	250	800		
Curtis, Harriot	Golf		195	395		
Curtis, Isaac	Football		3	15		NFL
Curtis, Margaret	Golf		188	450		
Curtright, Guy	Baseball		8	40		Debut 1943
Cushman, Calvin	Olympic		4	12		Hurdles
Cusick, Jack	Baseball		10	38		Debut 1951
Cutler, Wes	Football	+	10	22		1968 Canadian HOF
Cutshaw, George	Baseball		75	165		Debut 1912
Cutter, Slade	Football		12	40		CHOF Navy
Cuyler, Kiki	Baseball		267	425	2625	HOF 1968
Cypert, Al	Baseball		38	95		Debut 1914
Czarobski, Ziggie	Football	+	20	75		CHOF Notre Dame
Czyz, Bobby	Boxing		10	30		Lt. & Cruiser-Wt. Champ.

NAME	CATEGORY	+	SIG	SP	BALL	Comment
D'Antoni, Michael	Basketball		4	15		played NBA 73-76
Dabich, Michael	Basketball		4	18		played NBA 67
Dade, Paul	Baseball		3	12		Debut 1975
Dagenhard, John	Baseball		9			Debut 1943 Bost Braves
Daggett, Tim	Olympic		5	20		Gymnastics
Dagres, Angie	Baseball		4	15		Debut 1955
Dahlen, Ulf	Hockey		3	20		
Dahler, Edward	Basketball		10	50		played NBA 51
Dahlgren, Babe	Baseball		15	48		Debut 1935 RedSox
Dahlstrom, Carl	Hockey		5	18		1973 US HOF
Dailey, Quintin	Basketball		3	10		played NBA 82-83
Dalbey, Troy	Olympic		3	7		Swim/relay
Dale, Carroll	Football		6	16		CHOF Virginia Tech
Dalena, Pete	Baseball		3	10		Debut 1989
Daley, Arthur	Writer	+	10	22		1976 Ntl S&S HOF
Daley, Bill	Football		6	18		NFL
Daley, John	Baseball		30	95		Debut 1912
Dallessandro, Dom	Baseball		10	35		Debut 1937 RedSox
Dalrymple, Clay	Baseball		4	12		Debut 1960 Phillies
Dalrymple, Gerald	Football	+	15	45		CHOF Tulane
Dalton, John	Football		10	35		CHOF Navy
Daly, Charles	Football		10	35		CHOF Harvard/Army
Daly, Chuck	Basketball		5	18		HOF 1994. 2 NBA Titles
Daly, Derek	Auto Racing		4	8		
Daly, Fred	Golf		50	110		
Daly, John	Golf		10	25	30	
Dalziel, Doug	Golf		5	20	25	
Damaska, Jack	Baseball		4	15		Debut 1963 Cards
Dampier, Louie	Basketball		5	20		played NBA 67-78
Dancer, Stanley	Harness Racing		18	65		
Dandridge, Bob	Basketball		5	22		played NBA 69-81
Dandridge, Ray	Baseball					P-S HOF $30. HOF 1987
Dandridge, Ray	Baseball		20	40	55	Gold Pl. $20. Grt.Mo.$25
Danek, Ludvik	Olympic		30	60		Discus/World Rec.
Daniel, Beth	Golf		5	20	25	
Daniel, Dan	Writer		5	12		
Daniel, Ellie	Olympic		3	8		Swim/butterfly
Daniel, Jake	Baseball		4	12		Debut 1937 Brklyn Dodg.
Daniell, Averell	Football		7	25		CHOF Pittsburgh
Daniell, James	Football	+	15	45		CHOF Ohio State
Daniels, Clem	Football		4	22		NFL
Daniels, Essex	Football		3	7		NFL
Daniels, Fred	Baseball		7	32		Debut 1945

NAME	CATEGORY	+	SIG	SP	BALL	Comment
Daniels, Isabelle	Olympic		3	7		Track relay
Daniels, Jack	Baseball		4	15		Debut 1952
Daniels, Kal	Baseball		4	15		Debut 1986
Daniels, Mel	Basketball		5	25		played NBA 67-76
Danielson, Gary	Football		3	12		NFL
Danneberg, Rolf	Olympic		8	25		Discus
Danning, Harry	Baseball		15	55		Debut 1933 NY Giants
Danning, Ike	Baseball		25	60		Debut 1928
Danowski, Ed	Football		10	35		NFL
Dantley, Adrian	Basketball		6	20		played NBA 76-
Dantonio, John	Baseball		6	22		Debut 1944
Danzig, Allison	Tennis	+	25	75		HOF 1958
Danzig, Sarah Palfrey Cooke	Tennis		25	75		HOF 1963
Dapper, Cliff	Baseball		6	22		Debut 1942
Darcey, Peter	Basketball		16	45		played NBA 52
Darcy, Eamonn	Golf		10	25	25	
Darden, Oliver	Basketball		7	35		played NBA 57-63
Darden, James	Basketball		10	50		played NBA 48-49
Daringer, Cliff	Baseball		50	110		Debut 1914
Daringer, Rolla	Baseball		50	110		Debut 1914
Dark, Alvin	Baseball		5	18		Debut 1946
Dark, Jesse	Basketball		3	12		played NBA 74
Darling, Ron	Baseball		8	18		Debut 1983
Darnell, Rick	Basketball		3	12		played NBA 75
Darragh, Jack	Hockey		40	125		1962 HOF fwd
Darrow, James	Basketball		7	35		played NBA 61
Darwin, Bobby	Baseball		3	12		Debut 1962
Dascenzo, Doug	Baseball		3	10		Debut 1988
Dascoli, Frank	Baseball		3	8		Umpire
Dashiell, Wally	Baseball		30	85		Debut 1924
Date, Kamiko	Tennis		4	10		
Datz, Jeff	Baseball		3	10		Debut 1989
Dauer, Rich	Baseball		3	10		Debut 1976
Daugherty, Brad	Basketball		5	20		played NBA 86-
Daugherty, Duffy	Football		35	65		1984 CHOF coach
Daugherty, Harold "Doc"	Baseball		4	22		Debut 1951 Tigers
Daugherty, Jack	Baseball		3	10		Debut 1987
Daughters, Bob	Baseball		15	50		Debut 1937
Daughtry, Mack	Basketball		3	12		played NBA 70
Daulton, Darren	Baseball		4	20		Debut 1983
Dauss, George "Hooks"	Baseball		95	195		Debut 1912
Davalillo, Vic	Baseball		4	18		Debut 1963
DaVanon, Jerry	Baseball		4	15		Debut 1969 Cards
Davenport, Jim	Baseball		4	12		Debut 1958 Giants
Davenport, Lindsay	Olympic		5	5		Gold Med. Tennis
Davenport, Willie	Olympic		10	25		110 M Hurdles
Davey, Chuck	Boxing		10	22		
David, Andre	Baseball		3	10		Debut 1984
David, Jim	Football		5	20		NFL
Davidson, Ben	Football		5	20		NFL
Davidson, Bruce	Olympic		5	10		Equestrian
Davidson, Cotton	Football		3	18		NFL
Davidson, Gary	Executive		5	15		
Davidson, Mark	Baseball		3	10		Debut 1986
Davidson, Scotty	Hockey		45	150		1950 HOF fwd
Davies, Bob	Basketball	+	20	65	135	HOF 1969

NAME	CATEGORY	+	SIG	SP	BALL	Comment
Davies, Chick	Baseball		40	100		Debut 1914
Davies, Dr. Andrew	Football	+	10	22		1969 Canadian HOF
Davies, Karen	Golf		5	20	25	
Davies, Laura	Golf		10	25	30	
Davies, Richard	Golf		5	20	25	
Davies, Tom	Football	+	18	60		CHOF Pittsburgh
Davies, William	Golf		35	95		
Davis, Aaron	Boxing		7	15		
Davis, Al	Football		10	45	150	1992 HOF contributor
Davis, Alvin	Baseball		4	12		Debut 1984
Davis, Aubrey	Basketball		10	50		played NBA 46-48
Davis, Bill	Baseball		3	12		Debut 1965
Davis, Bob	Baseball		3	12		Debut 1973 S.D.
Davis, Brad	Basketball		3	10		played NBA 77-90
Davis, Brandy	Baseball		4	18		Debut 1952
Davis, Brock	Baseball		4	15		Debut 1963 Astros
Davis, Buddy	Basketball		10	40		played NBA 53-57
Davis, Butch	Baseball		3	10		Debut 1983
Davis, Calvin	Olympic		2	10		Medal 400 meter H
Davis, Charles	Basketball		3	12		played NBA 81-88
Davis, Charly	Basketball		3	14		played NBA 71-73
Davis, Chili	Baseball		4	15		Debut 1981
Davis, Clarence	Football		4	18		NFL
Davis, Dave	Bowling		6	14		1978 PBA, '90 ABC HOF
Davis, Dick	Baseball		3	10		Debut 1977
Davis, Doug	Baseball		3	10		Debut 1988
Davis, Dwight	Basketball		3	15		played NBA 72-76
Davis, Dwight	Tennis	+	30	75		HOF 1956
Davis, Eric	Baseball		4	12		Debut 1984
Davis, Ernie	Football	+	250	550		CHOF Syra.Heisman '61
Davis, Floyd E.	Auto Racing		20	75		
Davis, Gene	Olympic		3	6		Wrestling
Davis, George	Baseball					HOF 1998
Davis, George A.	Baseball		45			Debut 1912 Yankees
Davis, George W.	Baseball		30	70		Debut 1926
Davis, Glenn	Baseball		4	10		Debut 1984
Davis, Glenn	Football		10	35		CHOF Army. Heisman '46
Davis, Glenn	Olympic		10	22		400 M Hurdles
Davis, Harry	Baseball		30	70		Debut 1932
Davis, Hary	Basketball		3	15		played NBA 78-79
Davis, Isaac	Baseball		35	80		Debut 1919
Davis, Jack W.	Olympic		4	15		110 M Hurdles
Davis, Jacke	Baseball		3	12		Debut 1962
Davis, James	Basketball		10	40		played NBA 55
Davis, James W.	Basketball		3	18		played NBA 67-74
Davis, Jerry	Baseball		3	10		Debut 1983
Davis, Jody	Baseball		3	12		Debut 1981
Davis, John "Red"	Baseball		6	30		Debut 1941 NY Giants
Davis, Johnny	Basketball		3	15		played NBA 76-85
Davis, Josh	Olympic		3	7		Gold Medal. Swimming
Davis, Kenneth	Football		3	12		NFL
Davis, Lawrence	Baseball		7	30		Debut 1940
Davis, Lee	Basketball		5	15		played NBA 68-75
Davis, Mark	Basketball		3	10		played NBA 88-
Davis, Melvyn	Basketball		4	12		played NBA 73-76
Davis, Michael	Basketball		4	15		played NBA 69-72

NAME	CATEGORY	+	SIG	SP	BALL	Comment
Davis, Mickey	Basketball		4	15		played NBA 71-76
Davis, Mike	Baseball		3	10		Debut 1980
Davis, Milt	Football		6	15		NFL
Davis, Monti	Basketball		3	10		played NBA 80
Davis, Mouse	Football		3	8		NFL
Davis, Odie	Baseball		3	12		Debut 1980
Davis, Otis	Olympic		6	14		400 Meters
Davis, Ralph	Basketball		8	40		played NBA 60-61
Davis, Ray "Peaches"	Baseball		10			Debut 1936 Cin. Reds
Davis, Robert	Basketball		3	20		played NBA 72
Davis, Robert	Football		5	25		CHOF Georgia Tech
Davis, Rodger	Golf		5	20	25	
Davis, Ron	Baseball		5	15		Debut 1962
Davis, Ronald	Basketball		5	15		played NBA 76-81
Davis, Scott	Figure Skating		3	8		2x U.S. Champion
Davis, Steve	Baseball		4	10		Debut 1979
Davis, Storm	Baseball		4	12		Debut 1982
Davis, Terrell	Football		12	38	125	NFL Super Bowl MVP
Davis, Tod	Baseball		20	55		Debut 1949
Davis, Tommy	Baseball		5	10		Debut 1959
Davis, Tommy	Football		10	45		NFL
Davis, Trench	Baseball		3	10		Debut 1985
Davis, Virgil L. "Spud"	Baseball		30	75		Debut 1928 Phillies
Davis, Walter	Basketball		5	16		played NBA 77-?
Davis, Walter F.	Olympic		6	15		High Jump
Davis, Warren	Basketball		5	20		played NBA 67-72
Davis, William	Basketball		10	50		played NBA 45
Davis, Willie	Baseball		5	16		Debut 1960
Davis, Willie	Basketball		4	18		played NBA 70
Davis, Willie	Football		6	20	85	1981 HOF DL
Davis-Wrightsil, Clarissa	Basketball		2	5		Women's ABL
Daw, Charlie	Bowling	+	15	45		1941 ABC HOF
Dawes, Dominique	Olympic		5	38		Olymp.Gold.Gymnastics
Dawkins, Darryl	Basketball		10	18	100	played NBA 75-88
Dawkins, Johnny	Basketball		3	12		played NBA 86-
Dawkins, Paul	Basketball		5	25		played NBA 73
Dawkins, Pete	Football		10	24		CHOF Army. Heisman '58
Dawson, Andre	Baseball		4	18		Debut 1975
Dawson, James	Basketball		5	30		played NBA 67
Dawson, Joe	Auto Racing	+	22	70		
Dawson, John	Golf		25	75		
Dawson, Len	Football		5	20	85	1987 HOF QB
Dawson, Marco	Golf		5	20	25	
Day, Charles F. "Boots"	Baseball		3	10		Debut 1969 STL Cards
Day, Eagle	Football		5	12		NFL
Day, Hap	Hockey		6	25		1961 HOF fwd
Day, Leon	Baseball		15	45	95	HOF 1995
Day, Ned	Bowling	+	20	50		1952 ABC HOF
Day, Pat	Horse Racing		10	25		HOF 1991 jockey
Daye, Darren	Basketball		4	12		played NBA 83-87
Dayet, Brian	Baseball		3	10		Debut 1983
De la Chaume, Simone Thion	Golf		75	215		
De La Hoya, Oscar	Boxing		15	55		Jr.Welter-Wt. Champ.
De Leeuw, Diane	Olympic		8	24		Figure skating
De Marco, Paddy	Boxing		12	30		Light-Wt. Champ.
De St. Sauveur, Lally	Golf		10	35		

NAME	CATEGORY	+	SIG	SP	BALL	Comment
De Varona, Donna	Olympic		8	25		Swim/400 Ind. Medly
De Vicenzo, Roberto	Golf		10	25	35	PGA HOF 1989
Deal, Charlie	Baseball		35	95		Debut 1912 Tigers
Deal, Cot	Baseball		5	12		Debut 1947
Deal, F. Lindsay	Baseball		18	55		Debut 1939 Brklyn Dodg
Deal, Lance	Olympic		2	7		Medal; Hammer Throw
Dean, Alfred	Baseball		28	65		Debut 1936
Dean, Dizzy	Baseball		110	290	733	HOF '53. Gold Pl. S $175
Dean, Dizzy (Jay H.)	Baseball					B&W PC S $200
Dean, Everett	Basketball		12	45	100	HOF 1966-Coach
Dean, Man Mountain	Pro Wrestling		35	95		
Dean, Paul "Daffy"	Baseball		50	125		Debut 1934
Dean, Ted	Football		5	15		NFL
Dean, Tommy	Baseball		4	12		Debut 1967
Deane, Greg	Basketball		4	18		played NBA 73
DeAngelis, William	Basketball		3	18		played NBA 70
Dear, Buddy	Baseball		20	20		Debut 1927
Deardurff, Deena	Olympic		3	9		Swim/relay
DeBartolo, Ed	Football		3	10		NFL
DeBerg, Steve	Football		4	12		NFL
DeBernardi, Forrest	Basketball	+	15	45	125	HOF 1961
DeBerry, Fisher	Football		2	5		College Coach of Year
DeBus, Adam	Baseball		50	120		Debut 1917
DeBusschere, Dave	Basketball		6	22	125	HOF 1982
DeCinces, Doug	Baseball		4	12		Debut 1973
Decker (Slaney), Mary	Olympic		7	18		Track
Dedeaux, Rod	Baseball		5	25		Debut. 1935
Dee, Donald	Basketball		3	22		played NBA 68
Deer, Rob	Baseball		4	12		Debut 1984
Dees, Archie	Basketball		6	28		played NBA 58-61
Dees, Charlie	Baseball		4	22		Debut 1963
DeFord, Frank	Writer		3	6		
DeForest, John	Golf		60	135		
Degener, Richard	Olympic		30	70		Diving
DeGruchy, John	Football	+	10	22		1963 Canadian HOF
Dehnert, Henry "Dutch"	Basketball	+	30	90		HOF 1968. NBA 45
Deidel, Jim	Baseball		3	6		Debut 1974
DeJesus, Ivan	Baseball		4	8		Debut 1974
DeJohn, Mark	Baseball		3	6		Debut 1982
DeKoning, Bill	Baseball		15	35		Debut 1945
Del Greco, Bobby	Baseball		4	14		Debut 1952
Delahanty, Ed	Baseball		2850	4617		HOF 1945
Delahoussaye, Eddie	Horse Racing		12	35		HOF 1993 jockey
Delaney, F. James	Olympic		3	10		Shot Put
Delaney, Joe	Football		22	75		NFL
Delaney, Ron	Olympic		15	40		Track
DeLauro, Jack	Baseball		3			
DelGado, Carlos	Baseball		3	8		Debut
Delker, Eddie	Baseball		15	65		Debut 1929
Dellinger, Robert	Olympic		4	8		5,000 meters
Delmas, Bert C.	Baseball		15			Debut 1933 Brklyn Dodg.
Delnas, Bert	Baseball		20	55		Debut 1933
DeLoach, Joe	Olympic		6	15		200 Meters
DeLong, Nate	Basketball		8	45		played NBA 51
Delsing, Jay	Golf		3	20	25	
Delsing, Jim	Baseball		4	15		Debut 1948 ChiSox

NAME	CATEGORY	+	SIG	SP	BALL	Comment
Delvecchio, Alex	Hockey		5	18	20	1977 HOF fwd
DeMaestri, Joe	Baseball		4	15		Debut 1951
DeMane, Arthur	Golf		78	188		
DeMar, Clarence	Track		12	28		
DeMarco, Paddy	Boxing		12	30		
Demaret, Jimmy	Golf		125	375		PGA HOF 1983
DeMars, Billy	Baseball		4	15		Debut 1948 A's
Dembo, Fennis	Basketball		3	10		played NBA 88
DeMerit, John	Baseball		5	15		Debut 1957
Demeter, Don	Baseball		4	15		Debut 1956
Demeter, Steve	Baseball		4	12		Debut 1959 Tigers
Demic, Lawrence	Basketball		3	12		played NBA 79-81
Deming, Rolf	Golf		5	20	25	
DeMoulin, Seppi	Football	+	10	22		1963 Canadian HOF
Dempsey, George	Basketball		8	40		played NBA 54-63
Dempsey, Jack	Boxing		70	150		1919-26 H-Wt Champ
Dempsey, Rick	Baseball		4	12		Debut 1969 Twins
Dempsey, Tom	Football		6	22		NFL
Denkinger, Don	Baseball		4			Umpire
Dennard, Ken	Basketball		3	12		played NBA 81-83
Dennehey, Tod	Baseball		35	80		Debut 1923
Denneny, Cy	Hockey		40	110		1959 HOF fwd
Denning, Blaine	Basketball		10	50		played NBA 52
Denning, Otto	Baseball		8	25		Debut 1942
Denny, John	Baseball		5	15		Debut 1974
Denson, Drew	Baseball		3	19		Debut 1989
Dent, Bucky	Baseball		4	12		Debut 1973
Dent, Elliott	Baseball		15			Debut 1907
Dent, Jim	Golf		5	20	25	
Dent, Richard	Football		4	15		NFL
Dente, Sam	Baseball		4	22		Debut 1947
Denton, Randy	Basketball		3	18		played NBA 71-76
DePalma, Ralph	Auto Racing	+	75	200		HOF 1991, HOF 1992
DePaolo, Peter	Auto Racing	+	85	225		HOF 1995
DePhillips, Tony	Baseball		6	25		Debut 1943
DePre, Joe	Basketball		5	22		played NBA 70-71
Derby, Dean	Football		5	18		NFL
Derline, Rodney	Basketball		4	15		played NBA 74-75
Dernier, Bob	Baseball		3	10		Debut 1980
DeRogatis, Al	Football		10	25		CHOF Duke
Derrick, Jim	Baseball		4	12		Debut 1970
Derringer, Paul	Baseball		25	65		Debut 1931
Derry, Russ	Baseball		5	25		Debut 1944
Desautels, Gene	Baseball		8	38		Debut 1930 Tigers
Descampe, Florence	Golf		10	30	30	
Deshaies, Jim	Baseball		5	18		Debut 1984
DeShong, Jimmie	Baseball		18			Debut 1932 Phillies
DesJardien, Paul	Football	+	10	35		CHOF Chicago
Desjardins, Gerry	Hockey		5	9		
Desjardins, Peter	Olympic		8	25		Diving
DesJardins, Vic	Hockey		6	12		1974 US HOF
Desmond, Richard	Hockey		5	12		1988 US HOF
Detherage, Bob	Baseball		3	10		Debut 1980
Detmer, Ty	Football		10	35		Heisman Brig.Yng, '90
Detore, George	Baseball		12	45		Debut 1930 Indians
Dettweiler, Helen	Golf		35	90		

NAME	CATEGORY	+	SIG	SP	BALL	Comment
Detweiler, Robert	Baseball		4	10		Debut 1942
Deutsch, David	Basketball		5	25		played NBA 66
Devaney, Bob	Football		15	38		1981 CHOF coach
Devereaux, Mike	Baseball		3	10		Debut 1987
Devers, Gail	Olympic		5	25		Olymp.Gold. 100-Meters
Devine, Aubrey	Football	+	12	20		CHOF Iowa
Devine, Dan	Football		7	30		1985 CHOF coach
DeViveiros, Bernie	Baseball		15	60		Debut 1924 ChiSox
Devlin, Bruce	Golf		5	30	25	
Devlin, Corky	Basketball		8	42		played NBA 55-57
Devlin, Jim	Baseball		6	22		Debut 1944
Devore, Josh	Baseball		150	375		Debut 1908
DeWillis, Jeff	Baseball		3	10		Debut 1987
DeWitt, John	Football	+	20	85		CHOF Princeton
Dey, Joseph	Golf		30	125		PGA HOF 1975, Contrib.
DeZonie, Hank	Basketball		10	50		played NBA 48-50
Diaz, Mike	Baseball		3	10		Debut 1983
Dibble, Dorne	Football		5	12		NFL
Dibble, Ron	Baseball		3	10	25	Debut 1988
Dibiasi, Klaus	Olympic		15	35		Diving
DiCarlo, George	Olympic		5	12		Swim/400 free
Dicken, Paul	Baseball		3	14		Debut 1964
Dickerman, Leo	Baseball		18			Debut 1923 Brklyn Dodg.
Dickerson, Eric	Football		10	28	100	NFL
Dickerson, Henry	Basketball		3	14		played NBA 75-76
Dickey, Bill	Baseball					B&W PC $50.Grt.Mo. $80
Dickey, Bill	Baseball		30	60	137	Gold Pl. S $45.HOF 1954
Dickey, Bill	Baseball					P-S HOF $100
Dickey, Clyde	Basketball		3	12		played NBA 74
Dickey, Curtis	Football		3	12		NFL
Dickey, Derrek	Basketball		3	12		played NBA 73-77
Dickey, Dick	Basketball		10	50		played NBA 51
Dickey, George	Baseball		40	85		Debut 1935
Dickey, Lynn	Football		4	12		NFL
Dickinson, Gardner	Golf		5	20	25	
Dickinson, Gary	Bowling		5	12		1988 PBA, '92 ABC HOF
Dickinson, Judy	Golf		5	20	25	
Dickshot, Johnny	Baseball		30	65		Debut 1936 Pirates
Dickson, Bob	Golf		5	25	25	
Dickson, John	Basketball		3	18		played NBA 67
Dickson, Murry	Baseball		12			Debut 1939 STL Cards
Diddle, Ed	Basketball	+	25	65		HOF 1971 Coach
Didier, Bob	Baseball		3	10		Debut 1969
Didier, Clint	Football		3	10		NFL
Didrikson, Babe (Mildred)	Golf					(See Zaharias)
Diebel, Nelson	Olympic		3	10		Gold Medal. Swimming
Diegel, Leo	Golf		150	350		Old PGA HOF 1955
Diehl, Terry	Golf		5	20	25	
Diemer, Brian	Olympic		3	7		Steeplechase
Dierdorf, Dan	Football		6	25	85	1996 HOF
Diering, Chuck	Baseball		4	18		Debut 1947
Dierking, Connie	Basketball		7	25		played NBA 58-70
Dietrich, Bill	Baseball		5	20		Debut 1933
Dietrick, Coby	Basketball		4	18		played NBA 70-82
Dietz, Dick	Baseball		4	12		Debut 1966
Dietzel, Paul	Football		3	6		LSU-Army Coach

NAME	CATEGORY	+	SIG	SP	BALL	Comment
Dietzel, Roy	Baseball		3	14		Debut 1954
Difani, Jay	Baseball		4	18		Debut 1948
DiGregorio, Ernie	Basketball		6	18		played NBA 73-77
Dihigo, Martin	Baseball		800	1600	4030	HOF 1977
DiLauro, Jack	Baseball		2			Debut 1969 Giants
Dilfer, Trent	Football		5	15	100	NFL
Dill, Bob	Hockey	+	10	22		1979 US HOF
Dill, Craig	Basketball		4	18		played NBA 67
Dill, Mary Lou	Golf		5	20	25	
Dill, Terrance	Golf		5	20	25	
Dillard, Dave	Basketball		3	15		played NBA 75
Dillard, Don	Baseball		4	15		Debut 1959
Dillard, Harrison	Olympic		8	18		110 M Hurdles
Dillard, Mickey	Basketball		3	10		played NBA 81
Dillard, Steve	Baseball		4	12		Debut 1975
Dille, Oscar	Basketball		10	50		played NBA 40-46
Dillinger, Bob	Baseball		6	18		Debut 1946 Browns
Dillion, James L.	Olympic		3	12		Discus
Dillon, Bobby	Football		8	22		NFL
Dillon, Hooks	Basketball		10	50		played NBA 49
DiMaggio, Dom	Baseball		10	25		Debut 1940
DiMaggio, Joe	Baseball					P-S HOF $350.HOF 1955
DiMaggio, Joe	Baseball		80	145	225	Gold Pl $85,B&W PC$120
DiMaggio, Vince	Baseball		40	80		Debut 1937
Dimanchoff, Babe	Football		8	18		NFL
Dimas, Trent	Olympic		5	18		Gymnast. Gold Hor.Bars
Dimmel, Mike	Baseball		3	12		Debut 1977
Dineen, Gord	Hockey		4	15		
Dineen, Kerry	Baseball		3	12		Debut 1975
Dinges, Vance	Baseball		6	24		Debut 1945 Phillies
Dingley, Bert	Auto Racing	+	40	85		
Dinkins, Jackie	Basketball		3	12		played NBA 71
Dinnell, Harry	Basketball		5	22		played NBA 67
Dinwiddie, Bill	Basketball		5	22		played NBA 67-71
Dionne, Marcel	Hockey		7	22	25	1992 HOF
DiPietro, Bob	Baseball		4	15		Debut 1951
Disarcina, Gary	Baseball		3	10		Debut 1989
Dischinger, Terry	Basketball		7	20		played NBA 62-72
Disney, William	Olympic		3	6		Speed skating
Distefano, Benny	Baseball		3	16		Debut 1984
Ditka, Mike	Football		8	24	125	1988 HOF end/WB
Dittmer, Jack	Baseball		6	20		Debut 1952
Ditzen, Walt	Bowling	+	8	22		1973 ABC HOF-Mer.Serv.
Diute, Fred	Basketball		10	45		played NBA 54
Dixon, Diane	Olympic		3	7		Track relay
Dixon, George	Football	+	12	25		1974 Canadian HOF
Dixon, Leo	Baseball		35	90		Debut 1925 Browns
Dmitriev, A. & Kazakova, O.	Olympic		10	38		Gold Medal. Pairs fig. sktg
Dnlap, Bill	Baseball		22	65		Debut 1929
Doan, Catriona LeMay	Speed Skating		5	25		Olympic Gold
Dobb, John	Baseball		15			Debut 1924 ChiSox
Dobbek, Dan	Baseball		4	12		Debut 1953
Dobbs, Glenn	Football		6	20		CHOF Tulsa
Dobie, Gil	Football		75	165		1951 CHOF coach
Dobson, Helen	Golf		5	20	25	
Dobson, Joe	Baseball		10			Debut 1938 Indians

NAME	CATEGORY	+	SIG	SP	BALL	Comment
Doby, Larry	Baseball		9	25		Debut 1947, HOF 1998
Dod, Charlotte	Tennis	+	12	35		HOF 1983
Dod, Lottie	Golf		80	175		
Dodd, Bobby	Football	+	40	85		CHOF Tennessee
Dodd, Glenn	Basketball		10	50		played NBA 49
Dodd, Stephen	Golf		5	20	25	
Dodd, Tom	Baseball		3	10		Debut 1986
Dodrill, Dale	Football		4	15		NFL
Dodson, Leonard	Golf		35	95		
Dodson, Pat	Baseball		3	12		Debut 1986
Doeg, John	Tennis	+	20	65		HOF 1962
Doehrman, Bill	Bowling	+	8	22		1968 ABC HOF-Mer.Serv.
Doering, Art	Golf		10	45		
Doerr, Bobby	Baseball					P-S HOF $22, Grt.M0.$20
Doerr, Bobby	Baseball		10	20	20	Gold Pl. $10.HOF 1986
Doherty, John	Baseball		3	12		Debut 1974
Doherty, Lawrence	Tennis	+	12	40		HOF 1980
Doherty, Reginald	Tennis	+	12	40		HOF 1980
Dojack, Paul	Football		4	8		1978 Canadian HOF
Dokes, Michael	Boxing		15	30		1982-83 H-Wt Champ
Dolan, Tom	Olympic		3	12		Gold Med. Swimming
Doleman, Chris	Football		3	12		NFL
Dolhon, Joseph	Basketball		10	50		played NBA 49-50
Doll, Robert	Basketball		10	50		played NBA 46-49
Donahue, Mark	Auto Racing	+	70	165		HOF 1990, HOF 1990
Donahue, Pete	Baseball		30			Debut 1921 Cin.Reds
Donahue, Terry	Football		3	8		Longtime College Coach
Donahue, Tom	Baseball		3	12		Debut 1979
Donald, Mike	Golf		5	20	25	
Donaldson, James	Basketball		4	15		played NBA 80-
Donaldson, John	Baseball		3	10		Debut 1966
Donan, Holland	Football		6	25		CHOF Princeton
Donchess, Joseph	Football	+	15	55		CHOF Pittsburgh
Dondero, Lerl	Baseball		30	80		Debut 1929
Donham, Robert	Basketball		10	50		played NBA 50-53
Donnelly, Gord	Hockey		4	18		
Donohue, Michael	Football		15	40		1951 CHOF coach
Donovan, Anne	Olympic		5	15		HOF 1995. 2x Gold Med.
Donovan, Art	Football		7	22	100	1968 HOF DL
Donovan, Henry	Basketball		10	50		played NBA 49
Donovan, William	Basketball		3	12		played NBA 87
Donovan, Wm. E. "Wild Bill"	Baseball		75			Debut 1898 Brklyn. Dodg.
Dooin, Charles "Red"	Baseball		150	400		Debut 1902
Dooley, Vince	Football		3	10		College Coach of Year
Dorais, Gus	Football		65	175		1954 CHOF coach
Doran, Bill	Baseball		4	10		Debut 1982
Doran, Jim	Football		4	15		NFL
Dorfmeister, Michaela	Olympic		3	12		Medalist. Alpine Skiing
Dornblaser, Gertrude	Bowling	+	8	20		1979 Women's IBC HOF
Dornhoefer, Gary	Hockey		4	20		
Dorsett, Brian	Baseball		3	10		Debut 1987
Dorsett, Tony	Football		10	25	135	1994 HOF.Heisman'76.
Dorsey, Jacky	Basketball		4	15		played NBA 77-80
Dorsey, Ron	Basketball		4	15		played NBA 71
Doser, Clarence	Golf		45	125		
Dotter, Gary	Baseball		5			Debut 1961 Twins

NAME	CATEGORY	+	SIG	SP	BALL	Comment
Dotterer, Dutch	Baseball		5	18		Debut 1957
Dougherty, Ed	Golf		5	20	25	
Dougherty, Nathan	Football	+	6	28		CHOF Tennessee
Douglas (Chambers), Dorothy	Tennis	+	16	40		HOF 1981
Douglas, Bob	Basketball	+	18	45		HOF 1971
Douglas, Bruce	Basketball		4	12		played NBA 86
Douglas, Dave	Golf		15	40		
Douglas, Findlay	Golf		95	245		
Douglas, James "Buster"	Boxing		20	50		1990-91 H-Wt Champ
Douglas, John	Basketball		4	15		played NBA 81-82
Douglas, Katrina	Golf		5	20	25	
Douglas, Leon	Basketball		4	16		played NBA 76-82
Douglass, Bob	Golf		10	25	25	
Douglass, Bobby	Football		4	14		NFL
Douglass, Dale	Golf		5	20	25	
Douthit, Taylor	Baseball		35	90		Debut 1923 Cards
Dove, Sonny	Basketball		5	18		played NBA 67-71
Dover, Jerry	Basketball		4	15		played NBA 71
Dowd, James	Baseball		10	45		1910 Pitched 1 Phil. game
Dowell, Ken	Baseball		3	10		Debut 1987
Dowler, Boyd	Football		6	18		NFL
Dowling, Dave	Baseball		3			Debut 1964 Cards
Dowling, Jack	Golf		55	195		
Downes, Terry	Boxing		8	20		Middle-Wt. Champ.
Downey, Thomas	Baseball		25	55		Hit .270 for Reds 1910
Downey, William	Basketball		10	50		played NBA 47
Downing, Al	Baseball		8			Debut 1961 Yankees
Downing, Brian	Baseball		4	12		Debut 1973
Downing, Steve	Basketball		3	18		played NBA 73-74
Doyle, Alan	Golf		5	20	25	
Doyle, Brian	Baseball		3	12		Debut 1978
Doyle, Daniel	Basketball		8	38		played NBA 62
Doyle, Danny	Baseball		7	30		Debut 1943
Doyle, Denny	Baseball		3	12		Debut 1970
Doyle, Larry	Baseball		80	170		Debut 1907
Doyle, Patrick	Golf		25	60		
Doyle, Paul	Baseball		6			Debut 1969 ATL Braves
Drabek, Doug	Baseball		3	10	30	Debut 1986
Drabowsky, Moe	Baseball		6	20		Debut 1956
Drahas, Nick	Football		7	25		CHOF Cornell
Drake, Bruce	Basketball	+	20	45		HOF 1972 Coach
Drake, Darrell	Auto Racing	+	20	45		
Drake, Larry	Baseball		18	55		Debut 1945
Drake, Sammy	Baseball		4	15		Debut 1960
Drake, Solly	Baseball		6	15		Debut 1956
Dravecky, Dave	Baseball		5	15		Debut 1987
Draves, Vicky	Olympic		6	20		Diving
Drayton, Paul	Olympic		5	10		200 Meters
Drebinger, John	Writer		4	8		
Drechsler, Heike	Track		8	25		
Dreesen, Bill	Baseball		30	75		Debut 1931
Dreiling, Gregory	Basketball		4	16		played NBA 76-83
Dressen, Chuck	Baseball		55	150		Debut 1925
Drew, Cameron	Baseball		3	10		Debut 1988
Drew, John	Basketball		5	18		played NBA 74-84
Drew, Larry	Basketball		3	15		played NBA 80-87

NAME	CATEGORY	+	SIG	SP	BALL	Comment
Drew, Norman	Golf		5	20	25	
Drexler, Clyde	Basketball		8	30	125	played NBA 83-
Driesell, Lefty	Basketball		3	8		Legendary Coach
Driessen, Dan	Baseball		4	12		Debut 1973
Drillon, Gordie	Hockey		30	95		1975 HOF fwd
Drinkwater, Graham	Hockey		65	150		1950 HOF fwd
Driscoll, Jim	Baseball		3	425		Debut 1970
Driscoll, Paddy	Football	+	150	125		1965 HOF QB
Driscoll, Paddy	Football	+	50	15		CHOF Northwestern
Driscoll, Terrence	Basketball		3	50		played NBA 70-74
Drobny, Jaroslav	Tennis		12	50		HOF 1983
Drollinger, Ralph	Basketball		4	12		played NBA 80
Dropo, Walt	Baseball		6	14		Debut 1949 RedSox
Drouin, Jude	Hockey		4	20		
Drury, Morley	Football	+	12	55		CHOF So. California
Drut, Guy	Olympic		12	40		110 M Hurdles
Dryden, Charley	Writer		3	6		
Dryden, Ken	Hockey		8	40	55	1983 HOF goal
Dryer, Fred	Football		5	20	125	NFL
Dryer, Pat	Bowling		5	12		1978 Women's IBC HOF
Dryke, Matthew	Olympic		3	6		Skeet shooting
Drysdale, Cliff	Tennis		8	30		
Drysdale, Don	Baseball					P-S HOF $40. HOF 1984
Drysdale, Don	Baseball		22	58	63	Gold Pl. S $35
Dube, Joseph	Olympic		3	8		Weightlifting
Ducey, Rob	Baseball		3	10		Debut 1987
Duchesne, Gaetan	Hockey		4	18		
Duchesne, Steve	Hockey		4	1		
Duckett, Richard	Basketball		10	40		played NBA 57
Duckworth, Kevin	Basketball		4	12		played NBA 86-
Duden, Bob	Golf		10	45		
Dudley, Bill	Football		7	22	85	1966 HOF RB
Dudley, Charles	Basketball		4	15		played NBA 72-78
Dudley, Christopher	Basketball		3	10		played NBA 87-89
Dudley, Ed	Golf		75	185		Old PGA HOF 1964
Dudley, Ricky	Football		5	15	75	NFL
Duenkel, Virginia	Olympic		4	9		Swim/400 free
Duer, Al	Basketball	+	16	55		HOF 1981
Duerod, Terry	Basketball		3	12		played NBA 79-82
Duesenberg, Augie	Auto Racing	+	165			
Duesenberg, Fred	Auto Racing	+	200			HOF 1997
Duff, Dick	Hockey		5	20		
Duffy, Agnes	Bowling		5	10		1987 Women's IBC HOF
Duffy, Frank	Baseball		4	12		Debut 1970
Duffy, Hugh	Baseball		450	812	3083	B&W PC S $875.HOF '45
Duffy, Robert	Basketball		10	50		played NBA 46
Dugan, Joe	Baseball		38	125		Debut 1917 A's
Dugas, Gus			4	12		
Duggan, Anne Marie	Bowling		2	8		Bowler-of-Year
Duggan, Eric	Football	+	10	22		1981 Canadian HOF
Duguay, Ron	Hockey		4	18		
Duke, William	Horse Racing					HOF 1956 trainer
Dukes, Walter	Basketball		15	55		played NBA 55-62
Dumars III, Joe	Basketball		5	18		played NBA 85-
Dumas, Charles	Olympic		6	20		High Jump
Dumas, Rich	Basketball		5	30		played NBA 63

NAME	CATEGORY	+	SIG	SP	BALL	Comment
Dumovich, Nicholas	Baseball		15			Debut 1923 Cin. Reds
Dunbar, Tommy	Baseball		3	10		Debut 1983
Duncan, Andrew	Basketball		10	50		played NBA 47-50
Duncan, Dave	Baseball		4	12		Debut 1964
Duncan, George	Golf		150	395		
Duncan, Mariano	Baseball		3	12		Debut 1985
Duncan, Speedy	Football		4	14		NFL
Duncan, Taylor	Baseball		3	12		Debut 1977
Duncan, Tim	Basketball		6	28	100	'98 Rookie
Dundee, Angelo	Boxing		5	10		Manager
Dundee, Johnny	Boxing		95			Feather-Wt Champ.
Dunderdale, Tommy	Hockey		60	165		1974 HOF fwd
Dungy, Tony	Football		4	12		NFL Tampa Bay Coach
Dunlap, George Jr.	Golf		75	175		
Dunlap, Grant	Baseball		4	15		Debut 1953
Dunlap, Scott	Golf		5	20	25	
Dunleavy, Mike	Basketball		5	12		played NBA 76-88
Dunlop, George	Baseball		50	140		Debut 1913
Dunn, Jim Wiliam	Baseball		4			Debut 1952 Pirates
Dunn, Lin	Basketball		2	5		Women's ABL-Coach
Dunn, Patrick	Basketball		8	40		played NBA 57
Dunn, Ron	Baseball		3	10		Debut 1974
Dunn, T. R.	Basketball		3	12		played NBA 77-90
Dunn, Velma	Olympic		5	18		Diving
Dunn, Warrick	Football		6	32		NFL
Dunne, Mike	Baseball		4	15		Debut 1987
Dunphy, Don	Broadcaster		5	10		1986 Ntl S&S HOF
Dunston, Shawon	Baseball		4	12		Debut 1985
Duper, Mark	Football		4	15		NFL
Dupre, L.G.	Football		5	22		NFL
Duran, Dan	Baseball		3	12		Debut 1981
Duran, Roberto	Boxing		20	65		Mutiple Weight Champ.
Durant, Cliff	Auto Racing	+	50	110		
Durant, Joe	Golf		5	20	25	
Durbin, Mike	Bowling		5	18		1984 PBA HOF
Duren, John	Basketball		3	12		played NBA 80-82
Duren, Ryne	Baseball		5	15		Debut 1954
Durham, Jarrett	Basketball		3	15		played NBA 71
Durham, Joe	Baseball		4	15		Debut 1954 Orioles
Durham, Leon	Baseball		4	12		Debut 1980
Durnan, Bill	Hockey		60	175		1964 HOF goal
Durnbaugh, Bobby	Baseball		3	15		Debut 1957
Durning, George	Baseball		30	70		Debut 1925
Durocher, Leo	Baseball					B&W PC S $65
Durocher, Leo	Baseball		30	60	125	Debut 1925. HOF 1994
Durrant, Kevin	Basketball		3	10		played NBA 84-85
Durrett, Kenneth	Basketball		3	15		played NBA 71-74
Durrett, Red	Baseball		4	25		Debut 1944
Durst, Cedric	Baseball		32	75		Debut 1922
Dusak, Erv	Baseball		6	22		Debut 1941
Dusen, Fred Van	Baseball		4	18		Debut 1955
Dussere, Michelle	Olympic		3	8		Gymnastics
Dutra, Mortie	Golf		50	125		
Dutra, Olin	Golf		95	210		Old PGA HOF 1962
Dutton, Red	Hockey		30	90		1958 HOF def
Duval, David	Golf		5	20	25	

NAME	CATEGORY	+	SIG	SP	BALL	Comment
Duval, Dennis	Basketball		4	15		played NBA 74-75
Duval, Helen	Bowling		5	12		1970 Women's IBC HOF
Dwan, Jack	Basketball		10	50		played NBA 47-48
Dwight, James	Tennis	+	25	65		HOF 1955
Dwyer, Jim	Baseball		4	12		Debut 1973
Dwyer, Joe	Baseball		15	45		Debut 1937 Cin Reds
Dybzinski, Jerry	Baseball		3	10		Debut 1980
Dye, Babe	Hockey		55	160		1970 HOF fwd
Dye, Pete	Golf		5	20	25	
Dyer, Don Rober "Duffy"	Baseball		3	10		Debut 1968 NY Giants
Dyer, Eddie	Baseball		40	85		Debut 1922
Dykema, Craig	Basketball		3	10		played NBA 81
Dyker, Eugene	Basketball		8	40		played NBA 53
Dykes, Jimmy	Baseball		45	95		Debut 1918
Dykstra, Len	Baseball		4	12		Debut 1985

NAME	CATEGORY	+	SIG	SP	BALL	Comment
Eackles, Ledell	Basketball		3	10		played NBA 88-
Eaddy, Don	Baseball		5	15		Debut 1959
Eagan, H. Chandler	Golf		120	375		
Eagleson, Alan	Hockey		5	12		
Eakins, James	Basketball		3	18		played NBA 68-77
Earle, Ed	Basketball		10	45		played NBA 53
Earle, Scott	Baseball		3	10		Debut 1984
Early, Jake	Baseball		15	35		Debut 1939
Earnhardt, Dale	Auto Racing		10	30		
Earnshaw, George	Baseball		39	95		Debut 1928
Easler, Mike	Baseball		3	10		Debut 1973
Eason, Malcolm	Baseball		50			Debut 1900 Brooklyn
Eason, Tony	Football		3	12		NFL
East, Gordon Hugh	Baseball		8			Debut 1941 Yankees
Easter, Luke	Baseball		70	160		Debut 1949
Easter, Sarge	Bowling	+	12	25		1963 ABC HOF
Easterbrook, Syd	Golf		40	90		
Easterling, Paul	Baseball		30	70		Debut 1928
Easterwood, Roy	Baseball		8	25		Debut 1944
Eastman, Ben	Olympic		20	50		Track
Easton, John David	Baseball		3	20		Debut 1955 Phillies
Eastwood, Bob	Golf		5	20	25	
Eaton, Mark	Basketball		4	12		played NBA 82-
Eaton, Zell	Golf		25	75		
Eaves, Jerry	Basketball		3	12		played NBA 82-86
Ebben, William	Basketball		8	40		played NBA 57
Ebbets, Charlie H.	Baseball		150			"Ebbets Field"

NAME	CATEGORY	+	SIG	SP	BALL	Comment
Eberhard, Allen	Basketball		4	15		played NBA 74-77
Ebron, Roy	Basketball		4	15		played NBA 73
Echols, Sheila	Olympic		3	7		Track relay
Eckersall, Walter	Football	+	75	200		CHOF Chicago
Eckersley, Dennis	Baseball		4	12		Debut 1975
Edberg, Stefan	Tennis		8	25		
Eddleman, Dike	Basketball		10	50		played NBA 49-52
Edelin, Kent	Basketball		3	10		played NBA 84
Eden, Mike	Baseball		3	10		Debut 1976
Edenburn, Eddie	Auto Racing	+	30	65		
Ederle, Gertrude	Olympic		40	95		Swimming
Edgar, David	Olympic		3	6		Swim/relay
Edgar, J. D.	Golf		45	125		
Edge, Charles	Basketball		4	18		played NBA 73-74
Edge, Mitzi	Golf		5	20	25	
Edler, Dave	Baseball		3	10		Debut 1980
Edmonds, Bobby Joe	Basketball		6	38		played NBA 57-63
Edmonds, Jim	Baseball		10	34		
Edmonson, Keith	Basketball		3	12		played NBA 82-83
Edmonston, Sam	Baseball		12			Debut 1906 Senators
Edmunds, Ferrell	Football		3	10		NFL
Edmundson, John	Golf		45	130		
Edstrom, J. Sigfrid	Olympic		6	12		Dir. Swe. I.O.C.
Edwards, Bruce	Baseball		35	90		Debut 1946
Edwards, Danny	Golf		5	20	25	
Edwards, Dave	Baseball		3	10		Debut 1978
Edwards, David	Golf		5	20	25	
Edwards, Doc	Baseball		4	15		Debut 1962
Edwards, Don	Hockey		4	15		
Edwards, Foster	Baseball		15			Debut 1925 Bost. Braves
Edwards, Franklin	Basketball		3	12		played NBA 81-87
Edwards, Hank	Baseball		15	40		Debut 1941 Cle. Ind.
Edwards, James	Basketball		3	12		played NBA 77-
Edwards, Jim Joe	Baseball		10			Debut 1922 Indians
Edwards, Joel	Golf		5	20	25	
Edwards, Johnny	Baseball		4	15		Debut 1961
Edwards, Kevin	Basketball		3	12		played NBA 88-
Edwards, LaVell	Football		2	5		BYU Coach
Edwards, Marshall	Baseball		3	10		Debut 1981
Edwards, Mike	Baseball		3	10		Debut 1977
Edwards, Teresa	Basketball		2	7		Women's ABL
Edwards, Turk	Football	+	140	400		1969 HOF 2-way line
Edwards, William	Football	+	85	175		CHOF Princeton
Egan, John	Basketball		6	22		played NBA 61-71
Egan, Tom	Baseball		3	14		Debut 1965
Egerszegi, Krisztina	Olympic		8	32		Gold Med. Swimming
Eggeling, Dale	Golf		5	20	25	
Eggleston, Lonni	Basketball		10	50		played NBA 48
Ehlers, Edwin	Basketball		10	50		played NBA 47-48
Ehlo, Craig	Basketball		3	12		played NBA 83-
Ehrhardt, Welton C. "Rube"	Baseball		12			Debut 1924 Brklyn. Dodg.
Eichelberger, Dave	Golf		5	20	25	
Eichenlaub, Ray	Football	+	30	100		CHOF Notre Dame
Eichhorst, Richard	Basketball		6	35		played NBA 61
Eisenhauer, Larry	Football		4	14		NFL
Eisenreich, Jim	Baseball		3	12		Debut 1982

NAME	CATEGORY	+	SIG	SP	BALL	Comment
Eisenstat, Harry	Baseball		10			Debut 1935 Brklyn. Dodg.
Eklund, Pelle	Hockey		5	25		
El Cordoba, Manuel	Bull Fighting		15	45		
Elder, George	Baseball		6	30		Debut 1949
Elder, Lee	Golf		10	30	30	
Eldridge, Todd	Olympic		5	15		US Champ.Figure Skater
Elia, Lee	Baseball		3	8		Debut 1966
Elias, Eddie	Bowling		5	12		1976 PBA, '85 ABC HOF
Eliason, Donald	Basketball		10	50		played NBA 46
Eliowitz, Abe	Football	+	10	22		1969 Canadian HOF
Elizabeth, Miss	Pro Wrestling		7	25		
Elkington, Steve	Golf		10	25	25	
Elko, Pete	Baseball		6	32		Debut 1943
Ellard, Henry	Football		4	15	75	NFL
Ellefson, Ray	Basketball		10	50		played NBA 48-50
Eller, Carl	Football		7	20		NFL
Ellerbe, Frank	Baseball		15			Debut 1919 Senators
Ellerbe, Frank	Baseball		45	125		Debut 1919 Senators
Elliot, Larry	Baseball		4	15		Debut 1962
Elliott, Bill	Auto Racing		7	25		
Elliott, Bob	Baseball		50	125		Debut 1939
Elliott, Bump	Football		10	20		CHOF Michigan/Purdue
Elliott, Harry	Baseball		4	22		Debut 1953
Elliott, Herb	Olympic		10	45		Track
Elliott, Randy	Baseball		3	10		Debut 1972
Elliott, Robert	Basketball		3	15		played NBA 78-80
Ellis, Alexander	Basketball		7	38		played NBA 58-59
Ellis, Dale	Basketball		4	15		played NBA 83-
Ellis, Don	Bowling		5	12		1981 ABC HOF
Ellis, Gerry	Football		3	12		NFL
Ellis, Jimmy	Boxing		15	40		1968-70 H-Wt Champ
Ellis, John	Baseball		3	12		Debut 1969
Ellis, Joseph	Basketball		4	25		played NBA 66-73
Ellis, Kathleen	Olympic		3	10		Swim/100 free
Ellis, LeRon	Basketball		4	15		played NBA 91-
Ellis, LeRoy	Basketball		5	18		played NBA 62-75
Ellis, Maurice	Basketball		3	15		played NBA 77-79
Ellis, Rob	Baseball		3	12		Debut 1971
Ellis, Ron	Hockey		5	22		
Ellis, Sam	Baseball		4			Debut 1962 Cin. Reds
Ellis, Wes	Golf		10	45		
Ellison, Willie	Football		4	15		NFL
Ellsworth, Dick	Baseball		6			Debut 1958 Cubs
Elmore, Leonard	Basketball		5	15		played NBA 74-83
Els, Ernie	Golf		10	25	35	
Elsh, Roy	Baseball		40	95		Debut 1923
Elson, Bob	Broadcaster		5	10		
Elster, Kevin	Baseball		3	12		Debut 1986
Elston, Darrell	Basketball		4	15		played NBA 74-76
Elway, John	Football		15	45	140	NFL
Ely, Janet	Diving		3	15		World Champion
Embree, Chas. "Red"	Baseball		3			Debut 1941 Indians
Embry, Wayne	Basketball		4	18		played NBA 58-63
Emerson, Eddie	Football	+	10	22		1963 Canadian HOF
Emerson, Roy	Tennis		10	25		HOF 1982
Emery, Cal	Baseball		4	15		Debut 1963

NAME	CATEGORY	+	SIG	SP	BALL	Comment
Enberg, Dick	Broadcaster		4	8		
Endacott, Paul	Basketball		6	20	100	HOF 1971
Ender, Kornelia	Olympic		15	40		Swimming
Endicott, Bill	Baseball		7	30		Debut 1946
Endo, Yukio	Olympic		15	30		Gymnastics
Endress, Ned	Basketball		10	50		played NBA 43-46
Engelstad, Wayne	Basketball		3	10		played NBA 83
Engle, Charlie	Baseball		45	95		Debut 1925
Engle, Dave	Baseball		3	10		Debut 1981
Engle, Rip	Football	+	35	95		1973 CHOF coach
Engler, Christopher	Basketball		3	12		played NBA 82-87
English, Alex	Basketball		6	22		HOF 1997 NBA 76
English, Charlie	Baseball		30	75		Debut 1932
English, Claude	Basketball		3	12		played NBA 70
English, Gil	Baseball		20	80		Debut 1931
English, Scott	Basketball		3	18		played NBA 72-74
English, Woody	Baseball		25	75		Debut 1927 Cubs
Englund, Gene	Basketball		10	50		played NBA 41-49
Engram, Bobby	Football		5	20	100	NFL
Enis, Curtis	Football		4	22		Penn St. RB
Enke, Karin	Olympic		10	38		Speed skating
Ennis, Del	Baseball		12	35		Debut 1945
Enquist, Paul	Olympic		3	6		Rowing
Enqvist, Thomas	Tennis		3	9		
Enright, George	Baseball		3	12		Debut 1976
Enright, Jim	Basketball	+	18	50		HOF 1978 Referee
Ensor, Lavelle	Horse Racing					HOF 1962 jockey
Enzmann, Johnny"Gentleman"	Baseball		20	80		Debut 1914 Brklyn. Dodg.
Eppard, Jim	Baseball		3	10		Debut 1987
Epps, Aubrey	Baseball		30	85		Debut 1935
Epps, Hal	Baseball		25	75		Debut 1938
Epps, Ray	Basketball		4	15		played NBA 73
Epstein, Mike	Baseball		4	12		Debut 1966
Erautt, Joe	Baseball		25	85		Debut 1950
Erias, Bo	Basketball		8	40		played NBA 57
Erickson, Bob	Golf		5	20	25	
Erickson, Keith	Basketball		4	18		played NBA 65-76
Eriksen, Stein	Olympic		10	30		Alpine skiing
Erikson, Stephen	Olympic		3	6		Yachting
Ermer, Cal	Baseball		4	12		Debut 1947 Senators
Ernaga, Frank	Baseball		3	16		Debut 1957
Errickson, Dick "Leif"	Baseball		8			Debut 1938 Bost. Braves
Erskine, Carl	Baseball		4	16		Debut 1943
Ertl, Sue	Golf		5	20	25	
Erving, Julius	Basketball		10	35	175	HOF 1993. NBA 71-86
Esasky, Nick	Baseball		4	16		Debut1983
Escalera, Alfredo	Boxing		15	36		Jr. Lt-Wt Champ.
Eschen, Larry	Baseball		8	32		Debut 1942
Esiason, Boomer	Football		6	22	125	NFL
Eskridge, Jack	Basketball		10	50		played NBA 48
Espinosa, Abe	Golf		25	75		
Espinosa, Al	Golf		35	90		
Esposito, Frank	Bowling		5	18		1975 PBA HOF-Mer.Serv.
Esposito, Phil	Hockey		8	38	30	1984 HOF fwd
Esposito, Sammy	Baseball		6	22		Debut 1952
Esposito, Tony	Hockey		7	28	30	1988 HOF goal

NAME	CATEGORY	+	SIG	SP	BALL	Comment
Espy, Cecil	Baseball		3	10		Debut 1983
Essegian, Chuck	Baseball		4	15		Debut 1958
Esser, Mark	Baseball		3			Debut 1979 ChiSox
Essian, Jim	Baseball		4	12		Debut 1973
Estelle, Dick	Baseball		6			Debut 1964 S.F. Giants
Estes, Bob	Golf		5	20	25	
Estill, Michelle	Golf		5	20	25	
Estock, George J.	Baseball		8			Debut 1951 Bost. Braves
Etchebarren, Andy	Baseball		12	12		Debut 1962
Etchebaster, Pierre	Tennis	+	12	35		HOF 1978
Etcheverry, Sam	Football		6	18		1984 Canadian HOF
Etchison, Buck	Baseball		22	55		Debut 1945
Etheridge, Bobby	Baseball		3	12		Debut 1967
Etten, Nick	Baseball		7	17		Debut 1938 A's
Etzel, Edward	Olympic		3	6		Rifle
Eubanks, Chris	Boxing		15	32		
Evans, Al	Baseball		20	65		Debut 1939
Evans, Barry	Baseball		3	16		Debut 1978
Evans, Billy	Baseball		338	700	3267	HOF 1973 Umpire
Evans, Charles Chick Jr.	Golf		95	295		
Evans, Chick	Golf		5	20	25	PGA HOF 1975
Evans, Darrell	Baseball		4	12		Debut 1969
Evans, Dick	Bowling		5	12		1986 PBA HOF-Mer.Serv.
Evans, Duncan	Golf		5	20	25	
Evans, Dwayne	Olympic		4	9		200 meters
Evans, Dwight	Baseball		4	15		Debut 1972
Evans, Earl	Basketball		3	12		played NBA 79
Evans, J. Thomas	Olympic		3	6		Wrestling
Evans, Janet	Olympic		6	30		Swim/400 free
Evans, Lee	Olympic		6	22		Track
Evans, Max	Golf		10	35		
Evans, Michael	Basketball		4	15		played NBA 79-87
Evans, Ray	Football		8	22		CHOF Kansas
Evans, Robert	Basketball		10	50		played NBA 49
Evans, Vince	Football		5	12		NFL
Evans, William	Basketball		5	18		played NBA 69
Evanshen, Terry	Football		4	8		1974 Canadian HOF
Evenson, Cory	Bodybuilder		5	20		
Everett, Danny	Olympic		5	10		400 Meters
Everett, Doug	Hockey		5	15		1974 US HOF
Everett, Jim	Football		5	15	75	NFL
Evers, Hoot	Baseball		18	40		Debut 1941 Tigers
Evers, Johnny	Baseball		575	1225	4692	B&W PC S $1400.HOF'46
Evert, Chris	Tennis		12	30		HOF 1995
Ewbank, Weeb	Football		6	22	110	1978 HOF coach
Ewell, H. Norwood	Olympic		6	15		200 meters
Ewing, Buck	Baseball		2250	4250		HOF 1939
Ewing, Jack	Golf		10	35		
Ewing, Patrick	Basketball		10	40	175	played NBA 85-
Ewing, Sam	Baseball		3	15		Debut 1973
Ewoldt, Art	Baseball		45	110		Debut 1919
Exendine, Albert	Football	+	22	85		CHOF Carlisle
Ezersky, John	Basketball		10	50		played NBA 47-49

NAME	CATEGORY	+	SIG	SP	BALL	Comment

NAME	CATEGORY	+	SIG	SP	BALL	Comment
Fabel, Brad	Golf		5	20	25	
Fabel, Joseph	Basketball		35	75		played NBA 38-46
Faber, Urban "Red"	Baseball		45	125	1217	HOF 1964. Gold Pl. $135
Fabi, Teo	Auto Racing		5	25		
Face, Elroy	Baseball		4	18		Debut 1953
Faedo, Len	Baseball		3	10		Debut 1980
Fagen, Clifford B.	Basketball		6	25		HOF 1983-Contributor
Faggs, Mae	Olympic		3	7		Track relay
Fahey, Bill	Baseball		4	12		Debut 1971
Fain, Ferris	Baseball		12	38		Debut 1947
Fairbairn, Bill	Hockey		5	18		
Fairchild, John	Basketball		5	30		played NBA 65-69
Fairey, Jim	Baseball		3	12		Debut 1968
Fairfield, Don	Golf		10	35		
Fairly, Ron	Baseball		4	15		Debut 1958
Falaschi, Nello	Football		8	25		CHOF Santa Clara
Falcaro, Joe	Bowling	+	10	25		1968 ABC HOF
Faldo, Nick	Golf		10	50	35	
Falk, Bibb	Baseball		35	85		Debut 1920 ChiSox
Falkenburg, Bob	Tennis		12	35		HOF 1974
Fall, David	Olympic		7	28		Diving
Fallon, George	Baseball		7	28		Debut 1937
Falls, Mike	Football		4	12		NFL
Faloney, Bernie	Football		5	14		1974 Canadian HOF
Famechon, Johnny	Boxing		12	30		Feather-Wt Champ.
Famiglietti, Gary	Football		6	20		NFL
Famose, Annie	Olympic		10	25		Alpine skiing
Fangio, Juan-Manuel	Auto Racing	+	70	195		HOF 1990
Fanning, Jim	Baseball		4	10		Debut 1954
Fanzone, Carmen	Baseball		10	50		Debut 1970
Farbman, Philip	Basketball		5	10		played NBA 43
Fargis, Joe	Olympic		5	14		Equestrian
Farigalli, Lindy	Bowling		5	18		1968 ABC HOF
Farkas, Andy	Football		5	18		U. of Detroit
Farley, Bob	Baseball		4	15		Debut 1961
Farley, Dick	Basketball		6	40		played NBA 54-58
Farmer, James	Basketball		3	12		played NBA 87-
Farmer, Mike	Basketball		5	30		played NBA 58-64
Farr, Tommy	Boxing		100	200		Hvy-Wt Contender
Farrell, Arthur	Hockey		40	125		1965 HOF fwd
Farrell, Dick	Baseball		35	75		Debut 1956
Farrell, Johnny	Golf		95	195		Old PGA HOF 1961
Farrell, Kerby	Baseball		65	65		Debut 1943

NAME	CATEGORY	+	SIG	SP	BALL	Comment
Farrell, Thomas	Olympic		7	7		800 meters
Fator, Laverne	Horse Racing		95	95		HOF 1955 jockey
Fats, Minnesota	Pocket Billiards		40	90		
Faught, Robert	Basketball		10	50		played NBA 45
Faulk, Marshall	Football		6	24	125	NFL Colts Running Back
Faulk, Mary Lena	Golf		10	30	30	
Faulkner, Max	Golf		35	125		
Fauntz, Jane	Olympic		8	22		Diving
Faurot, Don	Football		10	25		1961 CHOF coach
Fausett, Buck	Baseball		7	32		Debut 1944
Favell, Doug	Hockey		4	18		
Favre, Brett	Football		20	55	145	NFL 3-Time MVP
Faxon, Brad	Golf		5	25	35	
Fazio, Buzz	Bowling		7	25		1963 ABC, '76 PBA HOF
Fazio, Ernie	Baseball		3	15		Debut 1962
Fazio, George	Golf		85	195		
Fazio, Tom	Golf		10	35		
Fear, A.H.	Football	+	10	22		1967 Canadian HOF
Fears, Tom	Football		12	25	95	1970 HOF end/WB
Federko, Bernie	Hockey		5	22		
Federoff, Al	Baseball		4	16		Debut 1951
Federov, Sergei	Hockey		8	38	35	
Fedor, Dave	Basketball		4	32		played NBA 62
Feerick, Robert	Basketball		10	50		played NBA 45-49
Feher, Butch	Basketball		3	18		played NBA 75
Feherty, David	Golf		5	20	25	
Fehr, Donald	Baseball		4	12		Executive
Fehr, Rick	Golf		5	20	25	
Fehring, Bill "Dutch"	Baseball		30	70		Debut 1934 Chi Sox
Feiereisel, Ron	Basketball		8	40		played NBA 55
Feigenbaum, George	Basketball		10	50		played NBA 49-52
Feitl, Dave	Basketball		3	10		played NBA 86-
Felder, Mike	Baseball		3	10		Debut 1985
Felderman, Marv	Baseball		7	28		Debut 1942
Felix, Junior	Baseball		4	10		Debut 1989
Felix, Ray	Basketball		22	50		played NBA 53-61
Fell, Jeff	Horse Racing		10	30		
Feller, Bob	Baseball					P-S HOF $30. HOF 1962
Feller, Bob	Baseball		10	25	22	Gold Pl $15, B&W PC $25
Feller, Jack	Baseball		4	16		Debut 1958
Fellmeth, Catherine	Bowling		5	15		1970 Women's IBC HOF
Felske, John	Baseball		3	12		Debut 1968 Chi Sox
Fendley, Jake	Basketball		10	45		played NBA 51-52
Fenech, Jeff	Boxing		12	30		Bantam-Fthr-Wt Champ
Fengler, Harlan	Auto Racing	+	30	60		
Fenimore, Bob	Football		10	30		CHOF Oklahoma State
Fenley, William	Basketball		10	50		played NBA 46
Fennell, Dave	Football		4	8		1990 Canadian HOF
Fenney, Rick	Football		5	12		NFL
Fenstermacher, Carol	Swimming		8	25		Breast Stroke
Fenton, Doc	Football	+	15	60		CHOF Louisiana State
Fenwick, Bobby	Baseball		4	12		Debut 1972
Fergerson, Mable	Olympic		3	8		Track relay
Fergon, Vicki	Golf		5	20	25	
Fergus, Keith	Golf		5	20	25	
Ferguson, Bob	Football		3	12		Ohio St. RB

NAME	CATEGORY	+	SIG	SP	BALL	Comment
Ferguson, Bob	Golf		775	1650		
Ferguson, Cathy	Olympic		3	10		Swim/backstroke
Ferguson, Joe	Baseball		4	12		Debut 1970
Ferguson, Joe	Football		4	12		NFL
Ferguson, John	Hockey		6	20		
Ferguson, Rufus "Roadrunner"	Football		3	10		NFL
Ferguson, Tom	Rodeo		5	12		
Fermin, Felix	Baseball		3	12		Debut 1987
Fernandez, Frank	Baseball		4	12		Debut 1967
Fernandez, Gigi	Tennis		5	18		
Fernandez, Mary Joe	Tennis		6	18		
Fernandez, Nanny	Baseball		6	22		Debut 1942
Fernandez, Tony	Baseball		6	18		Debut 1983
Fernandez, Vincente	Golf		5	20	25	
Fernie, Willie	Golf		775	1600		
Fernsten, Eric	Basketball		4	16		played NBA 75-83
Ferotte, Gus	Football		5	15	85	NFL
Ferragamo, Vince	Football		3	10		NFL
Ferrara, Al	Baseball		4	15		Debut 1963
Ferrarese, Don	Baseball		6			Debut 1968 Orioles
Ferrari, Albert	Basketball		6	35		played NBA 55-62
Ferrari, Enzo	Auto Racing		395			HOF 1994. Manufacturer
Ferraro, Dave	Bowling		2	8		1997 PBA HOF
Ferraro, John	Football		8	20		CHOF Southern California
Ferraro, John	Football	+	10	22		1966 Canadian HOF
Ferraro, Mike	Baseball		3	12		Debut 1966
Ferraro, Ray	Hockey		5	22		
Ferree, Jim	Golf		5	20	25	
Ferreira, Rolando	Basketball		8	15		played NBA 88
Ferreira, Wayne	Tennis		4	10		
Ferrell, Barbara	Olympic		3	10		Track sprints
Ferrell, Duane	Basketball		3	10		played NBA 88
Ferrell, Rick	Baseball					P-S HOF $35, Grt.Mo.$30
Ferrell, Rick	Baseball		12	30	36	Gold Pl. $15. HOF 1984
Ferrell, Wes	Baseball		70	155		Debut 1927
Ferrick, Tom	Baseball		5			Debut 1941 A's
Ferrier, Jim	Golf		95	200		
Ferrin, Arnie	Basketball		8	30		played NBA 48-50
Ferris, John	Olympic		3	6		Swim/butterfly
Ferriss, Dave "Boo"	Baseball		10	20		Debut 1945 Bost.Red Sox
Ferry, Bob	Basketball		7	30		played NBA 59-63
Ferry, Danny	Basketball		4	12		played NBA 89-
Fesler, Wes	Football	+	25	75		CHOF Ohio State
Fetchick, Mike	Golf		5	25	25	
Feustel, Louis	Horse Racing					HOF 1964 trainer
Fezler, Forrest	Golf		5	20	25	
Fibak, Wojtek	Tennis		4	8		
Fidrych, Mark	Baseball		4	12		Debut 1976
Fielder, Cecil	Baseball		5	25		Debut 1985
Fieldgate, Norm	Football		4	8		1979 Canadian HOF
Fields, Bruce	Baseball		4	10		Debut 1986
Fields, Jackie	Boxing		35	75		Welter-Wt Champ
Fields, Ken	Basketball		4	12		played NBA 84-87
Fields, Robert	Basketball		4	20		played NBA 71
Figg-Currier, Cindy	Golf		5	20	25	
Figini, Michela	Olympic		10	25		Alpine skiing

NAME	CATEGORY	+	SIG	SP	BALL	Comment
Figueras-Dotti, Marta	Golf		5	20	25	
Filchock, Frank	Football		12	32		NFL
Filipek, Ron	Basketball		5	25		played NBA 67
Filipski, Gene	Football		7	22		NFL
Fillmore, Greg	Basketball		4	18		played NBA 70-71
Fimple, Jack	Baseball		3	10		Debut 1983
Finch, Larry	Basketball		3	15		played NBA 73-74
Fincher, Bill	Football	+	20	60		CHOF Georgia Tech
Fingers, Rollie	Baseball					P-S HOF $25.Grt.Mo.$25
Fingers, Rollie	Baseball		9	19	25	Gold Pl. $15. HOF 1992
Finigan, Jim	Baseball		12	35		Debut 1954
Finke, Gertrude	Bowling		5	10		1990 Women's IBC HOF
Finkel, Hank	Basketball		3	25		played NBA 65-74
Finks, Jim	Football		30	145	225	NFL. HOF 1995
Finley, Charles O.	Baseball		10	55		Maverick Owner
Finley, Steve	Baseball		3	10		Debut 1989
Finn, Dan	Basketball		10	45		played NBA 52-61
Finneran, Sharon	Olympic		3	9		Swim/ind. medley
Finney, Allison	Golf		5	20	25	
Finney, Hal	Baseball		18	60		Debut 1931 Pirates
Finsterwald, Dow	Golf		10	25	25	
Fiore, Mike	Baseball		3	12		Debut 1968 Orioles
Fiori, Ed	Golf		5	20	25	
Firestone, Dennis	Auto Racing		5	10		
Firestone, Harvey Sr.	Auto Racing	+	175	425		
Firestone, Raymond	Bowling		5	15		1987 PBA HOF-Mer.Serv.
Firestone, Roy	Broadcaster		5	10		
Firova, Dan	Baseball		3	10		Debut 1981
Fischer, Bill	Football		6	18		CHOF Notre Dame
Fischer, Bobby	Chess		80	200		
Fischer, John	Golf		45	95		
Fischer, Pat	Football		7	18		NFL
Fischer, Reuben W. "Rube'	Baseball		8			Debut 1941 NY Giants
Fischlin, Mike	Baseball		3	10		Debut 1977
Fish, Hamilton	Football	+	25	80		CHOF Harvard
Fish, Jennifer	Olympic		3	9		Speed skating
Fishel, John	Baseball		4	10		Debut 1988
Fisher, Carl	Auto Racing	+	30	60		
Fisher, E.A.	Bowling		5	12		1984 PBA HOF-Mer.Serv.
Fisher, Eddie	Baseball		6			Debut 1959 SF Giants
Fisher, Harry	Basketball	+	18	45		HOF 1973
Fisher, Rick	Basketball		4	18		played NBA 71
Fisher, Robert	Football	+	25	75		CHOF Harvard
Fishwick, Diana	Golf		50	125		
Fisk, Carlton	Baseball		5	28	60	Debut 1969
Fisk, Rae	Bowling	+	8	20		1983 Women's IBC HOF
Fittipaldi, Emerson	Auto Racing		10	32		
Fitzgerald, Ed	Baseball		4			Debut 1948 Pirates
Fitzgerald, Mike	Baseball		4	10		Debut 1983
Fitzgerald, Richard	Basketball		10	50		played NBA 46-47
Fitzgerald, Robert	Basketball		10	50		played NBA 45-48
Fitzgerald-Brown, Benita	Olympic		4	18		100 Meter Hurdles
Fitzmann, Bill	Baseball		3			Cin. Reds
FitzRandolph, Casey	Speed Skating		3	8		World Champion
Fitzsimmons, "Fat Freddie"	Baseball		45	95		Debut 1925 NY Giants
Fitzsimmons, Bob	Boxing		550	950		1897-99 H-Wt Champ

NAME	CATEGORY	+	SIG	SP	BALL	Comment
Fitzsimmons, Cotton	Basketball		5	12		NBA Suns
Fitzsimons, Sunny Jim	Horse Racing		65	200		HOF 1958 trainer
Fitzsimons, Pat	Golf		5	20	25	
Flager, Wally	Baseball		6	22		Debut 1945
Flaherty, Ray	Football		12	35	175	1976 HOF player/coach
Flaim, Eric	Olympic		3	10		Speed skating
Flair, Al	Baseball		4			Debut 1941 Bost.Red Sox
Flair, Ric	Pro Wrestling		7	20		
Flaman, Fernie	Hockey		5	22		1990 HOF def
Flanagan, Del	Boxing		8	20		
Flannery, Tim	Baseball		3	10		Debut 1979
Flatley, Paul	Football		4	15		NFL
Flavin, John, Jr.	Baseball		4			Debut 1964 Cubs
Fleck, Jack	Golf		12	30	35	
Fleckman, Marty	Golf		5	20	25	
Fleischer, Chad	Skiing		3	6		Alpine Ski.World Cup Tour
Fleischmann, Torrance	Olympic		5	10		Equestrian
Fleisher, Bruce	Golf		5	20	25	
Fleisher, Larry	Basketball	+	25	60		HOF 1991
Fleishman, Jerry	Basketball		10	50		played NBA 45-52
Fleming, Albert	Basketball		4	18		played NBA 77
Fleming, Edward	Basketball		8	40		played NBA 55-59
Fleming, Les	Baseball		9			Debut 1939 Tigers
Fleming, Marv	Football		3	12		NFL
Fleming, Peggy	Olympic		9	28		Figure Skating
Fleming, Reggie	Hockey		4	16		
Fleming, Vern	Basketball		4	15		played NBA 84-
Flerning, Willie	Football		5	12		1982 Canadian HOF
Fletcher, Caroline	Olympic		10	30		Diving
Fletcher, Darrin	Baseball		3	10		Debut 1989
Fletcher, Elbie	Baseball		15	38		Debut 1934 Bost. Braves
Fletcher, Scott	Baseball		3	10		Debut 1981
Flett, Bill	Hockey		4	16		
Fleury, Theoron	Hockey		6	20	20	
Flick, Elmer	Baseball					B&W PC $450
Flick, Elmer	Baseball		72	200	2250	Gold Pl. $500. HOF 1963
Float, Jeff	Olympic		3	6		Swim/relay
Flock, Tim	Auto Racing		5	14		
Flood, Curt	Baseball		22	45		Debut 1956
Florence, Paul	Baseball		16	50		Debut 1926
Flores, Tom	Football		5	12		NFL
Flosadottir, Vala	Pole Vault		3	10		Women's World Record
Flowers, Allen	Football	+	20	75		CHOF Georgia Tech
Flowers, Bruce	Basketball		3	10		played NBA 82
Flowers, Wes	Baseball		10			Debut 1940 Brklyn. Dodg.
Floyd, Bobby	Baseball		3	10		Debut 1968
Floyd, Bubba	Baseball		8	30		Debut 1944
Floyd, Eric	Basketball		4	12		played NBA 82-
Floyd, Ray	Golf		10	35	35	PGA HOF 1989
Flutie, Doug	Football		10	40		Heisman Boston '84.NFL
Flynn, Doug	Baseball		3	10		Debut 1975
Flynn, Mike	Basketball		4	16		played NBA 75-77
Flynt, Bob	Golf		5	20	25	
Fogle, Larry	Basketball		4	16		played NBA 75
Foiles, Hank	Baseball		10	25		Debut 1953
Foley, John	Basketball		7	35		played NBA 62

NAME	CATEGORY	+	SIG	SP	BALL	Comment
Foley, Marv	Baseball		3	10		Debut 1978
Foley, Tom	Baseball		3	10		Debut 1983
Foli, Tim	Baseball		4	12		Debut 1970
Folley, Zora	Boxing		45	95		
Fondy, Dee	Baseball		6	18		Debut 1951
Fonseca, Lew	Baseball		30	65		Debut 1921 Cin. Reds
Fontaine, Levi	Basketball		4	20		played NBA 70
Fontes, Wayne	Football		4	12		NFL
Fonteyne, Val	Hockey		5	22		
Fontinato, Louie	Hockey		6	25		
Foote, Barry	Baseball		3	10		Debut 1973
Ford, Alan	Olympic		4	9		Swim/sprints
Ford, Chris	Basketball		3	10		played NBA 72-81
Ford, Curt	Baseball		3	10		Debut 1985
Ford, Dan	Baseball		3	10		Debut 1975
Ford, Danny	Football		2	5		College Coach of Year
Ford, Donald	Basketball		3	15		played NBA 75-81
Ford, Doug	Golf		9	25	35	Old PGA HOF 1975
Ford, Gene	Baseball		10			Debut 1905
Ford, Henry	Auto Racing	+	950	2500		
Ford, Jake	Basketball		5	22		played NBA 70-71
Ford, Len	Football	+	175	350		1976 HOF DL
Ford, Phil	Basketball		5	20		played NBA 78-84
Ford, Robert	Basketball		4	22		played NBA 72
Ford, Russell	Baseball		100			Debut 1909 Yankee Pitch.
Ford, Ted	Baseball		3	12		Debut 1970
Ford, Whitey	Baseball					P-S HOF $38. HOF 1974
Ford, Whitey	Baseball		10	22	30	Gold Pl. $15
Foreman, Chuck	Football		5	20		NFL
Foreman, George	Boxing		20	45		1973-74 H-Wt Champ
Forget, Guy	Tennis		5	16		
Forman, Donald	Basketball		10	50		played NBA 48
Forrest, Bayard	Basketball		4	18		played NBA 77-78
Forrester, Jack	Golf		45	120		
Forsberg, Peter	Hockey		7	32	35	
Forsbrand, Anders	Golf		5	20	25	
Forsman, Dan	Golf		5	20	25	
Forster, Terry	Baseball		5	12		Debut 1971
Forte, Aldo	Football		10	35		NFL
Fortmann, Dan	Football		25	80		1965 HOF. 2-way line
Fortunato, Joe	Football		5	18		NFL
Fosbury, Dick	Olympic		50	125		High Jump
Fosse, Ray	Baseball		3	12		Debut 1967
Foster, Bill	Baseball					HOF 1996
Foster, Bill	Basketball		3	6		NCAA USC
Foster, Bob	Boxing		18	38		Lt.Hvy-Wt Champ.
Foster, Fred	Basketball		4	15		played NBA 68-76
Foster, George	Baseball		5	20		Debut 1969
Foster, Greg	Olympic		4	18		Hurdles
Foster, Harold "Bud"	Basketball		30	55		HOF 1964. Wisc.
Foster, Jimmy	Basketball		4	20		played NBA 74-75
Foster, Leo	Baseball		3	14		Debut 1971
Foster, Martin	Golf		10	25		
Foster, Rod	Basketball		3	12		played NBA 83-85
Foster, Roy	Baseball		3	12		Debut 1970
Foster, Rube	Baseball		3500	6400	13000	HOF 1981

NAME	CATEGORY	+	SIG	SP	BALL	Comment
Foster, Todd "Kid"	Boxing		7	15		
Foster, Willie	Baseball		95	225		HOF 1996, Negro Leaguer
Fothergill, Dotty	Bowling		5	10		1980 Women's IBC HOF
Fotheringhan, George	Golf		65	185		
Fought, John	Golf		5	20	25	
Foulis, James	Golf		525	1250		
Foulis, Jim	Golf		35	95		
Foust, Larry	Basketball		10	22		played NBA 50-61
Fouts, Dan	Football		9	25	150	NFL
Fowler, Calvin	Basketball		5	25		played NBA 69
Fowler, Jerry	Basketball		10	50		played NBA 51
Fownes, W.C. Jr	Golf		150	395		
Fox, Catherine	Olympic		3	6		Gold Med. Swimming
Fox, Francine	Olympic		3	8		Kayak
Fox, Harold	Basketball		4	22		played NBA 72
Fox, James	Basketball		4	20		played NBA 67-76
Fox, Nellie	Baseball		150	275	2050	Debut 1947. HOF 1997
Foxx, Jimmie	Baseball					B&W PC S $700
Foxx, Jimmie	Baseball		250	1200	3000	Gold Pl. $2275. HOF1951
Foy, Joe	Baseball		8	18		Debut 1966
Foyston, Frank	Hockey		45	150		1958 HOF fwd
Foyt, A.J.	Auto Racing		7	25		HOF 1989
Frame, Fred	Auto Racing	+	30	70		
France, Bill Sr.	Auto Racing		6	18		founder/pres. of NASCAR
Francis, Ron	Hockey		6	20		
Francis, Russ	Football		3	16		NFL
Francis, Sam	Football		40	75		CHOF Nebraska
Franckhauser, Tom	Football		5	12		NFL
Franco, Ed	Football		6	25		CHOF Fordham
Franco, John	Baseball		4	15		Debut 1984
Franco, Julio	Baseball		4	12		Debut 1982
Francona, Terry	Baseball		5	15		Debut 1981
Francona, Tito	Baseball		7	18		Debut 1956
Frank, Clint	Football		18	38		CHOF Yale. Heisman '37
Frank, Tellis	Basketball		3	12		played NBA 87-
Frankel, Nat	Basketball		20	75		played NBA 39-46
Frankhouse, Fred M.	Baseball		15			Debut 1927 STL Cards
Franklin, Tony	Football		3	10		NFL
Franklin, Will	Basketball		3	15		played NBA 72-75
Franks, Herman	Baseball		7	22		Debut 1939 STL Cards
Frantz, Lou	Bowling		5	12		1978 PBA HOF-Mer.Serv.
Franz, Rod	Football		6	18		CHOF California
Franz, Ron	Basketball		4	20		played NBA 67-72
Fraser, Dawn	Olympic		20	45		Swimming
Fraser, Gretchen	Olympic		12	26		Alpine Skiing
Fraser, Neale	Tennis		5	25		HOF 1984
Fraser, Steven	Olympic		3	6		Wrestling
Fratiane, Linda	Olympic		6	18		Figure Skating
Frazer, Alexa Sterling	Golf		65	165		
Frazier, Amy	Tennis		4	10		
Frazier, Herman	Olympic		5	12		400 Meters
Frazier, Joe	Baseball		6	22		Debut 1947
Frazier, Joe	Boxing		15	40		1971-73 H-Wt Champ
Frazier, Marvis	Boxing		5	15		Hvy-Wt.
Frazier, Tommie	Football		3	10		Nebraska QB
Frazier, Walt	Basketball		10	32	125	HOF 1986-87

NAME	CATEGORY	+	SIG	SP	BALL	Comment
Frazier, Will	Basketball		4	22		played NBA 65-68
Frederick, Anthony	Basketball		3	10		played NBA 88
Frederickson, Frank	Hockey		65	150		1958 HOF fwd
Frederickson, Tucker	Football		3	12		NFL
Free, World B.	Basketball		7	16		played NBA 75-87
Freed, Roger	Baseball		3	10		Debut 1970
Freehan, Bill	Baseball		4	15		Debut 1961
Freeman, Antonio	Football		4	18	75	NFL
Freeman, Donnie	Basketball		5	18		played NBA 67-75
Freeman, Gary	Basketball		3	15		played NBA 70
Freeman, Kevin	Olympic		3	6		Equestrian
Freeman, Robin	Golf		5	20	25	
Freeman, Rodney	Basketball		3	18		played NBA 73
Freeman, Ron	Olympic		7	22		400 Meters
Freese, Gene	Baseball		4	12		Debut 1955
Freese, George	Baseball		3	12		Debut 1953
Fregosi, Jim	Baseball		4	12		Debut 1961 Angels
Freiburger, Vern	Baseball		6	25		Debut 1941
Freitas, Tony	Baseball		12			Debut 1932 Phil. A's
French, Emmet	Golf		45	160		
French, Jim	Baseball		3	12		Debut 1965
French, Larry	Baseball		30	70		Debut 1929
French, Ray	Baseball		35	80		Debut 1920 Yankees
French, Walter Fitz	Baseball		14	30		Debut 1923 Phil. A's
Frey, Frido	Basketball		10	50		played NBA 46
Frey, Lonny	Baseball		25	65		Debut 1933 Brklyn. Dodg.
Frick, Ford	Baseball					B&W PC $175
Frick, Ford	Baseball		60	165	800	Gold Pl. $135.HOF 1970
Fridley, Jim	Baseball		6	18		Debut 1952
Friedman, Benny	Football	+	60	125		CHOF Michigan
Friedman, Max "Marty"	Basketball	+	22	50		HOF 1971
Friend, Bob	Baseball		3	12		Debut 1951
Friend, Lawrence	Basketball		8	40		played NBA 57
Friend, Owen	Baseball		7	22		Debut 1949 STL Browns
Frierson, Buck	Baseball		8	28		Debut 1941
Friesz, John	Football		4	10		NFL
Frink, Fred	Baseball		8	35		Debut 1934
Frink, Patrick	Basketball		4	20		played NBA 68
Frisch, Frankie	Baseball		80	180	1650	Gold Pl. $185. HOF 1947
Frisch, Frisch	Baseball					B&W PC $175
Fritsche, James	Basketball		10	45		played NBA 53-54
Fritz, Deane	Bowling		8	28		1966 Women's IBC HOF
Fritz, Larry	Baseball		3	12		Debut 1975
Fromme, Art	Baseball		85			Debut 1906
Frost, David	Golf		5	20		
Fruhwith, Amy	Golf		5	20	25	
Fry Irvin, Shirley	Tennis		5	18		HOF 1970
Fry, Hayden	Football		2	5		Iowa Coach
Fry, Jerry	Baseball		3	10		Debut 1978
Fry, Mark	Golf		15	45		
Fryar, Irving	Football		4	15	80	NFL
Fryer, Bernie	Basketball		3	12		played NBA 73-74
Fryman, Travis	Baseball		10	36		Debut 1990
Ftorek, Robbie	Hockey		5	14		1991 US HOF
Fucarino, Frank	Basketball		10	50		played NBA 46
Fuchs, James	Olympic		4	16		Shot Put

NAME	CATEGORY	+	SIG	SP	BALL	Comment
Fuentes, Mike	Baseball		3	10		Debut 1983
Fuentes, Tito	Baseball		5	12		Debut 1965
Fuetsch, Herman	Basketball		10	50		played NBA 45-47
Fuhr, Grant	Hockey		6	32	35	
Fulcher, David	Football		3	10		NFL
Fulks, Joe	Basketball	+	40	90		HOF 1977
Fuller, Carl	Basketball		4	15		played NBA 70-71
Fuller, Jim	Baseball		3	10		Debut 1973
Fuller, John	Baseball		3	10		Debut 1974
Fuller, Tony	Basketball		3	10		played NBA 80
Fullerton, Hugh	Writer		60	95		Exposed 1919 WS Fix
Fullmer, Don	Boxing		15	27		
Fullmer, Gene	Boxing		15	35		Middle-Wt Champ.
Funaki, Kazuyoshi	Ski Jumping		4	18		Olympic Gold
Funderburk, Mark	Baseball		3	10		Debut 1981
Funk, Frank	Baseball		4			Debut 1960 Indians
Funk, Fred	Golf		5	20	25	
Funseth, Rod	Golf		5	20	25	
Fuqua, John	Football		6	18		NFL
Furby, Joanne	Golf		5	20	25	
Furgol, Ed	Golf		20	45	50	
Furgol, Marty	Golf		10	30	30	
Furillo, Carl	Baseball		38	102		Debut 1946
Furlow, Terry	Basketball		4	12		played NBA 76-79
Furniss, Bruce	Olympic		5	12		Swim/200 free
Furyk, Jim	Golf		5	20	25	
Fusari, Charlie	Boxing		35	75		

NAME	CATEGORY	+	SIG	SP	BALL	Comment
Gabl, Pepi	Skiing		6	18		
Gable, Dan	Olympic		6	12		Wrestling
Gabor, Bill	Basketball		10	50		played NBA 48-54
Gabriel, Roman	Football		6	15	85	CHOF N.C. St. NFL
Gabriel, Tony	Football		4	8		1985 Canadian HOF
Gabrielson, Len	Baseball		3	12		Debut 1960 Mil. Braves
Gadsby, Bill	Hockey		7	22		1970 HOF def
Gaetti, Gary	Baseball		4	12		Debut 1981
Gaffke, Fabian	Baseball		8	32		Debut 1936
Gagliano, Phil	Baseball		3	10		Debut 1963 Cards
Gagliano, Ralph	Baseball		3	10		Debut 1965
Gagne, Gresf	Baseball		4	10		Debut 1983
Gagner, Dave	Hockey		4	16		
Gailey, Chandler	Football		3	10		Cowboys coach
Gain, Bob	Football		6	20		CHOF Kentucky. NFL

NAME	CATEGORY	+	SIG	SP	BALL	Comment
Gainer, Elmer	Basketball		10	50		played NBA 41-49
Gaines, Ambrose "Rowdy"	Olympic		5	12		Swim/100 free
Gaines, Chryste	Olympic		3	6		Gold Medal. Track
Gaines, Clarence	Basketball		9	25		HOF 1981-Coach
Gaines, Corey	Basketball		3	10		played NBA 88
Gaines, David	Basketball		5	18		played NBA 67
Gaines, Joe	Baseball		3	15		Debut 1960
Gainey, Bob	Hockey		4	16	18	1992 HOF def
Gainey, Ty	Baseball		3	10		Debut 1985
Gaither, Jake	Football		8	22		1973 CHOF coach
Galan, Augie	Baseball		15	40		Debut 1934 Cubs
Galarraga, Andres	Baseball		4	28	28	Debut 1985
Galaxy, Khaosai	Boxing		12	30		Jr.Bantam-Wt Champ
Galbreath, Tony	Football		3	10		NFL
Gale, Lauren "Laddie"	Basketball		15	30		HOF 1976
Gale, Michael	Basketball		3	18		played NBA 71-81
Galehouse, Denny	Baseball		7	25		Debut 1934 Indians
Galento, Tony "Two Ton"	Boxing		70	145		Hvy-Wt Contender
Galfione, Jean	Olympic		5	22		Gold Medal. Pole Vault
Galiffa, Arnold	Football	+	22	75		CHOF Army
Galimore, Willie	Football		55	170		NFL
Galindo, Rudy	Figure Skating		3	10		U.S.Champion
Galitzen, Michael	Olympic		6	22		Diving
Gall, Hugh	Football	+	10	22		1963 Canadian HOF
Gallacher, Bernard	Golf		10	30	30	
Gallagher, Al	Baseball		3	10		Debut 1970
Gallagher, Bob	Baseball		3	10		Debut 1972 Bost. RedSox
Gallagher, Dave	Baseball		3	10		Debut 1987
Gallagher, Jim Jr.	Golf		5	20	25	
Gallagher, Joe	Baseball		8	40		Debut 1939 Yankees
Gallagher, Kim	Olympic		3	8		800 Meters
Gallant, Gerard	Hockey		4	16		
Gallarneau, Hugh	Football		6	25		CHOF Stanford
Gallatin, Harry	Basketball		5	16	100	HOF 1991
Galle, Stan	Baseball		6			Debut 1942 Senators
Gallego, Mike	Baseball		3	10		Debut 1985
Gallett, Francis	Golf		45	95		
Gallett, Leonard	Golf		45	95		
Galloway, Joey	Football		5	22	75	NFL Seattle Receiver
Galvin, Pud	Baseball		1983	4000	12000	Ball S $12000. HOF 1965
Gamache, Joey	Boxing		10	20		Lt-Wt Champ
Gambee, Dave	Basketball		5	20		played NBA 58-69
Gamble, Kevin	Basketball		3	10		played NBA 87-
Gamble, Lee	Baseball		7	30		Debut 1935
Gamble, Oscar	Baseball		4	12		Debut 1969
Gamez, Robert	Golf		5	20	25	
Gannon, Rich	Football		3	6		NFL
Gant, Harry	Auto Racing		10	45		
Gant, John	Bowling		2	8		Tourney winner
Gant, Ron	Baseball		4	12		Debut 1987
Gantenbein, Joe	Baseball		10	35		Debut 1939
Gantner, Jim	Baseball		3	10		Debut 1976
Gantt, Robert Jr.	Basketball		10	50		played NBA 46
Gaona, Bob	Football		5	15		NFL
Gaona, Robert	Golf		5	20	25	
Garagiola, Joe	Baseball		5	15		Debut 1946, Broadcasting HOF

NAME	CATEGORY	+	SIG	SP	BALL	Comment
Garbacz, Lori	Golf		5	20	25	
Garbark, Bob	Baseball		15	45		Debut 1934
Garbark, Mike	Baseball		4	20		Debut 1944
Garber, Gene	Baseball		4	12		Debut 1969 Pirates
Garbey, Barbaro	Baseball		3	12		Debut 1984
Garbisch, Ed	Football	+	15	80		CHOF Army
Garbowski, Ales	Baseball		4	18		Debut 1952
Garcia, Damaso	Baseball		3	10		Debut 1978
Garcia, Danny	Baseball		3	10		Debut 1981
Garcia, Kiko	Baseball		4	12		Debut 1976
Garcia, Leo	Baseball		3	10		Debut 1987
Garcia, Mike	Baseball		22	60		Debut 1948
Garcia, Pedro	Baseball		4	10		Debut 1973
Garciaparra, Nomar	Baseball		8	32		Rookie-of-Year
Gardella, Al	Baseball		6	22		Debut 1945 Giants
Gardella, Danny	Baseball		5	18		Debut 1944
Gardenhire, Ron	Baseball		3	10		Debut 1981
Gardiner, Chuck	Hockey		60	120		1945 HOF goal
Gardiner, Herb	Hockey		60	125		1958 HOF def
Gardner, Art	Baseball		3	10		Debut 1975
Gardner, Billy	Baseball		4	10		Debut 1954
Gardner, Buddy	Golf		5	20	25	
Gardner, Chuck	Basketball		3	22		played NBA 67
Gardner, Earl	Basketball		10	50		played NBA 48
Gardner, Floyd "Jelly"	Baseball		65	175		Played 15 Seasons, Negro League
Gardner, Jack	Basketball		7	20		HOF 1983 Coach
Gardner, Jimmy	Hockey		190	500		1962 HOF fwd
Gardner, Ken	Basketball		3	12		played NBA 75
Gardner, Larry	Baseball		40	85		Debut 1908
Gardner, Robert	Golf		125	300		
Gardner, Vern	Basketball		10	50		played NBA 49-51
Garfinkel, Jack	Basketball		10	50		played NBA 45-48
Garibaldi, Bob	Baseball		4	14		Debut 1962 SF Giants
Garland, Chuck	Tennis	+	15	42		HOF 1969
Garland, Gary	Basketball		3	10		played NBA 79
Garlits, Don	Auto Racing		7	20		HOF 1989
Garmaker, Dick	Basketball		6	20		played NBA 55-60
Garms, Debs	Baseball		20	60		Debut 1932 Browns
Garms, Shirley	Bowling		5	15		1971 Women's IBC HOF
Garnaas, Bill	Football		5	12		NFL
Garner, Andrew	Horse Racing					HOF 1969 jockey
Garner, Phil	Baseball		4	10		Debut 1973
Garner, William	Basketball		5	22		played NBA 67
Garnett, Bill	Basketball		3	14		played NBA 82-85
Garnett, Kevin	Basketball		10	32	125	NBA Wolves
Garr, Ralph	Baseball		5	15		Debut 1968
Garrett, Adrian	Baseball		3	15		Debut 1966
Garrett, Calvin	Basketball		3	12		played NBA 80-83
Garrett, Carl	Football		3	12		NFL
Garrett, Dick	Basketball		3	16		played NBA 69-73
Garrett, Mike	Football		15	30		CHOF USC. Heisman '65
Garrett, Rowland	Basketball		3	18		played NBA 72-76
Garrett, Wayne	Baseball		3	12		Debut 1969 Giants
Garrick, Thomas	Basketball		3	10		played NBA 88
Garrido, Gil	Baseball		4	12		Debut 1964
Garris, John	Basketball		3	10		played NBA 83

NAME	CATEGORY	+	SIG	SP	BALL	Comment
Garrison (Steeves), Kelly	Olympic		5	12		Skiing
Garrison, Ford	Baseball		6	25		Debut 1943
Garrison, Gary	Football		3	15		NFL
Garrison, John	Hockey	+	10	22		1974 US HOF
Garrison, Snapper	Horse Racing					HOF 1955 jockey
Garrison, Walt	Football		4	15		NFL
Garrison, Zina	Tennis		10	25		
Garrity, Jack	Hockey		5	14		1986 US HOF
Gartner, Mike	Hockey		3	22		
Garver, Ned	Baseball		4	16		Debut 1948 Browns
Garvey, Philomena	Golf		10	30	35	
Garvey, Steve	Baseball		7	20		Debut 1969
Garvin, James	Basketball		3	12		played NBA 73
Garza, Josele	Auto Racing		9	18		
Gaspar, Rod	Baseball		3	12		Debut 1969
Gaston, Alex	Baseball		20			Debut 1920 NY Giants
Gaston, Clarence "Cito"	Baseball		4	12		Debut 1967 Atl. Braves
Gaston, Milt	Baseball		12			Debut 1924 Yankees
Gates, Ben	Basketball		20	50		played NBA 46-49
Gates, Joe	Baseball		3	10		Debut 1978
Gates, Mike	Baseball		3	10		Debut 1981
Gates, William "Pop"	Basketball		12	35		HOF 1989
Gathers, James	Olympic		5	15		200 meters
Gatski, Frank	Football		6	18	80	1985 HOF OL
Gattison, Ken	Basketball		3	10		played NBA 86-
Gaudaur, J.G.	Football		4	8		1984 Canadian HOF
Gaudet, Jim	Baseball		3	10		Debut 1978
Gaunntt, Jim	Golf		15	50		
Gautreaux, Sid "Pudge"	Baseball		9			Debut 1936 Brklyn. Dodg.
Gaver, John M.	Horse Racing					HOF 1966 trainer
Gavilan, Kid	Boxing		18	35		Welter-Wt Champ
Gavin, Stewart	Hockey		5	22		
Gayda, Edward	Basketball		10	50		played NBA 50
Gaylord, Mitch	Olympic		8	20		Gymnastics
Gazella, Mike	Baseball		30	75		Debut 1923 Yanks.'26 WS
Gearhart, Lloyd	Baseball		4	15		Debut 1947
Geary, Huck	Baseball		22	55		Debut 1942
Gebhardt, Michael	Olympic		3	6		Yachting
Geddes, Jane	Golf		10	25	25	
Gedman, Rich	Baseball		3	7		Debut 1980
Gee, Johnny	Baseball		4			Debut 1939 Pirates
Gehrig, Lou	Baseball		1150	4400	5000	HOF 1939.
Gehringer, Charles	Baseball		20	50	120	Gold Pl.$30,B&W PC $55
Gehringer, Charlie	Baseball					P-S HOF $95,Grt.Mo. $90
Geiberger, Al	Golf		10	25	35	
Geiger, Gary	Baseball		4	15		Debut 1958 Indians
Geishert, Gary	Baseball		3			Debut 1969 Angels
Gelbert, Charles	Football	+	22	85		CHOF Pennsylvania
Gendron, Jean-Guy	Hockey		5	22		
Genewich, Joe	Baseball		10			Debut 1922 RedSox
Genter, Steven	Olympic		3	7		Swim/400 free
Gentile, Jim	Baseball		5	18		Debut 1957
Gentry, Harvey	Baseball		3	14		Debut 1954
Gentry, Rufe	Baseball		5			Debut 1943 Tigers
Geoffrion, Bernie	Hockey		10	25	30	1972 HOF fwd
Geoghegan, Bud	Golf		5	15		

NAME	CATEGORY	+	SIG	SP	BALL	Comment
George, Alex	Baseball		5	18		Debut 1955
George, Bill	Football	+	85	295		1974 HOF LB
George, Charles	Baseball		18	55		Debut 1935
George, Eddie	Football		15	45	165	1995 Heisman Trophy
George, Gorgeous	Pro Wrestling		50	95		
George, Jack	Basketball		8	45		played NBA 53-60
George, James	Olympic		3	6		Wrestling
George, Jeff	Football		6	18	85	NFL
Geraghty, Agnes	Olympic		7	29		Swim/breaststroke
Gerald, Ed Fitz	Baseball		4	14		Debut 1948
Gerard, Eddie	Hockey		225	550		1945 HOF fwd
Gerard, Gus	Basketball		3	14		played NBA 74-80
Gerber, Craig	Baseball		3	10		Debut 1985
Gerela, Roy	Football		3	12		NFL
Geren, Bob	Baseball		3	10		Debut 1981
Gerhart, Ken	Baseball		3	10		Debut 1986
Gerken, George	Baseball		35	95		Debut 1927
Germain, Dorothy	Golf		25	75		
Gernert, Dick	Baseball		4	15		Debut1952
Geronimo, Cesar	Baseball		4	12		Debut 1969
Gerratti, Eleanor	Olympic		7	18		Swim/100 M Free
Gerring, Cathy	Golf		5	25	25	
Gersonde, Russ	Bowling	+	12	25		1968 ABC HOF
Gerulaitas, Vitas	Tennis		7	22		
Gervin, George	Basketball		10	30	100	HOF 1996. NBA 72-85
Gestring, Marjorie	Olympic		8	24		Diving
Getchell, Charles	Basketball		20	65		played NBA 46
Getz, Gus	Baseball		85			Debut 1914 Inf Brooklyn
Geyer, Forest	Football	+	20	75		CHOF Oklahoma
Ghezzi, Victor	Golf		125	210		Old PGA HOF 1965
Giacomin, Eddie	Hockey		10	26	30	1987 HOF goal
Giambra, Joey	Boxing		8	22		Middle-Wt
Gianelli, John	Basketball		4	15		played NBA 72-79
Giardello, Joey	Boxing		12	36		Middle-Wt
Gibbon, Joe	Baseball		3			Debut 1960 Pirates
Gibbons, John	Baseball		3	10		Debut 1984
Gibbons, Tom J.	Boxing		75			Hvy-Wt Contender
Gibbs, Dick	Basketball		3	18		played NBA 71-75
Gibbs, Jake	Baseball		4	16		Debut 1962
Gibbs, Joe	Football		5	25	100	NFL
Gibron, Abe	Football		10	28		NFL
Gibson, Althea	Tennis		12	38		HOF 1971
Gibson, Bob	Baseball					P-S HOF $30.
Gibson, Bob	Baseball		9	22	25	HOF 1981. Gold Pl. $15
Gibson, Dee Jr.	Basketball		10	50		played NBA 48-49
Gibson, Greg	Olympic		3	6		Wrestling
Gibson, J.C.	Hockey	+	10	22		1973 US HOF admin
Gibson, Josh	Baseball		1142	1475	6500	HOF 1972
Gibson, Kelly	Golf		5	20	25	
Gibson, Kirk	Baseball		4	15		Debut 1979
Gibson, Leland	Golf		15	45		
Gibson, Melvin	Basketball		5	25		played NBA 63
Gibson, Michael	Basketball		3	10		played NBA 83-85
Gibson, Russ	Baseball		4	18		Debut 1967 RedSox
Gibson, Therm	Bowling	+	12	25		1965 ABC HOF
Gibson, Ward	Basketball		12	50		played NBA 48-49

The Sanders Price Guide to Sports Autographs 3rd Edition

NAME	CATEGORY	+	SIG	SP	BALL	Comment
Giebel, Diane	Olympic		3	6		Swim/butterfly
Giebell, Floyd	Baseball		3	10		Debut 1939
Giel, Paul	Baseball		5	15		Debut 1954
Giel, Paul	Football		6	20		CHOF Minnesota
Giertsen, Douglas	Olympic		3	6		Swim/relay
Gifford, Frank	Football		8	30	150	1977 HOF RB
Gigon, Norm	Baseball		3	15		Debut 1967
Gil, Benji	Baseball		3	8		
Gil, Gus	Baseball		3	15		Debut 1967
Gilbert, Andy	Baseball		15	35		Debut 1942
Gilbert, Charlie	Baseball		22	48		Debut 1940
Gilbert, Gibby	Golf		5	20	25	
Gilbert, Gilles	Hockey		4	20		
Gilbert, Mark	Baseball		3	10		Debut 1985
Gilbert, Rod	Hockey		6	20	25	1982 HOF fwd
Gilbert, Wally	Baseball		35			Debut 1928
Gilbert, Walter	Football	+	15	60		CHOF Auburn
Gilbreath, Rod	Baseball		3	10		Debut 1972
Gilchrist, Cookie	Football		35	75		NFL
Gilder, Bob	Golf		5	20	25	
Gilder, Virginia	Olympic		3	6		Rowing
Gile, Don	Baseball		4	15		Debut 1959
Giles, Brian	Baseball		3	10		Debut 1981
Giles, Curt	Hockey		4	18		
Giles, Vinny	Golf		5	20	25	
Giles, Warren	Baseball		55	168	875	HOF 1979. NL Pres.
Gilford, David	Golf		5	20	25	
Gill, Amory "Slats"	Basketball	+	22	50		HOF 1967 Coach
Gill, Johnny	Baseball		5	12		Debut 1987
Gillanders, J. David	Olympic		3	6		Swim/butterfly
Gillenwater, Carden	Baseball		15	45		Debut 1940
Gillery, Ben	Basketball		3	10		played NBA 88
Gillespie, Jack	Basketball		3	15		played NBA 69
Gillespie, Paul	Baseball		25	55		Debut 1942
Gillette, Gene	Basketball		10	50		played NBA 45
Gilliam, Armon	Basketball		4	12		played NBA 87-
Gilliam, Frank	Football		3	12		NFL
Gilliam, Herman	Basketball		4	12		played NBA 69-76
Gilliam, Horace	Football		3	12		NFL
Gilliam, Jim	Baseball		50	110		Debut 1953
Gillian, John	Football		4	9		NFL
Gillies, Clark	Hockey		4	19		
Gilligan, John	Baseball		15			Debut 1909
Gillis, Grant	Baseball		40	95		Debut 1927
Gillman, Sid	Football		6	18	80	1983 HOF coach
Gilmore, Artis	Basketball		8	28	120	played NBA 71-87
Gilmore, Earl	Auto Racing	+	30	60		
Gilmore, Mike	Golf		7	18		
Gilmore, Walt	Basketball		3	15		played NBA 70
Gilmour, Billy	Hockey		100	225		1962 HOF fwd
Gilmour, Doug	Hockey		6	25	30	
Gilmur, Charles	Basketball		10	50		played NBA 46-50
Ginsberg, Joe	Baseball		10	25		Debut 1948
Gionfriddo, Al	Baseball		10	35		Debut 1944 Pirates
Giordano, Tammy	Baseball		4	15		Debut 1953
Gipp, George	Football	+	550	1800		CHOF Notre Dame

NAME	CATEGORY	+	SIG	SP	BALL	Comment
Girardi, Joe	Baseball		3	10		Debut 1989
Giuliani, Tony	Baseball		10	28		Debut 1935
Giusti, Dave	Baseball		3			Debut 1962 Houston
Givens, Ernest	Football		4	15		NFL
Givens, Jack	Basketball		4	16		played NBA 78-79
Gjertsen, Doug	Olympic		3	6		Gold Medal. Swimming
Gladchuck, Chet	Football	+	15	50		CHOF Boston College
Gladd, Jim	Baseball		25	65		Debut 1946
Gladden, Dan	Baseball		4	10		Debut 1983
Gladding, Fred	Baseball		3			Debut 1961 Tigers
Glamack, George	Basketball		20	60		played NBA 41-48
Glance, Harvey	Olympic		5	15		Track sprints
Glaser, Jay	Olympic		3	6		Yachting
Glass, Bill	Football		6	18		CHOF Baylor
Glasson, Bill	Golf		5	20	25	
Glaviano, Tommy	Baseball		4	15		Debut 1949
Glavine, Tom	Baseball		10	55		Debut 1987
Glazner, C.F. "Whitey"	Baseball		9			Debut 1920 Pitt.
Gleaton, Jerry Don	Baseball		3			Debut 1979 TX Rangers
Gleeson, Jim	Baseball		10	38		Debut 1936
Glenesk, Dean	Olympic		3	6		Pentathlon
Glenn, Joe	Baseball		35	80		Debut 1932 Yankees
Glenn, John	Baseball		4	20		Debut 1960
Glenn, Mike	Basketball		3	12		played NBA 77-86
Glenn, Terry	Football		5	25	150	NFL
Glenn, Vencie	Football		3	10		NFL
Glick, Gary	Football		5	16		NFL
Glick, Normie	Basketball		10	50		played NBA 49
Glickman, Marty	Broadcaster		3	6		
Glisson, Gordon	Horse Racing		15	28		jockey
Gloor, Olga	Bowling		5	10		1976 Women's IBC HOF
Glossop, Al	Baseball		8	40		Debut 1939
Glouchkov, Georgi	Basketball		8	25		played NBA 85
Glover, Clarence	Basketball		3	16		played NBA 71
Glover, Randy	Golf		15	40		
Glynn, Bill	Baseball		6	18		Debut 1949
Gminski, Mike	Basketball		3	12		played NBA 80-88
Gnauck, Maxie	Olympic		12	38		Gymnastics
Goalby, Bob	Golf		10	30	35	
Godby, Danny	Baseball		3	10		Debut 1974
Goddard, Joe	Baseball		3	12		Debut 1972
Godfrey, Ernest	Football	+	15	35		1972 CHOF coach
Godina, John	Olympic		2	7		Medal; Shot Put
Godman, Jim	Bowling		5	10		1987 ABC, PBA HOF
Goebel, W. R.	Golf		45	195		
Goetz, Bob	Golf		10	25	30	
Goetz, Dick	Golf		5	20	25	
Goetze, Vicki	Golf		5	20	25	
Goggin, Chuck	Baseball		3	12		Debut 1972
Goggin, Willie	Golf		30	90		
Gogolak, Charlie	Football		3	12		NFL
Gogolak, Pete	Football		5	12		NFL
Goheen, F.X.	Hockey		40	85		1952 HOF def
Goheen, Frank	Hockey	+	7	25		1973 US HOF
Gola, Tom	Basketball		9	28	125	HOF 1975
Golab, Tony	Football		4	8		1964 Canadian HOF

NAME	CATEGORY	+	SIG	SP	BALL	Comment
Goldberg, Marshall	Football		12	35		CHOP Pittsburgh
Golden, Clyde	Baseball		8	30		Debut 1948, Negro League
Golden, Harry	Bowling		5	10		1983 PBA HOF-Mer.Serv.
Golden, Jim	Baseball		3			Debut 1960 L.A. Dodgers
Golden, John	Golf		125	250		
Golden, Kate	Golf		5	20	25	
Goldfaden, Ben	Basketball		10	50		played NBA 46
Goldsberry, Gordon	Baseball		10	25		Debut 1949 Chi Sox
Goldsmith, H.E. "Hal"	Baseball		7			Debut 1926 RedSox
Goldstein, Lonnie	Baseball		12	35		Debut 1943
Goldsworthy, Bill	Hockey		15	60		
Goldy, Purnal	Baseball		3	15		Debut 1962
Golembiewski, Billy	Bowling		6	15		1979 ABC HOF
Goletz, Stan	Baseball		8	35		Debut 1941
Goliat, Mike	Baseball		5	18		Debut 1949
Golvin, Walt	Baseball		40	90		Debut 1922
Gomes, Harold	Boxing		10	22		
Gomez, Andres	Tennis		5	12		
Gomez, Randy	Baseball		3	10		Debut 1984
Gomez, Vernon "Lefty"	Baseball					P-S HOF $95. HOF 1972
Gomez, Vernon "Lefty"	Baseball		22	65	150	Gold Pl. $28.Grt.Mo. $70
Gomez, Wilfredo	Boxing		15	40		Multiple Weight Champ.
Gonder, Jesse	Baseball		3	15		Debut 1960
Gondrezick, Glen	Basketball		6	12		played NBA 77-82
Gondrezick, Grant	Basketball		3	10		played NBA 86-88
Gonsoulin, Goose	Football		5	18		NFL
Gonzales, Tony	Football		5	22		NFL
Gonzalez, Dan	Baseball		3	10		Debut 1979
Gonzalez, Juan	Baseball		4	15		Debut 1989
Gonzalez, Pancho	Tennis		25	85		HOF 1968
Gooch, Johnny	Baseball		60	125		Debut 1921
Goodell, Brian	Olympic		5	12		Swim/400 free
Gooden, Dwight	Baseball		4	15		Debut 1984
Goodenbour, Molly	Basketball		2	5		Women's ABL
Goodfellow, Ebbie	Hockey		22	90		1963 HOF def
Goodman, Billy	Baseball		22	55		Debut 1947
Goodman, Ival	Baseball		25	65		Debut 1935 Cin. Reds
Goodman, Ival	Baseball		8			Debut 1935 Reds
Goodman, John	Golf		155	350		
Goodreault, Gene	Football		6	18		CHOF Boston College
Goodrich, Gail	Basketball		7	20		HOF 1996. NBA 65-73
Goodson, Ed	Baseball		3	10		Debut 1970
Goodwin, Danny	Baseball		3	10		Debut 1975
Goodwin, Wilfred	Basketball		10	50		played NBA 45-47
Goodyear, Scott	Auto Racing		4	12		
Goolagong, Evonne	Tennis		15	35		HOF 1988 (Cawley)
Goolsby, Ray	Baseball		6	22		Debut 1946
Goosen, Greg	Baseball		3	12		Debut 1965
Goosie, J.C.	Golf		5	20	25	
Goossen, Leo	Auto Racing	+	30	65		
Gorbous, Glen	Baseball		4	18		Debut 1955
Gordeeva, Ekaterina	Olympic		10	65		Olymp.Gold.Figure Skating
Gordien, Fortune	Olympic		15	35		Discus
Gordon, Jack	Golf		45	125		
Gordon, Jeff	Auto Racing		6	45		NASCAR.Record Setter
Gordon, Joe	Baseball		55	120		Debut 1938

NAME	CATEGORY	+	SIG	SP	BALL	Comment
Gordon, Lancaster	Basketball		3	10		played NBA 84-87
Gordon, Malcolm	Hockey	+	10	22		1973 US HOF coach
Gordon, Mike	Baseball		3	10		Debut 1977
Gordon, Paul	Basketball		10	50		played NBA 49
Gordon, Sid	Baseball		38	85		Debut 1941
Gordon, Walter	Football	+	15	45		CHOF California
Goren, Charles	Bridge		40	90		
Goring, Butch	Hockey		5	16		
Gorinski, Bob	Baseball		3	10		Debut 1977
Gorman, Francis	Olympic		3	8		Diving
Gorman, Howie	Baseball		12	38		Debut 1937
Gorski, Mark	Olympic		3	6		Cycling
Goryl, John	Baseball		4	12		Debut 1957
Gosger, Jim	Baseball		4	12		Debut 1963 RedSox
Goslin, Leon A. "Goose"	Baseball		100	375	2700	Gold Pl. $3000
Goss, Howie	Baseball		3	15		Debut 1962
Gossage, Goose	Baseball		4	12		Debut 1972
Gossett, Bruce	Football		7	14		NFL
Gossick, Sue	Olympic		4	9		Diving
Gotch, Frank	Pro Wrestling		38	85		
Gottfried, Baron	Golf		8	22		
Gottfried, Brian	Tennis		6	14		
Gottlieb, Eddie	Basketball	+	22	75		HOF 1971-Contributor
Gottlieb, Leo	Basketball		10	50		played NBA 46-47
Goukas, Al	Basketball		10	50		played NBA 48-49
Goukas, Matthew	Basketball		10	50		played NBA 45
Goukas, Matty	Basketball		4	15		played NBA 66-75
Gould, Alan	Writer		3	6		1990 Ntl S&S HOF
Gould, Shane	Olympic		10	28		Swim/200 free
Goulet, Michel	Hockey		6	18		
Goulish, Nick	Baseball		8	18		Debut 1944
Gourdine, Meredith	Olympic		4	15		Long Jump
Goux, Jules	Auto Racing	+	22	75		
Govan, Gerald	Basketball		5	22		played NBA 67-75
Govedarica, Bato	Basketball		8	45		played NBA 53
Governali, Paul	Football	+	20	75		CHOF Columbia
Gowan, Caroline	Golf		5	20		
Gowdy, Curt	Broadcaster		6	25		1981 Ntl S&S HOF
Gowdy, Hank	Baseball		50	120		Debut 1910
Goydos, Paul	Golf		5	20	25	
Goyette, Phil	Hockey		5	18		
Grabarkewitz, Billy	Baseball		3	10		Debut 1969
Graber, Rod	Baseball		3	12		Debut 1958
Graboski, Joseph	Basketball		10	50		played NBA 48-61
Grace, Bobby	Golf		10	25	35	
Grace, Earl	Baseball		30	95		Debut 1929 Cubs
Grace, Joe	Baseball		35	70		Debut 1938
Grace, Mark	Baseball		6	25		Debut 1988
Grace, Mike	Baseball		3	10		Debut 1978
Graddy, Sam	Olympic		5	12		100 Meters
Grady, Wayne	Golf		10	30	25	
Graef, Jed	Olympic		4	8		Swim/200 backstroke
Graf, Steffi	Tennis		10	40		
Graff, Milt	Baseball		4	12		Debut 1957
Graffis, Herb	Golf		40	95		PGA HOF 1977, Contrib.
Graham, Dirk	Hockey		3	12		

NAME	CATEGORY	+	SIG	SP	BALL	Comment
Graham, Calvin	Basketball		5	22		played NBA 67
Graham, Dan	Baseball		3	10		Debut 1979
Graham, David	Golf		5	25	20	
Graham, Frank	Writer		5	10		
Graham, Gail	Golf		5	20	20	
Graham, Jack	Baseball		4	18		Debut 1946
Graham, Kim	Olympic		3	6		Gold Medal. Track
Graham, Lee	Baseball		3	10		Debut 1983
Graham, Lou	Golf		5	25	25	
Graham, Mal	Basketball		5	25		played NBA 67-68
Graham, Mary	Golf		125	225		
Graham, Mary Lou	Bowling		5	12		1989 Women's IBC HOF
Graham, Orlando	Basketball		3	10		played NBA 88
Graham, Otto	Football		8	24	125	1965 HOF QB
Graham, Wayne	Baseball		3	15		Debut 1963
Grammas, Alex	Baseball		4	18		Debut 1954
Granato, Cammie	Olympic		3	9		Women's Hockey Pioneer
Granato, Tony	Hockey		3	15		
Grandison, Ron	Basketball		3	10		played NBA 88-
Graney, Jack	Baseball		60	125		Debut 1908
Grange, Red	Football	+	70	155	600	1963 HOF RB
Granger, Hoyle	Football		3	10		NFL
Granger, Stewart	Basketball		3	10		played NBA 83-86
Granger, Wayne	Baseball		3			Debut 1969 Cin
Grant, Brian	Basketball		3	15		NBA
Grant, Bryan	Tennis	+	12	45		HOF 1972
Grant, Bud	Football		5	20	95	1994 HOF. '83 Can. HOF
Grant, Danny	Hockey		4	18		
Grant, Gary	Basketball		3	10		played NBA 88-
Grant, Harry	Auto Racing	+	22	45		HOF 1982
Grant, Harvey	Basketball		4	18		played NBA 88-
Grant, Horace	Basketball		6	40	125	played NBA 87-
Grant, Jack	Golf		30	75		
Grant, James T. "Mudcat"	Baseball		4	18		Debut 1958 Cleve.
Grant, Jimmy	Baseball		35	85		Debut 1942
Grant, Mike	Hockey		120	350		1950 HOF def
Grant, Travis	Basketball		5	18		played NBA 72-75
Grant-Suttie, Elsie	Golf		95	175		
Grasso, Mickey	Baseball		40	85		Debut 1946
Grate, Donald	Basketball		10	50		played NBA 47-49
Graves, Adam	Hockey		5	25		
Graves, Butch	Basketball		3	10		played NBA 84
Graves, Joe	Baseball		38	80		Debut 1927 RedSox
Gray, David	Tennis	+	12	40		HOF 1985
Gray, Dick	Baseball		4	15		Debut 1958
Gray, Gary	Baseball		3	10		Debut 1977
Gray, Gary	Basketball		4	15		played NBA 67
Gray, Gordon	Horse Racing		10	20		jockey
Gray, Herbert	Football		4	8		1983 Canadian HOF
Gray, Jerry	Football		3	9		NFL
Gray, Leonard	Basketball		3	10		played NBA 74-76
Gray, Mel	Football		3	12		NFL
Gray, Pete	Baseball		7	20	35	Debut 1945
Gray, Stuart	Basketball		3	10		played NBA 84-
Gray, Sylvester	Basketball		3	10		played NBA 88-
Gray, Ted	Baseball		4			Debut 1948 Tigers

NAME	CATEGORY	+	SIG	SP	BALL	Comment
Gray, Wyndol	Basketball		10	50		played NBA 46-47
Grayer, Jeff	Basketball		3	10		played NBA 88-
Grayson, Dave	Football		5	16		NFL
Grayson, Robert	Football	+	30	90		CHOF Stanford
Graziano, Rocky	Boxing		40	110		Middle-Wt Champ
Grbac, Elvis	Football		5	22		NFL
Greacen, Robert	Basketball		4	20		played NBA 69-71
Greason, Bill	Baseball		4			Debut 1954 STL Cards
Green, A. C.	Basketball		4	20	100	played NBA 85-
Green, David	Baseball		3	10		Debut 1981
Green, Dick	Baseball		7	18		Debut 1963 K.C.
Green, Freddie	Baseball		4			Debut 1959 Pitt.
Green, Gary	Baseball		3	10		Debut 1986
Green, Gene	Baseball		12	42		Debut 1957
Green, Hubert	Golf		5	25	25	
Green, Jack	Football	+	12	35		CHOF Army
Green, Joe	Baseball		30	30		Debut1924
Green, John	Basketball		7	25		played NBA 59-72
Green, Ken	Basketball		3	10		played NBA 85
Green, Ken	Golf		5	20	25	
Green, Kenneth L.	Basketball		3	10		played NBA 85-86
Green, Lamar	Basketball		3	15		played NBA 69-74
Green, Lenny	Baseball		4	15		Debut 1957
Green, Luther	Basketball		3	18		played NBA 69-72
Green, Michael	Basketball		3	12		played NBA 73-83
Green, Pumpsie	Baseball		6	18		Debut 1959
Green, Rickey	Basketball		3	12		played NBA 77-
Green, Roy	Football		5	12		NFL
Green, Sidney	Basketball		3	10		played NBA 83-
Green, Sihugo	Basketball		10	30		played NBA 56-65
Green, Steven	Basketball		3	12		played NBA 75-83
Green, Tammie	Golf		5	20	25	
Green, Tommie	Basketball		3	15		played NBA 78
Green, Wilf	Hockey		110	300		1962 HOF def
Greenberg, Henry "Hank"	Baseball					HOF 1956. P-S HOF $450
Greenberg, Henry "Hank"	Baseball		45	175	600	Gold Pl.$90,B&W PC $95
Greene, Al	Baseball		3	10		Debut 1979
Greene, Al	Olympic		10	25		Diving
Greene, Bert	Golf		15	45		
Greene, Charles	Olympic		5	14		100 Meters
Greene, Joe	Football		10	28	135	1987 HOF DL
Greene, Joe	Olympic		2	7		Medal; Long Jump
Greene, June	Baseball		35	90		Debut 1928
Greene, Nancy	Olympic		7	25		Alpine Skiing
Greenfield, Kent	Baseball		32			Debut 1924 NY Giants
Greengrass, Jim	Baseball		10	30		Debut 1952
Greenleaf, Ralph	Pocket Billiards		90	195		
Greenspan, Bud	Olympic		3	12		Film maker (Olympics)
Greenspan, Jerry	Basketball		5	25		played NBA 63-64
Greenwald, Gilda	Bowling	+	10	35		1953 Women's IBC HOF
Greenwell, Mike	Baseball		4	15	32	Debut 1985
Greenwood, David	Basketball		3	12		played NBA 79-90
Greenwood, Jeff	Snowboarding		2	5		World Cup Champion
Greenwood, L.C.	Football		5	20	85	NFL
Greer, Brian	Baseball		3	10		Debut 1977
Greer, Hal	Basketball		10	25	110	HOF 1981

NAME	CATEGORY	+	SIG	SP	BALL	Comment
Gregg, Forrest	Football		7	25	75	1977 HOF OL
Gregg, Tommy	Baseball		3	10		Debut 1987
Gregor, Gary	Basketball		3	12		played NBA 68-73
Gregory, Claude	Basketball		3	10		played NBA 85-87
Gregory, Paul	Baseball		6			Debut 1932 ChiSox
Gregson, Malcolm	Golf		5	20	25	
Greig, John	Basketball		3	10		played NBA 82
Greiner, Otto	Golf		10	35		
Grekin, Normak	Basketball		10	45		played NBA 53
Gremp, Buddy	Baseball		8	38		Debut 1940 Braves
Greschner, Ron	Hockey		3	15		
Gretzky, Wayne	Hockey		20	50	75	
Grevey, Kevin	Basketball		4	12		played NBA 75-84
Grewel, Alexi	Olympic		3	6		Cycling
Grey, Dennis	Basketball		3	20		played NBA 68-69
Grey, Earl Lord	Football	+	25	75		1963 Canadian HOF
Grich, Bob	Baseball		4	12		Debut 1970
Griese, Bob	Football		10	32	135	1990 HOF QB
Grieve, Tom	Baseball		3	10		Debut 1970
Griffey Jr., Ken	Baseball		15	47	50	Debut 1989
Griffey Sr., Ken.	Baseball		4	15		Debut 1973
Griffin, Archie	Football		15	30		CHOF OSU.Heisman 2x
Griffin, Clarence	Tennis	+	10	30		HOF 1970
Griffin, Doug	Baseball		3	10		Debut 1970
Griffin, Greg	Basketball		4	15		played NBA 77
Griffin, Henry	Horse Racing					HOF 1956 jockey
Griffin, Ivy	Baseball		55	125		Debut 1919
Griffin, Paul	Basketball		4	15		played NBA 76-82
Griffing, Dean	Football		4	8		1965 Canadian HOF
Griffis, Si	Hockey		100	300		1950 HOF fwd
Griffith, Clark	Baseball		225	500	2150	HOF 1946. B&W PC $600
Griffith, Darrell	Basketball		6	18		played NBA 80-
Griffith, Derrell	Baseball		3	12		Debut 1963
Griffith, Emile	Boxing		18	38		Welter & Mid-Wt Champ
Griffith, Harry	Football	+	10	22		1963 Canadian HOF
Griffith-Joyner, Florence	Olympic	+	16	60		
Grigsby, Chuck	Basketball		10	35		played NBA 54
Grim, Bob	Baseball		10	30		Debut 1954
Grimes, Burleigh	Baseball					HOF 1964. P-S HOF $325
Grimes, Burleigh	Baseball		20	88	225	HOF Gold Pl. $30
Grimes, Ed	Baseball		35	80		Debut 1931
Grimes, Oscar	Baseball		20	50		Debut 1938
Grimm, Charlie	Baseball		24	68		Debut 1916 Phill. A's
Grimshaw, George	Basketball		10	50		played NBA 46
Grimsley, Will	Writer	+	6	12		1987 Ntl S&S HOF
Grinfelds, Vesma	Bowling		5	12		1991 Women's IBC HOF
Grinkov & Gordeeva	Olympic		40	175		Olymp.Gold.Figure Skating
Grinkov, Sergei	Olympic		20	75		Olymp.Gold.Figure Skating
Griscom, Frances C	Golf		100	225		
Grissom, Marquis	Baseball		4	15		Debut 1989
Grizuk, P. & Platov, Yevgeny	Ice Dancing		8	38		Olympic Gold
Grizuk, Pasha	Ice Dancing		5	30		Olympic Gold
Groat, Dick	Baseball		5	16		Debut 1952 Pirates
Grogan, Steve	Football		3	12		NFL
Groh, Heinie	Baseball		65	125		Debut 1912
Groman, Bill	Football		5	18		NFL

NAME	CATEGORY	+	SIG	SP	BALL	Comment
Gromek, Steve	Baseball		4			Debut 1941 Indians
Gros, Piero	Olympic		12	30		Alpine skiing
Gross, Bob	Basketball		4	12		played NBA 75-82
Gross, Greg	Baseball		3	10		Debut 1973
Gross, Michael	Olympic		8	30		Swimming
Gross, Wayne	Baseball		3	10		Debut 1976
Grossklos, Howdie	Baseball		28	65		Debut 1930
Grosso, Michael	Basketball		3	15		played NBA 71
Grote, Jerry	Baseball		4	9		Debut 1963
Grote, Jerry	Basketball		3	18		played NBA 64
Groth, Johnny	Baseball		4	18		Debut 1946
Grout, Jack	Golf		35	75		
Grove, Lefty	Baseball					B&W PC $125
Grove, Lefty	Baseball		50	175	1300	HOF 1947. Gold Pl. $110
Grove, Orval	Baseball		12			Debut 1940 ChiSox
Grover, Roy	Baseball		50	110		Debut 1916 Phil. A's
Groza, Alex	Basketball		20	45		played NBA 49-50
Groza, Lou	Football		8	22	100	1974 HOF OL
Grubar, Richard	Basketball		3	20		played NBA 69
Grubb, Harvey	Baseball		60	125		Debut 1912
Grubb, Johnny	Baseball		3	12		Debut 1972
Gruber, Kelly	Baseball		5	20		Debut 1984
Gruenig, Robert	Basketball	+	15	45		HOF 1963
Grunfeld, Ernest	Basketball		3	14		played NBA 77-85
Grylls, David	Olympic		3	6		Cycling
Gryska, Sig	Baseball		18	40		Debut1938
Guarilia, Eugene	Basketball		8	30		played NBA 59-62
Gudmundsson, Karl	Basketball		3	12		played NBA 81-88
Guenther, Johnny	Bowling		5	15		'86 PBA-Vet,'88 ABC HOF
Guerin, Eric	Horse Racing		15	25		HOF 1972 jockey
Guerin, Richie	Basketball		8	46		played NBA 56-63
Guerrero, Pedro	Baseball		4	12		Debut 1978
Guerrero, Roberto	Auto Racing		4	15		
Guest, Charles	Golf		10	35		
Guest, Irene	Olympic		7	25		Swim/100 M free
Guglielmi, Ralph	Football		6	18		NFL
Gugliotta, Tom	Basketball		6	22		NBA Bullets
Guidry, Ron	Baseball		4	15		Debut 1975
Guilford, Jesse	Golf		75	225		
Guillen, Ozzie	Baseball		4	15		Debut 1985
Guindon, Bob	Baseball		3	18		Debut 1964 RedSox
Guintini, Ben	Baseball		7	30		Debut 1946
Guisto, Lou	Baseball		40	95		Debut 1916
Guldahl, Ralph	Golf		125	275		PGA HOF 1981
Gulden, Brad	Baseball		3	10		Debut 1978
Gulick, Luther	Basketball	+	18	45		HOF 1971
Gulick, Merel	Football	+	15	45		CHOF Hobart
Gullic, Ted	Baseball		15	40		Debut 1930 STL Browns
Gulliver, Glenn	Baseball		3	10		Debut 1982
Gumbert, Harry	Baseball		8			Debut 1935 NY Giants
Gump, Scott	Golf		5	20		
Gumpert, Randy	Baseball		8			Debut 1936 A's
Gunn, Watts	Golf		50	125		
Gunther, Coulby	Basketball		10	50		played NBA 46-48
Gunther, David	Basketball		7	35		played NBA 62
Gurney, Dan	Auto Racing		10	30		HOF 1991

NAME	CATEGORY	+	SIG	SP	BALL	Comment
Gurney, Hilda	Olympic		3	8		Equestrian
Gusmeroli, Vanessa	Figure Skating		6	22		World medalist
Gustafson, Andy	Football	+	22	50		1985 CHOF coach
Gustafsson, Magnus	Tennis		6	12		
Gustav V, (King Sweden)	Tennis	+	100	225		HOF 1980
Gustavson, Linda	Olympic		3	8		Swim/100 free
Gustin, Jon	Golf		15	45		
Gustine, Frank	Baseball		7	28		Debut 1939 Pitt. Pirates
Guth, Bucky	Baseball		3	10		Debut 1972
Guthridge, Bill	Basketball		2	5		North Carolina Coach
Guthrie, Janet	Auto Racing		7	22		Woman Driver
Gutowski, Bob	Olympic		6	20		Pole Vault
Gutsu, Tatiana	Olympic		7	38		Gold Medal. Gymnastics
Gutteridge, Don	Baseball		7	25		Debut 1936
Guyon, Joe	Football	+	155	425		1966 HOF RB
Guzman, Jose	Baseball		5	12		Debut 1989
Gwosdz, Doug	Baseball		4	10		Debut 1981
Gwynn, Chris	Baseball		4	10		Debut 1987
Gwynn, Tony	Baseball		7	28		Debut 1982
Gyselman, Dick	Baseball		12	45		Debut 1933

NAME	CATEGORY	+	SIG	SP	BALL	Comment
Haas, Bert	Baseball		15	40		Debut 1937 Brklyn. Dodg.
Haas, Dorothy	Bowling	+	8	25		1977 Women's IBC HOF
Haas, Eddie	Baseball		6	22		Debut 1957
Haas, Fred	Golf		20	65	45	
Haas, George "Mule"	Baseball		43	90		Debut 1925
Haas, Jay	Golf		5	20	25	
Haas, Jerry	Golf		5	15		
Hack, Stan	Baseball		28	65		Debut 1932 Cubs
Hackbarth, Otto	Golf		40	125		
Hacker, Rich	Baseball		3	10		Debut 1971 Montreal
Hackett, Bobby	Olympic		3	7		Swim/1,500 free
Hackett, Harold	Tennis	+	12	40		HOF 1961
Hackett, Rudolph	Basketball		3	15		played NBA 75-76
Hackney, Clarence	Golf		35	125		
Hackney, Dave	Golf		25	60		
Haddix, Harvey	Baseball		18	45		Debut 1952
Haddix, Wayne	Football		3	12		NFL
Hadfield, Vic	Hockey		6	18		
Hadl, John	Football		6	15		NFL
Hadley, Kent	Baseball		3	10		Debut 1958 K.C.
Hadnot, James	Basketball		3	22		played NBA 67
Haeffner, Bill	Baseball		40	90		Debut 1915 Phil.

NAME	CATEGORY	+	SIG	SP	BALL	Comment
Haegg, Gunder	Track		30	65		
Hafey, Bud	Baseball		28	60		Debut 1935 Chi Sox
Hafey, Chick	Baseball		82	215	1500	HOF 1971. Gold Pl. $600
Hafey, Tom	Baseball		15	40		Debut 1939 NY Giants
Hagan, Cliff	Basketball		13	24	100	HOF 1977
Hagan, Glenn	Basketball		3	10		played NBA 81
Hagan, Thomas	Basketball		3	18		played NBA 69-70
Hagberg, Roger	Football		15	65		NFL
Hagen, Walter	Golf		450	1500		PGA HOF 1974
Hagerty, Jack	Bowling	+	10	28		1963 ABC HOF-Mer.Serv.
Hagge, Marlene	Golf		10	35	35	
Hagler, Marvin	Boxing		12	30		Middle-Wt Champ
Hague, Joe	Baseball		3	12		Debut 1968
Hahn, Don	Baseball		3	12		Debut 1969 Royals
Hahn, Paul	Golf		20	45		
Hahn, Robert	Basketball		15	65		played NBA 43
Haines, Hinkey	Baseball		20	45		Debut 1923 Yankees
Haines, Jesse	Baseball		40	130	935	HOF 1970. Gold Pl. $85
Hainsworth, George	Hockey		95	300		1961 HOF goal
Hairston, Alan	Basketball		5	22		played NBA 68-69
Hairston, Happy	Basketball		5	18		played NBA 64-74
Hairston, Jerry	Baseball		3	10		Debut 1973
Hairston, John	Baseball		3	12		Debut 1969
Hairston, Lindsay	Basketball		3	18		played NBA 75
Hairston, Sam	Baseball		6	25		Debut 1951
Haislett, Nicole	Olympic		3	10		Gold Medal. Swimming
Hajduk, Chet	Baseball		8	40		Debut 1941 Chi Sox
Haji-Sheikh, Al	Football		3	8		NFL
Halas, George	Football	+	65	195	500	1963 HOF player/coach
Halbert, Chuck	Basketball		10	50		played NBA 46-50
Halbrook, Swede	Basketball		10	40		played NBA 60-61
Hale Broun, Heywood	Writer		18	50		
Hale, Bob	Baseball		7	28		Debut 1955 Phillies
Hale, Chip	Baseball		3	10		Debut 1989
Hale, Edwin	Football	+	15	45		CHOF Mississippi College
Hale, Hal	Basketball		4	18		played NBA 67
Hale, John	Baseball		3	10		Debut 1974
Hale, Odell	Baseball		15	65		Debut 1931
Hale, Sammy	Baseball		28	70		Debut 1920
Hale, William	Basketball		10	50		played NBA 46-50
Haley, Charles	Football		4	16	75	NFL
Haley, Jack	Basketball		3	10		played NBA 88-
Haley, Ray	Baseball		35	80		Debut 1915
Haliburton, Thomas	Golf		5	20	25	
Halimon, Shaler	Basketball		3	12		played NBA 68-72
Hall, Albert	Baseball		3	10		Debut 1981
Hall, Bill	Baseball		10	38		Debut 1954
Hall, Bob	Baseball		25			Debut 1904 Phillies
Hall, Dean	Auto Racing		4	10		
Hall, Edward	Football	+	17	41		1951 CHOF coach
Hall, Ervin	Olympic		3	10		Hurdles
Hall, Gary	Olympic		3	8		Gold Med. Swimming
Hall, Gary	Olympic		4	15		Swim/butterfly
Hall, Gary, Jr.	Olympic		3	12		Gold Medal. Swimming
Hall, Glenn	Hockey		7	22	25	1975 HOF goal
Hall, Halsey	Broadcaster		5	15		

NAME	CATEGORY	+	SIG	SP	BALL	Comment
Hall, Irv	Baseball		6	28		Debut 1943
Hall, Jimmie	Baseball		5	15		Debut 1963
Hall, Joe	Hockey		45	180		1961 HOF def
Hall, Julie Wade	Golf		5	20	25	
Hall, Kaye	Olympic		3	9		Swim/backstroke
Hall, Mel	Baseball		3	10		Debut 1981
Hall, Samuel	Olympic		3	8		Diving
Hallberg, Gary	Golf		5	20	25	
Halldorson, Dan	Golf		5	20	25	
Haller, Tom	Baseball		4	10		Debut 1961 Giants
Hallet, Jim	Golf		5	20	25	
Hallett, Jack	Baseball		12			Debut 1940 ChiSox
Halliburton, Jeff	Basketball		3	18		played NBA 71-72
Halter, Sydney	Football	+	10	22		1966 Canadian HOF
Ham, Jack	Football		5	18	95	1988 HOF LB
Hambrock, Sharon	Olympic		5	10		Synch. Swimming
Hamill, Dorothy	Olympic		10	35		Figure Skating
Hamilton, Billy	Baseball		875	2375	5600	HOF 1961
Hamilton, Bob	Football		6	20		CHOF Stanford
Hamilton, Bob	Golf		45	195		
Hamilton, Dale	Basketball		22	70		played NBA 39-49
Hamilton, Darryl	Baseball		3	10		Debut 1988
Hamilton, Dennis	Basketball		4	18		played NBA 67-68
Hamilton, Jeff	Baseball		3	10		Debut 1986
Hamilton, Joe	Basketball		3	16		played NBA 70-75
Hamilton, Ralph	Basketball		10	50		played NBA 47-48
Hamilton, Roy	Basketball		3	15		played NBA 79-80
Hamilton, Scott	Olympic		8	32		Figure Skating
Hamilton, Steve	Basketball		4	25		played NBA 58-59
Hamilton, Tom	Baseball		4	16		Debut 1952
Hamlin, Ken	Baseball		3	12		Debut 1957
Hamlin, Luke	Baseball		6			Debut 1933 Tigers
Hamlin, Shelley	Golf		5	20	25	
Hamm, Mia	Soccer (US)		4	22		Olympic Gold
Hammel, Penny	Golf		5	20	25	
Hammond, Donnie	Golf		5	20	25	
Hammond, Julian	Basketball		3	18		played NBA 67-71
Hammond, Kathy	Olympic		3	7		Track relay
Hammond, Steve	Baseball		3	10		Debut 1982
Hamner, Garvin	Baseball		6	18		Debut 1945
Hamner, Granny	Baseball		12	32		Debut 1944
Hamood, Joe	Basketball		5	22		played NBA 67
Hampton, Dave	Football		6	16		NFL
Hampton, Harry	Golf		35	110		
Hampton, Ike	Baseball		3	12		Debut 1974
Hampton, Millard	Olympic		5	16		200 Meters
Hampton, Rodney	Football		4	15	85	NFL
Hamric, Bert	Baseball		9	25		Debut 1955
Hamrick, Ray	Baseball		7	30		Debut 1943
Hanauer, Chip	Boat Racing		6	25		
Hancken, Buddy	Baseball		7	22		Debut 1940 Phil. A's
Hancock, Fred	Baseball		10	32		Debut 1949 ChiSox
Hancock, Greg	Motorcyling		4	15		Speedway world title
Hancock, Phil	Golf		15	35		
Handley, Gene	Baseball		4	20		Debut 1946
Haney, Fred	Baseball		5	25		Debut '22 Mgr.LA Dodgers

NAME	CATEGORY	+	SIG	SP	BALL	Comment
Hankins, Cecil	Basketball		10	50		played NBA 46-47
Hankinson, Phil	Basketball		3	18		played NBA 73-74
Hanks, Sam	Auto Racing	+	22	60		
Hanlon, Glen	Hockey		3	15		
Hanlon, Ned	Baseball					Debut 1996
Hannah, John	Football		6	22	80	1991 HOF OL
Hannah, Truck	Baseball		55			Debut 1918 Yankees
Hannan, Jim	Baseball		4			Debut 1962 Senators
Hanner, Dave	Football		100	300		NFL
Hannibal, Frank	Football	+	10	22		1963 Canadian HOF
Hannum, Alex	Basketball		7	28		played NBA 48-56
Hanrahan, Don	Basketball		8	40		played NBA 52
Hans, Rollen	Basketball		8	40		played NBA 53-54
Hansell, Ellen	Tennis	+	12	35		HOF 1965
Hansen, Frederick M.	Olympic		5	18		Pole Vault
Hansen, Glenn	Basketball		3	15		played NBA 75-77
Hansen, Lars	Basketball		3	15		played NBA 78
Hansen, Ron	Baseball		5			Debut 1958 Orioles
Hanson, Beverly	Golf		35	60		
Hanson, Fritz	Football		4	8		1963 Canadian HOF
Hanson, Tracy	Golf		5	20	25	
Hanson, Vic	Football	+	35	70		CHOF Syracuse
Hanson, Victor	Basketball	+	20	50	150	HOF 1960
Hanzlik, Bill	Basketball		3	10		played NBA 80-
Harada, Masahiki	Ski Jumping		5	22		Olympic Gold
Harbaugh, Jim	Football		4	15	75	NFL
Harbert, Chick	Golf		10	30	35	Old PGA HOF 1968
Hard, Darlene	Tennis		5	22		HOF 1973
Hardaway, Anfernee	Basketball		15	55	150	NBA Magic
Hardaway, Tim	Basketball		5	30		NBA Heat
Harder, Mel "Chief"	Baseball		10	40		Debut 1928 Indians
Harder, Pat	Football		15	55		NFL
Hardin, Christian	Golf		5	20	25	
Hardin, Glenn	Olympic		25	60		Hurdles
Hardin, Jim	Baseball		4			Debut 1967 Orioles
Hardin, W.E. "Bud"	Baseball		4			Debut 1952 Cubs
Harding, Austie	Hockey		5	10		1975 US HOF
Harding, Jack	Football		15	35		1980 CHOF coach
Harding, Jeff	Boxing		12	32		Lt.Hvy-Wt Champ
Harding, Reggie	Basketball		4	22		played NBA 63-67
Harding, Tonya	Olympic		10	35		Figure Skating
Hardnett, Charles	Basketball		3	28		played NBA 62-64
Hardwick, Billy	Bowling		6	20		1977 PBA, '85 ABC HOF
Hardwick, Tack	Football	+	22	75		CHOF Harvard
Hardy, Alan	Basketball		3	12		played NBA 80-81
Hardy, Darrell	Basketball		4	22		played NBA 67
Hardy, James	Basketball		5	15		played NBA 78-81
Hardy, Kevin	Football		3	12		1995 Butkus Award
Hare, T. Truxton	Football	+	25	80		CHOF Pennsylvania
Hargan, Steve	Baseball		5			Debut 1965 Cleve.Pitcher
Harge, Ira	Basketball		4	20		played NBA 67-72
Hargis, John	Basketball		10	50		played NBA 47-50
Hargreaves, Charlie	Baseball		7			Debut 1923 Brklyn.Dodg.
Hargrove, Mike	Baseball		6	12		Cleveland Mgr.
Hark, Doris	Tennis		7	15		
Harkey, Mike	Baseball		3	10		Debut 1988

NAME	CATEGORY	+	SIG	SP	BALL	Comment
Harkness, Jerry	Basketball		4	22		played NBA 63-68
Harlan, Bruce	Olympic		4	18		Diving
Harley, Chick	Football	+	40	145		CHOF Ohio State
Harley, Katherine	Golf		75	175		
Harlicka, Jules	Basketball		4	20		played NBA 68
Harlow, Richard	Football	+	15	40		1954 CHOF coach
Harman, Harvey	Football	+	15	40		1981 CHOF coach
Harman, Janet	Bowling	+	8	22		1985 Women's IBC HOF
Harmon, Chuck	Baseball					Debut 1954 Cin. Reds
Harmon, Claude	Golf		175	550		
Harmon, Terry	Baseball		5			Debut 1967 Phil.
Harmon, Tom	Football	+	45	125		CHOF Mich.Heisman '40
Harmon, Tom	Golf		25	60		
Harney, Paul	Golf		15	45	45	
Harper, Brian	Baseball		3			Debut 1979 Cal. Angels
Harper, Chandler	Golf		15	25		Old PGA HOF 1969
Harper, Derek	Basketball		4	12		played NBA 83-
Harper, George W.	Baseball		30			Debut 1916 Tigers
Harper, Jesse	Football	+	18	40		1971 CHOF coach
Harper, Michael	Basketball		3	10		played NBA 80-81
Harper, Ron	Basketball		4	10		played NBA 86-
Harpster, Howard	Football	+	20	65		CHOF Carnegie
Harrell, Billy	Baseball		3			Debut 1957 S.D. Padres
Harrell, Ray "Cowboy"	Baseball		12			Debut 1935 Cards
Harrelson, Bud	Baseball		3	15		Debut 1965
Harrick, Jim	Basketball		2	5		NCAA Title
Harridge, Will	Baseball		142	275	2500	HOF 1972
Harrigan, Don	Olympic		3	9		Swim/200 backstroke
Harriman, H.M.	Golf		125	295		
Harrington, Micky	Baseball		15	35		Debut 1963
Harris, Arthur	Basketball		4	18		played NBA 68-71
Harris, Bernie	Basketball		4	18		played NBA 74
Harris, Billy	Basketball		4	18		played NBA 74
Harris, Bob	Golf		15	45		
Harris, Bucky	Baseball		60	225	1200	Gold Pl. $175. HOF 1975
Harris, Chris	Basketball		6	40		played NBA 55
Harris, Danny	Olympic		3	8		Hurdles
Harris, Del	Basketball		3	8		Lakers Coach
Harris, Franco	Football		10	25	150	1990 HOF RB
Harris, James	Football		4	12		NFL
Harris, Jimmy	Football		4	15		NFL
Harris, Labron Jr.	Golf		30	95		
Harris, Luman	Baseball		8			Debut 1941 Phil. A's
Harris, Lusia	Basketball		7	25		HOF 1992. Delta St.
Harris, Robert	Basketball		10	50		played NBA 49-53
Harris, Robert	Golf		45	125		
Harris, Roy	Boxing		8	18		
Harris, Steven	Basketball		3	10		played NBA 85-
Harris, Vic	Baseball					Debut 1972 Rangers
Harris, Wayne	Football		4	8		1976 Canadian HOF
Harrison, Alvin	Olympic		3	6		Gold Medal. Track
Harrison, E. J. "Dutch"	Golf		50	130		Old PGA HOF 1962
Harrison, Kenny	Olympic		3	12		Gold Med; Triple Jump
Harrison, Les	Basketball		6	22	115	HOF 1979. Owner-Coach
Harrison, Lisa	Basketball		2	5		Women's ABL
Harrison, Marvin	Football		4	15	75	NFL

NAME	CATEGORY	+	SIG	SP	BALL	Comment
Harrison, Robert	Basketball		8	45		played NBA 49-57
Harrison, Roric	Baseball					Debut 1972 Orioles
Harroun, Ray	Auto Racing	+	125	325		
Harshman, Marv	Basketball		7	20	100	HOF 1984-Coach
Harstad, Oscar T.	Baseball		25			Debut 1915 Cleveland
Hart, Doris	Tennis		6	28		HOF 1969
Hart, Dudley	Golf		5	20	25	
Hart, Eddie	Olympic		6	22		Track sprints
Hart, Edward	Football	+	22	65		CHOF Princeton
Hart, Jim	Football		4	14		NFL
Hart, Leon	Football		10	25		CHOF ND. Heisman '49
Hart, Marvin	Boxing		750	1250		1905-06 H-Wt Champ
Hart, Steve	Golf		5	20	25	
Hartack, Bill	Horse Racing		10	30		HOF 1959 jockey
Hartman, Bill	Football		10	30		CHOF Georgia
Hartman, Sid	Writer		3	6		
Hartnett, Leo "Gabby"	Baseball					B&W PC $400
Hartnett, Leo "Gabby"	Baseball		85	250	2000	HOF 1955. Gold Pl. $425
Hartrick, Stella	Bowling	+	8	20		1982 Women's IBC HOF
Hartsfield, Roy	Baseball		14			Debut 1950 Bost. Braves
Hartung, Clint	Baseball		15			Debut 1947 NY Giants
Hartung, Jim	Olympic		3	10		Gymnastics
Hartz, Harry	Auto Racing	+	25	85		
Harvey, Doug	Hockey		50	185		1973 HOF def
Harwell, Ernie	Broadcaster		5	12		1989 Ntl S&S HOF
Harwood, Mike	Golf		5	20	25	
Hasbrook, Robert "Ziggy"	Baseball		10	22		
Hasek, Dominik	Hockey		6	45	50	Goalie, MVP
Hash, Herb	Baseball		8			Debut 1940 Bost. RedSox
Haskell, Coburn	Golf		75	175		
Haskins, Clem	Basketball		4	15		played NBA 67-75
Haskins, Don	Basketball		3	10		1997 HOF Coach
Hassett, Buddy	Baseball		12			Debut 1936 Brklyn. Dodg.
Hassett, Joe	Basketball		4	15		played NBA 77-82
Hassett, William	Basketball		10	50		played NBA 46-50
Hassler, Andy	Baseball		4			Debut 1971 Angels
Hastings, Scott	Basketball		3	10		played NBA 82-
Hatalshy, Morris	Golf		5	20	25	
Hatch, Grace	Bowling	+	12	32		1953 Women's IBC HOF
Hatcher, Kevin	Hockey		4	20		
Hatcher, Mickey	Baseball		3	12		Debut 1979
Hatten, Joe	Baseball		8			Debut 1946 Brklyn.Dodg.
Hatton, Grady	Baseball		8			Debut 1946 Reds
Hatton, Vern	Basketball		6	32		played NBA 58-61
Hattori, Michiko	Golf		5	25	30	
Hattstrom, H.A.	Bowling	+	8	25		1980 ABC HOF
Haugen, Greg	Boxing		8	18		
Haughton, Percy	Football	+	50	125		1951 CHOF coach
Haughton, Will	Harness Racing		15	45		
Hauser, Joe	Baseball		18	32		Debut 1922 Phil. A's
Havers, Arthur	Golf		115	300		
Havlicek, John	Basketball		10	30	150	HOF 1983
Havlish, Jean	Bowling		5	10		1987 Women's IBC HOF
Hawerchuk, Dale	Hockey		5	22		
Hawes, Steve	Basketball		3	10		played NBA 74-83
Hawkins, Ben	Football		4	15		NFL

NAME	CATEGORY	+	SIG	SP	BALL	Comment
Hawkins, Connie	Basketball		6	22		HOF 1992
Hawkins, Fred	Golf		20	45		
Hawkins, Hersey	Basketball		4	12		played NBA 88-
Hawkins, James	Basketball		10	50		played NBA 48-49
Hawkins, Robert	Basketball		3	15		played NBA 75-78
Hawkins, Tom	Basketball		6	18		played NBA 59-68
Haworth, Alan	Hockey		3	18		
Hawthorne, Nate	Basketball		3	18		played NBA 73-75
Hay, George	Hockey		75	250		1958 HOF fwd
Hayden Jones, Ann	Tennis		5	18		HOF 1985
Hayes, Bruce	Olympic		3	6		Gold Medal. Swimming
Hayes, Elvin	Basketball		8	22	100	HOF 1989-90
Hayes, J.P.	Golf		5	25	20	
Hayes, Jim	Basketball		3	18		played NBA 73
Hayes, Lawrence	Olympic		3	6		Swim/relay
Hayes, Lester	Football		5	15		NFL
Hayes, Mark	Golf		5	20	25	
Hayes, Steven	Basketball		3	12		played NBA 81-85
Hayes, Von	Baseball		3	10		Debut 1981 Cleve. Ind.
Hayes, Woody	Football	+	50	12		1983 CHOF coach
Hayman, Lew	Football	+	10	125		1975 Canadian HOF
Haynes, Abner	Football		5	20		NFL
Haynes, Michael	Football		5	15	85	1997 HOF
Haynie, Sandra	Golf		5	15		
Hayward, Brian	Hockey		4	18		
Haywood, Bill	Baseball		5			Debut 1968 Senators
Haywood, Spencer	Basketball		8	25		played NBA 69-82
Hayworth, Ray	Baseball		20			Debut 1926 Tigers
Hazel, Homer	Football	+	15	45		CHOF Rutgers
Hazeltine, Matt	Football	+	25	90		CHOF California
Hazen, John	Basketball		10	50		played NBA 48
Hazle, Bob	Baseball		7			Debut 1955 Reds
Head, Ed	Baseball		10			Debut 1940 Brklyn.Dodg.
Heafner, Clayton	Golf		50	150		
Heafner, Vance	Golf		10	25	30	
Healey, Thomas	Horse Racing					HOF 1955 trainer
Healy, Ed	Football	+	60	275		1964 HOF,CHOF Dartmth
Healy, Glenn	Hockey		3	15		
Heaney, Brian	Basketball		4	18		played NBA 69
Heard, Garfield	Basketball		3	15		played NBA 70-80
Heard, Jerry	Golf		5	30	25	
Hearn, Chick	Basketball		3	10		Broadcaster
Hearn, Jim	Baseball		7	25		Debut 1947 STL Cards
Hearne, Eddie	Auto Racing	+	30	85		
Hearns, Tommy	Boxing		18	38		Middle-Wt Champ x4
Hearst, Garrison	Football		4	18	85	NFL
Heath, Michael	Olympic		3	7		Swim/200 free
Heathcote, Jud	Basketball		3	8		Coach
Hebenton, Andy	Hockey		5	20		
Hebert, Jay	Golf		15	40	50	
Hebert, Lionel	Golf		10	25	30	
Hebner, Richie	Baseball		15			Debut 1968 Pitt. Pirates
Hecker, Genevieve	Golf		63	250		
Hedberg, Anders	Hockey		3	20		
Hedderick, Herman	Basketball		8	40		played NBA 54
Hedgepeth, Whitney	Olympic		3	6		Medal Swimming

NAME	CATEGORY	+	SIG	SP	BALL	Comment
Heffelfinger, Pudge	Football	+	200	500		CHOF Yale
Heffner, Bob	Baseball		6			Debut 1963 RedSox
Heffner, Don	Baseball		15			Debut 1934 Yankees
Hegan, Jim	Baseball		9			Debut 1941 Cleveland
Hegan, Mike	Baseball		6			Debut 1964 Yankees
Hegg, Steve	Olympic		3	6		Cycling
Heidemann, Jack	Baseball		4			Debut 1969 Cleveland
Heiden, Beth	Olympic		5	10		Speed Skating
Heiden, Eric	Olympic		7	24		Speed Skating
Heidenreich, Jerry	Olympic		3	7		Swim/100 free
Heilmann, Harry	Baseball		365	875	2500	HOF 1952
Hein, Mel	Football	+	18	75	180	1963 HOF 2-way line
Heinrich, Don	Football		10	25		CHOF Washington
Heinsohn, Tom	Basketball		10	25	100	HOF 1985
Heintzelman, Ken	Baseball		10			Debut 1937 Pirates
Heise, Bob	Baseball		4			Debut 1967 Giants
Heiss, Carol	Olympic		8	30		Figure Skating
Heldman, Gladys	Tennis		5	22		HOF 1979
Helf, Hank	Baseball		4			Debut 1938 Indians
Hellickson, Russell	Olympic		3	6		Wrestling
Helms, Tommy	Baseball		10			Debut 1964 Reds
Helser, Brenda	Olympic		7	25		Swimming
Helser, Roy	Baseball		5	18		PCL-Pitching Great AAA
Helton, John	Football		4	8		1986 Canadian HOF
Hemery, David	Olympic		4	22		400 meter hurdles
Hemric, Dick	Basketball		8	40		played NBA 55-56
Hemus, Solly	Baseball		12			Debut 1949 Cards
Hencken, John	Olympic		7	14		Swim/100, 200 Back.
Henderson, Cedric	Basketball		3	10		played NBA 86
Henderson, David	Basketball		3	10		played NBA 87
Henderson, Gerald	Basketball		3	12		played NBA 79-
Henderson, Jerome	Basketball		3	10		played NBA 85-86
Henderson, John	Football		3	10		NFL
Henderson, Kevin	Basketball		3	10		played NBA 86-87
Henderson, Mark	Olympic		3	7		Gold Medal. Swimming
Henderson, Rickey	Baseball		5	18		Debut 1979
Henderson, Thomas	Basketball		3	14		played NBA 74-82
Hendrick, Harvey	Baseball		35			Debut 1923
Hendricks, Ted	Football		6	20	85	1990 HOF LB
Hendrickson, Dick	Golf		5	20	25	
Henie, Sonja	Olympic		50	175		Gold. Figure Skating
Henke, Nolan	Golf		5	20	25	
Henley, Garney	Football		4	8		1979 Canadian HOF
Hennessey, Tom	Bowling		5	12		1976 ABC HOF
Hennessy, Lawrence	Basketball		8	40		played NBA 55-56
Hennigan, Charley	Football		5	20		NFL
Henning, Anne	Olympic		6	22		500 M Speed Skating
Henning, Harold	Golf		5	20	25	
Henning, Harry	Auto Racing	+	30	75		
Henninger, Brian	Golf		5	20	25	
Henrich, Tom	Baseball		4	10		Debut 1937
Henriksen, Don	Basketball		10	45		played NBA 52-54
Henry, Albert	Basketball		3	18		played NBA 70-71
Henry, Armin	Olympic		10	35		100 Meters
Henry, Bill	Baseball		4			Debut 1952 RedSox
Henry, Bill	Basketball		10	50		played NBA 48-49

NAME	CATEGORY	+	SIG	SP	BALL	Comment
Henry, Camille	Hockey		5	28		
Henry, Carl	Basketball		3	10		played NBA 85
Henry, Conner	Basketball		3	10		played NBA 86-87
Henry, Earl	Baseball		4			Debut 1944 Indians
Henry, James	Olympic		3	8		Diving
Henry, Ken	Olympic		6	15		500 M Speed Skating
Henry, Wilbur Pete (Fats)	Football	+	150	625		1963 HOF 2-way line
Henry, Wilbur Pete (Fats)	Football	+	150	625		CHOF Wash-Jeff
Hentz, Charlie	Basketball		3	16		played NBA 70
Hepbron, George	Basketball	+	22	45		HOF 1960 Referee
Hepburn, Ralph	Auto Racing	+	28	95		
Hepp, Ferenc	Basketball	+	18	55		HOF 1980
Herbel, Ron	Baseball		5			Debut 1963 SF Giants
Herber, Arnie	Football	+	105	550		1966 HOF
Herber, Arnie	Football	+	85	225		1966 HOF QB
Herberich, Jim	Olympic		2	5		Bobsled
Herbert, Dick	Broadcaster		3	3		
Herbert, Ray	Baseball		8			Debut 1950 Tigers
Herd, Alexander	Golf		220	595		
Herd, Fred	Golf		150	400		
Herget, Mattias	Soccer		7	15		
Herman, Babe	Baseball		25	75		Debut 1926
Herman, Billy	Baseball					HOF 1975. P-S HOF $30
Herman, Billy	Baseball		15	45	50	Gold Pl. $20.GRT.MO.$25
Herman, William	Basketball		10	50		played NBA 49
Hermann, Al B.	Baseball		18			Debut 1923 Bost. Braves
Hermann, Cone	Bowling	+	8	20		1968 ABC HOF-Mer.Serv.
Hermanski, Gene	Baseball		7			Debut 1943 Brklyn.Dodg.
Hermsen, Clarence	Basketball		22	65		played NBA 43-52
Hern, Riley	Hockey		200	600		1962 HOF goal
Hernandez, Enzo	Baseball		6			Debut 1971 Padres
Hernandez, Genaro	Boxing		15	32		
Hernandez, Livan	Baseball		9	35		'97 World Series MVP
Hernandez, Willie	Baseball		6	12		
Herrmann, August "Garry"	Baseball		40	125		Executive
Herron, Davidson	Golf		125	335		
Herron, Keith	Basketball		3	12		played NBA 78-81
Herron, MacK	Football		6	18		NFL
Herron, Tim	Golf		5	20	25	
Hershberger, Mike	Baseball		7			Debut 1961 ChiSox
Hershiser, Orel	Baseball		5	25		Debut 1983
Hertzberg, Sidney	Basketball		10	50		played NBA 46-50
Herwig, Robert	Football	+	15	45		CHOF California
Hess, Erika	Olympic		10	30		Alpine skiing
Hester, Dan	Basketball		3	15		played NBA 70
Hester, W.E.	Tennis		5	22		HOF 1981
Heston, Willie	Football	+	250	800		CHOF Michigan
Hetherington, Jean	Golf		40	95		
Hetki, Johnny	Baseball		5			Debut 1945 Reds
Hetzel, Fred	Basketball		4	18		played NBA 65-70
Hewitt, Bill	Football	+	125	700		1971 HOF end/WB
Hewitt, Foster	Broadcaster		10	25		
Hewitt, William	Basketball		4	22		played NBA 68-74
Hewson, John	Basketball		10	50		played NBA 47
Hextall, Bryan	Hockey		25	95		1969 HOF fwd
Hextall, Dennis	Hockey		5	22		

NAME	CATEGORY	+	SIG	SP	BALL	Comment
Hextall, Ron	Hockey		5	32		
Heyliger, Vic	Hockey		4	10		1974 US HOF coach
Heyman, Arthur	Basketball		5	24		played NBA 63-69
Heyns, Penny	Olympic		5	22		Gold Medal. Swimming
Hezlet, May	Golf		100	225		
Hiasek, Jakob	Tennis		4	10		
Hiatt, Jack	Baseball		4			Debut 1964 L.A. Dodgers
Hickcox, Ed	Basketball	+	20	65		HOF 1959-Contributor
Hickey, Eddie	Basketball	+	18	40		HOF 1978-Coach
Hickey, Frank	Football	+	25	100		CHOF Yale
Hickey, Nat	Basketball		15	60		played NBA 44-47
Hickman, Greg	Golf		5	20	25	
Hickman, Herman	Football	+	75	200		CHOF Tennessee
Hickman, Jim	Baseball		5	15		Debut 1962
Hickok, William	Football	+	35	150		CHOF Yale
Hickox, Charles	Olympic		4	12		Swim/100 backstroke
Hicks, Betty	Golf		50	95		
Hicks, Helen	Golf		45	95		
Hicks, Joe	Baseball		4	12		Debut 1959
Hicks, Phillip	Basketball		4	15		played NBA 76-78
Higbe, Kirby	Baseball		22	55		Debut 1937 Cubs
Higgins, Earl	Basketball		3	15		played NBA 73
Higgins, Robert	Football	+	15	35		1954 CHOF coach
Higgins, Rod	Basketball		3	12		played NBA 82-
Higgins, William	Basketball		4	18		played NBA 71
Higgs, Kenneth	Basketball		4	15		played NBA 78-81
High, Andy	Baseball		22			Debut 1922 Brklyn.Dodg.
High, Johnny	Basketball		4	15		played NBA 79-83
Hightower, Wayne	Basketball		6	28		played NBA 62-71
Higley, Margaret	Bowling	+	8	20		1969 Women's IBC HOF
Higuera, Ted	Baseball		7	20		Debut 1985
Hildebrand, Oral			40	95		1931
Hildner, Ernest	Basketball		10	33	125	HOF
Hildreth, Samuel	Horse Racing					HOF 1955 trainer
Hilgenberg, Jay	Football		3	10		NFL
Hilgenberg, Jerry	Football		3	10		NFL
Hilgenberg, Wally	Football		3	14		NFL
Hill, Armond	Basketball		4	15		played NBA 76-83
Hill, C. Bunker	Baseball		35			Debut 1915 Pitt.
Hill, Carolyn	Golf		5	20	25	
Hill, Cleo	Basketball		3	28		played NBA 61
Hill, Cynthia	Golf		5	20	25	
Hill, Dave	Golf		5	20	25	
Hill, Don	Football		6	22		CHOF Duke
Hill, Dorothy	Olympic		8	28		Diving
Hill, Drew	Football		5	18		NFL
Hill, Gary	Basketball		5	20		played NBA 63-64
Hill, Graham	Auto Racing	+	60	65		
Hill, Grant	Basketball		15	48	150	NBA Pistons Standout
Hill, James	Olympic		3	6		Rifle
Hill, Jesse	Baseball		5	15		Debut 1935 Yankees
Hill, Ken	Baseball		3	9		Debut 1988
Hill, Mike	Golf		5	20	25	
Hill, Opal	Golf		50	100		
Hill, Phil	Auto Racing		7	28		HOF 1989
Hill, Ralph	Olympic		6	14		5,000 M run

NAME	CATEGORY	+	SIG	SP	BALL	Comment
Hill, Simmie	Basketball		4	22		played NBA 69-73
Hill, Thomas L.	Olympic		3	7		Hurdles
Hill, Tony	Football		3	12		NFL
Hill, Virgil	Boxing		10	23		Lt.Hvy-Wt
Hillebrand, Art	Football	+	25	100		CHOF Princeton
Hillegas, Shawn	Baseball		4	15		Debut 1987
Hiller, Chuck	Baseball		5			Debut 1961 SF Giants
Hillhouse, Arthur	Basketball		10	50		played NBA 46-47
Hillin, Bobby	Auto Racing		4	8		
Hillman, Darnell	Basketball		4	18		played NBA 71-79
Hillman, Larry	Hockey		4	22		
Hilton, Fred	Basketball		4	18		played NBA 71-72
Hilton, Harold	Golf		500	1395		PGA HOF 1978
Hinchman, Bill	Baseball		30			Debut 1905
Hines, James	Olympic		12	32		100 Meters
Hines, Jimmy	Golf		45	110		
Hingis, Martina	Tennis		15	55		Teen Sensation
Hinkle, Carl	Football		6	32		CHOF Vanderbilt
Hinkle, Clarke	Football	+	50	100	200	1964 HOF RB
Hinkle, Lon	Golf		5	20	25	
Hinkle, Paul "Tony"	Basketball		26	65		HOF 1965-Coach, Contrib.
Hinson, Larry	Golf		5	20	25	
Hinson, Roy	Basketball		3	12		played NBA 83-
Hinton, Tom	Football		4	8		1991 Canadian HOF
Hipple, Eric	Football		3	12		NFL
Hirase, Mayumi	Golf		5	20	25	
Hirsch, Elroy	Football		8	25	125	1968 HOF end/WB
Hirsch, Max	Horse Racing		10	35		HOF 1959 trainer
Hirsch, Melvin	Basketball		10	50		played NBA 46
Hirsch, W.J.	Horse Racing		10	20		HOF 1982 trainer
Hirschbeck, John	Baseball		4	12		Umpire
Hiskey, Babe	Golf		5	20	25	
Hitch, Lewis	Basketball		10	45		played NBA 51-56
Hitchcock Sr., Thomas	Horse Racing		65	170		HOF 1973 trainer
Hitchcock, Billy	Baseball		8			Debut 1942 Tigers
Hitchcock, James	Football	+	15	45		CHOF Auburn
Hitchcock, Tommy	Polo		48	125		"Star"! & HERO WW I & II
Hoad, Lew	Tennis		12	45		HOF 1980
Hoad, Paul	Golf		5	20	25	
Hoak, Dick	Football		5	16		NFL
Hobart, Bob	Football		4	10		NFL
Hobaugh, Ed	Baseball		4	9		Debut 1961
Hobbs, Sir John Berry	Cricket		5	10		
Hobday, Simon	Golf		5	25	30	
Hobens, Jack	Golf		45	125		
Hoblitzell, Dick	Baseball		30	75		Debut 1908
Hobson, Howard "Hobby"	Basketball	+	25	60		HOF 1965-Coach
Hoch, Scott	Golf		5	20	25	
Hochstadter, Bee	Bowling	+	8	32		1967 Women's IBC HOF
Hodge, Daniel	Olympic		3	6		Wrestling
Hodge, Gomer	Baseball		4			Debut 1971 Indians
Hodge, Ken	Hockey		5	20		
Hodges, Craig	Basketball		3	12		played NBA 82-
Hodges, Gil	Baseball		95	350		Debut 1943. Dodger Great
Hodges, Russ	Broadcaster	+	20	65		1975 Ntl S&S HOF
Hodkinson, Paul	Boxing		8	18		

NAME	CATEGORY	+	SIG	SP	BALL	Comment
Hoefer, Adolph	Basketball		15	55		played NBA 46-47
Hoeft, Billy	Baseball		5	16		Debut 1952
Hoepner, Willi	Boxing		8	18		
Hoernschmyer, Bob	Football		40	85		NFL
Hoffman Jr., Ted	Bowling		5	10		1985 PBA HOF
Hoffman, Frank	Football		6	25		CHOF Notre Dame
Hoffman, Martha	Bowling		5	15		1979 Women's IBC HOF
Hoffman, Paul	Basketball		10	50		played NBA 47-54
Hoffner, Charles	Golf		75	195		
Hofman, Bobby	Baseball		9			Debut 1949 NY Giants
Hogan, Ben	Golf		125	350	350	PGA HOF 1974
Hogan, Hulk	Pro Wrestling		10	30		
Hogan, James J.	Football	+	22	85		CHOF Yale
Hogsett, Elon "Chief"	Baseball		10	27		Debut 1929 Tigers
Hogsett, Robert	Basketball		8	25		played NBA 66-67
Hogshead, Nancy	Olympic		5	12		Swim/100 free
Hogue, Paul	Basketball		5	30		played NBA 62-63
Holcomb, Douglas	Basketball		10	50		played NBA 48
Holden, Joe "Sox"	Baseball		8			Debut 1934 Phil.
Holderness, Ernest	Golf		75	145		
Holdsworth, Fred	Baseball		4			Debut 1972 Tigers
Holingberry, Babe	Football	+	18	60		1979 CHOF coach
Holland, Brad	Basketball		4	15		played NBA 79-81
Holland, Brud	Football	+	25	95		CHOF Cornell
Holland, Joe	Basketball		10	50		played NBA 49-51
Holland, Wilbur	Basketball		4	15		played NBA 75-78
Holleder, Don	Football	+	35	125		CHOF Army
Hollenbeck, Bill	Football	+	30	75		CHOF Pennsylvania
Hollingsworth, Al	Baseball		7	10		Debut 1935 Reds
Hollingsworth, J.B. "Bonnie"	Baseball		15			Debut 1922 Pitt. Pirates
Hollins, Lionel	Basketball		4	14		played NBA 75-84
Hollins, Marion	Golf		75	175		
Hollis, Essie	Basketball		3	12		played NBA 78
Holm, Eleanor	Olympic		10	38		Swim/100 Back.
Holm, Helen	Golf		65	150		
Holm, Joan	Bowling		5	12		1974 Women's IBC HOF
Holman, Dennis	Basketball		4	20		played NBA 67
Holman, Marshall	Bowling		6	18		1990 PBA HOF
Holman, Nat	Basketball		30	75		HOF 1964
Holman, Rodney	Football		3	12		NFL
Holmes, Hap	Hockey		135	350		1972 HOF goal
Holmes, Larry	Boxing		15	35		1980-85 H-Wt Champ
Holmes, Phillie	Baseball		8	30		Debut 1938, Negro League
Holmes, Tommy	Baseball		14	32		Debut 1942 Braves
Holmgren, Mike	Football		5	18		NFL Packer Coach
Holovak, Mike	Football		6	18		CHOF Boston College, NFL
Holscher, Bud	Golf		15	45		
Holstein, James	Basketball		10	45		played NBA 52-55
Holt, A.W.	Basketball		4	18		played NBA 70
Holt, Jim	Baseball		5			Debut 1968 Minn.
Holton, Michael	Basketball		3	10		played NBA 84-
Holtz, Lou	Football		7	25		NFL
Holtz, Skip	Football		2	5		Connecticut Coach
Holtzman, Jerome	Writer		3	8		
Holtzman, Ken	Baseball		5	12		Debut 1965 Cubs
Holub, E.J.	Football		6	18		CHOF Texas Tech

NAME	CATEGORY	+	SIG	SP	BALL	Comment
Holub, Richard	Basketball		10	50		played NBA 47
Holum, Dianne	Olympic		7	22		1500 M Speed Skating
Holup, Joseph	Basketball		8	45		played NBA 56-58
Holyfield, Evander	Boxing		20	50		1991- H-Wt Champ
Holzman, Red	Basketball		10	25	100	HOF 1985-Coach
Homer, Trevor	Golf		5	20	25	
Homfeld, Conrad	Olympic		5	10		Equestrian
Honeycutt, Rick	Baseball		4	10		Debut 1977
Honeyghan, Lloyd	Boxing		7	16		
Honochick, Jim	Baseball		5	15		Umpire
Hook, Jay	Baseball		2	6		Debut 1957
Hooper, Bobby	Basketball		4	25		played NBA 68
Hooper, C. Darrow	Olympic		3	12		Shot Put
Hooper, Harry	Baseball		45	175	1200	HOF 1971. Gold Pl. $135
Hooper, Tom	Hockey		95	225		1962 HOF fwd
Hooser, Carroll	Basketball		4	25		played NBA 67
Hooton, Burt	Baseball		3	12		Debut 1971
Hoover, Dick	Bowling		6	18		1974 ABC HOF
Hoover, Thomas	Basketball		5	28		played NBA 63-68
Hope, Bob	Golf		35	75		PGA HOF 1983, Contrib.
Hopkins, Gail	Baseball		4			Debut 1968 Cubs
Hopkins, Robert	Basketball		5	30		played NBA 56-59
Hopman, Harry	Tennis	+	12	40		HOF 1978
Hopp, Johnny	Baseball		8			Debut 1939 Cards
Hoppe, Willie	Pocket billiards		85	195		
Hoppe, Wolfgang	Olympic		5	25		Olymp.Gold. Bobsled
Hoppen, David	Basketball		3	10		played NBA 87-
Horan, John	Basketball		18	55		played NBA 55
Hordges, Cedrick	Basketball		3	12		played NBA 80-81
Horford, Tito	Basketball		3	10		played NBA 88
Horgan, P.H. III	Golf		5	20	25	
Horlen, Joel	Baseball		10	35		Debut 1961. No-Hitter
Horn, Miriam Burns	Golf		90	175		
Horn, Ronald	Basketball		6	28		played NBA 61-67
Horn, Ted	Auto Racing	+	25	75		HOF 1993
Hornacek, Jeff	Basketball		4	20		played NBA 86-
Horne, Stanley	Golf		10	35		
Horner, Red	Hockey		10	32		1965 HOF def
Hornsby, Rogers	Baseball		270	568	2750	HOF 1942. B&W PC $700
Hornung, Paul	Football		10	30	145	1986 HOF. Heisman '56
Horrell, Edwin	Football		8	28		CHOF California
Horsley, Jack	Olympic		3	12		Swim/200 backstroke
Horton, Donna	Golf		5	25	25	
Horton, Tim	Hockey		75	350	385	1977 HOF def
Horton, Tommy	Golf		8	25	25	
Horton, Willie	Baseball		5	15		Debut 1963
Horvath, Les	Football		18	55		CHOF OSU. Heisman '44
Hosket, Bill	Basketball		3	18		played NBA 68-71
Hostak, Al	Boxing		30	60		Middle-Wt Champ
Hostetler, Jeff	Football		6	20	90	NFL
Hotchkiss, Hazel	Tennis	+	90	300		HOF 1957, "Wightman"
Houbregs, Bob	Basketball		7	22		HOF 1986-87
Hough, Charlie	Baseball		4	10		Debut 1970
Houk, Ralph	Baseball		4	15		Debut 1947. Catcher-Mgr.
House, Frank	Baseball		5	14		Debut 1950
House, Tom	Baseball		4			Debut 1971 Atl Braves

NAME	CATEGORY	+	SIG	SP	BALL	Comment
Houston, Ken	Football		7	22	85	1986 HOF DB
Hovey, Fred	Tennis	+	7	40		HOF 1974
Howard, Bruce	Baseball		5			Debut 1963 ChiSox
Howard, Dana	Football		3	7		1994 Butkus Award
Howard, Denean	Olympic		10	6		Track relay
Howard, Desmond	Football		6	30	80	Heisman Mich. '91. NFL
Howard, Doug	Baseball		4			Debut 1972 Cal Angels
Howard, Elston	Baseball		18			Debut 1955 Yankees
Howard, Erik	Football		3	9		NFL
Howard, Frank	Baseball		4	12		Debut 1958
Howard, Frank	Football		50	95		1989 CHOF coach
Howard, George	Bowling		5	15		1986 ABC HOF
Howard, Gregory	Basketball		3	25		played NBA 70-71
Howard, Juwan	Basketball		10	25		"Fab Five"
Howard, Maurice	Basketball		4	22		played NBA 76
Howard, Otis	Basketball		4	20		played NBA 78
Howard, Richard W.	Olympic		3	15		Hurdles
Howard, Sherri	Olympic		2	5		Gold Medal. Track
Howarth, Jimmy	Baseball		5			Debut 1971 SF Giants
Howe, Art	Baseball		7	20		Debut 1974
Howe, Arthur	Football	+	18	65		CHOF Yale
Howe, Gordie	Hockey		12	30	40	1972 HOF fwd
Howe, Mark	Hockey		5	22		
Howe, Marty	Hockey		3	18		
Howe, Steve	Baseball		8	22		Debut 1980
Howe, Syd	Hockey		50	165		1965 HOF fwd
Howell, Bailey	Basketball		8	28		HOF 1997 NBA 59-70
Howell, Harry	Hockey		6	20	25	1979 HOF def
Howell, Jim Lee	Football		15	45		NFL
Howell, Millard	Football	+	18	65		CHOF Alabama
Howley, Chuck	Football		5	16		NFL
Howley, Dan	Baseball		30			Debut 1913. Phills 1 year
Howley, Pete	Bowling	+	15	42		1941 ABC HOF-Mer.Serv.
Howton, Billy	Football		12	45		NFL
Hoy, William "Dummy"	Baseball	+	75	150		Debut 1888. Deaf
Hoyt, Beatrix	Golf		175	350		
Hoyt, George	Basketball	+	18	65		HOF 1961-Referee
Hoyt, Waite	Baseball					HOF 1969. P-S HOF $650
Hoyt, Waite	Baseball		22	80	465	Gold Pl. $35
Hoz, Mike de la	Baseball		4	12		Debut 1960
Hrabosky, Al	Baseball		4	12		Debut 1970
Hrbek, Kent	Baseball		4	14		Debut 1981
Hrudey, Kelly	Hockey		4	22		
Huarte, John	Football		10	20		Heisman ND '64. NFL
Hubbard, Cal	Baseball		75	250	985	HOF 1976. Gold Pl. $600
Hubbard, Cal	Football	+	75	250		1963 HOF 2-way line
Hubbard, John	Football	+	20	70		CHOF Amherst
Hubbard, Marv	Football		3	12		NFL
Hubbard, Phillip	Basketball		3	15		played NBA 79-88
Hubbard, Robert	Basketball		10	10		played NBA 47-48
Hubbell, Bill	Baseball		25			Debut 1919 NY Giants
Hubbell, Carl	Baseball			50		HOF 1947. P-S HOF $100
Hubbell, Carl	Baseball		22	65	175	Gold Pl.$25,B&W PC $40
Hubbs, Ken	Baseball		40	275		Debut 1961
Huber, Anke	Tennis		5	12		
Hubert, Allison	Football	+	15	45		CHOF Alabama

NAME	CATEGORY	+	SIG	SP	BALL	Comment
Huddy, Charlie	Hockey		3	20		
Hudepohl, Joe	Olympic		3	7		Gold Medal. Swimming
Hudlin, Willis	Baseball		6	10		Debut 1926 Indians
Hudson, Bob Jr.	Golf		5	20	25	
Hudson, Charles	Baseball		4			Debut 1972 Cards
Hudson, Lou	Basketball		6	18		played NBA 66-78
Hudson, Martha	Olympic		3	7		Track relay
Hudson, Sid	Baseball		8	18		Debut 1940 Senators
Hudson, Tommy	Bowling		5	10		1989 PBA HOF
Huega, Jimmy	Olympic		6	18		Alpine skiing
Huff, Sam	Football		6	20	85	1982 HOF LB
Huffman, Dick	Football	+	10	22		1987 Canadian HOF
Huggett, Brian	Golf		5	30	25	
Huggins, Miller	Baseball		1000	1925	6000	Debut 1904. Mgr.
Hughes, Al	Basketball		3	10		played NBA 85
Hughes, Eddie	Basketball		3	10		played NBA 87-
Hughes, Hillie	Horse Racing					HOF 1973 trainer
Hughes, Kate	Golf		5	25	25	
Hughes, Kim	Basketball		3	14		played NBA 75-80
Hughes, Roy	Baseball		3	12		Debut 1935
Hughes, Tommy	Baseball		5			Debut 1941 Phil.
Hughes, W.P.	Football	+	10	22		1974 Canadian HOF
Hughson, Tex	Baseball		10	24		Debut 1941 RedSox
Hulbert, Mike	Golf		5	20	25	
Hulbert, William A.	Baseball		500			HOF 1995 (Owner)
Hull, Bobby	Hockey		10	28	35	1983 HOF fwd
Hull, Brett	Hockey		12	32	35	
Hull, Dennis	Hockey		5	17		
Hull, Gina	Golf		5	20	25	
Hull, Kent	Football		3	10		NFL
Hulman, Tony	Auto Racing	+	95	265		HOF 1991
Humble, Weldon	Football		7	20		CHOF Rice
Humenik, Ed	Golf		5	20	25	
Hummer, John	Basketball		3	20		played NBA 70-75
Humphrey, Bobby	Football		4	12		NFL
Humphrey, Terry	Baseball		3			Debut 1971 Montreal
Humphreys, Birdie	Bowling	+	8	22		1979 Women's IBC HOF
Humphreys, Bob	Baseball		4			Debut 1962 Det. Tigers
Humphries, John	Basketball		3	10		played NBA 84-
Humphries, Stan	Football		6	18	100	NFL
Hundley, Rod	Basketball		6	15		played NBA 57-62
Hunt, Bernard	Golf		10	30	25	
Hunt, Guy	Golf		5	20	25	
Hunt, Joe	Football	+	15	40		CHOF Texas A&M
Hunt, Joe	Tennis	+	12	35		HOF 1966
Hunt, Ken	Baseball		4	12		Debut 1959
Hunt, Lamar	Football		10	25	80	1972 HOF contributor
Hunter, Art	Football		6	20		NFL
Hunter, Bob	Writer		4	8		
Hunter, Dale	Hockey		4	18		
Hunter, Dave	Hockey		4	15		
Hunter, Frank	Tennis	+	10	30		HOF 1961
Hunter, Jim "Catfish"	Baseball	+				P-S HOF $25. HOF 1987
Hunter, Jim "Catfish"	Baseball	+	8	20	25	Gold Pl. $12. Grt.Mo. $25
Hunter, Leslie	Basketball		3	18		played NBA 64-71
Hunter, Tim	Hockey		4	15		

NAME	CATEGORY	+	SIG	SP	BALL	Comment
Hunter, Willie	Golf		75	225		
Huntington, Ellery	Football		10	38		CHOF Colgate
Huntley, Joni	Olympic		3	12		High Jump
Huntzinger, Walter H.	Baseball		12			Debut 1923 NY Giants
Hurd, Dorothy Campbell	Golf		150	395		
Hurd, Tom	Baseball		4			Debut 1954 RedSox
Hurley, Roy	Basketball		10	50		played NBA 45-48
Hurst, Bruce	Baseball		6	14		Debut 1980
Hurst, Pat	Golf		5	20	25	
Hurtubise, Jim	Auto Racing		10	35		
Husing, Ted	Broadcaster	+	25	50		1963 Ntl S&S HOF
Husted, Dave	Bowling		4	8		1996 PBA HOF
Huston, Geoffrey	Basketball		3	12		played NBA 79-86
Huston, John	Golf		5	20	25	
Huston, Paul	Basketball		10	50		played NBA 47
Hutcheson, Joe	Baseball		3	9		Debut 1933
Hutchings, Charles	Golf		450	950		
Hutchins, Mel	Basketball		10	45		played NBA 51-57
Hutchinson, Horace	Golf		500	1250		
Hutchison, Jock, Jr.	Golf		150	275		Old PGA HOF 1959
Hutson, Don	Football		15	65	95	1963 HOF end/WB
Hutton, J.B.	Hockey		75	250		1962 HOF goal
Hutton, Joseph	Basketball		10	50		played NBA 50-51
Hyatt, Chuck	Basketball	+	30	60	150	HOF 1959
Hyder, Gregory	Basketball		4	15		played NBA 70
Hyland, Harry	Hockey		60	195		1962 HOF fwd
Hyland, John	Horse Racing					HOF 1956 trainer
Hyman, Flo	Olympic		35	125		Volleyball
Hymers, Charles	Golf		45	145		

Iavaroni, Marcus	Basketball		3	12		played NBA 82-
Iba, Hank	Basketball		10	35	125	HOF 1968 Coach
Ibbetson, Bruce	Olympic		3	6		Rowing
Ikola, Willard	Hockey		5	10		1990 US HOF
Ilman, Gary	Olympic		3	6		Swim/relay
Imhoff, Darrall	Basketball		4	18		played NBA 60-71
Imlach, Punch	Hockey		50	175		Coach. 4 Stanley Cups
Immerfall, Daniel	Olympic		3	7		Speed skating
Ina, Kyoko & Dungjen, Jason	Figure Skating		7	22		U.S. Pairs Champions
Incaviglia, Pete	Baseball		3	15		Debut 1986
Indurian, Miguel	Cycling		5	25		5x Tour de France
Iness, Sim	Olympic		6	18		Discus
Infante, Lindy	Football		3	6		NFL

NAME	CATEGORY	+	SIG	SP	BALL	Comment
Inglehart, Stewart	Hockey	+	5	10		1975 US HOF
Inglesby, Tom	Basketball		3	20		played NBA 73-75
Ingram, Bill	Football	+	15	35		1973 CHOF coach
Ingram, James	Football	+	20	70		CHOF Navy
Ingram, Joel	Basketball		8	40		played NBA 57-58
Ingram, Sheila	Olympic		3	7		Track relay
Inkster, Juli	Golf		5	20	25	
Inman, Joe	Golf		5	20	25	
Inman, John	Golf		5	20	25	
Inman, Stu	Basketball		3	8		Drafting genius
Inniger, Ervin	Basketball		5	28		played NBA 67-68
Irabu, Hideki	Baseball		8	32		Controversial Yankee
Irish, Ned	Basketball	+	50	140		HOF 1964-Contributor
Irvin, Ann	Golf		5	20	25	
Irvin, Dick	Hockey		60	225		1958 HOF fwd
Irvin, Ernie	Auto Racing		4	15		
Irvin, Michael	Football		10	30	150	NFL
Irvin, Monte	Baseball					HOF 1973. P-S HOF $25
Irvin, Monte	Baseball		10	22	20	Gold Pl. $12. Grt.Mo. $25
Irvine, George	Basketball		3	15		played NBA 70-75
Irwin, Hale	Golf		10	30	35	PGA HOF 1992
Irwin, Juno	Olympic		15	38		Diving
Isaminger, James	Writer		4	8		
Isbell, Cecil	Football	+	22	75		CHOF Purdue
Isbister, Bob Sr.	Football	+	10	22		1965 Canadian HOF
Ishi, David	Golf		5	20	25	
Ismail, Raghib "Rocket"	Football		6	25	100	NFL
Issel, Dan	Basketball		6	22	100	HOF 1993. NBA 70-84
Ito, Midori	Figure Skating		8	40		World Champion
Ivanisevic, Goran	Tennis		4	10		
Iverson, Allen	Basketball		12	32	125	Rookie-of-Year
Iverson, Don	Golf		15	35		
Iverson, Willie	Basketball		5	22		played NBA 68
Ives, Edward	Olympic		3	6		Rowing
Ivey, Mitchell	Olympic		3	7		Swim/200 backstroke
Ivory, Elvin	Basketball		3	6		played NBA 68
Ivy, Pop	Football		20	65		NFL
Izo, George	Football		4	15		NFL

Jabali, Warren	Basketball		3	6		played NBA 68-74
Jablonsky, J.	Football	+	15	45		CHOF Army/Washington
Jack, Beau	Boxing		12	35		Lt-Wt Champ
Jacklin, Tony	Golf		10	30	25	

NAME	CATEGORY	+	SIG	SP	BALL	Comment
Jackson, Alvin	Basketball		4	22		played NBA 67
Jackson, Anthony	Basketball		3	12		played NBA 80
Jackson, Bo	Baseball		8	35		Debut 1986
Jackson, Bo	Football-Baseball		10	75	150	Heisman Auburn '85
Jackson, Busher	Hockey		50	175		1971 HOF fwd
Jackson, Earnest	Football		3	12		NFL
Jackson, Eddie	Bowling		5	15		1988 ABC HOF
Jackson, Gregory	Basketball		4	18		played NBA 74
Jackson, Harold	Football		5	16		NFL
Jackson, Jim	Basketball		5	20		Ohio State Grad
Jackson, Joe "Shoeless Joe"	Baseball	+	19500	75000		Deb.'08."Black Sox" scandal
Jackson, Joe (Mrs.)	Baseball		125			"Joe Jackson" by Mrs. J.
Jackson, Keith	Football		5	25		NFL
Jackson, Larry	Baseball		8	22		Debut 1955
Jackson, Luke	Basketball		4	20		played NBA 64-71
Jackson, Madeline	Olympic		3	12		Track relay
Jackson, Mark	Basketball		4	12		played NBA 87-
Jackson, Mervin	Basketball		4	18		played NBA 68-72
Jackson, Michael	Basketball		4	18		played NBA 72-75
Jackson, Myron	Basketball		3	10		played NBA 86
Jackson, Phil	Basketball		6	20	100	played NBA 67-79-Coach
Jackson, Ralph	Basketball		3	10		played NBA 84
Jackson, Ransom	Baseball		6			Debut 1950 Cubs
Jackson, Reggie	Baseball					Gold Pl. $30
Jackson, Reggie	Baseball		20	35	60	HOF 1993.P-S HOF $65
Jackson, Ron	Baseball		4			Debut 1954 ChiSox
Jackson, Russ	Football		4	8		1973 Canadian HOF
Jackson, Sonny	Baseball		6			Debut 1963 Astros
Jackson, Tom	Football		4	15	85	NFL
Jackson, Tony	Basketball		4	20		played NBA 67-68
Jackson, Tracy	Basketball		3	10		played NBA 81-83
Jackson, Travis	Baseball		18	95	350	HOF 1982.P-S HOF $135
Jackson, Travis	Baseball		28	85		Debut 1922, Gold Pl. $35
Jackson, Trina	Olympic		3	9		Gold Medal. Swimming
Jackson, Wardell	Basketball		3	15		played NBA 74
Jacobs, Chris	Olympic		4	8		Swim/100 free
Jacobs, Fred	Basketball		4	12		played NBA 46
Jacobs, Helen Hull	Tennis		20	70		HOF 1962
Jacobs, Hirsch	Horse Racing		25	50		HOF 1958 trainer
Jacobs, Jack	Football	+	10	22		1963 Canadian HOF
Jacobs, Jim	Handball		7	16		
Jacobs, John	Golf		5	20		
Jacobs, Lamar Jake	Baseball		4			Debut 1960 Senators
Jacobs, N.S. "Bucky"	Baseball		5			Debut 1937 Senators
Jacobs, Tommy	Golf		5	20		
Jacobsen, Peter	Golf		5	25	25	
Jacobson, D.D.	Bowling		5	10		1981 Women's IBC HOF
Jacobson, Wm.C. "Baby Doll"	Baseball		60			Debut 1915. .300+ 7x
Jacobus, George	Golf		50	110		
Jacoby, Brook	Baseball		4	8		Debut 1981
Jacoby, Mike	Snowboarding		2	5		World Cup Champion
Jacoby, Oswald	Bridge		10	20		
Jacquin, Lisa	Olympic		5	10		Equestrian
Jaeckel, Barry	Golf		5	20	25	
Jaeger, Andrea	Tennis		6	20		
Jaeger, Emma	Bowling	+	12	28		1953 Women's IBC HOF

NAME	CATEGORY	+	SIG	SP	BALL	Comment
Jagade, Harry "Chic"	Football		15	50		NFL
Jager, Tom	Olympic		5	15		Swim/50 free
Jagr, Jaromir	Hockey		8	32	40	
James, Aaron	Basketball		4	18		played NBA 74-78
James, Bill (Wm. L.)	Baseball		40	85		Debut 1913
James, Billy	Basketball		4	18		played NBA 73
James, Charlie	Baseball		4			Debut 1960 Cards
James, Dick	Football		6	18		NFL
James, Don	Football		2	5		College Coach of Year
James, Eddie	Football	+	10	22		1963 Canadian HOF
James, G. Lawrence	Olympic		5	10		400 Meters
James, Gerry	Football		4	8		1981 Canadian HOF
James, Harold	Basketball		10	50		played NBA 48-50
James, Lionel	Football		7	15		NFL
James, Mark	Golf		5	20	25	
Jameson, Betty	Golf		25	75	50	LPGA HOF 1951
Jamieson, Charles	Baseball		75			Debut 1915. 18 yrs..303
Jamieson, Jim	Golf		5	20	25	
Janisch, John	Basketball		10	50		played NBA 46-47
Janotta, Howard	Basketball		10	50		played NBA 49
Janowicz, Vic	Football		15	45		CHOF OSU. Heisman '50
Jansen, Dan	Olympic		5	28		Olymp.Gold.Speed Skating
Jansen, Larry	Baseball		8	16		Debut 1947 NY Giants
January, Don	Golf		10	25	30	
Janvrin, Hal	Baseball		100	395		Debut 1911
Janzen, Lee	Golf		5	25	25	
Jaros, Anthony	Basketball		10	50		played NBA 46-50
Jarrett, Dale	Auto Racing		5	15		
Jarrett, Ned	Auto Racing		9	18		HOF 1997
Jarvis, James	Basketball		4	18		played NBA 67-68
Jastremski, Chet	Olympic		4	18		Swim/200 breast
Jaugstetter, Robert	Olympic		3	6		Rowing
Javier, Stan	Baseball		3	10		Debut 1984
Jaworski, Ron	Football		4	15		NFL
Jazy, Michel	Olympic		10	25		Track/Mile
Jean King, Billie	Tennis		10	32		HOF 1987
Jeannette, Harry "Buddy"	Basketball		8	25		HOF 1994. NBA 38-49
Jedrzejoska, Jedviga	Tennis		15	35		
Jeelani, Abdulf	Basketball		3	15		played NBA 79-80
Jeffcoat, Hal	Baseball		4			Debut 1948 Cubs
Jefferies, Gregg	Baseball		3	9		Debut 1987
Jefferson, John	Football		4	16		NFL
Jefferson, Roy	Football		4	16		NFL
Jefferson, Thomas	Olympic		5	10		200 Meters
Jeffries, James J.	Boxing		425	800		1899-05 H-Wt Champ
Jelacic, Jon	Football		5	14		NFL
Jenkins, Alfred	Football		3	12		NFL
Jenkins, Charlie	Olympic		6	20		400 M Dash
Jenkins, Dan	Writer		5	12		
Jenkins, Darold	Football	+	15	45		CHOF Missouri
Jenkins, David	Olympic		7	18		Figure Skating
Jenkins, Ferguson	Baseball				20	HOF 1991. P-S HOF $25
Jenkins, Ferguson	Baseball		9	15	30	Gold Pl. $15. Grt.Mo. $20
Jenkins, Hayes	Olympic		7	22		Figure Skating
Jenkins, J.L.C.	Golf		165	495		
Jenkins, Jack	Baseball		3			Debut 1962 Senators

NAME	CATEGORY	+	SIG	SP	BALL	Comment
Jenkins, Lew	Boxing		50	95		Lt-Wt Champ
Jenkins, Tom	Golf		10	50	35	
Jenner, Bruce	Olympic		8	20		Decathlon
Jennings, Hugh	Baseball		800	2250	6000	HOF 1945
Jennings, Morley	Football	+	15	35		1973 CHOF coach
Jennings, William	Hockey	+	10	22		1981 US HOF admin
Jensen, Jackie	Baseball		35	80		Debut 1950 Yankees
Jensen, Jackie	Football	+	35	80		CHOF California
Jensen, Steve	Hockey		3	15		
Jensen, Woody	Baseball		14			Debut 1931 Pitt. Pirates
Jeremiah, Eddie	Hockey	+	10	22		1973 US HOF coach
Jerkens, H. Allen	Horse Racing					HOF 1975 trainer
Jerome, Harry	Olympic		7	25		100 Meters
Jesczek, Linda	Olympic		3	6		Swim/relay
Jeter, Derek	Baseball		8	38		Rookie-of-Year
Jeter, Harold	Basketball		4	18		played NBA 69
Jethroe, Sam	Baseball		20			Debut 1950
Jewell, Lynne	Olympic		3	6		Yachting
Jewell, Wanda	Olympic		3	6		Rifle
Jiles, Pam	Olympic		3	7		Track relay
Jimenez, Joe	Golf		5	20	25	
Job, Brian	Olympic		3	6		Swim/200 breast
Jobe, Brandt	Golf		5	20	25	
Joesting, Herb	Football	+	20	70		CHOF Minnesota
Jofre, Eder	Boxing		12	30		Bantam & Fthr-Wt Champ
Johansson, Ingemar	Boxing		30	60		1959-60 H-Wt Champ
Johansson, Jim	Hockey		3	8		
John, Sabine	Olympic		10	28		Heptathlon
John, Tommy	Baseball		4	15	95	Debut 1963
Johncock, Gordon	Auto Racing		7	18		
Johnson, Albert	Horse Racing					HOF 1971 jockey
Johnson, Alex	Baseball		4			Debut 1964 Phillies
Johnson, Allen	Olympic		3	10		Gold Med. 110 Hurdles
Johnson, Andrew	Basketball		3	26		played NBA 58-61
Johnson, Arnie	Basketball		4	50		played NBA 46-52
Johnson, Art H.	Baseball		3			Debut 1940 RedSox
Johnson, Avery	Basketball		3	10		played NBA 88
Johnson, Ban	Baseball		425	1375	3500	HOF 1937.
Johnson, Bart	Baseball		4			Debut 1969 ChiSox
Johnson, Ben	Olympic		16	40		100 Meters
Johnson, Bill	Olympic		8	28		Alpine Ski/downhill
Johnson, Bill "Skinny"	Basketball	+	18	45		HOF 1976
Johnson, Bill L.	Baseball		24			Debut 1916 Phil.
Johnson, Billy	Baseball		5	20		Debut 1943 Yankees
Johnson, Billy	Football		4	16		NFL
Johnson, Bob	Football		6	22		CHOF Tennessee
Johnson, Bob	Hockey	+	15	35		1991 US HOF coach
Johnson, Bob Dale	Baseball		4			Debut 1969 Giants
Johnson, Bob Lee	Baseball		15			Debut 1933 Phil. A's
Johnson, Brad	Football		6	28		NFL Rising Young QB
Johnson, Buck	Basketball		3	10		played NBA 86-
Johnson, Charles	Baseball		4	22		Errorless game record
Johnson, Charles	Basketball		3	18		played NBA 72-78
Johnson, Charles	Writer		3	6		
Johnson, Charley	Football		4	15		NFL
Johnson, Chet	Baseball		3			Debut 1946 STL Browns

NAME	CATEGORY	+	SIG	SP	BALL	Comment
Johnson, Ching hof	Hockey		85	290		1958 HOF def
Johnson, Chris	Golf		5	20	25	
Johnson, Clay	Basketball		3	12		played NBA 81-83
Johnson, Clem	Basketball		3	12		played NBA 78-87
Johnson, Curtis	Baseball		8	20		1950, Negro League
Johnson, Davey	Baseball		4	15		Debut 1965
Johnson, David	Basketball		10	50		played NBA 47-52
Johnson, Dennis	Basketball		5	22		played NBA 76-89
Johnson, Don	Bowling		6	20		1977 PBA, '82 ABC HOF
Johnson, Earl	Baseball		7	15		Debut 1940 RedSox
Johnson, Earl	Bowling		5	10		1987 ABC HOF
Johnson, Earvin "Magic"	Basketball		22	60	250	played NBA 79-92
Johnson, Ed	Basketball		4	18		played NBA 68-70
Johnson, Eddie	Basketball		4	18		played NBA 77-86
Johnson, Edward A.	Basketball		3	12		played NBA 81-
Johnson, Ernie	Hockey		80	225		1952 HOF def
Johnson, Franklin	Basketball		3	10		played NBA 81-
Johnson, George	Basketball		3	15		played NBA 70-71
Johnson, George	Golf		15	35		
Johnson, George L.	Basketball		3	15		played NBA 78-85
Johnson, George T.	Basketball		3	15		played NBA 72-85
Johnson, Gus	Basketball		18	50		played NBA 63-72
Johnson, Harold	Basketball		10	50		played NBA 46
Johnson, Harold	Boxing		15	30		Lt.Hvy-Wt Champ
Johnson, Henry "Hank"	Baseball		12			Debut 1925 Yankees
Johnson, Howard	Baseball		4	16		Debut 1982
Johnson, Howie	Golf		15	35		
Johnson, J. J.	Basketball		3	15		played NBA 70-81
Johnson, Jack	Boxing					Letter Signed $1600
Johnson, Jack	Boxing		875	1500		1908-15 H-Wt Champ
Johnson, James	Football	+	20	70		CHOF Carlisle
Johnson, Jan	Olympic		3	8		Pole Vault
Johnson, Jenna	Olympic		3	7		Swim/butterfly
Johnson, Jimmy	Football		5	20	125	1994 HOF Coach
Johnson, John Henry	Football		3	10		1987 HOF RB
Johnson, Johnny	Football		6	18		NFL
Johnson, Junior	Auto Racing		7	28		HOF 1991
Johnson, Kannard	Basketball		3	10		played NBA 87
Johnson, Kathy	Olympic		6	25		Gymnastics
Johnson, Ken	Basketball		3	12		played NBA 85
Johnson, Kevin	Basketball		8	28		played NBA 87-
Johnson, Keyshawn	Football		6	25	125	NFL Jets Receiver
Johnson, Larry	Basketball		4	15		played NBA 77
Johnson, Larry	Basketball		8	25		played NBA 91-
Johnson, Larry Doby	Baseball		3			Debut 1972 Cle. Indians
Johnson, Lee	Basketball		3	12		played NBA 80
Johnson, Lynbert	Basketball		3	15		played NBA 79
Johnson, Marques	Basketball		5	16		played NBA 77-86
Johnson, Marvin	Boxing		14	30		Lt.Hvy-Wt Champ
Johnson, Michael	Olympic		8	40		Gold; 200 meters; WR
Johnson, Mickey	Basketball		4	9		played NBA 74-85
Johnson, Mike	Football		3	9		NFL
Johnson, Neil	Basketball	+	3	18		played NBA 66-72
Johnson, Niesa	Basketball		2	5		Women's ABL
Johnson, Ollie	Basketball		3	15		played NBA 72-81
Johnson, Pepper	Football		3	7		NFL

NAME	CATEGORY	+	SIG	SP	BALL	Comment
Johnson, Pete	Football		4	15		NFL
Johnson, Rafer	Olympic		12	40		Decathlon
Johnson, Randy	Baseball		5	55		Debut '88. Cy Young '94
Johnson, Reginald	Basketball		3	12		played NBA 80-83
Johnson, Richard L.	Basketball		4	16		played NBA 68-70
Johnson, Ron	Basketball		5	35		played NBA 60
Johnson, Ron	Football		4	15		NFL
Johnson, Ron	Golf		5	20	25	
Johnson, Roy	Baseball		9			Debut 1929 Tigers
Johnson, Scott	Olympic		3	8		Gymnastics
Johnson, Shannon	Basketball		2	8		Women's ABL
Johnson, Silas "Si"	Baseball		12			Debut 1928 Cin Reds
Johnson, Steffond	Basketball		3	10		played NBA 85
Johnson, Steve	Basketball		3	12		played NBA 81-89
Johnson, Stewart	Basketball		4	16		played NBA 67-75
Johnson, Sylvester	Baseball		22			Debut 1922 Tigers
Johnson, Teri	Golf		10	30		
Johnson, Tim	Baseball		2	5		Debut 1973 Mil.(Tor. Mgr.)
Johnson, Tish	Bowler		4	8		
Johnson, Tish	Bowling		2	8		Bowler-of-Year
Johnson, Tom	Hockey		5	20		1970 HOF def
Johnson, Trish	Golf		5	20	25	
Johnson, Vaughn	Football		3	9		NFL
Johnson, Vinnie	Basketball		4	15		played NBA 79-
Johnson, Virgil	Hockey		5	10		1974 US HOF
Johnson, Walter	Baseball		650	1100	3500	HOF 1936.
Johnson, William C.	Basketball		10	35	125	HOF 1976
Johnson, William R.	Horse Racing					HOF 1986 trainer
Johnson, Wm.J."Judy"	Baseball					HOF 1975. P-S HOF $110
Johnson, Wm.J."Judy"	Baseball		18	65	200	Gold Pl. $30
Johnson,Mark	Hockey		4	12		
Johnston, Bill	Golf		35	75		
Johnston, Bill	Tennis	+	12	40		HOF 1958
Johnston, Cathy	Golf		10	25		
Johnston, D. Neil	Basketball		20	65	100	HOF 1989
Johnston, Harrison	Golf		65	170		
Johnston, Wheeler "Doc"	Baseball		55	175		1920 WS for Cleveland
Johnstone, James	Basketball		3	10		played NBA 82
Johson, Bill L.	Baseball		12			Debut 1916 Phil. A's
Johson, Darrell	Baseball		7			Debut 1952 STL Browns
Joiner, Charlie	Football		5	25	85	1996 HOF
Joiner, Roy	Baseball		4			Debut 1934 Cubs
Joliat, Aurel	Hockey		90	225		1947 HOF fwd
Jolley, LeRoy	Horse Racing					HOF 1987 trainer
Jolley, Smead	Baseball		10			Debut 1930 ChiSox
Jolliff, Howard	Basketball		5	30		played NBA 60-62
Jolly, Allison	Olympic		3	6		Yachting
Jones, Andrew	Baseball		6	25		Braves Outfielder
Jones, Ann	Tennis		10	10		
Jones, Anthony	Basketball		3	12		played NBA 86-
Jones, Barbara P.	Olympic		3	8		Track relay
Jones, Ben A.	Horse Racing		100	200		HOF 1958 trainer
Jones, Bert	Football		5	15		NFL
Jones, Biff	Football	+	15	45		1954 CHOF coach
Jones, Bill	Basketball		3	10		played NBA 88
Jones, Bobby	Basketball		4	15		played NBA 74-85

NAME	CATEGORY	+	SIG	SP	BALL	Comment
Jones, Brian	Golf		5	20	25	
Jones, Caldwell	Basketball		3	15		played NBA 73-90
Jones, Calvin	Football	+	75	225		CHOF Iowa
Jones, Carolyn	Basketball		2	7		Women's ABL
Jones, Carroll E. "Deacon"	Baseball		15			Debut 1916 Tigers
Jones, Charles	Basketball		3	12		played NBA 83-
Jones, Charles A.	Basketball		3	12		played NBA 84-88
Jones, Chipper	Baseball		8	35		Atl. Braves Star
Jones, Clint	Football		4	15		NFL
Jones, Deacon	Football		6	22	110	1980 HOF DL
Jones, Dub	Football		7	17		NFL
Jones, Dwight	Basketball		3	15		played NBA 73-82
Jones, Earl	Baseball		5			Debut 1945 STL Browns
Jones, Earl	Basketball		3	12		played NBA 84-85
Jones, Earl	Olympic		4	12		800 meters
Jones, Ed "Too Tall"	Boxing		6	40		Hvy-Wt
Jones, Ed "Too Tall"	Football		6	40		NFL
Jones, Edgar	Basketball		3	15		played NBA 80-85
Jones, Gomer	Football	+	15	55		CHOF Ohio State
Jones, Gorilla	Boxing		100	225		
Jones, Greer	Golf		5	20	25	
Jones, H.A.	Horse Racing					HOF 1959 trainer
Jones, Hayes	Olympic		3	8		Hurdles
Jones, Homer	Football		4	8		NFL
Jones, Howard	Football	+	55	150		1951 CHOF coach
Jones, J. Collis	Basketball		3	18		played NBA 71-75
Jones, Jake	Basketball		3	15		played NBA 71
Jones, James	Basketball		3	15		played NBA 67-75
Jones, Jimmy	Broadcaster		3	6		
Jones, John	Basketball		4	25		played NBA 67-68
Jones, John	Olympic		3	6		Track sprints
Jones, John Paul	Baseball		8			Debut 1919 NY Giants
Jones, June	Football		3	6		NFL
Jones, K. C.	Basketball		6	18	100	HOF 1988-89
Jones, Larry	Basketball		3	15		played NBA 64-73
Jones, Mack	Baseball		3	10		Debut 1961 Mil
Jones, Major	Basketball		4	15		played NBA 79-84
Jones, Mark	Basketball		3	12		played NBA 83
Jones, Miller	Basketball		4	18		played NBA 71
Jones, Nick	Basketball		4	22		played NBA 67-72
Jones, Ozell	Basketball		3	12		played NBA 84-85
Jones, Parnelli	Auto Racing		7	22		HOF 1992
Jones, Perry	Tennis		10	35		HOF 1970
Jones, R. William	Basketball	+	22	50		HOF 1964-Contributor
Jones, Ralph "Tiger"	Boxing		14	30		
Jones, Rees	Golf		5	20	25	
Jones, Richard	Basketball		3	15		played NBA 69-76
Jones, Robert Trent	Golf		25	75	45	Designer of Golf Courses
Jones, Robert Tyre, Jr.	Golf			3500		Variant SP's $1650-3500
Jones, Robert Tyre, Jr.	Golf		1750	2500		Variant Sigs.$550-1750
Jones, Robin	Basketball		3	15		played NBA 76-77
Jones, Rosie	Golf		5	20	25	
Jones, Roy	Boxing		10	20		Super-Middle-Wt Champ
Jones, Sam	Basketball		85	250		HOF 1983
Jones, Shelton	Basketball		3	10		played NBA 88
Jones, Stan	Football		5	18	85	1991 HOF OL

NAME	CATEGORY	+	SIG	SP	BALL	Comment
Jones, Steve	Basketball		4	15		played NBA 67-75
Jones, Steve	Golf		10	25	35	
Jones, Stuart	Golf		5	20		
Jones, Tad	Football	+	35	90		1958 CHOF coach
Jones, Wali	Basketball		3	18		played NBA 64-75
Jones, Wallace	Basketball		10	50		played NBA 49-51
Jones, Wilbert	Basketball		4	18		played NBA 69-77
Jones, Willie	Basketball		5	25		played NBA 60-64
Jones, Willie D.	Basketball		3	12		played NBA 82-83
Joost, Eddie	Baseball		5	15		Debut 1936 Cin Reds
Jordan, Buck (B.B.)	Baseball		6			Debut 1927 NY Giants
Jordan, Charles	Basketball		3	12		played NBA 75
Jordan, Edward	Basketball		3	15		played NBA 77-83
Jordan, Henry	Football		175	450		1995 HOF
Jordan, Kathy	Tennis		5	10		
Jordan, Lee Roy	Football		6	18		CHOF Alabama
Jordan, Lloyd	Football	+	15	40		1978 CHOF coach
Jordan, Michael	Baseball		20	75		
Jordan, Michael	Basketball		35	100	300	played NBA 84-
Jordan, Pete	Golf		5	20		
Jordan, Ralph "Shug"	Football	+	18	40		1982 CHOF coach
Jordan, Steve	Football		4	14		NFL
Jordan, Walter	Basketball		3	12		played NBA 80
Jordon, Phil	Basketball		4	30		played NBA 56-62
Jorgens, Arndt	Baseball		14			Debut 1929 Yankees
Jorgensen, Janel	Olympic		3	6		Swim/relay
Jorgensen, John	Basketball		10	50		played NBA 47-48
Jorgensen, Noble	Basketball		10	50		played NBA 46-52
Jorgensen, Roger	Basketball		10	50		played NBA 46
Jorgensen, Spider	Baseball		8	18		Debut 1947 Brklyn. Dodg.
Joseph, Joe	Bowling	+	20	55		'69 ABC HOF, '85 PBA
Joseph, Yvon	Basketball		3	10		played NBA 85
Josephson, Sarah and Karen	Olympic		8	20		Synch. Swimming
Joshua, Von	Baseball		4			Debut 1969 Dodgers
Joss, Addie	Baseball		1950	3950	10000	Debut 1902. HOF 1978
Jouglard, Lee	Bowling	+	10	20		1979 ABC HOF
Jowdy, John	Bowling		5	10		1988 PBA HOF-Mer.Serv.
Joyce, Don	Football		5	20		NFL
Joyce, Joan	Softball		3	6		
Joyce, Kevin	Basketball		3	18		played NBA 73-75
Joyce, Mike	Golf		5	20	25	
Joyce, Mike Lewis	Baseball		3			Debut 1962 ChiSox
Joyce, Tom	Golf		5	20	25	
Joyner, Al	Olympic		6	15		Triple Jump
Joyner, Andrew	Horse Racing					HOF 1955 trainer
Joyner, Florence Griffith	Olympic		15	40		Track
Joyner, Harry	Basketball		3	25		played NBA 63
Joyner, Wally	Baseball		5	22		Debut 1986
Joyner-Kersee, Jackie	Olympic		12	38		Track
Juantorena, Alberto	Olympic		10	40		400 Meters
Judge, Joe	Baseball		125	375		Debut 1915. Future HOF?
Judkins, Jeffrey	Basketball		3	15		played NBA 78-82
Judson, Howie	Baseball		6			Debut 1948 ChiSox
Juhan, Frank	Football	+	20	65		CHOF U. of South
Julian, Alvin "Doggie"	Basketball		15	42		HOF 1967-Coach
Jungwirth, Tomas	Olympic		30	60		800 Meters

NAME	CATEGORY	+	SIG	SP	BALL	Comment
Jurgensen, Sonny	Football		7	25	125	1983 HOF QB
Jurges, Bill	Baseball		10	25		Debut 1931 Cubs
Justice, Charlie "Choo Choo"	Football		6	25		CHOF North Carolina
Justice, Dave	Baseball		8	55	40	Debut 1989

NAME	CATEGORY	+	SIG	SP	BALL	Comment
Kaat, Jim	Baseball		5	15		Debut 1959
Kabat, Greg	Football	+	10	22		1966 Canadian HOF
Kachan, Edwin	Basketball		10	50		played NBA 43
Kaer, Mort	Football		8	28		CHOF Southern California
Kaese, Harold	Writer		3	6		
Kafelnikov, Yevgeny	Tennis		3	9		
Kaftan, George	Basketball		10	50		played NBA 48-52
Kahanamoku, Duke	Olympic		90	250		Swim/sprints
Kahl, Nick	Baseball		40			Debut 1905. Very Rare
Kahler, Nick	Hockey	+	10	22		1980 US HOF admin
Kaighen, Raymond A.	Basketball		30			
Kaiser, Bill	Golf		50	95		
Kaiser, Bob	Baseball		4			Debut 1971 Indians
Kalafat, Ed	Basketball		6	20		played NBA 54-55
Kaline, Al	Baseball					HOF 1980. P-S HOF $28
Kaline, Al	Baseball		9	22	25	Gold Pl. $15.Grt.Mo. $35
Kallio, Rudy	Baseball		7			Debut 1918 Tigers
Kamm, Brian	Golf		5	20	25	
Kamm, Willie	Baseball		12	50		Debut 1923
Kampouris, Alex	Baseball		4	10		Debut 1934
Kaneko, Yoshinori	Golf		5	20	25	
Kaplowitz, Ralph	Basketball		4	10		played NBA 46-47
Kapp, Joe	Football		5	10		1984 Canadian HOF
Kappen, Anthony	Basketball		15	65		played NBA 45
Kappisch, Walt	Football	+	15	40		CHOF Columbia
Karakas, Mike	Hockey		5	10		1973 US HOF
Kariya, Paul	Hockey		12	38	45	Ducks Standout
Karl, George	Basketball		4	12		played NBA 73-77
Karlis, Rich	Football		3	12		NFL
Karoly, Bela	Olympic		5	22		Gymnastic Coach
Karpov, Anatoly	Chess		12	42		
Karpov, Anatoly	Chess		20	65		World Champion
Karras, Alex	Football		6	30	100	NFL
Karras, John	Football		5	18		NFL
Karros, Eric	Baseball		8	42		Debut 1991
Kartheiser, Frank	Bowling	+	12	32		1967 ABC HOF
Kashey, Abe	Pro Wrestling		5	15		
Kasid, Edward	Basketball		10	50		played NBA 46

NAME	CATEGORY	+	SIG	SP	BALL	Comment
Kasparov, Garry	Chess		20	65		World Champion
Kassulke, Karl	Football		6	20		NFL
Katkaveck, Leo	Basketball		10	50		played NBA 48-49
Katt, Ray	Baseball		4	12		Debut 1952
Kauffman, Ewing	Baseball		10	30		Baseball Exec.
Kauffman, Robert	Basketball		4	18		played NBA 68-75
Kaufman, Tony	Baseball		9			Debut 1921 Cubs
Kautz, Wilbert	Basketball		25	75		played NBA 39-46
Kavanaugh, Ken	Football		10	28		CHOF Louisiana State
Kaw, Edgar	Football	+	18	75		CHOF Cornell
Kawamoto, Evelyn	Olympic		3	7		Swim/400 free
Kawolics, Ed	Bowling	+	20	65		1968 ABC HOF
Kay, Nora	Bowling	+	10	30		1964 Women's IBC HOF
Kazak, Eddie	Baseball		4			Debut 1948 Cards
Kazmaier, Dick	Football		15	30		CHOF Princeton.Heisman
Kea, Clarence	Basketball		3	12		played NBA 80-81
Keagan, George	Basketball	+	22	55		HOF 1961 Coach
Kealoha, Pua	Olympic		12	28		Swim/sprints
Kean, Laurel	Golf		5	20	25	
Keaney, Frank	Basketball	+	18	40		HOF 1960 Coach
Kearns, Jack	Boxing		75	175		Mgr.Dempsey, Walker etc.
Kearns, Michael	Basketball		10	40		played NBA 54
Kearns, Thomas	Basketball		7	22		played NBA 58
Keaser, Lloyd	Olympic		3	6		Wrestling
Keats, Duke	Hockey		60	65		1958 HOF fwd
Keck, James	Football	+	15	40		CHOF Princeton
Keech, Ray	Auto Racing	+	30	75		
Keefe, Dave	Baseball		15			Debut 1917.Forkball Pitch.
Keefe, Tim	Baseball		1200	3833	7050	HOF 1964
Keegan, Bob	Baseball		4	16		Debut 1953
Keeler, O.B.	Golf		50	160		
Keeler, Wm."Wee Willie"	Baseball		1575	3200	8000	HOF 1939
Keeling, Harold	Basketball		3	10		played NBA 85
Keeling, Jerry	Football		4	8		1989 Canadian HOF
Keely, Bob	Baseball		4			Debut 1944 Cards
Keffer, Karl	Golf		65	195		
Keggi, Caroline	Golf		5	20	25	
Kehoe, Rick	Hockey		5	18		
Keino, Kipchoge	Olympic		80	200		Steeplechase
Keiser, Herman	Golf		75	150	100	
Kell, George	Baseball					HOF 1983. P-S HOF $20
Kell, George	Baseball		7	15	25	Gold Pl. $12, Grt.Mo. $25
Kelleher, Frankie	Baseball		4			Debut 1942 Reds
Kelleher, Mick	Baseball		3			Debut 1972 Cards
Keller, Charlie	Baseball		12	28		Debut 1939 Yankees
Keller, Gary	Basketball		3	18		played NBA 67-68
Keller, Kasey	Soccer		5	22		USA Goalie sensation
Keller, Kenneth	Basketball		22	65		played NBA 46
Keller, William	Basketball		3	18		played NBA 69-75
Kelley, Al	Golf		5	20	25	
Kelley, Joe	Baseball		1150	2650	8250	HOF 1971
Kelley, Joe	Bowling		5	15		1989 PBA HOF-Mer.Serv.
Kelley, John	Hockey	+	10	25		1974 US HOF coach
Kelley, Larry	Football		30	50		CHOF Yale. Heisman '36
Kelley, Richard	Basketball		4	15		played NBA 75-85
Kelley, Tom	Baseball		4			Debut 1964 Cleve.

NAME	CATEGORY	+	SIG	SP	BALL	Comment
Kellogg, Clark	Basketball		3	12		played NBA 82-86
Kelly Jr., John B.	Olympic		18	65		
Kelly Sr., John B.	Olympic		65	165		Rowing
Kelly, Annesse	Bowling		5	12		1985 Women's IBC HOF
Kelly, Arvesta	Basketball		3	18		played NBA 67-71
Kelly, Brian	Football		4	8		1991 Canadian HOF
Kelly, Ellen	Bowling	+	8	18		1979 Women's IBC HOF
Kelly, George	Baseball					HOF 1973.P-S HOF $550
Kelly, George	Baseball		24	75	300	Gold Pl. $50
Kelly, Jerry	Basketball		10	50		played NBA 46-47
Kelly, Jerry	Golf		5	20	25	
Kelly, Jim	Football		8	38	110	NFL
Kelly, LeRoy	Football		8	18	100	1994 HOF
Kelly, Mike "King"	Baseball		2375	7500		HOF 1945
Kelly, Pat	Baseball		5	15		Debut 1967 Minn.
Kelly, Ray	Writer		4	8		
Kelly, Red	Hockey		5	20	25	1969 HOF def
Kelly, Thomas	Basketball		10	50		played NBA 48
Kelly, Van	Baseball		3			Debut 1969 S.D.
Kelly, William	Football	+	15	40		CHOF Montana
Kelone, Theresa	Bowling		5	12		1978 Women's IBC HOF
Kelser, Gregory	Basketball		3	15		played NBA 79-84
Kelso, Ben	Basketball		3	18		played NBA 73
Keltner, Ken	Baseball		10	26		Debut 1937 Indians
Kemmerer, Russ	Baseball		4			Debut 1954 Bost. RedSox
Kemp, Jack	Football		15	45	175	NFL
Kemp, Jennifer	Olympic		3	6		Swim/relay
Kemp, Shawn	Basketball		12	32	125	NBA Knicks
Kempner, Patty	Olympic		3	8		Swim/relay
Kempton, Timothy	Basketball		3	10		played NBA 86-
Kendrick, Frank	Basketball		4	15		played NBA 74
Kenna, Ed	Football		6	20		CHOF Syracuse
Kennedy, Bill	Golf		5	20		
Kennedy, Bob	Bowling	+	8	22		1981 ABC HOF-Mer.Serv.
Kennedy, Cortez	Football		4	15	75	NFL
Kennedy, Edwina	Golf		5	20	25	
Kennedy, Eugene	Basketball		4	18		played NBA 71-76
Kennedy, J. Walter	Basketball	+	100	225		HOF 1980-Contributor
Kennedy, John	Baseball		3			Debut 1962 Senators
Kennedy, Joseph	Basketball		4	18		played NBA 68-70
Kennedy, Matthew Pat	Basketball	+	25	65		HOF 1959-Referee
Kennedy, R.D. "Bob"	Baseball		8			Debut 1939 ChiSox
Kennedy, Ted	Hockey		12	28		1966 HOF fwd
Kennedy, Vern	Baseball		5	20		Debut 1934 Cubs
Kennedy, William	Basketball		6	35		played NBA 60
Kennelly, Richard	Olympic		3	6		Rowing
Kenney, Art	Baseball		4			Debut 1938 Bost. Braves
Kenney, Bill	Football		3	12		NFL
Kennion, Mrs W.	Golf		95	175		
Kenon, Larry	Basketball		4	16		played NBA 73-82
Kenville, William	Basketball		6	35		played NBA 53-59
Kenworthy, Dick	Baseball		3			Debut 1962 Cubs
Keon, Dave	Hockey		10	28		1986 HOF fwd
Kercheval, Ralph	Football		18	45		NFL
Kerdyk, Tracy	Golf		5	20	25	
Kerfeld, Charlie	Baseball		3	9		Debut 1985

NAME	CATEGORY	+	SIG	SP	BALL	Comment
Kern, Rex	Football		5	16		NFL
Kerns, Russ	Baseball		5			Debut 1945 Tigers
Kerr, Alan	Hockey		3	15		
Kerr, Andy	Football	+	25	60		1951 CHOF coach
Kerr, Dick	Baseball		100	275		Debut 1919.
Kerr, George	Football	+	15	60		CHOF Boston College
Kerr, John	Basketball		5	22		played NBA 54-65
Kerr, Johnny	Baseball		5	12		Debut 1923 Tigers
Kerr, Steve	Basketball		4	18		played NBA 88-
Kerr, Tim	Hockey		5	18		
Kerrigan, George	Golf		50	125		
Kerrigan, Nancy	Olympic		10	40		Figure Skating
Kerrigan, Tom	Golf		50	125		
Kerris, Jack	Basketball		10	50		played NBA 49-52
Kersey, Jerome	Basketball		5	15		played NBA 84-
Kerwin, Thomas	Basketball		4	18		played NBA 67
Kessinger, Don	Baseball		3			Debut 1964 Cubs
Ketcham, Henry	Football	+	20	60		CHOF Yale
Key, Jimmy	Baseball		5	20		Debut 1984
Keye, Julius	Basketball		3	18		played NBA 69-74
Keys, Eagle	Football		5	15		1990 Canadian HOF
Keys, Randolph	Basketball		3	10		played NBA 88-
Kidd, Billy	Olympic		7	22		Alpine Skiing
Kidd, Jason	Basketball		6	25	125	Phoenix Point
Kidd, Tom	Golf		450	950		
Kiefel, Ronald	Olympic		3	6		Cycling
Kiefer, Jack	Golf		5	20	25	
Kiefer, Thomas	Olympic		3	6		Rowing
Kiehl, Marina	Olympic		10	32		Alpine skiing
Kieran, John	Writer	+	6	15		1971 Ntl S&S HOF
Kiesling, Walt	Football		100	475		1966 HOF 2-way line.NFL
Kiffin, Irv	Basketball		3	15		played NBA 79
Kiick, Jim	Football		7	22		NFL
Kiley, Jack	Basketball		10	50		played NBA 51-52
Killebrew, Harmon	Baseball					HOF 1984. P-S HOF $30
Killebrew, Harmon	Baseball		8	22	25	Gold Pl. $15. Grt.Mo. $30
Killefer, Bill	Baseball		25	85		Debut 1909
Killinger, Glenn	Football	+	20	60		CHOF Penn State
Killum, Earnest	Basketball		3	18		played NBA 70
Killy, Jean-Claude	Olympic		12	38		Alpine skiing
Kilmer, Billy	Football		4	16		NFL
Kilpatrick, Carl	Basketball		3	16		played NBA 79
Kilroy, Frank	Football		6	18		NFL
Kim, Nelli	Olympic		35	90		Gymnastics
Kimball, Bruce	Olympic		5	25		Diving
Kimball, Judy	Golf		10	25	25	
Kimball, Norman	Football		4	8		1991 Canadian HOF
Kimball, Toby	Basketball		3	20		played NBA 66-71
Kimble, Dick	Baseball		4			Debut 1945 Senators
Kimbrough, John	Football		8	28		CHOF Texas A&M
Kimmick, W.L. "Wally"	Baseball		12			Debut 1919 Cards
Kinard, Frank	Football	+	20	65		CHOF Mississippi
Kinard, Frank "Bruiser"	Football	+	75	425		1971 HOF 2-way line
Kinch, Chad	Basketball		3	10		played NBA 80
Kinder, John	Golf		65	175		
Kindrachuk, Orest	Hockey		3	18		

NAME	CATEGORY	+	SIG	SP	BALL	Comment
Kiner, Ralph	Baseball					HOF 1975. P-S HOF $30
Kiner, Ralph	Baseball		8	19	25	Gold Pl. $15. Grt.Mo. $30
King, Albert	Basketball		4	18		played NBA 81-
King, Bernard	Basketball		5	20		played NBA 77-
King, Betsy	Golf		5	25	35	LPGA HOF 1995
King, BillieJean	Tennis		10	35		HOF 1987
King, Charles G.	Baseball		4			Debut 1954 Tigers
King, Clyde	Baseball		6	14		Debut 1944. Player-Mgr.
King, Daniel	Basketball		10	45		played NBA 54
King, Don	Boxing		5	10		Boxing Promoter
King, George	Basketball		10	45		played NBA 51-57
King, James	Basketball		3	18		played NBA 63-71
King, Jim	Baseball		4			Debut 1955 Cubs
King, Leamon	Olympic		4	10		400 meter relay
King, Loyd	Basketball		4	18		played NBA 71-72
King, Maurice	Basketball		6	32		played NBA 59-62
King, Micki	Olympic		7	22		Diving
King, Phillip	Football	+	25	100		CHOF Princeton
King, Reggie	Basketball		3	15		played NBA 79-84
King, Ron	Basketball		4	18		played NBA 73
King, Sam	Golf		35	75		
King, Thomas	Basketball		10	50		played NBA 46
Kingdom, Roger	Olympic		8	22		110 M Hurdles
Kinmont (Boothe), Jill	Olympic		15	38		Skiing
Kinney, Robert	Basketball		15	55		played NBA 45-49
Kinnick, Nile	Football	+	600	1750		CHOF Iowa, Heisman '39
Kipke, Harry	Football	+	75	275		CHOF Michigan
Kiraly, Karch	Olympic		7	32		Volleyball
Kirby, Dorothy	Golf		20	50		
Kirk, Walter	Basketball		10	50		played NBA 47-51
Kirkaldy, Hugh	Golf		825	1750		
Kirkby, Oswald	Golf		45	125		
Kirkland, Wilbur	Basketball		3	22		played NBA 69
Kirkpatrick, Ed	Baseball		3			Debut 1962 L.A. Dodg.
Kirkpatrick, John	Football	+	25	80		CHOF Yale
Kirkwood, David	Olympic		3	6		Pentathlon
Kirkwood, Joe Jr.	Golf		10	45	35	
Kirkwood, Joe Sr.	Golf		45	170		
Kirrane, Jack	Hockey		5	10		1987 US HOF
Kirrene, Joe	Baseball		4			Debut 1950 ChiSox
Kirrine, Joe	Baseball		3			Debut 1950 ChiSox
Kish, Ernie	Baseball		3			Debut 1945 Phil. A's
Kissane, James	Basketball		3	20		played NBA 68
Kissoff, Joe	Bowling	+	12	30		1976 ABC HOF
Kistler, Douglas	Basketball		6	35		played NBA 61
Kitchen, Curtis	Basketball		3	10		played NBA 85
Kite, Greg	Basketball		4	15		played NBA 83-
Kite, Tom	Golf		10	30	35	
Kitner, Malcolm	Football		6	25		CHOF Texas
Kitzmiller, John	Football	+	15	50		CHOF Oregon
Kjus, Lasse	Olympic		4	12		Medalist. Alpine Skiing
Kjus, Lasse	Skiing		5	18		Alpine. World Cup Champ
Klammer, Franz	Olympic		12	40		Alpine skiing
Klares, John	Bowling		5	10		1982 ABC HOF
Klein, Chuck	Baseball		265	1800	3000	HOF 1980
Klein, Willie	Golf		45	165		

NAME	CATEGORY	+	SIG	SP	BALL	Comment
Kleine, Joe	Basketball		3	10		played NBA 85-
Klem, Bill	Baseball		450	1075	3400	HOF 1953
Klesko, Ryan	Baseball		7	38		Debut 1992
Klien, Emilee	Golf		5	20	25	
Klier, Leo	Basketball		10	50		played NBA 46-49
Klima, Petr	Hockey		4	22		
Klimchock, Lou	Baseball		4			Debut 1958 K.C.
Kline, Bobby	Baseball		4			Debut 1955 Senators
Klippstein, Johnny	Baseball		10			Debut 1950 Cubs
Klopp, Stan	Baseball		4			Debut 1944 Bost. Braves
Klotz, Louis	Basketball		10	50		played NBA 47
Klueh, Duane	Basketball		10	50		played NBA 49-50
Kluszewski, Ted	Baseball		6	25		Debut 1947
Kluttz, Clyde	Baseball		6			Debut 1942 Bost. Braves
Kluttz, Lonnie	Basketball		3	18		played NBA 70
Knafelc, Gary	Football		5	15		NFL
Knapp, Willie	Horse Racing					HOF 1969 jockey
Knechtges, Doris	Bowling	+	8	20		1983 Women's IBC HOF
Kneece, Harold	Golf		35	70		
Knepproth, Jeannette	Bowling	+	10	30		1963 Women's IBC HOF
Knerr, Lou	Baseball		3			Debut 1945 Phil. A's
Knetzer, Elmer	Baseball		15			1909 Brooklyn Pitcher
Knickman, Roy	Olympic		3	6		Cycling
Knievel Jr, Evel	Motor Cycling		10	20		Daredevil stunts
Knievel, Evel	Motor Cycling		15	45		Daredevil stunts
Knight, Billy	Basketball		4	15		played NBA 74-84
Knight, Bob	Basketball		6	25		HOF 1991-Coach
Knight, Robert	Basketball		8	40		played NBA 54
Knight, Ron	Basketball		4	15		played NBA 70-71
Knight, Toby	Basketball		3	12		played NBA 77-81
Knoblauch, Chuck	Baseball					Debut 1991
Knorek, Lee	Basketball		10	50		played NBA 46-49
Knostman, Richard	Basketball		8	45		played NBA 53
Knott, Jack	Baseball		9			Debut 1933 Browns
Knowles, Rodney	Basketball		3	18		played NBA 68
Knox, Billy	Bowling	+	15	50		1954 ABC HOF
Knox, Chuck	Football		3	7		NFL 3x Coach of Year
Knox, Kenny	Golf		5	20	25	
Knudson, George	Golf		10	35	35	
Kobayashi, Hiromi	Golf		5	25	25	
Koch, Barton	Football	+	15	45		CHOF Baylor
Koch, Carin Hj	Golf		5	20	25	
Koch, Gary	Golf		5	20	25	
Koch, Marita	Track		10	25		
Kode-Kilsch, Claudia	Tennis		8	25		
Kodes, Jan	Tennis		10	25		HOF 1990
Koenig, Mark	Baseball		20	55		Debut 1925 Yankees
Kofoed, Bart	Basketball		3	10		played NBA 87-
Kojis, Don	Basketball		4	16		played NBA 63-74
Kolb, Claudia	Olympic		4	18		Swim/breaststroke
Kolloway, Don	Baseball		8			Debut 1940 ChiSox
Komenich, Milo	Basketball		15	65		played NBA 46-49
Komives, Howard	Basketball		4	22		played NBA 64-73
Koncak, Jon	Basketball		3	12		played NBA 85-
Kondla, Tom	Basketball		4	15		played NBA 68
Konnick, Michael	Baseball		15			Debut 1909

NAME	CATEGORY	+	SIG	SP	BALL	Comment
Konno, Ford	Olympic		6	18		Swim/1,500 free
Konrads, John	Olympic		10	22		Swim/1,500 free
Konz, Ken	Football		6	15		NFL
Koonce, Cal	Baseball		4			Debut 1962 Cubs
Koosman, Jerry	Baseball		4	15		Debut 1967
Koper, Herbert	Basketball		4	28		played NBA 64
Kopf, Larry	Baseball		65			Debut 1913. SS WS '19
Kopicki, Joseph	Basketball		3	15		played NBA 82-84
Koppe, Joe	Baseball		3			Debut 1958 Mil.
Korab, Jerry	Hockey		4	18		
Korbut, Olga	Olympic		15	40		Gymnastics
Korda, Petr	Tennis		5	15		
Kordic, John	Hockey		4	20		
Kosar, Bernie	Football		6	22	100	NFL
Koski, Bill	Baseball		3			Debut 1951 Pirates
Koski, Tony	Basketball		3	22		played NBA 68
Koslowski, Dennis	Olympic		3	6		Wrestling
Kosmalski, Leonard	Basketball		3	18		played NBA 74-75
Koss, Johann Olav	Olympic		10	35		Olymp.Gold.Speed Skating
Kostecka, Andrew	Basketball		10	50		played NBA 48
Kostecki, John	Olympic		3	6		Yachting
Koster, John	Bowling	+	25	75		1941 ABC HOF
Kostka, Stan	Football		10	25		
Kostro, Frank	Baseball		4			Debut 1962 Tigers
Kottman, Harold	Basketball		10	50		played NBA 46
Koufax, Sandy	Baseball					HOF 1972. P-S HOF $70
Koufax, Sandy	Baseball		20	60	75	Gold Pl. $55. Grt.Mo. $65
Kowalczyk, Walt	Football		3	9		AA-Mich. St.
Koy, Ernie	Football		3	16		NFL
Kozak, Walter	Golf		45	125		
Kozar, Andy	Football		6	18		NFL
Kozelko, Tom	Basketball		3	15		played NBA 73-75
Kozlicki, Ronald	Basketball		3	20		played NBA 67
Koznick, Kristina	Skiing; Alpine		3	14		U.S. Champ. World Cup
Kraft, Greg	Golf		5	20	25	
Krajicek, Richard	Tennis		4	8		
Kramer, Arvid	Basketball		3	15		played NBA 79
Kramer, Barry	Basketball		3	25		played NBA 64-69
Kramer, Jack	Tennis		10	28		HOF 1968
Kramer, Jerry	Football		5	16		NFL
Kramer, Joel	Basketball		3	14		played NBA 78-82
Kramer, R.A.	Football		4	8		1987 Canadian HOF
Kramer, Ron	Football		6	22		CHOF Michigan
Kramer, Steven	Basketball		4	20		played NBA 67-69
Kramer, Tommy	Football		3	14		NFL
Kratzert, Bill	Golf		5	20	25	
Kraus, Daniel	Basketball		10	50		played NBA 48
Krause, Barbara	Olympic		10	30		Swim/100 free
Krause, Edward "Moose"	Basketball		15	38		HOF 1975. Notre Dame
Krause, Jerry	Basketball		1	2		Bulls Gen. Mgr.
Krause, Paul	Football		5	16		NFL
Krausse, Lew	Baseball		5	17		Debut 1961
Krautblatt, Herbert	Basketball		10	50		played NBA 48
Krebs, Jim	Basketball		18	50		played NBA 57-63
Kreevich, Mike	Baseball		8	20		Debut 1931 Cubs
Kreklow, Wayne	Basketball		3	12		played NBA 80

NAME	CATEGORY	+	SIG	SP	BALL	Comment
Kremer, Mitzi	Olympic		3	6		Swim/relay
Krems, Eddie	Bowling	+	10	28		1973 ABC HOF
Kreutzer, Frank	Baseball		4			Debut 1962 ChiSox
Krickstein, Aaron	Tennis		4	8		
Krieg, Dave	Football		4	12		NFL
Kriek, Johan	Tennis		7	18		
Krisiloff, Steve	Auto Racing		9	18		
Krist, Howie	Baseball		3			Debut 1937 Cards
Kristof, Joe	Bowling		5	10		1968 ABC HOF
Kroc, Joan	Baseball		5	20		Owner
Kroc, Ray	Baseball		10	45		Owner
Krol, Joe	Football		4	8		1963 Canadian HOF
Kroll, Ted	Golf		10	20	35	
Krone, Julie	Horse Racing		7	30		Woman jockey
Krongerger, Petra	Skiing		7	30		Alpine. World Cup Champ
Kropp, Thomas	Basketball		4	18		played NBA 75-76
Krueger, Al	Golf		35	85		
Krueger, Bill	Basketball		3	5		U. of Portland
Krueger, Charlie	Football		6	18		CHOF Texas A&M
Kruk, John	Baseball		5	15		Debut 1986
Krumske, Paul	Bowling	+	5	14		1968 ABC HOF
Krupa, Joe	Football		8	20		NFL
Kruse, Pamela	Olympic		3	8		Swim/800 free
Krushelnyski, Mike	Hockey		4	12		
Kryczka, Kelly	Olympic		5	10		Synch. Swimming
Kryhoski, Dick	Baseball		5			Debut 1949 Yankees
Krystkowiak, Larry	Basketball		3	12		played NBA 86-
Krzyzewski, Mike	Basketball		2	10		Duke Coach
Ku, Ok-Hee	Golf		5	20	25	
Kubek, Tony	Baseball		4	15		Debut 1957
Kuberski, Stephen	Basketball		3	14		played NBA 69-77
Kubiak, Leo	Basketball		10	50		played NBA 48-49
Kucks, Johnny	Baseball		6	18		Debut 1955
Kucynski, Betty	Bowling		5	12		1981 Women's IBC HOF
Kuczenski, Bruce	Basketball		3	10		played NBA 83
Kudelka, Frank	Basketball		10	50		played NBA 49-52
Kuehn, Louis	Olympic		8	30		Diving
Kuenn, Harvey	Baseball		25	55		Debut 1952
Kuerten, Gustavo	Tennis		4	18		French Open winner
Kuester, John	Basketball		3	15		played NBA 77-79
Kuharich, Joe	Football		20	60		NFL
Kuhel, Joe	Baseball		15			Debut 1930 Senators
Kuhn, Bowie	Baseball		12	40		Commissioner
Kuiper, Duane	Baseball		4	15		Debut 1974
Kuka, Ray	Basketball		10	50		played NBA 47-48
Kukoc, Toni	Basketball		8	25		Europe to Bulls
Kulwicki, Alan	Auto Racing		50	125		
Kummer, Clarence	Horse Racing					HOF 1972 jockey
Kundla, John	Basketball		6	22		1995 HOF- Coach
Kunes, Gene	Golf		35	110		
Kunkel, Bill	Baseball		3			Debut 1961 K.C.
Kunnert, Kevin	Basketball		3	15		played NBA 73-81
Kuntz, Rusty	Baseball		3			Debut 1979 ChiSox
Kunze, Terry	Basketball		4	18		played NBA 67
Kupchak, Mitch	Basketball		3	15		played NBA 76-85
Kupec, Charles	Basketball		3	15		played NBA 75-77

NAME	CATEGORY	+	SIG	SP	BALL	Comment
Kurland, Bob	Basketball		14	22		HOF 1961
Kurowski, Whitey	Baseball		12			Debut 1941 Cardinals
Kurri, Jari	Hockey		7	28		
Kursinski, Anne	Olympic		5	10		Equestrian
Kurtenbach, Orland	Hockey		4	18		
Kurtis, Frank	Auto Racing	+	45	95		
Kurtsinger, Charles	Horse Racing		15	50		HOF 1967 jockey
Kush, Frank	Football		4	8		NFL
Kusner, Kathryn	Olympic		5	10		Equestrian
Kutyna, Marty	Baseball		3			Debut 1959 K.C.
Kuzava, Bob	Baseball		6	18		Debut 1946
Kwalick, Ted	Football		6	16		CHOF Penn State
Kwan, Michelle	Figure Skating		10	50		World Champion
Kyle, Alexander	Golf		35	85		

NAME	CATEGORY	+	SIG	SP	BALL	Comment
Laabs, Chet	Baseball		5			Debut 1937 Tigers
LaBarba, Fidel	Boxing		12	25		Fly-Wt Champ
Labine, Clem	Baseball		3	12		Debut 1950 Brklyn.Dodg.
Labine, Leo	Hockey		4	16		
Labonte, Terry	Auto Racing		7	18		
Lacefield, Reggie	Basketball		4	22		played NBA 68
Lacey, Arthur	Golf		75	175		
Lacey, Charles	Golf		55	150		
Lacey, Sam	Basketball		5	20		played NBA 70-82
Lach, Elmer	Hockey		6	20		1966 HOF fwd
Lach, Steve	Football	+	15	40		CHOF Duke
Lachey, Jim	Football		3	9		NFL
Lackey, Bob	Basketball		4	18		played NBA 72-73
Lackhart, Tom	Hockey	+	10	22		1973 US HOF admin
Lackie, Ethel	Olympic		8	24		Swim/100 M Free
Lacoste, Catherine	Golf		40	95	50	
Lacoste, Rene	Tennis		30	100		HOF 1976
LaCour, Fred	Basketball		6	35		played NBA 60-62
Lacy, Edgar	Basketball		4	20		played NBA 68
Ladewig, Marion	Bowling		5	20		1964 Women's IBC HOF
Ladner, Wendell	Basketball		3	18		played NBA 70-74
Laettner, Christian	Basketball		8	28		played NBA 92-
Laffoon, Ky	Golf		50	125		
Lafleur, Guy	Hockey		8	22	25	1988 HOF fwd
LaFontaine, Pat	Hockey		7	25	30	
Lagarde, Thomas	Basketball		4	16		played NBA 77-84
Lagerblade, Herbert	Golf		75	195		
Laguna, Ismael	Boxing		15	32		

NAME	CATEGORY	+	SIG	SP	BALL	Comment
Laidlaw, Tom	Hockey		3	18		
Laidlay, Johnny	Golf		497	1095		
Laimbeer, Bill	Basketball		6	22		played NBA 80-
Laird, Ron	Olympic		4	10		Walker
Lajoie, Nap	Baseball		400	980	4575	HOF 1937.B&W PC $800
LaLanne, Jack	Body Building		5	22		
Lalich, Peter	Basketball		15	60		played NBA 42-46
Lally, Tom	Golf		65	150		
Lalonde, Donny	Boxing		8	16		
Lalonde, Newsy	Hockey		85	250		1950 HOF fwd
Lamabe, Jack	Baseball		3			Debut 1962 Pirates
LaMacchia, Al	Baseball		6			Debut 1943 Browns
Lamanno, Ray	Baseball		4			Debut 1941 Reds
Lamar, Bill	Baseball		45	110		.310 Avg. over 9 years
Lamar, Dwight	Basketball		3	15		played NBA 73-76
Lamb, Ray	Baseball		3			Debut 1969 Dodgers
Lambeau, Curly	Football	+	160	500		1963 HOF player/coach
Lambert, Gene	Baseball		5			Debut 1941 Phillies
Lambert, Jack	Football		6	28	135	1990 HOF LB
Lambert, John	Basketball		3	15		played NBA 75-81
Lambert, Ward "Piggy"	Basketball	+	18	50		HOF 1960-Coach
Lamonica, Daryl	Football		5	15		NFL
Lamont, Gene	Baseball		2	5		Detroit Mgr. 1992
Lamontage, Steve	Golf		5	20	25	
LaMotta, Jake	Boxing		12	30		Middle-Wt Champ
Lamp, Dennis	Baseball		4	15		Debut 1977
Lamp, Jeff	Basketball		3	12		played NBA 81-88
Lampley, Jim	Basketball		3	10		played NBA 86
Lampley, Jim	Broadcaster		2	5		Olympic Host-Boxing
Lampley, Jim	Broadcaster		4	8		
Lancaster, Neal	Golf		5	20	25	
Lancaster, Ron	Football		5	15		1982 Canadian HOF
Landetta, Sean	Football		4	9		NFL
Landis, Kenesaw Mountain	Baseball		350	725	3500	HOF 1944
Landrith, Hobie	Baseball		10			Debut 1950 Reds
Landry, Greg	Football		3	12		NFL
Landry, Tom	Football		8	25	145	1990 HOF coach
Landsberger, Mark	Basketball		3	15		played NBA 77-83
Landy, John	Olympic		35	75		Track/distance
Lane, Dick "NightTrain"	Football		6	20	85	1974 HOF DB
Lane, Frank	Baseball		25	45		Owner
Lane, Jerome	Basketball		3	10		played NBA 88-
Lane, McArthur	Football		4	12		NFL
Lane, Myles	Football	+	18	50		CHOF Dartmouth
Lane, Myles	Hockey		5	10		1973 US HOF
Laney, Al	Tennis	+	12	30		HOF 1979
Lang, Andrew	Basketball		3	10		played NBA 88-
Lang, Jack	Writer		3	6		
Lange, Dick	Baseball		3			Debut 1972 Cal. Angels
Lange, Herb	Bowling	+	15	55		1941 ABC HOF
Langer, Bernhard	Golf		15	30	40	
Langer, Jim	Football		5	16	85	1987 HOF OL
Langert, Eddie	Golf		5	20	25	
Langford, Sam	Boxing		145	350		Welter-Wt Champ
Langston, Mark	Baseball		4	15		Debut 1984
Langtry, Abe	Bowling	+	8	25		1963 ABC HOF-Mer.Serv.

NAME	CATEGORY	+	SIG	SP	BALL	Comment
Lanier, Bob	Basketball		8	22		HOF 1992
Lanier, Hal	Baseball		8			Debut 1964 SF Giants
Lanier, Max	Baseball		3	12		Debut 1938
Lanier, Willie	Football		7	22	85	1986 HOF LB
Lansford, Buck	Football		6	16		NFL
Lansford, Carney	Baseball		10	30		Debut 1978
Lantz, Stuart	Basketball		3	15		played NBA 68-75
Laoretti, Larry	Golf		5	20	25	
LaPalme, Paul	Baseball		4			Debut 1951 Pirates
Lapchick, Joe	Basketball	+	50	150		HOF 1966
Laperriere, Jacques	Hockey		5	18	20	1987 HOF
Lapointe, Guy	Hockey		6	20		
Lapp, Bernice	Olympic		3	7		Swim relay
Lardner, Ring	Writer	+	20	45		1967 Ntl S&S HOF
Larese, York	Basketball		3	30		played NBA 61
Largent, Steve	Football		10	30		NFL. HOF 1995
Larker, Norm	Baseball		4			Debut 1958 L.A. Dodgers
Larkin, Barry	Baseball		5	22	35	Debut 1986
Larmer, Steve	Hockey		4	14		
Larned, William	Tennis	+	15	40		HOF 1956
Larose, Claude	Hockey		5	18		
Larouche, Pierre	Hockey		5	18		
Larrabee, Mike	Olympic		6	14		400 Meters
Larsen, Art	Tennis		5	20		HOF 1969
Larsen, Don	Baseball		5	25		Debut '53.Pitched No Hit
Larsen, Gary	Football		5	12		NFL
Larson, David	Olympic		3	6		Gold Medal. Swimming
Larson, Frank	Football		5	10		
Larson, Greg	Football		3	10		NFL
Larson, Lance	Olympic		5	14		Swim/sprints
LaRussa, Tony	Baseball		5	25		Debut 1963. K.C. - Mgr.
LaRusso, Rudy	Basketball		5	20		played NBA 59-68
Lary, Frank	Baseball		3	12		Debut 1954
Lary, Yale	Football		5	20	85	1979 HOF DB
Lash, Don	Olympic		35	75		Track/Mile
Lash, Don	Track		6	14		
Lasher, Iolia	Bowling	+	10	28		1967 Women's IBC HOF
Lasker, Deedee	Golf		5	15		
Laskowski, John	Basketball		3	15		played NBA 75-76
Lasley, Bill	Baseball		8			Debut 1924 STL Browns
LaSorda, Tommy	Baseball		5	18	35	Debut 1954.Mgr. HOF '97
Lassen, E.A.	Golf		475	1150		
LaStarza, Roland	Boxing		12	32		Lt-Hvy-Wt Champ
Lattin, David	Basketball		4	18		played NBA 67-72
Lattner, Johnny	Football		10	30		CHOF ND. Heisman '53
Latzo, Pete	Boxing		75	150		Welter-Wt Champ
Laub, Larry	Bowling		5	16		1985 PBA HOF
Lauer, Bonnie	Golf		5	20	25	
Lauman, Hank	Bowling		5	15		1976 ABC HOF
Laurel, Rich	Basketball		3	12		played NBA 77
Lauricella, Hank	Football		6	18		CHOF Tennessee
Laurie, Don	Football		8	25		CHOF Princeton
Laurie, Harry	Basketball		3	16		played NBA 70
Laurin, Lucien	Horse Racing			25		HOF 1977 trainer
Laut, Dave	Olympic		3	8		Shot Put
Lautenbach, Walter	Basketball		10	50		played NBA 47-49

NAME	CATEGORY	+	SIG	SP	BALL	Comment
Lauterborn, William	Baseball		15			Maj. League 1904-05
Lauzerique, George	Baseball		4			Debut 1967 K.C.
Lavagetto, Cookie	Baseball		15			Debut 1934 Pirates
Lavelli, Dante	Football		8	20	85	1975 HOF end/WB
Lavelli, Tony	Basketball		10	50		played NBA 49-50
Laver, Rod	Tennis		7	22		HOF 1981
LaVine, Jacqueline	Olympic		5	12		Swimming relay
Laviolette, Jack	Hockey		55	160		1962 HOF def
Lavoy, Robert	Basketball		10	50		played NBA 50-53
Law, Vernon	Baseball		6	20		Debut 1950 Pirates
Lawrence, Andrea	Olympic		7	22		Alpine Skiing
Lawrence, Bill	Baseball		5			Debut 1932 Tigers
Lawrence, Edmund	Basketball		3	10		played NBA 80
Lawson, Earl	Writer		4	8		
Lawson, Smirle	Football	+	10	22		1963 Canadian HOF
Lawton, Brian	Hockey		4	18		
Layne, Bobby	Football	+	65	175	475	1957 HOF QB
Layne, Hillis "Hilly"	Baseball		4			Debut 1941 Senators
Layne, Rex	Boxing		8	20		
Layton, Dennis	Basketball		3	18		played NBA 71-77
Layton, Les	Baseball		4			Debut 1948 NY Giants
Laz, Donald D.R.	Olympic		5	10		Pole Vault
Lazar, Danny	Baseball		3			Debut 1968 ChiSox
Lazzeri, Tony	Baseball		375	825	4000	HOF 1991.
Lea, Langdon	Football	+	25	90		CHOF Princeton
Leach, Reggie	Hockey		5	20		
Leadbetter, David	Golf		5	20	25	
Leadlay, Frank	Football	+	10	22		1963 Canadian HOF
Leaf, Ryan	Football		5	25		QB
Leahy, Frank	Football	+	45	90		1970 CHOF coach
Leahy, Pat	Football		3	10		NFL
Leaks, Manny	Basketball		3	15		played NBA 68-73
Lear, Harold	Basketball		8	40		played NBA 56
Lear, Les	Football	+	10	22		1974 Canadian HOF
Leary, Tim	Baseball		4	12		Debut 1981
Leatherwood, Lillie	Olympic		3	7		Track relay
Leavell, Allen	Basketball		3	15		played NBA 79-88
LeBaron, Eddie	Football		6	20		CHOF Pacific
LeBeau, Dick	Football		4	15		NFL
LeBlan, Nanette	Golf		70	150		
Leckner, Eric	Basketball		3	10		played NBA 88-
LeClair, John	Hockey		7	22	25	
Leconte, Henri	Tennis		6	22		
LeDoux, Scott	Boxing		7	15		
Lee, Butch	Basketball		3	10		played NBA 78-79
Lee, Carl	Football		3	10		NFL
Lee, Clyde	Basketball		3	15		played NBA 66-75
Lee, David	Basketball		3	15		played NBA 67-68
Lee, Dick	Basketball		3	15		played NBA 67
Lee, George	Basketball		4	22		played NBA 60-67
Lee, Greg	Basketball		4	15		played NBA 74-75
Lee, Hal	Baseball		5			Debut 1930 Brklyn.Dodg.
Lee, Keith	Basketball		3	12		played NBA 85-88
Lee, Rock	Basketball		3	10		played NBA 81
Lee, Ronnie	Basketball		5	15		played NBA 76-81
Lee, Russell	Basketball		3	15		played NBA 72-74

NAME	CATEGORY	+	SIG	SP	BALL	Comment
Lee, Sammy	Olympic		5	14		Diving
Lee, Thornton	Baseball		15			Debut 1933 Cleve. Indians
Leech, James	Football	+	18	45		CHOF VMI
Leede, Edward	Basketball		10	50		played NBA 49-50
Leeman, Gary	Hockey		4	17		
Leemans, Tuffy	Football	+	85	300		1978 HOF RB
Lees, Art	Golf		45	95		
Leetch, Brian	Hockey		6	24	30	
Lefebvre, Bill	Baseball		4			Debut 1938 Bost. RedSox
Lefebvre, Jim	Baseball		4	15		Debut 1965. Mgr.
Lefkowitz, Henry	Basketball		15	65		played NBA 45
Lefler, Wade	Baseball		6			Debut 1924 Bost. Braves
Lehman, Hughie	Hockey		65	185		1958 HOF goal
Lehman, Tom	Golf		10	30	40	
Lehmann, George	Basketball		3	18		played NBA 67-73
Leinhauser, Bill	Baseball		12			Debut 1912 Tigers
Leitch, Cecil	Golf		95	175		
Leiter, Al	Baseball		3	10		Debut 1987
Leith, Lloyd	Basketball	+	22	55		HOF 1982
Lema, Tony	Golf		295	595		
Lemaire, Jacques	Hockey		5	18	20	1984 HOF fwd
Lemelin, Reggie	Hockey		4	18		
Lemieux, Claude	Hockey		6	25		
Lemieux, Mario	Hockey		15	40	50	1997 HOF fwd
Lemm, Wally	Football		15	38		NFL
Lemon, Bob	Baseball					HOF 1976. P-S HOF $25
Lemon, Bob	Baseball		7	15	22	Gold Pl.S $15.Grt.Mo.$25
LeMond, Greg	Cycling		10	28		
Lemonds, Dave	Baseball		3			Debut 1969 Cubs
Lempke, Mark	Baseball		4	12		Debut 1988
Lenczyk, Grace	Golf		45	95		
Lendl, Ivan	Tennis		10	28		
Lenglen, Suzanne	Tennis	+	165	375		HOF 1978
Lenhardt, Don	Baseball		4			Debut 1950 Browns
Lentz, Leary	Basketball		3	18		played NBA 67-68
Lenz, Sidney S.	Bridge		20	40		
Leoffler, Ken	Basketball	+	22	50		HOF 1964
Leon, Eddie	Baseball		3			Debut 1968 Cleve. Indians
Leonard, Benny	Boxing		250	500		Lt.-Wt Champ
Leonard, Bob	Basketball		6	22		played NBA 56-62
Leonard, Buck	Baseball					HOF 1972. P-S HOF $45
Leonard, Buck	Baseball		12	35	45	Gold Pl. $32.Grt.Mo.$50
Leonard, Emil "Dutch"	Baseball		20			Debut 1933 Brklyn.Dodg.
Leonard, Joe	Auto Racing		6	15		HOF 1991
Leonard, Justin	Golf		10	25	25	
Leonard, Stan	Golf		15	45		
Leonard, Sugar Ray	Boxing		20	40		Welter,Middle-Wt Champ
Leone, Baron	Wrestling-Pro		10	20		
Leperrier, Jacques	Hockey		5	18		1987 HOF def
Les, Jim	Basketball		3	10		played NBA 88
Leshnock, Don	Baseball		3			Debut 1972 Tigers
Leslie, Lisa	Basketball		12	45		Olympic
Leslie, Lisa	Olympic		3	15		Gold Med. Basketball
Lesnevich, Gus	Boxing		85	200		
Lesser, Patricia	Golf		10	35		
Lester, Darrell	Football		7	15		CHOF Texas Christian

NAME	CATEGORY	+	SIG	SP	BALL	Comment
Lester, Ronnie	Basketball		3	12		played NBA 80-85
LeSueur, Percy	Hockey		95	280		1961 HOF goal
Levane, Andrew	Basketball		10	50		played NBA 45-52
Levens, Dorsey	Football		5	22		NFL
Lever, Don	Hockey		4	15		
Lever, Lafayette	Basketball		3	12		played NBA 82-
Levi, Wayne	Golf		5	20	25	
Levin, Dave	Pro Wrestling		5	10		
Levine, Sam	Bowling	+	8	20		1971 ABC HOF-Mer.Serv.
Levingston, Cliff	Basketball		3	10		played NBA 82-
Levy, Marv	Football		3	8		NFL
Lewis Howard J.	Horse Racing					HOF 1969 trainer
Lewis, Albert	Football		3	12		NFL
Lewis, Allen	Writer		4	8		
Lewis, Bill	Football		2	5		College Coach of Year
Lewis, Bradley	Olympic		3	6		Rowing
Lewis, Buddy	Baseball		22			Debut 1935 Senators
Lewis, Carl	Olympic		10	40		Track/4 '84 Golds
Lewis, Ed "Strangler"	Pro Wrestling		40	110		
Lewis, Fred	Basketball		10	50		played NBA 46-49
Lewis, Fred L.	Basketball		3	15		played NBA 66-76
Lewis, Grady	Basketball		10	50		played NBA 46-48
Lewis, Hedgemon	Boxing		8	18		
Lewis, Herbie	Hockey		75	180		1989 HOF fwd
Lewis, John Henry	Boxing		40	85		Lt.Hvy-Wt Champ
Lewis, Johnny	Baseball		3			Debut 1964 Cards
Lewis, Lennox	Boxing		12	35		Hvy-Wt Champ
Lewis, Leo	Football		4	10		1973 Canadian HOF
Lewis, Michael	Basketball		3	15		played NBA 68-73
Lewis, Ralph	Basketball		3	10		played NBA 87-
Lewis, Randy	Auto Racing		4	8		
Lewis, Randy	Olympic		3	6		Wrestling
Lewis, Reggie	Basketball		27	90	350	played NBA 87-
Lewis, Robert	Basketball		3	12		played NBA 67-70
Lewis, Steve	Olympic		5	14		400 meters
Lewis, Ted "Kid"	Boxing		30	125		Welterwt.Champ.1915-19
Lewis, Woodley	Football		5	15		NFL
Libke, Al	Baseball		4			Debut 1945 Cin. Reds
Lickliter, Frank	Golf		20	20	25	
Lieberman, M.I.	Football	+	10	22		1973 Canadian HOF
Lieberman-Cline, Nancy	Basketball		7	23		Women's pioneer.HOF '96
Liebhardt, Glenn	Baseball		5			Debut 1930 A's
Liebowitz, Barry	Basketball		3	15		played NBA 67
Lietzke, Bruce	Golf		7	25	25	
Ligon, Jim	Basketball		3	15		played NBA 67-73
Ligon, William	Basketball		3	15		played NBA 74
Lillard, Bill	Baseball		4	10		Debut 1939 Phillies
Lillard, Bill	Bowling		5	12		1972 ABC HOF
Lillard, Gene	Baseball		4			Debut 1929 Cubs
Lillis, Bob	Baseball		8			Debut 1958 L.A. Dodgers
Lilly, Bob	Football		10	22	120	1980 HOF DL
Lincoln, Craig	Olympic		3	8		Diving
Lincoln, Keith	Football		5	15		NFL
Lind, Joan	Olympic		3	6		Rowing
Lindell, John	Baseball		15			Debut 1941 Yankees
Lindeman, Jim	Baseball		4	12		Debut 1986

NAME	CATEGORY	+	SIG	SP	BALL	Comment
Lindemann, Tony	Bowling		5	12		1979 ABC HOF
Linder, Joe	Hockey	+	10	22		1975 US HOF
Lindgren, H. Blaine	Olympic		3	7		Hurdles
Lindh, Hilary	Olympic		4	18		Medalist. Alpine Skiing
Lindquist, Carl	Baseball		4			Debut 1943 Bost. Braves
Lindros, Eric	Hockey		10	38	45	
Lindsay, Ted	Hockey		6	18	22	1966 HOF fwd
Lindsey, Mort	Bowling	+	15	42		1941 ABC HOF
Lindstrom, Fred	Baseball		35	150	675	HOF 1976. Gold Pl. $75
Lindstrom, Murle	Golf		10	30		
Lingenfelter, Steve	Basketball		3	10		played NBA 82-83
Linke, Ed	Baseball		6			Debut 1933 Senators
Linn, Jeremy	Olympic		3	7		Gold Medal. Swimming
Linseman, Ken	Hockey		4	15		
Lio, Augie	Football	+	15	40		CHOF Georgetown
Lipinski, Tara	Olympic		8	40		Gold.Fig.Skater.Wld Champ.
Lipon, Johnny	Baseball		4			Debut 1942 Tigers
Lippe, Larry	Bowling		5	10		1989 ABC HOF
Lipscomb, Big Daddy	Football		90	225		NFL
Liska, Adolph "Ad"	Baseball		4	10		Debut 1929 Senators
Listach, Pat	Baseball		2	8		Debut 1992
Lister, Alton	Basketball		3	12		played NBA 81-
Lister, John	Golf		10	35		
Liston, Emil "Liz"	Basketball	+	20	50		HOF 1974
Liston, Sonny	Boxing		250	500		1962-64 H-Wt Champ
Little, David	Football		3	7		NFL
Little, Floyd	Football		6	20		CHOF Syracuse
Little, George	Football	+	15	35		1955 CHOF coach
Little, Larry	Football		4	15	85	1993 HOF
Little, Lawson	Golf		85	165		PGA HOF 1980
Little, Lou	Football		40	125		1960 CHOF coach
Little, Sally	Golf		5	25	25	
Little, Samuel	Basketball		3	18		played NBA 69
Littlefield, Dick	Baseball		3			Debut 1950 Bost. RedSox
Littler, Gene	Golf		10	25	30	PGA HOF 1990
Littles, Eugene	Basketball		4	15		played NBA 69-74
Litwack, Harry	Basketball		10	22		HOF 1975-Coach
Litwhiler, Danny	Baseball		7			Debut 1940 A's
Liut, Mike	Hockey		5	18		
Livengood, Wes	Baseball		4			Debut 1939 Cin. Reds
Livingston, Mike	Football		3	9		NFL
Livingston, Paddy	Baseball		4	10		Debut 1901
Livingstone, Ron	Basketball		10	50		played NBA 49-50
Lloyd, Chuck	Basketball		3	15		played NBA 70
LLoyd, Earl	Basketball		8	40		played NBA 50-59
Lloyd, Joe	Golf		625	1250		
Lloyd, John	Tennis		5	15		
Lloyd, John Henry	Baseball		775	2750	7000	HOF 1977
Lloyd, Lewis	Basketball		3	10		played NBA 81-86
Lloyd, Robert	Basketball		4	18		played NBA 67-68
Lloyd, Scott	Basketball		3	15		played NBA 76-82
Lobo, Rebecca	Basketball		3	9		Pro player
Lochmann, Reinhold	Basketball		3	15		played NBA 67-69
Lochmueller, Robert	Basketball		10	45		played NBA 52
Lock, Don	Baseball		3	8		Debut 1962
Lock, Robert	Basketball		3	10		played NBA 88

NAME	CATEGORY	+	SIG	SP	BALL	Comment
Locke, Bobby	Golf		150	375		PGA HOF 1977
Locke, Charlie	Baseball		3			Debut 1955 Orioles
Locke, Gordon	Football	+	15	40		CHOF Iowa
Lockhart, Darrell	Basketball		3	10		played NBA 83
Lockhart, Frank	Auto Racing	+	25	70		
Lockhart, Spider	Football		15	55		NFL
Locklear, Gene	Baseball		3	10		Debut 1973
Locklin, Stu	Baseball		4	15		Debut 1955
Lockman, Whitey	Baseball		12	28		Debut 1945 NY Giants
Lockwood, Skip	Baseball		3	12		Debut 1965
Loder, Kevin	Basketball		3	10		played NBA 81-83
Lodigiani, Dario	Baseball		12	65		Debut 1938 A's
Loeffler, Emil	Golf		75	200		
Loeffler, Kenneth	Basketball		20	35		HOF 1964-Coach
Lofgran, Don	Basketball		18	65		played NBA 50-53
Lofland, Dana	Golf		5	20	25	
Lofton, James	Football		7	22	100	NFL
Lofton, Kenny	Baseball		8	35		Debut 1991
Loftus, John	Horse Racing		25	70		HOF 1959 jockey
Logan, Bob "Lefty"	Baseball		3			Debut 1935 Brklyn.Dodg.
Logan, Henry	Basketball		4	15		played NBA 68-69
Logan, John	Basketball		10	50		played NBA 46-50
Logan, Johnny	Baseball		8	22		Debut 1951
Lohaus, Brad	Basketball		3	10		played NBA 87-
Lohr, Bob	Golf		5	20	25	
Lohrke, Lucky	Baseball		6	18		Debut 1947
Lohrman, Bill	Baseball		3	10		Debut 1934
Loiselle, Claude	Hockey		4	18		
Lolich, Mickey	Baseball		4	12		Debut 1963
Lolich, Ron	Baseball		3	10		Debut 1971
Lollar, Sherm	Baseball		25	70		Debut 1946
Loman, Doug	Baseball		3	10		Debut 1984
Lomax, Neil	Football		4	12		NFL
Lombardi, Ernie	Baseball		75	287	1400	HOF 1986
Lombardi, Phil	Baseball		3	10		Debut 1986
Lombardi, Vince	Football	+	250	517	1850	1971 HOF coach
Lombardozzi, Steve	Baseball		3	10		Debut 1985
Lonberg, Dutch	Basketball	+	15	38		HOF 1972 Coach
Lonborg, Jim	Baseball		3	12		Debut 1965
London, Brian	Boxing		8	18		
Londos, Jim	Pro Wrestling		25	65		
Loney, Troy	Hockey		3	15		
Long, Chuck	Football		2	7		Maxwell Award
Long, Dale	Baseball		18	40		Debut 1951
Long, Dallas	Olympic		8	20		Shot Put
Long, Grant	Basketball		3	10		played NBA 88-
Long, Howie	Football		4	15		NFL
Long, Jeoff	Baseball		3	15		Debut 1963
Long, John	Basketball		4	15		played NBA 78-
Long, Paul	Basketball		3	18		played NBA 67-70
Long, Willie	Basketball		3	18		played NBA 71-73
Longden, Johnny	Horse Racing		10	35		HOF 1958 jockey
Longhurst, Henry	Golf		5	20	25	
Longhurst, Henry	Golf		50	135		
Lonnett, Joe	Baseball		4	15		Debut 1956
Lonsberry, Ross	Hockey		4	20		

NAME	CATEGORY	+	SIG	SP	BALL	Comment
Loob, Hakan	Hockey		4	25		
Look, Bruce	Baseball		3	15		Debut 1968
Look, Dean	Baseball		3	15		Debut 1961
Looney, Don Joe	Football		60	175		NFL
Loos, Eddie	Golf		70	195		
Lopat, Ed	Baseball		22	60		Debut 1944 ChiSox
Lopata, Stan	Baseball		9	25		Debut 1948 Phillies
Lopatka, Art	Baseball		3			Debut 1945 Cards
Lopes, Davey	Baseball		5	12		Debut 1972 Dodgers
Lopez, AL	Baseball					HOF 1977. P-S HOF $95
Lopez, Al	Baseball		15	50	85	Gold Pl.$45.Grt.Mo.$95
Lopez, Danny "Little Red"	Boxing		15	32		Fthr-Wt Champ
Lopez, Hector	Baseball		4	18		Debut 1955
Lopez, Javier	Baseball		5	22		Outstanding Catcher
Lopez, Marcelino	Baseball		15	30		Debut 1963 Phill. Pitcher
Lopez, Nancy	Golf		10	35		PGA,LPGA HOF '89, '87
LoPresti, Sam	Hockey	+	15	40		1973 US HOF
Lorentz, Jim	Hockey		4	18		
Lorenzen, Fred	Auto Racing		5	10		
Lorick, Tony	Football		3	12		NFL
Losch, Claudia	Olympic		7	26		Shot Put
Loscutoff, Jim	Basketball		6	30		played NBA 55-63
Losey, Robert	Olympic		3	6		Pentathlon
Lott, George	Tennis		6	22		HOF 1964
Lott, Lyn	Golf		10	35		
Lott, Plummer	Basketball		4	18		played NBA 67-68
Lott, Ronnie	Football		7	28	100	NFL
Lotz, Dick	Golf		10	35		
Loucks, Scott	Baseball		3	10		Debut 1980
Louganis, Greg	Olympic		8	20		4 Diving Golds
Loughery, Kevin	Basketball		4	20		played NBA 62-71
Loughlin, Larry	Baseball		3			Debut 1967 Phillies
Loughran, Tommy	Boxing		110	200		Lt.Hvy-Wt Champ
Louis, Joe	Boxing		250	400		1937-48 H-Wt Champ
Love, Bob	Basketball		6	20		played NBA 66-76
Love, Davis	Golf		25	50		
Love, Davis, III	Golf		5	25	30	
Love, Stan	Basketball		3	12		played NBA 71-74
Loveless, Lea	Olympic		3	9		Gold Medal. Swimming
Lovellette, Clyde	Basketball		15	25	125	HOF 1987-88
Loviglio, Jay	Baseball		3	10		Debut 1980
Lovitto, Joe	Baseball		3	10		Debut 1972
Lovrich, Pete	Baseball		3			Debut 1963 K.C.
Lovullo, Torey	Baseball		3	10		Debut 1988
Lowdermilk, Elmer	Baseball		15			1909 STL Pitcher
Lowe, Paul	Football		6	22		NFL
Lowe, Sidney	Basketball		3	10		played NBA 83-88
Lowe, Kevin	Hockey		4	18		
Lowenstein, John	Baseball		3	12		Debut 1970
Lowery, Chuck	Basketball		4	15		played NBA 71
Lowery, Nick	Football		4	14		NFL
Lowery, Steve	Golf		5	20	25	
Lowrey, Peanuts	Baseball		20	55		Debut 1942
Lowry, Dwight	Baseball		3	10		Debut 1984
Lozado, Willie	Baseball		3	10		Debut 1984
Lubanski, Ed	Bowling		12	38		1971 ABC HOF

NAME	CATEGORY	+	SIG	SP	BALL	Comment
Lubick, Sonny	Football		2	5		Colorado St. Coach
Lubratich, Steve	Baseball		3	10		Debut 1981
Lubsen Jr., Walter	Olympic		3	10		Rowing
Luby Jr., Mort	Bowling		8	20		1988 ABC HOF-Mer.Serv.
Luby Sr., Mort	Bowling	+	8	25		1974 ABC HOF-Mer.Serv.
Luby, David	Bowling	+	8	20		1969 ABC HOF-Mer.Serv.
Luby, Hugh	Baseball		20	60		Debut 1936
Lucadello, Johnny	Baseball		8	45		Debut 1938 Browns
Lucas, Albert	Basketball		12	55		played NBA 44-48
Lucas, Fred. W. "Fritz"	Baseball		5			Debut 1935 Phillies
Lucas, Jerry	Basketball		12	28	125	HOF 1979
Lucas, John	Basketball		4	15		played NBA 76-89
Lucas, Maurice	Basketball		5	15		played NBA 74-87
Lucas, Red	Baseball		30	70		Debut 1923
Lucas, Richie	Football		6	22		CHOF Penn State
Lucci Sr., Vince	Bowling		5	12		1978 ABC HOF
Luciano, Ron	Baseball		5	15		Umpire
Lucier, Lou	Baseball		3			Debut 1943 Bost. RedSox
Luckenbill, Ted	Basketball		5	40		played NBA 61-62
Luckman, Sid	Football		10	26	125	1965 HOF QB
Luderus, Fred	Baseball		15			1915 World Ser./Phillies
Luebbe, Roy	Baseball		25	80		Debut 1925
Luis-Clerc, Jose	Tennis		6	14		
Luisetti, Angello "Hank"	Basketball		28	85		HOF 1959
Luisi, James	Basketball		10	45		played NBA 53
Lujack, Al	Basketball		10	50		played NBA 46
Lujack, Johnny	Football		10	40		CHOF ND. Heisman '37
Lukon, Eddie	Baseball		6	40		Debut 1941
Lum, Mike	Baseball		3	12		Debut 1967
Lumley, Harry	Hockey		7	25	32	1980 HOF goal
Lumpe, Jerry	Baseball		4	15		Debut 1956
Lumpkin, Phil	Basketball		3	12		played NBA 74-75
Lumpp, Raymond	Basketball		4	10		played NBA 48-52
Lund, Don	Baseball		6	30		Debut 1945 Brklyn.Dodg.
Lund, Gordon	Baseball		3	12		Debut 1967
Lund, Pug	Football		20	45		CHOF Minnesota
Lundquist, Steve	Olympic		5	14		Swim/100 breast
Lundquist, Verne	Broadcaster		2	5		FB-Olympics
Lundstedt, Tom	Baseball		3	12		Debut 1973
Lunn, Bob	Golf		10	35		
Lunsford, Earl	Football		5	14		1983 Canadian HOF
Lunt, Michael	Golf		5	20	25	
Lupien, Tony	Baseball		8	32		Debut 1940
Luplow, Al	Baseball		3	15		Debut 1961
Luro, Horatio	Horse Racing		10	25		HOF 1980 trainer
Lusader, Scott	Baseball		3	10		Debut 1987
Lusch, Ernie	Pro Wrestling		4	8		
Lusk, Bernie	Broadcaster		3	6		
Luster, Marv	Football		5	14		1990 Canadian HOF
Luther, Ted	Golf		50	95		
Luttrell, Lyle	Baseball		4	14		Debut 1956
Lutz, Bob	Tennis		15	30		
Lutz, Joe	Baseball		4	15		Debut 1951
Luyendyk, Arie	Auto Racing		9	22		
Luzinski, Greg	Baseball		4	14		Debut 1970
Luzzi, Don	Football		4	8		1986 Canadian HOF

NAME	CATEGORY	+	SIG	SP	BALL	Comment
Lye, Mark	Golf		5	20	25	
Lyle, Sandy	Golf		10	25	35	
Lyle, Sparky	Baseball		5	20		Debut 1967
Lyman, Link	Football		95	350		1964 HOF
Lynam, Robert	Basketball		3	15		played NBA 67
Lynch, Dick	Football		30	85		NFL
Lynch, Jair	Olympic		3	12		Medal Gymnastics
Lynch, Jerry	Baseball		6	15		Debut 1954
Lyne, Phil	Rodeo		6	14		
Lynn, Fred	Baseball		3	15	25	Debut 1974
Lynn, Janet	Olympic		6	20		Figure skating
Lynn, Lonnie	Basketball		3	18		played NBA 69
Lynn, Michael	Basketball		3	18		played NBA 69-70
Lyon, Russ	Baseball		7	35		Debut 1944
Lyons, Barry	Baseball		3	10		Debut 1986
Lyons, Bill	Baseball		3	10		Debut 1983
Lyons, Ed	Baseball		6	25		Debut 1947
Lyons, George	Baseball		9			Debut 1920 Cards
Lyons, Steve	Baseball		3	10		Debut 1985
Lyons, Ted	Baseball		10	80	235	HOF 1955.P-S HOF $300
Lyons, Ted	Baseball		30	85		Gold Pl.$40,B&W PC $65
Lyssenko, Tatiana	Olympic		7	35		Gold Medal. Gymnastics
Lyttle, Jim	Baseball		3	12		Debut 1969 Yankees

Maas, Kevin	Baseball		4	12		Debut 1990
Macaluso, Michael	Basketball		3	15		played NBA 73
Macauley, Ed "Easy"	Basketball		7	25		HOF 1960
MacCann, Catherine	Golf		10	35		
Macdonald, C.B.	Golf		325	775		
MacDonald, Robert	Golf		85	195		
Macfarlane, Mike	Baseball		3	10		Debut 1987
MacFarlane, Willie	Golf		450	995		
MacFie, Allen	Golf		525	1250		
Macha, Ken	Baseball		3	12		Debut 1974
Machemer, Dave	Baseball		3	12		Debut 1978
MacInnis, Allan	Hockey		3	18		
Macionis, John	Olympic		4	8		Swim relay
Mack, Connie	Baseball		184	350	1000	HOF 1937.B&W PC $625
Mack, Joe	Baseball		7	25		Debut 1945
Mack, Ollie	Basketball		3	12		played NBA 79-81
Mack, Shane	Baseball		4	15		Debut. 1987
Mackall, Michelle	Golf		5	20	25	
Mackanin, Pete	Baseball		3	12		Debut 1973

NAME	CATEGORY	+	SIG	SP	BALL	Comment
MacKay, Mickey	Hockey		80	325		1952 HOF fwd
Mackay, Pauline	Golf		95	195		
Mackenzie, Alister	Golf		750	1500		
MacKenzie, Eric	Baseball		3	15		Debut 1955
MacKenzie, Gordon	Baseball		3	15		Debut 1961
Mackey, Cindy	Golf		5	20	25	
Mackey, John	Football		6	18	85	1992 HOF end/WB
Mackie, Issac	Golf		35	75		
Mackiewicz, F.T. "Felix"	Baseball		4	35		Debut 1941 A's
Macklin, Rudy	Basketball		3	10		played NBA 81-83
Macknowski, John	Basketball		10	50		played NBA 48-50
Macko, Steve	Baseball		18	60		Debut 1979
MacLean, John	Hockey		4	18		
MacLean, Paul	Hockey		4	15		
MacLeish, Rick	Hockey		5	20		
MacLellan, Brian	Hockey		3	15		
MacLeod, Robert	Football		6	25		CHOF Dartmouth
MacMitchell, Leslie	Track		6	18		
Macomber, Bart	Football	+	22	65		CHOF Illinois
Macon, Max	Baseball		20	50		Debut 1938 Cards
MacPhail, Larry S. Jr.	Baseball		15	30		HOF 1998 Owner
MacPhail, Larry S. Sr.	Baseball		15	30	1650	Debut 1947 HOF 1998
Macpherson, Wendy	Bowling		2	10		Leading money winner
MacTavish, Craig	Hockey		4	18		
Macy, Kyle	Basketball		3	12		played NBA 80-86
Madden, John	Football		6	20	150	NFL Coach
Madden, John	Horse Racing					HOF 1983 trainer
Maddern, Clarence	Baseball		20	55		Debut 1946
Maddix, Ray	Baseball		8	20		1949-50, Negro League
Maddox, Elliott	Baseball		3	12		Debut 1970
Maddox, Garry	Baseball		3	12		Debut 1972
Maddox, Jack	Basketball		10	45		played NBA 46-53
Maddox, Jerry	Baseball		3	12		Debut 1978
Maddux, Greg	Baseball		6	30		Debut 1986
Madigan, Slip	Football	+	35	125		1974 CHOF coach
Madill, Maureen	Golf		5	20	25	
Madison, Helene	Olympic		10	32		Swim relay
Madison, Scotti	Baseball		3	10		Debut 1985
Madlock, Bill	Baseball		8	18		Debut 1973
Madrid, Sal	Baseball		25	65		Debut 1947
Maegle, Dick	Football		7	22		CHOF Rice
Magadan, Dave	Baseball		3	10		Debut 1986
Magee, Andrew	Golf		5	20	25	
Mager, Norman	Basketball		10	45		played NBA 50
Maggard, Dave	Olympic		5	10		Shot Put
Maggert, Jeff	Golf		5	20	25	
Maginnes, John	Golf		5	20	25	
Magley, David	Basketball		3	10		played NBA 82
Maglie, Sal	Baseball		25	65		Debut 1945 NY Giants
Magnussen, Karen	Olympic		6	16		Figure skating
Magrane, Joe	Baseball		5	15		Debut 1987
Maguire, Edith	Olympic		3	9		Track sprints
Maguire, Jack	Baseball		4	25		Debut 1950
Mahaffey, John	Golf		5	25	35	
Mahaffey, Randy	Basketball		3	18		played NBA 67-70
Mahan, Art	Baseball		4			Debut 1940 Phillies

NAME	CATEGORY	+	SIG	SP	BALL	Comment
Mahan, Larry	Rodeo		6	20		
Mahan, Ned	Football	+	15	45		CHOF Harvard
Maher, Danny	Horse Racing		5	15		HOF 1955 jockey
Mahlberg, Greg	Baseball		3	12		Debut 1978
Mahler, John	Auto Racing		9	18		
Mahnken, John	Basketball		10	50		played NBA 45-52
Mahoney, Bob	Baseball		3			Debut 1951 ChiSox
Mahoney, Brian	Basketball		3	18		played NBA 72
Mahoney, Francis	Basketball		10	45		played NBA 52-53
Mahoney, Jim	Baseball		3	15		Debut 1959
Mahorn, Rick	Basketball		4	18		played NBA 80-90
Mahovlich, Frank	Hockey		7	22	28	1981 HOF fwd
Mahovlich, Pete	Hockey		6	18		
Mahre, Phil	Olympic		8	18		Alpine Skiing
Mahre, Steve	Olympic		6	16		Alpine Skiing
Maier, Bob	Baseball		9			Debut 1945 Tigers
Maier, Hermann	Skiing		4	25		Olymp.Gold Alpine Skiing
Majerle, Dan	Basketball		5	25		played NBA 88-
Majerus, Rick	Basketball		3	8		Utah Coach
Majeski, Hank	Baseball		9	40		Debut 1939 Bost. Braves
Majkowski, Don	Football		5	15		NFL
Majoli, Iva	Tennis		4	20		Beat Hingis
Majors, John	Football		6	15		CHOF Tennessee
Makarov, Sergei	Hockey		6	30		
Maki, Chico	Hockey		4	22		
Maki, Wayne	Hockey		4	18		
Mako, Gene	Tennis		6	20		HOF 1973
Malamed, Lionel	Basketball		10	50		played NBA 48
Malarcher, Dave	Baseball		90	225		Player-Manager, Negro League
Malarchuk, Clint	Hockey		4	18		
Malavasi, Ray	Football		9	24		NFL
Maldonado, Candy	Baseball		3	12		Debut 1981
Maleeva, Katerina	Tennis		7	16		
Maleeva, Magdalena	Tennis		5	20		
Maler, Bob	Baseball		4	22		Debut 1945
Maler, Jim	Baseball		3	10		Debut 1981
Malinosky, Tony	Baseball		20	55		Debut 1937
Malkmus, Bobby	Baseball		4	18		Debut 1957
Mallett, Jerry	Baseball		3	15		Debut 1959
Mallon, Les	Baseball		10	38		Debut 1931 Phillies
Mallon, Meg	Golf		10	25	35	
Mallonee, H.B. Ben	Baseball		8			Debut 1921 A's
Mallory, Jim	Baseball		6	24		Debut 1940 Senators
Mallory, Sheldon	Baseball		3	12		Debut 1977
Mallory, William	Football	+	25	100		CHOF Yale
Malmberg, Harry	Baseball		20	50		Debut 1955
Malone, Eddie	Baseball		6	20		Debut 1949
Malone, Jeff	Basketball		5	16		played NBA 83-
Malone, Joe	Hockey		90	200		1950 HOF fwd
Malone, Karl	Basketball		10	38	150	played NBA 85-
Malone, Maicel	Olympic		3	6		Gold Medal. Track
Malone, Mark	Football		3	10		NFL
Malone, Moses	Basketball		10	40		played NBA 74-
Maloney, Jim	Baseball		7			Debut 1960 Cin. Reds
Maloney, Jim	Horse Racing		4	22		HOF 1989 trainer
Malovic, Steve	Basketball		3	10		played NBA 79

NAME	CATEGORY	+	SIG	SP	BALL	Comment
Maloy, Michael	Basketball		3	15		played NBA 70-72
Maltbie, Roger	Golf		5	20	25	
Malzone, Frank	Baseball		5	15		Debut 1955
Mamiit, Cecil	Tennis		3	6		1996 NCAA Champion
Manakas, Theodore	Basketball		3	12		played NBA 73
Mancha, Vaughn	Football		6	18		CHOF Alabama
Mancini, Ray "Boom Boom"	Boxing		12	25		Lt.-Wt Champ
Mancuso, Frank	Baseball		8	22		Debut 1944 Browns
Mancuso, Gus	Baseball		15			Debut 1928 Cards
Mandell, Sammy	Boxing		10	20		
Mandic, John	Basketball		10	50		played NBA 47-49
Mandlikova, Hana	Tennis		7	24		HOF 1994
Manero, Tony	Golf		225	475		
Mangan, Jim	Baseball		4	18		Debut 1952
Mangiapane, Frank	Basketball		10	50		played NBA 46
Mangrum, Lloyd	Golf		95	225		Old PGA HOF 1964
Mangrum, Ray	Golf		45	90		
Maniago, Cesare	Hockey		4	18		
Mankowski, Phil	Baseball		3	10		Debut 1976
Manley, Elizabeth	Olympic		7	22		Figure skating
Mann, Ben	Baseball		6	20		Debut 1944
Mann, Carol	Golf		10	30	35	LPGA HOF 1977
Mann, Gerald	Football	+	7	25		CHOF Southern Methodist
Mann, Ralph	Olympic		6	25		Hurdles
Mann, Shelley	Olympic		10	25		Swim/100 Butterfly
Manning, Archie	Football		6	18		CHOF Mississippi
Manning, Danny	Basketball		5	18		played NBA 88-
Manning, Ed	Basketball		3	12		played NBA 67-75
Manning, Guy	Basketball		4	15		played NBA 67-68
Manning, Madeline	Olympic		4	18		Track 800 meters
Manning, Peyton	Football		5	28		Tennessee QB
Manning, Rick	Baseball		3	10		Debut 1975
Mannion, Pace	Basketball		3	10		played NBA 83-88
Manno, Don	Baseball		7	25		Debut 1940 Bost. RedSox
Manrique, Fred	Baseball		3	10		Debut 1981
Mansell, Nigel	Auto Racing		6	25		
Manske, Edgar	Football		7	22		CHOF Northwestern
Mantha, Moe	Hockey		5	18		
Mantha, Sylvia	Hockey		65	175		1960 HOF def
Mantilla, Felix	Baseball		4	15		Debut 1956
Mantis, Nicholas	Basketball		4	25		played NBA 59-62
Mantle, Mickey	Baseball					HOF 1974.P-S HOF $350
Mantle, Mickey	Baseball		85	150	225	Gold Pl. $80.Grt.Mo.$200
Manuel, Chuck	Baseball		3	12		Debut 1969 Minn.
Manuel, Jerry	Baseball		3	10		Debut 1975
Manush, Heinie	Baseball		80	300	2325	HOF 1964.Gold Pl.S $375
Manwaring, Kirt	Baseball		3	10		Debut 1987
Mapes, Cliff	Baseball		7	28		Debut 1948 Yankees
Maple, Howard	Baseball		35	85		Debut 1932
Maples, Ellis	Golf		5	30	25	
Mara, Tim	Football	+	225	450		1963 HOF contributor
Mara, Wellington	Football		5	15	75	NFL Owner NY Giants
Maradona, Diego	Soccer		5	22		
Maranda, Geroges	Baseball		3			Debut 1960 S.F. Giants
Maranville, Rabbit	Baseball		347	450	2000	HOF 1954
Maravich, "Pistol Pete"	Basketball	+	70	150	475	Signed "Pistol Pete" only

NAME	CATEGORY	+	SIG	SP	BALL	Comment
Maravich, Pete	Basketball	+	130	285	600	HOF 1986
Maravich, Press	Basketball		15	45		played NBA 45-46
Marberry, Firpo	Baseball		55	130		Debut 1923
Marble, Alice	Tennis	+	40	85		HOF 1964
Marbury, Stephon	Basketball		12	30	125	NBA
Marcenac, Jean	Auto Racing	+	25	70		
Marchetti, Gino	Football		7	22	85	1972 HOF DL
Marchibroda, Ted	Football		5	15		NFL
Marciano, Rocky	Boxing		325	700		1952-55 H-Wt Champ
Marciniak, Michelle	Basketball		2	8		Women's ABL
Marcis, Dave	Auto Racing		5	10		
Marcol, Chester	Football		3	9		NFL
Marcum, Johnny	Baseball		15	40		Debut 1933 A's
Mariaschin, Saul	Basketball		10	50		played NBA 47
Marichal, Juan	Baseball					HOF 1983.P-S HOF $25
Marichal, Juan	Baseball		10	25	30	Gold Pl. $12.Grt.Mo.$25
Marin, Jack	Basketball		5	18		played NBA 66-76
Marino, Dan	Football		12	50	250	NFL
Marino, Hank	Bowling	+	22	65		1941 ABC HOF
Marion, Marty	Baseball		7	20		Debut 1940 Cards
Marion, Red	Baseball		8	32		Debut 1935
Maris, Roger	Baseball		110	312		Debut 1957
Mariucci, John	Hockey	+	10	28		1973 US HOF
Markland, Gene	Baseball		4			Debut 1950 A's
Markov, Vic	Football		7	22		CHOF Washington
Marlatt, Harvey	Basketball		3	18		played NBA 70-72
Marnie, Hal	Baseball		7	30		Debut 1940
Marotte, Gilles	Hockey		4	18		
Marquard, Rube	Baseball		40	140	700	HOF 1971. Gold Pl. $70
Marquez, Luis	Baseball		25	55		Debut 1951
Marquis, Bob	Baseball		4	22		Debut 1953 Cin. Reds
Marquis, Roger	Baseball		4	22		Debut 1955
Marr, Dave	Golf		5	25	25	
Marrs, Mabel	Bowling		5	15		1979 Women's IBC HOF
Marsh, Eric	Basketball		3	14		played NBA 77
Marsh, Fred	Baseball		4	22		Debut 1949 Cleve.
Marsh, Graham	Golf		5	25		
Marsh, James	Basketball		3	15		played NBA 71
Marshall, Bobb	Football	+	22	70		CHOF Minnesota
Marshall, Charlie	Baseball		8	35		Debut 1941
Marshall, Dave	Baseball		3	15		Debut 1967
Marshall, George Preston	Football	+	150	500		1963 HOF contributor
Marshall, Henry	Football		3	12		NFL
Marshall, Jack	Hockey		100	230		1965 HOF fwd
Marshall, Jim	Baseball		3	18		Debut 1958
Marshall, Jim	Football		7	20		NFL
Marshall, Keith	Baseball		3	12		Debut 1973
Marshall, Leonard	Football		4	10		NFL
Marshall, Max	Baseball		7	30		Debut 1942
Marshall, Mike	Auto Racing		5	10		
Marshall, Mike	Baseball		4	12		Debut 1981
Marshall, Rube (Roy) "Cy"	Baseball		12			Debut 1912 Phillies
Marshall, Tom	Basketball		7	40		played NBA 54-58
Marshall, Vester	Basketball		3	15		played NBA 73
Marshall, Willard	Baseball		8	30		Debut 1942 NY Giants
Marsikova, Regina	Tennis		6	14		

NAME	CATEGORY	+	SIG	SP	BALL	Comment
Marston, Max	Golf		125	250		
Marti, Fred	Golf		10	35		
Martin, Alastair	Tennis		5	20		HOF 1973
Martin, Babe	Baseball		7	25		Debut 1944
Martin, Billy	Baseball		65	125		Debut 1950
Martin, Bob	Golf		465	950		
Martin, Brian	Basketball		3	10		played NBA 85
Martin, Casey	Golf		6	25		Handicapped Golfer
Martin, Curtis	Football		6	22	125	NFL
Martin, Don	Basketball		10	50		played NBA 46-48
Martin, Donald	Basketball		10	50		played NBA 46-47
Martin, Doug	Golf		5	20	25	
Martin, Eric	Football		8	12		NFL
Martin, Fernando	Basketball		3	18		played NBA 86
Martin, Frank	Horse Racing		3	12		HOF 1981 trainer
Martin, Fred	Baseball		4			Debut 1946 Phillies
Martin, Harvey	Football		5	15		NFL
Martin, Hersh	Baseball		18	45		Debut 1937 Phillies
Martin, Hutt	Golf		10	35		
Martin, J. C.	Baseball		3	15		Debut 1959 ChiSox
Martin, Jerry	Baseball		3	12		Debut 1974
Martin, Jim	Football		7	22		NFL
Martin, Joe	Baseball		25			ML 1 year. 1903
Martin, LaRue	Basketball		5	18		played NBA 72-75
Martin, Mark	Auto Racing		4	15		
Martin, Maurice	Basketball		3	10		played NBA 86-87
Martin, Pepper	Baseball		110	285		Debut 1928
Martin, Philip	Basketball		8	45		played NBA 54
Martin, Pit	Hockey		5	20		
Martin, Rick	Hockey		5	22		
Martin, Rod	Football		4	12		NFL
Martin, Ronald	Basketball		4	30		played NBA 61
Martin, Slater	Basketball		9	32		HOF 1981
Martin, Stu	Baseball		8	32		Debut 1936 Cards
Martin, Sylvia Wene	Bowling		5	18		1966 Women's IBC HOF
Martin, Todd	Tennis		4	20		
Martin, William	Basketball		3	10		played NBA 85-87
Martindale, Bill	Golf		10	35		
Martinez, Buck	Baseball		3	12		Debut 1969
Martinez, Carmelo	Baseball		3	12		Debut 1983
Martinez, Conchita	Tennis		7	16		
Martinez, Dave	Baseball		3	10		Debut 1986
Martinez, Dennis	Baseball		7	38		Debut 1976
Martinez, Edgar	Baseball		7	35		Debut 1987
Martinez, James	Olympic		3	6		Wrestling
Martinez, Jose	Baseball		3			Debut 1969 Pirates
Martinez, Mario	Olympic		3	8		Weightlifting
Martinez, O. "Marty"	Baseball		4			Debut 1969 Hou. Astro
Martinez, Pedro	Baseball		7	30		Cy Young winner
Martinez, Tino	Baseball		5	35		Debut 1990
Martino, Angel	Olympic		3	8		Gold Med. Swimming
Martino, John	Bowling	+	10	28		1969 ABC HOF
Martorella, Millie	Bowling		5	15		1975 Women's IBC HOF
Marty, Joe	Baseball		15	42		Debut 1937
Martyn, Bob	Baseball		4	10		Debut 1957
Martz, Gary	Baseball		3	10		Debut 1975

NAME	CATEGORY	+	SIG	SP	BALL	Comment
Maruk, Dennis	Hockey		5	22		
Marvin, Cal	Hockey		5	10		1982 US HOF admin
Marvin, John	Olympic		3	6		Yachting
Maryland, Russell	Football		3	12		NFL
Marzano, John	Baseball		3	10		Debut 1987
Marzich, Andy	Bowling		5	10		1990 PBA, '93 ABC HOF
Masamino, Rollie	Basketball		5	15		Veteran Coach
Mashburn, Jamaal	Basketball		8	22	100	NBA Mavs
Mashburn, Jesse	Olympic		3	7		Track relays
Mashore, Clyde	Baseball		3	10		Debut 1969
Masi, Phil	Baseball		10	24		Debut 1939 Bost. Braves
Masino, Alfred	Basketball		10	45		played NBA 52-53
Mason, Don	Baseball		3	15		Debut 1966
Mason, Jim	Baseball		3	12		Debut 1971
Mason, Tommy	Football		5	16		NFL
Massa, Gordon	Baseball		3	15		Debut 1957
Massengale, Don	Golf		5	20	25	
Massengale, Rick	Golf		5	20	25	
Massey, Debbie	Golf		5	20	25	
Massy, Arnaud	Golf		175	350		
Mast, Edward	Basketball		3	15		played NBA 70-72
Master, Edith	Olympic		3	6		Equestrian
Masterson, Paul "Lefty"	Baseball		5			Debut 1949 A's
Masterson, Walt	Baseball		8			Debut 1939 Senators
Masterton, Bill	Hockey		30	150		Fatally Injured in Game
Matarazzo, Len	Baseball		3			Debut 1952 A's
Matchefts, John	Hockey		5	10		1991 US HOF
Matchick, Tom	Baseball		3	10		Debut 1967
Mathews, Eddie	Baseball					P-S HOF $25,Grt.Mo.$30
Mathews, Eddie	Baseball		10	22	30	Gold Pl. $15. HOF 1978
Mathews, Nelson	Baseball		3	15		Debut 1960
Mathewson, Christy	Baseball		1450	4000	13000	HOF 1936
Mathias, Bob	Olympic		7	25		Decathlon
Mathis, Bill	Football		4	14		NFL
Mathis, Buster, Sr.	Boxing		8	20		Fought Ali & Frazier
Mathis, John	Basketball		3	15		played NBA 67
Matias, John	Baseball		3	12		Debut 1970
Matson, Len	Golf		10	25		
Matson, Ollie	Football		7	20	85	1972 HOF RB
Matson, Randy	Olympic		6	20		Shot Put
Matte, Tom	Football		6	18		NFL
Matthes, Roland	Olympic		10	35		Swim/100 M Back.
Matthews, Bruce	Football		3	8		NFL
Matthews, Gary	Baseball		3	12		Debut 1972
Matthews, Merle	Bowling	+	8	20		1974 Women's IBC HOF
Matthews, Ray	Football		7	25		CHOF Texas Christian
Matthews, Sir Stanley	Soccer		15	45		
Matthews, Vince	Olympic		6	18		400 Meters
Matthews, Wes	Basketball		3	12		played NBA 80-87
Mattiace, Len	Golf		5	20	25	
Mattick, Bobby	Baseball		8	38		Debut 1938
Mattingly, Don	Baseball		10	40		Debut 1982
Matuszak, John	Football		30	70	175	NFL
Matuszek, Len	Baseball		3	10		Debut 1981
Matuzak, Harry G.	Baseball		4			Debut 1934 A's
Mauch, Gene	Baseball		4	15		Debut 1944

NAME	CATEGORY	+	SIG	SP	BALL	Comment
Maughan, Ariel	Basketball		10	50		played NBA 46-50
Maulbetsch, John	Football	+	15	50		CHOF Michigan
Maura, McHugh	Basketball		2	5		Women's ABL-Coach
Mauro, Carmen	Baseball		8	25		Debut 1948
Mauthe, Pete	Football	+	18	55		CHOF Penn State
Mavis, Bob	Baseball		6	22		Debut 1949
Maxim, Joey	Boxing		12	25		Lt.Hvy-Wt Champ
Maxvill, Dal	Baseball		5	15		Debut 1962 Cards(4 W.S.)
Maxwell, Billy	Golf		10	35	35	
Maxwell, Cedric	Basketball		6	15		played NBA 77-87
Maxwell, Charlie	Baseball		4	18		Debut 1950
Maxwell, Fred	Hockey		40	145		1962 HOF fwd
Maxwell, Norman	Golf		55	125		
Maxwell, Robert	Football	+	22	70		CHOF Swarthmore
Maxwell, Robert	Golf		450	1395		
Maxwell, Vernon	Basketball		3	10		played NBA 88-
May, Carlos	Baseball		3	12		Debut 1968
May, Dave	Baseball		3	12		Debut 1967
May, Donald	Basketball		3	15		played NBA 68-74
May, George	Golf		65	125		
May, Jerry	Baseball		3	12		Debut 1964
May, Lee	Baseball		4	16		Debut 1965
May, Merrill	Baseball		7	25		Debut 1939
May, Milt	Baseball		3	12		Debut 1972
May, Scott	Basketball		3	10		played NBA 76-82
May, William L.	Olympic		3	8		Hurdles
Mayasich, John	Hockey		5	12		1976 US HOF
Maybank, Anthuan	Olympic		3	6		Gold Medal. Track
Mayberry, John	Baseball		4	12		Debut 1968 Houston
Maye, Lee	Baseball		7	18		Debut 1959 Mil.
Mayer, Dick	Golf		10	35		
Mayes, Clyde	Basketball		3	15		played NBA 75-76
Mayfair, Billy	Golf		5	20	25	
Mayfield, Ken	Basketball		3	15		played NBA 75
Mayfield, Shelley	Golf		10	35		
Mayfield, William	Basketball		3	10		played NBA 80
Maynard, Buster	Baseball		30	85		Debut 1940
Maynard, Don	Football		7	20	125	1987 HOF end/WR
Mayo, Charles Jr.	Golf		35	85		
Mayo, Eddie	Baseball		15	55		Debut 1936
Mayo, Jackie	Baseball		7	28		Debut 1948
Mayo, Paul	Golf		5	20	25	
Mayotte, Tim	Olympic		3	9		Medalist Tennis
Mayotte, Tim	Tennis		10	22		
Mays, Carl	Baseball		85	228		Debut 1915
Mays, Rex	Auto Racing	+	165	400		
Mays, Willie	Baseball					HOF 1979. P-S HOF $70
Mays, Willie	Baseball		22	45	55	Gold Pl. $40.Grt.Mo.$35
Mazeroski, Bill	Baseball		6	18		Debut 1956
Mazza, Matthew	Basketball		10	50		played NBA 49
Mazzera, Mel	Baseball		10	42		Debut 1935
Mazzilli, Lee	Baseball		3	10		Debut 1976
McAdoo, Bob	Basketball		8	22		played NBA 72-85
McAfee, George	Football		7	20	85	1966 HOF RB
McAnally, Ernie	Baseball		4			Debut 1971 Montreal
McAnally, Ron	Horse Racing					HOF 1990 trainer

NAME	CATEGORY	+	SIG	SP	BALL	Comment
McAnany, Jim	Baseball		3	12		Debut 1958
McArthur, O.A. "Dixie"	Baseball		10			Debut 1914 Pittsburgh
McAtee, Linus	Horse Racing					HOF 1956 jockey
McAuliffe, Dick	Baseball		3	16		Debut 1960
McAvoy, Tom	Baseball		4			Debut 1959 Senators
McBee, Rives	Golf		5	20	25	
McBreen, Tom	Olympic		3	7		Swim/400 free
McBride, Bake	Baseball		3	10		Debut 1973
McBride, Bertha	Bowling	+	8	20		1968 Women's IBC HOF
McBride, George	Baseball		55	125		Debut 1901
McBride, Ken	Baseball		7	30		Debut 1959 ChiSox
McBride, Kenneth	Basketball		10	40		played NBA 54
McBride, Tom	Baseball		7	28		Debut 1943
McBrien, Harry	Football	+	10	22		1978 Canadian HOF
McCabe, Joe	Baseball		3	12		Debut 1964
McCafferty, Don	Football		15	50		NFL
McCaffrey, Jimmy	Football	+	10	22		1967 Canadian HOF
McCahan, Bill	Baseball		5			Debut 1946 A's
McCall, Brian	Baseball		3	15		Debut 1962
McCall, J.W. "Windy"	Baseball		9			Debut 1948 Bost. RedSox
McCall, Oliver	Boxing		10	20		
McCallister, Blaine	Golf		5	20	25	
McCallister, Bob	Golf		10	35		
McCallum, Mike	Boxing		8	18		
McCance, Ches	Football	+	10	22		1976 Canadian HOF
McCann, Bill	Baseball					
McCann, Brendan	Basketball		6	25		played NBA 57-59
McCann, Dave	Football	+	10	22		1966 Canadian HOF
McCarron, Chris	Horse Racing		10	35		HOF 1989 jockey
McCarron, Michael	Basketball		10	50		played NBA 46-49
McCarron, Scott	Golf		5	20	25	
McCartan, Jack	Hockey		5	18		1983 US HOF
McCarter, Andre	Basketball		3	15		played NBA 76-80
McCarter, Willie	Basketball		3	15		played NBA 69-71
McCarthy, Alex	Baseball		45	90		Debut 1910 Pitt. Pirates
McCarthy, Clem	Broadcaster	+	35	85		1970 Ntl S&S HOF
McCarthy, Joe	Baseball		35	150	1000	HOF 1957.Gold Pl. $85
McCarthy, Joe	Baseball		50	175		B&W PC $100
McCarthy, John	Baseball		40	95		Debut 1934
McCarthy, John	Basketball		7	30		played NBA 56-63
McCarthy, Tom	Baseball		1733	4500		Debut 1908. HOF 1946
McCarthy,Tommy	Hockey		7	25		
McCartney, Bill	Football		5	20		Colorado;Promise Keeper
McCarty, Howard	Basketball		10	50		played NBA 45-46
McCarver, Tim	Baseball		4	15		Debut 1959 Cards
McCary, Nikki	Basketball		3	15		Women's NBA
McCaskill, Kirk	Baseball		4	12		Debut
McClain, Dwayne	Basketball		3	10		played NBA 85
McClain, Katrina	Olympic		2	8		2x Gold Med. Basketball
McClain, Theodore	Basketball		3	15		played NBA 71-78
McClendon, Charley	Football		6	6		1986 CHOF coach
McClendon, Lloyd	Baseball		3	10		Debut 1987 1985
McClinton, Curtis	Football		7	18		NFL
McCloskey, Jack	Basketball		10	45		played NBA 52
McClung, Thomas	Football		25	85		CHOF Yale
McCluskey, Roger	Auto Racing		9	22		

NAME	CATEGORY	+	SIG	SP	BALL	Comment
McColl, Alex	Baseball		4			Debut 1933 Senators
McColl, Bill	Football		6	25		CHOF Stanford
McConathy, John	Basketball		10	45		played NBA 51
McConnell, Bucky	Basketball		10	45		played NBA 52
McConnell, George	Baseball		100			Debut 1909
McCord, Gary	Golf		10	20	25	
McCord, Keith	Basketball		3	10		played NBA 80
McCormack, Don	Baseball		3	10		Debut 1980
McCormack, Mark	Agent		3	6		
McCormack, Mark	Golf		10	25	25	
McCormack, Mike	Football		5	18	85	1984 HOF OL
McCormick, Frank	Baseball		25	60		Debut 1934 Reds
McCormick, Jim	Football	+	20	75		CHOF Princeton
McCormick, Kelly	Olympic		3	14		Diving
McCormick, Mike	Baseball		30	85		Debut 1940
McCormick, Pat	Olympic		6	20		4 Diving Golds
McCormick, Tim	Basketball		3	10		played NBA 84-
McCorrey, Bill	Baseball		30			Debut 1909 Browns
McCosky, Barney	Baseball		11	30		Debut 1939 Tigers
McCovey, Willie	Baseball		10	25	150	HOF 1986.Gold Pl.S $15
McCovey, Willie	Baseball		15	30		P-S HOF $25,Grt.Mo.$30
McCoy, Al	Boxing		55	125		
McCoy, Benny	Baseball		10	40		Debut 1938
McCrabb, Les	Baseball		5			Debut 1939 A's
McCracken, Branch	Basketball	+	50	125		HOF 1960
McCracken, Herb	Football		6	15		1973 CHOF coach
McCracken, Jack	Basketball	+	20	45		HOF 1962
McCracken, Paul	Basketball		3	15		played NBA 72-76
McCraw, Tcm	Baseball		3	12		Debut 1963 ChiSox
McCray, Carlton	Basketball		3	10		played NBA 83-86
McCray, Rodney	Basketball		3	10		played NBA 83-
McCready, Samuel	Golf		25	65		
McCreary, Conn	Horse Racing		10	20		HOF 1974 jockey
McCrimmon,Brad	Hockey		3	18		
McCrory, Steve	Boxing		8	18		
McCullers, Lance	Baseball		3	10		Debut 1985
McCullough, Clyde	Baseball		15	48		Debut 1940 Cubs
McCullough, Howard	Bowling	+	8	20		1971 ABC HOF-Mer.Serv.
McCullough, John	Basketball		3	10		played NBA 81
McCullough, Mike	Golf		5	20	25	
McCumber, Mark	Golf		5	20	25	
McCune, Don	Bowling		5	10		1991 PBA HOF-Vet.
McCurdy, Harry	Baseball		55	125		Debut 1922
McCutchan, Arad	Basketball		20	50		HOF 1980 Coach
McCutcheon, Floretta	Bowling	+	10	25		1956 Women's IBC HOF
McDaniel, Henry	Horse Racing					HOF 1956 trainer
McDaniel, Mildred	Olympic		4	18		High Jump
McDaniel, Randall	Football		4	15		NFL
McDaniel, Xavier	Basketball		5	18		played NBA 85-
McDaniels, James	Basketball		3	15		played NBA 71-77
McDermott, Bobby	Basketball		6	18		HOF 1987
McDermott, John	Golf		495	975		Old PGA HOF 1940
McDermott, Terry	Baseball		15	15		Debut 1972
McDermott, Terry	Olympic		7	20		500 M Speed Skating
McDonald, Ab	Hockey		4	18		
McDonald, Ben	Baseball		3	12		Debut 1989

NAME	CATEGORY	+	SIG	SP	BALL	Comment
McDonald, Benjamin	Basketball		3	10		played NBA 85-
McDonald, Dave	Baseball		4	12		Debut 1969
McDonald, Glenn	Basketball		3	12		played NBA 74-76
McDonald, Hank	Baseball		5			Debut 1931 A's
McDonald, Jiggs	Broadcaster		3	6		
McDonald, Lanny	Hockey		6	25	30	1992 HOF
McDonald, Rod	Basketball		4	15		played NBA 70-72
McDonald, Tom	Football		7	22		CHOF Oklahoma
McDonnell, Jim	Baseball		7	30		Debut 1943
McDonough, Bill	Golf		5	20	25	
McDonough, Patrick	Olympic		3	6		Cycling
McDougald, Gil	Baseball		5	15		Debut 1951
McDowall, Jack	Football	+	15	40		CHOF North Carolina St.
McDowell, Hank	Basketball		3	10		played NBA 81-86
McDowell, Jack	Baseball		8	30		Debut 1987
McDowell, Marc	Bowling		4	8		
McDowell, Roger	Baseball		6	15		Debut 1985
McDowell, Sam	Baseball		5	12		Debut 1961
McDyess, Antonio	Basketball		4	22		NBA
McElhenny, Hugh	Football		8	22	95	1970 HOF RB
McElroy, James	Basketball		3	15		played NBA 75-81
McElroy, Leland	Football		4	15	75	NFL
McElyea, Frank	Baseball		10	40		Debut 1942
McEnroe, John	Tennis		10	35		
McEver, Gene	Football	+	15	40		CHOF Tennessee
McEvoy, Peter	Golf		5	20	25	
McEwan, John	Football	+	22	45		CHOF Army
McFadden, Banks	Football		6	20		CHOF Clemson
McFadden, Leon	Baseball		3	12		Debut 1968
McFadin, Bud	Football		6	18		CHOF Texas
McFarland, Patrick	Basketball		4	15		played NBA 75-81
McFarlane, Tracy	Olympic		3	6		Swim/relay
McFaull, David	Olympic		3	6		Yachting
McGah, Ed	Baseball		7	20		Debut 1946
McGaha, Fred	Basketball		10	50		played NBA 48
McGann, Michelle	Golf		5	25	35	
McGee, Bill	Baseball		7			Debut 1935 Cards
McGee, Frank	Hockey		250	700		1945 HOF fwd
McGee, Jerry	Golf		5	25	25	
McGee, Max	Football		5	16		NFL
McGee, Michael	Basketball		3	10		played NBA 81-
McGee, Mike	Football		6	15		CHOF Duke
McGee, Willie	Baseball		4	12		Debut 1982
McGeorge, Missy	Golf		5	20	25	
McGhee, Bill	Baseball		7	25		Debut 1944
McGhee, Ed	Baseball		6	25		Debut 1950
McGill, Bill	Basketball		3	20		played NBA 62-69
McGill, Frank	Football	+	10	22		1965 Canadian HOF
McGilvray, Ronnie	Basketball		10	45		played NBA 54
McGimpsey, Garth	Golf		5	20	25	
McGimsie, Billy	Hockey		90	200		1962 HOF fwd
McGinley, Edward	Football	+	22	50		CHOF Pennsylvania
McGinn, Dan	Baseball		3			Debut 1968 Reds
McGinnis, George	Basketball		5	18		played NBA 71-81
McGinnity, Joe	Baseball		1500	5000	9150	HOF 1946
McGlocklin, Jon	Basketball		4	18		played NBA 65-75

NAME	CATEGORY	+	SIG	SP	BALL	Comment
McGovern, Jim	Golf		5	20	25	
McGovern, John	Football	+	38	95		CHOF Minnesota
McGovern, Terry	Boxing		195	350		
McGowan, Bill	Baseball		375	2000	5000	HOF 1992
McGowan, Frank	Baseball		18			Debut 1922 A's
McGowan, Jack	Golf		10	35		
McGowan, Pat	Golf		5	20	25	
McGrady, Tracy	Basketball		5	25		NBA 1st round pick
McGrath, Jack	Auto Racing	+	35	90		
McGrath, Matt	Olympic		10	25		Wld. Rec. Hammer Throw
McGrath, Mike	Bowling		5	10		1988 PBA, '93 ABC HOF
McGraw, Bob	Baseball		15			Debut 1917 Yankees
McGraw, John	Baseball		850	2250	6000	HOF 1937
McGraw, Thurman	Football		6	18		CHOF Colorado State
McGraw, Tug	Baseball		700	1600		Debut 1965
McGregor, Gilbert	Basketball		3	15		played NBA 71
McGriff, Elton	Basketball		4	20		played NBA 67-68
McGriff, Fred	Baseball		5	22		Debut 1986
McGriff, Terry	Baseball		3	10		Debut 1987
McGuff, Joe	Writer		4	8		
McGugin, Don	Football	+	15	35		1951 CHOF coach
McGuigan, Barry	Boxing		25	65		
McGuire, Al	Basketball		6	22		HOF 1992. NBA 51-54
McGuire, Allie	Basketball		3	10		played NBA 73
McGuire, Bill	Baseball		3	10		Debut 1988
McGuire, Dick	Basketball		7	25		HOF 1993. NBA 49-59
McGuire, Frank	Basketball		7	22		HOF 1976
McGuire, Marnie	Golf		5	20	25	
McGuire, Mickey	Baseball		3	15		Debut 1962
McGuire, Willa Worthington	Water Skiing		3	8		
McGwigan, Barry	Boxing		28	65		Fthr-Wt Champ
McGwire, Mark	Baseball		100	220		70 homers '98 ... see page 86!
McHaffie, Deborah	Golf		5	20	25	
McHale, John	Baseball		4	22		Debut 1943
McHale, Kevin	Basketball		5	20		played NBA 80-
McHartley, Maurice	Basketball		4	18		played NBA 67-69
McHenry, Vance	Baseball		3	10		Debut 1981
McIngvale, Cynthia	Olympic		5	12		Diving
McInnis, John "Stuffy"	Baseball		40			Debut 1909
McIntire, Barbara	Golf		10	35	35	
McIntosh, Kennedy	Basketball		3	15		played NBA 71-74
McIntyre, Guy	Football		3	10		NFL
McIntyre, Liz	Olympic		3	14		Olymp.Med.Mogul Ski
McIntyre, Robert	Basketball		4	18		played NBA 67
McKane-Godfree, Kathleen	Tennis		10	25		HOF 1978
McKay, Antonio	Olympic		5	10		400 Meters
McKay, Dave	Baseball		3	12		Debut 1975
McKay, Jim	Broadcaster		6	18		1987 Ntl S&S HOF
McKay, John	Football		8	18		1988 CHOF coach
McKean, Clive	Olympic		5	12		Swim relay
McKechnie, Bill	Baseball		212	375	1975	HOF 1962.B&W PC $500
McKechnie, Walt	Hockey		4	20		
McKee, Charlie	Olympic		3	6		Yachting
McKee, Gerald	Basketball		4	18		played NBA 69
McKee, Tim	Olympic		3	6		Swim/ind. medley
McKeever, Mike	Football	+	22	75		CHOF Southern California

The Sanders Price Guide to Sports Autographs

NAME	CATEGORY	+	SIG	SP	BALL	Comment
McKenna, Kevin	Basketball		3	12		played NBA 81-87
McKenzie, Don	Olympic		4	9		Swim/100 breast
McKenzie, Forrest	Basketball		3	10		played NBA 86
McKenzie, John	Hockey		4	20		
McKenzie, Stan	Basketball		3	12		played NBA 67-73
McKey, Derrick	Basketball		4	12		played NBA 87-
McKim, Josephine	Olympic		5	12		Swim/relay
McKinley, Chuck	Tennis	+	20	65		HOF 1986
McKinney, Horace	Basketball		10	50		played NBA 46-51
McKinney, Rich	Baseball		3	12		Debut 1970
McKinney, Richard	Olympic		3	6		Archery
McKinney, Rigan	Horse Racing					HOF 1968 jockey
McKinney, Tamara	Skiing		6	20		
McKinney, William	Basketball		3	12		played NBA 78-85
McKnight, Jeff	Baseball		3	10		Debut 1989
McKnight, Jim	Baseball		3	15		Debut 1960
McLain, Denny	Baseball		8	22		Debut 1963
McLane, James	Olympic		5	12		Swim/1,500 free
McLaren, Bruce	Auto Racing	+	50	125		HOF 1995
McLaren, George	Football	+	20	60		CHOF Pittsburgh
McLarney, Art	Baseball		5			Debut 1932 NY Giants
McLarnin, Jimmy	Boxing		20	42		Lt.-Wt Champ
McLaughlin, James	Horse Racing					HOF 1955 jockey
McLaughlin, Jeff	Olympic		3	6		Rowing
McLaughlin, Leon	Football		5	15		NFL
McLaughry, Tuss	Football	+	15	35		1962 CHOF coach
McLean, George	Golf		75	150		
McLemore, Mark	Baseball		3	10		Debut 1986
McLemore, McCoy	Basketball		3	18		played NBA 64-71
McLendon, John B.	Basketball		12	25		HOF 1978-Contributor
McLendon, John B., Jr.	Basketball		20	45		
McLendon, Mac	Golf		5	20		
McLeod, Fred	Golf		125	295		Old PGA HOF 1960
McLeod, George	Basketball		10	45		played NBA 52
McLeod, Jim	Baseball		4			Debut 1930 Senators
McLish, Cal	Baseball		8			Debut 1944 Brklyn.Dodg.
McLoughlin, Maurice	Tennis	+	18	40		HOF 1957
McLouglin, Maurice	Tennis		12	25		
McMahon, Jack	Basketball		8	40		played NBA 52-59
McMahon, Jim	Football		7	22		NFL
McMahon, Junie	Bowling	+	12	30		1967 ABC HOF
McMahon, Vince	Promoter		3	12		Wrestling
McMartin, William	Tennis		5	15		HOF 1982
McMath, Jimmy	Baseball		3	15		Debut 1968
McMillan, Don	Football	+	18	45		CHOF Southern Cal/Cal
McMillan, Kathy	Olympic		3	8		Long Jump
McMillan, Nathaniel	Basketball		4	15		played NBA 86-
McMillan, Randy	Football		3	10		NFL
McMillan, Roy	Baseball		8	22		Debut 1951
McMillan, Shannon	Olympic		4	10		US Gold. Soccer
McMillan, Tommy	Baseball		3	12		Debut 1977
McMillen, Tom	Basketball		6	20		played NBA 75-85
McMillian, James	Basketball		4	15		played NBA 70-78
McMillin, Bo	Football	+	55	125		CHOF Centre
McMillon, Shellie	Basketball		8	35		played NBA 58-61
McMullen, John	Golf		10	35		

NAME	CATEGORY	+	SIG	SP	BALL	Comment
McMullen, Kathy	Golf		5	20	25	
McMullen, Ken	Baseball		3	12		Debut 1962 L.A. Dodgers
McMullen, Malcolm	Basketball		10	50		played NBA 49-50
McNab, Peter	Hockey		6	20		
McNabb, Chester	Basketball		10	50		played NBA 47
McNair, Steve	Football		7	22	85	NFL Oilers QB
McNall, Bruce	Hockey		4	12		
McNally, Dave	Baseball		3	15		Debut 1962
McNally, Johnny Blood	Football		45	225	500	1963 HOF RB
McNally, Mike	Baseball		85	195		Debut 1915. Inf Yankees
McNamara, Bob	Baseball		10	45		Debut 1939
McNamara, Bob	Football		4	18		NFL
McNamara, Dick	Football		2	6		NFL
McNamara, Frank	Golf		65	195		
McNamara, George	Hockey		100	275		1958 HOF def
McNamara, John	Baseball		3	8		Coach
McNamara, Julieanne	Olympic		8	40		Gymn./Uneven bars
McNamara, Mark	Basketball		3	10		played NBA 82-89
McNamara, Melissa	Golf		5	20	25	
McNamara, Tim	Baseball		8			Debut 1922 Bost. Braves
McNamara, Tom	Golf		65	195		
McNamee, Graham	Broadcaster		20	45		Radio Sports Legend
McNamee, Graham	Broadcaster	+	25	65		1964 Ntl S&S HOF
McNamee, Joe	Basketball		10	50		played NBA 50-51
McNealy, Christopher	Basketball		3	10		played NBA 85-87
McNeeley, Tom	Boxing		10	20		
McNeely, Earl	Baseball		35	95		Debut 1924
McNeil, Freeman	Football		6	18		NFL
McNeil, Lori	Tennis		4	8		
McNeill, Don	Tennis		5	20		HOF 1965
McNeill, Larry	Basketball		3	15		played NBA 73-78
McNeill, Robert	Basketball		5	30		played NBA 60-61
McNertny, Jerry	Baseball		3	12		Debut 1964
McNulty, Bill	Baseball		3	12		Debut 1969
McNulty, Carl	Basketball		8	40		played NBA 54
McNulty, Mark	Golf		5	25	25	
McPeak, Bill	Football		15	38		NFL
McPeak, Holly "Twin"	Volleyball		2	15		
McPherson, Don	Football		2	7		Maxwell Award
McPherson, Don	Football	+	10	22		1983 Canadian HOF
McPipe, Koy	Basketball		4	18		played NBA 71
McQuarters, Ed	Football		4	8		1988 Canadian HOF
McQueen, Cozell	Basketball		3	10		played NBA 86
McQuillen, Glenn	Baseball		5			Debut 1938 Browns
McQuinn, George	Baseball		18	45		Debut 1936 Cin. Reds
McRae, Basil	Hockey		4	18		
McRae, Hal	Baseball		4	14		Debut 1968
McReynolds, Kevin	Baseball		4	12		Debut 1983
McReynolds, Thales	Basketball		4	18		played NBA 65
McSorley, Marty	Hockey		5	22		
McSpaden, Harold	Golf		75	225		
McWhorter, Bob	Football	+	20	55		CHOF Georgia
McWilliams, Eric	Basketball		3	15		played NBA 72
Meacham, Bobby	Baseball		3	10		Debut 1983
Mead, Charlie	Baseball		7	28		Debut 1943
Meador, Ed	Football		3	15		NFL

NAME	CATEGORY	+	SIG	SP	BALL	Comment
Meadows, Earle	Olympic		18	65		Pole Vault
Meadows, Louie	Baseball		3	10		Debut 1986
Meagher, Mary	Olympic		8	12		Swim/Butterfly
Meagher, Rick	Hockey		4	14		
Meaney, Tom	Writer		3	6		
Means, Natrone	Football		10	35	125	NFL
Meanwell, Walter "Doc"	Basketball	+	18	50		HOF 1959-Coach
Meany, Helen	Olympic		8	22		Diving
Mearns, George	Basketball		10	50		played NBA 46-47
Mears, Rick	Auto Racing		10	35		
Mecir, Miloslav	Olympic		4	10		Gold Medal. Tennis
Medeiros, Ray	Baseball		7	25		Debut 1945
Mediate, Rocco	Golf		5	20	25	
Medica, Jack	Olympic		5	15		Swim/1,500 free
Medina, Luis	Baseball		3	12		Debut 1988
Medwick, Joe	Baseball		77	200	1575	HOF 1968.Gold Pl.S $175
Meeks, Eric	Golf		5	20	25	
Meeks, Sammy	Baseball		7	28		Debut 1948
Meely, Cliff	Basketball		4	15		played NBA 71-75
Mees, Kevin	Baseball		3	10		
Meggett, Dave	Football		4	12		NFL
Mehen, Richard	Basketball		10	50		played NBA 47-51
Mehlhorn, Bill	Golf		75	225	95	
Meier, Dave	Baseball		3	10		Debut 1984
Meineke, Donald	Basketball		10	45		played NBA 52-57
Meinhold, Carl	Basketball		10	50		played NBA 47-48
Meissnitzer, Alexandra	Olympic		3	12		Medalist. Alpine Skiing
Mejias, Rcman	Baseball		7	16		Debut 1955
Melchionni, Gary	Basketball		3	15		played NBA 73-74
Melchionni, William	Basketball		4	15		played NBA 66-74
Mele, Sam	Baseball		5	16		Debut 1947 Bost. RedSox
Melnyk, Steve	Golf		5	20	25	
Meloche, Gilles	Hockey		4	18		
Melton, Bill	Baseball		4	12		Debut 1968
Melton, Dave	Baseball		3	12		Debut 1956
Melvin, Bob	Baseball		3	10		Debut 1985
Melvin, Edward	Basketball		10	50		played NBA 46
Meminger, Dean	Basketball		3	15		played NBA 71-76
Mencel, Chuck	Basketball		7	25		played NBA 55-56
Mendoza, Mike	Baseball		3	12		Debut 1979
Menendez, Luis	Pro Wrestling		5	10		
Mengelt, John	Basketball		3	12		played NBA 71-80
Menke, Denis	Baseball		5	14		Debut 1962 Mil. Braves
Menke, Frank G.	Writer		8	15		Baseball & Sports Writer
Menke, Kenneth	Basketball		10	50		played NBA 47-49
Menne, Catherine	Bowling	+	8	18		1979 Women's IBC HOF
Menno, Jenni & Sand, Todd	Figure Skating		2	15		U.S. Champions
Menosky, Mike	Baseball		15			Debut 1914 Pitt.
Menyard, DeWitt	Basketball		4	18		played NBA 67
Meoli, Rudi	Baseball		3	18		Debut 1971
Mercer, LeRoy	Football	+	20	16		CHOF Pennsylvania
Mercer, Ray	Boxing		12	25		
Mercer, Ron	Basketball		5	25		NBA
Mercer, Sid	Writer		3	50		
Merchant, Andy	Baseball		3	6		Debut 1975
Mercurio, Skang	Bowling	+	8	22		1967 ABC HOF

NAME	CATEGORY	+	SIG	SP	BALL	Comment
Meredith, Don	Football		7	22	110	CHOF Southern Methodist
Meriweather, Joe C.	Basketball		3	12		played NBA 75-84
Meriwether, Porter	Basketball		5	20		played NBA 62
Merkle, Fred	Baseball		300			Major World Series Error
Merrick, Marge	Bowling		5	12		1980 Women's IBC HOF
Merriman, Lloyd	Baseball		6	25		Debut 1949
Merriott, Ron	Olympic		3	7		Diving
Merson, Jack	Baseball		6	22		Debut 1951 Pirates
Merten, Lauri	Golf		5	25	25	
Merullo, Lennie	Baseball		8	35		Debut 1941 Cubs
Merullo, Matt	Baseball		3	10		Debut 1989
Merz, Sue	Olympic		2	7		Olympic Hockey Pioneer
Meschery, Tom	Basketball		4	15		played NBA 61-70
Meskhi, Lelia	Tennis		4	8		
Mesner, Steve	Baseball		18	65		Debut 1938
Messersmith, Andy	Baseball		3	12		Debut 1963
Messier, Mark	Hockey		15	50	55	
Messing, Shep	Soccer		5	18		
Metcalf, Eric	Football		4	15	75	NFL
Metcalf, Terry	Football		3	12		NFL
Metcalfe, Ralph	Olympic		80	225		100 meters
Metheny, Bud	Baseball		7	32		Debut 1943 Yankees
Metkovich, George "Catfish"	Baseball		22	65		Debut 1943 Bost. RedSox
Metras, Johnny	Football	+	10	22		1980 Canadian HOF
Metro, Charlie	Baseball		7	22		Debut 1943 Tigers
Metz, Dick	Golf		45	95	65	
Metzger, Bert	Football	+	22	60		CHOF Notre Dame
Metzger, Roger	Baseball		5	12		Debut 1970
Metzig, Bill	Baseball		7	28		Debut 1944
Metzler, Alex	Baseball		40	95		Debut 1925
Meulens, Hensley "Bam Bam"	Baseball		3	10		Debut 1989
Meusel, Bob	Baseball		42	152		Debut 1920
Meusel, Chuck	Basketball		4	15		NBA
Meusel, Emil F. "Irish"	Baseball	+	175			Debut 1914 for J.McGraw
Meyer, Benny	Baseball		45	125		Debut 1913
Meyer, Bob	Baseball		4			Debut 1964 Yankees
Meyer, Dan	Baseball		3	10		Debut 1974
Meyer, Debbie	Olympic		6	24		Swim/200 M free
Meyer, Dutch	Football	+	25	75		1956 CHOF coach
Meyer, Joey	Baseball		3	10		Debut 1988
Meyer, Louis	Auto Racing		25	65		HOF 1993
Meyer, Ray	Basketball		10	22		HOF 1978-Coach
Meyer, Ron	Football		3	7		NFL
Meyer, Russ	Baseball		7			Debut 1946 Cubs
Meyer, Scott	Baseball		3	10		Debut 1978
Meyer, William	Basketball		3	18		played NBA 67
Meyers, Ann	Basketball		6	20		HOF 1993
Meyers, David	Basketball		4	18		played NBA 75-79
Meyers, Mary	Olympic		4	18		Speed skating
Meyers, Norm	Bowling	+	8	20		1984 ABC HOF
Meyfarth, Ulrike	Olympic		10	32		High Jump
Miasek, Stanley	Basketball		10	50		played NBA 46-52
Miceli, Joe	Boxing		8	16		Welter-Wt Contender
Micelotta, Bob	Baseball		8	22		Debut 1954
Michael, Gene	Baseball		3	12		Debut 1966
Michaels, Al	Broadcaster		2	7		".....Believe in Miracles?"

NAME	CATEGORY	+	SIG	SP	BALL	Comment
Michaels, Cass	Baseball		18	45		Debut 1943 ChiSox
Michaels, Johnny	Baseball		5			Debut 1932 Bost. RedSox
Michaels, Lou	Football		5	15		NFL
Michaels, Ralph	Baseball		22	65		Debut 1924
Michalske, Mike	Football	+	50	175	425	1964 HOF 2-way line
Micheaux, Larry	Basketball		3	10		played NBA 83-84
Mickal, Abe	Football		6	20		CHOF Louisiana State
Mickelson, Ed	Baseball		7	32		Debut 1950
Mickelson, Phil	Golf		10	30	35	
Middlecoff, Cary	Golf		15	30	35	PGA HOF 1986
Middleton, Rick	Hockey		6	22		
Mierkowicz, Ed	Baseball		7	30		Debut 1945
Miggins, Larry	Baseball		7	30		Debut 1948
Mihalic, John	Baseball		18	45		Debut 1935 Senators
Mihalik, Zigmund J."Red"	Basketball		10	50		HOF 1985-Referee
Mikan, Edward	Basketball		10	50		played NBA 48-53
Mikan, George L.	Basketball		15	35	100	HOF 1959
Mikan, George, III	Basketball		3	12		played NBA 70
Mikita, Stan	Hockey		8	28	30	1983 HOF fwd
Mikkelsen, Pete	Baseball		6			Debut 1964 Yankees
Mikkelsen, Vern	Basketball		7	20	125	HOF 1995. NBA 49-58
Mikkiel, Val	Bowling	+	8	18		1979 Women's IBC HOF
Miksis, Al	Basketball		10	50		played NBA 49
Miksis, Eddie	Baseball		8	25		Debut 1944 Brklyn. Dodg.
Milan, Clyde	Baseball		75			Record Stolen Bases '12-
Milbourne, Larry	Baseball		3	10		Debut 1974
Milbrett, Tiffany	Olympic		4	10		US Gold. Soccer
Milburn, Rod	Olympic		7	30		110 Meter hurdles
Miles, Don	Baseball		3	15		Debut 1958
Miles, Eddie	Basketball		3	22		played NBA 63-71
Miles, Jearl	Olympic		3	6		Gold Medal. Track
Miles, Rollie	Football		4	8		1980 Canadian HOF
Miley, Marion	Golf		50	125		
Miley, Mike	Baseball		30	75		Debut 1975
Militzok, Nathan	Basketball		10	50		played NBA 46
Mill, Peter	Golf		5	20	25	
Millan, Felix	Baseball		3	15		Debut 1966
Millard, Keith	Football		3	12		NFL
Millen, Greg	Hockey		3	12		
Miller, Alice	Golf		5	25	25	
Miller, Allen	Golf		10	30		
Miller, Anthony	Football		4	12	75	NFL
Miller, Bill	Football		4	14		NFL
Miller, Bruce	Baseball		3	10		Debut 1973
Miller, Cheryl	Basketball		10	25		HOF 1995
Miller, Chris	Football		6	14		NFL
Miller, Creighton	Football		10	40		CHOF Notre Dame
Miller, Darrell	Baseball		3	10		Debut 1984
Miller, Dean, Dr.	Sports Physician		5	10		
Miller, Dorothy	Bowling	+	12	28		1954 Women's IBC HOF
Miller, Eddie	Baseball		3	10		Debut 1977
Miller, Edwin	Basketball		8	40		played NBA 52-53
Miller, Elmer	Baseball		25	55		Debut 1929
Miller, Eugene	Football	+	20	75		CHOF Penn State
Miller, Fred	Football	+	20	70		CHOF Notre Dame
Miller, Harry	Auto Racing	+	35	85		

NAME	CATEGORY	+	SIG	SP	BALL	Comment
Miller, Harry	Basketball		10	50		played NBA 45
Miller, Inger	Olympic		3	6		Gold Medal. Track
Miller, Jay	Basketball		3	15		played NBA 67-70
Miller, John	Baseball		3	10		Debut 1966 Yankees
Miller, Johnny	Golf		10	30	35	
Miller, Keith	Baseball		3	10		Debut 1987
Miller, Keith	Baseball		3	10		Debut 1988
Miller, Lawrence	Basketball		3	15		played NBA 68-74
Miller, Lemmie	Baseball		3	10		Debut 1984
Miller, Lennox	Olympic		7	20		100 Meters
Miller, MacKenzie	Horse Racing					HOF 1987 trainer
Miller, Marvin	Union Official		12	30		
Miller, Norm	Baseball		3	12		Debut 1965
Miller, Ralph	Basketball		6	12		HOF 1987-Coach
Miller, Red	Football		3	7		NFL
Miller, Reggie	Basketball		12	35	125	played NBA 87-
Miller, Richard	Basketball		3	10		played NBA 80
Miller, Rick	Baseball		5	12		Debut 1971 Bost. RedSox
Miller, Rip	Football		10	40		CHOF Notre Dame
Miller, Robert	Basketball		3	10		played NBA 83
Miller, Shannon	Olympic		10	50		Gymnastics
Miller, Walter	Basketball		20	75		played NBA 37-45
Miller, Walter	Horse Racing					HOF 1955 jockey
Miller, William	Basketball		10	50		played NBA 48
Miller, William	Olympic		6	20		Javelin
Miller, William W.	Olympic		10	38		Pole Vault
Millies, Wally	Baseball		12			Debut 1934 Brklyn. Dodg.
Milligan, Randy	Baseball		3	10		Debut 1987
Millner, Wayne	Football		80	350		1968 HOF end/WB
Millon, Harry	Baseball		8	22		1946-47, Negro League
Mills, Bill	Baseball		8	25		Debut 1944
Mills, Billy	Olympic		8	26		IOK run
Mills, Brad	Baseball		3	10		Debut 1980
Mills, Buster	Baseball		10			Debut 1934 Cards
Mills, Derek	Olympic		3	6		Gold Medal. Track
Mills, Frank L.	Baseball		8			Debut 1914 Cleve. Indians
Mills, Freddie	Boxing		20	50		
Mills, John	Basketball		12	55		played NBA 44-46
Mills, Mary	Golf		5	20	25	
Mills, Phoebe	Olympic		7	25		Gymnastics
Milnar, Al	Baseball		4	9		Debut 1936 Cleve. Indians
Milne, Pete	Baseball		6	22		Debut 1948
Milner, Eddie	Baseball		3	10		Debut 1980
Milner, John	Baseball		3	12		Debut 1971
Milner, Wayne	Football	+	75	150		1968 HOF end/WB
Milosovici, Lavinia	Olympic		7	38		Gold Medal. Gymnastics
Milstead, C.A.	Football	+	15	45		CHOF Wabash/Yale
Milton, DeLisha	Basketball		2	5		Women's ABL
Milton, Tommy	Auto Racing	+	50	165		
Mincher, Don	Baseball		6	18		Debut 1960 Senators
Minds, John	Football	+	25	90		CHOF Pennsylvania
Mingzia, Fu	Olympic		10	50		Gold Medal. Swimming
Minisi, Skip	Football		6	20		CHOF Pennsylvania/Navy
Minniefield, Dirk	Basketball		3	12		played NBA 85-87
Minor, Dave	Basketball		10	45		played NBA 51-52
Minor, Mark	Basketball		3	18		played NBA 72

NAME	CATEGORY	+	SIG	SP	BALL	Comment
Minoso, Minnie	Baseball		7	20		Debut 1949 Cleve. Indians
Minter, Alan	Boxing		12	28		
Miranda, Willie	Baseball		8	25		Debut 1951
Mirer, Rick	Football		5	18	100	NFL
Misaka, Wataru	Basketball		12	65		played NBA 47
Mitchell, Abe	Golf		200	450		
Mitchell, Betsy	Olympic		3	10		Swim/backstroke
Mitchell, Bobby	Baseball		3	10		Debut 1980
Mitchell, Bobby	Football		7	20	85	1983 HOF end/WB
Mitchell, Bobby	Golf		10	35		
Mitchell, Dale	Baseball		10	40		Debut 1946
Mitchell, Jeff	Golf		10	35		
Mitchell, Kevin	Baseball		4	12		Debut 1984
Mitchell, Leland	Basketball		3	18		played NBA 67
Mitchell, Lydell	Football		4	14		NFL
Mitchell, Michael	Basketball		4	14		played NBA 78-87
Mitchell, Michele	Olympic		4	16		Diving
Mitchell, Murray	Basketball		10	50		played NBA 49
Mitchell, Scott	Football		4	15	75	NFL
Mitchell, Stump	Football		3	12		NFL
Mitchell, Todd	Basketball		3	10		played NBA 88-
Mitchell, Willie	Baseball		30			CLE-DET Pitch.1909-'19
Mittermaier, Rosi	Olympic		12	32		Alpine skiing
Mitterwald, George	Baseball		3	12		Debut 1966
Mivelaz, Betty	Bowling		5	10		1991 Women's IBC HOF
Mix, Ron	Football		6	22	85	1979 HOF OL
Mix, Steve	Basketball		4	12		played NBA 69-82
Mize, Johnny	Baseball					P-S HOF $25,Grt.Mo.$35
Mize, Johnny	Baseball		15	35	65	HOF 1981.Gold Pl.S $20
Mize, Larry	Golf		10	25	25	
Mizell, Wilmer "Vinegar Bend"	Baseball		4	14		Debut 1952
Mizerock, John	Baseball		3	10		Debut 1983
Mlkvy, Bill	Basketball		8	45		played NBA 52
Moates, Dave	Baseball		3	10		Debut 1974
Moceanu, Dominique	Olympic		7	55		Olymp.Gold.Gymnastics
Mochrie, Dottie	Golf		10	30	35	
Modak, Mike	Baseball		4			Debut 1945 Cin. Reds
Modano, Mike	Hockey		6	25	30	
Modzelewski, Dick	Football		5	15		NFL
Modzelewski, Ed	Football		5	15		NFL
Moe, Bill	Hockey		5	10		1974 US HOF
Moe, Doug	Basketball		4	18		played NBA 67-71-Coach
Moe, Karen	Olympic		5	15		Swim/butterfly
Moe, Tommy	Olympic		5	28		Olympic Gold.Alpine Skiing
Moeller, Joe	Baseball		3	8		Debut 1962 Dodgers
Moffatt, Alex	Football	+	25	100		CHOF Princeton
Moffett, Larry	Basketball		3	12		played NBA 77
Moffitt, Robert	Golf		5	20	25	
Mogilny, Alexander	Hockey		7	25	30	
Mogus, Leo	Basketball		10	50		played NBA 45-50
Mohns, Doug	Hockey		6	22		
Mokan, Johnny	Baseball		8			Debut 1921 Pirates
Mokeski, Paul	Basketball		3	12		played NBA 79-
Mokray, Bill	Basketball	+	15	35		HOF 1985
Mole, Fenton	Baseball		6	20		Debut 1949
Molinaro, Bob	Baseball		3	12		Debut 1975

NAME	CATEGORY	+	SIG	SP	BALL	Comment
Molinas, Jack	Basketball		10	40		played NBA 53-
Molinski, Ed	Football	+	15	50		CHOF Tennessee
Molis, Wayne	Basketball		3	15		played NBA 66-67
Molitor, Paul	Baseball		7	30		Debut 1978
Mollenkopf, Jack	Football	+	15	35		1988 CHOF coach
Molson, Percy	Football	+	10	22		1963 Canadian HOF
Molter Jr., William	Horse Racing					HOF 1960 trainer
Monacelli, Amleto	Bowler		5	10		1997 PBA HOF
Monchak, Al	Baseball		8	20		Debut 1940 Phillies
Moncrief, Sidney	Basketball		4	15		played NBA 79-
Monday, Kenneth	Olympic		3	6		Wrestling
Monday, Rick	Baseball		3	12		Debut 1966
Mondesi, Raul	Baseball		6	33		
Money, Don	Baseball		3	10		Debut 1968 Phillies
Money, Eric	Basketball		3	12		played NBA 74-83
Monk, Art	Football		6	28	145	NFL
Monroe, Earl "Pearl"	Basketball		7	20	100	HOF 1990
Monson, Don	Basketball		2	6		Coach UO
Montague, John	Golf		50	125		Trick shot hustler
Montana, Joe	Football		20	75	175	NFL
Montgomerie, Colin	Golf		10	25	35	
Montgomery, Bob	Baseball		3	10		Debut 1970
Montgomery, Bob	Boxing		15	30		2x Lt-Wt Champ
Montgomery, Cliff	Football		7	28		CHOF Columbia
Montgomery, Howard	Basketball		3	20		played NBA 62
Montgomery, Jack	Golf		10	35		
Montgomery, Jim	Olympic		5	12		Swim/100 free
Montgomery, Ken	Football	+	10	22		1970 Canadian HOF
Montgomery, Mike	Basketball		2	5		Stanford Coach
Monti, Eric	Golf		15	45		
Montross, Eric	Basketball		8	25		NBA Celtics
Monzon, Carlos	Boxing		25	70		Middle-Wt Champ 1970-77
Monzon, Danny	Baseball		4			Debut 1972 Minn. Twins
Moody, Orville	Golf		5	25	25	
Moog, Andy	Hockey		4	20		
Moomaw, Donn	Football		6	22		CHOF UCLA
Moon, Wally	Baseball		4	16		Debut 1954
Moon, Warren	Football		6	30	125	NFL
Mooney, James	Basketball		8	45		played NBA 52
Mooney, Jim	Baseball		9			Debut 1930 ChiSox
Moore, Andre	Basketball		3	10		played NBA 87
Moore, Archie	Baseball		3	12		Debut 1964
Moore, Archie	Boxing		15	30		Lt.Hvy-Wt Champ
Moore, Bernie	Football	+	15	35		1954 CHOF coach
Moore, Billy	Baseball		3	10		Debut 1986
Moore, Charles	Olympic		3	10		Track relay
Moore, Charlie	Baseball		3	7		Debut 1973
Moore, Davey	Boxing		18	38		Fthr-Wt
Moore, Dee	Baseball		12	42		Debut 1936
Moore, Dickie	Hockey		6	18		1974 HOF fwd
Moore, Eddie	Baseball		40	85		Debut 1923
Moore, Elisabeth	Tennis	+	12	32		HOF 1971
Moore, Eugene	Basketball		3	14		played NBA 68-74
Moore, Frank	Golf		25	60		
Moore, Gene	Baseball		40	90		Debut 1931
Moore, Herman	Football		4	22	100	NFL Reception Leader

NAME	CATEGORY	+	SIG	SP	BALL	Comment
Moore, Jackie	Baseball		3	12		Debut 1965
Moore, Jackie	Basketball		7	38		played NBA 54-56
Moore, James	Olympic		3	6		Pentathlon
Moore, Joe	Baseball		12	32		Debut 1930 NY Giants
Moore, John	Basketball		3	10		played NBA 80-87
Moore, Johnny	Baseball		15	40		Debut 1928 Cubs
Moore, Junior	Baseball		3	10		Debut 1976
Moore, Kelvin	Baseball		3	10		Debut 1981
Moore, Larry	Basketball		5	25		played NBA 67
Moore, Lenny	Football		7	20	85	1975 HOF RB
Moore, Lou	Auto Racing	+	30	75		
Moore, Lowes	Basketball		3	10		played NBA 80-82
Moore, Nat	Football		3	8		NFL
Moore, Otto	Basketball		3	12		played NBA 68-76
Moore, Randy	Baseball		8			Debut 1927 ChiSox
Moore, Richie	Basketball		3	10		played NBA 67
Moore, Ron	Basketball		3	10		played NBA 87
Moore, Scrappy	Football	+	15	35		1980 CHOF coach
Moore, Tad	Golf		10	25		
Moore, Terry	Baseball		10	25		Debut 1935 Cards
Moorehead, Grant	Golf		5	20	25	
Moorer, Michael	Boxing		12	25		
Morales, Jerry	Baseball		4	12		Debut 1969
Morales, Jose	Baseball		3	12		Debut 1973
Morales, Pablo	Olympic		4	18		Swim/butterfly
Morales, Rich	Baseball		3	12		Debut 1967
Moran, Al	Baseball		3	12		Debut 1963
Moran, Billy	Baseball		3	15		Debut 1958
Moran, Gussy	Tennis		12	35		
Moran, Paddy	Hockey		95	260		1958 HOF goal
More, Forrest	Baseball		20	55		Boston, STL Pitch. 1909
Moreau, Janet	Olympic		10	20		Track/100 M relay
Morehart, Ray	Baseball		30	65		Debut 1924
Morehead, Dave	Baseball		10			Debut 1963 Bost. RedSox
Moreland, Jack	Basketball		22	50		played NBA 60-69
Moreland, Keith	Baseball		3	10		Debut 1978
Moren, Lew	Baseball		15			Won 16 for 1909 Phillies
Moreno, Jose	Baseball		3	10		Debut 1980
Moreno, Omar	Baseball		3	10		Debut 1975
Morenz, Howie	Hockey		950	1400		1945 HOF fwd
Morerod, Lise-Marie	Skiing		5	18		Alpine. World Cup Champ
Morgan, Bobby	Baseball		6	17		Debut 1950
Morgan, Chet	Baseball		6			Debut 1935 Tigers
Morgan, Ed	Baseball		12	40		Debut 1928
Morgan, Eddie	Baseball		22	65		Debut 1936
Morgan, Gil	Golf		5	20	25	
Morgan, Joe	Baseball					P-S HOF $25,Grt.Mo.$25
Morgan, Joe	Baseball		8	20	25	HOF 1990. Gold Pl.S $15
Morgan, Joe M.	Baseball		3	6		Debut 1959 Mil.-Phillies
Morgan, Munden	Basketball		3	10		played NBA 82
Morgan, Ralph	Basketball	+	18	55		HOF 1959-Contributor
Morgan, Rex	Basketball		3	15		played NBA 70-71
Morgan, Stanley	Football		5	12		NFL
Morgan, Tom	Baseball		4	10		Debut 1951
Morgan, Vern	Baseball		25	55		Debut 1954
Morgan, Walter	Golf		5	20	25	

NAME	CATEGORY	+	SIG	SP	BALL	Comment
Morgan, Wanda	Golf		75	150		
Morgenthaler, Elmore	Basketball		10	50		played NBA 45-48
Morgenweck, Frank"Pop"	Basketball	+	22	55		HOF 1962
Morhardt, Moe	Baseball		3	15		Debut 1961
Morkis, Dorothy	Olympic		3	6		Eguestrian
Morley, Mike	Golf		5	20	25	
Morley, William	Football	+	20	65		CHOF Columbia
Morman, Russ	Baseball		3	10		Debut 1986
Moronko, Jeff	Baseball		3	10		Debut 1984
Morrall, Earl	Football		6	18	85	NFL
Morris, Bam	Football		4	15	85	NFL
Morris, Betty	Bowling		5	10		1983 Women's IBC HOF
Morris, Christopher	Basketball		3	12		played NBA 88-
Morris, Doyt	Baseball		16	42		Debut 1937
Morris, Frank	Football		4	8		1983 Canadian HOF
Morris, G. Max	Basketball		10	50		played NBA 46-49
Morris, George	Football		6	22		CHOF Georgia Tech
Morris, George	Olympic		5	10		Equestrian
Morris, Glenn	Olympic		40	90		Decathlon
Morris, Hal	Baseball		3	10		Debut 1988
Morris, Jack	Baseball		5	15		Debut 1977
Morris, Joe	Football		6	18		NFL
Morris, John	Baseball		3	10		Debut 1986
Morris, Johnny	Football		5	16		NFL
Morris, Marianne	Golf		5	20	25	
Morris, Mercury	Football		8	20		NFL
Morris, Ronald H.	Olympic		5	12		Pole Vault
Morris, Teddy	Football	+	10	22		1964 Canadian HOF
Morris, Tom	Golf		1500	3500		PGA HOF 1976
Morris, Tom Jr.	Golf		2250	5500		PGA HOF 1975
Morrish, Jay	Golf		5	20	25	
Morrison, Dwight	Basketball		8	40		played NBA 54-57
Morrison, Fred	Golf		15	45		
Morrison, Jim	Baseball		3	10		Debut 1977
Morrison, Joe	Football		20	45		NFL
Morrison, John R.	Basketball		3	18		played NBA 67
Morrison, Ray	Football	+	15	40		1954 CHOF coach
Morrison, Tommy	Boxing		12	25		
Morrow, Bobby	Olympic		6	20		100 M Dash
Morse, John	Golf		5	20	25	
Morton, Bill	Football	+	6	15		CHOF Dartmouth
Morton, Bubba	Baseball		5	15		Debut 1961
Morton, Craig	Football		4	12		NFL
Morton, Richard	Basketball		3	10		played NBA 88
Moryn, Walt	Baseball		8	22		Debut 1954
Mosbacher, Bus	Yachting		5	16		
Mosca, Angelo	Football		5	14		1987 Canadian HOF
Moschitto, Ross	Baseball		3	12		Debut 1965
Mosconi, Willie	Pocket billiards		20	50		
Moscrip, Monk	Football	+	22	55		CHOF Stanford
Mosebar, Don	Football		3	8		NFL
Moseby, Lloyd	Baseball		3	10		Debut 1980
Moseley, Fred	Hockey		5	10		1975 US HOF
Moseley, Jonny	Olympic		3	18		Gold Medal.Mogul Skiing
Moseley, Jonny	Skiing; Freestyle		2	6		World Champion
Moseley, Mark	Football		4	10		NFL

The Sanders Price Guide to Sports Autographs 3rd Edition

NAME	CATEGORY	+	SIG	SP	BALL	Comment
Moses, Edwin	Olympic		20	50		Track/Hurdles
Moses, Gerry	Baseball		3	12		Debut 1965
Moses, Haven	Football		3	10		NFL
Moses, John	Baseball		3	10		Debut 1982
Moses, Wally	Baseball		15	35		Debut 1935 Phil. A's
Mosienko, Bill	Hockey		22	65		1965 HOF fwd
Mosley, Glenn	Basketball		3	10		played NBA 77-78
Mosolf, Jim	Baseball		28	65		Debut 1929
Moss, Charlie	Baseball		12	40		Debut 1934
Moss, Howie	Baseball		10	28		Debut 1942
Moss, Les	Baseball		6	18		Debut 1946 Browns
Moss, Perry	Basketball		3	10		played NBA 85-86
Moss, Stirling	Auto Racing		25	60		
Most, Johnny	Broadcaster		7	22		
Mota, Manny	Baseball		3	12		Debut 1962
Mota, Rosa	Olympic		10	24		Decathlon
Mothersel, Charles	Golf		75	195		
Motley, Darryl	Baseball		3	10		Debut 1981
Motley, Marion	Football		8	22	85	1968 HOF RB
Mott, Bitsy	Baseball		10	28		Debut 1945
Motta, Dick	Basketball		5	15		NBA Kings
Motton, Curt	Baseball		3	12		Debut 1967
Moulds, Eric	Football		4	15	75	NFL
Mount, Rick	Basketball		5	18		played NBA 70-74
Mourning, Alonzo	Basketball		5	25	125	
Mowry, Larry	Golf		5	20	25	
Moyer, Denny	Boxing		12	25		
Moyer, Phil	Boxing		10	20		
Mraz, Jo	Bowling	+	10	22		1959 Women's IBC HOF
Mrazovich, Charles	Basketball		10	50		played NBA 50
Mucha, Barb	Golf		5	20	25	
Mudd, Jodie	Golf		5	25	25	
Mueller, Don	Baseball		8	22		Debut 1948 NY Giants
Mueller, Emmett	Baseball		12	38		Debut 1938
Mueller, Erwin	Basketball		3	18		played NBA 66-73
Mueller, Gordy	Baseball		3			Debut 1950 Bost. RedSox
Mueller, Leah	Olympic		5	12		Speed skating
Mueller, Peter	Olympic		7	25		Alpine skiing
Mueller, Ray	Baseball		10	35		Debut 1935
Mueller, Walter	Baseball		25	65		Debut 1922
Muha, Joe	Football		8	25		NFL
Muhammad, Eddie Mustapha	Boxing		15	32		Lt.Hvy-Wt
Muhammed, Matthew Saad	Boxing		15	35		
Muir, Joe	Baseball		4			Debut 1951 Pirates
Mulcahy, Hugh	Baseball		5			Debut 1935 Phillies
Muldoon, William	Wrestler		65			And J.L.Sullivan's Trainer
Muldowney, Shirley	Auto Racing		8	22		HOF 1990
Mulford, Ralph	Auto Racing	+	40	40		
Mulholland, Winbert	Horse Racing					HOF 1967 trainer
Mullaney, Joseph	Basketball		10	50		played NBA 49
Mulleavy, Greg	Baseball		15	32		Debut 1930 ChiSox
Mullen, Billy	Baseball		35	75		Debut 1920
Mullen, Ford "Moon"	Baseball		8	22		Debut 1944 Phillies
Mullen, Joe	Hockey		5	25		
Mullens, Robert	Basketball		10	50		played NBA 46
Muller, Harold "Brick"	Football	+	80	140		CHOF California

NAME	CATEGORY	+	SIG	SP	BALL	Comment
Muller, Kirk	Hockey		4	18		
Mulligan, Eddie	Baseball		12			Debut 1915 Cubs
Mulligan, Joe	Baseball		4			Debut 1934 Bost. RedSox
Mullikan, William	Olympic		3	8		Swim/breaststroke
Mullin, Chris	Basketball		8	28		played NBA 85-
Mullin, Pat	Baseball		12	32		Debut 1940 Tigers
Mulliniks, Rance	Baseball		3	10		Debut 1977
Mullins, Fran	Baseball		3	10		Debut 1980
Mullins, Jeff	Basketball		5	15		played NBA 64-75
Mulloy, Gardner	Tennis		7	22		HOF 1972
Mumphrey, Jerry	Baseball		3	12		Debut 1974
Muncey, Bill	Boat Racing		30	75		
Munchak, Mike	Football		3	8		NFL
Muncie, Chuck	Football		5	14		NFL
Muncrief, Bob	Baseball		6			Debut 1943 Cards
Muncy, Bill	Auto Racing	+	22	55		HOF 1989
Munger, George "Red"	Football	+	15	35		1976 CHOF coach
Mungo, Van Lingle	Baseball		40	95		Debut 1931 Brklyn Dodg.
Munkelt, Thomas	Olympic		7	18		110 M Hurdles
Munn, Clarence	Football	+	18	60		1959 CHOF coach
Munns, Les	Baseball		3	9		Debut 1934
Munoz, Anthony	Football		4	16	85	NFL
Munro, George	Basketball		10	50		played NBA 46-47
Munson, Bill	Football		4	12		NFL
Munson, Edith C.	Golf		75	150		
Munson, Joe	Baseball		20			Debut 1925 Cubs
Munson, Thurman	Baseball		110	250	25	Debut 1969
Muntz, Rolf	Golf		5	20	25	
Munzel, Edgar	Writer		3	6		
Murcer, Bobby	Baseball		3	12		Debut 1965
Murchison, Ira	Olympic		8	25		400 meter relay
Murdock, Margaret	Shooting		3	6		
Murnane, Tim	Writer		4	8		
Murphy, Allen	Basketball		3	12		played NBA 75
Murphy, Bob	Golf		5	20	25	
Murphy, Calvin	Basketball		8	22	135	HOF 1993. NBA 70-82
Murphy, Charles "Stretch"	Basketball		10	32		HOF 1960
Murphy, Dale	Baseball		7	28		Debut 1976
Murphy, Danny	Baseball		3	12		Debut 1960
Murphy, Danny F.	Baseball		95	350		Debut 1900 NY Giants
Murphy, Dwayne	Baseball		3	10		Debut 1978
Murphy, Isaac	Horse Racing		200	400		HOF 1955 jockey
Murphy, Jack	Writer	+	12	25		1988 Ntl S&S HOF
Murphy, Jay	Basketball		3	10		played NBA 84-87
Murphy, Jimmy	Auto Racing	+	22	50		
Murphy, John	Basketball		10	50		played NBA 45
Murphy, John	Olympic		3	6		Swim/relay
Murphy, Johnny	Baseball		30	68		Debut 1932
Murphy, Richard	Basketball		10	50		played NBA 46
Murphy, Ron	Basketball		3	10		played NBA 87
Murphy, Tod	Basketball		3	10		played NBA 87
Murphy, Tom	Baseball		5			Debut 1968 Cal. Angels
Murray, Bill	Football	+	30	60		1974 CHOF coach
Murray, Eddie	Baseball		7	32		Debut 1977
Murray, Eddie	Football		5	14		NFL
Murray, Frank	Football	+	15	35		1983 CHOF coach

NAME	CATEGORY	+	SIG	SP	BALL	Comment
Murray, Hugh, Sir	Hockey		10	22		1987 US HOF
Murray, Jim	Writer		8	20		1978 Ntl S&S HOF
Murray, John Red	Baseball		75	225		Debut 1906
Murray, Kenneth	Basketball		10	50		played NBA 50-54
Murray, Larry	Baseball		3	12		Debut 1974
Murray, Lindley	Tennis	+	12	35		HOF 1958
Murray, Ray	Baseball		7	22		Debut 1948
Murray, Rich	Baseball		3	10		Debut 1980
Murray, Ross	Golf		5	20	25	
Murray, Troy	Hockey		4	12		
Murrell, Ivan	Baseball		3	12		Debut 1963
Murrell, Willie	Basketball		4	16		played NBA 67-69
Murrey, Dorie	Basketball		3	18		played NBA 66-71
Murtaugh, Danny	Baseball		40	85		Debut 1941
Musberger, Brent	Broadcaster		4	8		
Muser, Tony	Baseball		3	12		Debut 1969
Musi, Angelo	Basketball		10	50		played NBA 46-48
Musial, Stan	Baseball					P-S HOF $85,Grt.Mo.$90
Musial, Stan	Baseball		18	45	65	HOF 1969. Gold Pl.S $30
Musselman, Bill	Basketball		3	7		NBA College Coach
Mussina, Mike	Baseball		5	15		Debut 1991
Musso, George	Football		8	22	85	1982 HOF 2-way line
Muster, Thomas	Tennis		4	10		
Mutombo, Dikembe	Basketball		5	15	100	NBA Nuggets
Mutscheller, Jim	Football		4	12		NFL
Myatt, George	Baseball		10	32		Debut 1938 NY Giants
Myer, Buddy	Baseball		40	85		Debut 1925
Myers, Billy	Baseball		12	30		Debut 1935
Myers, Billy, Jr.	Bowling		2	8		Rookie-of-Year
Myers, Peter	Basketball		3	10		played NBA 86-
Myers, Randy	Baseball		5	12		Debut 1985
Myers, T. E.	Auto Racing	+	50	125		
Mykkanen, John	Olympic		4	8		Swim/400 free
Mylin, Ed	Football	+	15	35		1974 CHOF coach
Myrick, Julian	Tennis	+	12	24		HOF 1963
Myricks, Larry	Olympic		3	12		Long Jump

NAME	CATEGORY	+	SIG	SP	BALL	Comment
Naber, John	Olympic		7	16		Swim/100 M Back.
Naber, Robert	Basketball		10	45		played NBA 52
Nabholtz, Larry	Golf		75	195		
Nachamkin, Boris	Basketball		8	45		played NBA 54
Nadig, Marie-Therese	Olympic		12	32		Alpine skiing
Nafzger, Carl A.	Horse Racing		5	10		Trainer
Nagel, Bill	Baseball		22	45		Debut 1939
Nagel, Gerry	Basketball		10	50		played NBA 49
Nagelson, Russ	Baseball		3	12		Debut 1968
Nagle, Kel	Golf		10	35	35	
Nagler, Gern	Football		5	15		NFL
Nagurski, Bronko	Football	+	60	165	395	1963 HOF RB
Nagy, Charles	Baseball		3	10		Debut 1990
Nagy, Fred	Basketball		10	50		played NBA 47-48
Nagy, Steve	Bowling	+	25	65		1963 ABC HOF-Mer.Serv.
Nahorodny, Bill	Baseball		3	10		Debut 1976 Phillies
Naismith, James	Basketball	+	400	850		HOF 1959
Nall, Anita	Olympic		3	12		Gold Medal. Swimming
Namath, Joe	Football		20	60	175	1985 HOF QB
Nance, Jim	Football		60	150		NFL
Nance, Larry	Basketball		5	14		played NBA 81
Nanne,Lou	Hockey		4	15		
Nannini, Alessandro	Auto Racing		4	12		
Nantz, Jim	Broadcaster		2	5		Olympic Host
Napoleon, Danny	Baseball		3	12		Debut 1965
Napoles, Jose	Boxing		18	28		Welter-Wt Champ (4Yrs)
Napolitano, Pau1	Basketball		10	50		played NBA 47-48
Naragon, Hal	Baseball		5	20		Debut 1951
Narleski, Bill	Baseball		12	45		Debut 1929
Narron, Jerry	Baseball		3	10		Debut 1979
Narron, Sam	Baseball		10	30		Debut 1935
Nary, Bill	Golf		15	40		
Nash, Cotton	Baseball		3	15		Debut 1967
Nash, Cotton	Basketball		3	15		played NBA 64-67
Nash, Robert	Basketball		3	12		played NBA 72-78
Naslund, Mats	Hockey		4	24		
Nastase, Ilie	Tennis		20	45		HOF 1991
Nater, Swen	Basketball		3	12		played NBA 73-83
Nathan, Tony	Football		3	10		NFL
Natt, Calvin	Basketball		3	12		played NBA 79-83
Natt, Kenneth	Basketball		3	10		played NBA 80-84
Naulls, Willie	Basketball		5	16		played NBA 56-65
Nause, Martha	Golf		5	20	25	

NAME	CATEGORY	+	SIG	SP	BALL	Comment
Navratilova, Martina	Tennis		12	38		
Naylor, Earl	Baseball		10	30		Debut 1942
Naymick, Mike	Baseball		8			Debut 1939
Ndiaye, Astou	Basketball		2	5		Women's ABL
Neal, Charlie	Baseball		12	28		Debut 1956
Neal, Craig	Basketball		3	10		played NBA 88
Neal, James	Basketball		10	45		played NBA 53-54
Neal, Lloyd	Basketball		3	12		played NBA 72-78
Neale, Earle "Greasy"	Football	+	100	395		1967 CHOF coach
Neale, Earle "Greasy"	Football	+	100	395		1969 HOF coach
Nealy, Eddie	Basketball		3	12		played NBA 82-83
Neeley, Jess	Football	+	28	65		1971 CHOF coach
Neely, Cam	Hockey		5	22		
Neeman, Cal	Baseball		3	18		Debut 1957
Negratti, Al	Basketball		10	50		played NBA 45-46
Negro, Vincent Del	Basketball		3	10		played NBA 88-
Nehf, Art	Baseball		15	40		21 game pitcher '18/Giants
Neill, Tommy	Baseball		7	20		Debut 1946
Neilson, Sandra	Olympic		5	12		Swim/100 free
Nelford, Jim	Golf		5	20	25	
Neloy, Eddie	Horse Racing					HOF 1983 trainer
Nelsen, Bill	Football		4	12		NFL
Nelson, Andy	Football		5	16		NFL
Nelson, Azurnah	Boxing		10	20		
Nelson, Barry	Basketball		3	10		played NBA 71
Nelson, Bob	Baseball		3	15		Debut 1955
Nelson, Byron	Golf		20	35	45	PGA HOF 1974
Nelson, Cindy	Olympic		6	18		Alpine skiing
Nelson, Darrin	Football		3	12		NFL
Nelson, Dave	Baseball		3	12		Debut 1968 Indians
Nelson, David	Football		8	15		1987 CHOF coach
Nelson, Don	Basketball		4	18		played NBA 62-75
Nelson, Hub	Hockey	+	10	22		1978 US HOF
Nelson, Jamie	Baseball		3	10		Debut 1983
Nelson, John	Olympic		3	7		Swim/1,500 free
Nelson, Larry	Golf		10	30	35	
Nelson, Lindsey	Broadcaster		6	25		1979 Ntl S&S HOF
Nelson, Louis	Basketball		3	12		played NBA 73-77
Nelson, Mel	Baseball		6			Debut 1960 Cards
Nelson, Oscar "Battling"	Boxing		250			Lt.-Wt Champ 1906
Nelson, Ricky	Baseball		3	10		Debut 1983
Nelson, Rob	Baseball		3	10		Debut 1986
Nelson, Rocky	Baseball		6	20		Debut 1949
Nelson, Roger	Football		4	8		1986 Canadian HOF
Nelson, Ron	Basketball		3	12		played NBA 70
Nelson, Tom	Baseball		22	50		Debut 1945
Nemelka, Richard	Basketball		3	12		played NBA 70
Nen, Dick	Baseball		3	15		Debut 1963
Nerud, John	Horse Racing					HOF 1972 trainer
Nessley, Martin	Basketball		3	10		played NBA 87
Nesterenko, Eric	Hockey		4	22		
Netolicky, Bob	Basketball		3	12		played NBA 67-75
Netter, Mildrette	Olympic		3	7		Track relay
Nettles, Graig	Baseball		4	15		Debut 1967
Nettles, Jim	Baseball		3	10		Debut 1970
Nettles, Morris	Baseball		3	10		Debut 1974

NAME	CATEGORY	+	SIG	SP	BALL	Comment
Neuheisel, Rick	Football		3	7		Colorado Coach
Neumann, Johnny	Basketball		4	12		played NBA 71-77
Neumann, Liselotte	Golf		5	25	25	
Neumann, Paul	Basketball		4	18		played NBA 61-66
Neumann, Peter	Football		4	8		1979 Canadian HOF
Neun, Johnny	Baseball		35	60		Debut 1925 Tigers
Nevers, Ernie	Football	+	75	250		1963 HOF RB
Neves, Ralph	Horse Racing					HOF 1960 jockey
Nevil, Dwight	Golf		10	35		
Neville, Jack	Golf		75	165		
Nevin, Bob	Hockey		5	18		
Nevitt, Charles	Basketball		3	10		played NBA 82-
Newberry, Jimmy	Baseball		8	30		Debut 1942, Negro League
Newcombe, Don	Baseball		7	18		Debut 1949
Newcombe, John	Tennis		8	26		HOF 1986
Newell, Betty Hicks	Golf		50	95		
Newell, Marshall	Football	+	25	65		CHOF Harvard
Newell, Pete	Basketball		7	20		HOF 1978-Contributor
Newhouse, Fred	Olympic		4	8		400 meters
Newhouse, Robert	Football		3	10		NFL
Newhouser, Hal	Baseball					P-S HOF $25,Grt.Mo.$20
Newhouser, Hal	Baseball		8	20	25	HOF 1992.Gold Pl.S $18
Newlin, Mike	Basketball		4	12		played NBA 71-81
Newman, Al	Baseball		3	12		Debut 1985
Newman, Anthony	Football		3	12		NFL
Newman, Fred	Baseball		4			Debut 1962 L.A. Angels
Newman, Harry	Football		50	100		CHOF Michigan
Newman, Jeff	Baseball		3	10		Debut 1976
Newman, John	Basketball		3	10		played NBA 86-
Newmark, David	Basketball		3	15		played NBA 68-70
Newsome, Ozzie	Football		4	14	85	NFL
Newsome, Skeeter	Baseball		15	45		Debut 1935
Newton, Bill	Basketball		15	15		played NBA 72-73
Newton, Jack	Football	+	22	22		1964 Canadian HOF
Newton, Jack	Golf		30	30		
Neyland, Robert	Football	+	40	100		1956 CHOF coach
Niarhos, Gus	Baseball		3	15		Debut 1946
Niccolai, Armand	Football		8	22		NFL
Nicholas, Alison	Golf		5	20	25	
Nicholas, Don	Baseball		3	18		Debut 1952
Nicholls, Bernie	Hockey		5	24		
Nichols, Bobby	Golf		10	25	35	
Nichols, Carl	Baseball		3	10		Debut 1986
Nichols, Charles "Kid"	Baseball		325	700	3200	HOF '49. B&W PC $1200
Nichols, Gil	Golf		75	225		
Nichols, Jack	Basketball		10	50		played NBA 48-57
Nichols, Lorrie	Bowling		5	10		1989 Women's IBC HOF
Nichols, Reid	Baseball		3	10		Debut 1980
Nichols, Roy	Baseball		8	22		Debut 1944
Nicholson, Bill	Baseball		15	38		Debut 1936 A's
Nicholson, Dave	Baseball		5	15		Debut 1960
Nicklaus, Gary	Golf		5	20	25	
Nicklaus, Jack	Golf		75	150	125	PGA HOF 1974
Nicklaus, Jack Jr	Golf		5	25	25	
Nicks, Orlando	Basketball		3	10		played NBA 80-82
Nicolette, Mike	Golf		5	20	25	

NAME	CATEGORY	+	SIG	SP	BALL	Comment
Nicosia, Steve	Baseball		3	10		Debut 1978
Nieder, Bill	Olympic		7	20		Shot Put
Niekro, Joe	Baseball		3	15		Debut 1967 Cubs
Niekro, Phil	Baseball		10	20	25	HOF 1997 Debut 1964
Nielsen, Arthur	Tennis	+	12	38		HOF 1971
Nielsen, Milt	Baseball		6	20		Debut 1949
Nieman, Bob	Baseball		15	38		Debut 1951 Browns
Nieman, Butch	Baseball		7	30		Debut 1943
Niemann, Richard	Basketball		3	14		played NBA 68-71
Niemiera, Dick	Basketball		10	50		played NBA 46-49
Nieporte, Tom	Golf		10	35		
Nieto, Tom	Baseball		3	10		Debut 1984
Nieuwendyk, Joe	Hockey		4	20		
Nieves, Juan	Baseball		5	15		Debut 1986
Nighbor, Frank	Hockey		70	225		1947 HOF fwd
Nilan,Chris	Hockey		3	20		
Niles, Harry	Baseball		95	225		Debut 1906
Niles, Michael	Basketball		3	10		played NBA 80
Nilsmark, Catrin	Golf		5	20	25	
Nimphius, Kurt	Basketball		3	12		played NBA 81-87
Ninowski, Jim	Football		4	15		NFL
Nitschke, Ray	Football		6	20	110	1978 HOF LB
Nitz, Leonard	Olympic		3	6		Cycling
Nix, Sunder	Olympic		3	7		Track relay
Nixon, Donell	Baseball		3	10		Debut 1987
Nixon, Norm	Basketball		4	15		played NBA 77-88
Nixon, Otis	Baseball		3	15		Debut 1983
Nixon, Russ	Baseball		3	14		Debut 1957
Noah, Yannick	Tennis		10	20		
Nobillo, Frank	Golf		5	20	25	
Nobis, Tommy	Football		6	20		CHOF Texas
Noble, Chuck	Basketball		7	38		played NBA 55-61
Noble, Karen	Golf		5	20	25	
Noble, Reg	Hockey		70	275		1962 HOF fwd
Noble, Richard	Auto Racing		7	15		
Noel, Paul	Basketball		10	50		played NBA 47-51
Nokes, Matt	Baseball		3	12		Debut 1985
Nolan, Gary	Baseball		5			Debut 1967 Reds
Nolan, James	Basketball		10	50		played NBA 49
Nolan, Joe	Baseball		3	12		Debut 1972 Yankees
Nold, Dick	Baseball		4			Debut 1967 Senators
Nolen, Paul	Basketball		10	45		played NBA 53
Noll, Chuck	Football		7	18	85	1993 HOF. NFL
Nolon, Dennis	Auto Racing		6	15		
Nolting, Ray	Football		12	35		NFL
Nomellini, Leo	Football		10	22	85	1969 HOF DL
Nomo, Hideo	Baseball		8	50		Dodger Pitcher
Nonenkamp, Les "Red"	Baseball		3	8		Debut 1933
Nonnenkamp, Leo	Baseball		10			Debut 1933 Pirates
Nordbrook, Tim	Baseball		3	12		Debut 1974
Nordell, Peter	Olympic		3	6		Rowing
Nordhagen, Wayne	Baseball		3	12		Debut 1976
Nordmann, Robert	Basketball		6	28		played NBA 61-64
Nordone, Augie	Golf		20	50		
Norelius, Martha	Olympic		5	12		Swim relay
Noren, Irv	Baseball		3	14		Debut 1950

NAME	CATEGORY	+	SIG	SP	BALL	Comment
Norlander, John	Basketball		10	50		played NBA 46-50
Norman, Coniel	Basketball		3	12		played NBA 74-78
Norman, Dan	Baseball		3	10		Debut 1977
Norman, Fred	Baseball		6			Debut 1962 K.C.
Norman, Greg	Golf		20	45	45	
Norman, Kenneth	Basketball		4	10		played NBA 87-
Norman, Nelson	Baseball		3	10		Debut 1978
Norris, Audie	Basketball		3	10		played NBA 82-84
Norris, Jim	Baseball		3	10		Debut 1977
Norris, Joe	Bowling		7	22		1954 ABC HOF
Norris, Sylvester	Basketball		3	10		played NBA 79
Norris, Terry	Boxing		12	22		
Norris, Tim	Golf		10	35		
North, Andy	Golf		10	35		
North, Billy	Baseball		3	12		Debut 1971
Northey, Ron	Baseball		30	65		Debut 1942
Northey, Scott	Baseball		3	12		Debut 1969
Northrop, Jim	Baseball		3	12		Debut 1964
Northway, Douglas	Olympic		3	7		Swim/1,500 free
Norton, Homer	Football	+	15	40		1971 CHOF coach
Norton, Jerry	Football		5	12		NFL
Norton, Ken	Boxing		20	60		1978-80 H-Wt Champ
Norton, Ken	Football		5	18	85	NFL
Norton, Virginia	Bowling		5	10		1988 Women's IBC HOF
Norwood, Scott	Football		3	8		NFL
Norwood, Willie	Baseball		3	10		Debut 1977
Norwood, Willie	Basketball		3	12		played NBA 71-77
Nossek, Joe	Baseball		3	12		Debut 1964 Minn. Twins
Nostrand, George	Basketball		10	50		played NBA 46-49
Noszka, Stanley	Basketball		10	50		played NBA 45-48
Notaro, Phyllis	Bowling		5	10		1979 Women's IBC HOF
Nottebart, Don	Baseball		7			Debut 1960 Atl. Braves
Notter, Joe	Horse Racing					HOF 1963 jockey
Nottingham, Don	Football		3	12		NFL
Nova, Lou	Boxing		15	35		Hvy-Wt Contender
Novacek, Jay	Football		4	15	75	NFL
Novacek, Karel	Tennis		5	18		
Novak, Michael	Basketball		15	60		played NBA 39-53
Novikoff, Lou	Baseball		46	95		Debut 1941
Novotna, Jana	Tennis		7	22		
Novotney, Rube	Baseball		7	27		Debut 1949
Nowell, Melvyn	Basketball		3	18		played NBA 62-67
Nucatola, John	Basketball		10	24		HOF 1977-Referee
Nunn, Michael	Boxing		8	18		
Nurmi, Paavo	Olympic		125	350		Track/distance
Nuthall Shoemaker, Betty	Tennis	+	15	30		HOF 1977
Nutt, Dennis	Basketball		3	12		played NBA 86
Nuxhall, Joe	Baseball		3	10		Debut 1941
Nyad, Diane	Olympic		5	10		Swim
Nye, Rich	Baseball		3			Debut 1966 Cubs
Nykanen, Matti	Olympic		15	35		Ski jump
Nylund, Gary	Hockey		4	22		
Nyman, Chris	Baseball		3	10		Debut 1982
Nyman, Nyls	Baseball		3	12		Debut 1974

NAME	CATEGORY	+	SIG	SP	BALL	Comment

NAME	CATEGORY	+	SIG	SP	BALL	Comment
O'Berry, Mike	Baseball		3	12		Debut 1979
O'Boyle, John	Basketball		10	45		played NBA 52
O'Bradovich, Jim	Baseball		3	10		Debut 1978
O'Brien, Charlie	Baseball		3	10		Debut 1985
O'Brien, Davey	Football	+	125	395		CHOF TCU. Heisman '38
O'Brien, Eddie	Baseball		5	18		Debut 1953
O'Brien, J.J.	Golf		75	105		
O'Brien, James	Basketball		3	16		played NBA 73-74
O'Brien, James J.	Basketball		3	15		played NBA 71-74
O'Brien, John J. "Jack"	Basketball	+	22	45		HOF 1961-Contributor
O'Brien, Johnny	Baseball		5	18		Debut 1953
O'Brien, Ken	Football		5	12		NFL
O'Brien, Larry	Basketball	+	30	80		HOF 1991-Contributor
O'Brien, Michael	Olympic		4	10		Swim/1,500 free
O'Brien, Parry	Olympic		8	20		Shot Put
O'Brien, Pete	Baseball		3	12		Debut 1982
O'Brien, Ralph	Basketball		10	45		played NBA 51-52
O'Brien, Robert	Basketball		10	50		played NBA 47-48
O'Brien, Syd	Baseball		4	15		Debut 1969
O'Brien, Tommy	Baseball		25	60		Debut 1943
O'Connell, Danny	Baseball		38	85		Debut 1950
O'Connell, Dermott	Basketball		10	50		played NBA 48-49
O'Connell, Jimmy	Baseball		35	75		Debut 1923
O'Connor, Buddy	Hockey		40	175		1988 HOF fwd
O'Connor, Christy	Golf		20	35	45	
O'Connor, Christy Jr	Golf		5	30	25	
O'Connor, John J.	Golf		15	45		
O'Connor, Winnie	Horse Racing					HOF 1956 jockey
O'Dea, Ken	Baseball		18	40		Debut 1935
O'Dea, Pat	Football	+	125	300		CHOF Wisconsin
O'Dea, Paul	Baseball		18	45		Debut 1944
O'Donnell, Andrew	Basketball		10	50		played NBA 49
O'Donnell, Chuck	Bowling		5	20		1968 ABC HOF
O'Donnell, Neil	Football		4	15	75	NFL
O'Doul, Lefty	Baseball		75	200		Debut 1919
O'Farrell, Bob	Baseball		45	95		Debut 1915 Cubs
O'Grady, Francis	Basketball		10	50		played NBA 45-48
O'Grady, Mac	Golf		5	20	25	
O'Hanlon, Francis	Basketball		3	12		played NBA 70
O'Hara, Patrick	Golf		75	195		
O'Hara, Peter	Golf		75	195		
O'Hearn, Jack	Football	+	18	45		CHOF Cornell
O'Hern, Jim	Golf		5	20	25	

NAME	CATEGORY	+	SIG	SP	BALL	Comment
O'Keefe, Richard	Basketball		10	50		played NBA 47-50
O'Keefe, Thomas	Basketball		10	50		played NBA 50
O'Koren, Michael	Basketball		3	12		played NBA 80-87
O'Leary, John	Golf		5	20	25	
O'Leary, Paul	Golf		10	35		
O'Loughlin, Martin	Golf		45	140		
O'Malley, Peter	Baseball		4	12		Dodger Owner (ex)
O'Malley, Tom	Baseball		3	10		Debut 1982
O'Malley, V. Grady	Basketball		3	16		played NBA 69
O'Malley, Walter	Baseball		75	200		Dodger Owner (ex)
O'Mara, Ollie	Baseball		3	10		Debut 1989
O'Meara, Mark	Golf		5	25	25	
O'Neal, Jermaine	Basketball		10	36		NBA Portland
O'Neal, Jermaine	Basketball		12			NBA Portland
O'Neal, Shaquille	Basketball		10	65	200	NBA Top 50
O'Neal, Steve	Football		3	8		NFL
O'Neil, John	Baseball		7	20		Debut 1946
O'Neill, Frank	Football	+	18	35		1951 CHOF coach
O'Neill, Frank	Horse Racing					HOF 1956 jockey
O'Neill, Mike	Basketball		10	45		played NBA 52
O'Neill, Paul	Baseball		4	18		Debut 1985
O'Quinn, John "Red"	Football		4	8		1981 Canadian HOF
O'Ree, Willie	Hockey		8	35		
O'Reilly, Terry	Hockey		4	12		
O'Rourke, Charles	Football		6	15		CHOF Boston College
O'Rourke, Frank	Baseball		50	125		Debut 1912
O'Rourke, Jim	Baseball	+	2500	4000	10000	HOF 1945
O'Rourke, Joe	Baseball		45	85		Debut 1929
O'Shea, Kevin	Basketball		10	45		played NBA 50-52
O'Shields, Garland	Basketball		10	50		played NBA 46-47
O'Sullivan, Keala	Olympic		5	12		Diving
Oakley, Charles	Basketball		4	18		played NBA 85-
Oates, Adam	Hockey		6	28	32	
Oates, Bart	Football		3	8		NFL
Oates, Johnny	Baseball		3	10		Debut 1970
Oberkfell, Ken	Baseball		3	10		Debut 1977
Oberlander, Andrew	Football	+	15	45		CHOF Dartmouth
Ocasio, Osvaldo	Boxing		15	35		
Oda, Mikio	Olympic		10	20		Swim
Odam, George	Horse Racing					HOF 1955 jockey
Odom, J.L. "Blue Moon"	Baseball		12			Debut 1964 K.C.
Oertel, Chuck	Baseball		3	14		Debut 1958
Oerter, Al	Olympic		8	22		Discus
Oeschger, Joe	Baseball		40	90		Debut 1914 Phillies
Oester, Ron	Baseball		3	12		Debut 1978 Reds
Offenhauser, Fred	Auto Racing	+				
Offerdahl, John	Football		3	8		NFL
Office, Rowland	Baseball		3	10		Debut 1972
Ogden, Carlos	Basketball		3	15		played NBA 69-70
Ogden, Jonathon	Football		3	9		1995 Outland Winner
Ogden, Ralph	Basketball		3	15		played NBA 70
Ogg, Willie	Golf		75	195		
Oglivie, Ben	Baseball		3	10		Debut 1971
Ogrin, David	Golf		5	20	25	
Ogrodnick, John	Hockey		4	16		
Oh, Sadaharu	Baseball		50	125		

NAME	CATEGORY	+	SIG	SP	BALL	Comment
Ohl, Don	Basketball		5	22		played NBA 60-69
Ojeda, Bob	Baseball		4	16		Debut 1980
Okamoto, Ayako	Golf		10	25	25	
Okker, Tom	Tennis		5	15		
Okoye, Christian	Football		6	15		NFL
Okrie, Len	Baseball		7	20		Debut 1948
Olajuwon, Hakeem	Basketball		13	38	175	played NBA 84-
Olazabal, Jose Maria	Golf		10	30	45	
Olberding, Mark	Basketball		4	10		played NBA 75-86
Oldfield, Barney	Auto Racing	+	225	550		HOF 1989. 1st mile/min
Oldham, Jawann	Basketball		3	15		played NBA 80-87
Oldham, John	Baseball		3	14		Debut 1956
Oldham, John	Basketball		10	50		played NBA 49-50
Oldis, Bob	Baseball		8	22		Debut 1953
Olds, Robin	Football		10	35		CHOF Army
Olerud, John	Baseball		6	28		Debut 1989
Oleynick, Frank	Basketball		3	10		played NBA 75-76
Olin, Bob	Boxing		35	75		
Oliphant, Elmer	Football	+	30	95		CHOF Army/Purdue
Oliva, Patrizio	Boxing		15	32		
Oliva, Tony	Baseball		6	14		Debut 1962
Olivares, Ruben	Boxing		18	38		Bantam & Fthr-Wt Champ
Olive, John	Basketball		3	12		played NBA 78-79
Oliver, Al	Baseball		4	12		Debut 1968
Oliver, Bob	Baseball		3	12		Debut 1965
Oliver, Dave	Baseball		3	12		Debut 1977
Oliver, Dean	Rodeo		7	22		
Oliver, Ed	Golf		125	275		
Oliver, Gene	Baseball		10	22		Debut 1959
Oliver, Harry	Hockey		45	150		1967 HOF fwd
Oliver, Joe	Baseball		3	10		Debut 1989
Oliver, Nate	Baseball		3	12		Debut 1963
Oliver, Tom	Baseball		18	45		Debut 1930 Bost. RedSox
Ollrich, Gene	Basketball		10	50		played NBA 49
Olmedo, Alex	Tennis		12	35		HOF 1987
Olmo, Luis	Baseball		40	85		Debut 1943
Olmstead, Bert	Hockey		7	22		1985 HOF fwd
Olsen, Enoch	Basketball		3	16		played NBA 62-69
Olsen, Harold G.	Basketball	+	22	50		HOF 1959-Contributor
Olsen, Jon	Olympic		3	7		Gold Medal. Swimming
Olsen, Merlin	Football		7	20	100	1982 HOF DL
Olsen, Zoe Ann	Olympic		7	18		Diving
Olson, Barney	Baseball		17	42		Debut 1941
Olson, Bobo (Carl)	Boxing		20	40		Middle-Wt Champ
Olson, Eddie	Hockey		5	10		1977 US HOF
Olson, Greg	Baseball		3	10		Debut 1989
Olson, Karl	Baseball		7	18		Debut 1951
Olson, Lute	Basketball		2	6		Arizona Coach
Olson, Marv	Baseball		18	40		Debut 1931
Olszewski, John	Football		8	22		NFL
Ongais, Danny	Auto Racing		4	15		
Ontiveros, Steve	Baseball		3	12		Debut 1973
Oosterbaan, Bennie	Football	+	25	70		CHOF Michigan
Oosterhuis, Peter	Golf		5	25	25	
Oppemman, Steve	Golf		10	35		
Oquendo, Jose	Baseball		3	10		Debut 1983

NAME	CATEGORY	+	SIG	SP	BALL	Comment
Orantes, Manuel	Tennis		7	22		
Oravetz, Ernie	Baseball		7	18		Debut 1955
Orengo, Joe	Baseball		18	45		Debut 1939 Cards
Orms, Barry	Basketball		3	15		played NBA 68-69
Orr, Bobby	Hockey		22	90	95	1979 HOF def
Orr, Edith C.	Golf		150	275		
Orr, Jimmy	Football		6	16		NFL
Orr, John	Basketball		10	50		played NBA 49, Coach
Orr, Louis	Basketball		3	12		played NBA 80-87
Orser, Brian	Olympic		6	18		Figure skating
Orsi, John	Football	+	15	35		CHOF Colgate
Orsino, John	Baseball		3	14		Debut 1961
Orsulak, Joe	Baseball		3	10		Debut 1983
Orta, Jorge	Baseball		3	12		Debut 1972
Ortenzio, Fran	Baseball		3	12		Debut 1973
Ortiz, Carlos	Boxing		12	25		
Ortiz, Jose	Baseball		3	12		Debut 1969
Ortiz, Jose	Basketball		3	10		played NBA 88-
Ortiz, Junior	Baseball		3	10		Debut 1982
Ortner, Bev	Bowling		5	10		1972 Women's IBC HOF
Orton, John	Baseball		3	10		Debut 1989
Osborn, Dave	Football		5	14		NFL
Osborne duPont, Margaret	Tennis		25	50		HOF 1967 (DuPont)
Osborne, Bobo	Baseball		5	18		Deubt 1957
Osborne, Charles	Basketball		6	28		played NBA 61
Osborne, Mark	Hockey		3	12		
Osborne, Tom	Football		5	15		Nebraska Coach
Osborne, Wayne	Baseball		7			Debut 1935 Pirates
Osgood, Win	Football	+	25	75		CHOF Cornell
Osipowich, Albina	Olympic		5	10		Swim relay
Osmanski, Bill	Football		12	35		CHOF Holy Cross
Osteen, Claude	Baseball		3	12		Debut 1957
Ostergard, Red	Baseball		35	85		Debut 1921
Osterkorn, Walter	Basketball		10	45		played NBA 51-54
Osterloh, Lilia	Tennis		3	6		1997 NCAA Champion
Ostrosser, Brian	Baseball		3	12		Debut 1973
Ostrowski, Joe	Baseball		5			Debut 1948 Browns
Ostrowski, John	Baseball		9	28		Debut 1943
Osuna, Rafael	Tennis	+	15	35		HOF 1979
Otero, Reggie	Baseball		10	32		Debut 1945
Otis, Amos	Baseball		4	12		Debut 1967
Otis, Jirn	Football		5	14		NFL
Otis, Paul F. "Bill"	Baseball		18			Debut 1912 Yankees
Ott, Billy	Baseball		3	15		Debut 1962
Ott, Ed	Baseball		3	10		Debut 1974
Ott, Mel	Baseball		317	650	3550	HOF '51.B&W PC S $650
Otten, Donald	Basketball		10	50		played NBA 46-52
Otten, Mac	Basketball		10	50		played NBA 49
Ottey, Merlene	Track		8	20		
Otto, Jim	Football		6	20	95	1980 HOF OL
Otto, Joel	Hockey		5	20		
Otto, Kristin	Olympic		12	32		Swim/50 free
Ouelette, G.R.	Olympic		10	20		Rifle
Ouelette, Phil	Baseball		3	10		Debut 1986
Ouimet, Francis	Golf		350	750		PGA HOF 1974
Outerbridge, Mary	Tennis	+	12	25		HOF 1981

NAME	CATEGORY	+	SIG	SP	BALL	Comment
Outlaw, Jimmy	Baseball		15	40		Debut 1937 Reds
Overton, Claudell	Basketball		10	45		played NBA 52
Owen, Bennie	Football	+	15	35		1951 CHOF coach
Owen, Dave	Baseball		3	10		Debut 1983
Owen, George	Football	+	20	50		CHOF Harvard
Owen, George	Hockey	+	10	22		1973 US HOF
Owen, Larry	Baseball		3	10		Debut 1981
Owen, Marv	Baseball		12	30		Debut 1931
Owen, Mickey	Baseball		8	22		Debut 1937 Cards
Owen, Spike	Baseball		3	12		Debut 1983
Owen, Steve	Football	+	275	700		1966 HOF player/coach
Owens, Billy	Basketball		7	20		NBA Warrior
Owens, Charles	Golf		10	30	35	
Owens, Eddie	Basketball		3	12		played NBA 77
Owens, James	Basketball		10	32		played NBA 49-51
Owens, Jesse	Olympic		85	275		Track
Owens, Jim	Basketball		3	12		played NBA 73-74
Owens, Jim	Football		6	18		CHOF Oklahoma
Owens, Laurence	Figure Skating	+	50	125		Died '61 Air Disaster
Owens, R.C. "Alley Oop"	Football		7	18		NFL
Owens, Steve	Football		10	20		Heisman OK '69
Owens, Thomas	Basketball		4	15		played NBA 71-82
Oxley, Dinah	Golf		5	20	25	
Oyler, Ray	Baseball		8	15		Debut 1965
Ozaki, Joe	Golf		5	20	25	
Ozaki, Jumbo	Golf		10	35	35	
Ozio, David	Bowler		5	10		1995 PBA HOF

Pace, Darrell	Olympic		5	10		Archery
Pace, Joe	Basketball		3	12		played NBA 76-77
Pace, Orlando	Football		4	18		Lombardi Trophy
Pace, Roy	Golf		10	35		
Pacillo, Joanne	Golf		5	20	25	
Paciorek, Jim	Baseball		3	12		Debut 1987
Paciorek, John	Baseball		3	12		Debut 1963
Paciorek, Tom	Baseball		3	12		Debut 1970
Pack, Robert	Basketball		7	22		NBA Nuggets
Pack, Wayne	Basketball		3	12		played NBA 74
Padden, Tom	Baseball		28	60		Debut 1932
Paddock, Charles	Olympic		40	95		200 Meters
Padgett, Don	Baseball		18	45		Debut 1937
Padgham, Alf	Golf		95	225		
Paepke, Dennis	Baseball		3	12		Debut 1969

NAME	CATEGORY	+	SIG	SP	BALL	Comment
Pafko, Andy	Baseball		5	15		Debut 1943 Cubs
Pagan, Jose	Baseball		10			Debut 1959 S.F. Giants
Page, Alan	Football		10	20	85	1988 HOF DL
Page, Estelle Lawson	Golf		45	95		
Page, Greg	Boxing		15	30		1984-85 H-Wt Champ
Page, Harlan "Pat"	Basketball	+	18	40		HOF 1962
Page, Michael	Olympic		3	6		Equestrian
Page, Mike	Baseball		3	10		Debut 1968
Page, Mitchell	Baseball		3	10		Debut 1977
Pagel, Karl	Baseball		3	10		Debut 1978 Cubs
Pagett, Dana	Basketball		3	12		played NBA 71
Pagliarulo, Mike	Baseball		3	12		Debut 1984
Pagliorini, Jim	Baseball		4	18		Debut 1955
Pagnozzi, Tom	Baseball		3	10		Debut 1987
Paiernent, Wilf	Hockey		4	18		
Paige, Sachel	Baseball					HOF '71. P-S HOF $3500
Paige, Satchel	Baseball		97	222	950	Gold Pl.S $175
Paine, Frederick	Basketball		10	50		played NBA 48
Pajaczkowski, Tony	Football		4	8		1988 Canadian HOF
Palacios, Rey	Baseball		3	10		Debut 1988
Palazzi, Togo	Basketball		8	40		played NBA 54-59
Palica, Erv	Baseball		22	48		Debut 1947 Brklyn. Dodg.
Palli, Anne Marie	Golf		5	20	25	
Palmeiro, Rafael	Baseball		6	22		Debut 1986
Palmer, Arnold	Golf		25	75	50	PGA HOF 1974
Palmer, Bud	Basketball		10	35		played NBA 46-48
Palmer, Dean	Baseball		4	20		Debut 1989
Palmer, Eddie "Baldy"	Baseball		22			Debut 1917 Phil. A's
Palmer, Errol	Basketball		3	15		played NBA 67
Palmer, James	Basketball		7	22		played NBA 58-60
Palmer, Jim	Baseball					HOF 1990. P-S HOF $30
Palmer, Jim	Baseball		10	20	25	Gold Pl. $22. Grt.Mo. $30
Palmer, Johnny	Golf		35	95		
Palmer, Sandra	Golf		5	25	25	
Palmer, Winthrop	Hockey		10	22		1973 US HOF
Palmisano, Joe	Baseball		35	70		Debut 1931
Palmroth, Tera	Auto Racing		4	10		
Palomino, Carlos	Boxing		14	30		Welter-Wt Champ
Palys, Stan	Baseball		4			Debut 1953 Phillies
Pankovits, Jim	Baseball		3	10		Debut 1984
Panther, Jim	Baseball		3			Debut 1971 Oakland
Panton, Catherine	Golf		5	20	25	
Panton, John	Golf		15	45		
Pape, Ken	Baseball		3	10		Debut 1976
Papi, Stan	Baseball		3	10		Debut 1974
Pappas, George	Bowling		5	15		1986 PBA, '89 ABC HOF
Pappas, Milt	Baseball		3	14		Debut 1957
Pappin, Jim	Hockey		4	15		
Parades, Johnny	Baseball		3	10		Debut 1988
Paradise, Bob	Hockey		5	12		1989 US HOF
Parcells, Bill	Football		5	16	125	NFL Coach
Pardee, Jack	Football		7	18		CHOF Texas A&M, NFL
Pardo, Al	Baseball		3	10		Debut 1985
Parent, Bernie	Hockey		10	25	28	1984 HOF goal
Parent, Freddy	Baseball		45	95		Debut 1899
Parent, Mark	Baseball		3	10		Debut 1986

NAME	CATEGORY	+	SIG	SP	BALL	Comment
Parham, Estes	Basketball		10	50		played NBA 48-50
Parilli, Babe	Football		7	20		CHOF Kentucky
Parise, J.P.	Hockey		4	15		
Parish, Lance	Baseball		4	14		Debut 1977
Parish, Robert	Basketball		9	22		played NBA 76-
Park, Brad	Hockey		5	25	30	1988 HOF def
Park, Chan Ho	Baseball		8	38		
Park, Medford	Basketball		8	40		played NBA 55-59
Park, Mungo	Golf		450	950		
Park, Willie	Golf		495	950		
Park, Willie, Jr.	Golf		350	795		
Parke, Ivan	Horse Racing					HOF 1978 jockey
Parker, Billy	Baseball		3	6		Debut 1971
Parker, Buddy	Football		55	125		NFL
Parker, Clarence "Ace"	Baseball		3			Debut 1937 Phil. A's
Parker, Clarence "Ace"	Football		10	22		1972 HOF QB
Parker, Dan	Writer	+	10	22		1975 Ntl S&S HOF
Parker, Dave	Baseball		4	18		Debut 1973
Parker, Denise	Olympic		3	15		Medalist-Archery
Parker, Dixie	Baseball		35	70		Debut 1923
Parker, Francis James "Salty"	Baseball		20	40		Debut 1936 Tigers
Parker, Frank	Tennis		6	22		HOF 1966
Parker, Jackie	Football		7	22		CHOF MS St.,'71 HOF Can.
Parker, Jim	Football		7	22	85	1973 HOF OL
Parker, Wes	Baseball		4	15		Debut 1964
Parkhill, Barry	Basketball		3	12		played NBA 73-75
Parkin, Philip	Golf		5	20	25	
Parkinson, Jack	Basketball		10	50		played NBA 49
Parks, Charley	Basketball		3	15		played NBA 68
Parks, Dave	Football		3	12		NFL
Parks, Maxie	Olympic		3	7		Track relay
Parks, Richard	Basketball		3	15		played NBA 67
Parks, Sam, Jr.	Golf		50	150		1935 Nat'l Open winner
Parnell, Mel	Baseball		7	20		Debut 1947 Bost. RedSox
Parnevik, Jesper	Golf		10	30	35	
Parr, Jack	Basketball		8	35		played NBA 58
Parrack, Doyle	Basketball		10	50		played NBA 46
Parrilla, Sam	Baseball		3	10		Debut 1970
Parrish, Lance	Baseball		5	15		Debut 1977
Parry, Craig	Golf		5	20	25	
Parseghian, Ara	Football		10	30		1980 CHOF coach
Parsley, Charles	Basketball		10	50		played NBA 48
Parsons, Benny	Auto Racing		10	25		
Parsons, Bill	Baseball		4			Debut 1971 Mil.
Parsons, Casey	Baseball		3	10		Debut 1981
Parsons, Dixie	Baseball		14	42		Debut 1939
Parsons, Johnny	Auto Racing	+	30	75		
Parsons, Phil	Auto Racing		4	9		
Partee, Roy	Baseball		10	22		Debut 1943 Bost. RedSox
Partridge, Jay	Baseball		28	65		Debut 1927
Pasarell, Charlie	Tennis		6	17		
Pasarella, Joe	Baseball		4	12		Umpire
Paschal, Ben	Baseball		42	90		Debut 1915
Paschall, Bill	Baseball		3			Debut 1978 K.C. A's
Pascoe, Amy	Golf		125	250		
Pascual, Camilo	Baseball		6	18		Debut 1954

NAME	CATEGORY	+	SIG	SP	BALL	Comment
Pasek, Johnny	Baseball		30	65		Debut 1933
Pasero, George	Writer		3	6		
Paslawski, Greg	Hockey		3	12		
Pasley, Kevin	Baseball		3	10		Debut 1974
Pasqua, Dan	Baseball		3	10		Debut 1985
Passaglia, Martin	Basketball		10	50		played NBA 46-48
Pastorini, Dan	Football		4	12		NFL
Pastornicky, Cliff	Baseball		3	10		Debut 1983
Pastrano, Willie	Boxing		12	30		Lt.Hvy-Wt Champ
Pastushok, George	Basketball		10	50		played NBA 46
Pate, Bob	Baseball		3	12		Debut 1980
Pate, Jerry	Golf		5	25	25	
Pate, Steve	Golf		5	20	25	
Patek, Freddie	Baseball		3	10		Debut 1968
Paterno, Joe	Football		5	15		Penn State Coach
Paterson, Moira	Golf		10	35		
Patrese, Riccardo	Auto Racing		5	10		
Patrick, Bob	Baseball		12	25		Debut 1941
Patrick, Craig	Hockey		4	12		Player-Executive
Patrick, Gil	Horse Racing					HOF 1970 jockey
Patrick, Lester	Hockey		50	125		1947 HOF def
Patrick, Lynn	Hockey		45	95		1980 HOF fwd
Patrick, Myles	Basketball		3	10		played NBA 80
Patrick, Stanley	Basketball		10	50		played NBA 44-49
Patterson, Daryl	Baseball		6			Debut 1968 Tigers
Patterson, Floyd	Boxing		15	30		56-59/60-62 H-Wt Champ
Patterson, George	Basketball		4	18		played NBA 67
Patterson, Gerald	Tennis	+	12	30		HOF 1989
Patterson, Hal	Football		4	8		1971 Canadian HOF
Patterson, Mike	Baseball		3	10		Debut 1981
Patterson, Morehead	Bowling	+	8	18		1985 ABC HOF-Mer.Serv.
Patterson, Pat	Bowling	+	8	20		1974 ABC HOF
Patterson, Steve	Basketball		3	12		played NBA 71-75
Patterson, Tommy	Basketball		3	12		played NBA 72-73
Patterson, Worthington	Basketball		8	30		played NBA 57
Pattin, Marty	Baseball		16			Debut 1968 Cal.
Patton, Bill	Baseball		30	55		Debut 1935
Patton, Billy Joe	Golf		10	30	25	
Patton, Chris	Golf		5	20	25	
Patton, Gene	Baseball		8	25		Debut 1944 Bost. Braves
Patton, Jimmy	Football		28	60		NFL
Patton, Mel	Olympic		7	18		200 Dash
Patton, Ted	Olympic		3	6		Rowing
Patton, Tom	Baseball		3	12		Debut 1957
Pauca, Simona	Olympic		15	45		Gymn./Bal. Beam
Paul, Don	Football		7	18		NFL (Browns, Rams)
Paul, Mike	Baseball		4			Debut 1968 Indians
Paul, Tommy	Boxing		35	75		
Paulk, Charles	Basketball		4	18		played NBA 68-71
Paulsen, Paul	Baseball		15			Debut 1928 Tigers
Paulson, Jerry	Basketball		7	38		played NBA 57
Paultz, William	Basketball		4	14		played NBA 70-84
Pavin, Corey	Golf		10	25	35	
Pavletich, Dan	Baseball		3	14		Debut 1957
Pawloski, Stan	Baseball		4	18		Debut 1955
Paxson, James E.	Basketball		6	28		played NBA 56-57

NAME	CATEGORY	+	SIG	SP	BALL	Comment
Paxson, James J.	Basketball		6	15		played NBA 79-89
Paxson, John	Basketball		6	22		played NBA 83-
Payak, John	Basketball		10	45		played NBA 49-52
Payne, Thelma	Olympic		10	35		Diving
Payne, Tom	Basketball		3	18		played NBA 71
Payton, Gary	Basketball		5	28	100	NBA Sonics
Payton, George	Golf		30	65		
Payton, Melvin	Basketball		8	45		played NBA 51-52
Payton, Walter	Football		10	30	150	1993 HOF
Pazienza, Vinny	Boxing		12	30		Lt-Wt & Jr.Mid.-Wt Champ
Pazzetti, V.J.	Football	+	15	35		CHOF Lehigh
Peabody, Chub	Football	+	15	45		CHOF Harvard
Peacock, Johnny	Baseball		22	45		Debut 1937
Peaks, Clarence	Football		5	15		NFL
Pearce, Eddie	Golf		10	35		
Pearcy, George	Basketball		10	50		played NBA 46
Pearcy, Henry	Basketball		10	50		played NBA 46
Pearson, Albie	Baseball		8	22		Debut 1958
Pearson, Becky	Golf		5	20	25	
Pearson, David	Auto Racing		7	25		HOF 1993
Pearson, Drew	Football		5	15		NFL
Pearson, Ike	Baseball		8			Debut 1939 Phillies
Pearson, Monte	Baseball		25	50		Debut 1932 Indians
Pearson, Preston	Football		5	14		NFL
Peck, Hal	Baseball		10	35		Debut 1943 Brklyn. Dodg.
Peck, Robert	Football	+	15	40		CHOF Pittsburgh
Peck, Wiley	Basketball		3	12		played NBA 79
Peckinpaugh, Roger	Baseball		40	80		Debut 1910
Pecota, Bill	Baseball		3	10		Debut 1986
Peden, Les	Baseball		3	15		Debut 1953
Pedersen, Susan	Olympic		3	7		Swim/100 free
Pederson, Stu	Baseball		3	10		Debut 1985
Pedrique, Al	Baseball		3	10		Debut 1987
Pedroza, Eusebia	Boxing		15	40		Fthr-Wt Champ
Peebles, Bob	Golf		75	150		
Peek, Richard	Basketball		3	15		played NBA 67
Peel, Homer	Baseball		30	65		Debut 1927 Cards
Peeples, George	Basketball		3	15		played NBA 67-72
Peete, Calvin	Golf		5	20	25	
Peeters, Pete	Hockey		4	15		
Peitrangeli, Nicola	Tennis		5	18		HOF 1986
Pele	Soccer		35	75		
Pelkington, John	Basketball		12	55		played NBA 40-48
Pell, Theodore	Tennis	+	12	35		HOF 1965
Pellagrini, Eddie	Baseball		6	18		Debut 1946 Bost. RedSox
Pellegrini, Bob	Football		3	12		NFL
Pellom, Samuel	Basketball		3	12		played NBA 79-82
Pemberton, Brock	Baseball		3	10		Debut 1974
Pena, Bert	Baseball		3	10		Debut 1981
Pena, Tony	Baseball		4	12		Debut 1980
Pender, Jerry	Basketball		3	12		played NBA 73
Pender, Mel	Olympic		8	22		Track sprints
Pender, Paul	Boxing		15	32		Middle-Wt
Pendleton, Jim	Baseball		10	25		Debut 1953
Pendleton, Terry	Baseball		4	12		Debut 1984
Penick, Harvey	Golf		35	75	75	

NAME	CATEGORY	+	SIG	SP	BALL	Comment
Penna Sr., Angel	Horse Racing					HOF 1988 trainer
Penna, Toney	Golf		40	95		
Pennock, Herb	Baseball		265	388	2200	HOF 1948
Pennock, Stan	Football	+	20	40		CHOF Harvard
Penny, Christopher	Olympic		3	6		Rowing
Penske, Roger	Auto Racing		7	30		HOF 1995
Peoples, David	Golf		5	20	25	
Pep, Willie	Boxing		10	35		Fthr-Wt Champ
Pepitone, Joe	Baseball		5	15		Debut 1962
Peplinski,Jim	Hockey		3	15		
Pepper, Don	Baseball		3	12		Debut 1966 Tigers
Pepper, Dottie	Golf		10	30	35	
Pepper, Ray	Baseball		10			Debut 1932 Cards
Perconte, Jack	Baseball		3	10		Debut 1980 L.A.
Perdue, Will	Basketball		3	12		played NBA 88-
Perelli, John	Golf		10	35		
Perez, Marty	Baseball		3	12		Debut1969
Perez, Tony	Baseball		5	25		Debut 1964
Perkins, Broderick	Baseball		3	10		Debut 1978
Perkins, Don	Football		6	16		NFL
Perkins, Phil	Golf		15	45		
Perkins, Ray	Football		3	10		NFL
Perkins, Sam	Basketball		7	22		played NBA 84-
Perkins, Thomas	Golf		45	95		
Perkins, Warren	Basketball		10	50		played NBA 49-50
Perlozzo, Sam	Baseball		3	10		Debut 1977
Perreault, Gilbert	Hockey		6	20	25	1990 HOF fwd
Perret, Craig	Horse Racing		15	35		jockey
Perrier, Glorianne	Olympic		3	6		Kayak
Perry, Alf	Golf		125	250		
Perry, Aulcie	Basketball		3	12		played NBA 74
Perry, Bob	Baseball		3	12		Debut 1963
Perry, Boyd	Baseball		10	38		Debut 1941
Perry, Curtis	Basketball		4	12		played NBA 70-77
Perry, Doyt	Football		6	15		1988 CHOF coach
Perry, Fred	Tennis		18	45		HOF 1975
Perry, Gaylord	Baseball					HOF 1991. P-S HOF $25
Perry, Gaylord	Baseball		10	20	20	Gold Pl.S $12.Grt.Mo.$20
Perry, Gerald	Baseball		3	7		Debut 1983
Perry, Gordon	Football		4	8		1970 Canadian HOF
Perry, Jim	Baseball		10	12		Debut 1959 Indians
Perry, Joe	Football		8	25	125	1969 HOF RB
Perry, Kenny	Golf		5	20	25	
Perry, Michael Dean	Football		4	10		NFL
Perry, Norm	Football	+	10	22		1963 Canadian HOF
Perry, Ron	Basketball		3	15		played NBA 67-69
Perry, Timothy	Basketball		3	10		played NBA 88-
Person, Chuck	Basketball		4	10		played NBA 86-
Persons, Peter	Golf		5	20	25	
Pescatore, John	Olympic		3	6		Rowing
Pesky, Johnny	Baseball		10	22		Debut 1942 Bost. RedSox
Pesthy, Paul	Olympic		3	6		Pentathlon
Peteralli, Geno	Baseball		3	10		Debut 1982
Peterman, Bill	Baseball		12	35		Debut 1942
Peters, Gary	Baseball		10	20		Debut 1959 ChiSox
Peters, Ricky	Baseball		3	16		Debut 1979

NAME	CATEGORY	+	SIG	SP	BALL	Comment
Peters, Rusty	Baseball		15	45		Debut 1936
Petersen, Jim	Basketball		3	10		
Petersen, Louie	Bowling	+	10	25		1963 ABC HOF-Mer.Serv.
Petersen, Loy	Basketball		3	15		played NBA 68-69
Peterson, Amy	Olympic		3	15		Olymp.Med.Speed Skating
Peterson, Ben	Olympic		3	6		Wrestling
Peterson, Buddy	Baseball		6	20		Debut 1955
Peterson, Cap	Baseball		18	45		Debut 1962 S.F.Giants
Peterson, Edward	Basketball		10	50		played NBA 48-50
Peterson, Hardy	Baseball		6	18		Debut 1955
Peterson, John	Olympic		3	6		Wrestling
Peterson, Kent	Baseball		4			Debut 1944 Reds
Peterson, Melvin	Basketball		6	22		played NBA 63-69
Peterson, Robert	Basketball		8	42		played NBA 53-55
Petillo, Kelly C.	Auto Racing		60	100		
Petitbon, Richie	Football		3	12		NFL
Petoskey, Fred "Ted"	Baseball		25	55		Debut 1934 Reds
Petraglia, John	Bowling		5	18		1982 PBA HOF
Petrenko, Victor	Olympic		5	25		Olymp.Gold.Figure Skating
Petrie, Geoff	Basketball		5	12		played NBA 70-82
Petrocelli, Rico	Baseball		3	14		Debut 1963
Petrovic, Drazen	Basketball		20	75		
Pettini, Joe	Baseball		3	10		Debut 1980
Pettis, Gary	Baseball		3	10		Debut 1982
Pettit, Bob	Basketball		17	35	150	HOF 1970
Pettite, Andy	Baseball		10	50		
Pettitt, Tom	Tennis	+	12	30		HOF 1982
Pettitte, Andy	Baseball		4	28		
Pettway, Jerry	Basketball		3	8		played NBA 67-68
Petty, Kyle	Auto Racing		5	25		
Petty, Lee	Auto Racing		20	48		legendary stock car racer
Petty, Richard	Auto Racing		10	30		winningest NASCAR driver
Pevey, Marty	Baseball		3	10		Debut 1989
Peyton, Kim	Olympic		10	38		Swim/relay
Pezzano, Chuck	Bowling		5	12		1975 PBA, '82 ABC HOF
Pfann, George	Football		7	28		CHOF Cornell
Pfeil, Bobby	Baseball		3	12		Debut 1969
Pfeil, Mark	Golf		5	20	25	
Pfister, George	Baseball		7	32		Debut 1941
Pfund, Lee	Baseball		5			Debut 1945 Bklyn. Dodg.
Phaler, Emma	Bowling	+	8	22		1965 Women's IBC HOF
Phegley, Roger	Basketball		3	10		played NBA 78-83
Phelan, Art	Baseball		35			Maj. League 1910-12
Phelan, James	Basketball		10	50		played NBA 53
Phelan, Jimmy	Football	+	22	75		1973 CHOF coach
Phelan, John	Basketball		10	50		played NBA 49
Phelps, Digger	Basketball		7	14		Coach-Notre Dame
Phelps, G. "Babe"	Baseball		35	80		Debut 1931 Senators
Phelps, Jaycee	Olympic		4	38		Gold Medal. Gymnastics
Phelps, Ken	Baseball		3	10		Debut 1980
Phelps, Michael	Basketball		3	10		played NBA 85-
Philley, Dave	Baseball		8	25		Debut 1941 Cubs
Phillip, Andrew	Basketball		10	22		played NBA 47-57
Phillip, Andy	Basketball		8	45		HOF 1961
Phillips, Adolfo	Baseball		3	15		Debut 1964
Phillips, Andre	Olympic		4	9		Hurdles

NAME	CATEGORY	+	SIG	SP	BALL	Comment
Phillips, Bubba	Baseball		6	18		Debut 1955
Phillips, Damon	Baseball		8	25		Debut 1942
Phillips, Dick	Baseball		3	10		Debut 1962 S.F. Giants
Phillips, Eddie	Basketball		3	10		played NBA 82
Phillips, Gary	Basketball		3	18		played NBA 61-65
Phillips, Gene	Basketball		3	15		played NBA 71-72
Phillips, H.D.	Football	+	22	60		CHOF U of South
Phillips, Jack	Baseball		6	22		Debut1947
Phillips, Jimmy	Football		4	15		NFL
Phillips, Lawrence	Football		5	18	110	NFL
Phillips, Mike	Baseball		3	12		Debut 1973
Phillips, Tom	Hockey		250	700		1945 HOF fwd
Phillips, Tony	Baseball		3	10		Debut 1982
Phinney, Connie Carpenter	Cycling		4	10		
Phinney, Davis	Olympic		3	7		Cycling
Phinney, Elihu	Baseball		55			Cooperstown HOF Field
Phipps, Mike	Football		3	12		NFL
Phoebus, Keri	Tennis		3	6		1995 NCAA Champion
Piatkowski, Walter	Basketball		3	12		played NBA 68-71
Piazza, Mike	Baseball		10	45		Dodger Catcher
Picard, Henry	Golf		100	225	200	Old PGA HOF 1961
Picard, Noel	Hockey		3	12		
Piccard, Franck	Olympic		10	25		Alpine skiing
Picciolo, Rob	Baseball		3	10		Debut 1977
Picciuto, Nick	Baseball		6	25		Debut 1945
Piccolo, Brian	Football		250	395		NFL
Pickens, Carl	Football		4	15	75	NFL
Piechota, Al "Pie"	Baseball		4			Debut 1940 Bost. RedSox
Pierce, Billy	Baseball		4	15		Debut 1945
Pierce, Caroline	Golf		5	20	25	
Pierce, Jack	Baseball		3	10		Debut 1973
Pierce, James H.	Football		35	80		NFL
Pierce, Mary	Tennis		6	22		
Pierce, Ricky	Basketball		4	10		played NBA 82-
Piers, Julie	Golf		5	20	25	
Piersall, Jimmy	Baseball		6	15		Debut 1950
Piet, Tony	Baseball		32	70		Debut 1931 Pirates
Pietkiewicz, Stanley	Basketball		3	10		played NBA 78-80
Pietrosante, Nick	Football		25	85		NFL
Pignatano, Joe	Baseball		8	20		Debut 1957 Brklyn.Dodg.
Pihos, Pete	Football		10	22	85	1970 HOF end/WB
Pike, Jess	Baseball		15	35		Debut 1946
Pilarcik, Al	Baseball		3	12		Debut 1956
Pilch, John	Basketball		10	45		played NBA 51
Pillette, Duane	Baseball		6			Debut 1949 Yankees
Pillsbury, Art	Auto Racing	+	40	80		
Pilney, Andy	Baseball		15	35		Debut 1936
Pilote, Pierre	Hockey		6	20		1975 HOF def
Pincay, Laffit, Jr.	Horse Racing		7	24		HOF 1975 jockey
Pinckert, Erny	Football	+	38	90		CHOF Southern California
Pinckney, Ed	Basketball		3	10		played NBA 85-
Pincus, Jacob	Horse Racing					HOF 1988 trainer
Pinelli, Babe	Baseball		35	85		Debut 1918 ChiSox
Pingel, John	Football		25	50		CHOF Michigan State
Piniella, Lou	Baseball		4	15		Debut 1964
Pinkston, Elizabeth	Olympic		10	28		Diving

NAME	CATEGORY	+	SIG	SP	BALL	Comment
Pinone, John	Basketball		3	10		played NBA 83
Pinson, Vada	Baseball		18	38		Debut 1958
Piontek, David	Basketball		7	38		played NBA 56-62
Piotrowski, Thomas	Basketball		3	10		played NBA 83
Piper, Rowdy Roddy	Pro Wrestling		7	28		
Pipgras, George	Baseball		35	95		Debut 1923 Yankees
Pipp, Wally	Baseball		80	215		Debut 1913
Pippen, Scottie	Basketball		8	40	150	played NBA 87-
Piquet, Nelson	Auto Racing		5	12		
Pisoni, Jim	Baseball		3	15		Debut 1953
Pitcock, Joan	Golf		5	20		
Pitino, Rick	Basketball		2	10		Celtics Coach
Pitino, Rick	Basketball		4	12		NBA & College
Pitko, Alex	Baseball		10	35		Debut 1938
Pitler, Jake	Baseball		42	90		Debut 1917
Pitre, Didier	Hockey		200	500		1962 HOF def
Pittaro, Chris	Baseball		3	10		Debut 1985
Pittenger, Pinky	Baseball		40	80		Debut 1921
Pittman, Charles	Basketball		3	10		played NBA 82-85
Pittman, Jerry	Golf		10	35		
Pittman, Joe	Baseball		3	10		Debut 1981
Pitts, Gaylen	Baseball		3	12		Debut 1974
Pizzaro, Juan	Baseball		4	8		Debut 1957
Plank, Ed	Baseball		1850	3800	8000	HOF 1946
Plante, Jacques	Hockey		60	250	300	1978 HOF goal
Plante, Pierre	Hockey		4	18		
Plantier, Phil	Baseball		4	25		Debut 1990
Plarski, Don	Baseball		15	35		Debut 1955
Plaskett, Elmo	Baseball		3	15		Debut 1962
Platt, Whitey	Baseball		35	75		Debut 1942
Platte, Al	Baseball		42	90		Debut 1913
Player, Gary	Golf		15	40	50	PGA HOF 1974
Pleban, Connie	Hockey		5	20		1990 US HOF coach
Plesac, Dan	Baseball		4	9		Debut 1986
Pless, Rance	Baseball		3	15		Debut 1956
Plette, Willi	Hockey		4	22		
Plews, Herb	Baseball		3	14		Debut 1956
Plimpton, George	Writer		6	15		
Ploen, Ken	Football		5	16		1975 Canadian HOF
Ploujoux, Phillipe	Golf		5	20	25	
Pluckhahn, Bruce	Bowling		5	12		1989 ABC HOF-Mer.Serv.
Plum, Milt	Football		4	14		NFL
Plumb, J. Michael	Olympic		3	6		Equestrian
Plumer, Bill	Baseball		3	12		Debut 1968
Plummer, Gary	Basketball		3	10		played NBA 84
Plummer, Jake	Football		5	28		NFL
Plunk, Eric	Baseball		4	10		Debut 1986
Plunkett, Jim	Football		10	30	125	CHOF Stanfd.Heisman '70
Poat, Ray	Baseball		3			Debut 1942 Indians
Pocoroba, Biff	Baseball		3	10		Debut 1975
Poddubny, Walt	Hockey		4	18		
Podkopayeva, Lilia	Olympic		7	40		Gold Medal. Gymnastics
Podolak, Ed	Football		4	15		NFL
Podoloff, Maurice	Basketball	+	100	250		HOF 1973-Contributor
Podres, Johnny	Baseball		10	22		Debut 1953 Dodgers
Poepping, Mike	Baseball		3	10		Debut 1975

NAME	CATEGORY	+	SIG	SP	BALL	Comment
Poetsch, Annet	Olympic		10	35		Figure skating
Pofahl, Jimmy	Baseball		24	60		Debut 1940
Poff, John	Baseball		3	12		Debut 1979
Poffenberger, Cletus "Boots"	Baseball		5	12		Debut 1937
Pohl, Dan	Golf		5	20	25	
Pointer, Aaron	Baseball		3	15		Debut 1963
Pokey, Allen	Football		2	8		College Player & Coach
Poland, Hugh	Baseball		25	50		Debut 1943
Polee, Dwayne	Basketball		3	10		played NBA 85
Polidor, Gus	Baseball		3	10		Debut 1985
Pollack, Andrea	Olympic		5	20		Gold Medal. Swimming
Pollard, Frederick	Olympic		4	10		110 meter hurdles
Pollard, Fritz	Football	+	75	200		CHOF Brown
Pollard, Jim	Basketball		14	30		HOF 1977
Polly, Nick	Baseball		28	60		Debut 1937
Polonia, Luis	Baseball		3	12		Debut 1987
Polson, Ralph	Basketball		10	45		played NBA 52
Polynice, Olden	Basketball		3	12		played NBA 87-
Ponce, Carlos	Baseball		3	12		Debut 1985
Pondexter, Cliff	Basketball		3	15		played NBA 75-77
Pont, John	Football		2	5		College Coach of Year
Pool, Tommy	Olympic		3	6		Rifle
Poole, Barney	Football		8	25		CHOF Miss/No. Car/Army
Poole, Jim	Baseball		32	75		Debut 1925
Poole, Jim	Football		12	35		NFL
Poole, Ray	Baseball		9	38		Debut 1941
Pooley, Don	Golf		5	20	25	
Pope, Dave	Baseball		7	24		Debut 1952
Pope, David	Basketball		3	10		played NBA 84-85
Pope, Eddie	Soccer		3	12		USA Player of Year
Pope, Paula	Olympic		6	22		Diving
Popov, Aleksander	Olympic		7	28		Gold Medal. Swimming
Popovich, Paul	Baseball		3	12		Debut 1964
Popson, David	Basketball		3	10		played NBA 88
Poquette, Benedict	Basketball		3	14		played NBA 77-86
Poquette, Tom	Baseball		3	14		Debut 1973
Porter, Bob	Baseball		3	10		Debut 1981
Porter, Cora	Bowling		5	12		1986 Women's IBC HOF
Porter, Dan	Baseball		3	20		Debut 1951
Porter, Darrell	Baseball		3	12		Debut 1971
Porter, Dick	Baseball		35	75		Debut 1929
Porter, Henry "H.V."	Basketball	+	18	45		HOF 1960-Contributor
Porter, Howard	Basketball		3	14		played NBA 71-77
Porter, Irv	Baseball		45	95		Debut 1914
Porter, J. W.	Baseball		5	18		Debut 1952
Porter, Kevin	Basketball		3	14		played NBA 72-82
Porter, Lee	Golf		5	20	25	
Porter, Terry	Basketball		5	12		played NBA 85-
Porter, William	Olympic		5	15		110 meter hurdles
Porter, Willie	Basketball		3	18		played NBA 67-68
Portman, Robert	Basketball		3	15		played NBA 69-72
Posada, Leo	Baseball		4	15		Debut 1960 K.C.
Posedel, Bill	Baseball		9			Debut 1938 Bklyn. Dodg.
Post, Sandra	Golf		10	25	25	
Post, Wally	Baseball		22	48		Debut 1949 Reds
Postema, Pam	Baseball		5	20		1st Fem. Ump.

NAME	CATEGORY	+	SIG	SP	BALL	Comment
Postlewait, Kathy	Golf		5	20	25	
Postley, John	Basketball		3	16		played NBA 67
Postma, Ids	Speed Skating		3	15		Olympic Gold
Pott, Johnny	Golf		20	45		
Potter, Barbara	Tennis		5	12		
Potter, Cynthia	Olympic		5	14		Diving
Potter, Maryland D.	Baseball		5	15		Debut 1938 Bklyn Dodg.
Potter, Mike	Baseball		3	12		Debut 1976
Potter, Nelson "Nels"	Baseball		12			Debut 1936 Cards
Potvin, Denis	Hockey		5	20	25	1991 HOF def
Potvin, Felix	Hockey		7	22	25	
Poulin, Dave	Hockey		3	14		
Poulson, Ken	Baseball		3	15		Debut 1967
Povich, Shirley	Writer		4	8		1984 Ntl S&S HOF
Powell, Alonzo	Baseball		3	10		Debut 1987
Powell, Art	Football		5	16		NFL
Powell, Bob	Baseball		3	18		Debut 1955
Powell, Boog	Baseball		5	16		Debut 1961
Powell, Cincy	Basketball		4	18		played NBA 67-74
Powell, Hosken	Baseball		3	10		Debut 1978 Minn. Twins
Powell, Jimmy	Golf		5	25	25	
Powell, John	Olympic		3	14		Discus
Powell, Mike	Olympic		10	35		Long Jump
Powell, Paul Ray	Baseball		3	12		Debut 1971
Power, Vic	Baseball		8	25		Debut 1954
Powers, Connie	Bowling		5	12		1973 Women's IBC HOF
Powers, Greg	Golf		5	20	25	
Powers, Jimmy	Writer		6	14		
Powers, Johnny	Baseball		5	18		Debut 1955
Powers, Les	Baseball		25	60		Debut 1938
Powers, Mike	Baseball		32	68		Debut 1932 Indians
Powers, Ross	Snowboarding		2	5		World & World Cup Champ
Powis, Carl	Baseball		3	15		Debut 1957
Poynton, Dorothy	Olympic		8	22		Diving
Pradd, Mal	Basketball		3	18		played NBA 67-68
Pramesa, Johnny	Baseball		4	24		Debut 1948
Pratt, Babe	Hockey		95	225		1966 HOF def
Pratt, Del	Baseball		60	125		Debut 1912
Pratt, Frank	Baseball		45	95		Debut 1921
Pratt, Larry	Baseball		45	100		Debut 1914
Pratt, Michael	Basketball		3	14		played NBA 70-71
Prefontaine, Steve	Track		100	225		Distance Legend
Pregulman, Merv	Football		7	22		CHOF Michigan
Preibisch, Mel	Baseball		22	45		Debut 1940 Bost. RedSox
Prentice, Dean	Hockey		5	24		
Prescott, Bobby	Baseball		3	15		Debut 1961
Presko, Joe	Baseball		4			Debut 1951 Cards
Presley, Jim	Baseball		3	10		Debut 1984
Presnell, Tot	Baseball		4	8		Debut 1938
Pressey, Paul	Basketball		3	10		played NBA 82-
Pressley, Dominic	Basketball		3	10		played NBA 88
Pressley, Harold	Basketball		3	10		played NBA 86-
Preston, Ken	Football		4	8		1990 Canadian HOF
Previs, Stephen	Basketball		3	14		played NBA 72
Price, Anthony	Basketball		3	10		played NBA 83
Price, C.M. "Nibs"	Basketball		5	15		Coach-Cal

NAME	CATEGORY	+	SIG	SP	BALL	Comment
Price, Eddie	Football	+	40	110		CHOF Tulane
Price, Elizabeth	Golf		10	35		
Price, James	Basketball		3	15		played NBA 72-78
Price, Jim	Baseball		4	15		Debut 1967
Price, Joe	Baseball		3			Debut 1980 Reds
Price, John	Olympic		3	6		Yachting
Price, Michael	Basketball		4	14		played NBA 70-71
Price, Mike	Football		2	6		Washington St. Coach
Price, Nick	Golf		10	35	45	
Price, William	Basketball		3	10		played NBA 86-
Prichard, Bob	Baseball		22	48		Debut 1939
Priddy, Bob	Baseball		6			Debut 1962 Pirates
Priddy, Gerry	Baseball		20	65		Debut 1941 Yankees
Priddy, Robert	Basketball		10	45		played NBA 52
Pride, Dicky	Golf		5	20	25	
Priest, Johnnie	Baseball		50	110		Debut 1911 Yankees
Primeau, Joe	Hockey		95	275		1963 HOF fwd
Prince, Bob	Broadcaster	+	15	35		1986 Ntl S&S HOF
Prince, Lindsay	Tennis		4	10		Arkansas star
Prince, Tom	Baseball		3	10		Debut 1987
Pritchard, Buddy	Baseball		4	15		Debut 1957
Pritchard, John	Basketball		10	50		played NBA 49
Probert, Bob	Hockey		5	25		
Pronovost, Jean	Hockey		5	18		
Pronovost, Marcel	Hockey		6	20	20	1978 HOF def
Propp, Brian	Hockey		5	18		
Prost, Alain	Auto Racing		5	12		
Prothro, Doc	Baseball		50	95		Debut 1920
Prothro, Tommy	Football		5	15		1991 CHOF
Protopopov, Alec	Olympic		15	35		Figure Skating
Provis, Nicole	Tennis		4	8		
Provost, Claude	Hockey		4	16		
Prudhomme, Don	Auto Racing		6	18		HOF 1991
Pruess, Earl "Gibby"	Baseball		15			Debut 1920 Browns
Pruett, Jim	Baseball		6	24		Debut 1944
Pruett, Scott	Auto Racing		4	18		
Pruitt, Dillard	Golf		5	20	25	
Pruitt, Greg	Football		4	12		NFL
Pruitt, Mike	Football		4	12		NFL
Pruitt, Ron	Baseball		3	10		Debut 1975
Pryor, Aaron	Boxing		10	22		
Pryor, Greg	Baseball		3	10		Debut 1976
Puckett, Kirby	Baseball		12	40		Debut 1984
Pugh, Leslie	Basketball		10	50		played NBA 48-49
Pugh, Roy	Basketball		10	50		played NBA 47-48
Puhl, Terry	Baseball		3	10		Debut 1977
Puica, Maricica	Olympic		10	22		800 Meters
Puig, Rich	Baseball		3	10		Debut 1974
Pujols, Luis	Baseball		3	12		Debut 1977
Pulford, Bob	Hockey		7	20	22	1991 HOF fwd
Pulford, Harvey	Hockey		125	390		1945 HOF def
Pund, Peter	Football	+	15	40		CHOF Georgia Tech
Pung, Jackie	Golf		10	35	45	
Punsalan, E. & Swallow, J.	Ice Dancing		4	22		USA Champions
Puppa, Daren	Hockey		4	18		
Purdy, Sam	Horse Racing					HOF 1970 jockey

NAME	CATEGORY	+	SIG	SP	BALL	Comment
Purpur, Clifford	Hockey		5	10		1974 US HOF
Pursey, Walter	Golf		65	170		
Purtzer, Tom	Golf		5	25	25	
Purvis, Duane	Football		7	20		Purdue
Putman, Ed	Baseball		3	10		Debut 1976
Putnam, Don	Basketball		10	50		played NBA 46-49
Putnam, Pat	Baseball		3	10		Debut 1977
Pyburn, Jim	Baseball		3	14		Debut 1955
Pye, Fred	Golf		75	175		
Pyle, C.C.	Promoter		20	55		
Pytlak, Frankie	Baseball		35	75		Debut 1932
Pyznarski, Tim	Baseball		3	10		Debut 1986

Quackenbush, Bill	Hockey		10	24		1976 HOF def
Qualls, Jimmy	Baseball		3	12		Debut 1969
Quarrie, Donald	Olympic		10	22		200 Meters
Quarry, Jerry	Boxing		12	30		Hvy-Wt Contender
Quast, Anne	Golf		10	35		
Queen, Billy	Baseball		3	18		Debut 1954
Queen, Melvin Joseph	Baseball		6	22		Debut 1942 Yankees
Quick, Hal	Baseball		40	95		Debut 1939
Quick, Mike	Football		3	12		NFL
Quick, Robert	Basketball		3	16		played NBA 68-71
Quick, Smiley	Golf		10	35		
Quigley, Brett	Golf		5	20	25	
Quigley, Ernest "Quig"	Basketball	+	22	48		HOF 1961
Quilici, Frank	Baseball		3	10		Debut 1963
Quillen, Glenn	Baseball		20	42		Debut 1938
Quilty, S.P.	Football	+	10	22		1966 Canadian HOF
Quinn, Dan	Hockey		4	12		
Quinn, Jack P.	Baseball		150	375		Still valid ML records
Quinn, Zoe	Bowling	+	8	18		1979 Women's IBC HOF
Quinones, Luis	Baseball		3	10		Debut 1983
Quinones, Rey	Baseball		3	10		Debut 1986
Quintana, Carlos	Baseball		3	10		Debut 1988
Quirk, Jamie	Baseball		3	10		Debut 1975
Quist, Adrian	Tennis		5	12		HOF 1984
Qway, Dwight Braxton	Boxing		12	30		Lt.-Hvy-Wt Champ

NAME	CATEGORY	+	SIG	SP	BALL	Comment
Rabb, Johnny	Baseball		3	10		Debut 1982
Rackley, Luke	Basketball		3	15		played NBA 69-73
Rackley, Marv	Baseball		6	24		Debut 1947
Radbourn, Charles	Baseball		2033	4233		HOF 1939
Rademacher, Pete	Boxing		5	10		Hvy-Wt Contender
Rader, Dave	Baseball		3	10		Debut 1971
Rader, Don	Baseball		38	80		Debut 1913 ChiSox
Rader, Doug	Baseball		3	12		Debut 1967
Rader, Howard	Basketball		10	50		played NBA 46-48
Radford, Floyd	Baseball		3	10		Debut 1980
Radford, Mark	Basketball		3	10		played NBA 81-82
Radford, Wayne	Basketball		3	12		played NBA 78
Radosavljevic, Preki	Soccer		4	15		USA Scoring threat
Radovich, Frank	Basketball		3	22		played NBA 61
Radovich, George	Basketball		10	45		played NBA 52
Radtke, Jack	Baseball		20	40		Debut 1936
Radzisewski, Raymond	Basketball		8	40		played NBA 57
Raffensberger, Ken	Baseball		7			Debut 1939 Cards
Rafferty, Ronan	Golf		5	25	25	
Rafter, Pat	Tennis		5	22		
Ragan, Dave	Golf		10	35		
Ragelis, Raymond	Basketball		10	45		played NBA 51
Ragland, Tom	Baseball		3	14		Debut 1971
Rahal, Bobby	Auto Racing		8	25		
Rahlves, Daron	Skiing		3	9		Alpine, Team USA
Raiken, Sherwin	Basketball		10	45		played NBA 52
Raines, Larry	Baseball		18	40		Debut 1957
Raines, Tim	Baseball		4	14		Debut 1979
Rains, Edward	Basketball		3	10		played NBA 81-82
Rajsich, Gary	Baseball		3	10		Debut 1982
Ralston, Dennis	Tennis		7	22		HOF 1987
Ralston, John	Football		3	6		NFL Coach of Yr. '73
Ramage, Rob	Hockey		3	18		
Ramazzoti, Bob	Baseball		8	28		Debut 1946 Brklyn Dodg.
Rambis, Kurt	Basketball		3	12		played NBA 81-
Rambo, John	Olympic		5	18		High Jump
Ramenofsky, Marilyn	Olympic		3	7		Swim/400 free
Ramey, Nancy	Olympic		3	7		Swim/butterfly
Ramirez, Manny	Baseball		8	30		
Ramirez, Mario	Baseball		3	10		Debut 1980
Ramirez, Milt	Baseball		3	14		Debut 1970
Ramirez, Orlando	Baseball		3	12		Debut 1974
Ramirez, Rafael	Baseball		3	12		Debut 1980

NAME	CATEGORY	+	SIG	SP	BALL	Comment
Ramos, Bobby	Baseball		3	12		Debut 1978
Ramos, Domingo	Baseball		3	12		Debut 1978
Ramos, Sugar (Ultiminio)	Boxing		22	48		Fthr-Wt Champ
Ramsay, Jack	Basketball		7	22		HOF 1992 Coach
Ramsbottom, Nancy	Golf		5	20	25	
Ramsey, Bill	Baseball		9	28		Debut 1945
Ramsey, Calvin	Basketball		7	25		played NBA 59-60
Ramsey, Frank	Basketball		8	20		HOF 1981
Ramsey, G.	Football		7	20		CHOF William and Mary
Ramsey, Jack	Basketball		4	10		NBA
Ramsey, Mike	Baseball		3	10		Debut 1978
Ramsey, Mike	Baseball		3	10		Debut 1987
Ramsey, Raymond	Basketball		10	50		played NBA 47-48
Rand, Dick	Baseball		6	25		Debut 1953
Rand, Mary	Olympic					Long jump
Randall, Bob	Baseball		3	10		Debut 1976
Randall, Jim	Baseball		3	10		Debut 1988
Randle, Lenny	Baseball		3	14		Debut 1971 Senators
Randle, Sonny	Football		4	15		NFL
Randolph, John "Dutch"	Baseball		15			Cubs 1904
Randolph, Mason	Golf		5	20	25	
Randolph, Sam	Golf		5	20	25	
Randolph, Willie	Baseball		3	14		Debut 1975
Ranew, Merritt	Baseball		3	14		Debut 1962
Ranford, Bill	Hockey		3	12		
Rank, Wallace	Basketball		3	10		played NBA 80
Rankin, Frank	Hockey		260	750		1961 HOF fwd
Rankin, Judy	Golf		10	25	30	
Ransey, Kelvin	Basketball		3	12		played NBA 80-85
Ransom, Henry	Golf		50	95		
Ransom, Jeff	Baseball		3	10		Debut 1981
Ranzino, Samuel	Basketball		10	45		played NBA 51
Rapp, Earl	Baseball		4	24		Debut 1949 Tigers
Rapp, Susan	Olympic		3	7		Swim/breaststroke
Rarick, Cindy	Golf		5	20	25	
Rarnsey, Mike	Hockey		3	14		
Raschi, Vic	Baseball		16	38		Debut 1946 Yankees
Rascoe, Robert	Basketball		3	18		played NBA 67-69
Rashad, Ahmad	Football		5	20	125	NFL
Rasmussen, Blair	Basketball		3	10		played NBA 85-
Rasmussen, Eric	Baseball		4	10		Debut 1975
Rasmussen, Kyle	Skiing		2	7		Alpine, Team USA
Rassmussen, Bill	Broadcasting		5	20		Founder ESPN
Ratelle, Jean	Hockey		6	18	22	1985 HOF fwd
Rathman, Tom	Football		3	12		NFL
Rathmann, Jim	Auto Racing		22	50		
Ratkovicz, George	Basketball		12	55		played NBA 41-54
Ratleff, Ed	Basketball		3	16		played NBA 73-77
Ratliff, Gene	Baseball		3	12		Debut 1965
Ratliff, Michael	Basketball		3	14		played NBA 72-73
Ratliff, Paul	Baseball		3	12		Debut 1963
Ratterman, George	Football		4	15		NFL
Rauch, Johnny	Football		4	14		NFL
Raudman, Bob	Baseball		3	12		Debut 1966
Rautins, Leo	Basketball		3	10		played NBA 83-84
Ravenscroft, Gladys	Golf		95	175		

NAME	CATEGORY	+	SIG	SP	BALL	Comment
Rawlings, Johnny	Baseball		45	90		Debut 1914
Rawlins, Horace	Golf		525	1100		
Rawls, Betsy	Golf		30	65	45	PGA, LPGA HOF '87, '77
Rawls, Katherine	Olympic		8	25		Diving
Ray, Clifford	Basketball		3	12		played NBA 71-80
Ray, Donald	Basketball		10	50		played NBA 48-49
Ray, Edward	Golf		150	365		
Ray, Hugh "Shorty"	Football	+	260	840		1966 HOF contributor
Ray, James	Basketball		8	40		played NBA 56-59
Ray, Johnny	Baseball		3	10		Debut 1981
Ray, Larry	Baseball		3	10		Debut 1982
Rayl, James	Basketball		3	18		played NBA 67-68
Raymer, Milt	Bowling		5	12		1972 ABC HOF-Mer.Serv.
Raymond, Claude	Baseball		6			Debut 1959 ChiSox
Raymond, Craig	Basketball		3	18		played NBA 68-72
Rayner, Chuck	Hockey		5	20		1973 HOF goal
Rea, Connie	Basketball		10	45		played NBA 53
Read, Don	Football		2	5		College Nat'l Title
Ready, Randy	Baseball		3	10		Debut 1983
Reams, Leroy	Baseball		3	14		Debut 1969
Reardon, Jeff	Baseball		3	14		Debut 1979
Reardon, Kenny	Hockey		10	24		1966 HOF def
Reaves, Joe	Basketball		3	10		played NBA 73
Rebegliati, Ross	Olympic		3	15		Snowboarding
Rebel, Art	Baseball		25	25		Debut 1938
Rebholz, Russ	Football		4	8		1963 Canadian HOF
Recchi, Mark	Hockey		5	18		
Rechichar, Bert	Football		6	12		NFL
Reddout, Franklin	Basketball		10	45		played NBA 53
Reder, Johnny	Baseball		15	50		Debut 1932
Redfern, Buck	Baseball		40	85		Debut 1928
Redfield, Joe	Baseball		3	10		Debut 1988
Redman, Michele	Golf		5	20	25	
Redman, Susie	Golf		5	20	25	
Redmond, Jack	Baseball		40	80		Debut 1935
Redmond, Marlon	Basketball		3	10		played NBA 78-79
Redmond, Wayne	Baseball		3	12		Debut 1965
Redus, Gary	Baseball		3	10		Debut 1982
Reece, Bob	Baseball		3	10		Debut 1978
Reece, Gabrielle	Volleyball		5	35		Model-Athlete
Reed, Andre	Football		5	14	100	NFL
Reed, Bill	Baseball		3	15		Debut 1952
Reed, Elmer	Bowling	+	8	18		1978 ABC HOF-Mer.Serv.
Reed, George	Football		4	8		1979 Canadian HOF
Reed, Hub	Basketball		7	28		played NBA 58-64
Reed, Jack	Baseball		3	12		Debut 1961
Reed, Jake	Football		6	20		NFL Vikings WR
Reed, Jody	Baseball		3	12		Debut 1987
Reed, Ron	Basketball		4	18		played NBA 65-66
Reed, Willis	Basketball		10	22	125	HOF 1981
Reedmon, Glenn	Baseball		3	12		Debut 1974
Reeds, Claude	Football	+	20	45		CHOF Oklahoma
Rees, Dai	Golf		75	165		
Reese, Jimmy	Baseball		7	20		Debut 1930 Yankees
Reese, Pee Wee	Baseball					HOF 1984,Gold Pl.S $28
Reese, Pee Wee	Baseball		15	30	50	P-S HOF $45,Grt.Mo.$45

NAME	CATEGORY	+	SIG	SP	BALL	Comment
Reese, Rich	Baseball		3	12		Debut 1964 Minn.
Reeve, Ted	Football	+	10	22		1963 Canadian HOF
Reeves, Bobby	Baseball		30	65		Debut 1926
Reeves, Dan	Football		5	18	100	NFL Coach
Reeves, Dan	Football	+	85	350		1967 HOF contributor
Refram, Dean	Golf		10	35		
Regalado, Rudy	Baseball		7	22		Debut 1954
Regalado, Victor	Golf		10	35		
Regan, Bill	Baseball		35	80		Debut 1926
Regan, Phil	Baseball		4			Debut 1960 Tigers
Regan, Richie	Basketball		7	32		played NBA 55-57
Rego, Tony	Baseball		28	60		Debut 1924
Rehfeldt, Donald	Basketball		10	50		played NBA 50-51
Reiber, Frank	Baseball		20	45		Debut 1933
Reich, Herm	Baseball		6	22		Debut 1949
Reichardt, Bill	Football		15	32		NFL
Reichardt, Rick	Baseball		3	12		Debut 1964
Reichler, Joe	Writer		3	6		
Reichow, Jerry	Football		5	12		NFL
Reid, Floyd	Football		9	35		NFL
Reid, Jessie	Baseball		3	10		Debut 1987
Reid, Jim	Basketball		3	16		played NBA 67
Reid, John	Olympic		3	6		Yachting
Reid, Kerry Melville	Tennis		5	14		
Reid, Mike	Football		8	20		CHOF Penn State
Reid, Mike	Golf		5	25	25	
Reid, Robert	Basketball		3	14		played NBA 77-
Reid, Scott	Baseball		3	12		Debut 1969
Reid, Steve	Football		6	22		CHOF Northwestern
Reid, Steve	Golf		5	20	25	
Reid, William	Basketball		3	10		played NBA 80
Reid, William	Football	+	20	45		CHOF Harvard
Reid, William A.	Basketball	+	22	65		HOF 1963-Contributor
Reid, Wilred	Golf		75	195		
Reiff, John	Horse Racing					HOF 1956 jockey
Reimer, Kevin	Baseball		3	10		Debut 1988
Reinbach, Mike	Baseball		3	10		Debut 1974
Reinholz, Art	Baseball		25	60		Debut 1928
Reinsdorf, Jerry	Basketball		3	12		2-sport owner
Reis, Bobby	Baseball		32	70		Debut 1931
Reiser, "Pistol" Pete	Baseball		38	90		Debut 1940
Reiser, Chick	Basketball		15	60		played NBA 43-49
Reiss, Al	Baseball		25	55		Debut 1932
Reith, Bob	Golf		5	20	25	
Reitz, Ken	Baseball		3	12		Debut 1972
Rellford, Richard	Basketball		3	10		played NBA 87
Remigino, Lindy	Olympic		3	7		400 meter relay
Remy, Jerry	Baseball		3	12		Debut 1975
Renberg, Mikael	Hockey		6	18	22	
Renfro, Mel	Football		6	20	100	CHOF Oregon. '96 HOF
Renfro, Ray	Football		12	30		NFL
Renick, Rick	Baseball		3	12		Debut 1968 Minn.
Renna, Bill	Baseball		4	18		Debut 1953
Renner, Jack	Golf		5	20	25	
Rennicke, John	Basketball		10	45		played NBA 51
Renolds, Danny	Baseball		6	22		Debut 1945

NAME	CATEGORY	+	SIG	SP	BALL	Comment
Rensa, Tony	Baseball		12	55		Debut 1930 Tigers
Renserger, Robert	Basketball		10	50		played NBA 45-46
Renshaw, Ernest	Tennis	+	12	25		HOF 1983
Renshaw, William	Tennis	+	12	25		HOF 1983
Renteria, Rich	Baseball		3	10		Debut 1986
Rentner, Pug	Football	+	20	45		CHOF Northwestern
Rentzel, Lance	Football		5	16		NFL
Repass, Bob	Baseball		9	38		Debut 1939
Repoz, Roger	Baseball		3	12		Debut 1964
Repulski, Rip	Baseball		12	28		Debut 1953
Rerych, Stephen	Olympic		3	8		Swim/relay
Resch, Glenn	Hockey		5	20		
Resta, Dario	Auto Racing	+	35	75		
Restani, Kevin	Basketball		3	12		played NBA 74-81
Restelli, Dino	Baseball		7	24		Debut 1949 Pirates
Rettenmund, Merv	Baseball		5	18		Debut 1968 Balt. Orioles
Retton, Mary Lou	Olympic		7	30		Gymn/All Around
Retzer, Ken	Baseball		3	12		Debut 1961
Retzlaff, Pete	Football		5	15		NFL
Reulbach, Ed	Baseball		180			CHI Cubs Pitch.1905-13
Reuschel, Rick	Baseball		4	10		Debut 1972
Reutemann, Carlos	Auto Racing		5	12		
Revering, Dave	Baseball		3	10		Debut 1978
Revolta, Johnny	Golf		50	125	75	Old PGA HOF 1963
Revson, Peter	Auto Racing		75	165		HOF 1996 sports cars
Reyes, Gilberto	Baseball		3	10		Debut 1983
Reyna, Claudio	Soccer		3	10		Team USA standout
Reynolds, Allie	Baseball		12	35		Debut 1942 Indians
Reynolds, Bob	Football		7	25		CHOF Stanford
Reynolds, Bobby	Football	+	22	75		CHOF Nebraska
Reynolds, Butch	Track		6	25		400 Meters World Record
Reynolds, Carl	Baseball		45	90		Debut 1927 ChiSox
Reynolds, Cathy	Golf		5	20	25	
Reynolds, Craig	Baseball		3	12		Debut 1975
Reynolds, Don	Baseball		3	10		Debut 1978 S.D. Padres
Reynolds, George	Basketball		3	12		played NBA 69
Reynolds, Harold	Baseball		5	12		Debut 1983
Reynolds, Harry	Olympic		3	12		400 Meters
Reynolds, Jerry	Basketball		3	10		played NBA 85-
Reynolds, R. J.	Baseball		3	10		Debut 1983
Reynolds, Ronn	Baseball		3	10		Debut 1982
Reynolds, Tommie	Baseball		3	12		Debut 1963
Rhawn, Bobby	Baseball		22	48		Debut 1947
Rheaume, Manon	Hockey		5	25		Women's Pioneer
Rhett, Eric	Football		4	15	75	NFL
Rhine, Kendall	Basketball		3	18		played NBA 67-68
Rhoden, Rick	Baseball		5	12		Debut 1974
Rhodes, Dusty	Baseball		8	25		Debut 1952
Rhodes, Eugene	Basketball		8	45		played NBA 52
Rhodes, Ray	Football		3	7		NFL Player & Coach
Rhomberg, Kevin	Baseball		3	12		Debut 1982
Rhyan, Richard	Golf		5	20	25	
Rhyne, Hal	Baseball		32	70		Debut 1926
Rice, Bob	Baseball		30	65		Debut 1926
Rice, Del	Baseball		18	38		Debut 1945 Cards
Rice, Glen	Basketball		6	25		NBA-Heat

NAME	CATEGORY	+	SIG	SP	BALL	Comment
Rice, Grantland	Writer	+	95	200		1962 Ntl S&S HOF
Rice, Greg	Track		7	16		
Rice, Hal	Baseball		4	18		Debut 1948
Rice, Harry	Baseball		30	70		Debut 1923
Rice, Jerry	Football		12	50	195	NFL
Rice, Jim	Baseball		4	15		Debut 1974
Rice, Len	Baseball		4	18		Debut 1944
Rice, Sam	Baseball					B&W PC $165
Rice, Sam	Baseball		70	192	1500	HOF 1963, Gold Pl.S $145
Richard, Deb	Golf		5	20	25	
Richard, Henri	Hockey		6	20	25	1979 HOF fwd
Richard, Jacques	Hockey		3	7		
Richard, Lee	Baseball		3	10		Debut 1971
Richard, Maurice	Hockey		7	22	30	1961 HOF fwd
Richards, Bob	Olympic		6	25		Pole Vault
Richards, Fred	Baseball		3	18		Debut 1951
Richards, Gene	Baseball		3	10		Debut 1977
Richards, Gordon, Sir	Horse Racing		65	225		Acclaimed British Jockey
Richards, Joe	Bowling	+	8	22		1976 PBA HOF-Mer. Serv.
Richards, Paul	Baseball		16	48		Debut 1932
Richards, Vincent	Tennis	+	65	155		HOF 1961
Richardson, Bobby	Baseball		4	12		Debut 1955
Richardson, Clint	Basketball		3	6		played NBA 79-86
Richardson, Dot, Dr.	Olympic		3	15		Gold Med. Softball
Richardson, George	Hockey		295	1250		1950 HOF fwd
Richardson, Ham	Tennis		35	80		
Richardson, Jeff	Baseball		3	10		Debut 1989
Richardson, Ken	Baseball		20	65		Debut 1942
Richardson, Michael Ray	Basketball		3	10		played NBA 78-85
Richardson, Michele	Olympic		3	10		Swim/800 free
Richardson, Nolan	Basketball		3	7		Arkansas Coach
Richardson, Steven	Golf		5	20	25	
Richardt, Mike	Baseball		3	10		Debut 1980
Richbourg, Lance	Baseball		40	85		Debut 1921
Richer, Stephane	Hockey		5	18		
Richey, Nancy	Tennis		6	18		
Richie, Bob	Baseball		3	10		Debut 1989
Richman, Milt	Writer		3	6		
Richmond, Don	Baseball		22	65		Debut 1941
Richmond, Mitch	Basketball		5	20	100	played NBA 88-
Richmond, Tim	Auto Racing		5	12		
Richter, Al	Baseball		4	18		Debut 1951
Richter, Annagret	Olympic		6	30		Gold Medal. Track
Richter, John	Basketball		8	38		played NBA 59
Richter, Les	Football		8	22		CHOF California
Richter, Mike	Hockey		3	22		
Richter, Ulrike	Olympic		6	28		Gold Medal. Swimming
Rickard, Tex	Promoter		40	95		
Rickenbacker, Eddie	Auto Racing	+	90	195		HOF 1994
Ricker, Chester	Auto Racing	+	30	85		
Rickert, Marv	Baseball		32	75		Debut 1942
Ricketts, Dave	Baseball		6	16		Debut 1963
Ricketts, Dick	Basketball		18	38		played NBA 55-57
Rickey, Branch	Baseball		203	575	2500	HOF 1967
Rickon, Kelly	Olympic		3	6		Rowing
Rico, Fred	Baseball		3	12		Debut 1969

NAME	CATEGORY	+	SIG	SP	BALL	Comment
Ridder, Bob	Hockey		5	10		1976 US HOF admin
Riddick, Steve	Olympic		10	22		Track sprints
Riddle, Elmer	Baseball		10			Debut 1939 Reds
Riddle, Johnny	Baseball		18	55		Debut 1930 Cubs
Riddles, Libby	Dog Sled Racing		6	16		
Rider, Isaiah	Basketball		5	20		5
Rider, J.R.	Basketball		7	30		NBA-Wolves
Ridgeway, Angie	Golf		5	20	25	
Ridgle, Jackie	Basketball		3	10		played NBA 71
Ridley, Fred	Golf		5	20	25	
Ridley, Mike	Hockey		4	12		
Riebe, Hank	Baseball		7	22		Debut 1942
Riebe, Melvin	Basketball		22	75		played NBA 43-48
Riedel, Lars	Olympic		4	15		Gold Medal. Discus
Riedy, Robert	Basketball		5	29		played NBA 67
Riegel, Skee	Golf		50	95		
Riesen, Marty	Tennis		5	12		
Rifenburg, Dick	Football		4	14		NFL
Riffey, James	Basketball		10	50		played NBA 50
Rigby, Cathy	Olympic		6	22		Gymnastics
Riger, Robert	Artist-Photographer		10	40		Depicted Sports
Riggert, Joe	Baseball		35	95		Debut 1911
Riggin, Aileen	Olympic		10	28		Diving
Riggins, John	Football		12	35	150	1992 HOF RB
Riggs, Bobby	Tennis		10	30		HOF 1957
Riggs, Gerald	Football		5	12		NFL
Riggs, Lew	Baseball		35	85		Debut 1934
Rigney, Bill	Baseball		4	14		Debut 1946 NY Giants
Rigney, Frank	Football		5	10		1985 Canadian HOF
Rigney, Johnny	Baseball		10			Debut 1937 ChiSox
Rigney, Topper	Baseball		35	80		Debut 1922
Rikard, Cully	Baseball		8	30		Debut 1941
Riker, Tom	Basketball		3	10		played NBA 72-74
Riles, Ernest	Baseball		3	10		Debut 1985
Riley, Bill	Hockey		5	10		1977 US HOF
Riley, Jack	Football		6	18		CHOF Northwestern
Riley, Jack	Hockey		5	10		1979 US HOF coach
Riley, Jim	Baseball		24	80		Debut 1921
Riley, Mike	Football		2	5		Oregon St. Coach
Riley, Pat	Basketball		5	25	125	played NBA 67-75-Coach
Riley, Polly	Golf		35	75		
Riley, Robert	Basketball		3	10		played NBA 70
Riley, Ron	Basketball		3	10		played NBA 72-75
Rinaldi, Richard	Basketball		3	10		played NBA 71-73
Rinehart, Charles	Football		15	55		CHOF Lafayette
Ringo, Jim	Football		6	18	85	1981 HOF OL
Rinker, Bob	Baseball		4	18		Debut 1950
Rinker, Larry	Golf		5	20	25	
Riordan, Mike	Basketball		4	14		played NBA 68-76
Rios, Juan	Baseball		3	12		Debut 1969
Rios, Marcelo	Tennis		4	18		
Ripken, Billy	Baseball		3	9		Debut 1987
Ripken, Cal Jr.	Baseball		15	50		Debut 1981
Ripken, Cal Sr.	Baseball		5	10		Coach
Ripley, Elmer	Basketball	+	18	40		HOF 1972
Ripple, Jimmy	Baseball		25	55		Debut 1936

NAME	CATEGORY	+	SIG	SP	BALL	Comment
Ripplemeyer, Ray	Baseball		4			Debut 1962 Senators
Ris, Walter	Olympic		5	14		Swim/sprints
Risen, Arnie	Basketball		10	35		played NBA 45-57
Rishling, Gertrude	Bowling	+	8	18		1972 Women's IBC HOF
Rison, Andre	Football		6	18	100	NFL
Ritchie, Alvin	Football	+	10	22		1963 Canadian HOF
Ritchie, Willie	Boxing		65			Lt.-Wt Champ
Ritger, Dick	Bowling		5	10		1978 PBA, '84 ABC HOF
Ritter, Goebel	Basketball		10	50		played NBA 48-50
Ritter, Louise	Olympic		5	15		High Jump
Rittner, Barbara	Tennis		4	8		
Ritzman, Alice	Golf		5	20	25	
Rivas, Ramon	Basketball		3	10		played NBA 88
Rivera, Bombo	Baseball		3	10		Debut 1975
Rivera, German	Baseball		3	10		Debut 1983
Rivera, Jim	Baseball		7	22		Debut 1952
Rivera, Luis	Baseball		3	10		Debut 1986
Rivers, David	Basketball		3	10		played NBA 88-
Rivers, Doc	Basketball		4	14		played NBA 83-
Rivers, Mickey	Baseball		3	12		Debut 1970
Rixey, Eppa	Baseball		208	450	3500	HOF 1963
Rizzo, Johnny	Baseball		25	65		Debut 1938
Rizzo, Patti	Golf		5	20	25	
Rizzuto, Phil	Baseball					Gold Pl.$15,P-S HOF $35
Rizzuto, Phil	Baseball		9	20	25	Debut 1941, HOF 1994
Roach, Mel	Baseball		4	15		Debut 1953
Roarke, Mike	Baseball		3	12		Debut 1961 Tigers
Robb, James	Golf		475	995		
Robbins, Hillman	Golf		10	35		
Robbins, Kelly	Golf		5	20	25	
Robbins, Lee Roy	Basketball		10	50		played NBA 47-48
Robbins, Red	Basketball		3	14		played NBA 67-74
Robello, Tommy	Baseball		12	38		Debut 1933
Roberge, Skippy	Baseball		10	35		Debut 1941
Roberson, Bo	Olympic		5	16		Long Jump
Roberson, Dick	Basketball		4	16		played NBA 69-75
Roberts, Anthony	Basketball		3	10		played NBA 77-83
Roberts, Bip	Baseball		3	10		Debut 1986
Roberts, Clifford	Golf		125	250		
Roberts, Curt	Baseball		15	48		Debut 1954
Roberts, Dave L.	Baseball		3	10		Debut 1962 Hou. Astros
Roberts, Dave W.	Baseball		3	10		Debut 1972 S.D.Padres
Roberts, David	Olympic		5	17		Pole Vault
Roberts, Floyd	Auto Racing	+	85	190		
Roberts, Fred	Basketball		3	10		played NBA 83-
Roberts, Gordie	Hockey		55	175		1971 HOF fwd
Roberts, Joseph	Basketball		4	22		played NBA 60-67
Roberts, Kenny	Auto Racing		5	15		HOF 1990
Roberts, Leon	Baseball		3	10		Debut 1974
Roberts, Loren	Golf		5	20	25	
Roberts, Marvin	Basketball		3	16		played NBA 71-76
Roberts, Robin	Baseball					HOF 1976. P-S HOF $25
Roberts, Robin	Baseball		10	20	25	Gold Pl. $12, Grt.Mo.$20
Roberts, William	Basketball		10	50		played NBA 48-49
Robertson, Alfred	Horse Racing					HOF 1971 jockey
Robertson, Alvin	Basketball		4	12		played NBA 84-

NAME	CATEGORY	+	SIG	SP	BALL	Comment
Robertson, Andre	Baseball		3	10		Debut 1981
Robertson, Belle	Golf		5	20	25	
Robertson, Bob	Baseball		3	10		Debut 1967 Pirates
Robertson, Daryl	Baseball		3	15		Debut 1962
Robertson, Dave	Baseball		55	125		Debut 1912
Robertson, Don	Baseball		4	15		Debut 1954
Robertson, Gene	Baseball		40	90		Debut 1919
Robertson, George	Auto Racing	+	30	65		
Robertson, Jim	Baseball		4	17		Debut 1954 Phil. A's
Robertson, Oscar	Basketball		20	60	135	HOF 1979
Robertson, Rich	Baseball		3			Debut 1966 S.F. Giants
Robertson, Sherry	Baseball		25	65		Debut 1940
Robertson, Tony	Basketball		3	10		played NBA 77-78
Robey, Rick	Basketball		3	10		played NBA 78-85
Robidoux, Billy Jo	Baseball		3	10		Debut1985
Robie, Carl	Olympic		4	8		Swim/200 fly
Robinson, Aaron	Baseball		32	65		Debut 1943
Robinson, Arnie	Olympic		3	8		Long Jump
Robinson, Bill	Baseball		3	12		Debut 1966
Robinson, Brooks	Baseball					HOF 1983. P-S HOF $30
Robinson, Brooks	Baseball		7	20	25	Gold Pl. $12, Grt.Mo.$25
Robinson, Bruce	Baseball		3	12		Debut 1978 Oakland
Robinson, Cliff	Basketball		3	10		played NBA 79-
Robinson, Cliff	Basketball		3	10		played NBA 89-
Robinson, Craig	Baseball		3	10		Debut 1972
Robinson, Dave	Baseball		3	10		Debut 1970
Robinson, Dave	Basketball		10	28	150	NBA-Spurs
Robinson, Davé	Football		4	14		NFL
Robinson, E.N.	Football	+	18	40		1955 CHOF coach
Robinson, Earl	Baseball		3	15		Debut 1958
Robinson, Eddie	Baseball		7	24		Debut 1942 Indians
Robinson, Elizabeth	Olympic		3	6		Track relay
Robinson, Floyd	Baseball		3	15		Debut 1960 ChiSox
Robinson, Flynn	Basketball		3	14		played NBA 66-73
Robinson, Frank	Baseball					HOF 1982. P-S HOF $35
Robinson, Frank	Baseball		12	25	30	Gold Pl. $18. Grt.Mo. $30
Robinson, Glenn	Basketball		4	22	125	NBA-Bucks
Robinson, Jack "Jackie"	Baseball		367	800	2500	Gold Pl.$700,B&W PC $600
Robinson, Jackie	Basketball		4	12		played NBA 78-79
Robinson, Johnny	Football		5	18		NFL
Robinson, Larry	Hockey		4	18		
Robinson, Leona	Bowling	+	8	20		1969 Women's IBC HOF
Robinson, Mack	Olympic		25	60		200 Meters
Robinson, Oliver	Basketball		3	10		played NBA 82
Robinson, Ronnie	Basketball		3	10		played NBA 73-74
Robinson, Samuel Lee	Basketball		4	18		played NBA 70-71
Robinson, Sugar Ray	Boxing		100	225		Middle&Welter-Wt Champ
Robinson, Truck	Basketball		5	16		played NBA 74-84
Robinson, Wayne	Basketball		3	10		played NBA 80
Robinson, Wayne	Football		7	22		NFL
Robinson, Wil	Basketball		3	12		played NBA 73
Robinson, Wilbert	Baseball		933	2500	6000	HOF 1945
Robinzine, Bill	Basketball		3	12		played NBA 75-81
Robinzine, Kevin	Olympic		3	7		Track relay
Robisch, David	Basketball		3	10		played NBA 71-83
Robitaille, Luc	Hockey		5	22		

NAME	CATEGORY	+	SIG	SP	BALL	Comment
Robson, Tom	Baseball		3	10		Debut 1974
Robustelli, Andy	Football		5	18	100	1971 HOF DL
Rocca, Contantino	Golf		5	20	25	
Rocca, Peter	Olympic		3	7		Swim/200 backstroke
Rocco, Mickey	Baseball		6	20		Debut 1943 Indians
Rocha, Red	Basketball		7	22		played NBA 47-56
Roche, John	Basketball		3	12		played NBA 71-81
Roche, Tony	Tennis		6	20		HOF 1986
Rochelli, Lou	Baseball		7	25		Debut 1944
Rock, Eugene	Basketball		10	50		played NBA 47
Rock, Les	Baseball		15	45		Debut 1936
Rocker, Jack	Basketball		10	50		played NBA 47
Rockett, Pat	Baseball		3	10		Debut 1976
Rockne, Knute	Football		750	2500		TLS/Content $2,000
Rodden, Michael	Football	+	10	22		1964 Canadian HOF
Rodgers, Bill	Baseball		35	85		Debut 1915
Rodgers, Bob "Buck"	Baseball		4	12		Debut 1961 L.A.
Rodgers, Guy	Basketball		8	25		played NBA 58-69
Rodgers, Ira	Football		15	45		CHOF West Virginia
Rodgers, Johnny	Football		7	30		Heisman Nebr. '72. NFL
Rodgers, Phil	Golf		5	20	25	
Rodin, Eric	Baseball		3	15		Debut 1954
Rodman, Dennis	Basketball		15	54	150	played NBA 86-
Rodnina, Irina	Olympic		10	50		Olymp.Gold.Figure Skating
Rodriguez, Aurelio	Baseball		3	10		Debut 1967
Rodriguez, Chi Chi	Golf		5	20	25	PGA HOF 1992, Contrib.
Rodriguez, Ellie	Baseball		3	12		Debut 1968
Rodriguez, Luis	Boxing		15	40		Welter-Wt Champ
Rodriguez, Raoul	Olympic		3	5		Rowing
Rodriquez, Alex	Baseball		10	40		Debut
Rodriquez, Frank	Basketball		3	18		Twins young pitcher
Rodriquez, Jennifer	Speed Skating		3	9		US Record breaker
Roe, Elwin "Preacher"	Baseball		8	18		Debut 1933
Roelants, Gaston	Olympic		75	150		Distance
Roenick, Jeremy	Hockey		5	22	30	
Roenicke, Gary	Baseball		3	10		Debut 1976
Roenicke, Ron	Baseball		3	10		Debut 1976
Roettger, Oscar	Baseball		28	60		Debut 1923 Yankees
Roffe-Steinrotter, Diann	Olympic		4	18		Olymp.Gold.Alpine Skiing
Rogan, Bullet Joe	Baseball					HOF 1998
Rogel, Fran	Football		4	14		NFL
Rogell, Billy	Baseball		18	42		Debut 1925 Bost. Braves
Rogers, Andre	Baseball		4	14		Debut 1957
Rogers, Annette	Olympic		3	6		Track relay
Rogers, Bill	Golf		5	20	25	
Rogers, Edward	Football		22	75		CHOF Minnesota
Rogers, George	Football		10	30		Heisman So.Car. '80
Rogers, Harry	Basketball		3	12		played NBA 75
Rogers, John	Basketball		3	10		played NBA 86-87
Rogers, John	Golf		75	165		
Rogers, John	Horse Racing					HOF 1955 trainer
Rogers, Marshall	Basketball		3	10		played NBA 76
Rogers, Packy	Baseball		9	32		Debut 1938
Rogers, Steve	Baseball		3	8		Debut 1973
Rogers, Willie	Basketball		5	16		played NBA 68
Roges, Albert	Basketball		10	22		played NBA 53-54

NAME	CATEGORY	+	SIG	SP	BALL	Comment
Rogodzinski, Mike	Baseball		3	10		Debut 1973
Rohde, Kim	Olympic		2	6		Gold Med. Trap Shooting
Rohde, Lisa	Olympic		3	6		Rowing
Rohloff, Ken	Basketball		7	35		played NBA 63-64
Rohn, Dan	Baseball		3	10		Debut 1983
Rohwer, Ray	Baseball		30	70		Debut 1921 Pirates
Roig, Tony	Baseball		3	16		Debut 1953
Rojas, Cookie	Baseball		3	12		Debut 1962
Rojek, Stan	Baseball		7	20		Debut 1942 Brklyn. Dodg.
Roland, Jim	Baseball		3			Debut 1962 Minn.
Roland, Johnny	Football		5	14		NFL
Rolfe, Red	Baseball		65	150		Debut 1931
Rolling, Ray	Baseball		35	85		Debut 1912
Rollings, Red	Baseball		30	75		Debut 1927
Rollins, Ken	Basketball		10	50		played NBA 48-52
Rollins, Philip	Basketball		8	35		played NBA 58-60
Rollins, Rich	Baseball		4	14		Debut 1961 Minn.
Rollins, Wayne	Basketball		3	12		played NBA 77-
Romack, Barbara	Golf		10	35	35	
Roman, Bill	Baseball		3	14		Debut 1964
Romano, Johnny	Baseball		4	14		Debut 1958
Romano, Tom	Baseball		3	10		Debut 1987
Romar, Lorenzo	Basketball		3	10		played NBA 80-84
Romario	Soccer		4	15		Brazil
Romeo, Robin	Bowler		4	8		
Romero, Ed	Baseball		3	10		Debut 1977
Romero, Eduardo	Golf		5	20	25	
Romig, Joe	Football		6	15		CHOF Colorado
Romine, Kevin	Baseball		3	10		Debut 1985
Romme, Gianne	Speed Skating		8	28		Gold Medal Olympic WR
Romnes, Elwin	Hockey	+	10	22		1973 US HOF
Romney, Dick	Football	+	18	40		1954 CHOF coach
Romonosky, John	Baseball		4			Debut 1953 Cards
Ronaldo	Soccer		4	18		Player of Year
Rondeau, Dick	Hockey		5	10		1985 US HOF
Roof, Gene	Baseball		3	10		Debut 1981
Roof, Phil	Baseball		3	12		Debut 1961 Mil.
Rook, Jerry	Basketball		4	18		played NBA 69
Roomes, Rolando	Baseball		3	10		Debut 1988
Rooney, Art	Football	+	30	95	275	1964 HOF contributor
Rooney, Pat	Baseball		3	10		Debut 1981
Roosevelt, Ellen	Tennis	+	16	40		HOF 1975
Roosma, John	Basketball	+	28	60		HOF 1961
Root, Charlie	Baseball		40	95		Debut 1923
Root, Elbert	Olympic		6	22		Diving
Roper, Bill	Football	+	18	40		1951 CHOF coach
Rosar, Buddy	Baseball		12	45		Debut 1939 Yankees
Rosario, Edwin "El Chapo"	Boxing		25	65		4x Lt.-Wt. World Champ
Rosario, Jimmy	Baseball		3	10		Debut 1971
Rosburg, Bob	Golf		10	25	35	
Rose, Bob	Basketball		3	9		played NBA 88
Rose, Bobby	Baseball		3	10		Debut 1989
Rose, Clarence	Golf		5	20	25	
Rose, George	Football		3	9		NFL
Rose, Lionel	Boxing		12	30		Bantam-Wt Champ
Rose, Mauri	Auto Racing	+	150	350		HOF 1996

NAME	CATEGORY	+	SIG	SP	BALL	Comment
Rose, Murray	Olympic		10	40		Swimming
Rose, Pete	Baseball		10	25		Debut 1963
Roseboro, Johny	Baseball		5	15		Debut 1957
Roselli, Bob	Baseball		3	14		Debut 1955
Rosello, Dave	Baseball		3	10		Debut 1972
Rosen, Al	Baseball		14	28		Debut 1947 Indians
Rosen, Goody	Baseball		6	25		Debut 1937
Rosenberg, Aaron	Football		18	60		CHOF Southern California
Rosenberg, Harry	Baseball		15	40		Debut 1930
Rosenberg, Lou	Baseball		35	75		Debut 1923
Rosenberg, Petey	Basketball		10	50		played NBA 46
Rosenbloom, Maxie "Slapsy"	Boxing		55	120		HOF Lt.Hvy-Wt Champ
Rosenbluth, Lenny	Basketball		8	25		played NBA 57-58
Rosenfeld, Max	Baseball		35	80		Debut 1931
Rosenstein, Hank	Basketball		10	50		played NBA 46
Rosenthal, Jody	Golf		5	20	25	
Rosenthal, Larry	Baseball		10	25		Debut 1936
Rosenthal, Richard	Basketball		10	45		played NBA 54-56
Rosenthal, Si	Baseball		40	95		Debut 1925
Roser, Jack	Baseball		35	80		Debut 1922
Rosewall, Ken	Tennis		10	40		HOF 1980
Ross, Alex	Golf		995	2250		
Ross, Art	Hockey		60	300		1945 HOF def
Ross, Barney	Boxing		85	185		Welter & Lt-Wt Champ
Ross, Bob	Baseball		3			Debut 1950 Senator
Ross, Bobby	Football		3	8		NFL Lions Coach
Ross, Chet	Baseball		15	40		Debut 1939
Ross, Dan	Football		3	10		NFL
Ross, Don	Baseball		9	30		Debut 1938
Ross, Donald	Golf		750	1595		PGA HOF 1977, Contrib.
Ross, Larry	Hockey		5	10		1988 US HOF coach
Ross, Lee "Buck"	Baseball		5			Debut 1936 A's
Rosset, Marc	Olympic		4	12		Gold Medal. Tennis
Rossman, Mike	Boxing		12	35		Lt-Hvy-Wt
Rote, Kyle	Football		8	25		CHOF Southern Methodist
Rote, Kyle, Jr.	Soccer		4	10		
Rote, Tobin	Football		4	15		NFL
Roth, Joe	Football		18	40		
Roth, Mark	Bowling		6	15		1987 PBA HOF
Roth, Richard	Olympic		4	8		Swim/ind. medley
Roth, Scott	Basketball		3	10		played NBA 87-
Rothel, Bob	Baseball		8	25		Debut 1945
Rothenberg, Irv	Basketball		10	50		played NBA 46-48
Rothhammer, Keena	Olympic		4	12		Swim/800 free
Rothrock, Jack	Baseball		35	70		Debut 1925
Rothwell, Michael	Olympic		3	8		Yachting
Rottner, Mickey	Basketball		10	50		played NBA 45-47
Rotz, John L.	Horse Racing					HOF 1983 jockey
Round (Little), Dorothy	Tennis	+	12	32		HOF 1985
Roundfield, Danny	Basketball		4	14		played NBA 75-86
Rouse, Jeff	Olympic		3	7		Gold Medal. Swimming
Rouser, Jason	Olympic		3	6		Gold Medal. Track
Roush, Edd	Baseball					HOF 1962. P-S HOF $110
Roush, Edd	Baseball		18	75	155	Gold Pl. $35,B&W PC$85
Rousseau, Bobby	Hockey		4	12		
Routt, Joe	Football		15	45		CHOF Texas A&M

NAME	CATEGORY	+	SIG	SP	BALL	Comment
Roux, Gifford	Basketball		10	50		played NBA 46-48
Rowan, Ron	Basketball		3	10		played NBA 86
Rowdon, Wade	Baseball		3	10		Debut 1984
Rowe Sr, James	Horse Racing					HOF 1955 trainer
Rowe, Charles	Golf		75	195		
Rowe, Curtis	Basketball		3	10		played NBA 71-78
Rowe, Paul	Football	+	10	22		1964 Canadian HOF
Rowell, Bama	Baseball		9	38		Debut 1939 Bost. Braves
Rowinski, Jim	Basketball		3	10		played NBA 88
Rowland, Chuck	Baseball		35	85		Debut 1923 Phil. A's
Rowland, Derrick	Basketball		3	9		played NBA 85
Rowsom, Brian	Basketball		3	9		played NBA 87-
Roy, Luther	Baseball		35	90		Cle-Brooklyn Pitch '24-'29
Roy, Patrick	Hockey		12	38	45	
Royal, Darrell	Football		6	20		1983 CHOF coach
Royals, Reggie	Basketball		3	10		played NBA 74
Royer, Hugh	Golf		10	35		
Royer, Hugh III	Golf		5	20	25	
Royer, Robert	Basketball		10	50		played NBA 49
Royser, Willie	Baseball		3	10		Debut 1981
Royster, Jerry	Baseball		3	12		DEbut 1973
Rozelle, Pete	Football		14	40	125	1985 HOF contributor
Rozier, Mike	Football		10	25		Heisman Nebr. '83. NFL
Roznovsky, Vic	Baseball		5	16		Debut 1964
Rubeling, Al	Baseball		24	40		Debut 1940 Phil. A's
Ruberto, Sonny	Baseball		3	14		Debut 1969
Ruby, Lloyd	Auto Racing		18	65		
Ruby, Martin	Football		4	8		1974 Canadian HOF
Rucker, Johnny	Baseball		12	42		Debut 1940 NY Giants
Rucker, Reggie	Football		3	10		NFL
Rudd, John	Basketball		3	10		played NBA 78
Rudd, Ricky	Auto Racing		7	15		
Rudi, Joe	Baseball		3	10		Debut 1967
Rudo, Milt	Bowling		5	10		1984 ABC HOF-Mer.Serv.
Rudolph, Dick	Baseball		125			1914 27 game winner
Rudolph, Ernie	Baseball		4			Debut 1945 Brklyn. Dodg.
Rudolph, Ken	Baseball		4	14		Debut 1969
Rudolph, Mason	Golf		10	30	35	
Rudolph, Wilma	Olympic		40	85		100 Dash
Rudometkin, John	Basketball		6	22		played NBA 62-64
Ruel, Muddy	Baseball		55	125		Debut 1915
Ruether, Dutch	Baseball		42	90		Debut 1917
Rufer, Rudy	Baseball		4	15		Debut 1949
Ruffing, Red	Baseball					HOF 1967. Gold Pl.$110
Ruffing, Red	Baseball		40	140	500	P-S HOF $650
Ruffner, Paul	Basketball		3	16		played NBA 70-75
Ruiz (Conforto), Tracie	Olympic		7	22		Synch. Swimming
Ruiz, Chico	Baseball		38	80		Debut 1964
Ruiz, Chico	Baseball		4	12		Debut 1978
Ruklick, Joseph	Basketball		6	25		played NBA 59-61
Ruland, Jeff	Basketball		4	10		played NBA 81-86
Rule, Bob	Basketball		4	15		played NBA 67-74
Rule, Jack	Golf		10	30		
Rullo, Jerry	Basketball		10	50		played NBA 46-49
Rullo, Joe	Baseball		35	75		Debut 1943
Rumler, Bill	Baseball		45	95		Debut 1914

NAME	CATEGORY	+	SIG	SP	BALL	Comment
Rummells, Dave	Golf		5	20	25	
Rump, Anita	Bowling	+	8	20		1962 Women's IBC HOF
Runge, Paul	Baseball		3	10		Debut 1981
Runnells, Pete	Baseball		16	38		Debut 1951
Runnells, Tom	Baseball		3	10		Debut 1985
Runyan, Damon	Writer	+	65	150		1964 Ntl S&S HOF
Runyan, Joe	Dog Sled Racing		4	12		
Runyan, Paul	Golf		55	125	75	
Ruotsalainen, Reijo	Hockey		4	9		
Rupp, Adolph	Basketball	+	85	175		HOF 1968-Coach
Ruppert, Jacob	Baseball		75	195		Owner
Ruschmeyer, Addie	Bowling	+	10	22		1961 Women's IBC HOF
Rush, Bob	Baseball		10			Debut 1948 Cubs
Rusher, John	Olympic		3	6		Rowing
Rusie, Amos	Baseball		950	2500	5000	HOF 1977
Russel, Blair	Hockey		70	250		1965 HOF fwd
Russel, Jeff	Football	+	19	22		1963 Canadian HOF
Russell, Bill	Baseball		3	10		Debut 1969
Russell, Bill	Basketball		175	275	550	HOF 1974
Russell, Cazzie	Basketball		6	18		played NBA 66-77
Russell, Douglas	Olympic		4	12		Swim/100 fly
Russell, Ernie	Hockey		65	200		1965 HOF fwd
Russell, Frank	Basketball		3	18		played NBA 72
Russell, Fred	Writer		3	6		1988 Ntl S&S HOF
Russell, Harvey	Baseball		48	100		Debut 1914 Balt.(Federal)
Russell, Jim	Baseball		12	30		Debut 1942 Pirates
Russell, John	Baseball		3	10		Debut 1984
Russell, John "Honey"	Basketball	+	20	45		HOF 1964
Russell, Lloyd	Baseball		22	45		Debut 1968
Russell, Michael	Basketball		3	10		played NBA 74-84
Russell, Pierre	Basketball		3	10		played NBA 71-72
Russell, Reb	Baseball		40	95		Debut 1913
Russell, Rip	Baseball		18	45		Debut 1939
Russell, Rube	Basketball		4	18		played NBA 67
Russell, Walker	Basketball		3	10		played NBA 82-87
Russi, Bernhard	Olympic		10	28		Alpine Skiing
Russo, Andy	Basketball		5	10		Coach-UW
Russo, Marius	Baseball		12			Debut 1939 Yankees
Ruszkowski, Hank	Baseball		8	25		Debut 1944
Ruth, Babe	Baseball		1000	2800	4500	HOF 1936.B&W PC$4750
Rutherford, Jim	Baseball		40	95		Debut 1910
Rutherford, Johnny	Auto Racing		10	20		HOF1996
Rutigliano, Sam	Football		3	6		NFL & Colleg Coach
Rutledge, Jeff	Football		3	10		NFL
Rutner, Mickey	Baseball		6	22		Debut 1947
Rutschman, Ad			2	6		NAIA HOF
Ruttan, Jack	Hockey		50	180		1962 HOF fwd
Ruttman, Troy	Auto Racing		15	45		
Ruuska, Sylvia	Olympic		3	7		Swim relay
Ruuttu, Christian	Hockey		4	15		
Ruzici, Virginia	Tennis		5	12		
Ryal, Mary	Baseball		3	10		Debut 1982
Ryan, Blondy	Baseball		42	90		Debut 1930
Ryan, Bud	Baseball		48	100		Debut 1912
Ryan, Buddy	Football		5	20	100	NFL Coach
Ryan, Connie	Baseball		8	22		Debut 1942 NY Giants

NAME	CATEGORY	+	SIG	SP	BALL	Comment
Ryan, Elizabeth	Tennis	+	12	25		HOF 1972
Ryan, Esther	Bowling	+	12	32		1963 Women's IBC HOF
Ryan, Frank	Football		4	10		NFL
Ryan, Jack	Baseball		32	70		Debut 1929
Ryan, Joe B.	Football	+	10	22		1968 Canadian HOF
Ryan, Mike	Baseball		3	10		Debut 1964
Ryan, Nolan	Baseball		18	45	55	Debut 1966
Ryan, W.P.D. "Rosy"	Baseball		25			Debut 1919 NY Giants
Rydze, Richard	Olympic		3	8		Diving
Rye, Gene	Baseball		22	55		Debut 1931
Rymer, Charlie	Golf		5	20	25	
Rypien, Mark	Football		4	10		NFL
Ryun, Jim	Olympic		8	25		1,500 meters

Saam, Byrum	Broadcaster		5	12		
Saari, Roy	Olympic		3	7		Swim/ind. medley
Sabatini, Gabriela	Tennis		15	50		
Saberhagen, Bret	Baseball		5	10		Debut 1984
Sablatnik, Ethel	Bowling	+	8	18		1979 Women's IBC HOF
Sabo, Alex	Baseball		8	28		Debut 1936
Sabo, Chris	Baseball		3	10	20	Debut 1988
Sabourin, Gary	Hockey		4	15		
Sachs, Leonard	Basketball	+	22	45		HOF 1961-Coach
Sacka, Frank	Baseball		6	15		Debut 1951
Saddler, Sandy	Boxing		15	32		Fthr-Wt Champ
Sadek, Mike	Baseball		3	10		Debut 1973
Sadowski, Bob	Baseball		3	14		Debut 1960
Sadowski, Ed	Baseball		3	12		Debut 1960
Sadowski, Ed	Basketball		12	50		played NBA 40-49
Saffell, Tom	Baseball		4	16		Debut 1949
Saier, Vic	Baseball		40	85		Debut 1911
Saiki, Kim	Golf		5	20	25	
Sailer, Toni	Olympic		15	42		Alpine skiing
Sailors, Ken	Basketball		10	50		played NBA 46-50
Sain, John	Baseball		4	14		Debut 1942
Sakata, Lenn	Baseball		3	10		Debut 1977
Sakic, Joe	Hockey		8	25	30	
Salaam, Rashaan	Football		10	40	90	'94 Heisman Colo.
Salas, Lauro	Boxing		18	38		
Salas, Mark	Baseball		3	10		Debut 1984
Salazar, Alberto	Marathon		6	20		
Salazar, Angel	Baseball		3	10		Debut 1983
Salazar, Luis	Baseball		3	10		Debut 1980

NAME	CATEGORY	+	SIG	SP	BALL	Comment
Salisbury, Sean	Football		4	9		NFL
Salkeld, Bill	Baseball		30	70		Debut 1945
Salley, John	Basketball		4	15		played NBA 86-
Salman, Louis	Football		22	65		CHOF Notre Dame
Salmon, Chico	Baseball		4	15		Debut 1964
Salsinger, H.G.	Writer		3	6		
Saltzgaver, Jack (Otto H.)	Baseball		30	65		Debut 1932 Yankees
Salvadori, Al	Basketball		3	12		played NBA 67
Salvino, Carmen	Bowling		7	22		1975 PBA, '79 ABC HOF
Salvo, Manny	Baseball		4			Debut 1939 NY Giants
Samaranch, Juan A.	Olympic		5	10		Pres. I.O.C.
Samcoff, Ed	Baseball		4	15		Debut 1951
Samford, Ron	Baseball		4	15		Debut 1954
Sample, Billy	Baseball		3	10		Debut 1978
Sampras, Pete	Tennis		12	55		
Sampson, Harold	Golf		65	195		
Sampson, Ralph	Basketball		5	14		played NBA 83-
Samuel, Juan	Baseball		3	10		Debut 1983
Samuelsson, Kjell	Hockey		4	15		
Sanchez, Emilio	Tennis		5	14		
Sand, Heinie	Baseball		45	95		Debut 1923
Sandberg, Ryne	Baseball		10	35		Debut 1981
Sande, Earl	Horse Racing		100	40		HOF 1955 jockey
Sander, Anne Quast	Golf		5	20	25	
Sander, Bill	Golf		5	20	25	
Sanders, Al	Basketball		3	12		played NBA 72
Sanders, Barry	Football		14	55	150	Heisman OK St. '88. NFL
Sanders, Deion	Baseball		12	25		Debut 1989
Sanders, Deion	Football		10	35	150	NFL
Sanders, Doug	Golf		5	25	25	
Sanders, Frankie	Basketball		3	10		played NBA 78-80
Sanders, George	Baseball	+	20	35		Minor League, Broadcaster
Sanders, George	Broadcaster	+	10	20		
Sanders, John	Baseball		4	14		Debut 1965
Sanders, Mike	Basketball		3	10		played NBA 82-
Sanders, Ray	Baseball		12	32		Debut 1942 Cards
Sanders, Reggie	Baseball		3	10		Debut 1974
Sanders, Rick	Olympic		18	45		Wrestling
Sanders, Ricky	Football		6	15		NFL
Sanders, Spec	Football		30	85		NFL
Sanders, Tom	Basketball		7	22		played NBA 60-72
Sanderson, Derek	Hockey		4	18		
Sandlock, Mike	Baseball		5	22		Debut 1942 Bost. Braves
Sandow	Weightlifting		60	125		
Sands, Charlie	Baseball		3	12		Debut 1967 Yankees
Sandstrom, Tomas	Hockey		5	16		
Sandt, Tom	Baseball		3	10		Debut 1975
Sandusky, John	Football		3	12		NFL
Sanford, Fred	Baseball		6			Debut 1943 Browns
Sanford, George	Football	+	15	35		1971 CHOF coach
Sanford, Jack	Baseball		4	14		Debut 1940
Sanford, Ron	Basketball		3	10		played NBA 71
Sanguillen, Manny	Baseball		4	12		Debut 1967
Sanicki, Ed	Baseball		4	18		Debut 1949
Sankey, Ben	Baseball		20	45		Debut 1929
Santana, Manuel	Tennis		7	22		HOF 1984

NAME	CATEGORY	+	SIG	SP	BALL	Comment
Santee, Wes	Olympic		15	35		Track
Santiago, Benito	Baseball		4	10		Debut 1986
Santini, Robert	Basketball		8	40		played NBA 55
Santo, Ron	Baseball		5	14		Debut 1960
Sanudo, Cesar	Golf		10	30		
Sapenter, Debra	Olympic		3	7		Track relay
Saperstein, Abe	Basketball	+	175	365		HOF 1970-Contributor
Sappleton, Wayne	Basketball		3	10		played NBA 84
Sarazen, Gene	Golf		10	35	35	PGA HOF 1974
Sargent, George	Golf		195	495		
Sargissian, Sargis	Tennis		3	6		1995 NCAA Champion
Sarni, Bill	Baseball		15	35		Debut 1951
Sasser, Mackey	Baseball		5	12	20	Debut 1987
Sather, Glenn	Hockey		5	18		1997 HOF. Builder
Satriano, Tom	Baseball		3	12		Debut 1961
Saubert, Jean	Olympic		5	20		Alpine skiing
Saucier, Frank	Baseball		4	16		Debut 1951 Browns
Sauer, George	Football		7	18		CHOF Nebraska
Sauer, George, Jr.	Football		4	12		NFL
Sauer, Hank	Baseball		7	18		Debut 1941 Reds
Sauers, Gene	Golf		5	20	25	
Saul, Pep	Basketball		10	40		played NBA 49-54
Sauldsberry, Woody	Basketball		6	28		played NBA 57-65
Saulters, Glynn	Basketball		4	18		played NBA 68
Saunders, Fred	Basketball		3	14		played NBA 74-77
Saunders, Rusty	Baseball		30	75		Debut 1927
Savage, Don	Baseball		28	60		Debut 1944
Savage, Don	Basketball		10	45		played NBA 51-56
Savage, John Robert "Bob"	Baseball		4			Debut 1942 Phil. A's
Savage, Ted	Baseball		3	14		Debut 1962
Savard, Denis	Hockey		5	20		
Savard, Serge	Hockey		5	22		1986 HOF def
Savchenko-Neiland, Larisa	Tennis		4	10		
Saverine, Bob	Baseball		4	14		Debut 1959 Balt. Orioles
Saville, Eleanor	Olympic		6	18		Swim/100 M Free
Savio, Garton Del	Baseball		7	24		Debut 1943
Savitt, Dick	Tennis		8	25		HOF 1976
Sawatski, Carl	Baseball		12	35		Debut 1948
Sawchuk, Terry	Hockey		100	300	350	1971 HOF goal
Sawyer, Alan	Basketball		10	50		played NBA 50
Sawyer, Carl	Baseball		40	80		Debut 1915
Sawyer, D. E.	Golf		50	125		
Sax, Dave	Baseball		3	10		Debut 1982
Sax, Ollie	Baseball		25	65		Debut 1928
Sax, Steve	Baseball		6	16		Debut 1981
Saxton, Johnny	Boxing		15	36		Welter-Wt Champ
Sayers, Gale	Football		8	25	125	1977 HOF RB
Sayles, Bill	Baseball		4			Debut 1939 Bost. RedSox
Sazio, Ralph	Football		4	8		1988 Canadian HOF
Scahill, Stephen	Golf		5	20	25	
Scala, Jerry	Baseball		4	18		Debut 1948
Scales, DeWayne	Basketball		3	10		played NBA 80-83
Scalzi, Frank	Baseball		8	22		Debut 1939
Scalzi, Johnny	Baseball		30	65		Debut 1931
Scanlan, Frank	Baseball		15			Debut 1909
Scanlan, Fred	Hockey		75	250		1965 HOF fwd

NAME	CATEGORY	+	SIG	SP	BALL	Comment
Scanlon, Pat	Baseball		3	10		Debut 1974
Scarbath, Jack	Football		6	18		CHOF Maryland
Scarlett, Hunter	Football		20	60		CHOF Pennsylvania
Scarritt, Russ	Baseball		35	75		Debut 1929
Scarsella, Les	Baseball		30	60		Debut 1935
Schaal, Paul	Baseball		3	12		Debut 1964
Schabinger, Arthur	Basketball	+	22	45		HOF 1961
Schacht, Al	Baseball		20	45		Debut 1919. BBball Clown
Schade, Frank	Basketball		3	12		played NBA 72
Schadler, Ben	Basketball		10	50		played NBA 47-48
Schaefer, Herman	Basketball		15	60		played NBA 41-49
Schaefer, Jeff	Baseball		3	10		Debut 1989
Schaeffer, Billy	Basketball		3	12		played NBA 73-75
Schaeffer, Carl	Basketball		12	50		played NBA 49-50
Schafer, Robert	Basketball		8	40		played NBA 55-56
Schaffer, Jimmie	Baseball		3	14		Debut 1961 Cards
Schaive, Johnny	Baseball		3	12		Debut 1958
Schalk, Ray	Baseball					Gold Pl. $335
Schalk, Ray	Baseball					HOF 1955. Gold Pl. $375
Schalk, Ray	Baseball		75	185		HOF 1955, B&W PC $450
Schalk, Roy	Baseball		5	12		Debut 1932
Schang, Bobby	Baseball		45	75		Debut 1914
Schang, Wally	Baseball		52	120		Debut 1913
Schardt, Wilburt	Baseball		20	45		1911-12 Brooklyn Pitcher
Scharein, George	Baseball		20	48		Debut 1937
Scharnus, Ben	Basketball		10	50		played NBA 46-48
Schatzman, Marvin	Basketball		10	50		played NBA 49
Schaus, Fred	Basketball		18	38		played NBA 49-53
Schayes, Danny	Basketball		3	10		played NBA 81-
Schayes, Dolph	Basketball		8	20		HOF 1972
Scheckter, Jody	Auto Racing		5	12		
Schectman, Ossie	Basketball		10	50		played NBA 46
Scheer, Heinie	Baseball		32	70		Debut 1922
Scheeren, Fritz	Baseball		40	85		Debut 1914
Scheffing, Bob	Baseball		16	35		Debut 1941 Cubs
Scheffler, Thomas	Basketball		3	10		played NBA 84
Scheib, Carl	Baseball		8	18		Debut 1943 A's
Scheinblum, Richie	Baseball		3	10		Debut 1965
Schell, Danny	Baseball		18	48		Debut 1954
Schellhase, Dave	Basketball		4	18		played NBA 66-67
Schemansky, Norbert	Olympic		3	10		Weightlifting
Schembechler, Bo	Football		3	10		Michigan Coach
Schemer, Mike	Baseball		8	28		Debut 1945
Schenk, Ard	Olympic		15	35		Olymp.Gold.Speed skating
Schenk, Christian	Olympic		10	22		Decathlon
Schenkel, Chris	Bowling		6	15		1976 PBA, '88 ABC HOF
Schenkel, Chris	Broadcaster		6	15		1981 Ntl S&S HOF
Schenz, Hank	Baseball		9	28		Debut 1946
Scherbarth, Bob	Baseball		4	16		Debut 1950
Scherbo, Vitaly	Olympic		7	38		Olymp.Gold.Gymnastics
Scherer, Herbert	Basketball		10	50		played NBA 50-51
Scherr, William	Olympic		3	6		Wrestling
Scherrer, Tom	Golf		5	20	25	
Schick, Morrie	Baseball		40	95		Debut 1917
Schilling, Carroll	Horse Racing					HOF 1970 jockey
Schilling, Chuck	Baseball		4	10		Debut 1961 RedSox

NAME	CATEGORY	+	SIG	SP	BALL	Comment
Schindler, Bill	Baseball		38	85		Debut 1920
Schiraldi, Cal	Baseball		5	12		Debut 1984
Schissler, Les	Bowling		5	10		1979 ABC HOF
Schlee, John	Golf		5	20	25	
Schlesinger, Rudy	Baseball		3	12		Debut 1965
Schliebner, Dutch	Baseball		32	70		Debut 1923
Schloredt, Bob	Football		4	14		CHOF Washington
Schlueter, Dale	Basketball		3	10		played NBA 68-77
Schlueter, Jay	Baseball		3	10		Debut 1971
Schlueter, Norm	Baseball		14	38		Debut 1938
Schmandt, Ray	Baseball		38	80		Debut 1915
Schmautz, Bobby	Hockey		4	14		
Schmautz, Cliff	Hockey		4	14		
Schmees, George	Baseball		3	16		Debut 1952
Schmeling, Max	Boxing		35	60		1930-32 H-Wt Champ
Schmid, Harald	Olympic		7	22		400 M Hurdles
Schmidt, Bob	Baseball		3	12		Debut 1958 Reds
Schmidt, Dave	Baseball		3	10		Debut 1981
Schmidt, Ernest J.	Basketball	+	18	40		HOF 1973
Schmidt, Francis	Football	+	50	100		1971 CHOF coach
Schmidt, Fred	Olympic		3	6		Swim/butterfly
Schmidt, Joe	Football		10	20	85	1973 HOF LB
Schmidt, Kathy	Olympic		3	7		Javelin
Schmidt, Mike	Baseball					P-S HOF $80
Schmidt, Mike	Baseball		12	40	55	HOF 1995. Gold Pl. $45
Schmidt, Milt	Hockey		6	18		1961 HOF fwd
Schmidt, Walter	Baseball		42	90		Debut 1916
Schmidt, William	Olympic		3	9		Javelin
Schmidt. Willard	Baseball		4			Debut 1952 Cards
Schmitz, Johnny	Baseball		6			Debut 1941 Cubs
Schmulbach, Hank	Baseball		4	22		Debut 1943
Schnabl, Karl	Olympic		10	30		Ski jumping
Schneck, Dave	Baseball		3	10		Debut 1972
Schneider, Petra	Olympic		12	35		Swimming
Schneider, Vreni	Olympic		10	30		Alpine skiing
Schneiter, George	Golf		45	95		
Schnellbacher, Otto	Basketball		7	50		played NBA 48
Schnittker, Dick	Basketball		7	45		played NBA 50-57
Schoendienst, Red	Baseball					HOF 1989. Gold Pl. $15
Schoendienst, Red	Baseball		10	20	25	P-S HOF $30.Grt.Mo. $25
Schoene, Russ	Basketball		3	10		played NBA 82-
Schoenfield, Dana	Olympic		3	7		Swim/breaststroke
Schofield, Dick	Baseball		3	10		Debut 1983
Scholes, C. Clarke	Olympic		5	14		Swim/sprints
Schollander, Don	Olympic		10	25		Swim/100 Free
Scholz, David	Basketball		4	16		played NBA 69
Scholz, Jackson	Olympic		35	90		200 M Dash
Schommer, John	Basketball	+	18	40		HOF 1959
Schonley, Bill	Broadcaster		3	6		
Schoon, Milton	Basketball		10	50		played NBA 46-49
Schoonmaker, Jerry	Baseball		4	14		Debut 1955
Schoonover, Wear	Football		15	45		CHOF Arkansas
Schott, Gene	Baseball		4			Debut 1935 Reds
Schott, Marge	Baseball		5	15		Owner (Reds)
Schottenheimer, Marty	Football		5	20	100	NFL Coach
Schoux, George	Golf		45	90		

NAME	CATEGORY	+	SIG	SP	BALL	Comment
Schrader, Ken	Auto Racing		4	14		
Schramka, Paul	Baseball		3	16		Debut 1953
Schramm, Tex	Football		6	22	85	1991 HOF contributor
Schranz, Karl	Olympic		10	35		Skiing
Schreiber, Paul	Baseball		6			Debut 1922 NY Giants
Schreiber, Ted	Baseball		3	15		Debut 1963
Schreiner, Dave	Football	+	125	300		CHOF Wisconsin
Schrempf, Detlef	Basketball		4	15		played NBA 85-
Schreyer, Cindy	Golf		5	20	25	
Schridde, Herman	Olympic		5	10		Equestrian
Schriner, Sweeney	Hockey		45	165		1962 HOF fwd
Schroder, Bob	Baseball		3	14		Debut 1965
Schroeder, Bill	Baseball		3	10		Debut 1983
Schroeder, Jim	Bowling		5	10		1990 ABC HOF
Schroeder, John	Golf		5	30	25	
Schroeder, Richard	Olympic		3	7		Swim/relay
Schroeder, Ted	Tennis		10	28		HOF 1966
Schroth, Frances	Olympic		5	14		Swim/100 M Free
Schu, Rick	Baseball		3	10		Debut 1984
Schuba, Beatrix	Olympic		12	32		Figure skating
Schuble, Heinie	Baseball		15	55		Debut 1927
Schul, Robert	Olympic		4	10		1,500 & 5,000 Meters
Schuler, Carolyn	Olympic		4	9		Swim/butterfly
Schulmerich, Wes	Baseball		15	45		Debut 1931 Bost.Braves
Schult, Art	Baseball		4	16		Debut 1953
Schult, Jurgen	Olympic		8	24		Discus
Schulte, Fred	Baseball		30	65		Debut 1927 Cards
Schulte, Herman "Ham"	Baseball		8	30		Debut 1940 Phillies
Schulte, Jack	Baseball		60	125		Debut 1906
Schulte, Johnny	Baseball		45	90		Debut 1923
Schulte, Len	Baseball		14	40		Debut 1944
Schulte, Myrtle	Bowling	+	8	22		1965 Women's IBC HOF
Schultz, Dave	Olympic	+	20	50		Wrestling (murdered)
Schultz, Eddie	Golf		50	125		
Schultz, Germany	Football	+	90	325		CHOF Michigan
Schultz, Howard	Basketball		16	45		played NBA 46-52
Schultz, Howie	Baseball		7	25		Debut 1943
Schultz, Joe C., Jr.	Baseball		7	25		Debut 1939 Pirates
Schultz, Joe C., Sr.	Baseball		15			Debut 1912 Bost. Braves
Schultz, Mark	Olympic		3	10		Wrestling
Schultz, Webb	Baseball		5			Debut 1924 ChiSox
Schulz, Jeff	Baseball		3	10		Debut 1989
Schulz, Richard	Basketball		15	65		played NBA 42-49
Schulz, Ted	Golf		5	20	25	
Schumacher, Bradley	Olympic		3	7		Gold Medal. Swimming
Schumacher, Hal	Baseball		15	38		Debut 1931 NY Giants
Schurig, Roger	Basketball		3	16		played NBA 67
Schuster, Bill	Baseball		15	38		Debut 1937
Schwab, Frank	Football		15	60		CHOF Lafayette
Schwandt, Rhonda	Gymnastics		4	12		
Schwartz, Izzy	Boxing		14	40		Fly-Wt Champ
Schwartz, Marchy	Football		35	80		CHOF Notre Dame
Schwartz, Randy	Baseball		3	10		Debut 1965
Schwartzwalder, Ben	Football		7	22		1982 CHOF coach
Schwegler, Paul	Football		15	45		CHOF Washington
Schweitz, John	Basketball		3	10		played NBA 84-86

NAME	CATEGORY	+	SIG	SP	BALL	Comment
Schwoegler, Connie	Bowling	+	8	20		1968 ABC HOF
Schypinski, Jerry	Baseball		5	18		Debut 1955
Scioscia, Mike	Baseball		3	10		Debut 1980
Scoffic, Lou	Baseball		15	40		Debut 1936
Scolari, Fred	Basketball		10	45		played NBA 46-54
Sconiers, Daryl	Baseball		3	10		Debut 1981
Score, Herb	Baseball		5	18		Debut 1955 Indians
Scott, Alvin	Basketball		3	10		played NBA 77-84
Scott, Barbara Ann	Olympic		10	35		Figure Skating
Scott, Byron	Basketball		4	12		played NBA 83-
Scott, Charlie	Basketball		5	16		played NBA 70-79
Scott, Clyde	Football		6	15		CHOF Arkansas
Scott, Dick	Baseball		3	10		Debut 1989
Scott, Everett	Baseball		90	185		Debut 1914
Scott, George	Baseball		3	12		Debut 1966
Scott, Jake	Football		5	12		NFL
Scott, Jim	Baseball		40	85		Debut 1914
Scott, John	Baseball		3	10		Debut 1974
Scott, Lady Margaret	Golf		150	325		
Scott, LeGrant	Baseball		15	45		Debut 1933
Scott, Michael	Golf		45	125		
Scott, Mike	Baseball		7	18		Debut 1979
Scott, Ray	Basketball		4	18		played NBA 61-71
Scott, Ray	Broadcaster		6	18		1982 Ntl S&S HOF
Scott, Rodney	Baseball		3	10		Debut 1975
Scott, Tom	Football		6	18		CHOF Virginia
Scott, Tony	Baseball		3	10		Debut 1973
Scott, Vince	Football		4	8		1982 Canadian HOF
Scott, Willie	Basketball		3	12		played NBA 69
Scranton, Jim	Baseball		3	10		Debut 1984
Scranton, Nancy	Golf		5	20	25	
Scranton, Paul	Basketball		3	15		played NBA 67
Scrivener, Chuck	Baseball		3	10		Debut 1975
Scully, Vin	Broadcaster		6	20		1991 Ntl S&S HOF
Scurry, Carey	Basketball		3	10		played NBA 85-87
Sczabo, Ecatarine	Olympic		15	40		Gymn./Floor
Seagren, Bob	Olympic		7	18		Pole Vault
Seals, Bruce	Basketball		3	10		played NBA 73-77
Searcy, Edwin	Basketball		3	10		played NBA 76
Sears, Eleanora	Tennis	+	12	25		HOF 1968
Sears, Ken	Baseball		32	70		Debut 1943
Sears, Ken	Basketball		8	30		played NBA 55-63
Sears, Mary	Olympic		3	6		Swim/butterfly
Sears, Richard	Tennis	+	20	55		HOF 1955
Seau, Junior	Football		5	25	100	NFL
Seaver, Tom	Baseball					P-S HOF $45.Grt.Mo.$40
Seaver, Tom	Baseball		15	32	85	HOF 1992. Gold Pl. $25
Secory, Frank	Baseball		6	22		Debut 1940 Tigers
Sedgman, Frank	Tennis		7	20		HOF 1979
Sedran, Barney	Basketball	+	15	35		HOF 1962
See, Larry	Baseball		5	18		Debut 1986
See, Marshall	Basketball		10	50		played NBA 49
Seeds, Bob	Baseball		12	38		Debut 1930
Seerey, Pat	Baseball		16	42		Debut 1943
Segrist, Kal	Baseball		5	15		Debut 1952
Segui, Diego	Baseball		5			Debut 1962 K.C.

NAME	CATEGORY	+	SIG	SP	BALL	Comment
Segura, Pancho	Tennis		10	38		HOF 1984
Seibels, Henry	Football		25	80		CHOF Sewanee
Seibert, Earl	Hockey		25	140		1963 HOF def
Seibert, Kurt	Baseball		3	10		Debut 1979
Seibert, Oliver	Hockey		150	375		1961 HOF fwd
Seifert, George	Football		4	25	125	NFL Coach
Seikaly, Rony	Basketball		4	15		played NBA 88-
Seilheimer, Rick	Baseball		3	10		Debut 1980
Seitzer, Kevin	Baseball		3	10		Debut 1986
Seixas, Vic	Tennis		10	28		HOF 1971
Seizinger, Katja	Skiing		5	25		Alpine.World Cup Champ.
Selanne, Teemu	Hockey		6	20	25	
Selbo, Glen	Basketball		10	50		played NBA 47-49
Seldon, Bruce	Boxing		10	20		
Seles, Monica	Tennis		12	48		
Selig, Bud	Baseball		5	15		Acting Commissioner
Selkirk, George	Baseball		15	42	375	Debut 1934 Yankees
Sellers, Brad	Basketball		3	10		played NBA 86-
Sellers, Gib	Golf		10	35		
Sellers, Philip	Basketball		3	12		played NBA 76
Sellers, Ron	Football		6	15		CHOF Florida State
Selmon, Lee Roy	Football		7	18	85	CHOF Oklahoma
Selph, Carey	Baseball		35	75		Debut 1929
Seltz, Rollie	Basketball		10	50		played NBA 46-49
Seltzer, Leo	Roller Derby		25	50		
Selvage, Lester	Basketball		4	15		played NBA 67-69
Selvy, Frank	Basketball		7	22		played NBA 54-63
Sember, Mike	Baseball		3	10		Debut 1977
Seminick, Andy	Baseball		7	10		Debut 1943 Phillies
Seminoff, James	Basketball		10	50		played NBA 46-49
Semiz, Teata	Bowling		5	10		1991 ABC HOF
Semple, Carol	Golf		5	30	30	
Semproch, Ray	Baseball		5			Debut 1958 Phillies
Senerchia, Sonny	Baseball		3	15		Debut 1952
Senesky, George	Basketball		10	45		played NBA 46-53
Senna, Ayrton	Auto Racing		70	225		
Sepkowski, Ted	Baseball		9	36		Debut 1942
Septien, Rafael	Football		5	10		NFL
Serafin, Felix	Golf		35	95		
Serebryanskaya, Ekaterina	Olympic		3	15		Gold Medal. Rhythm.Gym
Serena, Bill	Baseball		3	15		Debut 1949
Serna, Paul	Baseball		3	10		Debut 1981
Servo, Marty	Boxing		22	45		
Sessi, Walter	Baseball		10	25		Debut 1941 Cards
Setson, Mrs. G. Henry	Golf		95	175		
Seufert, Christina	Olympic		3	7		Diving
Sevcik, John	Baseball		4	14		Debut 1965
Severeid, Hank	Baseball		45	95		Debut 1911
Severson, Rich	Baseball		3	12		Debut 1970
Sewell, Harley	Football		5	12		NFL
Sewell, Joe	Baseball					HOF 1977. Gold Pl.$20
Sewell, Joe	Baseball		18	45	85	P-S HOF$80.Grt.Mo.$100
Sewell, Luke	Baseball		10	25		Debut 1921
Sewell, Tom	Basketball		3	10		played NBA 84
Sewell, Truett "Rip"	Baseball		20	55		Debut 1932 Tigers
Sexton, Jimmy	Baseball		3	10		Debut 1977

NAME	CATEGORY	+	SIG	SP	BALL	Comment
Seymour, Paul	Basketball		7	20		played NBA 46-59
Seymour, Steve	Olympic		3	10		Javelin
Shaback, Nicholas	Basketball		10	50		played NBA 46
Shablis, Helen	Bowling	+	8	18		1977 Women's IBC HOF
Shackelford, Lynn	Basketball		3	12		played NBA 69
Shadden, John	Olympic		3	6		Yachting
Shafer, Art "Tillie"	Baseball		75			Debut 1909
Shaffer, Lee	Basketball		8	22		played NBA 61-63
Shakespeare, Bill	Football		30	75		CHOF Notre Dame
Shamsky, Art	Baseball		3	14		Debut 1965
Shanahan, Brendan	Hockey		4	20	25	
Shanahan, Mike	Football		3	8		NFL Broncos Coach
Shaner, Wally	Baseball		32	70		Debut 1923
Shannon, Earl	Basketball		10	50		played NBA 46-48
Shannon, Howard	Basketball		10	50		played NBA 48-49
Shannon, Mike	Baseball		4	14		Debut 1962
Shannon, Red	Baseball		40	85		Debut 1915
Shannon, Wally	Baseball		4	16		Debut 1959
Shantz, Billy	Baseball		4	15		Debut 1954
Shantz, Bobby	Baseball		10	35		Debut 1949 Phil. A's
Share, Charles	Basketball		10	40		played NBA 51-59
Sharkey, Jack	Boxing		60	175		1932-33 H-Wt Champ
Sharman, Bill	Basketball		8	20		HOF 1975
Sharockman, Ed	Football		3	16		NFL
Sharon, Dick	Baseball		3	10		Debut 1973
Sharp, Bill	Baseball		3	10		Debut 1973
Sharpe, Shannon	Football		6	25	80	NFL Broncos Standout
Sharpe, Sterling	Football		7	28	150	NFL
Sharperson, Mike	Baseball		5	15		Debut 1987
Shasky, John	Basketball		3	10		played NBA 88-
Shatto, Dick	Football		5	10		1975 Canadian HOF
Shaughnessy, Clark	Football	+	35	75		1968 CHOF coach
Shaughnessy, Frank	Football	+	15	40		1963 Canadian HOF
Shave, Bob	Golf		10	35		
Shavers, Earnie	Boxing		10	30		Hvy-Wt
Shavlik, Ronnie	Basketball		15	38		played NBA 56-57
Shaw, Al	Baseball		30			Debut 1901 for 4 years
Shaw, Al S.	Baseball		65	130		Debut 1907
Shaw, Brian	Basketball		4	10		played NBA 88-
Shaw, Buck	Football	+	35	75		1972 CHOF coach
Shaw, Don	Baseball		4			Debut 1967 NY Giants
Shaw, George	Football		10	25		NFL
Shaw, Tim	Olympic		3	10		Swim/400 free
Shaw, Tom	Golf		5	20	25	
Shaw, Wilbur	Auto Racing	+	325	750		HOF 1991
Shawkey, Bob	Baseball		45	90		Debut 1913 Phil. A's
Shea, Francis J. "Spec"	Baseball		10			Debut 1947 Yankees
Shea, John "Jack"	Olympic		12	40		500 Speed Skating
Shea, Robert	Basketball		10	50		played NBA 46
Sheaffer, Danny	Baseball		3	10		Debut 1987
Shean, Dave	Baseball		25			1918 World Ser./Red Sox
Shearer, Bob	Golf		5	20	25	
Shearer, Ray	Baseball		10	24		Debut 1957
Sheehan, Jack	Baseball		40	80		Debut 1920 Cards
Sheehan, Patty	Golf		10	30	35	LPGA HOF 1993
Sheehan, Tom	Baseball		15			Debut 1915 Phil. A's

NAME	CATEGORY	+	SIG	SP	BALL	Comment
Sheehy, Neil	Hockey		3	10		
Sheely, Bud	Baseball		8	20		Debut 1951
Sheer, Gordy & Thorpe, Chris	Luge		5	12		1st US Olymp. Medals
Sheerin, Charlie	Baseball		14	38		Debut 1936
Sheets, Larry	Baseball		3	10		Debut 1984
Sheffield, Fred	Basketball		10	50		played NBA 46
Sheffield, Gary	Baseball		6	22		Debut 1988
Shelby, Carroll	Auto Racing		6	22		HOF 1991 Manufacturer
Shelby, John	Baseball		3	10		Debut 1981
Sheldon, Bob	Baseball		3	12		Debut 1974
Shell, Art	Football		10	22	100	1989 HOF OL
Shelley, Hugh	Baseball		28	68		Debut 1935
Shelley, Ken	Figure Skating		2	5		US Men's Champion
Shelton, Craig	Basketball		3	10		played NBA 80-81
Shelton, Everett	Basketball	+	19	40		HOF 1979-Coach
Shelton, Lonnie	Basketball		3	10		played NBA 76-85
Shelton, Murray	Football		18	60		CHOF Cornell
Shemo, Stan	Baseball		4	25		Debut 1944
Shepard, Bert	Baseball		4			Debut 1945 Senators
Shepard, Jack	Baseball		6	22		Debut 1953
Shepardson, Ray	Baseball		40	85		Debut 1924
Shepherd, Billy	Basketball		3	15		played NBA 72-74
Shepherd, Morgan	Auto Racing		4	15		
Shepherd, Ron	Baseball		3	10		Debut 1984
Sheppard, Jonathon	Horse Racing					HOF 1990 trainer
Sheppard, Steve	Basketball		3	12		played NBA 77-78
Sheridan, Neill	Baseball		6	22		Debut 1948
Sheridan, Pat	Baseball		3	10		Debut 1981
Sheridan, Red	Baseball		42	90		Debut 1918
Sherk, Cathy	Golf		5	20	25	
Sherlock, Monk	Baseball		38	80		Debut 1930 Phillies
Sherlock, Vince	Baseball		35	80		Debut 1935
Sherman, Allie	Football		5	15		NFL Coach of Yr.'61 & '62
Sherman, Willard	Football		4	12		NFL
Sherod, Edmund	Basketball		3	10		played NBA 82
Sherrill, Dennis	Baseball		3	12		Debut 1973
Sherrod, Blackie	Writer		3	6		1991 Ntl S&S HOF
Sherry, Larry	Baseball		8			Debut 1958 L.A. Dodgers
Sherry, Norm	Baseball		4	12		Debut 1959 L.A. Dodgers
Shetrone, Barry	Baseball		4	14		Debut 1959 Balt. Orioles
Shevlin, Jimmy	Baseball		40	85		Debut 1930
Shevlin, Tom	Football		18	60		CHOF Yale
Shields, Ben C.	Baseball		10			Debut 1924 Yankees
Shields, Frank	Tennis	+	15	38		HOF 1964
Shields, Pete	Baseball		45	95		Debut 1915
Shields, Susan	Olympic		3	7		Swim/butterfly
Shilling, Jim	Baseball		16	38		Debut 1939
Shimer, Brian	Olympic		2	8		Bobsled
Shine, Michael	Olympic		3	8		Hurdles
Shines, Razor	Baseball		3	10		Debut 1983
Shipley, Craig	Baseball		3	10		Debut 1986
Shipley, Joe	Baseball		4			Debut 1958 S.F. Giants
Shipp, Charles	Basketball		22	65		played NBA 37-49
Shires, Art	Baseball		45			Cocky 20's BB & Boxer
Shirley, Bart	Baseball		4	15		Debut 1964
Shirley, J. Dallas	Basketball		18	36		HOF 1979-Referee

NAME	CATEGORY	+	SIG	SP	BALL	Comment
Shirley, Tex	Baseball		6			Debut 1941 Phil. A's
Shively, Bernie	Football		15	50		CHOF Illinois
Shiver, Ivey	Baseball		38	80		Debut 1931
Shockley, Costen	Baseball		4	15		Debut 1964
Shoemaker, Bill	Horse Racing		30	75		HOF 1958 jockey
Shoemaker, Charlie	Baseball		3	14		Debut 1961
Shofner, Del	Football		4	14		NFL
Shofner, Jimmy	Football		5	12		NFL
Shofner, Strick	Baseball		6	18		Debut 1947
Shokes, Eddie	Baseball		7	25		Debut 1941 Reds
Shoop, Ron	Baseball		4	15		Debut 1959
Shopay, Tom	Baseball		4	12		Debut 1967
Shore, Eddie	Hockey		100	250		1947 HOF def
Shore, Ernie	Baseball	+	20			Debut 1912 NY Giants
Shore, Ray	Baseball		4			Debut 1946 Browns
Short, Dave	Baseball		18	38		Debut 1940 ChiSox
Short, Eugene	Basketball		3	12		played NBA 75
Short, Purvis	Basketball		3	15		played NBA 78-88
Shorter, Frank	Olympic		7	22		Marathon
Shotton, Burt	Baseball	+	42	100		Debut 1909
Shoulders, Jim	Rodeo		15	35		
Shouldice, W.T.	Football	+	10	22		1977 Canadian HOF
Show, Eric	Baseball		4	10		Debut 1981
Shrider, Richard	Basketball		10	50		played NBA 48
Shriver, Pam	Tennis		7	25		
Shuba, George "Shotgun"	Baseball		4	12		Debut 1948 Brklyn. Dodg.
Shue, Gene	Basketball		5	22		played NBA 54-63
Shula, Don	Football		12	25	140	NFL
Shuler, Mickey	Football		3	15	95	NFL
Shumate, John	Basketball		3	10		played NBA 75-80
Shute, Denny	Golf		150	350		Old PGA HOF 1957
Shutt, Steve	Hockey		4	16		
Sibert, Sam	Basketball		3	12		played NBA 72
Sibley, Mark	Basketball		3	12		played NBA 73
Sichting, Jerry	Basketball		3	12		played NBA 80-81
Siderowf, Dick	Golf		5	20	25	
Sidle, Don	Basketball		4	14		played NBA 68-71
Siebern, Norm	Baseball		3	12		Debut 1956
Siebert, Babe	Hockey		250	800		1964 HOF fwd
Siebert, Dick	Baseball		25	50		Debut 1932
Sieckmann, Tom	Golf		5	20	25	
Siegfried, Larry	Basketball		4	18		played NBA 63-71
Sierra, Ruben	Baseball		5	18		Debut 1986
Sievers, Roy	Baseball		8	22		Debut 1949 Browns
Siewert, Ralph	Basketball		10	50		played NBA 46
Sifford, Charles	Golf		5	20	25	
Sigel, Jay	Golf		5	20	25	
Sikes, Dan	Golf		5	20	25	
Sikes, R. H.	Golf		5	20	25	
Sikma, Jack	Basketball		4	14		played NBA 77-
Silas, James	Basketball		3	14		played NBA 72-81
Silas, Paul	Basketball		4	18		played NBA 64-79
Silber, Eddie	Baseball		35	75		Debut 1937
Silivas, Daniela	Olympic		7	35		Gold Medal. Gymnastics
Sill, Aleta	Bowling		2	8		Tourney winner
Silliman, Michael	Basketball		3	12		played NBA 70

NAME	CATEGORY	+	SIG	SP	BALL	Comment
Sills, Tony	Golf		5	20	25	
Silvera, Al	Baseball		3	15		Debut 1955
Silvera, Charlie	Baseball		4	14		Debut 1948 Yankees
Silvester, Jay	Olympic		10	25		Discus
Silvestri, Ken	Baseball		5	15		Debut 1939 ChiSox
Sime, Dave	Olympic		8	18		100 Meters
Simmer, Charlie	Hockey		4	20		
Simmons, Al	Baseball		300	550	2800	HOF 1953. B&W PC $850
Simmons, Connie	Basketball		10	45		played NBA 46-55
Simmons, Curt	Baseball		4	14		Debut 1947 Phillies
Simmons, Floyd	Olympic		4	12		Decathlon
Simmons, Grant	Basketball		3	14		played NBA 67-68
Simmons, John	Baseball		6	20		Debut 1949
Simmons, John	Basketball		10	50		played NBA 46
Simmons, Ted	Baseball		5	15		Debut 1968 Cards
Simms, Phil	Football		10	30	125	NFL
Simms, Willie	Horse Racing					HOF 1977 jockey
Simon, Dick	Auto Racing		6	15		
Simon, Syl	Baseball		40	85		Debut 1923
Simon, Violet	Bowling	+	10	28		1960 Women's IBC HOF
Simon, Walter	Basketball		3	14		played NBA 67-73
Simone, Anne	Bowling		5	10		1991 Women's IBC HOF
Simons, Jim	Golf		5	20	25	
Simons, Mel	Baseball		32	70		Debut 1931
Simons, Monk	Football		15	40		CHOF Tulane
Simons, Nancy	Olympic		4	8		Swim relay
Simpson, Ben	Football	+	10	22		1963 Canadian HOF
Simpson, Bob	Football		4	8		1976 Canadian HOF
Simpson, Craig	Hockey		4	10		
Simpson, Dick	Baseball		3	15		Debut 1962 L.A. Angels
Simpson, George	Golf		50	125		
Simpson, Harry	Baseball		16	50		Debut 1951
Simpson, Jack	Golf		625	1395		
Simpson, Jimmie	Football	+	10	22		1986 Canadian HOF
Simpson, Joe	Baseball		3	10		Debut 1975
Simpson, Joe	Hockey		50	175		1962 HOF def
Simpson, O.J.	Football		20	75	250	'85 HOF. Heisman '68
Simpson, Ralph	Basketball		3	12		played NBA 70-79
Simpson, Scott	Golf		5	20	25	
Simpson, Tim	Golf		5	20	25	
Sims, Billy	Football		10	30		Heisman OK '78. NFL
Sims, Douglas	Basketball		3	12		played NBA 68
Sims, Duke	Baseball		3	12		Debut 1964
Sims, Greg	Baseball		3	12		Debut 1966
Sims, Robert	Basketball		4	18		played NBA 61-67
Sims, Scott	Basketball		3	12		played NBA 77
Sindelar, Joey	Golf		5	20	25	
Sinden, Harry	Hockey		5	15	18	1983 HOF
Siner, Hosea	Baseball		75			Debut 1909 10 ML games
Singer, Al	Boxing		65	110		Lt-Wt Champ. 1930
Singh, Vijay	Golf		5	20	25	
Singletary, Mike	Football		10	25	100	NFL
Singleton, Ken	Baseball		3	12		Debut 1970
Singleton, McKinley	Basketball		3	10		played NBA 86
Sington, Fred	Baseball		16	40		Debut 1934 Senators
Sington, Fred	Football		7	20		CHOF Alabama

NAME	CATEGORY	+	SIG	SP	BALL	Comment
Sinicola, Emilio	Basketball		10	45		played NBA 51-53
Sinkwich, Frank	Football	+	60	125		CHOF GA. Heisman '42
Sinn, Pearl	Golf		5	20	25	
Sipe, Brian	Football		3	10		NFL
Sipek, Dick	Baseball		6	20		Debut 1945 Reds
Sipin, John	Baseball		3	12		Debut 1969
Sisk, Tommie	Baseball		5			Debut 1962 Pirates
Sisler, Dick	Baseball		8	20		Debut 1946 Cards
Sisler, George	Baseball					B&W PC $160
Sisler, George	Baseball		72	175	1275	HOF 1939. Gold Pl. $165
Sisti, Sibby	Baseball		10	27		Debut 1939 Bost. Braves
Sitko, Emil	Football		38	80		CHOF Notre Dame
Sittler, Darryl	Hockey		5	18	22	1989 HOF fwd
Sitton, Charlie	Basketball		3	12		played NBA 84
Sitzberger, Ken	Olympic		50	110		Diving
Sizemore, Ted	Baseball		3	10		Debut 1969
Skaff, Frank	Baseball		16	38		Debut 1935
Skaggs, Dave	Baseball		3	12		Debut 1977
Sketchley, Bud	Baseball		18	40		Debut 1942
Skidmore, Roe	Baseball		3	12		Debut 1970
Skiff, Bill	Baseball		38	80		Debut 1921
Skiles, Scott	Basketball		3	12		played NBA 86-
Skinatro, Matt	Baseball		3	20		Debut 1981
Skinner, Albert	Basketball		3	12		played NBA 74-79
Skinner, Bob	Baseball		4	15		Debut 1954
Skinner, Joel	Baseball		3	10		Debut 1983
Skinner, Talvin	Basketball		3	10		played NBA 74-75
Skinner, Val	Golf		5	20	25	
Skizas, Lou	Baseball		3	14		Debut 1956
Skladany, Joe	Football		15	40		CHOF Pittsburgh
Skoog, Whitey	Basketball		7	25		played NBA 51-56
Skorich, Nick	Football		7	20		NFL
Skoronski, Bob	Football		9	20		NFL
Skov, Glen	Hockey		4	15		
Skowron, Bill "Moose"	Baseball		5	15		Debut 1954 Yankees
Skube, Bob	Baseball		3	10		Debut 1982
Slade, Gordon	Baseball		32	70		Debut 1930
Slade, Jeff	Basketball		6	22		played NBA 62
Slater, Duke	Football	+	42	110		CHOF Iowa
Slater, Jackie	Football		4	12		NFL
Slattery, James	Boxing		140	170		Lt-Hvywt. World Champ.
Slaught, Don	Baseball		3	10		Debut 1982
Slaughter, Enos	Baseball					P-S HOF $25, Grt.Mo. $25
Slaughter, Enos	Baseball		12	25	20	HOF 1985. Gold Pl. $15
Slaughter, James	Basketball		10	50		played NBA 51
Slaughter, Jose	Basketball		3	10		played NBA 82
Slayback, Scottie	Baseball		35	75		Debut 1926
Sloan, Bruce	Baseball		25	60		Debut 1944
Sloan, Catherine	Bowling		8	15		1985 Women's IBC HOF
Sloan, Jerry	Basketball		5	14		played NBA 65-75
Sloan, Todhunter	Horse Racing		300			HOF 1955 jockey
Slocomb, Karl	Football	+	10	22		1989 Canadian HOF
Slocum, Henry	Tennis	+	12	35		HOF 1955
Slocum, Ron	Baseball		3	14		Debut 1969
Sluby, Tom	Basketball		3	10		played NBA 84
Sluman, Jeff	Golf		5	20	25	

NAME	CATEGORY	+	SIG	SP	BALL	Comment
Slusarski, Tadeusz	Olympic		10	30		Pole Vault
Smajstrla, Craig	Baseball		3	12		Debut 1988
Small, Hank	Baseball		3	10		Debut 1973
Small, Jim	Baseball		5	16		Debut 1955
Small, Tess	Bowling	+	8	18		1971 Women's IBC HOF
Smalley, Roy III	Baseball		3	16		Debut 1975
Smalley, Roy Jr.	Baseball		3	10		Debut 1948
Smart, Jonathan	Basketball		3	10		played NBA 88
Smawley, Belus	Basketball		10	50		played NBA 46-51
Smaza, Joe	Baseball		22	55		Debut 1946
Smid, Tomas	Tennis		4	10		
Smiley, John	Basketball		10	50		played NBA 47-49
Smith Astaire, Robyn	Horse Racing		10	20		Jockey(Mrs. Fred Astaire)
Smith Court, Margaret	Tennis		10	28		HOF 1979
Smith, Adrian	Basketball		3	14		played NBA 61-71
Smith, Al	Golf		45	95		
Smith, Al	Hockey		100	350		1962 HOF fwd
Smith, Al E. "Fuzzy"	Baseball		5	18		Debut 1953 Indians
Smith, Al K.	Baseball		6			Debut 1926 NY Giants
Smith, Alan	Basketball		3	12		played NBA 71-75
Smith, Alex	Golf		500	1295		Old PGA 1940
Smith, Andy	Football	+	15	35		1951 CHOF coach
Smith, Art	Baseball		4			Debut 1932 ChiSox
Smith, Ben	Golf		5	30	25	
Smith, Bernie	Baseball		3	10		Debut 1970
Smith, Billy	Baseball		3	10		Debut 1975
Smith, Billy	Hockey		4	20		
Smith, Bob	Baseball		40	85		Debut 1923
Smith, Bob	Golf		10	35		
Smith, Bobby	Basketball		3	14		played NBA 69-79
Smith, Bobby	Hockey		4	15		
Smith, Bobby Gene	Baseball		10	25		Debut1957
Smith, Bonecrusher	Boxing		15	30		1986-87 H-Wt Champ
Smith, Brick	Baseball		3	10		Debut 1987
Smith, Bruce	Football		5	18	100	NFL
Smith, Bruce	Football	+	550	825		CHOF MN. Heisman '41
Smith, Bubba	Football		6	22		CHOF Michigan State
Smith, Calvin	Olympic		5	20		100 Meters
Smith, Caroline	Olympic		8	22		Diving
Smith, Cecil	Polo		25	50		"Star"
Smith, Charles	Basketball		3	15		played NBA 88-
Smith, Charley	Baseball		3	10		Debut 1960
Smith, Chris	Baseball		3	10		Debut 1981
Smith, Clint	Hockey		5	18		1991 HOF fwd
Smith, Clinton	Basketball		3	10		played NBA 86
Smith, Clipper	Football		35	85		CHOF Notre Dame
Smith, Dallas	Hockey		3	12		
Smith, Dave	Baseball				20	Debut 1980
Smith, Dean	Basketball		13	29	100	HOF 1982-Coach
Smith, Delbert	Basketball		10	50		played NBA 46
Smith, Dennis	Football		3	14		NFL
Smith, Derek	Basketball		3	12		played NBA 82-
Smith, Des	Basketball		10	50		played NBA 42-48
Smith, Dick	Baseball		3	12		Debut 1969
Smith, Dick	Baseball		3	15		Debut 1963
Smith, Dick	Baseball		6	18		Debut 1951

NAME	CATEGORY	+	SIG	SP	BALL	Comment
Smith, Donald	Basketball		3	12		played NBA 74
Smith, Dwight	Baseball		3	10		Debut 1989
Smith, Earl	Baseball		5	16		Debut 1955
Smith, Ed "Gunboat"	Boxing		40	100		Hvy-Wt
Smith, Edward	Basketball		10	45		played NBA 53
Smith, Elmer E.	Baseball		75	250		Debut 1886 Cin. AA
Smith, Elmer J.	Baseball		48	100		Debut 1914 Indians
Smith, Elmore	Basketball		4	12		played NBA 71-78
Smith, Emmitt	Football		10	40		NFL
Smith, Eric	Golf		75	150		
Smith, Ernie	Baseball		32	70		Debut 1930
Smith, Ernie	Football		15	45		CHOF Southern California
Smith, F. Dean	Olympic		3	8		400 meter relay
Smith, Garfield	Basketball		3	12		played NBA 70-72
Smith, George	Baseball		10	25		Debut 1963
Smith, Grace	Bowling	+	8	20		1968 Women's IBC HOF
Smith, Greg	Baseball		3	10		Debut 1989
Smith, Greg	Basketball		3	12		played NBA 68-75
Smith, Hal R.	Baseball		3	15		Debut 1956 Cards
Smith, Hal W.	Baseball		12	25		Debut 1955 Orioles
Smith, Harry	Football		7	25		CHOF Southern California
Smith, Hooley	Hockey		70	240		1972 HOF fwd
Smith, Horton	Golf		400	950		PGA HOF 1990
Smith, J. D.	Football		6	15		NFL
Smith, J. T.	Football		3	12		NFL
Smith, Jack	Baseball		42	90		Debut 1915
Smith, Jackie	Football		4	18	85	1994 HOF. NFL
Smith, James	Basketball		15	30		played NBA 81-82
Smith, James "Bonecrusher"	Boxing		3	10		
Smith, Jerry	Football		25	60		NFL
Smith, Jim Ray	Football		6	15		CHOF Baylor
Smith, Jimmy	Baseball		3	10		Debut 1982
Smith, Jimmy	Bowling	+	25	55		1941 ABC HOF
Smith, Joe	Baseball		42	85		Debut 1913
Smith, Joe	Basketball		5	28	125	NBA-Warriors
Smith, John	Baseball		25	50		Debut 1931
Smith, John	Basketball		5	16		played NBA 68-69
Smith, John	Olympic		3	6		Rowing
Smith, John	Olympic		3	6		Wrestling
Smith, Katie	Basketball		2	7		Women's ABL
Smith, Keith	Baseball		3	10		Debut 1984
Smith, Keith	Baseball		3	12		Debut 1977
Smith, Keith	Basketball		3	10		played NBA 86
Smith, Ken	Baseball		3	10		Debut 1981
Smith, Ken	Basketball		3	12		played NBA 75
Smith, Ken	Writer		8	18		
Smith, Kenny	Basketball		3	10		played NBA 87-
Smith, Lamont	Olympic		3	6		Gold Medal. Track
Smith, Larry	Basketball		3	10		played NBA 80-
Smith, Lee	Baseball		4	15		Debut 1980
Smith, Lonnie	Baseball		3	12		Debut 1978
Smith, Luke	Tennis		3	6		1997 NCAA Champion
Smith, Macdonald	Golf		125	325		Old PGA HOF 1954
Smith, Margaret	Golf		10	35	35	
Smith, Marilyn	Golf		10	35	35	
Smith, Mayo	Baseball		25	55		Debut 1945

NAME	CATEGORY	+	SIG	SP	BALL	Comment
Smith, Melanie	Olympic		5	10		Equestrian
Smith, Michelle	Olympic		4	28		3 Gold Med. Swimming
Smith, Mike	Baseball		40	85		Debut 1926
Smith, Mike	Golf		5	20		
Smith, Milt	Baseball		3	15		Debut 1955
Smith, Neil	Football		4	15	75	NFL
Smith, O. Guinn	Olympic		6	14		Pole Vault
Smith, Otis	Basketball		3	10		played NBA 86-
Smith, Ozzie	Baseball		4	24		Debut 1978
Smith, Paul	Baseball		5	15		Debut 1953
Smith, Pete	Basketball		3	12		played NBA 72
Smith, Philip	Basketball		3	10		played NBA 74-82
Smith, Randy	Basketball		4	16		played NBA 71-82
Smith, Ray	Baseball		3	10		Debut 1981
Smith, Red	Baseball		35	70		Debut 1917
Smith, Red	Baseball		35	70		Debut 1927
Smith, Reggie	Baseball		3	14		Debut 1966
Smith, Riley	Football		40	80		CHOF Alabama
Smith, Robert	Basketball		6	35		played NBA 59-61
Smith, Robert	Football		7	22		NFL Vikings RB
Smith, Robert A.	Horse Racing					HOF 1976 trainer
Smith, Robert L.	Basketball		3	10		played NBA 77-84
Smith, Ronnie Ray	Olympic		3	12		Track sprints
Smith, Sam	Basketball		3	12		played NBA 78-79
Smith, Sam	Basketball		3	15		played NBA 67-70
Smith, Sherman	Football		3	10		NFL
Smith, Stan	Tennis		10	25		HOF 1987
Smith, Taylor	Golf		5	20	25	
Smith, Thomas	Basketball		10	50		played NBA 51
Smith, Timmy	Football		3	12		NFL
Smith, Tommie	Olympic		12	32		200 M Dash
Smith, Tommy	Baseball		3	12		Debut 1973
Smith, Tommy	Hockey		50	175		1973 HOF fwd
Smith, Vernon	Football		15	45		CHOF Georgia
Smith, Vinnie	Baseball		18	40		Debut 1941
Smith, Wallace "Bud"	Boxing		18	38		
Smith, Walter "Red"	Writer		22	50		1977 Ntl S&S HOF
Smith, William	Basketball		3	12		played NBA 71-72
Smith, William F.	Basketball		3	22		played NBA 61
Smith, Willie	Baseball		3	12		Debut 1963
Smith, Willie	Basketball		3	12		played NBA 76-79
Smith, Willie	Golf		195	450		
Smith, Zane	Baseball		4	10		Debut 1984
Smithwick, A. Patrick	Horse Racing					HOF 1973 jockey
Smithwick, Mike	Horse Racing					HOF 1976 trainer
Smits, Rik	Basketball		3	20		played NBA 88-
Smoltz, John	Baseball		10	45		Debut 1988
Smrek, Mike	Basketball		3	10		played NBA 85-
Smyres, Clancy	Baseball		8	25		Debut 1944
Smyth, Joseph	Basketball		8	45		played NBA 53
Smythe, Randy	Olympic		3	6		Yachting
Snavely, Carl	Football	+	20	45		1965 CHOF coach
Snead, J. C.	Golf		5	20	25	
Snead, Norm	Football		4	12		NFL
Snead, Sam	Golf		20	50	65	PGA HOF 1974
Sneed, Ed	Golf		5	20	25	

NAME	CATEGORY	+	SIG	SP	BALL	Comment
Snell, Charlie	Baseball		35	75		Debut 1912 Browns
Snell, Matt	Football		30	85		NFL
Snell, Peter	Olympic		15	40		800 M Run
Snell, Wally	Baseball		38	85		Debut 1913
Snepsts, Harold	Hockey		3	15		
Sneva, Tom	Auto Racing		9	18		
Snider, Duke	Baseball					P-S HOF $40,Grt.Mo. $35
Snider, Duke	Baseball		12	25	30	HOF 1980. Gold Pl. $15
Snider, Van	Baseball		3	10		Debut 1988
Snodgrass, Fred C.	Baseball		48	100		Debut 1908
Snow, J.T.	Baseball		8	35		Debut 1992
Snow, Neil	Football		25	75		CHOF Michigan
Snuka, Jimmy	Pro Wrestling		5	12		
Snyder, Bernie	Baseball		16	35		Debut 1935
Snyder, Cory	Baseball		3	10		Debut 1986
Snyder, Dick	Basketball		3	15		played NBA 66-78
Snyder, Frank	Baseball		30			Debut 1912. Four WS
Snyder, Gene	Baseball		3			Debut 1959 L.A. Dodgers
Snyder, George	Auto Racing		12	32		
Snyder, Jack	Baseball		42	90		Debut 1914
Snyder, Jery	Baseball		3	16		Debut 1952
Snyder, Jimmy	Auto Racing	+	35	85		
Snyder, Jimmy	Baseball		4	15		Debut 1961
Snyder, Jimmy "The Greek"	Broadcaster		6	20		
Snyder, Russ	Baseball		4	14		Debut 1959 K.C.
Sobek, George	Basketball		10	50		played NBA 45-49
Sobers, Ricky	Basketball		3	12		played NBA 76-85
Sobie, Ron	Basketball		8	30		played NBA 56-59
Sodd, Bill	Baseball		20	42		Debut 1937
Soderholm, Eric	Baseball		3	10		Debut 1971 Minn.
Sofield, Rick	Baseball		3	12		Debut 1979
Sohl, Robert	Olympic		3	7		Swim/breaststroke
Sojourner, Mike	Basketball		3	16		played NBA 74-76
Sojourner, Willie	Basketball		3	16		played NBA 71-74
Solaita, Tony	Baseball		3	12		Debut 1968
Solheim, Karsten	Golf		15	35		
Solomon, Freddie	Football		4	14		NFL
Solomon, Harold	Tennis		20	45		
Soltau, Gordon	Football		5	15		NFL
Soltau, Jimmy	Football		3	10		NFL
Solters, Julius	Baseball		40	85		Debut 1934
Somerset, Willie	Basketball		3	16		played NBA 65-68
Sommers, Bill	Baseball		4	14		Debut 1950
Sommerville, Ross	Golf		125	295		
Soose, Billy	Boxing		35	80		Middle-Wt Champ
Sorenson, Carol	Golf		5	20	25	
Sorenson, David	Basketball		3	12		played NBA 70-72
Sorenstam, Annika	Golf		5	25	25	
Sorrell, Bill	Baseball		3	12		Debut 1965
Sorrells, Chick	Baseball		38	80		Debut 1922
Sorrento, Paul	Baseball		3	18		Debut 1989
Sosa, Sammy	Baseball		70	175		66 HR 1998... See page 86!
Sothern, Denny	Baseball		32	65		Debut 1926
Souchak, Mike	Golf		20	30	35	
Souchock, Steve	Baseball		10	22		Debut 1946
Souders, George	Auto Racing		55	110		

NAME	CATEGORY	+	SIG	SP	BALL	Comment
Soutar, Dave	Bowling		5	16		1979 PBA, '85 ABC HOF
Soutar, Judy	Bowling		5	12		1976 Women's IBC HOF
Southern, Eddie	Olympic		5	15		Hurdles
Southworth, Bill	Baseball		3	12		Debut 1964
Southworth, Billy	Baseball		50	110		Debut 1913
Sovran, Gino	Basketball		10	50		played NBA 46
Spahn, Warren	Baseball					P-S HOF $25, Grt.Mo.$25
Spahn, Warren	Baseball		10	25	20	HOF 1973. Gold Pl. $15
Spain, Ken	Basketball		3	12		played NBA 70
Spalding, Albert G.	Baseball	+	1200	4500	12000	HOF 1939
Spanarkel, James	Basketball		3	12		played NBA 79-83
Spangler, Al	Baseball		4	10		Debut 1959 Mil.
Sparando, Tony	Bowling	+	8	30		1968 ABC HOF
Sparks, Art	Auto Racing	+	30	65		
Sparks, Dan	Basketball		4	15		played NBA 68-69
Sparlis, Al	Football		6	18		CHOF UCLA
Sparrow, Guy	Basketball		7	30		played NBA 59-59
Sparrow, Rory	Basketball		3	10		played NBA 80-
Spassky, Boris	Chess		40	90		
Speake, Bob	Baseball		3	14		Debut 1955
Speaker, Tris	Baseball		362	742		HOF 1937.B&W PC $650
Spearman, Marley	Golf '		5	20	25	
Spears, Clarence	Football	+	75	200		CHOF Dartmouth
Spears, Odie	Basketball		8	40		played NBA 48-56
Spears, W. D.	Football		8	25		CHOF Vanderbilt
Speck, Birdie	Bowling	+	8	25		1966 Women's IBC HOF
Spector, Arthur	Basketball		10	50		played NBA 46-49
Speed, Horace	Baseball		3	10		Debut 1975
Speedie, Mac	Football		7	20		NFL
Speier, Chris	Baseball		4	14		Debut 1971 S.F. Giants
Spelstra, Arthur	Basketball		4	16		played NBA 54-57
Spence, Bob	Baseball		3	12		Debut 1969
Spence, Stan	Baseball		14	28		Debut 1940 Bost. RedSox
Spencer, Ben	Baseball		42	90		Debut 1913
Spencer, Daryl	Baseball		3	10		Debut 1952
Spencer, Jim	Baseball		3	12		Debut 1968
Spencer, Roy	Baseball		30	65		Debut 1925
Spencer, Vern	Baseball		22	48		Debut 1932
Spencer-Devlin, Muffin	Golf		5	20	25	
Sperber, Ed	Baseball		30	65		Debut 1924
Sperber, Paula	Bowler		5	16		
Sperring, Roy	Baseball		3	10		Debut 1974
Sperry, Stan	Baseball		32	65		Debut 1936
Spicer, Lou	Basketball		10	50		played NBA 46
Spiers, Bill	Baseball		3	10		Debut 1989
Spiezio, Ed	Baseball		3	12		Debut 1964
Spikes, Charlie	Baseball		3	10		Debut 1972
Spikes, Jack	Football		3	15		NFL
Spilman, Harry	Baseball		3	12		Debut 1978
Spindel, Hal	Baseball		15	30		Debut 1939
Spinella, Barney	Bowling		5	12		1968 ABC HOF
Spink, J.G. Taylor	Writer-Publisher	+	30	75		1969 Ntl S&S HOF
Spinks, Leon	Boxing		20	45		1978 H-Wt Champ
Spinks, Michael	Boxing		50			Hvy-Wt
Spitz, Mark	Olympic		10	30		Swim/7 Golds 1972
Spitzer, Craig	Basketball		3	15		played NBA 67

NAME	CATEGORY	+	SIG	SP	BALL	Comment
Spoelstra, Watson	Writer		3	6		
Spognardi, Andy	Baseball		18	40		Debut 1932
Spohrer, Al	Baseball		25	60		Debut 1928
Spotts, Jim	Baseball		30	65		Debut 1930
Sprackling, William	Football	+	20	65		CHOF Brown
Spraggins, Warren	Basketball		3	15		played NBA 67
Sprague, Bud	Football	+	15	50		CHOF Texas
Sprague, David	Football	+	10	22		1963 Canadian HOF
Sprague, Ed	Baseball		4	12		Debut 1991 Toronto
Spratt, Harry	Baseball		45	95		Debut 1911
Spray, Steve	Golf		10	30		
Sprewell, Latrell	Basketball		4	10		Controversial suspension
Spriggs, George	Baseball		3	14		Debut 1965
Spriggs, Larry	Basketball		3	12		played NBA 81-85
Spring, Alma	Bowling	+	8	18		1979 Women's IBC HOF
Spring, Harry	Football	+	10	22		1976 Canadian HOF
Springer, Gregory	Olympic		3	6		Rowing
Springer, Jim	Basketball		10	50		played NBA 47-48
Springer, Mike	Golf		5	25	25	
Springs, Shawn	Football		5	22		NFL
Sprinz, Joe	Baseball		20	45		Debut 1930
Sproul, Charlie	Baseball		4			Debut 1945 Phillies
Spruill, James	Basketball		10	50		played NBA 48
Spurgeon, Freddy	Baseball		35	75		Debut 1924
Spurrier, Steve	Football		10	22		CHOF FL. Heisman '66
Spuzich, Sandra	Golf		5	25	25	
Squires, Mike	Baseball		3	10		Debut 1975
St. Clair, Bob	Football		6	25	85	1990 HOF OL
St. James, Lyn	Auto Racing		6	20		
St. John, Jim	Bowling	+	10	25		1989 PBA HOF
St. John, Lynn W.	Basketball	+	22	60		HOF 1962
St. Marseille, Frank	Hockey		4	20		
Stabler, Ken	Football		6	25	100	NFL
Stack, Allen	Olympic		4	14		Swim- backstroke
Stackhouse, Jerry	Basketball		5	35	125	
Stacom, Kevin	Basketball		3	12		played NBA 74-81
Stacy, Hollis	Golf		5	25	25	
Stadler, Craig	Golf		5	25	05	
Staehle, Marv	Baseball		3	14		Debut 1964
Stafford, Harrison	Football		6	18		CHOF Texas
Stafford, Heinie	Baseball		38	80		Debut 1916
Stagg, Amos Alonzo	Basketball	+	150	275		HOF 1959
Stagg, Amos Alonzo	Football	+	150	275		1951 CHOF coach
Staggs, Erv	Basketball		3	15		played NBA 69
Staggs, Steve	Baseball		3	12		Debut 1977
Stahl, Larry	Baseball		3	12		Debut 1964
Stahley, Skip	Athletic Director		4	8		
Staiger, Roy	Baseball		3	10		Debut 1975
Stainback, Tuck	Baseball		22	48		Debut 1934
Staley, Gale	Baseball		35	70		Debut 1925
Staley, Gerry	Baseball		5	15		Debut 1947 Cards
Stallard, Tracy	Baseball		3	8		Debut 1960
Stallcup, Virgil	Baseball		12	30		Debut 1947
Staller, George	Baseball		12	30		Debut 1943 Phil. A's
Stallworth, Bud	Basketball		3	12		played NBA 72-76
Stallworth, Dave	Basketball		3	15		played NBA 65-74

NAME	CATEGORY	+	SIG	SP	BALL	Comment
Stallworth, John	Football		5	16	100	NFL
Stamn, Mike	Olympic		3	7		Swim/200 backstr.
Stanage, Oscar	Baseball		60	125		Debut 1906
Stanczak, Edmund	Basketball		10	50		played NBA 46-50
Stanczyk, Stanley	Olympic		3	6		Wrestling
Standaert, Jerry	Baseball		35	75		Debut 1925
Standly, Mike	Golf		5	20	25	
Stanfel, Dick	Football		3	14		NFL
Stanfield, Andrew	Olympic		5	15		200 Meters
Stanfield, Fred	Hockey		4	15		
Stang, Lee	Baseball		5			Debut 1961 Minn.
Stanhouse, Don	Baseball		4			Debut 1972 Tex
Stanicek, Pete	Baseball		3	10		Debut 1987
Stanicek, Steve	Baseball		3	10		Debut 1987
Stanka, Joe	Baseball		3			Debut 1959 ChiSox
Stankiewicz, Andy	Baseball		4	15		Debut 1992 Yankees
Stankovic, Boris	Basketball		6	18		HOF 1991
Stankowski, Paul	Golf		5	20	25	
Stanky, Eddie	Baseball		6	16		Debut 1943
Stanley, Allan	Hockey		10	24		1981 HOF def
Stanley, Barney	Hockey		60	200		1962 HOF fwd
Stanley, Fred	Baseball		3	12		Debut 1969
Stanley, Joe	Baseball		75	145		Debut 1897
Stanley, Mickey	Baseball		3	12		Debut 1964
Stanley, Mike	Baseball		3	10		Debut 1986
Stansbury, John	Baseball		38	80		Debut 1918
Stansbury, Terence	Basketball		3	10		played NBA 84-86
Stanton, Bob	Golf		10	30		
Stanton, Buck	Baseball		20	42		Debut 1931
Stanton, Leroy	Baseball		3	10		Debut 1970
Starbird, Kate	Basketball		3	10		Pro Pioneer
Starbuck & Shelley	Figure Skating		8	20		US Pairs Champions
Starbuck, JoJo	Figure Skating		3	12		US Pairs
Stargell, Willie	Baseball					P-S HOF $25,Grt.Mo. $25
Stargell, Willie	Baseball		8	20	20	HOF 1988. Gold Pl.$15
Stark, Matt	Baseball		3	10		Debut 1987
Stark, Rohn	Football		3	10		NFL
Starks, John	Basketball		3	14		played NBA 88-
Starling, Marlon	Boxing		10	22		
Starr, Bart	Football		10	28	140	1977 HOF QB
Starr, Chick	Baseball		22	50		Debut 1935
Starr, Keith	Basketball		3	12		played NBA 76
Starring, Stephen	Football		3	12		NFL
Stasiuk, Vic	Hockey		5	18		
Stassforth, Bowen	Olympic		3	8		Swim 200 M breaststr
Stastny, Peter	Hockey		4	18		
Staton, Joe	Baseball		3	10		Debut 1972
Statz, Arnold J. "Jigger"	Baseball		28	70		Debut 1919
Staub, Rusty	Baseball		4	12		Debut 1963
Staubach, Roger	Football		10	30	150	1985 HOF.Heisman '63
Stautner, Ernie	Football		10	22	85	1969 HOF DL
Staverman, Lawrence	Basketball		7	30		played NBA 58-63
Stearnes, Turkey	Baseball		225	600		Negro League
Stearns, John	Baseball		3	10		Debut 1974
Stebbins, Richard	Olympic		3	7		400 meter relay
Steding, Katy	Olympic		2	5		Gold Med. Basketball

NAME	CATEGORY	+	SIG	SP	BALL	Comment
Stedman, Alex	Golf		45	95		
Steeb, Charly	Tennis		10	20		
Steele, Larry	Basketball		3	10		played NBA 71-79
Steele, Randall	Olympic		3	5		Yachting
Steele, William S.	Olympic		7	16		Long jump
Steels, James	Baseball		3	10		Debut 1987
Steelsmith, Jerry	Golf		10	35		
Steen, Thomas	Hockey		3	12		
Steers, Harry	Bowling	+	15	42		1941 ABC HOF
Stefanich, Jim	Bowling		5	12		1980 PBA, '83 ABC HOF
Stefero, John	Baseball		3	10		Debut 1987
Steffen, Walter	Football	+	22	75		CHOF Chicago
Steffy, Joe	Football		6	15		CHOF Army
Stegman, Dave	Baseball		3	12		Debut 1978 Tigers
Stein Jr., Otto	Bowling	+	8	20		1971 ABC HOF
Stein, Bill	Baseball		3	10		Debut 1972
Stein, Herbert	Football	+	18	60		CHOF Pittsburgh
Steinbach, Terry	Baseball		3	15		Debut 1986
Steinbacher, Hank	Baseball		30	60		Debut 1937
Steinbrenner, Gene	Baseball		42	85		Debut 1912
Steinbrenner, George	Baseball		5	20		Yankee Owner
Steinecke, Bill	Baseball		25	55		Debut 1931
Steiner, Anton	Olympic		10	28		Alpine skiing
Steiner, Ben	Baseball		14	32		Debut 1945
Steiner, Red	Baseball		14	32		Debut 1945
Steinhauer, Sherri	Golf		5	25	25	
Steinkraus, William	Olympic		5	10		Equestrian
Steinmetz, Christian	Basketball	+	18	40		HOF 1961
Steinseifer, Carrie	Olympic		4	12		Swim/100 Free
Steitz, Ed	Basketball	+	18	40		HOF 1983-Contributor
Stellbauer, Bill	Baseball		38	80		Debut 1916
Stelmaszek, Rick	Baseball		3	10		Debut 1971
Stemkowski, Pete	Hockey		4	14		
Stenerud, Jan	Football		5	18	85	1991 HOF kicker
Stengel, Casey	Baseball					P-S HOF$25,B&W PC$150
Stengel, Casey	Baseball		95	215	1000	HOF 1966, Gold Pl. $125
Stenhouse, Mike	Baseball		3	10		Debut 1982
Stenmark, Ingamar	Olympic		10	38		Alpine Skiing
Stennett, Rennie	Baseball		3	12		Debut 1971
Stepan, Marilee	Olympic		4	8		Swim/relay
Stephens, Country Jake	Baseball		75	175		Played 17 Seasons
Stephens, Everette	Basketball		3	10		played NBA 88
Stephens, Frances	Golf		10	35		
Stephens, Gene	Baseball		3	16		Debut 1952
Stephens, Helen	Olympic-Track		15	35		
Stephens, Jack	Basketball		8	35		played NBA 55
Stephens, Jim	Baseball		55	110		Debut 1907
Stephens, Vern	Baseball		50	125		Debut 1941
Stephens, Woody	Horse Racing		22	50		HOF 1976 trainer
Stephenson, Bobby	Baseball		3	15		Debut 1955
Stephenson, Jan	Golf		5	25	25	
Stephenson, Joe	Baseball		12	30		Debut 1943
Stephenson, Johnny	Baseball		3	12		Debut 1964
Stephenson, Phil	Baseball		3	10		Debut 1989
Stephenson, Riggs	Baseball		45	85		Debut 1921 Indians
Stephenson, Walter	Baseball		18	35		Debut 1935 Cubs

NAME	CATEGORY	+	SIG	SP	BALL	Comment
Steppe, Brook	Basketball		3	10		played NBA 82-
Sterkel, Jill	Olympic		3	10		Swim- relay
Stern, Bill	Broadcaster	+	30	75		1974 Ntl S&S HOF
Stern, David	Basketball		5	12		NBA Commissioner
Sterrett, Dutch	Baseball		40	85		Debut 1912
Steuber, Robert	Football		6	15		CHOF Missouri
Stevens, Bobby	Baseball		18	38		Debut 1931 Phillies
Stevens, Chuck	Baseball		7	35		Debut 1941
Stevens, Ed	Baseball		7	30		Debut 1945 Brklyn. Dodg.
Stevens, Mal	Football	+	18	55		CHOF Yale
Stevens, Myron	Auto Racing	+	25	50		
Stevens, R. C.	Baseball		3	12		Debut 1958 Pirates
Stevens, Rochelle	Olympic		3	6		Gold Medal. Track
Stevens, Wayne	Basketball		7	28		played NBA 59
Stevenson, Art	Football		4	8		1969 Canadian HOF
Stevenson, Vincent	Football	+	25	75		CHOF Pennsylvania
Stewart, Bill	Baseball		3	14		Debut 1955
Stewart, Bill	Hockey	+	10	22		1982 US HOF coach
Stewart, Dave	Baseball		4	12		Debut 1978
Stewart, Dennis	Basketball		3	10		played NBA 70
Stewart, Earl Jr.	Golf		20	50		
Stewart, Edward "Bud"	Baseball		10	30		Debut 1941 Pirates
Stewart, Glen	Baseball		3			Debut 1940 NY Giants
Stewart, J.F. "Stuffy"	Baseball		10			Debut 1916 Cards
Stewart, Jack	Hockey		60	175		1964 HOF def
Stewart, Jackie	Auto Racing		12	35		
Stewart, Jimmy	Baseball		3	15		Debut 1963 Cubs
Stewart, Kordell	Football		7	25	125	NFL Steelers QB
Stewart, Marlene	Golf		10	35		
Stewart, Melvin	Olympic		3	15		Gold Med. Swimming
Stewart, Neb	Baseball		9	25		Debut 1940
Stewart, Nels	Hockey		110	300		1962 HOF fwd
Stewart, Norman	Basketball		8	40		played NBA 56
Stewart, Payne	Golf		5	30	35	
Stewart, Ron	Football		4	8		1977 Canadian HOF
Stewart, Ron	Hockey		4	18		
Stewart, Stuffy	Baseball		40	85		Debut 1916
Stich, Michael	Tennis		15	35		
Stickles, Terri	Olympic		3	7		Swim/400 free
Stieb, Dave	Baseball		3	12		Debut 1979
Stiegler, Pepi	Olympic		7	25		Skiing
Stigman, Dick	Baseball		4			Debut 1960 Indians
Stiles, Rollie	Baseball		5			Debut 1930 Browns
Still, Ken	Golf		5	20	25	
Still, Valerie	Basketball		2	5		Women's ABL
Stillings, John	Olympic		3	6		Rowing
Stillman, Royle	Baseball		3	10		Debut 1975
Stillwell, Kurt	Baseball		3	10		Debut 1986
Stillwell, Ron	Baseball		3	12		Debut 1961
Stimac, Craig	Baseball		3	10		Debut 1980
Stinchcomb, Pete	Football	+	18	50		CHOF Ohio State
Stingley, Darryl	Football		35	95		NFL
Stinson, Bob	Baseball		3	12		Debut 1969
Stipanovich, Steve	Basketball		3	10		played NBA 83-87
Stirling, Hugh	Football		4	8		1966 Canadian HOF
Stirnweiss, George	Baseball		35	80		Debut 1943

NAME	CATEGORY	+	SIG	SP	BALL	Comment
Stith, Samuel	Basketball		3	22		played NBA 61
Stits, Bill	Football		3	14		NFL
Stitzlein, Lorraine	Bowling		5	10		1980 PBA HOF-Mer.Serv.
Stives, Karen	Olympic		3	6		Equestrian
Stivrins, Alex	Basketball		3	10		played NBA 85
Stobbs, Chuck	Baseball		3	12		Debut 1947
Stock, Leonard	Olympic		10	32		Alpine skiing
Stock, Milt	Baseball		32	65		Debut 1913
Stock, Wes	Baseball		4			Debut 1959 Orioles
Stockdale, Louise	Bowling	+	12	40		1953 Women's IBC HOF
Stockton, Dave	Golf		5	25	25	
Stockton, Dave, Jr.	Golf		5	20	25	
Stockton, Dick	Tennis		5	18		
Stockton, J. Roy	Writer		5	15		
Stockton, John	Basketball		8	35	125	played NBA 84-
Stojko, Elvis	Olympic		5	25		Olymp.Med.Figure Skating
Stokes, Al	Baseball		25	65		Debut 1925
Stokes, Greg	Basketball		3	10		played NBA 85
Stokes, J.J.	Football		5	20	75	NFL
Stokes, Maurice	Basketball		150	600		played NBA 55-57
Stolkey, Arthur	Basketball		10	50		played NBA 46
Stoll, Randy	Basketball		3	14		played NBA 67
Stolle, Fred	Tennis		10	22		HOF 1985
Stone, Ed	Baseball		25	80		1931-50, Negro League
Stone, Gene	Baseball		3	12		Debut 1969
Stone, George	Baseball		6			Debut 1967 Atl. Braves
Stone, George	Basketball		3	14		played NBA 68-71
Stone, Jeff	Baseball		3	10		Debut 1983
Stone, Nikki	Skiing		3	14		Freestyle, Olympic Gold
Stone, Ron	Baseball		3	12		Debut 1966
Stoneham, Horace C.	Baseball Owner		50	150		Moved NY Giants
Stoneham, John	Baseball		15	40		Debut 1933
Stonehouse, Ralph	Golf		50	125		
Stoneman, Bill	Baseball		3			Debut 1967 Cubs
Stones, Dwight	Olympic		10	22		Track
Stonesifer, Don	Football		6	16		NFL
Storie, Howie	Baseball		30	65		Debut 1931
Storm, Michael	Olympic		3	6		Pentathlon
Storti, Lin	Baseball		16	45		Debut 1930 Browns
Stottlemyre, Mel	Baseball		3	12		David 1964
Stotz, Carl E.	Baseball		5	15		Little League
Stoudamire, Damon	Basketball		12	38	125	Rookie-of-Year
Stouder, Sharon	Olympic		3	7		Swim/100 free
Stoudt, Bud	Bowling		5	10		1991 ABC HOF
Stout, James	Horse Racing		10	25		HOF 1968 jockey
Stovall, Paul	Basketball		3	12		played NBA 72-73
Stoviak, Ray	Baseball		18	40		Debut 1938
Stracey, John	Boxing		10	22		
Strachan, Rod	Olympic		4	10		Swim/ind. medley
Strahs, Dick	Baseball		3			Debut 1954 ChiSox
Strain, Joe	Baseball		3	12		Debut 1979
Stram, Brock	Football		6	15		CHOF Air Force
Stram, Hank	Football		6	16		AFL-NFL Won Super Bwl
Strampe, Bob	Bowling		5	10		1977 ABC, '87 PBA HOF
Stranahan, Frank	Golf		30	80		
Strand, Paul	Baseball		35	75		Debut 1913

NAME	CATEGORY	+	SIG	SP	BALL	Comment
Strange, Alan	Baseball		15	45		Debut 1934
Strange, Curtis	Golf		10	30	40	
Strange, Doug	Baseball		3	10		Debut 1989
Strath, Andrew	Golf		450	950		
Stratton, Monty	Baseball		40	80		Debut 1934 ChiSox
Strawberry, Darryl	Baseball		6	25		Debut 1983
Strawder, Joe	Basketball		5	15		played NBA 65-67
Strech, Ron	Golf		5	20	25	
Street, Picabo	Olympic		10	35		Olymp.Gold.Alpine Skiing
Streuli, Walt	Baseball		3	15		Debut 1954
Stricker, Andrew	Golf		5	20	25	
Stricker, William	Basketball		3	12		played NBA 70
Strickland, George	Baseball		6	15		Debut 1950
Strickland, Rod	Basketball		4	18		played NBA 88-
Strickland, Roger	Basketball		4	16		played NBA 63
Stricklett, Elmer	Baseball		50	95		Inventor of "Spitball"
Strincevich, Nick	Baseball		4	10		Debut 1940
Stringer, Lou	Baseball		14	32		Debut 1941
Stripp, Joe	Baseball		25	50		Debut 1928 Reds
Strobel, Albert	Baseball		25			Maj. League 1905-06
Strobel, Eric	Olympic		3	10		Ice Hockey
Stroble, Bobby	Golf		5	20	25	
Strode, Woody	Football		15	75		NFL Pioneer. Film Actor
Stroeder, John	Basketball		3	10		played NBA 87-
Strolz, Hubert	Olympic		10	30		Alpine skiing
Stroner, Jim	Baseball		32	70		Debut 1929
Strong, Herbert	Golf		50	100		
Strong, Ken	Football	+	60	195		1967 HOF RB
Strong, Lewis	Auto Racing	+	25	50		
Stroud, Ed	Baseball		3	12		Debut 1966
Stroud, John	Basketball		3	10		played NBA 80
Stroud, Red	Basketball		3	16		played NBA 67
Stroughter, Steve	Baseball		3	10		Debut 1982
Strug, Keri	Olympic		8	55		Olymp.Gold.Gymnastics
Strunk, Amos	Baseball		60	125		Debut 1908
Strupper, George	Football	+	22	60		CHOF Georgia Tech
Strzykalski, John	Football		12	40		NFL
Stuart, Bruce	Hockey		110	350		1961 HOF fwd
Stuart, Dick	Baseball		8	20		Debut 1958
Stuart, Hod	Hockey		500	1250		1945 HOF def
Stubbs, Franklin	Baseball		3	10		Debut 1984
Stubing, Larry	Baseball		3	12		Debut 1967
Studstill, Pat	Football		4	14		NFL
Stuhldreher, Harry	Football		60			One of the "Four Horsemen"
Stukus, Annis	Football		4	8		1974 Canadian HOF
Stulce, Mike	Olympic		3	15		Olymp.Gold. Shot Put
Stump, Eugene	Basketball		10	50		played NBA 47-49
Stumpf, Bill	Baseball		40	85		Debut 1912
Stumpf, George	Baseball		18	45		Debut 1931 Bost. RedSox
Stunyo, Jeanne	Olympic		12	38		Diving
Stuper, John	Baseball		5			Debut 1982 Cards
Sturdivant, Tom	Baseball		3	14		Debut 1955
Sturdy, Guy	Baseball		28	60		Debut 1927
Sturgeon, Bobby	Baseball		16	38		Debut 1940
Sturhan, Herb	Football	+	18	50		CHOF Yale
Sturm, Johnny	Baseball		10	30		Debut 1941

NAME	CATEGORY	+	SIG	SP	BALL	Comment
Stutz, Henry	Auto Racing	+				
Stutz, Stanley	Basketball		10	50		played NBA 46-48
Stydahar, Joe	Football	+	50	225		1967 HOF 2-way line
Suarez, Ken	Baseball		3	14		Debut 1966
Suckow, Wendell	Luge		3	10		World Champion
Sudakis, Bill	Baseball		3	10		Debut 1968
Sudduth, Andrew	Olympic		3	6		Rowing
Suder, Pete	Baseball		7	20		Debut 1941 Phil. A's
Suffridge, Bob	Football	+	22	75		CHOF Tennessee
Suggs, Louise	Golf		20	35	45	PGA, LPGA HOF '79,'51
Suhey, Steve	Football	+	15	45		CHOF Penn State
Suhr, Gus	Baseball		22	65		Debut 1930 Pirates
Suiter, Gary	Basketball		3	14		played NBA 70
Sukeforth, Clyde	Baseball		10	24		Debut 1926 Reds
Sukova, Helena	Tennis		10	32		
Sularz, Gy	Baseball		3	10		Debut 1980
Sullivan, Billy	Baseball		18	45		Debut 1931
Sullivan, Danny	Auto Racing		7	22		
Sullivan, Frank	Baseball		3	14		Debut 1953
Sullivan, Haywood	Baseball		3	14		Debut 1955
Sullivan, Jack	Baseball		15	35		Debut 1944
Sullivan, Joe	Baseball		5			Debut 1935 Tigers
Sullivan, John	Baseball		15	32		Debut 1942
Sullivan, John	Baseball		3	14		Debut 1963
Sullivan, John L.	Boxing		600	1150		1885-92 H-Wt Champ
Sullivan, Marc	Baseball		3	10		Debut 1982
Sullivan, Mike	Golf		5	20	25	
Sullivan, Pat	Football		5	20		Heisman Aub. '71. NFL
Sullivan, Russ	Baseball		3	18		Debut 1951
Summerall, Pat	Football		6	22	100	NFL
Summerhays, Bruce	Golf		5	20	25	
Summers, Champ	Baseball		3	10		Debut 1974
Summit, Pat H.	Basketball		6	20		NCAA Coach UT
Sumners, Rosalyn	Olympic		6	18		Figure Skating
Sumpter, Barry	Basketball		3	10		played NBA 88
Sunday, Billy	Baseball		162	575		Debut 1883. Evangelist
Sundberg, Jim	Baseball		3	12		Debut 1974
Sunderlage, Don	Basketball		12	45		played NBA 53-54
Sundstram, Frank	Football	+	20	55		CHOF Cornell
Sundstrom, Patrik	Hockey		4	20		
SundvoLd, Jon	Basketball		3	10		played NBA 83-
Surhoff, B. J.	Baseball		3	12		Debut 1987
Surhoff, Richard	Basketball		10	45		played NBA 52-53
Susce, George	Baseball		28	60		Debut 1929
Susko, Pete	Baseball		18	45		Debut 1934
Susman, Karen	Tennis		6	18		
Sutcliffe, Butch	Baseball		16	35		Debut 1933
Sutcliffe, Rick	Baseball		5	10		Debut 1976
Suter, Gary	Hockey		5	16		
Sutherland, Gary	Baseball		3	12		Debut 1966
Sutherland, Jock	Football	+	40	100		1951 CHOF coach
Sutherland, Kevin	Golf		5	20	25	
Sutherland, Leo	Baseball		3	10		Debut 1980
Sutor, George	Basketball		3	14		played NBA 67-69
Sutter, Brent	Hockey		4	20		
Sutter, Brian	Hockey		4	20		

NAME	CATEGORY	+	SIG	SP	BALL	Comment
Sutter, Bruce	Baseball		4	15		Debut 1976
Sutter, Darryl	Hockey		4	20		
Sutter, Duane	Hockey		4	20		
Sutter, Rich	Hockey		4	22		
Sutter, Ron	Hockey		4	22		
Suttle, Dane	Basketball		4	12		played NBA 83-84
Sutton Bundy, May	Tennis	+	30	60		HOF 1956
Sutton, Don	Baseball		7	22	25	Debut 1966, HOF 1998
Sutton, Eddie	Basketball		4	15		Coach-OKU
Sutton, Hal	Golf		5	30	25	
Sveum, Dale	Baseball		3	10		Debut 1986
Svoboda, Peter	Hockey		3	16		
Swagerty, Keith	Basketball		3	12		played NBA 68-69
Swaggerty, Jane	Olympic					Swim/backstroke
Swain, Bennie	Basketball		8	35		played NBA 58
Swain, Michael	Olympic		3	5		Judo
Swann, Lynn	Football		9	20	125	NFL
Swanson, Clarence	Football	+	18	50		CHOF Nebraska
Swanson, Evar	Baseball		35	75		Debut 1929
Swanson, Karl	Baseball		35	75		Debut 1928
Swanson, Norman	Basketball		10	45		played NBA 53
Swanson, Stan	Baseball		3	12		Debut 1971
Swartz, Daniel	Basketball		4	18		played NBA 62
Sweeney, Ennis	Bowling	+	8	18		1974 ABC HOF-Mer. Serv.
Sweeney, Hank	Baseball		18	45		Debut 1944
Sweeny, Robert Jr	Golf		75	150		
Sweet, Rick	Baseball		3	10		Debut 1978
Sweetser, Jess	Golf		150	325		
Swenson, Rick	Dog Sled Racing		4	12		
Swiacki, Bill	Football	+	22	75		CHOF Columbia/Holy Cross
Swift, Bob	Baseball		30	65		Debut 1940
Swift, Harley	Basketball		3	14		played NBA 69-73
Swilling, Pat	Football		3	18		NFL
Swindell, Greg	Baseball		3	10		Debut 1986
Swink, Jim	Football		7	20		CHOF Texas Christian
Swisher, Steve	Baseball		3	10		Debut 1974
Switzer, Barry	Football		9	20	100	NFL Coach
Switzer, Pearl	Bowling	+	8	20		1973 Women's IBC HOF
Swoboda, Ron	Baseball		3	12		Debut 1965
Swoopes, Sheryl	Olympic		2	6		Gold Med. Basketball
Sydnor, Buck	Basketball		10	50		played NBA 46
Syms, Nancy Roth	Golf		5	20	25	
Szabo, Ecaterina	Olympic		12	38		Gymnastics
Szczerbiak, Walt	Basketball		3	12		played NBA 71
Szekely, Joe	Baseball		3	15		Debut 1953
Szewinska, Irene	Track		10	22		
Szotkiewicz, Ken	Baseball		3	12		Debut 1970

NAME	CATEGORY	+	SIG	SP	BALL	Comment
Tabb, Jerry	Baseball		3	10		Debut 1976
Tabler, Pat	Baseball		3	10		Debut 1981
Tabor, Greg	Baseball		3	10		Debut 1987
Tafoya, Michelle	Broadcaster		2	7		Olympic Host
Tagliabue, Paul	Football		5	12		NFL Commissioner
Tait, Freddie	Golf		750	1995		
Taitt, Doug	Baseball		30	65		Debut 1928
Talbert, Bill	Tennis		10	35		HOF 1967
Talbot, Bob	Baseball		4			Debut
Talbot, Dale	Baseball		3	14		Debut 1953
Taliafarro, George	Football		15	30		CHOF Indiana
Talman, M.	Golf		75	195		
Talton, Tim	Baseball		3	12		Debut 1966
Tamargo, John	Baseball		3	12		Debut 1976
Tanana, Frank	Baseball		3	12		Debut 1973
Tanenbaum, Sidney	Basketball		10	50		played NBA 47-48
Tankersley, Leo	Baseball		32	70		Debut 1925
Tannehill, Jesse	Baseball		60	150		Debut 1894
Tanner, Chuck	Baseball		3	10		Debut 1955
Tanner, Roscoe	Tennis		7	20		
Tanti,Tony	Hockey		4	15		
Taorima, Sheila	Olympic		3	9		Gold Medal. Swimming
Tapie, Alan	Golf		10	30		
Tappan, Walter	Baseball		40	85		Debut 1914
Tappe, Elvin	Baseball		3	16		Debut 1954
Tappe, Ted	Baseball		3	15		Debut 1950
Taral, Fred	Horse Racing					HOF 1955 jockey
Tarkanian, Jerry	Basketball		5	14		UNLV Coach
Tarkenton, Fran	Football		10	30	145	1986 HOF QB
Tarpley, Roy	Basketball		3	12		played NBA 86-90
Tart, LeVern	Basketball		3	12		played NBA 67-70
Tartabull, Danny	Baseball		4	24		Debut 1984
Tartabull, Jose	Baseball		4	16		Debut 1962
Tarver, LaSchelle	Baseball		3	10		Debut 1986
Tasby, Willie	Baseball		3	14		Debut 1958
Tasker, Steve	Football		4	15		NFL
Tataurangi, Phil	Golf		5	20	25	
Tate, Bennie	Baseball		30	65		Debut 1924
Tate, Frank	Boxing		10	22		
Tate, John "Big John"	Boxing		15	40		1979-80 H-Wt Champ
Tate, Lee	Baseball		4	15		Debut 1958
Tatum, Earl	Basketball		3	12		played NBA 76-79
Tatum, Jack	Football		5	20		NFL

NAME	CATEGORY	+	SIG	SP	BALL	Comment
Tatum, Jarvis	Baseball		3	12		Debut 1968
Tatum, Jim	Football	+	35	85		1984 CHOF coach
Tatum, Tani	Golf		5	20		
Tatum, Tommy	Baseball		12	35		Debut 1941
Taussig, Don	Baseball		3	15		Debut 1958
Tauziaf, Nathalie	Tennis		4	8		
Tavener, Jackie	Baseball		38	80		Debut 1921
Taveras, Alex	Baseball		3	12		Debut 1976
Taveras, Frank	Baseball		3	12		Debut 1971
Taylor, Altie	Football		3	14		NFL
Taylor, Anthony	Basketball		3	10		played NBA 88
Taylor, Bennie	Baseball		4	15		Debut 1951
Taylor, Bill	Baseball		4	15		Debut 1954
Taylor, Bob	Baseball		3	12		Debut 1970
Taylor, Bob	Baseball		3	14		Debut 1957
Taylor, Brian	Basketball		3	12		played NBA 72-81
Taylor, C. L.	Baseball		30	65		Debut 1925
Taylor, Carl	Baseball		3	14		Debut 1968 Pirates
Taylor, Charley	Football		10	22	85	1984 HOF end/WB
Taylor, Chuck	Basketball	+	25	55		HOF 1968-Contributor
Taylor, Chuck	Football		6	18		CHOF Stanford
Taylor, Danny	Baseball		38	75		Debut 1926
Taylor, Dave	Hockey		3	14		
Taylor, Dwight	Baseball		3	10		Debut 1986
Taylor, Eddie	Baseball		28	60		Debut 1926
Taylor, Fred	Baseball		4	15		Debut 1950
Taylor, Fred	Basketball		6	18		HOF 1985. Coach
Taylor, Fred	Hockey		150	400		1947 HOF fwd
Taylor, Harry	Baseball		28	60		Debut 1932
Taylor, Harry	Golf		5	20		
Taylor, Hugh "Bones"	Football		22	45		NFL
Taylor, Jack	Olympic		3	8		Swim/backstroke
Taylor, Jeffrey	Basketball		3	10		played NBA 82-86
Taylor, Jim	Football		6	22	85	1976 HOF RB
Taylor, Joe	Baseball		3	14		Debut 1951
Taylor, John	Football		5	18	85	NFL
Taylor, John H.	Golf		445	1100		PGA HOF 1975
Taylor, Lawrence	Football		8	28	120	NFL
Taylor, Leo	Baseball		28	65		Debut 1923
Taylor, Lionel	Football		7	20		NFL
Taylor, Meldrick	Boxing		10	22		
Taylor, N.J.	Football	+	10	22		1963 Canadian HOF
Taylor, Ollie	Basketball		3	14		played NBA 70-73
Taylor, Robert	Olympic		3	7		Track sprints
Taylor, Roland	Basketball		3	14		played NBA 69-75
Taylor, Ronald	Basketball		3	14		played NBA 69-71
Taylor, Sammy	Baseball		4	15		Debut 1958
Taylor, Tony	Baseball		4	14		Debut 1958
Taylor, Vernon C. "Pete"	Baseball		3			Debut 1952 Brown
Taylor, Vincent	Basketball		3	10		played NBA 82
Taylor, Zack	Baseball		45	85		Debut 1920
Teaff, Grant	Football		2	5		College Coach of Year
Teagle, Terry	Basketball		3	10		played NBA 82-
Teague, Bertha	Basketball	+	20	45		HOF 1984
Teal, Glenn	Golf		10	30		
Tebbetts, Birdie	Baseball		8	22		Debut 1936 Tigers

NAME	CATEGORY	+	SIG	SP	BALL	Comment
Teed, Dick	Baseball		4	16		Debut 1953
Tejada, Wil	Baseball		3	10		Debut 1986
Tellier, Louis	Golf		75	195		
Temple, Collis	Basketball		3	12		played NBA 74
Temple, Johnny	Baseball		7	22		Debut 1952
Templeton, Garry	Baseball		3	14		Debut 1976
Ten Broeck, Lance	Golf		5	20	25	
Tenace, Gene	Baseball		3	12		Debut 1969
Tennyson, Brian	Golf		5	20	25	
Tepedino, Frank	Baseball		3	12		Debut 1967
Terney, Bob	Golf		5	20	25	
Terrell, Ernie	Boxing		15	40		1965-67 H-Wt Champ
Terrell, Ira	Basketball		3	12		played NBA 76-78
Terrell, Jerry	Baseball		3	10		Debut 1975
Terrell, Kim	Bowler		4	8		
Terreri, Chris	Hockey		3	10		
Terry, Carlos	Basketball		3	10		played NBA 80-82
Terry, Chuck	Basketball		3	12		played NBA 72-76
Terry, Claude	Basketball		3	12		played NBA 72-77
Terry, Ralph	Baseball		3	14		Debut 1955
Terry, Wm. H, "Bill"	Baseball			55		HOF 1954. B&W Pl.$95
Terry, Wm. H. "Bill"	Baseball		15			Gold Pl.$40,P-S HOF$105
Terry, Zeb	Baseball		35	75		Debut 1916 ChiSox
Terwilliger, John	Olympic		3	6		Rowing
Terwilliger, Wayne	Baseball		4	12		Debut 1949 Cubs
Testa, Nick	Baseball		3	14		Debut 1958
Testaverde, Vinny	Football		5	35		Heisman Miami '86. NFL
Testeverde, Vinny	Football		6	30	95	NFL
Teti, Mike	Olympic		3	7		Rowing
Tettelbach, Dick	Baseball		3	14		Debut 1955
Tettleton, Mickey	Baseball		4	18		Debut 1984
Teufel, Tim	Baseball		3	10		Debut 1983
Tewell, Doug	Golf		5	20		
Tewksbury, J.W.B.	Olympic		25	50		Track
Tewksbury, Mark	Olympic		4	12		Gold Medal. Swimming
Thacker, Moe	Baseball		3	14		Debut 1958
Thacker, Thomas	Basketball		3	14		played NBA 63-70
Theard, Floyd	Basketball		4	15		played NBA 69
Theismann, Joe	Football		5	18	125	NFL
Thelen, Dave	Football		4	8		1989 Canadian HOF
Theobald, Ron	Baseball		3	12		Debut 1971
Theodore, George	Baseball		3	12		Debut 1973
Theumer, Petra	Olympic		15	38		Swimming
Theus, Reggie	Basketball		4	15		played NBA 78-88
Thevenow, Tommy	Baseball		35	90		Debut 1924
Theys, Dider	Auto Racing		4	8		
Thibaudeau, Gilles	Hockey		3	10		
Thibeaux, Peter	Basketball		3	10		played NBA 84-85
Thieben, William	Basketball		7	30		played NBA 56-57
Thiel, Bert	Baseball		4			Debut 1952 Bost. Braves
Thigpen, Bobby	Baseball		3	10		Debut 1986
Thigpen, Justus	Basketball		3	12		played NBA 69-73
Thirdkill, David	Basketball		3	10		played NBA 82-86
Thobois, Jayne	Golf		5	20	25	
Thoeni, Gustav	Olympic		12	32		Alpine skiing
Thomas, Andres	Baseball		3	12		Debut 1985

NAME	CATEGORY	+	SIG	SP	BALL	Comment
Thomas, Aurelius	Football		6	15		CHOF Ohio State
Thomas, Bud	Baseball		3	14		Debut 1951 Browns
Thomas, Danny	Baseball		15	32		Debut 1976
Thomas, Dave	Golf		5	20	25	
Thomas, Debi	Olympic		6	20		Figure skating
Thomas, Derrel	Baseball		3	12		Debut 1971
Thomas, Derrick	Football		3	20	85	NFL
Thomas, Duane	Football		12	25		NFL
Thomas, Emmitt	Football		5	15		NFL
Thomas, Frank	Baseball		4	14		Debut 1951
Thomas, Frank	Baseball		6	38		Debut 1990
Thomas, Frank	Football	+	30	50		1951 CHOF coach
Thomas, Fred	Baseball		40	85		Debut 1918
Thomas, George	Baseball		3	14		Debut 1957
Thomas, Gorman	Baseball		3	10		Debut 1973
Thomas, Herb	Baseball		30	65		Debut 1924
Thomas, Ira	Baseball		60	125		Debut 1906
Thomas, Isiah	Basketball		10	36		played NBA 81-
Thomas, James	Basketball		3	10		played NBA 83-85
Thomas, John	Olympic		8	24		High Jump
Thomas, Joseph	Basketball		3	14		played NBA 70
Thomas, Keith	Baseball		4	15		Debut 1952
Thomas, Kurt	Olympic		5	14		Gymnastics
Thomas, Lee	Baseball		3	14		Debut 1961 Yankees
Thomas, Leo	Baseball		4	16		Debut 1950
Thomas, Luther B. "Bud"	Baseball		7			Debut 1932 Senators
Thomas, Mike	Football		3	8		NFL
Thomas, Pinklon	Boxing		15	30		1984-86 H-Wt Champ
Thomas, Ray	Baseball		18	40		Debut 1938
Thomas, Ren,	Auto Racing		45	95		
Thomas, Ron	Basketball		3	12		played NBA 72-75
Thomas, Sykes	Bowling	+	10	22		1971 ABC HOF
Thomas, Terry	Basketball		3	12		played NBA 75
Thomas, Thurman	Football		8	28	125	NFL
Thomas, Tommy (Alphonse)	Baseball		9	35		Debut 1926 ChiSox
Thomas, Valmy	Baseball		5	16		Debut 1957
Thomas, Willis	Basketball		3	15		played NBA 67
Thomasson, Gary	Baseball		3	12		Debut 1972
Thome, Jim	Baseball		6	29		Debut 1991
Thompson, Al	Bowling		5	10		1991 PBA HOF-Mer.Serv.
Thompson, Bernard	Basketball		3	10		played NBA 84-
Thompson, Bertha	Golf		85	175	25	
Thompson, Bobby	Baseball		3	14		Debut 1978
Thompson, Cliff	Hockey	+	10	22		1973 US HOF coach
Thompson, Cornelius	Basketball		3	10		played NBA 82
Thompson, Daley	Olympic		10	25		Decathlon
Thompson, Danny	Baseball		25	65		Debut 1970
Thompson, David	Basketball		7	24		HOF 1996. NBA 75-83
Thompson, Don	Baseball		12	36		Debut 1949 Bost. Braves
Thompson, Eugene "Junior"	Baseball		6			Debut 1939 Reds
Thompson, Fresco	Baseball		30	60		Debut 1925
Thompson, George	Basketball		5	16		played NBA 69-74
Thompson, H.J.	Horse Racing					HOF 1969 trainer
Thompson, Hank	Baseball		35	75		Debut 1947
Thompson, Jason	Baseball		3	10		Debut 1976
Thompson, Jenny	Olympic		3	10		Gold Med. Swimming

NAME	CATEGORY	+	SIG	SP	BALL	Comment
Thompson, Jimmy	Golf		45	95		
Thompson, Joe	Football	+	25	75		CHOF Pittsburgh
Thompson, John	Basketball		7	20		played NBA 64-65
Thompson, John A."Cat"	Basketball	+	25	55		HOF 1962
Thompson, John S.	Basketball		3	14		played NBA 68
Thompson, LaSalle	Basketball		3	10		played NBA 82-
Thompson, Leonard	Football		3	10		NFL
Thompson, Leonard	Golf		5	20	25	
Thompson, Martin	Golf		5	20	25	
Thompson, Mickey	Auto Racing	+	60	135		HOF 1990
Thompson, Mychal	Basketball		3	12		played NBA 78-90
Thompson, Paul	Basketball		3	10		played NBA 83-85
Thompson, Reyna	Football		3	8		NFL
Thompson, Robby	Baseball		3	10		Debut 1986
Thompson, Rocky	Golf		5	20	25	
Thompson, Sam	Baseball		3100	6000	10000	HOF 1974
Thompson, Scot	Baseball		3	10		Debut 1978
Thompson, Tim	Baseball		3	14		Debut 1954
Thompson, Tiny	Hockey		100	325		1959 HOF goal
Thompson, Tommy	Baseball		35	75		Debut 1933
Thompson, Wilbur	Olympic		7	18		Shot put
Thompson, William	Basketball		3	18		played NBA 86-
Thomson, Bobby	Baseball		7	15		Debut 1946 NY Giants
Thomson, Hector	Golf		35	85		
Thomson, Jimmy	Golf		45	95		
Thomson, Lena	Golf		75	170		
Thomson, Peter	Golf		20	45	45	PGA HOF 1988
Thon, Dickie	Baseball		3	10		Debut 1979
Thoren, Duane	Basketball		3	14		played NBA 67-69
Thorn, Rodney	Basketball		4	15		played NBA 63-70
Thorne, Samuel	Football	+	25	75		CHOF Yale
Thornhill, Jill	Golf		5	20	25	
Thornton, Andre	Baseball		3	10		Debut 1973
Thornton, Dallas	Basketball		4	14		played NBA 68-69
Thornton, Karen Mae	Olympic		3	10		Swimming
Thornton, Lou	Baseball		3	10		Debut 1985
Thornton, Otis	Baseball		3	10		Debut 1973
Thornton, Rogert	Basketball		3	10		played NBA 85-
Thorpe, Bob	Baseball		4	18		Debut 1951
Thorpe, Jim	Football		500	1400		1963 HOF RB
Thorpe, Jim	Golf		5	20	25	
Thorpe, Otis	Basketball		4	15		played NBA 84-
Threatt, Sedale	Basketball		3	12		played NBA 83-
Throneberry, Faye	Baseball		12	38		Debut 1952
Throneberry, Marv	Baseball		4	14		Debut 1955
Thum, Joe	Bowling	+	8	18		1980 ABC HOF-Mer.Serv.
Thuman, Lou	Baseball		5			Debut 1939 Senators
Thurman, Bob	Baseball		3	15		Debut 1955
Thurman, Gary	Baseball		3	10		Debut 1987
Thurmond, Nate	Basketball		8	20		HOF 1984
Thurston, Fuzzy	Football		5	15		NFL
Thurston, Hollis	Baseball		40	85		Debut 1923
Thurston, Mel	Basketball		10	50		played NBA 46-47
Tiant, Luis	Baseball		6	20		Debut 1964
Tibbs, Casey	Rodeo		7	18		
Tickner, Charles	Olympic		5	14		Figure skating

NAME	CATEGORY	+	SIG	SP	BALL	Comment
Ticknor, Ben	Football	+	15	45		CHOF Harvard
Tidrick, Hal	Basketball		10	50		played NBA 44-48
Tieman, Daniel	Basketball		3	25		played NBA 62
Tigert, John	Football	+	25	75		CHOF Vanderbilt
Tikkanen, Esa	Hockey		4	24		
Tilden, Bill	Tennis	+	195	425		HOF 1959
Tilley, Pat	Football		3	10		NFL
Tillinghast, Albert.W	Golf		350	750		
Tillis, Darren	Basketball		3	10		played NBA 82-83
Tillman, Bob	Baseball		3	14		Debut 1962
Tillman, Rusty	Baseball		3	10		Debut 1982
Timmerman, Ulf	Olympic		8	28		Shot Put
Timmis, Brian	Football	+	10	22		1969 Canadian HOF
Timmons, Steve	Olympic		3	18		Volleyball
Tincup, Ben	Baseball		25			Debut 1914 Phillies
Tindall, Frank	Football		4	8		1985 Canadian HOF
Tingay, Lance	Tennis	+	12	32		HOF 1982
Tingle, Jack	Basketball		10	50		played NBA 47-48
Tinglehoff, Mick	Football		4	15		NFL
Tingley, Ron	Baseball		3	10		Debut 1982
Tinker, Gerald	Olympic		3	7		Track sprints
Tinker, Joe	Baseball		525	1250	6000	HOF '46. B&W PC $1000
Tinling, Ted	Tennis	+	20	45		HOF 1986
Tinnell, Carol	Pole Vault		18	45		
Tinordi, Mark	Hockey		4	18		
Tinsley, Bud	Football		4	8		1982 Canadian HOF
Tinsley, Gaynell	Football		6	15		CHOF Louisiana State
Tinsley, George	Basketball		3	12		played NBA 69-71
Tippett, Andre	Football		3	12		NFL
Tippett, Dave	Hockey		3	10		
Tipton, Eric	Baseball		10			Debut 1939 A's
Tipton, Eric	Football		6	15		CHOF Duke
Tipton, Joe	Baseball		6	20		Debut 1948 Indians
Tischinski, Tom	Baseball		3	12		Debut 1969
Tisdale, Wayman	Basketball		5	14		played NBA 85-
Titterton, Maud	Golf		95	195		
Tittle, Y.A.	Football		10	20	100	1971 HOF QB
Tkachuk, Keith	Hockey		8	28	30	
Tkaczuk, Walt	Hockey		4	25		
Tnompson, Milt	Baseball		3	10		Debut 1984
Tobey, Dave	Basketball		10	32		HOF 1961-Referee
Tobian, Gary	Olympic		4	12		Diving
Tobin, Jack	Baseball		45	95		Debut 1914
Tobin, Jim	Baseball		30	65		Debut 1937
Tobin, John	Baseball		10	32		Debut 1945
Tobin, Johnny	Baseball		15	45		Debut 1932
Tocchet, Rick	Hockey		4	18		
Todd, Al	Baseball		18	45		Debut 1932
Todd, Harry	Golf		25	75		
Todd, Richard	Football		3	12		NFL
Todorovich, Mike	Basketball		10	50		played NBA 47-50
Todt, Phil	Baseball		28	60		Debut 1924
Toepfer, Elvira	Bowling		5	12		1976 Women's IBC HOF
Toft, Rod	Bowling		5	12		1991 ABC HOF
Tokle, Roger	Skiing		10	20		
Tolan, Bobby	Baseball		3	10		Debut 1965

NAME	CATEGORY	+	SIG	SP	BALL	Comment
Tolan, Eddie	Olympic		30	60		200 Dash
Tolbert, Ray	Basketball		3	10		played NBA 81-
Tolbert, Tom	Basketball		3	10		played NBA 88-
Tolles, Tommy	Golf		5	25	25	
Tolleson, Wayne	Baseball		3	10		Debut 1981
Tolley, Cyril	Golf		95	235		
Tolliver, Billy Joe	Football		3	10		NFL
Tolman, Tim	Baseball		3	10		Debut 1981
Tolson, Byron	Basketball		3	12		played NBA 74-77
Tomba, Alberto	Olympic		10	38		Alpine skiing
Tomer, George	Baseball		35	75		Debut 1913
Tomjanovich, Rudy	Basketball		4	15		played NBA 70-80
Tommy, Andy	Football	+	10	22		1989 Canadian HOF
Tompkins, Harry	Rodeo		10	20		
Toms, David	Golf		5	20	25	
Tonelli, John	Hockey		4	16		
Toney, Andrew	Basketball		4	12		played NBA 80-87
Toney, James "Lights Out"	Boxing		15	40		Middle-Wt Champ
Toney, Sedric	Basketball		3	10		played NBA 85-
Tonkovich, Andrew	Basketball		10	50		played NBA 48
Tonnemaker, Clayton	Football		7	20		CHOF Minnesota
Tooley, Bert	Baseball		42	85		Debut 1911
Toomay, John	Basketball		10	50		played NBA 47-49
Toomey, Bill	Olympic		8	18		Decathlon
Toon, Al	Football		4	12		NFL
Toone, Bernard	Basketball		3	12		played NBA 79
Toporcer, Specs	Baseball		40	75		Debut 1921
Torborg, Jeff	Baseball		3	10		Debut 1964
Torgeson, Earl	Baseball		12	28		Debut 1947 Bost. Braves
Torgoff, Irving	Basketball		20	75		played NBA 39-48
Tormohlen, Eugene	Basketball		6	22		played NBA 62-69
Torphy, Red	Baseball		35	75		Debut 1920
Torrance, Sam	Golf		5	20	25	
Torre, Frank	Baseball		5	17		Debut 1956
Torre, Joe	Baseball		4	14		Debut 1960
Torrence, Gwen	Olympic		5	25		Olymp.Gold. 200-Meters
Torres, Dara	Olympic		3	12		Swim/relay
Torres, Enrique	Pro Wrestler		7	22		
Torres, Hector	Baseball		3	14		Debut 1968
Torres, Rusty	Baseball		3	12		Debut 1971
Torretta, Gino	Football		6	22		'92 Heisman Miami
Torrey, Bob	Football	+	25	75		CHOF Pennsylvania
Torrez, Mike	Baseball		15	40		Debut 1967 Cards
Torve, Kelvin	Baseball		3	10		Debut 1988
Torville and Dean	Olympic		22	60		Figure skating
Tosheff, William	Basketball		10	45		played NBA 51-53
Toski, Bob	Golf		10	30	35	
Toth, Zollie	Football		4	15		NFL
Tough, Red	Basketball		10	50		played NBA 45-49
Tountas, Pete	Bowling		5	12		1989 ABC HOF
Tovar, Cesar	Baseball		14	31		Debut 1965
Towe, Monte	Basketball		3	12		played NBA 75-76
Toweel, Vic	Boxing		15	40		Bantam-Wt Champ
Tower, Oswald	Basketball	+	20	45		HOF 1959-Contributor
Towery, William	Basketball		18	75		played NBA 41-49
Towler, Dan	Football		12	28		NFL

NAME	CATEGORY	+	SIG	SP	BALL	Comment
Townes, E. D.	Golf		65	125		
Townes, Linton	Basketball		3	12		played NBA 82-84
Towns, Forrest G.	Olympic		8	25		110 M Hurdles
Townsend Toulmin, Bertha	Tennis	+	12	30		HOF 1974
Townsend, Greg	Football		4	12		NFL
Townsend, Raymond	Basketball		3	12		played NBA 78-79
Traber, Jim	Baseball		2	10		Debut 1984
Trabert, Tony	Tennis		10	26		HOF 1970
Tracewski, Dick	Baseball		3	14		Debut 1962
Tracy, Jim	Baseball		3	10		Debut 1980
Trafton, George	Football	+	75	325		1964 HOF 2-way line
Trageser, Walt	Baseball		40	80		Debut 1913
Tramback, Red	Baseball		25	55		Debut 1940
Trammell, Alan	Baseball		5	15		Debut 1977
Trapp, George	Basketball		3	12		played NBA 71-76
Trapp, John	Basketball		3	12		played NBA 68-72
Trautwig, Al	Broadcaster		2	5		Olympic Host
Travers, Jerome	Golf		495	995		
Travers, Jerry	Golf		495	995		PGA HOF 1976
Travis, Brick	Football	+	22	60		CHOF Missouri
Travis, Cecil	Baseball		10	35		Debut 1933 Senators
Travis, Walter	Golf		495	995		PGA HOF 1979
Trawick, Herb	Football	+	10	22		1975 Canadian HOF
Traynor, Pie	Baseball		160	400	1250	HOF 1948.B&W PC $6250
Traynor, Pie	Baseball					Gold Pl. $575
Treadway, Jeff	Baseball		3	10		Debut 1987
Treadway, Red	Baseball		8	22		Debut 1944
Treblehorn, Tom	Baseball		3	10		Brewers Mgr.
Trechock, Frank	Baseball		15	35		Debut 1937
Tremark, Nick	Baseball		15	35		Debut 1934 Brklyn. Dodg.
Tremblay, Gilles	Hockey		4	20		
Tremblay, J.C.	Hockey		4	22		
Tremblay, Mario	Hockey		5	20		
Tremper, Overton	Baseball		35	75		Debut 1927
Trenary, Jill	Olympic		5	25		Figure Skating
Tresh, Mike	Baseball		38	80		Debut 1938
Tresh, Tom	Baseball		4	14		Debut 1961
Trester, Arthur "A.L."	Basketball	+	18	40		HOF 1961-Contributor
Tresvant, John	Basketball		3	15		played NBA 64-72
Tretiak, Vladislav	Hockey		22	50		1989 HOF goal
Trevino, Alex	Baseball		3	12		Debut 1978
Trevino, Bobby	Baseball		3	14		Debut 1963
Trevino, Lee	Golf		15	35	35	PGA HOF 1981
Triandos, Gus	Baseball		4	14		Debut 1953
Trickle, Dick	Auto Racing		4	12		
Trihey, Harry	Hockey		175	600		1950 HOF fwd
Trillo, Manny	Baseball		3	12		Debut 1973
Trinkl, Hannes	Olympic		4	12		Medalist. Alpine Skiing
Triplet, Kirk	Golf		5	20	25	
Triplett, Coaker	Baseball		15	38		Debut 1938
Trippi, Charley	Football		8	22	85	1968 HOF RB
Triptow, Richard	Basketball		10	50		played NBA 44-49
Tripucka, Frank	Football		6	16		NFL
Tripucka, Kelly	Basketball		4	12		played NBA 81-
Trosky, Hal	Baseball		35	70		Debut 1933
Trotsek, Harry	Horse Racing					HOF 1984 trainer

NAME	CATEGORY	+	SIG	SP	BALL	Comment
Trotter, Bill	Baseball		6			Debut 1937 Browns
Trottier, Bryan	Hockey		6	20		1997 HOF fwd
Trouppe, Quincy	Baseball		3	15		Debut 1952
Trout, Paul "Dizzy"	Baseball		30	72		Debut 1939
Trovinger, W. H.	Golf		75	172		
Troy, Michael	Olympic		3	9		Swim/200 fly
Trucks, Virgil	Baseball		10	25		Debut 1941 Tigers
Truitt, Ansley	Basketball		3	12		played NBA 72
Trumble, Hal	Hockey		5	10		1970 US HOF admin
Tryba, Ted	Golf		5	20	25	
Tryon, Edward	Football	+	18	50		CHOF Colgate
Tschetter, Kris	Golf		5	20	25	
Tschogl, John	Basketball		3	12		played NBA 72-74
Tsioropoulos, Louis	Basketball		4	28		played NBA 56-58
Tubbs, Billy	Basketball		4	12		Coach
Tubbs, Jerry	Football		3	12		NFL
Tubman, Joe	Football	+	10	22		1976 Canadian HOF
Tucker, Albert	Basketball		3	12		played NBA 67-71
Tucker, Bill	Bowling		5	12		1988 ABC HOF
Tucker, Bob	Football		3	12		NFL
Tucker, Chris	Golf		5	20	25	
Tucker, James	Basketball		8	40		played NBA 54-56
Tucker, Thurman	Baseball		14	32		Debut 1942 ChiSox
Tucker, Tony	Boxing		15	30		1986-87 H-Wt Champ
Tucker, Trent	Basketball		3	10		played NBA 82-
Tuckman, Bayard Jr.	Horse Racing					HOF 1973 jockey
Tudor, John	Baseball		5	18		Debut 1979
Tueting, Sarah	Hockey		2	10		Women's Goalie
Tufts, Richard	Golf		75	160		PGA HOF 1992, Contrib.
Tully, Mike	Olympic		4	14		Pole Vault
Tunnell, Emlen	Football	+	75	240		1967 HOF DB
Tunney, Gene	Boxing		130	250		1926-28 H-Wt Champ
Turchin, Eddie	Baseball		16	40		Debut 1943
Turcotte, Ron	Horse Racing		8	32		HOF 1979 jockey
Turgeon, Pete	Baseball		35	80		Debut 1923
Turgeon, Pierre	Hockey		4	18	22	
Turgeon, Sylvain	Hockey		4	16		
Turley, Bob	Baseball		4	12		Debut 1951
Turnbull, Perry	Hockey		3	10		
Turnbull, Wendy	Tennis		6	16		
Turner, Andre	Basketball		3	10		played NBA 86-
Turner, Bake	Football		4	14		NFL
Turner, Bulldog	Football		12	35	150	1966 HOF 2-way line
Turner, Cathy	Olympic		4	22		Olymp.Gold.Speed Skating
Turner, Earl	Baseball		12	30		Debut 1948
Turner, Elston	Basketball		3	10		played NBA 81-
Turner, Gary	Basketball		3	15		played NBA 67
Turner, Gil	Boxing		12	30		Welter-Wt Contender
Turner, Greg	Golf		5	20	25	
Turner, Herschell	Basketball		3	18		played NBA 67
Turner, Jackie	Basketball		8	42		played NBA 54
Turner, Jeffrey	Basketball		3	10		played NBA 84-86
Turner, Jerry	Baseball		3	10		Debut 1974
Turner, Jim	Baseball		15	38		Debut 1937 Bost. Braves
Turner, Jim	Football		5	15		NFL
Turner, John	Basketball		4	22		played NBA 61

NAME	CATEGORY	+	SIG	SP	BALL	Comment
Turner, Kim	Olympic		3	7		100 meter Hurdles
Turner, Nash	Horse Racing					HOF 1955 jockey
Turner, Roscoe	Auto Racing	+	45	100		And Pilot
Turner, Shane	Baseball		3	10		Debut 1988
Turner, Sherri	Golf		5	20	25	
Turner, Ted	Golf		10	30		
Turner, Ted	Yachting		6	16		
Turner, Terry	Baseball		75	150		Debut 1901
Turner, Torn	Baseball		15	40		Debut 1940
Turner, William	Basketball		3	14		played NBA 67-72
Turnesa, Jim	Golf		50	95		
Turnesa, Joe	Golf		45	90		
Turnesa, Mike	Golf		35	85		
Turnesa, Willie	Golf		50	95		
Turpin, Melvin	Basketball		3	12		played NBA 84-87
Turpin, Randy	Boxing		125	250		
Tutt, Thayer	Hockey	+	10	22		1973 US HOF admin
Tuttle, Bill	Baseball		3	12		Debut 1952
Twardzik, Dave	Basketball		3	12		played NBA 72-79
Tway, Bob	Golf		5	25	25	
Tweedell, William	Golf		95	195		
Twibell, Roger	Broadcaster		3	8		
Twigg, Rebecca	Olympic		3	10		Cycling
Twiggs, Greg	Golf		5	20	25	
Twitty, Howard	Golf		5	20	25	
Twombly, Clarence	Baseball		42	85		Debut 1920
Twombly, George	Baseball		45	90		Debut 1914
Twyford, Sally	Bowling	+	10	24		1964 Women's IBC HOF
Twyman, Jack	Basketball		9	20		HOF 1982
Twyman, Jack	Tennis		4	8		
Tyack, Jim	Baseball		8	35		Debut 1943
Tyler, Frederick	Olympic		3	6		Swim/relay
Tyler, Johnnie	Baseball		40	80		Debut 1934
Tyler, Terry	Basketball		3	10		played NBA 78-
Tyler, Wendell	Football		5	15		NFL
Tyra, Charley	Basketball		6	25		played NBA 57-61
Tyrone, Jirn	Baseball		3	12		Debut 1972
Tyrone, Wayne	Baseball		3	12		Debut 1976
Tyson, Mike	Baseball		3	12		Debut 1972
Tyson, Mike	Boxing		35	100		1988-90 H-Wt Champ
Tyson, Ty	Baseball		5	12		HOF Broadcaster
Tyus, Wyomia	Olympic		10	40		100 M Dash

NAME	CATEGORY	+	SIG	SP	BALL	Comment

NAME	CATEGORY	+	SIG	SP	BALL	Comment
Ueberroth, Peter	Baseball		8	18		BB Comm. & Olymp. Hd.
Uecker, Bob	Baseball		10	30		Debut 1962
Uhlaender, Ted	Baseball		3	12		Debut 1965
Uhle, George	Baseball		40	95		Debut 1919
Uhlir, Charlie	Baseball		12	38		Debut 1931
Ulion, Gretchen	Olympic		2	7		Olympic Hockey Pioneer
Ulisney, Mike	Baseball		10	28		Debut 1945
Ullger, Scott	Baseball		3	10		Debut 1983
Ullman, Norm	Hockey		6	20	28	1982 HOF fwd
Ullrich, Jan	Cycling		4	15		Tour de France Champion
Ulrich, Walt	Golf		15	45		
Umphlett, Tom	Baseball		3	15		Debut 1953
Underhill, Ruth	Golf		75	172		
Unger, Gary	Hockey		6	22		
Unitas, Johnny	Football		14	38	135	1979 HOF QB
Unseld, Wes	Basketball		8	22		HOF 1987
Unser, Al	Auto Racing		7	22		HOF 1991
Unser, Al	Baseball		6	20		Debut 1947
Unser, Al, Jr.	Auto Racing		7	28		
Unser, Bobby	Auto Racing		7	25		HOF 1990, HOF 1994
Unser, Del	Baseball		4	14		Debut 1968 Senators
Upchurch, Rick	Football		3	15		NFL
Upham, John	Baseball		3	14		Debut 1967
Uplinger, Hal	Basketball		8	45		played NBA 53
Upright, Dixie	Baseball		8	25		Debut 1953 Browns
Upshaw, Cecil	Baseball		6			Debut 1966 Atl. Braves
Upshaw, Gene	Football		7	20	75	1987 HOF OL
Upshaw, Kelvin	Basketball		3	10		played NBA 88-
Upshaw, Willie	Baseball		3	12		Debut 1978
Upton, Torn	Baseball		4	16		Debut 1950
Uram, Andy	Football		12	30		NFL
Urban, Luke	Baseball		38	80		Debut 1927
Urbanski, Billy	Baseball		40	80		Debut 1931
Uresti, Omar	Golf		5	20	25	
Uribe, Jose	Baseball		3	10		Debut 1984
Urness, Ted	Football		4	8		1989 Canadian HOF
Urzetta, Sam	Golf		25	75		
USA Magnificent Seven	Olympic		75	500		Gold Medal '96. Gymn.
Usher, Bob	Baseball		4	22		Debut 1946
Ussery, Robert	Horse Racing		10	25		HOF 1980 jockey
Utay, Joe	Football	+	25	75		CHOF Texas A&M
Utley, Sam	Golf		5	20	25	
Uzcudun, Paolino	Boxing		35			Lost to Louis & Carnera

NAME	CATEGORY	+	SIG	SP	BALL	Comment
Uzielli, Angela	Golf		5	20	25	

V

NAME	CATEGORY	+	SIG	SP	BALL	Comment
Vacario, Arancha Sanchez	Tennis		4	18		
Vacendak, Stephen	Basketball		3	18		played NBA 67-69
Vachon, Rogatien	Hockey		5	20		
Vadnais, Carol	Hockey		4	18		
Vail, Mike	Baseball		3	12		Debut 1975
Vails, Nelson	Olympic		3	6		Cycling
Vaive, Rick	Hockey		4	14		
Valdespino, Sandy	Baseball		4	18		Debut 1965
Valdez, Julio	Baseball		3	10		Debut 1980
Valdivielso, Jose	Baseball		5	14		Debut 1955
Valentine, Bobby	Baseball		3	10		Debut 1969
Valentine, Darnell	Basketball		3	10		played NBA 81-90
Valentine, Ellis	Baseball		3	10		Debut 1975
Valentine, Fred	Baseball		4	15		Debut 1953 Orioles
Valentine, Jessie	Golf		10	35		
Valentine, Ronnie	Basketball		3	10		played NBA 80
Valentine, Tommy	Golf		5	20	25	
Valenzuela, Fernando	Baseball		5	16		Debut 1980
Valle, Dave	Baseball		3	10		Debut 1984
Vallely, John	Basketball		3	12		played NBA 70-71
Valliancourt, Michael	Olympic		5	10		Equestrian
Valo, Elmer	Baseball		5	15		Debut 1940 A's
Valvano, Jim	Basketball		15	35		N.C. State #1! Coach
Van Alen, James	Tennis	+	12	38		HOF 1965
Van Arsdale, Dick	Basketball		4	14		played NBA 65-76
Van Arsdale, Tom	Basketball		4	14		played NBA 65-76
Van Berg, Jack	Horse Racing					HOF 1985 trainer
Van Berg, Marion	Horse Racing					HOF 1970 trainer
Van Biesbrouck, John	Hockey		10	30	35	
Van Boxmeer, John	Hockey		4	18		
Van Breda Kolff, Butch	Basketball		10	50		played NBA 46-49
Van Breda Kolff, Jan	Basketball		3	10		played NBA 74-82
Van Brocklin, Norm	Football	+	55	250	350	1971 HOF. NFL QB
Van Buren, Steve	Football		7	22	85	1965 HOF RB
Van Camp, AL	Baseball		30	85		Debut 1928
Van Cuyk, John	Baseball		4	10		Debut 1947
Van De Weghe, Albert	Olympic		4	12		Swim/backstroke
Van Dyken, Amy	Olympic		4	20		4 Gold Med. Swimming
Van Eeghen, Mark	Football		7	15		NFL
Van Exel, Nick	Basketball		5	25		NBA-Lakers
Van Gorder, Dave	Baseball		3	10		Debut 1982

NAME	CATEGORY	+	SIG	SP	BALL	Comment
Van Horn, Keith	Basketball		5	30		NBA '97-'98 rookie
Van Lier, Norm	Basketball		4	14		played NBA 69-78
Van Noy, Jay	Baseball		6	18		Debut 1951
Van Poppel, Todd	Baseball		3	10		Debut 1991
Van Ryn, John	Tennis		10	25		HOF 1963
Van Sickel, Dale	Football	+	18	50		CHOF Florida
Van Slyke, Andy	Baseball		4	15		Debut 1983
Van Surdam, H.	Football	+	25	75		CHOF Wesleyan
Van Wie, Virginia	Golf		50	95		
Van Zant, Dennis	Basketball		3	12		played NBA 75
Vance, Dazzy	Baseball		275	650	3200	HOF 1955.B&W PC $650
Vance, Gene	Basketball		10	50		played NBA 47-51
Vander Meer, Johnny	Baseball		30	55		Debut 1937 Reds
VanDer Veer, Tara	Basketball		2	6		Coach. Olympic Gold
Vanderbeck, Florence	Golf		95	175		
Vanderbilt, Harold S.	Yachting		35	75		
Vanderbilt, William K.	Auto Racing	+	45	125		
Vandeweghe, Ernie	Basketball		7	30		played NBA 49-55
Vandeweghe, Kiki	Basketball		3	12		played NBA 80-
Vandivier, Robert "Fuzzy"	Basketball	+	22	50		HOF 1974
Vann, Thadd	Football	+	15	35		1987 CHOF coach
Vanos, Nicholas	Basketball		3	10		played NBA 85-86
Vanover, Tamarik	Football		4	15	75	NFL
Varangot, Brigitte	Golf		5	20	25	
Vardon, Harry	Golf		750	1750		PGA HOF 1974
Vare, Glenna Collett	Golf		125	295		PGA HOF 1975
Vargas, Hedi	Baseball		3	10		Debut 1982
Varipapa, Andy	Bowling	+	25	65		1957 ABC HOF
Varner, Buck	Baseball		3	15		Debut 1952
Varney, Pete	Baseball		3	12		Debut 1973
Varsho, Gary	Baseball		3	10		Debut 1988
Vataha, Randy	Football		3	12		NFL
Vaughan, Arky	Baseball		325	1700	3500	HOF 1985
Vaughan, Glenn	Baseball		4	15		Debut 1963
Vaughan, Kaye	Football		4	8		1978 Canadian HOF
Vaughn, Charlie	Baseball		4			Debut 1966 Atl. Braves
Vaughn, Chico	Basketball		4	20		played NBA 62-69
Vaughn, David	Basketball		0	12		played NBA 74-75
Vaughn, Greg	Baseball		3	20		Debut 1989
Vaughn, Mo	Baseball		5	30		Debut 1991
Vaughn, Virgil	Basketball		10	50		played NBA 46-47
Vaught, John	Football		6	20		1979 CHOF coach
Veal, Orville "Coot"	Baseball		4	15		Debut 1958 Tigers
Veatch, Georgia	Bowling	+	8	18		1974 Women's IBC HOF
Veeck, Bill	Baseball		75	250	2000	Executive
Veitch, Darren	Hockey		3	12		
Veitch, Sylvester	Horse Racing					HOF 1977 trainer
Velarde, Randy	Baseball		3	10		Debut 1987
Velasquez, Jorge	Horse Racing		8	30		HOF 1990 jockey
Velez, Otto	Baseball		3	12		Debut 1973
Veltman, Art	Baseball		35	75		Debut 1926
Venable, Max	Baseball		3	12		Debut 1979
Ventura, Robin	Baseball		6	22		Debut 1989
Ventura, Vince	Baseball		4	10		Debut 1945
Venturi, Ken	Golf		10	30	35	
Venzke, Jene	Track		20	40		

NAME	CATEGORY	+	SIG	SP	BALL	Comment
Verban, Emil	Baseball		14	30		Debut 1944
Verbeek, Pat	Hockey		4	18		
Verble, Gene	Baseball		3	14		Debut 1951
Verdeur, Joseph	Olympic		5	14		Swim/breast stroke
Verdi, Frank	Baseball		3	14		Debut 1953
Verdin, Clarence	Football		3	10		NFL
Verga, Robert	Basketball		4	16		played NBA 67-73
Vergez, Johnny	Baseball		22	50		Debut 1931 NY Giants
Verhoeven, Peter	Basketball		3	12		played NBA 81-86
Vermeil, Dick	Football		3	10		NFL
Vernon, Mickey	Baseball		10	25		Debut 1939 Senators
Vernon, Mike	Hockey		4	18		
Verplank, Scott	Golf		5	20	20	
Versalles, Zoilo	Baseball		15	45		Debut 1959
Verwey, Bob	Golf		5	20	25	
Very, Dexter	Football	+	20	60		CHOF Penn State
Veryzer, Tom	Baseball		3	12		Debut 1973
Vessels, Billy	Football		10	25		CHOF OK. Heisman '52
Vezina, Georges	Hockey		500	2000		1945 HOF goal
Vicario, Arantxa Sanchez	Tennis		5	16		
Vick, Ernie	Baseball		35	75		Debut 1922
Vick, Ernie	Football	+	20	60		CHOF Michigan
Vick, Sammy	Baseball	+	38	80		Debut 1917
Vico, George	Baseball		6	30		Debut 1948
Vidal, Jose	Baseball		3	14		Debut 1966
Vidali, Lynn	Olympic		3	6		Swim/ind. medley
Vidmar, Peter	Olympic		5	18		Gymnastics
Vilas, Guillermo	Tennis		8	20		HOF 1991
Villa, Pancho	Boxing		150	325		
Villeneuve, Jacques	Auto Racing		7	38		Indy 500 Winner
Vilwock, Dave	Power Boat Racing		5	22		Gold Cup winner
Vincent, Fay	Baseball		10	25		MLB Commissioner
Vincent, James	Basketball		3	10		played NBA 85-
Vincent, Jay	Basketball		3	10		played NBA 81-
Vines, Ellsworth	Golf		35	95		
Vines, Ellsworth	Tennis		35	95		HOF 1962
Vinson, Charlie	Baseball		3	14		Debut 1966
Vinson, Maribel Y.	Olympic		55	125		Figure Skating
Vinton, Donald	Golf		75	195		
Viola, Frank	Baseball		5	12	36	Debut 1982
Viox, Jim	Baseball		45	85		Debut 1912
Virden, Claude	Basketball		3	14		played NBA 72
Virdon, Bill	Baseball		3	12		Debut 1955
Viren, Lasse	Olympic		10	28		Track
Virgil, Ozzie	Baseball		4	15		Debut 1956
Virgil, Ozzie Jr.	Baseball		3	10		Debut 1989
Vitt, Ossie	Baseball	+	45	90		Debut 1912
Vizcaino, Jose	Baseball		3	10		Debut 1989
Vizquel, Omar	Baseball		3	10		Debut 1989
Vogel, Matt	Olympic		4	12		Swim/100 fly
Vogel, Otto	Baseball		38	80		Debut 1923
Voges, Mitch	Golf		5	20	25	
Voigt, George	Golf		75	195		
Voiselle, Bill	Baseball		8			Debut 1942 NY Giants
Volker, Floyd	Basketball		10	50		played NBA 47-49
Volkov, Alexander	Tennis		4	8		

NAME	CATEGORY	+	SIG	SP	BALL	Comment
Vollmer, Clyde	Baseball		8	22		Debut 1942
Von Appen, Fred	Football		2	5		Hawaii Coach
Von Cramm, Gottfried	Tennis	+	18	45		HOF 1977
Von Elm, George	Golf		75	195		
Von Hagge, Bob	Golf		5	20	25	
Von Nida, Norm	Golf		20	35	35	
Von Nieda, Whitey	Basketball		10	50		played NBA 47-49
Von Saltza, Chris	Olympic		4	20		Swim/400 free
Von Schamann, Uwe	Football		3	10		NFL
Vosmik, Joe	Baseball		40	85		Debut 1930
Voss, Bill	Baseball		3	15		Debut 1965
Vossler, Ernie	Golf		15	45		
Voyles, Phil	Baseball		35	70		Debut 1929
Vranes, Dan	Basketball		3	10		played NBA 81-87
Vroman, Brett	Basketball		3	10		played NBA 80
Vukovich, Bill Sr.	Auto Racing	+	225	550		HOF 1991, HOF 1992
Vukovich, George	Baseball		3	10		Debut 1980
Vukovich, John	Baseball		3	12		Debut 1970

Wachter, Anita	Olympic		12	32		Alpine skiing
Wachter, Ed	Basketball	+	18	40		HOF 1961
Waddell, Rube	Baseball		1767	5250	12000	HOF 1946
Waddey, Frank	Baseball		20	45		Debut 1931 Browns
Wade, Ben	Baseball		7			Debut 1948 Cubs
Wade, Bill	Football		6	18		NFL
Wade, Gale	Baseball		3	15		Debut 1955
Wade, Ham	Baseball		60	125		Debut 1907
Wade, Margaret	Basketball		10	30		HOF 1984 Coach
Wade, Mark	Basketball		3	10		played NBA 87
Wade, Virginia	Tennis		10	38		HOF 1989
Wade, Wallace	Football	+	25	50		1955 CHOF coach
Wadkins, Bobby	Golf		5	20	25	
Wadkins, Lanny	Golf		5	25	25	
Wager, Clinton	Basketball		15	65		played NBA 43-49
Wagner, Allison	Olympic		3	6		Medal Swimming
Wagner, Charlie	Baseball		6			Debut 1938 Bost. RedSox
Wagner, Daniel	Basketball		10	50		played NBA 47-49
Wagner, Fred	Auto Racing	+	40	85		
Wagner, Hal	Baseball		18	45		Debut 1937
Wagner, Honus	Baseball		450	1075	4000	HOF 1936.B&W PC$1250
Wagner, Huber	Football	+	22	65		CHOF Pittsburgh
Wagner, Leon	Baseball		10	20		Debut 1958
Wagner, Marie	Tennis	+	12	25		HOF 1969

NAME	CATEGORY	+	SIG	SP	BALL	Comment
Wagner, Mark	Baseball		3	12		Debut 1976
Wagner, Milton	Basketball		3	10		played NBA 87
Wagner, Philip	Basketball		4	18		played NBA 68
Wagner, Virgil	Football		4	10		1980 Canadian HOF
Wahl, Kermit	Baseball		12	32		Debut 1944
Wainwright, Helen	Olympic		16	45		Diving
Waite, Grant	Golf		5	20	25	
Waiters, Granville	Basketball		3	10		played NBA 83-87
Waitkus, Eddie	Baseball		40	80		Debut 1941
Waitz, Greta	Olympic		12	25		Marathon
Wakefield, Andre	Basketball		3	12		played NBA 78-79
Wakefield, Dick	Baseball		20	42		Debut 1941 Tigers
Walcott, Jersey Joe	Boxing		15	35		1951-52 H-Wt Champ
Walczak, Ed	Baseball		8	25		Debut 1945 Phillies
Walden, Robert	Horse Racing					HOF 1970 trainer
Waldo, Carolyn	Olympic		5	15		Synch. Swimming
Waldorf, Duffy	Golf		5	20	25	
Waldorf, Lynn	Football	+	50	125		1966 CHOF coach
Walewander, Jim	Baseball		3	10		Debut 1987
Walk, Neal	Basketball		3	14		played NBA 69-76
Walker, Andrew	Basketball		3	12		played NBA 76
Walker, Antoine	Basketball		7	32	100	NBA
Walker, Barry	Baseball		3	10		Debut 1989
Walker, Brady	Basketball		10	50		played NBA 48-51
Walker, Chet	Basketball		7	25		played NBA 62-74
Walker, Chico	Baseball		3	10		Debut 1980
Walker, Colleen	Golf		5	20	25	
Walker, Cyril	Golf		75	195		
Walker, Darrell	Basketball		3	14		played NBA 83-
Walker, Dixie	Baseball		25	55		Debut 1931
Walker, Doak	Football		35	60	175	'86 HOF.Heisman SMU'48
Walker, Duane	Baseball		3	10		Debut 1982
Walker, Foots	Basketball		3	12		played NBA 74-83
Walker, Frank	Baseball		40	85		Debut 1917
Walker, Fulton	Football		3	10		NFL
Walker, Gerald "Gee"	Baseball		40	80		Debut 1931 Tigers
Walker, Greg	Baseball		3	12		Debut 1982
Walker, Harry "The Hat"	Baseball		4	15		Debut 1940 Cards
Walker, Herschel	Football		12	35	125	Heisman GA '82. NFL
Walker, Horace	Basketball		4	20		played NBA 61
Walker, Hub	Baseball		22	50		Debut 1931
Walker, Jack	Hockey		150	400		1960 HOF fwd
Walker, James	Basketball		4	14		played NBA 67-75
Walker, Johnny	Baseball		40	85		Debut 1919
Walker, Ken	Basketball		3	10		played NBA 86-
Walker, Larry	Baseball		5	32		1997 NL MVP
Walker, Laura	Olympic		3	8		Swim/relay
Walker, Michelle	Golf		5	20	25	
Walker, Mickey	Boxing		85	200		Middle,Welter-Wt Champ
Walker, Phillip	Basketball		3	12		played NBA 77
Walker, Rube	Baseball		5	22		Debut 1943
Walker, Tony	Baseball		3	10		Debut 1946
Walker, Wally	Basketball		3	10		played NBA 76-83
Walker, Wesley	Football		7	15		NFL
Wall, Art	Golf		5	20	25	
Wallace, Bill	Football		6	18		CHOF Rice

NAME	CATEGORY	+	SIG	SP	BALL	Comment
Wallace, Bobby	Baseball		350	900	4250	HOF 1953.B&W PC$1000
Wallace, Don	Baseball		3	14		Debut 1969
Wallace, Jack	Baseball		15			Debut 1915 Cubs
Wallace, Red	Basketball		10	50		played NBA 46
Wallace, Rusty	Auto Racing		10	20		
Wallach, Tim	Baseball		3	14		Debut 1980
Wallaesa, Jack	Baseball		12	28		Debut 1980
Wallen, Norm	Baseball		10	25		Debut 1956
Waller, Dwight	Basketball		3	10		played NBA 68-71
Waller, Jamie	Basketball		3	10		played NBA 87
Waller, Tye	Baseball		3	10		Debut 1980
Walling, Denny	Baseball		3	10		Debut 1975
Wallis, Joe	Baseball		3	10		Debut 1975
Walliser, Maria	Olympic		10	30		Alpine skiing
Walls, Everson	Football		4	16		NFL
Walls, Lee	Baseball		3	14		Debut 1952
Walsh, Adam	Football	+	40	85		CHOF Notre Dame
Walsh, Bill	Football		7	30	135	1993 HOF. NFL
Walsh, Christy	Writer		28	65		
Walsh, David	Basketball	+	20	45		HOF 1961 Referee
Walsh, Dee	Baseball		45	95		Debut 1913
Walsh, Ed "Big Ed"	Baseball		275	600	3500	HOF 1946.B&W PC $600
Walsh, Frank	Golf		75	172		
Walsh, James	Basketball		10	40		played NBA 57
Walsh, Joe	Baseball		15	35		Debut 1938
Walsh, Ken	Olympic		4	8		Swim/100 free
Walsh, Marty	Hockey		150	375		1962 HOF fwd
Walsh, Stella	Olympic		60	125		100 Dash
Walston, Bobby	Football		30	65		NFL
Walter, Bernard	Baseball		8			Debut 1930 Pirates
Walters, Bucky	Baseball		22	48		Debut 1931 Bost. Braves
Walters, Fred	Baseball		15	38		Debut 1945
Walters, Ken	Baseball		3	14		Debut 1960
Walters, Lisa	Golf		5	20	25	
Walther, Paul	Basketball		10	45		played NBA 49-54
Walthour, Isaac	Basketball		8	40		played NBA 53
Walton, Bill	Basketball		8	22		HOF 1993. NBA 74-86
Walton, Danny	Baseball		3	10		Debut 1968 Houston
Walton, Dwight	Baseball		4	10		
Walton, Jerome	Baseball		4	10	28	Debut 1989
Walton, Lloyd	Basketball		3	12		played NBA 76-80
Walton, Mike	Hockey		4	15		
Walton, Reggie	Baseball		3	10		Debut 1980
Waltrip, Darrell	Auto Racing		10	22		
Waltrip, Michael	Auto Racing		5	15		
Walzel, Bobby	Golf		10	35		
Wambsganss, Bill	Baseball	+	25	60		Debut 1914
Wampler, Fred	Golf		10	35		
Wamsley,Rick	Hockey		3	12		
Waner, Lloyd	Baseball					P-S HOF $3250
Waner, Lloyd	Baseball		35	105	550	HOF 1967.Gold Pl. S $45
Waner, Paul	Baseball		155	350	2500	HOF 1952.B&W PC $400
Waninger, Pee Wee	Baseball		28	60		Debut 1925
Wannstedt, Dave	Football		3	18	100	NFL Bears Coach
Wanzer, Bobby	Basketball		6	18		HOF 1987
Warbington, Perry	Basketball		3	12		played NBA 74

NAME	CATEGORY	+	SIG	SP	BALL	Comment
Warburton, Cotton	Football	+	50	125		CHOF Southern California
Ward, Aaron	Baseball		40	85		Debut 1917
Ward, Arch	Writer	+	25	65		1973 Ntl S&S HOF
Ward, Bob	Football		3	9		NFL
Ward, Bud	Golf		50	95		
Ward, Charles	Golf		35	75		
Ward, Charlie	Basketball		6	28	100	NBA
Ward, Charlie	Football		10	25		Heisman FL St. '93. NBA
Ward, Chris	Baseball		3	12		Debut 1972
Ward, Chuck	Baseball		35	75		Debut 1917
Ward, Gary	Baseball		3	12		Debut 1979
Ward, Gerry	Basketball		3	18		played NBA 63-65
Ward, Hap	Baseball		40	85		Debut 1912
Ward, Harvey	Golf		20	35	45	
Ward, Henry	Basketball		3	12		played NBA 75-76
Ward, Holcombe	Tennis	+	15	40		HOF 1956
Ward, Jay	Baseball		4	15		Debut 1963
Ward, Jimmy	Hockey		40	90		Montreal Maroons
Ward, John Monte	Baseball		1633	4975	12000	HOF 1964
Ward, Pete	Baseball		3	12		Debut 1962 Orioles
Ward, Preston	Baseball		4	18		Debut 1948 Brklyn. Dodg.
Ward, Robert	Football		20	45		CHOF Maryland
Ward, Rodger	Auto Racing		20	45		HOF 1992, HOF 1995
Ward, Sherrill	Horse Racing					HOF 1978 trainer
Ward, Walter	Bowling	+	10	35		1959 ABC HOF
Ward, Willis	Football		5	10		
Warden, Jon	Baseball		5			Debut 1968 Tigers
Ware, Andre	Football		10	25		Heisman Houston '89
Ware, James	Basketball		3	18		played NBA 66-68
Warfield, Paul	Football		7	20	80	1983 HOF 2-way line
Warga, Steve	Golf		35	85		
Wargo, Tom	Golf		5	20	25	
Warley, Benjamin	Basketball		5	20		played NBA 62-69
Warlick, Robert	Basketball		4	20		played NBA 65-69
Warmath, Murray	Football		2	8		College Coach of Year
Warmbier, Marie	Bowling	+	12	32		1953 Women's IBC HOF
Warmerdam, Cornelius	Olympic		20	50		Pole Vault
Warneke, Lon	Baseball		30	65		Debut 1930
Warner, Clair	Football	+	10	22		1965 Canadian HOF
Warner, Cornell	Basketball		3	14		played NBA 70-76
Warner, Curt	Football		5	14		NFL
Warner, Glenn "Pop"	Football	+	135	275		1951 CHOF coach
Warner, Jackie	Baseball		3	15		Debut 1966
Warner, John R. "Jack"	Baseball		25	55		Debut 1925 Tigers
Warner, William	Football	+	25	80		CHOF Cornell
Warnock, Hal	Baseball		25	55		Debut 1935
Warren, Bennie	Baseball		25	50		Debut 1939 Phillies
Warren, Bill	Baseball		45	95		Debut 1914
Warren, Chris	Bowler		4	8		
Warren, Chris	Football		5	18	85	NFL
Warren, John	Basketball		3	14		played NBA 69-73
Warren, Robert	Basketball		3	24		played NBA 68-75
Warrick, Bryan	Basketball		3	20		played NBA 82-85
Warstler, Harold "Rabbit"	Baseball		45	90		Debut 1930
Warwick, Bert	Football	+	10	22		1964 Canadian HOF
Warwick, Bill	Baseball		35	80		Debut 1921 Pirates

NAME	CATEGORY	+	SIG	SP	BALL	Comment
Warwick, Carl	Baseball		3	15		Debut 1961 L.A. Dodgers
Wasdell, Jimmy	Baseball		14	38		Debut 1937 Senators
Wasem, Link	Baseball		20	45		Debut 1937
Washam, Jo Ann	Golf		5	20	25	
Washburn, Chris	Basketball		3	10		played NBA 86-87
Washburn, Ray	Baseball		8	24		Debut 1961 Cards
Washburn, Watson	Tennis	+	12	35		HOF 1965
Washington, Claudell	Baseball		3	12		Debut 1974
Washington, Don	Basketball		3	12		played NBA 74-75
Washington, Dwayne	Basketball		3	12		played NBA 86-
Washington, Gene	Football		5	16		NFL
Washington, George	Baseball		20	45		Debut 1935
Washington, Herb	Baseball		3	12		Debut 1974
Washington, James	Basketball		3	14		played NBA 65-74
Washington, Joe	Football		4	14		NFL
Washington, Kenny	Football	+	80	175		CHOF UCLA
Washington, Kermit	Basketball		3	14		played NBA 74-87
Washington, LaRue	Baseball		3	12		Debut 1978
Washington, Malival	Tennis		4	10		
Washington, Richard	Basketball		3	12		played NBA 76-81
Washington, Robert	Basketball		3	15		played NBA 69-71
Washington, Ron	Baseball		3	12		Debut 1977
Washington, Stanley	Basketball		3	14		played NBA 74
Washington, Thomas	Basketball		3	14		played NBA 67-72
Washington, U. L.	Baseball		3	12		Debut 1977
Washington, Vernon (Sloan)	Baseball		12	30		Debut 1935 ChiSox
Washington, Wilson	Basketball		3	12		played NBA 77-78
Wasinger, Mark	Baseball		3	10		Debut 1986
Waterfield, Bob	Football	+	65	225	325	1965 HOF QB
Wathan, John	Baseball	–	3	10		Debut 1976
Watkins, Dave	Baseball		3	12		Debut 1969
Watkins, George	Baseball		28	60		Debut 1930
Watlington, Neal	Baseball		5	18		Debut 1953 A's
Watrous, Al	Golf		45	160		
Watson, A.J.	Auto Racing		5	10		HOF 1996
Watson, Bob	Baseball		4	12		Debut 1966
Watson, Denis	Golf		5	20	25	
Watson, Harry	Hockey		100	350		1962 HOF fwd
Watson, Johnny	Baseball		28	60		Debut 1930
Watson, Lillian	Olympic		3	15		Swim/backstroke
Watson, Robert	Basketball		8	40		played NBA 54
Watson, Steve	Football		3	12		NFL
Watson, Tom	Golf		15	40	45	PGA HOF 1988
Watt, Allie	Baseball		35	70		Debut 1920
Watt, Eddie	Baseball		7	22		Debut 1966 Orioles
Watters, Ricky	Football		5	15	85	NFL
Watts, Brian	Golf		5	20	25	
Watts, Ronald	Basketball		3	15		played NBA 65-66
Watts, Slick	Basketball		4	14		played NBA 73-78
Watts, Stan	Basketball		3	14		HOF 1985. Coach
Watts, Stan	Basketball		6	20		HOF 1985
Watwood, Cliff	Baseball		35	75		Debut 1929
Way, Bob	Baseball		35	80		Debut 1927
Wayne, Marshall	Olympic		10	30		Diving
Wayte, Mary	Olympic		5	12		Swim/200 free
Weatherly, Roy "Stormy"	Baseball		18	45		Debut 1935 Indians

NAME	CATEGORY	+	SIG	SP	BALL	Comment
Weatherspoon, Nick	Basketball		3	14		played NBA 73-79
Weatherspoon, Tim	Boxing		15	30		1984 H-Wt Champ
Weaver, Andrew	Olympic		3	6		Cycling
Weaver, Bert	Golf		5	25	25	
Weaver, Dewitt	Golf		5	20	25	
Weaver, Earl	Baseball		7	22	25	HOF 1964. Mgr.
Weaver, Jim	Baseball		3	10		Debut 1985
Weaver, Jim D.	Baseball		30	65		Debut 1925 Senators
Weaver, Mike	Boxing		15	35		1980-82 H-Wt Champ
Weaver, Monte	Baseball		25	60		Debut 1931 Senators
Weaver, Robert	Olympic		3	6		Wrestling
Webb, Del	Baseball		25	75		Owner Yankees
Webb, Earl	Baseball		40	85		Debut 1925
Webb, Jeffrey	Basketball		3	14		played NBA 70-71
Webb, Karri	Golf		5	25	25	
Webb, Richmond	Football		3	9		NFL
Webb, Skeeter	Baseball		18	45		Debut 1932
Webb, Spud	Basketball		5	20		played NBA 85-
Webb, Tweed	Baseball		5			Negro League
Webber, Chris	Basketball		10	28	125	"Fab Five"
Weber, Dick	Bowling		6	22		1970 ABC HOF
Weber, Forest	Basketball		10	50		played NBA 45-46
Weber, Pete	Bowler		4	12		
Webster, Alex	Football		7	18		NFL
Webster, Elnardo	Basketball		3	14		played NBA 71
Webster, George	Football		7	18		CHOF Michigan State
Webster, Lenny	Baseball		3	10		Debut 1989
Webster, Marvin	Basketball		3	14		played NBA 75-86
Webster, Mike	Football		5	15	95	1997 HOF, NFL
Webster, Mitch	Baseball		3	10		Debut 1983
Webster, Ramon	Baseball		3	14		Debut 1967
Webster, Ray	Baseball		3	12		Debut 1959
Webster, Robert	Olympic		6	18		Diving
Wedemeyer, Herman	Football		8	24		CHOF St. Mary's
Wedman, Scott	Basketball		3	12		played NBA 74-86
Weekes, Harold	Football	+	25	75		CHOF Columbia
Weekly, Johnny	Baseball		12	28		Debut 1962
Weetman, Harry	Golf		20	45		
Wehr, Richard	Basketball		10	50		played NBA 48
Wehselau, Mariechen	Olympic		6	15		Swim/100 M Free
Weibring, D. A.	Golf		5	20	25	
Weidner, Brant	Basketball		3	10		played NBA 83
Weigel, Ralph	Baseball		8	25		Debut 1946
Weigert, Zach	Football		3	9		1994 Outland Winner
Weik, Dick "Legs"	Baseball		6	18		Debut 1948 Senators
Weiland, Bob	Baseball		14	32		Debut 1928 ChiSox
Weiland, Cooney	Hockey		50	200		1971 HOF fwd
Weill, David	Olympic		3	6		Discus
Weinberg, Wendy	Olympic		3	7		Swim/800 free
Weinbrecht, Donna	Olympic		6	22		Mogul Skiing. Gold Med.
Weingartner, Elmer	Baseball		8	25		Debut 1945
Weinmeister, Arnie	Football		5	20	85	1984 HOF DL
Weinstein, Sam	Bowling		5	10		1970 ABC HOF-Mer.Serv.
Weintraub, Phil	Baseball		22	50		Debut 1933
Weir, Ed	Football		10	28		CHOF Nebraska
Weis, Al	Baseball		3	12		Debut 1962

NAME	CATEGORY	+	SIG	SP	BALL	Comment
Weis, Arthur "Butch"	Baseball		25	55		Debut 1922 Cubs
Weiskopf, Tom	Golf		10	25	35	
Weiss, Gary	Baseball		3	10		Debut 1983
Weiss, George	Baseball		100	325	3500	HOF 1971
Weiss, Joe	Baseball		45	85		Debut 1915
Weiss, Michael	Olympic		3	8		Figure Skating
Weiss, Robert	Basketball		3	14		played NBA 65-76
Weiss, Walt	Baseball		3	12		Debut 1987
Weissmuller, Johnny	Olympic		100	350		Swimming
Weitzman, Rick	Basketball		3	18		played NBA 67
Welaj, Johnny	Baseball		25	50		Debut 1939 Senators
Welch, Bob	Baseball		4	10		Debut 1978
Welch, Gus	Football	+	25	80		CHOF Carlisle
Welch, Hawley	Football	+	10	22		1964 Canadian HOF
Welch, Herb	Baseball		18	38		Debut 1925
Welch, Lew	Auto Racing	+	20	45		
Welch, Mickey	Baseball		2150	4000	8500	HOF 1973
Welch, Milt	Baseball		12	28		Debut 1945
Welchonce, Harry	Baseball		45	85		Debut 1911
Welf, Ollie	Baseball		45	85		Debut 1916
Weller, John	Football	+	15	45		CHOF Princeton
Wellman, Bob	Baseball		8	22		Debut 1948
Wellman, Brad	Baseball		3	10		Debut 1982
Wells, Boomer	Baseball		3	10		Debut 1981
Wells, Cliff	Basketball	+	20	40		HOF 1971-Contributor
Wells, Eddie	Baseball		27	55		Debut 1923 Tigers
Wells, Leo	Baseball		10	30		Debut 1942
Wells, Owen	Basketball		3	12		played NBA 74
Wells, Ralph	Basketball		3	18		played NBA 62
Wells, Willie	Basebal		225	600		BB HOF 1997. Negro League
Welp, Christian	Basketball		3	12		played NBA 87-
Welsh, George	Football		3	6		College Player-& Coach
Welsh, Jimmy	Baseball		35	70		Debut 1925
Welu, Billy	Bowling	+	30	65		1975 PBA, '75 ABC HOF
Wendell, Percy	Football	+	25	75		CHOF Harvard
Wennington, William	Basketball		3	12		played NBA 85-
Wentz, Carol	Bowling		5	16		NW Sensation
Wentzel, Stan	Baseball		7	25		Debut 1945
Wenzel, Hanni	Olympic		12	30		Alpine skiing
Wera, Julie	Baseball		45	95		Debut 1927
Werber, Bill	Baseball		18	45		Debut 1930 Yankees
Werhas, John	Baseball		3	12		Debut 1964
Werle, Bill	Baseball		5	12		Debut 1949 Pirates
Werner, Don	Baseball		3	10		Debut 1975
Wersching, Ray	Football		3	10		NFL
Wert, Don	Baseball		3	12		Debut 1963
Werth, Dennis	Baseball		3	12		Debut 1979
Wertis, Ray	Basketball		10	50		played NBA 46-47
Wertz, Vic	Baseball		18	40		Debut 1947 Tigers
Wesley, Glen	Hockey		3	16		
Wesley, Walter	Basketball		3	14		played NBA 66-75
Wessinger, Jim	Baseball		3	12		Debut 1979
West, Belford	Football	+	15	45		CHOF Colgate
West, Charlie	Football		3	10		NFL
West, Dick	Baseball		22	50		Debut 1938
West, James	Golf		50	125		

NAME	CATEGORY	+	SIG	SP	BALL	Comment
West, Jerry	Basketball		11	30	150	HOF 1979
West, Mark	Basketball		3	12		played NBA 83-
West, Max	Baseball		18	48		Debut 1938
West, Roland	Basketball		3	15		played NBA 67
West, Sammy	Baseball		28	60		Debut 1927
Westbrook, Dexter	Basketball		3	14		played NBA 67
Westbrook, Michael	Football		6	20	85	NFL
Westfall, Bob	Football	+	15	45		CHOF Michigan
Westfall, Ed	Hockey		4	12		
Westlake, Jim	Baseball		4	14		Debut 1955 Phillies
Westlake, Wally	Baseball		3	14		Debut 1947
Westland, Jack	Golf		15	45		
Weston, Al	Baseball		12	55		Debut 1929
Westphal, Paul	Basketball		4	14		played NBA 72-83
Westrop, Jackie	Horse Racing		20	40		jockey
Westrum, Wes	Baseball		6	18		Debut 1947 NY Giants
Westwick, Harry	Hockey		125	365		1962 HOF fwd
Wetherby, Jeff	Baseball		3	10		Debut 1989
Wethered, Joyce	Golf		95	195		PGA HOF 1975
Wethered, Roger	Golf		45	95		
Wetzel, John	Basketball		3	14		played NBA 67-75
Weyand, Alex	Football	+	25	75		CHOF Army
Whaling, Bert	Baseball		45	90		Debut 1913
Wharram, Kenny	Hockey		4	14		
Wharton, Buck	Football	+	35	100		CHOF Pennsylvania
Wharton, David	Olympic		3	6		Swim/ind. medley
Whatley, Ennis	Basketball		3	12		played NBA 83-
Wheat, Mack	Baseball		45	95		Debut 1915
Wheat, Zack						HOF 1959. Gold Pl.$400
Wheat, Zack	Baseball	+	101	300	1670	B&W PC $300
Wheaton, Woody	Baseball		8	25		Debut 1943
Wheeler, Arthur	Football	+	35	100		CHOF Princeton
Wheeler, Clinton	Basketball		3	10		played NBA 87-
Wheeler, Dick	Baseball		42	85		Debut 1918
Wheeler, Don	Baseball		8	25		Debut 1949
Whigham, J.H.	Golf		125	322		
Whisenant, Pete	Baseball		6	18		Debut 1952
Whisenton, Larry	Baseball		3	10		Debut 1977
Whisman, Greg	Golf		5	20	25	
Whitaker, Lou	Baseball		3	18		Debut 1977
Whitaker, Lucian	Basketball		10	45		played NBA 54
Whitaker, Pernell	Boxing		20	55		Welter-Wt Champ
Whitaker, Steve	Baseball		3	12		Debut 1965
Whitcombe, Charles A.	Golf		75	150		
Whitcombe, Ernest R.	Golf		50	95		
Whitcombe, Reginald A.	Golf		50	95		
Whitcroft, Fred	Hockey		275	850		1962 HOF fwd
White, Albert	Olympic		10	35		Diving
White, Albert "Fuzz"	Baseball		9	22		Debut 1940
White, Amy	Olympic		3	6		Swim/backstroke
White, Bill	Baseball		7	18		Debut 1956
White, Bill	Baseball		7	22		Debut 1945
White, Bob	Football		3	14		Ohio St. RB
White, Buck	Golf		35	85		
White, Byron	Football		18	50		CHOF Colorado
White, Charles	Football		20	40		Heisman USC '79

NAME	CATEGORY	+	SIG	SP	BALL	Comment
White, Charlie	Baseball		10	25		Debut 1954
White, Danny	Football		6	18		NFL
White, Devon	Baseball		3	12		Debut 1985
White, Don	Baseball		12	28		Debut 1948
White, Donna	Golf		5	25	25	
White, Ed	Baseball		10	28		Debut 1955
White, Ed	Football		5	12		NFL
White, Elder	Baseball		3	14		Debut 1962
White, Eric	Basketball		3	10		played NBA 87-
White, Frank	Baseball		3	14		Debut 1973
White, Guy "Doc"	Baseball		60	125		Debut 1901
White, Herbert	Basketball		3	12		played NBA 70
White, Hubie	Basketball		3	15		played NBA 62-70
White, Jack	Baseball		35	70		Debut 1927
White, Jack	Golf		150	400		
White, Jerry	Baseball		3	10		Debut 1974
White, Jo Jo	Basketball		6	18		played NBA 69-80
White, Joyner "Jo-Jo"	Baseball		20	48		Debut 1932 Tigers
White, Marilyn	Olympic		3	9		Track/relay
White, Mike	Baseball		3	14		Debut 1963
White, Mike	Football		3	6		NFL
White, Mildred	Bowling	+	8	18		1975 Women's IBC HOF
White, Myron	Baseball		3	10		Debut 1978
White, Orville	Golf		10	35		
White, Randy	Football		5	18	125	1994 HOF. NFL
White, Reggie	Football		5	24	125	NFL
White, Rory	Basketball		3	10		played NBA 82-86
White, Roy	Baseball		3	12		Debut 1965
White, Rudolph	Basketball		3	12		played NBA 75-80
White, Sammie	Football		4	14		NFL
White, Sammy	Baseball		15	30		Debut 1951
White, Tony	Basketball		3	10		played NBA 87
White, Willie	Basketball		3	10		played NBA 84-85
White, Willye	Olympic		4	18		Track/sprints
Whited, Ed	Baseball		3	10		Debut 1989
Whitehead, Barb	Golf		5	20	25	
Whitehead, Burgess	Baseball		20	42		Debut 1933 Cards
Whitehead, Jerome	Basketball		3	12		played NBA 78-
Whiteley, Frank, Jr.	Horse Racing					HOF 1978 trainer
Whitfield, Beverly	Olympic		8	22		Swim/breaststroke
Whitfield, Fred	Baseball		3	14		Debut 1962
Whitfield, Mal	Olympic		7	18		800 Run
Whitfield, Terry	Baseball		3	12		Debut 1974
Whitman, Dick	Baseball		6	22		Debut 1946
Whitman, Frank	Baseball		6	22		Debut 1946
Whitman, Malcolm	Tennis	+	20	48		HOF 1955
Whitmer, Dean	Baseball		3	10		Debut 1980
Whitmire, Don	Football		10	25		CHOF Navy/Alabama
Whitney, Arthur "Pinky"	Baseball		16	38		Debut 1928 Phillies
Whitney, Charles	Basketball		3	10		played NBA 80-81
Whitney, Hank	Basketball		3	16		played NBA 67-69
Whitsett, Bob	Basketball-NFL		1	3		2-sport exec.
Whitt, Don	Golf		10	35		
Whitt, Ernie	Baseball		3	10		Debut 1976
Whittaker, James	Mountain Climbing		12	25		
Whitted, George "Possum"	Baseball		45	95		Debut 1912

NAME	CATEGORY	+	SIG	SP	BALL	Comment
Whittingham, Charlie	Horse Racing		8	25		HOF 1974 trainer
Whitworth, Kathy	Golf		20	35	45	PGA, LPGA HOF '82, '75
Wiberg, Pernilla	Skiing		5	22		Alpine. World Cup Champ
Wichman, Sharon	Olympic		4	9		Swim/breaststroke
Wicker, Floyd	Baseball		3	12		Debut 1968 Cards
Wickersham, Dave	Baseball		8	25		Debut 1960 K.C.
Wickhorst, Frank	Football	+	20	55		CHOF Navy
Wickland, Al	Baseball		42	85		Debut 1913
Wicks, Sidney	Basketball		12	24		played NBA 71-80
Widby, Ron	Basketball		2	14		played NBA 67
Widing, Juha	Hockey		3	22		
Widmar, Al	Baseball		5	18		Debut 1947 Bost. RedSox
Widseth, Ed	Football		4	25		CHOF Minnesota
Wiebe, Mark	Golf		7	20	25	
Wiecher, Jim	Golf		5	20	25	
Wiedenbauer, Tom	Baseball		3	20		Debut 1973
Wieman, E.E.	Football	+	18	40		1956 CHOF coach
Wier, Murray	Basketball		10	50		played NBA 48-49
Wiesenhahn, Robert	Basketball		6	28		played NBA 61
Wiesner, Kenneth	Olympic		3	12		High Jump
Wietelmann, Whitey	Baseball		7	28		Debut 1939 Bost. Braves
Wigger, Lones	Olympic		3	6		Rifle
Wiggin, Paul	Football		4	12		NFL
Wiggins, Alan	Baseball		15	32		Debut 1981
Wiggins, Mitchell	Basketball		3	12		played NBA 83-86
Wilander, Mats	Tennis		10	24		
Wilber, Del	Baseball		7	22		Debut 1946
Wilborn, Claude	Baseball		8	30		Debut 1940
Wilborn, Ted	Baseball		3	12		Debut 1979
Wilbur, Doreen	Olympic		3	10		Archery
Wilburn, Barry	Football		3	8		NFL
Wilburn, Ken	Basketball		3	14		played NBA 67-68
Wilce, John	Football	+	3	35		1954 CHOF coach
Wilcox, Dave	Football		15	15		NFL
Wilcox, Howard	Auto Racing	+	25	50		
Wilcutt, D. C.	Basketball		10	50		played NBA 48-49
Wilde, Jimmy	Boxing		140	330		Grt.Fly-Wt Champ.'16-'23
Wilder, James	Football		3	12		NFL
Wilding, Anthony	Tennis	+	12	25		HOF 1978
Wildung, Dick	Football	+	12	22		CHOF Minnesota
Wiley, Eugene	Basketball		3	22		played NBA 62-67
Wiley, Michael	Basketball		3	10		played NBA 80-81
Wiley, Morlon	Basketball		3	10		played NBA 88-
Wilfong, Rob	Baseball		3	10		Debut 1977
Wilfong, Win	Basketball		5	26		played NBA 57-60
Wilhelm, Charles "Spider"	Baseball		6	18		Debut 1953
Wilhelm, Hoyt	Baseball					P-S HOF $25,Grt.Mo. $20
Wilhelm, Hoyt	Baseball		8	18	22	HOF 1997, Gold Pl. $12
Wilhelm, Jim	Baseball		40	80		Debut 1978
Wilke, Harry	Baseball		18	40		Debut 1927
Wilke, Lou	Basketball	+	6	20		HOF 1982-Contributor
Wilkens, Lenny	Basketball		3	10	100	HOF 1989
Wilkerson, Curtis	Baseball		3	12		Debut 1983
Wilkerson, Robert	Basketball		3	12		played NBA 76-82
Wilkes, Jamaal	Basketball		6	22		played NBA 74-85
Wilkes, James	Basketball		3	10		played NBA 80-82

NAME	CATEGORY	+	SIG	SP	BALL	Comment
Wilkie, David	Olympic		9	20		Swim/breaststroke
Wilkins, Bobby	Baseball		7	24		Debut 1944
Wilkins, Eddie	Basketball		3	10		played NBA 84-
Wilkins, Gerald	Basketball		4	10		played NBA 85-
Wilkins, Jacques	Basketball		3	10		played NBA 82-
Wilkins, Jeffrey	Basketball		3	10		played NBA 80-85
Wilkins, Mac	Olympic		8	26		Discus
Wilkinson, Bud	Football		35	70		1969 CHOF coach
Wilkinson, Dale	Basketball		5	10		played NBA 84
Wilkinson, Dorothy	Bowling		3	10		1990 Women's IBC HOF
Wilkinson, Martha	Golf		5	20	25	
Wilkinson, Tom	Football		4	8		1987 Canadian HOF
Will, Bob	Baseball		7	18		Debut 1957
Will, Maggie	Golf		5	20	25	
Willard, Jerry	Baseball		3	10		Debut 1984
Willard, Jess	Boxing		275	500		1916-19 H-Wt Champ
Willard, Ken	Football		3	14		NFL
Willard, Mary	Olympic		4	10		Diving
Willey, Norman	Football		4	14		NFL
Williams, Alfred	Basketball		3	14		played NBA 70
Williams, Archie	Olympic		15	30		400 Meters
Williams, Arthur	Basketball		3	14		played NBA 67-74
Williams, Bernard	Basketball		3	14		played NBA 69-73
Williams, Bernie	Baseball		3	12		Debut 1979
Williams, Beverly	Basketball		2	5		Women's ABL
Williams, Billy	Baseball					P-S HOF $25,Grt.Mo. $20
Williams, Billy	Baseball		7	18	25	HOF 1987. Gold Pl. $12
Williams, Bob	Baseball		45	95		Debut 1911
Williams, Bob	Football		6	18		CHOF Notre Dame
Williams, Buck	Basketball		6	20		played NBA 81-
Williams, Charles	Basketball		3	12		played NBA 76
Williams, Chuck	Basketball		3	12		played NBA 70-77
Williams, Cleveland	Boxing		12	30		Hvy-Wt
Williams, Clifford	Basketball		3	12		played NBA 68
Williams, Dallas	Baseball		3	10		Debut 1981
Williams, Dan	Golf		30	80		
Williams, Dana	Baseball		3	10		Debut 1989
Williams, Davey	Baseball		5	22		Debut 1943
Williams, Delvin	Football		3	9		NFL
Williams, Dewey	Baseball		6	22		Debut 1944
Williams, Dib	Baseball		20	48		Debut 1930
Williams, Dick	Baseball		3	12		Debut 1951
Williams, Donald	Basketball		3	12		played NBA 79
Williams, Doug	Football		5	14		NFL
Williams, Earl	Baseball		3	10		Debut 1970
Williams, Earl	Basketball		3	12		played NBA 74-78
Williams, Ed. Bennett	Baseball		10	25		Executive
Williams, Eddie	Baseball		3	10		Debut 1986
Williams, Eddie	Golf		10	30		
Williams, Eugene	Basketball		3	14		played NBA 69
Williams, Fred	Baseball		7	22		Debut 1945
Williams, Fred "Cy"	Baseball		45	125		Debut 1912
Williams, Freeman	Basketball		4	14		played NBA 78-85
Williams, George	Baseball		6	18		Debut 1961
Williams, Gus	Basketball		12	28		played NBA 75-86
Williams, Guy	Basketball		3	10		played NBA 84-85

NAME	CATEGORY	+	SIG	SP	BALL	Comment
Williams, Hank	Basketball		3	10		played NBA 74
Williams, Henry	Football	+	40	85		1951 CHOF coach
Williams, Henry	Golf		10	30		
Williams, Herbert	Basketball		3	10		played NBA 81-
Williams, Ike	Boxing		22	35		Lt-Wt Champ
Williams, James	Football		6	15		CHOF Rice
Williams, Jim	Baseball		3	14		Debut 1969
Williams, Jimy	Baseball		3	14		Debut 1966
Williams, John	Olympic		4	12		Archery
Williams, John (Hot Rod)	Basketball		3	10		played NBA 86-
Williams, John L.	Football		3	9		NFL
Williams, John S.	Basketball		3	10		played NBA 86-
Williams, Ken	Baseball		3	10		Debut 1986
Williams, Ken	Baseball		60	125		Debut 1915
Williams, Kevin	Basketball		3	10		played NBA 83-
Williams, Lucinda	Olympic		3	8		Track/relay
Williams, Mark	Baseball		3	10		Debut 1977
Williams, Matt	Baseball		6	30		Debut 1987
Williams, Michael	Basketball		3	10		played NBA 88-
Williams, Milt	Basketball		3	12		played NBA 70-74
Williams, Mitch	Baseball		3	10		Debut 1986
Williams, Natalie	Basketball		2	5		Women's ABL
Williams, Nate	Basketball		3	12		played NBA 71-78
Williams, Pete	Basketball		3	10		played NBA 85-86
Williams, Randy	Olympic		3	8		Long Jump
Williams, Reggie	Baseball		3	10		Debut 1985
Williams, Reggie	Basketball		3	10		played NBA 87-
Williams, Richard, 2nd	Tennis	+	22	48		HOF 1957
Williams, Rickey	Basketball		3	10		played NBA 82
Williams, Rob	Basketball		3	10		played NBA 82-83
Williams, Robert	Basketball		7	42		played NBA 55-56
Williams, Ron	Basketball		3	14		played NBA 68-75
Williams, Sam	Basketball		3	12		played NBA 68-73
Williams, Samuel	Basketball		3	10		played NBA 81-84
Williams, Serena	Tennis		5	22		Exciting new player
Williams, Sly	Basketball		3	14		played NBA 79-85
Williams, Stan	Baseball		5	14		Debut 1953 L.A. Dodgers
Williams, Ted	Baseball					P-S HOF$300,Grt.Mo$275
Williams, Ted	Baseball		60	210	250	HOF 1966. Gold Pl $100
Williams, Thomas	Basketball		3	10		played NBA 77-86
Williams, Tommy	Hockey	+	28	65		1981 US HOF
Williams, Toothpick	Basketball		3	14		played NBA 67-72
Williams, Travis	Football		45	90		NFL
Williams, Venus	Tennis		6	28		Exciting new player
Williams, Walt	Baseball		3	12		Debut 1964
Williams, Walter R.	Bowling		2	10		1995 PBA HOF
Williams, Ward	Basketball		10	50		played NBA 48
Williams, Wendy	Olympic		6	22		Diving
Williams, Willie	Basketball		3	14		played NBA 70
Williams, Woody	Baseball		12	32		Debut 1938 Brklyn. Dodg.
Williamson, Fred	Football		5	18		NFL
Williamson, John	Basketball		3	12		played NBA 73-80
Williford, Vann	Basketball		3	12		played NBA 70
Willing, Oscar	Golf		150	350		
Willingham, Hugh	Baseball		20	45		Debut 1930
Willis, Bill	Football		6	20	85	1977 HOF DL

NAME	CATEGORY	+	SIG	SP	BALL	Comment
Willis, Kevin	Basketball		4	14		played NBA 84-
Willis, Vic	Baseball		400	850		HOF 1995
Willoughby, Claude	Baseball		5			Phillies 15 game winner '73
Willoughby, William	Basketball		3	12		played NBA 75-83
Wills, (Moody, Roark) Helen	Tennis		35	90		HOF 1959
Wills, Bump	Baseball		3	10		Debut 1977
Wills, Maury	Baseball		4	14		Debut 1959
Wilman, Joe	Bowling	+	10	32		1951 ABC HOF
Wilson, Archie	Baseball		6	18		Debut 1951
Wilson, Art	Baseball		60	125		Debut 1908
Wilson, Artie	Baseball		4	18		Debut 1951
Wilson, Bill	Baseball		5	22		Debut 1950
Wilson, Billy	Football		5	15		NFL
Wilson, Bob	Baseball		3	14		Debut 1953
Wilson, Bob "Red"	Baseball		3	14		Debut 1951
Wilson, Bobby	Football		6	15		CHOF SMU
Wilson, Charlie	Baseball		30	65		Debut 1931
Wilson, Coatlen	Basketball		3	10		played NBA 84-86
Wilson, Craig	Baseball		3	10		Debut 1989
Wilson, Dan	Baseball		8	29		Debut 1992
Wilson, Deborah Keplar	Olympic		4	12		Diving
Wilson, Enid	Golf		50	125		
Wilson, Frank	Baseball		30	65		Debut 1924
Wilson, George	Football		10	22		NFL
Wilson, George	Football	+	20	45		CHOF Washington
Wilson, George "Icehouse"	Baseball		30	60		Debut 1934
Wilson, Glenn	Baseball		3	10		Debut 1982
Wilson, Gordon	Hockey		50	250		1962 HOF def
Wilson, Grady	Baseball		10	28		Debut 1948
Wilson, Hack	Baseball		400	975		HOF 1979
Wilson, Harry	Football		10	35		CHOF Army/Penn State
Wilson, Isaiah	Basketball		3	12		played NBA 71-72
Wilson, James	Basketball		3	12		played NBA 70
Wilson, Jasper	Basketball		3	14		played NBA 68-69
Wilson, Jiff	Basketball		4	14		played NBA 64-70
Wilson, Jim	Baseball		6	18		Debut 1985 Indians
Wilson, Jim	Golf		50	100		
Wilson, Jimmie	Baseball		25			Debut 1923
Wilson, John	Golf		5	20	25	
Wilson, Larry	Football		10	22	85	1978 HOF DB
Wilson, Les	Baseball		45	90		Debut 1911
Wilson, Linetta	Olympic		3	6		Gold Medal. Track
Wilson, Marc	Football		3	10		NFL
Wilson, Michael	Basketball		3	12		played NBA 83-86
Wilson, Mike	Baseball		40	85		Debut 1921
Wilson, Mike	Football		8	20		CHOF Lafayette
Wilson, Mookie	Baseball		3	12		Debut 1980
Wilson, Neil	Baseball		3	14		Debut 1960
Wilson, Nikita	Basketball		3	10		played NBA 87
Wilson, Rick	Basketball		3	12		played NBA 78-79
Wilson, Ricky	Basketball		3	10		played NBA 87
Wilson, Robert E.	Basketball		3	14		played NBA 74-77
Wilson, Robert F.	Basketball		3	12		played NBA 67
Wilson, Robert, Jr.	Basketball		10	50		played NBA 51
Wilson, Seymour	Football		10	22		1984 Canadian HOF
Wilson, Shelby	Olympic		3	6		Wrestling

NAME	CATEGORY	+	SIG	SP	BALL	Comment
Wilson, Stephen	Basketball		3	14		played NBA 70-71
Wilson, Tack	Baseball		3	10		Debut 1983
Wilson, Ted	Baseball		12	30		Debut 1952
Wilson, Thomas	Basketball		3	10		played NBA 79
Wilson, Tom	Basketball		1	2		Pistons Owner
Wilson, Tom	Football		10	22		NFL
Wilson, Wade	Football		3	8		NFL
Wilson, Willie	Baseball		3	14		Debut 1976
Wilt, Fred	Track		7	15		
Winandy, Cecilia	Bowling	+	8	18		1975 Women's IBC HOF
Winceniak, Ed	Baseball		3	16		Debut 1955
Winder, Sammy	Football		3	12		NFL
Windhorn, Gordie	Baseball		3	16		Debut 1959
Windis, Tony	Basketball		7	32		played NBA 59
Windle, Bill	Baseball		42	90		Debut 1923
Wine, Bobby	Baseball		3	15		Debut 1960
Wine, Robbie	Baseball		3	10		Debut 1986
Winegarner, Ralph	Baseball		32	65		Debut 1932 Indians
Winfield, Dave	Baseball		7	30		Debut 1973
Winfield, Ed	Auto Racing	+	20			
Winfield, LeRoy	Basketball		3	14		played NBA 69-75
Winfrey, Carey	Horse Racing					HOF 1971 trainer
Wingate, David	Basketball		3	10		played NBA 86-
Wingo, Harthorne	Basketball		3	14		played NBA 72-75
Wininger, Bo	Golf		20	45		
Winkler, Hans	Olympic		10	20		Equestrian
Winkler, Yarvin	Basketball		3	14		played NBA 70-71
Winningham, Herm	Baseball		3	10		Debut 1984
Winsett, Tom	Baseball		15	48		Debut 1930
Winslow, Kellen	Football		10	20	100	1995 HOF. NFL
Winslow, Rickie	Basketball		3	10		played NBA 87
Winsor, Ralph	Hockey		10	22		1973 US HOF coach
Winters, Brian	Basketball		3	14		played NBA 74-82
Winters, Frank	Hockey	+	10	22		1973 US HOF
Winters, Matt	Baseball		3	10		Debut 1989
Winters, Voise	Basketball		3	10		played NBA 85
Wirtz, William	Hockey		20	40		1967 US HOF admin
Wise, Allen	Basketball		3	10		played NBA 85
Wise, Casey	Baseball		3	16		Debut 1957
Wise, Hughie	Baseball		20	45		Debut 1930
Wise, Willie	Basketball		3	14		played NBA 69-77
Wismer, Harry	Baseball		25	40		Broadcaster
Wisner, John	Baseball		40	85		Debut 1919 Pirates
Wisniewski, Steve	Football		3	9		NFL
Wissman, Dave	Baseball		3	12		Debut 1964
Wistert, Albert	Football		10	25		CHOF Michigan
Wistert, Alvin	Football		10	25		CHOF Michigan
Wistert, Francis	Football	+	25	50		CHOF Michigan
Witek, Mickey	Baseball		12	38		Debut 1940 Yankees
Withrow, Corky	Baseball		3	12		Debut 1963
Witt, Bobby	Baseball		3	10		Debut 1986
Witt, Bobby	Basketball		3	9		NBA
Witt, Katarina	Olympic		20	50		Figure skating
Witt, Mike	Baseball		4	16		Debut 1981
Witt, Whitey	Baseball		40	85		Debut 1916
Witte, Jerry	Baseball		12	30		Debut 1946 Browns

NAME	CATEGORY	+	SIG	SP	BALL	Comment
Witte, Luke	Basketball		3	12		played NBA 73-75
Wittman, Gregory	Basketball		3	12		played NBA 69-70
Wittman, Randy	Basketball		3	10		played NBA 83-
Witts, Garry	Basketball		3	10		played NBA 81
Witty, Christine	Speed Skating		3	15		World Champion.Olympic
Wockenfuss, John	Baseball		3	10		Debut 1974
Woehr, Andy	Baseball		30	65		Debut 1923 Phillies
Wofford, James	Olympic		3	6		Equestrian
Wohl, David	Basketball		3	12		played NBA 71-77
Wohlford, Jim	Baseball		3	10		Debut 1972
Wohlhuter, Richard	Olympic		4	10		800 meters
Wojciechowicz, Alex	Football		20	45	250	1968 HOF 2-way line
Wojcik, John	Baseball		3	12		Debut 1962
Wolf, Fred	Bowling		5	10		1976 ABC HOF-Mer.Serv.
Wolf, Joseph	Basketball		3	10		played NBA 87-
Wolf, Phil	Bowling	+	8	20		1961 ABC HOF
Wolf, Ray	Baseball		35	75		Debut 1927
Wolfe, Harry	Baseball		42	85		Debut 1917
Wolfe, Larry	Baseball		3	10		Debut 1977
Wolford, Will	Football		3	8		NFL
Wolgast, Ad	Boxing		150	325		
Wolter, Harry	Baseball		60	125		Debut 1907
Womack, Dooley	Baseball		7	18		Debut 1966 Yankees
Wonders, Rich	Bowling		5	10		1990 ABC HOF
Wood, Ann	Bowling	+	8	18		1970 Women's IBC HOF
Wood, Barry	Football	+	15	40		CHOF Harvard
Wood, Charles "Doc"	Baseball		35	75		Debut 1923
Wood, Craig	Golf		350	700		Old PGA HOF 1952
Wood, David	Basketball		3	10		played NBA 86-
Wood, Gar	Powerboat Racing	+	30	75		HOF 1990
Wood, Jake	Baseball		3	15		Debut 1961
Wood, James	Basketball		3	10		played NBA 81
Wood, Joe P.	Baseball		12	28		Debut 1943 Tigers
Wood, Ken	Baseball		8	25		Debut 1943
Wood, Martin	Basketball		3	10		played NBA 81-86
Wood, Norman	Golf		5	20	25	
Wood, Osie	Basketball		3	10		played NBA 84-87
Wood, Robert	Basketball		10	50		played NBA 40
Wood, Roy	Baseball		40	85		Debut 1913
Wood, Sidney	Tennis		12	40		HOF 1964
Wood, Smoky Joe	Baseball		30	125		Debut 1908
Wood, Tim	Figure Skating		3	12		2x U.S. Champion
Wood, Wilbur	Baseball		3	12		Debut 1961
Wood, Willie	Football		10	20	85	1989 HOF DB
Wood, Willie	Golf		5	20	25	
Woodall, Larry	Baseball		42	85		Debut 1920
Woodard, Darrell	Baseball		3	10		Debut 1973
Woodard, Lynette	Olympic		3	15		Gold Med; Globetrotters
Woodard, Mike	Baseball		3	10		Debut 1985
Woodbridge, Todd	Tennis		3	8		
Wooden, John	Basketball		10	30	125	HOF 1960 & '72 as Coach
Woodeschick, Tom	Football		4	15		NFL
Woodhead, Cynthia	Olympic		4	15		Swim- 200 free
Woodling, Gene	Baseball		4	14		Debut 1943 Indians
Woodruff, George	Football	+	15	35		1963 CHOF coach
Woods, Al	Baseball		3	10		Debut 1977

NAME	CATEGORY	+	SIG	SP	BALL	Comment
Woods, Gary	Baseball		3	10		Debut 1976
Woods, George R.	Olympic		3	9		Shot Put
Woods, Jim	Baseball		4	15		Debut 1957
Woods, Ron	Baseball		3	12		Debut 1969
Woods, Tiger	Golf		100	350	300	Masters Winner 1997
Woods, Tommy	Basketball		3	12		played NBA 67
Woodson, Abe	Football		10	20		Heisman Mich. '97
Woodson, Abe	Football		6	18		NFL 1958-64
Woodson, Michael	Basketball		3	10		played NBA 80-
Woodson, Rod	Football		6	28	100	NFL
Woodson, Tracy	Baseball		3	10		Debut 1987
Woodson, Warren	Football		6	15		1989 CHOF coach
Woodward, Jim	Golf		5	20	25	
Woodward, Stanley	Writer	+	20	45		1974 Ntl S&S HOF
Woodward, Woody	Baseball		3	10		Debut 1963
Woolard, Robert	Basketball		4	18		played NBA 63
Woolfe, George	Horse Racing		100	200		HOF 1955 jockey
Woolridge, Orlando	Basketball		3	14		played NBA 81-
Woosnam, Ian	Golf		10	30	35	
Wooten, Earl	Baseball		5	18		Debut 1947
Worden, Neil	Football		3	12		NFL
Workman, Chuck	Golf		5	15		
Workman, Hank	Baseball		6	22		Debut 1950
Workman, Mark	Basketball		10	25		played NBA 52-53
Workman, Raymond	Horse Racing		100	200		HOF 1955 jockey
Workman, Thomas	Basketball		3	14		played NBA 67-70
Worrell, Todd	Baseball		3	10		Debut 1985
Worsham, Lew Jr.	Golf		75	150		
Worsley, Gump	Hockey		10	25	30	1980 HOF goal
Worsley, Willie	Basketball		3	18		played NBA 68
Worters, Roy	Hockey		75	300		1969 HOF goal
Worthen, Sam	Basketball		3	12		played NBA 80-81
Worthington, Al	Baseball		3	10		Debut 1953
Worthington, Craig	Baseball		3	10		Debut 1988
Worthington, J. S.	Golf		65	125		
Worthy, James	Basketball		6	25		played NBA 82-
Wortman, Chuck	Baseball		42	90		Debut 1916
Wosham, Jo Ann	Golf		10	30	30	
Wotherspoon, Jeremy	Speed Skating		3	10		World Record
Wottle, Dave	Olympic		10	22		800 meters
Wotus, Ron	Baseball		3	10		Debut 1983
Wrenn, Robert	Golf		5	20	25	
Wrenn, Robert	Tennis	+	15	40		HOF 1955
Wright, Ab	Baseball		25	55		Debut 1935
Wright, Al	Baseball		30	60		Debut 1933
Wright, Beals	Tennis	+	20	45		HOF 1956
Wright, Bradford	Basketball		3	10		played NBA 86-87
Wright, Clyde	Baseball		6	20		Debut 1966 Cal. Angels
Wright, Ed	Baseball		6	25		Debut 1945 Bost. Braves
Wright, Ernie	Football		7	15		NFL
Wright, George	Baseball		1200	2800	8500	HOF 1937
Wright, George	Baseball		3	10		Debut 1982
Wright, Glenn	Baseball		50	125		Debut 1924
Wright, Harry	Baseball		2000	3600		HOF 1953
Wright, Howard	Basketball		3	12		played NBA 70-71
Wright, Jim	Baseball		4	12		Debut 1978 Bost. RedSox

NAME	CATEGORY	+	SIG	SP	BALL	Comment
Wright, Joseph	Basketball		3	12		played NBA 72-75
Wright, Larry	Basketball		3	12		played NBA 76-81
Wright, Lawrence	Basketball		3	14		played NBA 67-71
Wright, LeRoy	Basketball		3	14		played NBA 67-73
Wright, Lorenzo	Olympic		5	10		Track sprints
Wright, Lyle	Hockey	+	10	22		1973 US HOF admin
Wright, Mickey	Golf		20	35	45	PGA, LPGA HOF '76, '64
Wright, Pamela	Golf		5	20	25	
Wright, Taft	Baseball		22	48		Debut 1938
Wright, Tom	Baseball		10	22		Debut 1948 Bost. RedSox
Wrightson, Bernard	Olympic		4	12		Diving
Wrightstone, Russ	Baseball		40	80		Debut 1920
Wrigley, Philip K.	Baseball		65			Owner (Cubs)
Wrigley, William	Baseball		125			Owner (Cubs)
Wrigley, William, Jr.	Baseball		95			Owner (Cubs)
Writer, John	Olympic		4	8		Rifle
Wrona, Rick	Baseball		3	10		Debut 1988
Wuerffel, Danny	Football		10	30		Heisman FL '96
Wuestling, George "Yats"	Baseball		35	70		Debut 1929
Wulf, Lee	Outdoorsman		7	15		
Wuycik, Dennis	Basketball		3	12		played NBA 72-74
Wyant, Andy	Football	+	30	100		CHOF Chicago/Bucknell
Wyatt, Bowden	Football	+	25	75		CHOF Tennessee
Wyatt, Jennifer	Golf		5	20	25	
Wyatt, Joe	Baseball		35	70		Debut 1924
Wyche, Sam	Football		4	12		NFL
Wyckoff, Clint	Football	+	30	100		CHOF Cornell
Wyland, Wendy	Olympic		4	22		Diving
Wylie, Harvey	Football		4	8		1980 Canadian HOF
Wylie, Paul	Olympic		10	25		Figure Skating
Wynegar, Butch	Baseball		3	10		Debut 1976
Wynn, Bob	Golf		5	20	25	
Wynn, Early	Baseball					P-S HOF $30,Grt.Mo.$25
Wynn, Early	Baseball		10	20	25	HOF 1972.Gold Pl. S $12
Wynn, Jimmy	Baseball		4	15		Debut. 1963
Wynne, Marvell	Baseball		3	10		Debut 1983
Wyrostek, Johnny	Baseball		14	29		Debut 1942 Pirates
Wysong, Dudley	Golf		5	20	25	

NAME	CATEGORY		SIG	SP	BALL	Comment
Xwong, Normie	Football		5	10		1969 Canadian HOF

NAME	CATEGORY	+	SIG	SP	BALL	Comment
Yackel, Ken	Hockey	+	9	10	22	1986 US HOF
Yamaguchi, Kristi	Olympic		15	48		Figure Skating
Yancey, Bert	Golf		20	35	45	
Yancy, Hugh	Baseball		4	12		Debut 1972
Yang, C. K.	Olympic		10	35		Decathlon
Yankowski, George	Baseball		7	22		Debut 1942
Yantz, George	Baseball		42	90		Debut 1912
Yarborough, Cale	Auto Racing		7	16		HOF 1993, HOF 1994
Yarborough, Lee Roy	Auto Racing		7	16		
Yardley, George	Basketball		7	22		HOF 1996. NBA 53-59
Yarr, Tommy	Football	+	25	60		CHOF Notre Dame
Yary, Ron	Football		6	16		NFL
Yary, Ron	Football		7	16		CHOF Southern California
Yasztremski, Carl	Baseball					P-S HOF $50,Grt.Mo. $45
Yasztremski, Carl	Baseball		10	30	40	HOF 1989. Gold Pl. $30
Yates, Al	Baseball		3	12		Debut 1971
Yates, Barry	Basketball		7	30		played NBA 61
Yates, Charles	Golf		30	75		
Yawkey, Tom	Baseball		200	550	2350	HOF 1980
Ycaza, Manuel	Horse Racing		10	20		HOF 1977 trainer
Yde, Emil	Baseball		35	70		Debut 1924
Yeager, Steve	Baseball		3	10		Debut 1972
Yelding, Eric	Baseball		3	10		Debut 1983
Yelle, Archie	Baseball		42	85		Debut 1917
Yelverton, Charles	Basketball		3	10		played NBA 71
Yepremian, Garo	Football		4	12		NFL
Yerkes, Steve	Baseball		55	125		Debut 1909
Yerman, Jack	Olympic		3	7		Track sprints
Yewcic, Tom	Baseball		3	12		Debut 1957
Yochim, Lenny	Baseball		4	10		Debut 1951 Pirates
Yoder, Lloyd	Football	+	15	40		CHOF Carnegie
Yonakor, Richard	Basketball		3	10		played NBA 81
York, Rudy	Baseball		60	125		Debut 1934
Yorzyk, Michael	Olympic		4	10		Swim/200 fly
Yost, Eddie	Baseball		8	20		Debut. 1944 Senators
Yost, Fielding	Football	+	85	175		1951 CHOF coach
Yost, Ned	Baseball		3	10		Debut 1980
Yoter, Elmer	Baseball		38	80		Debut 1921
Youmans, Floyd	Baseball		3	10		Debut 1985
Young, Bobby	Baseball		12	30		Debut 1948
Young, Buddy	Football	+	30	90		CHOF Illinois
Young, Connie	Olympic		3	6		Cycling
Young, Cy	Baseball		550	1088	3500	HOF '37.B&W PC $1300

NAME	CATEGORY	+	SIG	SP	BALL	Comment
Young, Cy	Olympic		6	15		Javelin
Young, Danny	Basketball		4	12		played NBA 81-
Young, Del	Baseball		20	45		Debut 1937
Young, Dick	Baseball		6	18		Debut 1951
Young, Dick	Writer		7	18		
Young, Don	Baseball		3	12		Debut 1965
Young, Earl	Olympic		3	7		Track sprints
Young, Edwin	Olympic		3	8		Diving
Young, George	Bowling	+	10	25		1959 ABC HOF
Young, George	Olympic		3	7		Steeplechase
Young, Gerald	Baseball		3	10		Debut 1987
Young, Harry	Football	+	18	45		CHOF Washington & Lee
Young, Herman	Baseball		45	100		Debut 1911
Young, Jim	Football		4	8		1991 Canadian HOF
Young, John	Baseball		3	10		Debut 1971
Young, Kathy	Golf		5	20	25	
Young, Kim	Golf		5	20	25	
Young, Michael	Basketball		3	10		played NBA 84-85
Young, Mike	Baseball		3	10		Debut 1982
Young, Norman "Babe"	Baseball		18	45		Debut 1936
Young, Perry	Basketball		3	10		played NBA 86
Young, Rickey	Football		3	10		NFL
Young, Russ	Baseball		18	45		Debut 1931
Young, Sheila	Olympic		7	18		500 M Speed Skating
Young, Steve	Football		12	45	150	NFL
Youngblood, Jack	Football		3	10		NFL
Youngblood, Jim	Football		3	10		NFL
Youngblood, Joel	Baseball		4	15		Debut 1976
Younger, Paul	Football		10	25		NFL
Youngs, Ross	Baseball		1350	2500	7000	HOF 1972
Yount, Eddie	Baseball		25	60		Debut 1937
Yount, Robin	Baseball		7	22		Debut 1974
Youso, Frank	Football		5	10		NFL
Yowell, Carl	Baseball		14	30		Debut 1924 Indians
Yunnick, Smokey	Auto Racing		5	10		HOF 1990
Yurak, Jeff	Baseball		3	10		Debut 1978
Yvars, Sal	Baseball		6	20		Debut 1947
Yzerman, Steve	Hockey		8	32	35	

NAME	CATEGORY	+	SIG	SP	BALL	Comment
Zabriski, Bruce	Golf		5	20	25	
Zaby, John	College Sports		4	15		UCLA HOF
Zagalo, Mario	Soccer		5	12		
Zaharias, Babe (Didrikson)	Golf		650	1400		PGA, LPGA HOF '74, '51

NAME	CATEGORY	+	SIG	SP	BALL	Comment
Zahn, Wayne	Bowling		5	12		1980 ABC, '81 PBA HOF
Zak, Frankie	Baseball		22	45		Debut 1944
Zalapski, Zarley	Hockey		3	10		
Zale, Tony	Boxing		15	35		Middle-Wt Champ
Zamboni, Frank	Inventor		15	32		Ice-Maker
Zamora, Alfonso	Boxing		12	30		Bantam-Wt Champ
Zamperini, Louis	Olympic		25	50		Track
Zanni, Dom	Baseball		8	24		Debut 1958 S.F. Giants
Zapustas, Joe	Baseball		20	48		Debut 1938
Zaragoza, Daniel	Boxing		10	22		
Zarate, Carlos	Boxing		8	16		
Zarhardt, Joe	Golf		35	75		
Zarilla, Al	Baseball		10	22		Debut 1943 Browns
Zarley, Kermit	Golf		5	20	25	
Zarnas, Gus	Football		7	20		CHOF Ohio State
Zaslofsky, Max	Basketball		18	55		played NBA 46-55
Zatopek, Emil	Olympic		65	150		Track
Zauchin, Norm	Baseball		3	14		Debut 1951
Zawoluk, Zeke	Basketball		10	45		played NBA 52-54
Zayak, Elaine	Figure Skating		3	18		World Champion
Zdeb, Joe	Baseball		3	10		Debut 1977
Zeber, George	Baseball		3	10		Debut 1977
Zedlitz, Jean	Golf		5	20		
Zeile, Todd	Baseball		3	12		Debut 1989
Zeller, Bart	Baseball		3	10		Debut 1973
Zeller, David	Basketball		5	20		played NBA 61
Zeller, Gary	Basketball		3	14		played NBA 70-71
Zeller, Hank	Basketball		10	50		played NBA 46
Zembriski, Walter	Golf		5	20	25	
Zeno, Tony	Basketball		3	12		played NBA 79
Zernial, Gus	Baseball		4	14		Debut 1949
Zevenbergen, Phil	Basketball		3	10		played NBA 87
Ziegelmeyer, Nikki	Olympic		3	10		Olymp.Med.Speed Skater
Ziegler, John	Hockey		5	12		NHL Commissioner
Ziegler, Larry	Golf		5	20	25	
Zientara, Benny	Baseball		18	42		Debut 1941
Zikes, Les	Bowling		5	12		1983 ABC HOF
Zimmer, Don	Baseball		3	12		Debut 1954
Zimmerman, Alf	Golf		60	125		
Zimmerman, Donna	Bowling		5	10		1982 Women's IBC HOF
Zimmerman, Egon	Olympic		10	26		Alpine skiing
Zimmerman, Gary	Football		5	14		NFL
Zimmerman, Heinie	Baseball		60	125		Debut 1907
Zimmerman, Jerry	Baseball		3	10		Debut 1961 Reds
Zimmerman, Mary Beth	Golf		18	45		LPG record. Birdies (8)
Zimmerman, Roy	Baseball		8	20		Debut 1945
Zipfel, Bud	Baseball		3	14		Debut 1961
Zisk, Richie	Baseball		3	10		Debut 1971
Zitzmann, Billy	Baseball		35	70		Debut 1919 Pirates
Zivic, Fritzie	Boxing		40	59		
Zmeskal, Kim	Gymnastics		3	25		World Champion
Zock, William	Football	+	10	22		1985 Canadian HOF
Zoeller, Fuzzy	Golf		10	30	35	
Zoet, Jim	Basketball		3	10		played NBA 82
Zokol, Richard	Golf		5	20	25	
Zombo, Rick	Hockey		3	10		

NAME	CATEGORY	+	SIG	SP	BALL	Comment
Zopf, Zip	Basketball		3	12		played NBA 70
Zorich, Chris	Football		3	9		Lombardi Trophy
Zorn, Jim	Football		6	15		NFL
Zsivotsky, Gyula	Olympic		30	60		Hammer throw
Zunic, Matthew	Basketball		10	50		played NBA 47-48
Zunker, Gil	Bowling	+	15	35		1941 ABC HOF
Zuppke, Bob	Football	+	175	400		1951 CHOF coach
Zurbriggen, Pirmin	Olympic		14	38		Alpine skiing

George Sanders during his radio and TV days in Los Angeles with Olympic swimming gold medalist and silver screen legend Johnny "Tarzan" Weissmuller. Johnny, in this photo, is helping promote George's sports programs on Los Angeles' first successful commercial FM station in the 1950s.

The

SANDERS

Price Guide to

SPORTS
AUTOGRAPHS

Section 3:

FACSIMILES

Facsimile Contents

FACSIMILES

Anyone can sign Babe Ruth's name, or Mark McGwire's, or Sammy Sosa's, or Joe Montana's, and many do! A person of low morals might invest $2 in an 8x10 glossy of home run slugger McGwire, sign it with Mark's supposed signature, and sell it at a collectibles show for a seemingly bargain price of $35 or $40. If this unprincipled thief got a good deal on an assortment of unsigned photographs of sports and other stars he might come away with several hundred dollars from the pockets of unsuspecting autograph collectors. This forged trash is, of course, worthless!

You've no doubt seen or heard of segments on such hard-hitting news shows as "60 Minutes" or "20/20"–both of which have addressed the problem of out and out fakes and forgeries in the sports autograph field in recent years. Unless you get it signed in person and (by doing so) *know* the piece is authentic because you witnessed it signed by the athlete or other celebrity, our best advice is to buy autographs only from reputable dealers (such as the ones advertising in this book). These fine professionals guarantee the authenticity of the autographs they sell.

Yet, we all dream of finding that signed Babe Ruth or Shoeless Joe Jackson photograph at the flea market for $5. It's good to dream, but how do you know what's authentic and what's just so much ink on paper? The answer is having known authentic examples of signatures available. These are called *facsimile signatures*. They are simply copies of real signatures of the celebrity. Compare your "find" to a known good sig and, if it matches, you're much more likely to have an authentic autograph!

The following pages are a good start to developing your own reference library of facsimiles. This book presents you with several thousand facsimiles known to be good. While our attorney screams if we try to say anything absolute (i.e. we make no warranties either express or implied), the sigs in this book are good to the best of our knowledge.

Use this book and the other Sanders guides as a start in amassing a reference library of facsimiles. Enlarge the library with other facsimile books (we have a few of those in the works ourselves) and by keeping (*never* throwing away!) all the dealer catalogs you can find. Please write the dealers advertising in these pages.;, many of them put out most useful and interesting catalogs, chock full of facsimiles. Then when you come across a questionable signature, a few minutes of browsing through your facsimile library can answer the question of authenticity by simple comparison with a known good example.

Which is not to say all of this is easy. Over the course of years, a person's signature changes with age and through other factors such as injury or just the technology of writing instruments. You'll want to accumulate, wherever possible, the facsimiles of an individual's autograph at differing ages.

There is no such thing as having too many facsimiles!

We hope these that follow prove helpful.

Finally, a few words about the nature of this facsimile section as opposed to that of our *Sanders Price Guide to Autographs* (4th edition)–i.e. the general price guide as opposed to just sports as this one is. In the general guide, beginning with its third edition (1994), we moved the pricing section from categories (Artists & Authors, Entertainment, U.S. Presidents, etc.) to a straight alphabetical listing of names. This has been hailed enthusiastically from everyone we've heard from on the subject. However, in that 1994 edition, we kept the facsimiles in the old categories simply because we did not have time to totally re-scan and re-alphabetize. By the fourth edition of the general guide (issued fall of 1996), everything was in alphabetical order, as it will be in the forthcoming fifth edition (scheduled for release in early 1999–see page 448 for a special offer).

The same situation exists for this third edition of *The Sanders Price Guide to Sports Autographs*. We have moved all names into alphabetical order instead of by category (Baseball, Basketball, Football, etc.). In doing so, we've added many more names. This makes the price guide far easier to work with but, like above, the facsimiles (while extensive) are still categorized. [TIP: Don't forget to check the Miscellaneous category for any name that does not fit in a major category.] By the next edition of the sports price guide (as we did with the general guide) we'll try to have everything in alphabetical order.

In short, we continue to improve the world's best autograph price guides to better serve autograph collectors and dealers everywhere.

Finally, there is one more general difference between facsimiles here and in our general guides. Most of the signatures depicted in the following section obviously came from photographs as opposed to SIGs as in the general guides. This has a lot to do with the nature of sports collecting which tends more toward the signed photograph. However, in the next edition–thanks to improving technology–we'll probably pull the signatures out and discard the background. We certainly welcome your comments on this.

In closing–while still putting forth the lawyerly disclaimers already voiced–the following facsimiles are an invaluable tool in your quest to authenticate signatures you did not see signed in person. It is not the only tool you should have, but it's a darn good start.

AUTO RACING

NOTE: Check the Miscellaneous section for additional Auto Racing facsimiles.

Bobby Allison

Davey Allison

Mario Andretti

Michael Andretti

Buddy Baker

Gary Bettenhausen

Tony Bettenhausen

Tom Bigelow

Neal Bonnett

Craig Breedlove

Louis Chevrolet

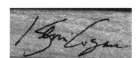

Kevin Cogan

Scott Crossfield

Peter DePaolo

Dale Earnhardt

Bill Elliott

Emerson Fittepaldi

A.J. Foyt

Bill France, Jr.

Josele Garza

Dan Gurney

Janet Guthrie

Sam Hawks

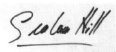

Graham Hill

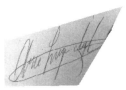

Arie Luyendyk

John Mahler

Dave Marcis

Mike Marshall

Jim McElrath

Rick Mears

Sterling Moss

Lou Meyer

Richard Noble

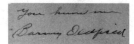

Barney Oldfield

Benny Parsons

David Pearson

Roger Penske

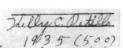

Kelly C. Petillo

King Richard Petty

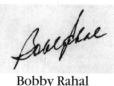

Bobby Rahal

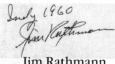

Jim Rathmann

Lloyd Ruby

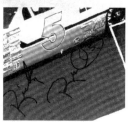

Ricky Rudd

Johnny Rutherford

Troy Ruttman

Wilbur Shaw

Tom Sneva

George Snyder

Jackie Stewart

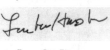

Lyn St. James

Danny Sullivan

Rene Thomas

Al Unser, Sr.

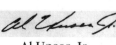

Al Unser, Jr.

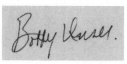

Bobby Unser

BASEBALL

Bill Vukovich

Rusty Wallace

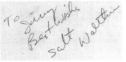

Salt Walther

Darrell Waltrip

Roger Ward

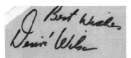

Desiré Wilson

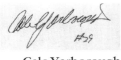

Cale Yarborough

Hank Aaron

Shawn Abner

Joe Adcock

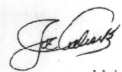

Mel Allen

Grover Cleveland
Alexander (3 variants)

Rick Aguilera

Sparky Anderson

Walt Alston

Luis Aparicio

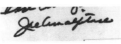

Joe Amalfitano

Luke Appling

Richie Ashburn

Elden Auker

Earl Averill

Harold Baines

Wally Backman

J. Franklin Baker

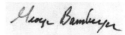

George Bamberger

Sol Bando

Dave Bancroft

Scott Bankhead

Ernie Banks

Hank Bauer

Juan R. Bernhardt

Al Barlick

"Chief" Bender

Charles "Red" Barrett

Dick Bartell

"Buzzie" Bavasi

George Bell

Matt Batts

Johnny Bench

Steve Blass

Vida Blue

Ron Blomberg

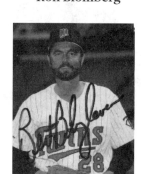
Bert Blylevin

Wade Boggs

Barry Bonds

Milt Bolling

Ray Boone

Zeke Bonura

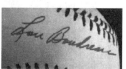
Lou Boudreau

Bobby Bonds

"Oil Can" Boyd

Jim Bouton

Bobby Bonila

Clete Boyer

Ralph Branca

Scott Bradley

Bobby Bragin

Harry Boyles

Tom Brewer

Lou Brock

George Brett

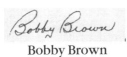

Bobby Brown

Tom Browning

Tom Brunansky

Jerry Bucher

John Berardino

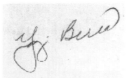

Yogi Berra

Vern Benson

Ewell Blackwell

Al Bumbry

Don Buford

Joe Bunning

Lou Burdette

Smoky Burgess

Guy Bush

Owen Donie Bush

Bob Cain

Dolph Camilli

Roy Campanella

Al Campanis

Jose Canseco

Harry Caray

Max Carey

Rod Carew

Steve Carlton

"Tex" Carleton

Joe Carter

George Case

Clyde Castleman

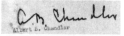

Albert B.
"Happy" Chandler

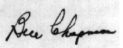

Ben Chapman

Phil Cavaretta

Orlando Cepeda

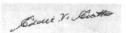

Eddie V. Cicotte

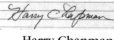

Harry Chapman

Oscar Charleston

Sam Chapman

Jack Clark

Will Clark

Roberto Clemente

Roger Clemmens

"Flea" Clifton

Harland Clifton

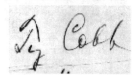

Ty Cobb

Vince Coleman

Mickey Cochrane

Eddie Collins

Earle Combs

Dave Cone

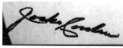

Jocko Conlan

Tony Conigliaro

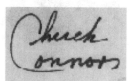

Chuck Connors

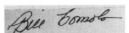
Bill Consolo

Cecil Cooper

Walker Cooper

Ed Correa

Stan Coveleski

Roger Craig

Roger "Doc" Cramer

Del Crandall

Wahoo Sam Crawford

"Shag" Crawford

Tim Crews

Joe Cronin

Joseph E. Cronin

George Crowe

Mike Cuellar

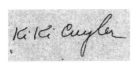
Ki Ki Cuyler

Ray Dandridge

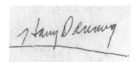
Harry Danning

Ron Darling

Mark Davidson

Alvin Davis

Frank Dascoli

Eric Davis

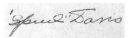
"Spud" Davis

Andre Davison

Dizzy Dean

Paul Dean

Glenn Davis

Ron Deer

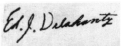
Ed J. Delahanty

Don Denkinger

Bucky Dent

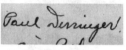

Paul Derringer

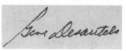

Gene Desautels

Jim Deshaies

Mike Devereaux

Ron Dibble

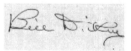

Bill Dickey

Bill Dietrich

Dom DiMaggio

Joe DiMaggio

Vince DiMaggio

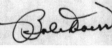

Larry Doby

Bobby Doerr

Taylor Douthit

Doug Drabek

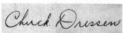

Dave Dravecky

Chuck Dressen

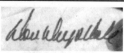

Moe Drobowsky

Don Drysdale

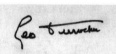

Mike Dunne

Leo Durocher

Leon Durham

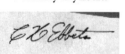

Lenny Dykstra

Charlie Ebbetts

Dennis Eckersley

Del Ennis

Carl Erskine

Darrell Evans

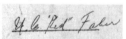

Dwight Evans

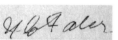

Urban "Red" Faber

Urban "Red" Faber (variant)

Ferris Fain

Bob Feller

Sid Fernandez

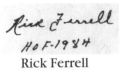

Rick Ferrell

Mark Fidrick

Cecil Fielder

Rollie Fingers

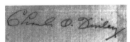

Charles O. Finley

Carlton Fisk

Fred Fitzsimmons

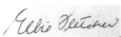

Elbie Fletcher

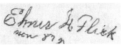

Elmer Flick

Curt Flood

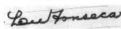

Lew Fonseca

Whitey Ford

Terry Forster

George Foster

John Franco

Julio Franco

Tito Francona

Herman Franks

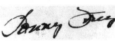

Lonny Frey

Nelson Fox

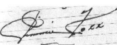

Jimmie Foxx

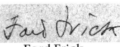

Ford Frick

Bob Friend

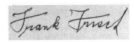

Frank Frisch

Carl Furillo

Phil Gagliano

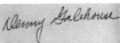

Denny Galehouse

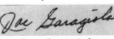

Joe Garagiola

Mike Garcia

Billy Gardner

Ned Garver

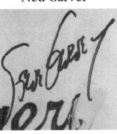

Steve Garvey

Lou Gehrig

Charles Gehringer

Dick Gernert

Bob Gibson

Kirk Gibson

Floyd Giebell

A. Bartlett Giamatti

Paul Giel

Lefty Gomez

Ival Goodman

"Goose" Goslin

Dwight Goodman

Mark Grace

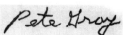
Jim "Mudcat" Grant

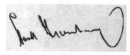
Pete Gray

Hank Greenberg
(Two Variants)

Mike Greenwell

Ken Griffey Sr. &
Ken Griffey Jr.

Clark Griffith

Burleigh A. Grimes

Charlie Grimm

Dick Groat

Lefty Grove

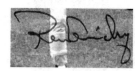
Ron Guidry

Ozzie Guillen

Don Gutteridge

Jose Guzman

Chris Gwynn

Tony Gwynn

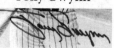
Tony Gwynn
(Variant)

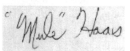
"Mule" Haas

Stan Hack

Harvey Haddix

Chick Hafey

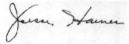

Hinkey Haines

Jesse Haines

Mel Harder

Fred Harding

Harry Heilman

Will Harridge

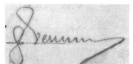

Bud Harrelson

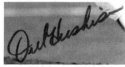

"Bucky" Harris

Leo "Gabby" Hartnett

Joe Hauser

Von Hayes

Rickey Henderson

Tom Henrich

Babe Herman

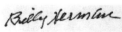

Billy Herman

August Herrmann

Orel Hershiser

Kent Hrbek

Jim Hickman

Joe Hicks

Kirby Higbe

Ted Higuera

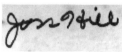

Jess Hill

Shawn Hillegas

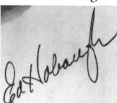

Ed Hobaugh

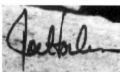

Joel Horlen

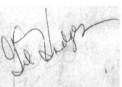

Gil Hodges

Elon "Chief" Hogsett

Al Hollingsworth

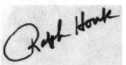
Tommy Holmes

Rick Honeycutt

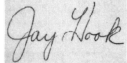
Ralph Hauk

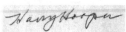
Jim Honochick

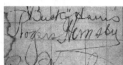
Jay Hook

Harry Hooper

Rogers Hornsby

Rogers Hornsby
(Variant)

Charles Hough

Frank Howard

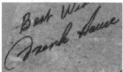
Frank House

Art Howe

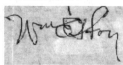
William E.
"Dummy" Hoy

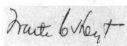
Waite Hoyt

Cal Hubbard

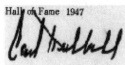
Carl Hubbell

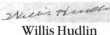
Willis Hudlin

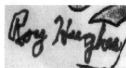
Sid Hudson

Roy Hughes

Tex Hughson

Jim "Catfish" Hunter

Jim "Catfish" Hunter
(Variant)

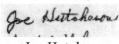
Bruce Hurst

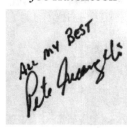
Joe Hutcheson

Pete Incaviglia

Monte Irvin

Bo Jackson

Reggie Jackson

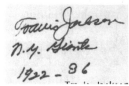
Travis Jackson

Brook Jacoby

Larry Jansen

Gregg Jeffries

Ferguson Jenkins

Tommy John

Billy Johnson

Davey Johnson

Earl Johnson

Judy Johnson

"Si" Johnson

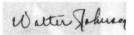

Walter
"Big Train" Johnson

Mack Jones

Spider Jorgensen

Wally Joyner

Bill Jurges

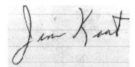

Jim Kaat

Al Kaline

Ray Katt

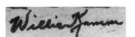

Willie Kamm

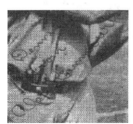

Alex Kampouris

Ewing Kauffman

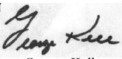

George Kell

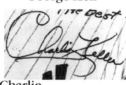

Charlie
"King Kong" Keller

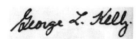

George L. Kelly

Ken Keltner

Vernon Kennedy

Charlie Kerfeld

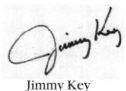

Jimmy Key

Harmon Killebrew

Ralph Kiner

Claude King

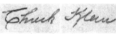

Chuck Klein

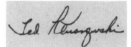

Ted Kluzsewski

Mark Koenig

Jerry Koosman

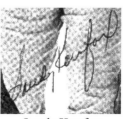

Sandy Koufax

Lew Krausse

Mike Kreevich

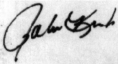

Joan Kroc

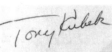

John Kruk

Tony Kubek

Harvey Kuenn

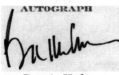

Joe Kuhel

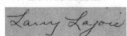

Bowie Kuhn

Larry "Nap" Lajoie

Dennis Lamp

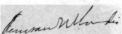

Kenesaw
Mountain Landis

Mark Langston

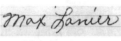

Max Lanier

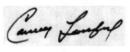

Carney Lansford

Barry Larkin

Don Larsen

Tom Lasorda

Vernon Law

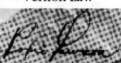

Roxie Lawson

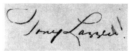

Tony Lazzell

John Lefebre

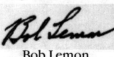

Bob Lemon

Chet Lemon

Buck Leonard

Bill Lillard

Jim Lindeman

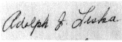

Freddy Lindstrom

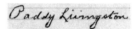

Adolph "Ad" J. Liska

Paddy Livingston

Whitey Lockman

Dario Lodigiani

Bill Lohrman

Ron Lolich

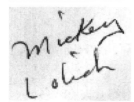

Mickey Lolich

Ernie Lombardi

Dale Long

Ed Lopat

Al Lopez

Ron Luciano

Mike Lum

Sparky Lyle

Ted Lyons

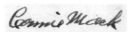

Connie Mack

Greg Maddox

Dave Magadan

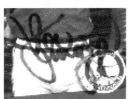

Joe Magrane

Sal Maglie

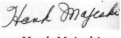

Hank Majeski

Frank Malzone

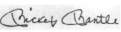

Mickey Mantle

Heinie Manush

Rabbit Maranville

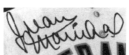

Juan Marichal

Marty Marion

Harry "Hal" Marnie

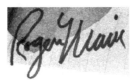

Roger Maris

Rube Marquard

Mike Marshall

Billy Martin

"Pepper" Martin

Tom Matchick

Ed Mathews

Don Mattingly

Gene Mauch

Carmen Mauro

(Baseball)

Willie Mays

Bill Mazeroski

Joe McCarthy

Mark McCaskill

Frank McCormick

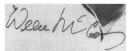

Willie McCovey

Lance McCullers

Roger McDowell

Sam McDowell

Willie McGee

Fred McGriff

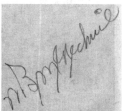

Mark McGwire

Wm."Bill" McKechnie

Denny McLain

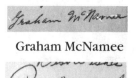

Graham McNamee

Joe Medwick

Bobby Mercer

Eddie Miksis

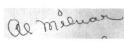

Al Milnar

Minnie Minoso

Kevin Mitchell

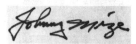

Johnny Mize

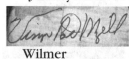

Wilmer
"Vinegar Bend"
Mizell

Paul Molitor

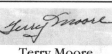

Terry Moore

Keith Moreland

Tom Morgan

Jack Morris

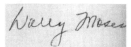

Wally Moses

Manny Mota

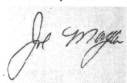

Joe Morgan

Bill Mullen

Jerry Mumphrey

Les Munns

Van Lingle Mungo

Thurman Munson

Dale Murphy

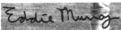
Eddie Murray

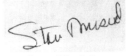
Stan Musial

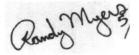
Randy Myers

Graig Nettles

Don Newcombe

Hal Newhouser

Charles A. "Kid" Nichols

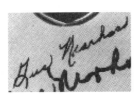
Gus Niarhos

Joe Niekro

Phil Niekro

Juan Nieves

Les "Red" Nonnenkamp

Irv Noren

Bob Ojeda

Tony Oliva

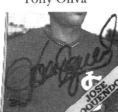
Jose Oquendo

Gene Oliver

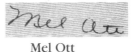
Mel Ott

Mickey Owen

Johnny Podres

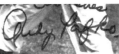
Andy Pafko

Satchel Paige

Jim Palmer

Dave Parker

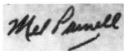
Mel Parnell

Lance Parrish

Joe Pascarella

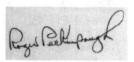
Monte Pearson

Roger Peckinpaugh

Herb Pennock

Tony Perez

Gaylord Perry

Jim Perry

Johnny Pesky

Billy Pierce

Jimmy Piersell

Lou Piniella

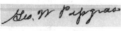
George W. Pipgras

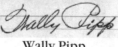
Wally Pipp

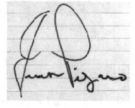
Juan Pizarro

Dan Plesac

Eric Plunk

Cletus "Boots"
Poffenberger

Pam Postema

Doug Powell

Forest C. "Tot"
Pressnell

Kirby Puckett

Terry Puhl

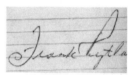
Frank Pytlak

Doug Rader

Tim Raines

Vic Raschi

Jeff Reardon

"Pee Wee" Reese

Rick Reuschel

Allie Reynolds

Jim Rice

Sam Rice

Bill Rigney

Bill Ripken

Cal Ripken, Sr.

Cal Ripken Jr.

Eppe Rixey, Jr.

Phil Rizzuto

Robin Roberts

Billy Jo Robidoux

Brooks Robinson

Frank Robinson

Jackie Robinson

Eddie Robinson

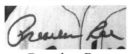

Preacher Roe

Bill Rogell

Steve Rogers

Charlie Root

Pete Rose

Al Rosen

Edd J. Roush

Red Ruffing

Jacob Ruppert

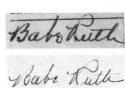

Babe Ruth
(Variants)

Nolan Ryan

Bret Saberhagen

Johnny Sain

Mark Salas

Juan Samuel

Ryne Sandburg

Hank Sauer

Dave Sax

Richie Scheinblum

Cal Schiraldi

Mike Schmidt

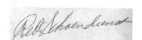

Red Schoendienst

Hal Schumacher

Herb Score

Marge Schott

Mike Scott

Tom Seaver

Kevin Seitzer

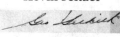

George Selkirk

Joe Sewell

"Rip" Sewell

Bobby Shantz

Eric Show

Al H. Simmons

Ken Singleton

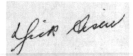

Dick Sister

George Sister

Bill "Moose" Skowron

Enos Slaughter

Enos Slaughter
(Variant)

Roy Smalley

Roy Smalley, Jr.

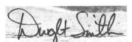

Dwight Smith

Hal Smith

Les Smith

Ozzie Smith

Reggie Smith

Zane Smith

Duke Snider

Fred C. Snodgrass

Cory Snyder

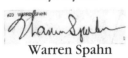

Warren Spahn

Bob Speake

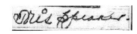

Tris Speaker

Daryl Spencer

Hal Spindel

Jerry Staley

Tracy Stallard

Pete Stanicek

Eddie Stanky

Fred Stanley

Willie Stargell

Rusty Staub

Terry Steinbach

George Steinbrenner

Casey Stengel

Riggs Stephenson

Dave Stieb

Horace Stoneham

Carl E. Stotz

Monty Stratton

Franklin Stubbs

Kirk Strincevich

Darryl Strawberry

B. J. Surhoff

Charlie "Butch" Sutcliffe

Rick Sutcliffe

Don Sutton

Mel Stottlemyre

Dale Sveum

Ron Swoboda

Dan Tartabull

Gary Templeton

Wm. "Bill" Terry

Andres Thomas

Frank Thomas

Bobby Thomson

Luis Tiant

Jeff Torborg

Earl Torgeson

Joe Torre

Alan Trammell

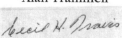

Cecil H. Travis

Cliff Travis

Harold "Pie" Traynor (Variants)

Tom Trebelhorn

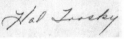

Hal Trosky

Virgil Trucks

John Tudor

Bob Turley

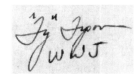

"Ty " Tyson

Peter Ueberroth

Fernando Valenzuela

Elmer Valo

John Van Cuyk

Johnny Vander Meer

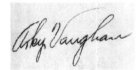

Arky Vaughan

Bill Veeck

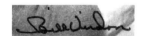

Bill Virdon

Mickey Vernon

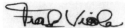

Frank Viola

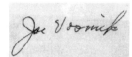

Joe Vosmik

Honus Wagner

"Gee" Walker

Harry "the Hat"
Walker

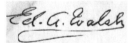

Big Ed Walsh

Bucky Walters

Jerome Walton

Bill Wambsganss

Lloyd Waner

Paul Waner

Pete Ward

Lon Warneke

Ron Washington

Earl Weaver

"Tweed" Webb

Walt Weiss

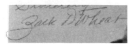

Zack Wheat

Bill White

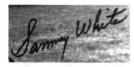

Sammy White

Hoyt Wilhelm

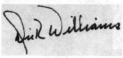

Dick Williams

Billy Williams

Ken Williams

Mitch Williams

Reggie Williams

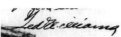

Ted Williams

Jimmie Wilson

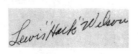

Lewis "Hack" Wilson

Maury Wills

Mookie Wilson

Dave Winfield

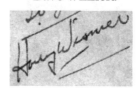

Harry Wismer

Mike Witt

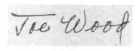

"Smokey Joe" Wood

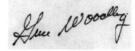

Gene Woodling

Todd Worrell

Philip K. Wrigley

Early Wynn

Carl Yasztremski

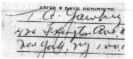

Tom Yawkey

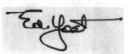

Eddie Yost

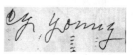

Cy Young

Robin Yount

Norm Zauchin

Gus Zernial

Don Zimmer

The great Carl Furillo patrolled the Brooklyn outfield for 15 years and starred in seven World Series. Furillo and author Sanders appeared in a Paramount movie together in 1958.

BASKETBALL

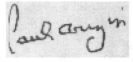

Kareem Abdul-Jabbar

Rick Barry

Larry Bird

Lou Carnesecca

Bernard L. Carnevale

Paul Arizin

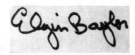

Elgin Baylor

Sam Bowie

Bill Bradley

Wilt Chamberlain

Al Attles

Mel Counts

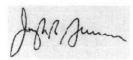

Joseph R. Brennan

Red Auerbach

Bernie Borgmann

Mark Bryant

Bob Cousy

Charles Barkley

Bernie Bicherstaff

Dave Bing

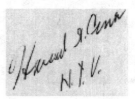

Howard G. Cann

Denny Crum

Billy Cunningham

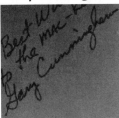

Gary Cunningham

Bob Davies

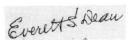

Everett S. Dean

Dave DeBusschere

Terry Dischinger

Len Elmore

Julius "Dr. J" Erving

Clifford B. Fagan

Bill Foster

H. E. "Bud" Foster

Walt Frazier

Lauren Laddie Gale

Harry Gallatin

George Gervin

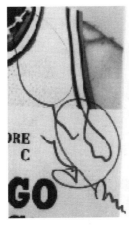

Artis Gilmore

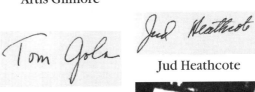

Tom Gola

A. C. Green

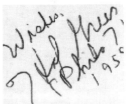

Hal Greer

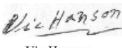

Vic Hanson

Joe Havlicek

Elvin Hayes

Chick Hearn

Jud Heathcote

Tom Heinsohn

Paul "Tony" Hinkle

Howard A. Hobson

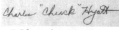
Nat Holman

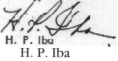
"Chuck" Hyatt

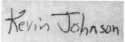
H. P. Iba

Edward S. Irish

Kevin Johnson

K. C. Jones

Steve Jones

Michael Jordan

Magic Johnson

Caldwell Jones

Jerome Kersey
(Variants)

Bobby Knight

Bill Krueger

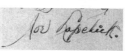
Bob Kurland

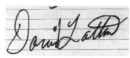
Joe Lapchick

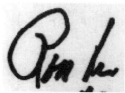
David Lattin

Ron Lee

Harry Litwack

Ken Loeffler

Jerry Lucas

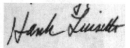
Hank Luisetti

Easy Ed Macauley

Moses Malone

Eph. 2:8,9
John 3:3
John 14:6
Rom. 10:9,10
"Pistol Pete" Maravich

Press Maravich

Slater Martin

Roland Massimino

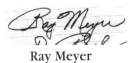

Chuck Meucel

Ray Meyer

Ralph H. Miller

Doug Moe

Don Monson

Norm Nixon

Lawrence O'Brien

Lute Olson

Coach Johnny Orr

Robert Parrish

Jim Paxson

Sam Perkins

Drazen Petrovic

Bob Pettit

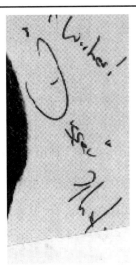

"Digger" Phelps

Andy Phillip

Jack Ramsey

Willis Reed

Pat Riley

Oscar Robertson

David Robinson

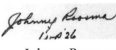

Johnny Roosma

Adolph Rupp

Bill Russell

Andy Russo

Dolph Schayes

Bill Sharman

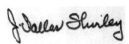

J. Dallas Shirley

(Basketball)

Dean Smith

Larry Smith

Edward S. Steitz

Jerry Tarkanian

Isiah Thomas

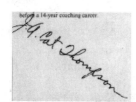

John A.
"Cat" Thompson

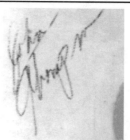

John Thompson

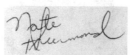

Nate Thurmond

Wayman Tisdale

Kelly Tripucka

Jack Twyman

Wes Unseld

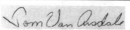

Tom Van Arsdale

Jim Valvano

Kiki Vandeweghe

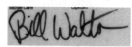

Bill Walton

Spud Webb

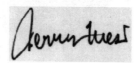

Jerry West

Sidney Wicks

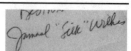

Jamaal "Silk" Wilkes

Dominque Wilkins

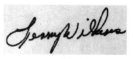

Lenny Wilkins

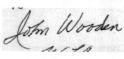

John Wooden

James Worthy

Danny Young

Basketball Hall of Fame immortal Elgin Baylor joins author George Sanders for an Oregon sports program in 1963.

BOXING

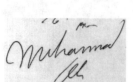

Carmen Basilio

Cesar Brion

Tony Canzonari

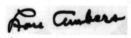

Muhammad Ali

Lou Brouillard

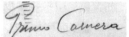

Primo Carnera

Lou Ambers

Joe Brown

Georges Carpentier

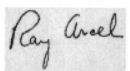

Vito Antuofermo

Wilfred Benitez

Dan Bucceroni

Rubin
"Hurricane" Carter

Ray Arcel

Paul Berlenbach

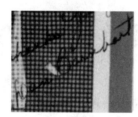

Dan Barnhart,
Manager

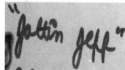

Joltin' Jeff Chandler

Henry Armstrong

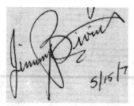

Jimmy Bivins

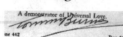

Tommy Burns

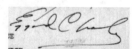

Ezzard Charles

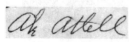

Alexis Arquella

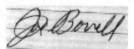

Joe Bovell

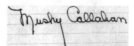

Mushy Callahan

Hector "Macho"
Camacho

Abe Attell

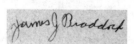

James J. Braddock

George Chuvalo

Billy Conn

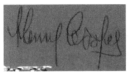

Henry Cooper

James J. Corbett

Pipino Cuevas

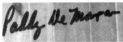

Paddy DeMarco

Jack Dempsey

James "Buster" Douglas

Angelo Dundee

Roberto Duran

Jimmy Ellis

Jackie Fields

George Foreman

Bob Foster

Todd "Kid" Foster

Joe Frazier

Don Fullmer

Gene Fullmer

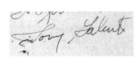

Tony "Two Ton" Galanto

Kid Gavilan

Joey Giambra

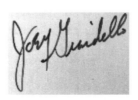

Joey Giardello

Rocky Graziano

Emile Griffith

Marvelous Marvin Hagler

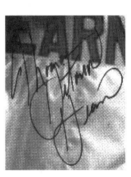

Thomas "Hitman" Hearns

Larry Holmes

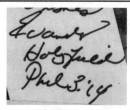

Evander Holyfield

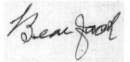

Beau Jack

James J. Jeffries

Ingemar Johansson

Harold Johnson

Jack Johnson

Ed "Too Tall" Jones

Don King

Jake La Motta and George Sanders (1939)

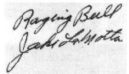

Jake La Motta

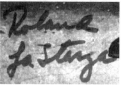

Roland La Starza

Pete Latzo

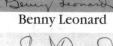

Benny Leonard

Sugar Ray Leonard

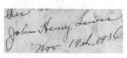

John Henry Lewis

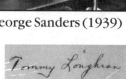

Tommy Loughran

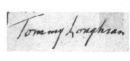

Tommy Loughran
(variant)

Joe Louis, George
Sanders, and Sandy
Sanders (1958)

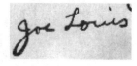

Joe Louis

Barry McGuigan

Jimmy McLamin

Ray "Boom Boom"
Mancini

Rocky Marciano

Vince Martinez

Joey Maxim

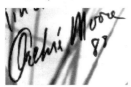

Archie Moore

Matthew Saad
Muhammad

Jose Napoles

Carl "Bobo" Nelson

Lou Nova

Floyd Patterson

Eusebio Pedroza

Paul Pender

Willie Pep

Pete Rademacher

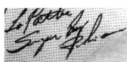

Sugar Ray Robinson

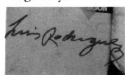

Luis Rodriguez

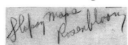

Slapsy Maxie
Rosenbloom

Barney Ross

Mike Rossman

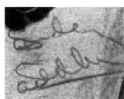

Sandy Sadler

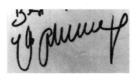

Max Schmeling

Izzy Schwartz

Jack Sharkey

James
"Bonecrusher" Smith

Billy Soose

Leon Spinks

Michael Spinks

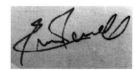

Ernie Terrell

Gene Tunney

Mike Tyson

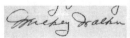

Jersey Joe Walcott

Mickey Walker

Cleveland Williams

Ike Williams

Tony Zale

The author's father, George R. Sanders, Sr., the 1951-52 World Lightweight Boxing Champion James "Jimmy" Carter, and Hollywood sportscaster George Sanders. The restaurant in Los Angeles they are posing in front of was owned by the authors, George and Helen Sanders, for over 30 years.

FOOTBALL

Frank Albert

Ki Aldrich

Ron Acks

George H. Allen

Herb Adderley

Steve Alwak

Ben Agajanian

Lance Alworth

Alex Agase

Lou Agase

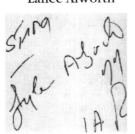

Lyle Alzado

Troy Aikman

Dick Alban

Bobby Anderson

Eddie Anderson

Donny Anderson

Ken Anderson

Fred Arbanas

Mike Archer

Jerry Argowitz

Bill Arnsparger

Frank K. Aschenbrenner

Doug Atkins

Charles W. Bachman

Morris "Red" Badgro

Johnny Baker

Ralph "Moon" Baker

Gary Ballman

Pete Banaszak

Carl Banks

Vince Banonis

George Barclay

Steve Bartkowski

Lem Barney

Mike James Basrak

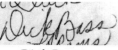
Dick Bass

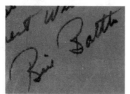
Bill Battle

Sammy Baugh

Maxie Baughan

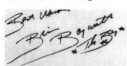
Bill Baywater

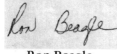
Ron Beagle

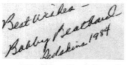
Bobby Beathard

Gary Beban

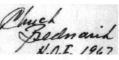
Chuck Bednarik

Forrest Behm

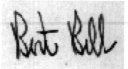
Bert Bell

Eddie Bell

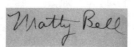
Matty Bell

Emory Bellard

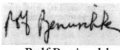
Cornelius Bennett

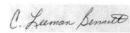
Rolf Benirschke

C. Leeman Bennett

Raymond Berry

Dana X. Bible

Dick Bielski

Bernie Bierman

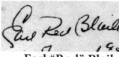
Chris Binford

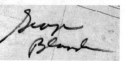
George Blanda

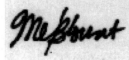
Mel Blount

J. R. Boone

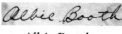
Albie Booth

Robbie Bosco

Bobby Bowden

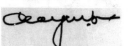
Cloyce Box

Bob Boyd

Earl "Red" Blaik

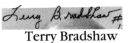

Terry Bradshaw

Clifford Branch

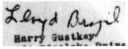

Mel Branch

Lloyd Brazil

Berke Breathern

Bob Breunig

Stan Brock

Dieter Brock

John Brockington

John Brodie

Tommy Brooker

Bill Brooks

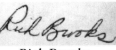

Rich Brooks

Tom Brookshier

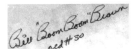

Bill "Boom Boom" Brown

Jim Brown

Larry Brown

Paul E. Brown

Roosevelt "Rosie" Brown Sr.

Willie Brown

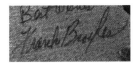

Frank Broyles

Earle Bruce

Ed Bruce

Bob Bruggers

Kelvin Bryant

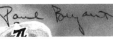

Paul Bryant

Buck Buchanan

Ed Budde

Joe Bugel

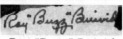

Ray "Buzz" Buivid

Ronnie Bell

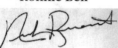

Nick Buoniconti

Jerry Burns

Paul "Buddy" Burris

Jim Burt

Leon Burtrott

Dick Butkus

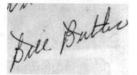

Bill Butler

Dave Butz

Walter Camp

Earl Campbell

Hugh Campbell

Marion Campbell

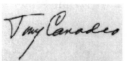

Tony Canadeo

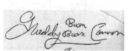

Freddy "Boom Boom" Cannon

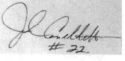

John Cappelletti

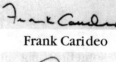

Frank Carideo

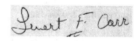

Harold Carmichael

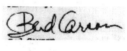

Lenert F. Carr

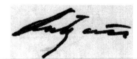

Bud Carson

Anthony Carter

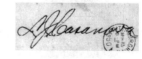

Jim Carter

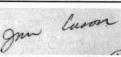

Len Casanova

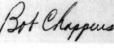

Jim Cason

Bob Chappuis

Jack Christiansen

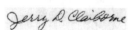

Paul Christman

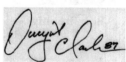

Jerry D. Claiborne

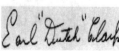

Dwight Clark

Earl "Dutch" Clark

Don Cockroft

Don E. Coleman

Bobby Collins

Charlie Conerly

Clyde Conner

George Connor

Jack Kent Clarke

Bruce Coslet

Robly Cox

Carey Cozza

Roger Craig

Jeff Cravath

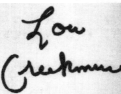

Dick Crayne

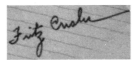

Lou Creekmur

Fritz Crisler

H. O. Crisler

John David Crow

Jimmy Crowley

Larry Csonka

Gary Cuozzo

Curley Culp

Randall Cunningham

Bill Curry

Carroll Dale

Larry Dalton

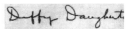

Duffy Daugherty

Cotton Davidson

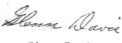

Glenn Davis

Mouse Davis

Willie Davis

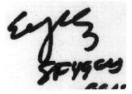

Ed DeBartalo

Steve DeBerg

Fisher DeBerry

Joe DeLamelleur

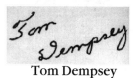
Rey Dempsey

Tom Dempsey

Bob Devaney

Dan Devine

Dorne Dibble

Eric Dickerson

Lynn Dickey

Mike Ditka

Glenn Dobbs

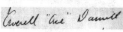
Dale Dodrill

Averell "Ave" Donnell

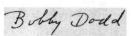
Conrad Dobbler

Bobby Dodd

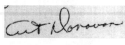
Aldo "Buff" Donelli

Art Donovan

Bill Dooley

Jim Doran

Tony Dorsett

Bobby Douglass

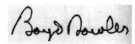
Harry Dowda

Boyd Dowler

John L.
"Paddy" Driscoll

Fred Dryer

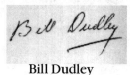
Bill Dudley

Tony Dungy

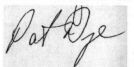
Pat Dye

Ken Easley

Ron East

Lavell Edwards

Doug Eggers

Joe Ehrmann

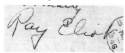
Larry Eisenhauer

Ray Eliot

Carl Eller

"Bump" Elliott

Pete Elliott

Jack Elway

John Elway

"Ox" Emerson

Dennis Erickson

Boomer (Esiason)

Coach Weeb Eubank

Forest Evashevski

Jim Everett

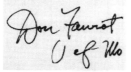
Mel Farr

Don Faurot

Gerry Faust

Tom Fears

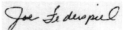
Beattie Feathers

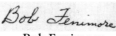
Joe Federspiel

Bob Fenimore

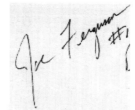
Rick Fenney

Joe Ferguson

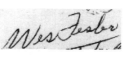
Manny Fernandez

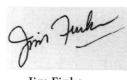
Wes Fesler

Jim Finks

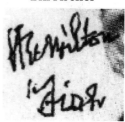
Bill Fischer

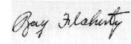
Hamilton Fish

Ray Flaherty

Paul Flatley

Marv Fleming

Reg Fleming

Tom Floras

Doug Flutie

Danny Ford

Gerald R. Ford

Dan Fouts

Sam Francis

Rod Franz

Benny Friedman

Roman Gabriel

Verne Gagne

Bob Gain

Bob Gaona

Ed Garbisch

Bill Garnaas

Frank Gatski

Roy Gerela

Joe Gibb

Abe Gibson

Paul Giel

Frank Gifford

Sid Gillman

Bob Gladieux

Jerry Glanville

Bill Glass

Gary Glick

Peter Gogolack

Marshall Goldberg

Bruce Gossett

Mike Gottfried

Paul Governali

Jim Grabowski

Randy Gradishar

Otto Graham

"Red" Grange

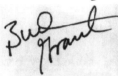

Bud Grant

Bobby Grayson

"Mean" Joe Greene

L. C. Greenwood

Forrest Gregg

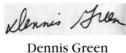

Dennis Green

Roosevelt "Rosey" Grier

Bob Griese

Bob Grim

Steve Grogan

Bill Groman

Lou Groza

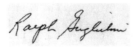

Ralph Guglielmi

John Gutekunst

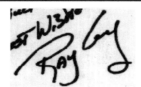

Ray Guy

Dale Hackbart

Pat Haden

John Hadl

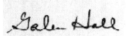

Galen Hall

George Halas

Jack Ham

Jim Hanifan

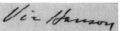

Vic Hanson

Dan Hampton

Pat Harder

Cliff Harris

Franco Harris

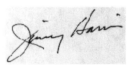

Jimmy Harris

Jim Hart

Leon Hart

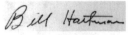

Bill Hartman

Ken Hatfield

Ed Healey

"Bullet Bob" Hayes

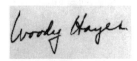

Woody Hayes

Bobby Hebert

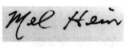

Mel Hein

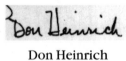

Don Heinrich

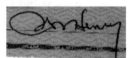

Dan Henning

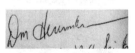

Wilbur "Fats" Henry

Don Hermann

Willie Heston

Herman Hickman

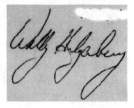

Wally Hilgaberg

Jay Hilgenberg

Calvin Hill

Drew Hill

Harlon Hill

Clarke Hinkle

Elroy
"Crazylegs" Hirsch

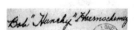

Bob "Hunchy"
Hoernschemeyer

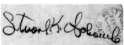

Stuart K.
Holcomb

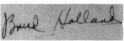

Jerome "Brud"
Holland

Lou Holtz

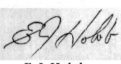

E. J. Holub

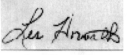

Les Horvath

Jeff Hostetler

Kenny Houston

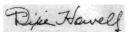

Frank Howard

Dixie Howell

John Huarte

Cal Hubbard

Arnie Herber

Sam Huff

Bobby Humphry

Lamar Hunt

Don Hutson

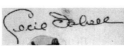

Cecil Isbell

Raghib "Rocket" Ismail

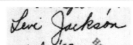

Levi Jackson

Craig James

Don James

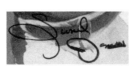

Lionel James

Vic Janowicz

Ron Jaworski

Roy Jefferson

Jim Johnson

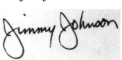

Jimmy Johnson

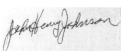

John Henry Johnson

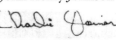

Charlie Joiner

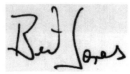

Bert Jones

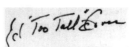

Ed "Too Tall" Jones

Howard Jones

Jerry Jones

Lee Roy Jordan

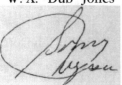
Pat Jones

W. A. "Dub" Jones

Sonny Jurgensen

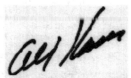
Charlie "Choo Choo" Justice

Joe Kapp

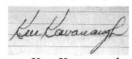
Alex Karras

Dave Karourek

Ken Kavanaugh

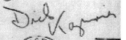
Dick Kazmaier

Louis Kelcher

Jim Kelly

Larry Kelley

Ralph G. Kercheval

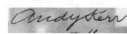
Andy Kerr

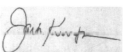
Jack Kemp

Jeff Kemp

Rex Kern

Jim Kiick

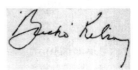
"Bucko" Kilroy

John Kimbrough

Frank M. "Bruiser" Kinard

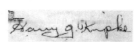
Harry G. Kipke

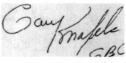
Gary Knafele

Chuck Knox

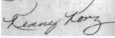
Kenny Korz

Bernie Kosar

Stan Kostka

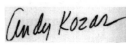
Andy Kozar

Dave Kragthorpe

Jerry Kramer

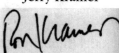
Ron Kramer

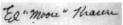
Ed "Moose" Krause

Paul Krause

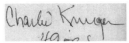

Charlie Kruger

Bob Kuechenberg

George Kunz

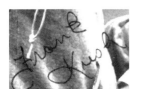

Frank Kush

Ted Kwalik

Curly Lambeau

Daryl Lamonica

Greg Landry

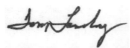

Tom Landry

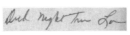

Dick "Night Train" Lane

Jim Langer

Willie Lanier

Steve Largent

Gary Larsen

Greg Larson

Yale Lary

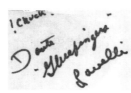

Hank Lauricella

Dante "Gluefingers" Lavelli

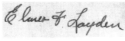

Elmer F. Layden

Bobby Layne

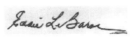

Eddie LeBaron

Frank Leahy

D. D. Lewis

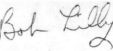

Bob Lilly

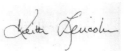

Keith Lincoln

Floyd Little

Larry Little

Louie Lipps

Lou Little

Ronny Lott

Sid Luckman

Ronny Lott

Francis "Pug" Lund

James Lofton

Neil Lomax

Vince Lombardi

Chuck Long

Art Luppino

Bill Maas

George McAfee

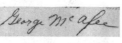
Napoleon
McCallum

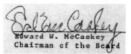
Bill McCartney

Edward McCaskey

Bill McColl

Mike McCormack

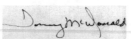
Sam McCullum

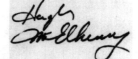
Tommy McDonald

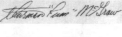
Hugh McElhenny

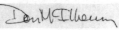
Thurman McGraw

Don McIlhenny

George MacIntyre

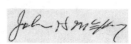
John McKay

Jim McMahon

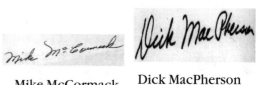
Dick MacPherson

Bill "Red" Mack

Freeman McNeil

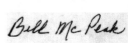
Bill McPeak

John Mackey

John Mackovic

John Madden

E. P. Madigan

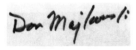

Don Majkowski

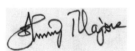

Johnny Majors

Coach Bill Mallory

Tony Mandarich

Dave Manders

Jack Manders

Dexter Manly

Archie Manning

Gino Marchetti

Ted Marchibroda

Dan Marino

Larry Marmie

Ray Marshall

Bernie Masterson

Ollie Matson

John Matuszak

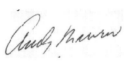

Andy Maurer

Don Maynard

Ken Mecklenberg

"Dandy Don" Meredith

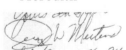

Jerry Mertens

Ron Meyer

Lou Michaels

Walt Michaels

Mike Michalske

Keith Millard

Matt Millen

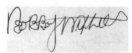
Chris Miller

Bobby Mitchell

Lydell Mitchell

Ron Mix

Art Monk

Cliff Montgomery

Wilbert Montgomery

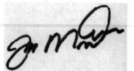
Joe Montana

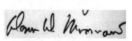
Donn Moomaw

Warren Moon

Lenny Moore

Earl Morrall

Joe Morris

Mercury Morris

Craig Morton

"Monk" Moscrip

Marion Motley

Harold "Brick" Muller, M.D.

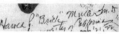
George Munger

Clarence "Biggie" Munn

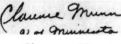
Eddie Murray

George Musso

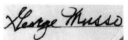
Gern Nagler

Bronko Nagurski (Variants)

"Broadway Joe"
Namath

Jim Nance

Earle "Greasy" Neale

Jess Neely

Don Nehlen

Ernie Nevers

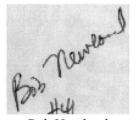

Bob Newland

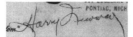

Harry Newman

Ozzie Newsome

John Niland

Ray Nitschke

Tommy Nobis

Dick Nolan

Chuck Noll

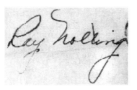

Ray Nolting

Leo Nomellini

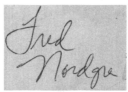

Fred Nordgren

Tom Nowatzke

Ken O'Brien

Christian Okoya

Jordan Olivar

Merlin Olsen

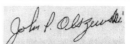

John P.
Olszewski

Bennie
Oosterbaan

Dave Osborn

Chet Ostrowski

Jim Otis

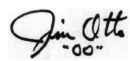

Jim Otto

R. C. "Alley
Oop" Owens

Steve Owens

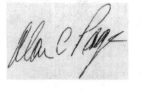

Alan C. Page

Jim Parker

Bill Parcells

Jack Pardee

Jackie Parker

Babe Parilli

Buddy Parker

Clarence "Ace" Parker

Ara Parseghian

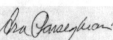

Joe Paterno

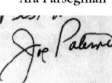

Billy Patterson

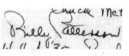

Eddie Payton

Walter Payton

Drew Pearson

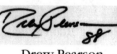

Preston Pearson

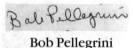

Rodney Peete

Bob Pellegrini

Don Perkins

Ray Perkins

George Perles

Joe Perry

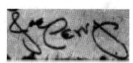

Jimmy Phelan

"Bum" Phillips

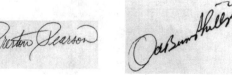

Jim Phillips

John Pingel

Pete Pihos

Doug Plank

Milt Plum

Jim Plunkett

Ed Podolak

Fritz Pollard, Jr.

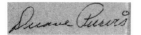
Glenn Presnell

Tommy Prothro

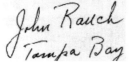
Duane Purvis

Tom Rathman

John Rauch

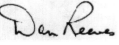
John Reaves

Don Read

Dan Reeves

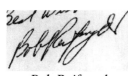
Bob Reifsnyder

Robert O. Reynolds

Jim Ricca

Grantland Rice

Jerry Rice

Les Richter

John Riggins

Jim Ringo

André Rison

Eddie Robinson

Paul Robeson

Andy Robustelli

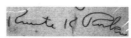
Knute K. Rockne

Fran Rogel

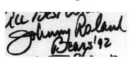
Johnny Roland

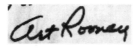
Art Rooney

Bobby Ross

Kyle Rote

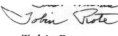
Tobin Rote

Darrell Royal

Pete Rozelle

Mike Rozier

Coach Buddy Ryan

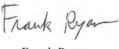
Frank Ryan

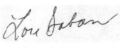
Lou Saban

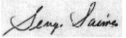
George Saimes

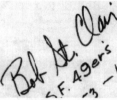
Bob St. Claire

Barry Sanders

Deion Sanders

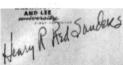
Henry R. "Red" Sanders

Orban "Speck" Sanders

Ricky Sanders

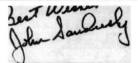
John Sandusky

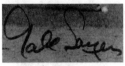
Gale Sayers

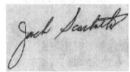
Jack Scarbath

Bo Schembeckler

Bob Schloredt

Francis Schmidt

Joe Schmidt

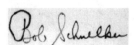
Bob Schnelker

Howard Schnellenberger

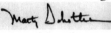
Marty Schottenheimer

Tex Schramm

Jay Schroeder

Marchmont "Marchie" Schwartz

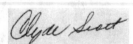
Clyde Scott

Lee Roy Selmon

Rafael Septien

Harley Sewell

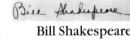
Bill Shakespeare

Ed Sharockman

Art Shell

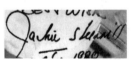
Jackie Sherrill

Clark Shaughnessy

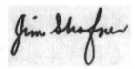
Jim Shofner

Don Shula

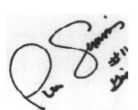

Jeff Siemon

Phil Simms

O. J. Simpson

Mike Singletary

Emil Sitko

Bob Skoranski

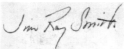

Bubba Smith

Jim Ray Smith

Riley Smith

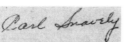

Carl Snavely

Norm Snead

Matt Snell

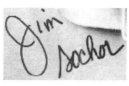

Jim Sochor

Gordy Soltau

Jack Spikes

Steve Spurrier

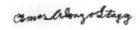

Ken "Snake" Stabler

Amos Alonzo Stagg

Jim Stanley

Bart Starr

Ernie Stautner

Jan Stenerud

Bill Stits

Steve Stonebreaker

Hank Stram

Matt Suhey

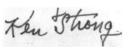

Ken Strong

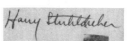

Harry Stuhldreher

Pat Summerall

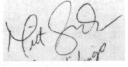

Milt Sunde

Lynn Swann

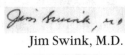

Jim Swink, M.D.

Barry Switzer

Mosi Tatupu

George Taliaferro

Fran Tarkenton

Charley Taylor

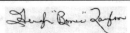

Hugh "Bones" Taylor

Jim Taylor

Lawrence Taylor

Otis Taylor

Vinny Testaverde

Corky Thays

Joe Theismann

Frank Thomas

Harry J. Thompson

Jim Thorpe

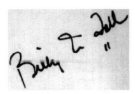

Mick Tinglehoff

Eric Tipton

Y. A. Tittle

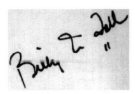

Billy Joe Tolliver

Ted Tollner

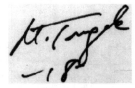

Mike Tomczak

Dan "Deacon" Towler

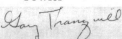

Gary Tranquill

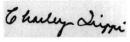

Charley Trippi

Arnold Tucker

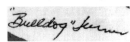

Clyde "Bulldog" Turner

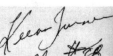

Keena Turner

Wendell Tyler

Pat Uebel

Johnny Unitas

Gene Upshaw

Andy Uram

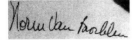

Norm Van Brocklin

Steve Van Buren

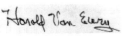

Mark Van Eeghen

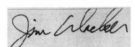

Harold Van Every

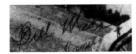

Jim Wacker

Wallace Wade

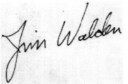

Bobby Walden

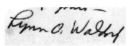

Jim Walden

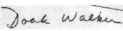

Lynn O. "Pappy" Waldorf

Doak Walker

Herschel Walker

Wesley Walker

Bill Wade

Ron Waller

Bill Walsh

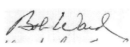

Joe Walton

Bob Ward

Cotton Warburton

Willis F. Ward

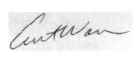

Paul Warfield

Curt Warner

Glenn S. "Pop" Warner

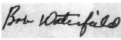

Kenny Washington

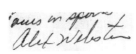

Bob Waterfield

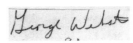

Alex Webster

George Webster

Arnie Weinmeister

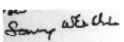

Herman Wedemeyer

Sonny Werbin

Byron White

Mike White

Woody Widenhofer

Ed Widseth

Paul Wiggins

Dick Wildung

Bud Wilkinson

Ken Willard

Bob Williams

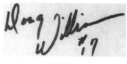

Doug Williams

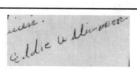

Eddie Williamson

Fred "The Hammer" Williamson

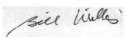

Bill Willis

Billy Wilson

Larry Wilson

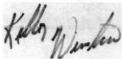

Kellon Winslow

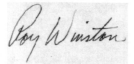

Roy Winston

Former President Gerald Ford during his college football days.

Legendary pro football Hall of Famer Bronko Nagurski with George Sanders at Nagurski's gas station in International Falls, Minnesota. This photograph was taken in 1966.

GOLF

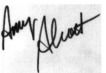

Tommy Aaron

Amy Alcott

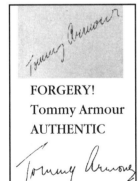

George Archer

FORGERY!
Tommy Armour
AUTHENTIC

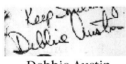

Tommy Armour III

Debbie Austin

Paul Azinger

Kathy Baker

Ian Baker-Finch

Seve Ballesteros

Jerry Barber

Miller Barber

Dave Barr

Alice Bauer

Dave Bauer

Marlene Bauer

Laura Baugh

Frank Beard

Chip Beck

Deane Beman

Patty Berg

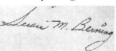

Susie M. Berning

Al Besselink

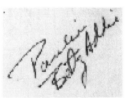

Pauline Betz Addie

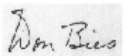

Don Bies

Jay Don Blake

Homero Blancas

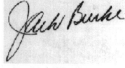
Jack Burke

Charles Coody

Beth Daniel

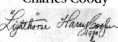
"Lighthorse"
Harry Cooper

Tommy Bolt

Sam Byrd

Henry Cotton

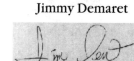
Roberto
de Vincenzo

Jimmy Demaret

Julius Boros

John Paul Cain

Bruce Crampton

Jim Dent

Bruce Devlin

Mark Calcavecchia

Ben Crenshaw

Pat Bradley

Donna Caponi

John Cook

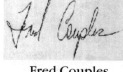
Joseph C. Dey

Gardner Dickenson

Fred Couples

Gay Brewer

Jo Anne Carner

Babe Didrikson
(early & later variants)

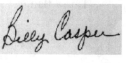
Mark Brooks

Billy Casper

John Daly

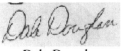

Dale Douglass

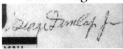

George Dunlap Jr.

George Sanders with famous golfer and president, Dwight D. Eisenhower

Lee Elder

Bob Estes

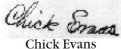

Chick Evans

Nick Faldo

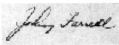

George Fazio

Johnny Farrell

Brad Faxon

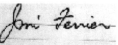

Jim Ferree

Jim Ferrier

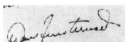

Mike Fetchick

Dow Finsterwald

Jack Fleck

Ray Floyd

Doug Ford

Ed Furgol

Jim Gallagher Jr.

Jane Geddes

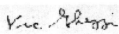

Al Geiberger

Vic Ghezzi

Gibby Gilbert

Bob Goalby

Johnny Goodman

Wayne Grady

Herb Graffis

David Graham

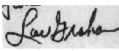

Lou Graham

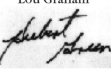

Hubert Green

Tammie A. Green

Ralph Guldahl

Freddie Haas

Jay Haas

Walter Hagen

Marlene Bauer Hagge

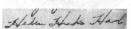

Helen Hicks Harb

"Chick" Harbert

Claude Harmon

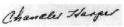

Chandler Harper

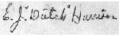

E. J. "Dutch"
Harrison

Lionel Hebert

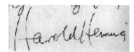

Harold Henning

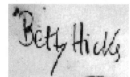

Betty Hicks

Dave Hill

Mike Hill

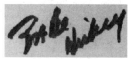

Babe Hiskey

Scott Hoch

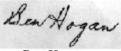

Ben Hogan

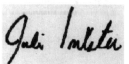

Juli Inkster

Hale Irwin

Tony Jacklin

Peter Jacobsen

Don January

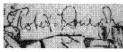

Joe Jimenez

Robert T. Jones

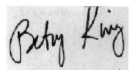

Rosie Jones

Betsy King

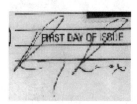

Tom Kite

Kenny Knox

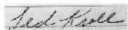

Ted Kroll

Catherine Lacoste

Bernhard Langer

Wayne Levi

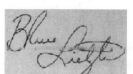

Bruce Lietzke

Lawson Little

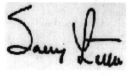

Sally Little

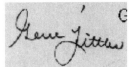

Gene Littler

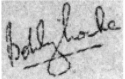

Bobby Locke

Nancy Lopez

Davis Love III

Sandy Lyle

Willie MacFarlane

John Mahaffey

Meg Mallon

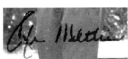

Roger Maltbe

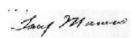

Tony Manero

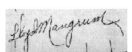

Lloyd Mangrum

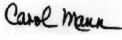

Carol Mann

Dave Marr

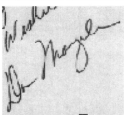

Don Massengale

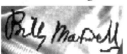

Billy Maxwell

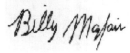

Billy Mayfair

Rives McBee

Mark McCumber

Dottie Mochrie

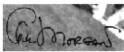

Gil Morgan

Orville Moody

Mike Morley

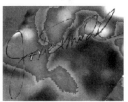

Jodie Mudd

Byron Nelson

Larry Nelson

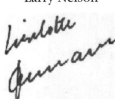

Liselotte Neumann

Bobby Nichols

Jack Nicklaus

Greg Norman

Andy North

Mark O'Meara

Asako Okamoto

Charles Owens

Francis Ouimet

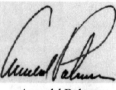
Arnold Palmer

Johnny Palmer

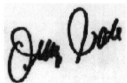
Jerry Pate

Corey Pavin

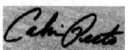
Calvin Peete

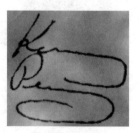
Ken Perry

Henry G. Picard

Gary Player

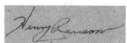
Dan Pohl

Henry Ransom

Betsy Rawls

Mike Reid

Johnny Revolta

Patti Rizzo

Phil Rodgers

Chichi Rodriguez

Bill Rogers

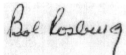
Bob Rosburg

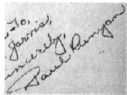
Paul Runyan

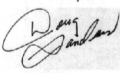
Doug Sanders

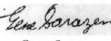
Gene Sarazen

Patty Sheehan

Cathy Reynolds

U.S. Ryder Cup Team

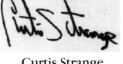

Curtis Strange

Louise Suggs

Hal Sutton

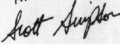

Denny Shute

Charles Sifford

Scott Simpson

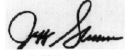

Tim Simpson

J. C. Snead

Sam Snead

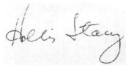

Mike Souchak

Jan Stephenson

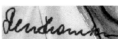

Peter Thompson

Rocky Thompson

Payne Stewart

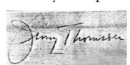

Jimmy Thomson

Hollis Stacy

Ken Still

Joey Sindelar

Dave Stockton

Jeff Sluman

Craig Stadler

Frank Stranahan

Bob Toski

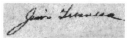
Jerry Travers

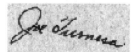
Lee Trevino

Sherri Turner

Jim Turnesa

Joe Turnesa

Mike Turnesa

Willie Turnesa

Bob Tway

Ken Venturi

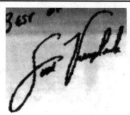
Scott Verplank

Lanny Wadkins

Colleen Walker

Art Wall

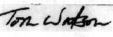
Tom Watson

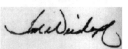
Tom Weiskopf

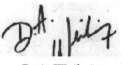
D. A. Weibring

Kathy Whitworth

Oscar F. Willing

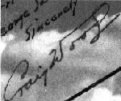
Craig Wood

Ian Woosnam

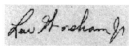
Lew Worsham Jr.

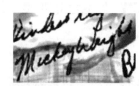
Mickey Wright

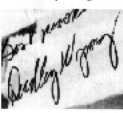
Dudley Wysong

Bert Yancey

Kathryn A. Young

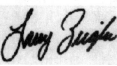
Larry Zeigler

Fuzzy Zoeller

MISCELLANEOUS

Sid Abel
Hockey

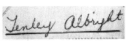

Tenley Albright
Ice Skating

Bobby Allison
Auto

Davey Allison
Auto

Andre the Giant
Pro Wrestling

Mario Andretti
Auto

Michael Andretti
Auto

Earl Anthony
Bowling

Eddie Arcaro
Jockey

Debbie Armstrong
Skiiing

Evelyn Ashford
Track

Horace Ashenfelter
Track

Robyn Smith-Astaire
Jockey

Ted Atkinson
Jockey

Tai Babilonia
Skating

Braulio Baeza
Jockey

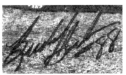

Buddy Baker
Auto

Thane Baker
Track

Dave Balon
Hockey

Ed Banach
Wrestling

Roger Bannister
Track
(Variants)

Hank Bassen
Hockey

Bob Beamon
Track

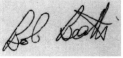
Bob Beattie

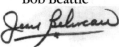
Jean Beliveau
Hockey

Brian Bellons

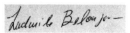
Ludmilla Belousova
Ice Skater

Bruce Bennett
(Tarzan)
(see Herman Brix)

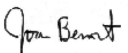
Joan Benoit
Marathon

Gary Bettenhausen
Auto Racing

Tony Bettenhausen
Auto Racing

Tom Bigelow
Auto Racing

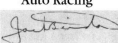
Jack Bionda
Lacrosse & Hockey

Matt Biondi
Swimming

Bonnie Blair
Speed Skating

Fanny Blankers-Koen
Track

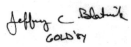
Jeffrey C. Blatnick
Wrestling

Ray Bluth
Bowling

Brian Boitano
Ice Skating

Neil Bonnett
Auto Racing

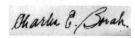
Charles E. Borah
Track

Mike Bossy
Hockey

Ralph Boston
Track

Henry Boucha
Hockey

Christi Bowman
Ice Skating

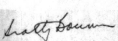
Scotty Bowman
Hockey

Donald G. Bragg
Olympic Pole Vault

Jack Brabham
Auto Racing

Craig Breedlove
Auto Racing

Jack Brickhouse
Broadcaster

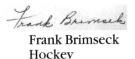

Frank Brimseck
Hockey

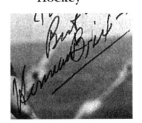

Herman Brix
Olympics
(AKA Bruce Bennett)

Avery Brundage
Olympic President

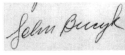

John Bucyk
Hockey

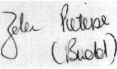

Zola Budd
Track

Lord Burghley
Olympics

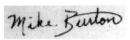

Mike Burton
Swimming

Susan Butcher
Dog Sled

Dick Button
Ice Skating

Gina Campbell
Power Boat

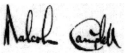

Malcolm Campbell
Speed Boat

Kitty
& Peter Carruthers
Ice Skating

Don Carter
Bowling

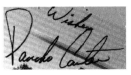

Pancho Carter
Bowling

John R. Case
Olympics

Steve Cauthen
Jockey

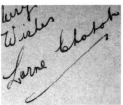

Lorne Chabot
Hockey

Florence Chadwick
Swimming

Suzy Chaffee
Skiing

Joe Chamaco
Billiards

Bobby Charlton
Soccer

Chris Chelios
Hockey

(Miscellaneous)   FACSIMILES   421

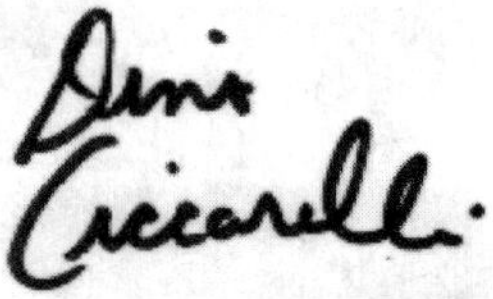

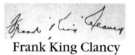

Dino Ciccarelli
Hockey

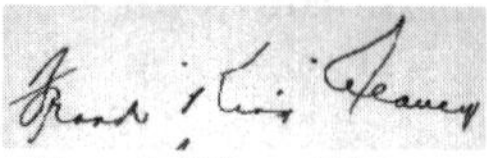

Frank King Clancy
Hockey

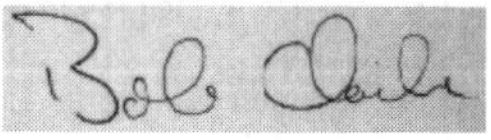

Bob Clarke
Hockey

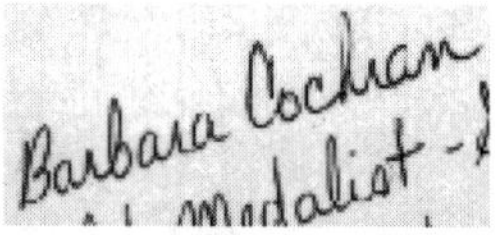

Barbara Cochran
Skiing

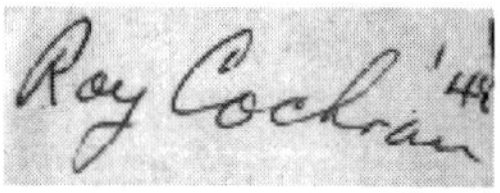

Roy Cochran
Track

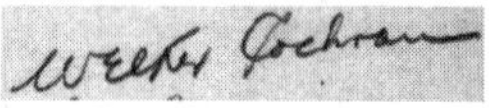

Welker Cochran
Billiards

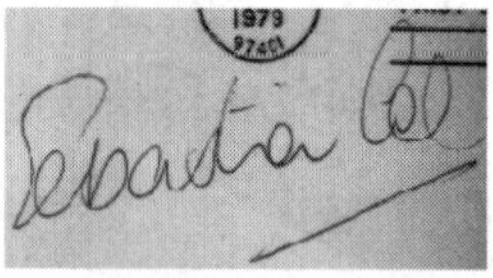

Sebastian Coe
Track

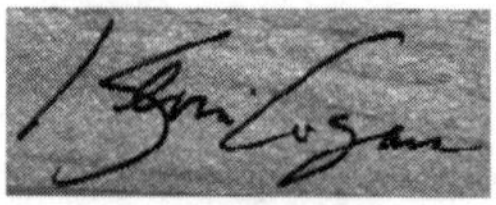

Kevin Cogan
Auto Racing

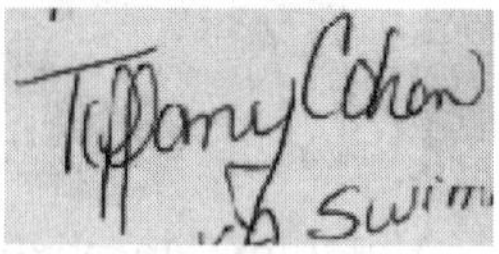

Tiffany Cohen
Swimming

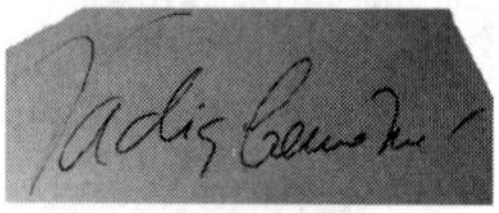

Nadia Comaneci
Gymnast

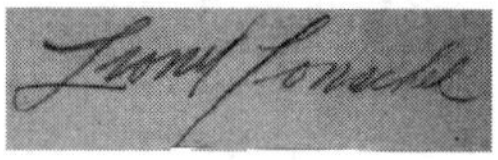

Lionel Conacher
Hockey

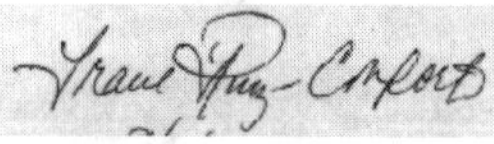

Tracie Ruiz-Conforto
Marathon

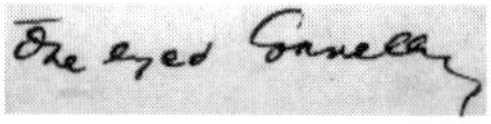

One Eyed Connally
Gate Crasher

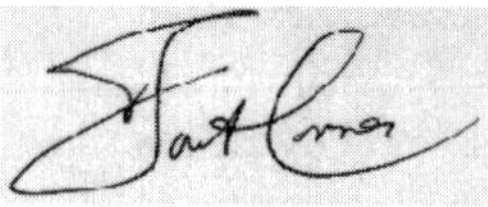

Bart Conner
Gymnast

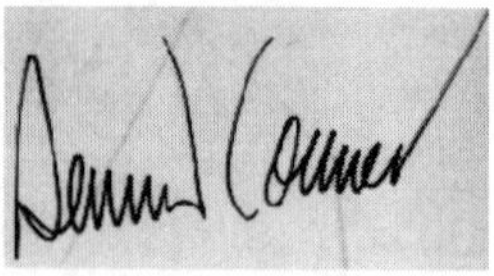

Dennis Conner
Yacht Racing

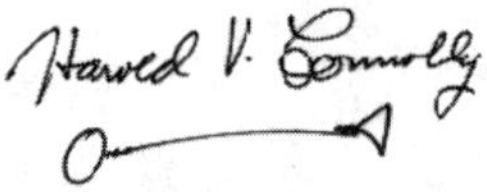

Harold V. Connolly
Olympic Track

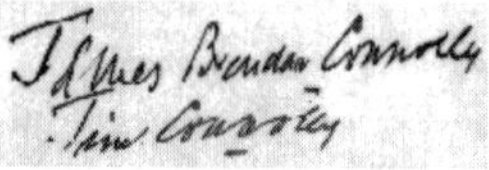

James B. Connolly
1st USA Olympics

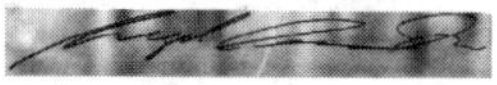

Angel Cordero, Jr.
Jockey

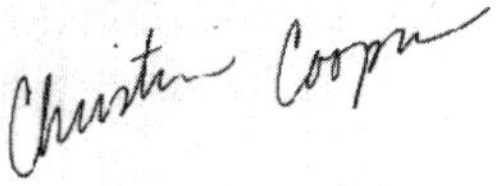

Christie Cooper
Skiing

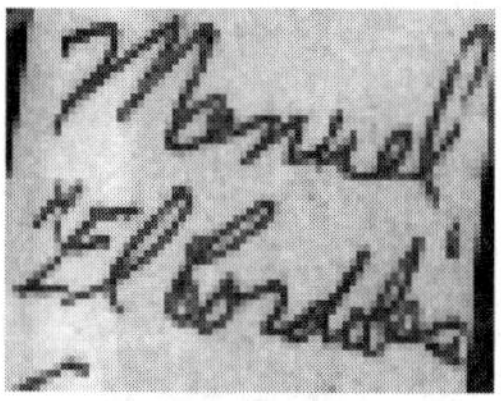

Manuel "El Cordoba"
Bullfighting

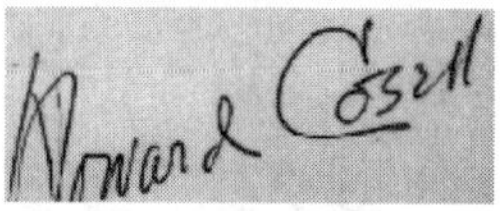

Howard Cosell
Broadcaster

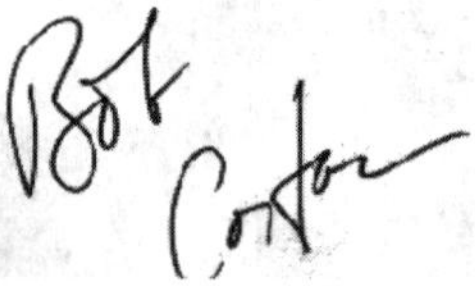

Bob Costas
Broadcaster

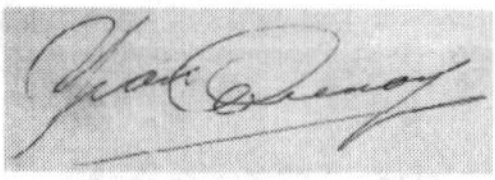

Yuan Couroget
Hockey

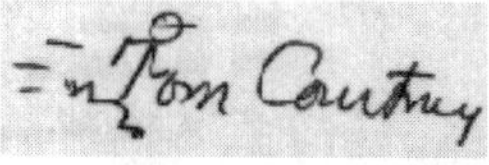

Tom Courtney
Track

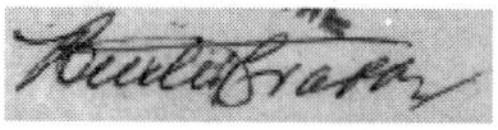

Buster Crabbe
Swimming

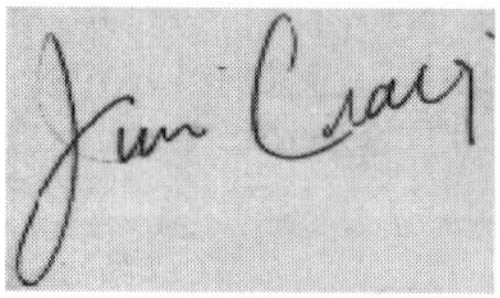

Jim Craig
Hockey

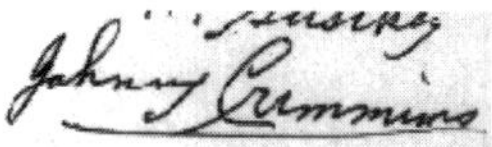

Johnny Crimmins
Bowling

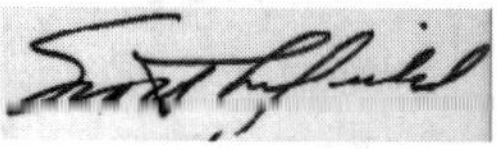

Scott Crossfield
Auto Racing

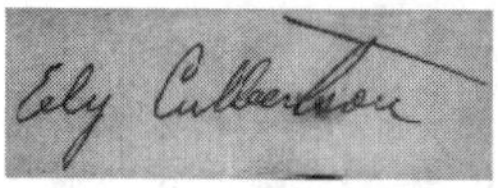

Ely Culbertson
Bridge

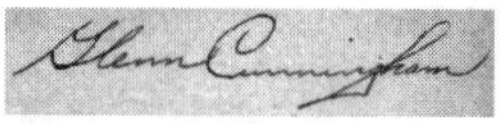

Glenn
Cunningham
Track

Willie D. Davenport
Track

Floyd Davis
Auto Racing

Glenn Davis
Track

Willi Daume
General Sports Exec

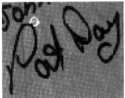

Pat Day
Jockey

Peter De Paolo
Auto Racing

Donna de Verona
Swimming

Mary Decker-Slaney
Track

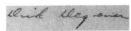

Dick Degener
Diving

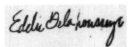

Eddie Delahoussaye
Jockey

Ron Delany
Miler

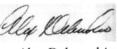

Alex Delvecchio
Jockey

Harrison Dillard
Track

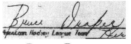

Bruce Draper
Hockey

Ron Duguay
Hockey

Charlie Duma
Track

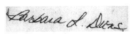

Barbara L. Duns
Bowling

Dale Earnhardt
Auto Racing

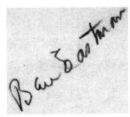

Ben Eastman
Track

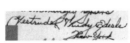

Gertrude "Trudy"
Ederle
Swimming

J.S. Edstrom
Olympic Exec

Bill Elliott
Auto Racing

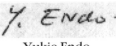

Yukio Endo
Gymnast

Mike Eruzione
Hockey

Phil Esposito
Hockey

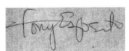

Tony Esposito
Hockey

Janet Evans
Swimming

Barney Ewell
Track

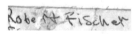

Joe Fargis
Equestrian

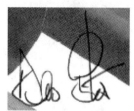

Dennis Firestone
Auto Racing

Robert "Bobby"
Fischer
Chess
(Variants)

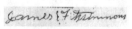

Emerson Fittepaldi
Auto Racing

James E. "Sunny
Jim" Fitzsimmons
Trainer

Peggy Fleming
(Jenkins)
Ice Skating

William
Clay Ford
Team Owner

A.J. Foyt
Auto Racing

Bill France Jr.
Auto Racing

Dawn Fraser
Swimming

Gretchen Fraser
Skiing

Randy Gardner
Skating

Bob Gaines
Hockey

Kelly
Garrison-Steves
Skiing

Josele Garza
Auto

Bernie Geoffrion
Hockey

Charles Goren
Bridge

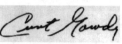

Curt Gowdy
Broadcaster

Bud Greenspan

Ralph Greenleaf
Billiards

Wayne Gretsky
Hockey

Florence
Griffith Joyner
Track

Dan Gurney
Auto Racing

Janet Guthrie
Auto Racing

Vic Hadfield
Hockey

Dorothy Hamill
Ice Skating

Scott Hamilton
Ice Skating

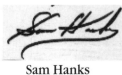

Sam Hanks
Auto Racing

Ted Harris
Hockey

Eddie Hart
Track

Bill Hartack
Jockey

Jim Hartung
Gymnast

Michel Harvey
Hockey

Ernie Harwell
Broadcaster

Bill Haughton
Harness Racing

Fred Hausen
Pole Vault

Beth Heiden
Speed Skating

Eric Heiden
Speed Skating

Matthias Herget
Soccer

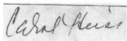

Carol Heiss
Olympic Gold
Ice Skating

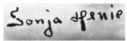

Sonja Henie
Ice Skating

Ken Henry
Speed Skating

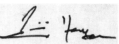

Jim Heuga
Skiing

Bill Hicke
Hockey

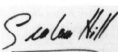

Graham Hill
Auto Racing

Ken Hodge
Hockey

Hulk Hogan
Pro Wrestling

Nancy Hogshead
Swimming

Eleanor Holm
Swimming

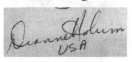

Deanne Holum
Speed Skater

Willie Hoppe
Billiards

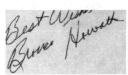

Bronco Horvath
Hockey

Gordy Howe
Hockey

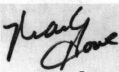

Mark Howe
Hockey

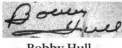

Bobby Hull
Hockey

Parnelli Jones
Auto Racing

Duke P.
Kahanamoku
Swimming

Bela Karolyi
Gymnastics Coach

Kip Keino
Distance Runner

Annette Kellermann
Swimming

John B. Kelly, Jr.
Rowing

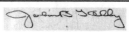

John B. Kelly, Sr.
Rowing

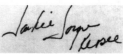

Jackie Joyner
Kersee
Track

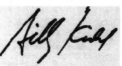

Billy Kidd
Skiing

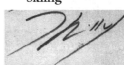

Jean-Claude Killy
Skiing

Jill Kinmont
Skiing

John Kinsella
Olympics

Joe Kittinger
Balloonist

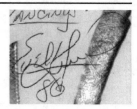

Evel Knievel
Motorcycling

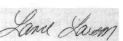

Lance Larson
Olympics

Don Lash
Track Miler

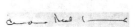

Andrea Mead
Lawrence
Skiing

Sammy Lee, M.D.
Diving

Mario Lemieux
Hockey

Greg Lemond
Bicycle Racing

Sidney S. Lenz
Bridge

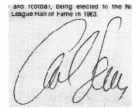

Carl Lewis
Track

Jim Londos
Pro Wrestling

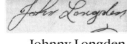

Johnny Longden

Greg Louganis
Diving

Arie Luyendyk
Auto Racing

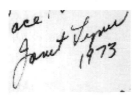

Janet Lynn
Ice Skating

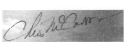

Chris McCarren
Jockey

Roger McCluskey

Pat McCormack
Diving

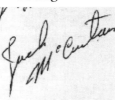

Jack
McCutcheon
Hockey

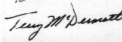

Terry
McDermott
Speed Skater

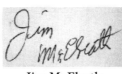

Jim McElrath
Auto Racing

John E. Magasich
Olympics

Dave Maggard
Shot

Larry Mahan

John Mahler
Auto

Phil Mahre
Skiing

Steve Mahre
Skiing

Frank Mahovlich
Hockey

Liz Manley
Olympics

Dave Marcis
Auto Racing

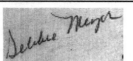

Hank Marino
Bowling

Mike Marshall
Auto Racing

Bob Mathias
Track

Randy Matson
Olympic Shot

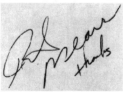

Mary T. Meagher
Swimming

Rick Mears
Auto Racing

Ralph Metcalfe
Track

Debbie Meyer
Swimming

Lou Meyer
Auto Racing

Al Michaels
Hockey

Stan Mikita
Hockey

Billy Mills
Track

Phoebe Mills
Gymnast

Minnesota Fats
Billiards

Jim Montgomery
Olympics

Janet Moreau
Olympic
Relay-Track

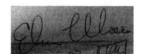

Howie Morenz
Hockey

Willie Mosconi
Billiards

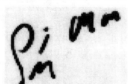

Edwin Moses
Track

Sterling Moss
Auto Racing

Shirley
Muldowney
Auto Racing

Peter Mueller
Olympics

Brent Musberger
Broadcaster

John Naber

Sandy Neilson
Olympics

Richard Noble
Auto

Paavo Nurmi
Track

Diane Nyad
Swimming

Parry O'Brien
Shot Put

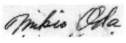

Mikio Oda

Al Oerter
Shot

Barney Oldfield
Auto Racing

Bobby Orr
Hockey

Gerald R.
Ouellette
Olympic Rifle

Jesse Owens
Track

Darrell O. Pace
Olympic Archery

Benny Parsons
Auto Racing

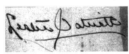

Lester Patrick
Hockey

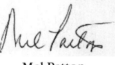

Mel Patton
Track

David Pearson
Auto Racing

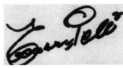

Pelé
Soccer

Mel Pender
Track

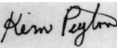

Kim Peyton
Olympics

Roger Penske
Auto Racing

Craig Perrett
Jockey

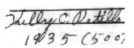

Kelly C. Petillo
Auto Racing

Richard Petty
Auto Racing

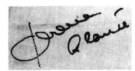

Jacques Plante
Hockey

Laffit Pincay
Jockey

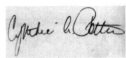

Cynthie Potter
Diving

Alec Protopopov
Ice Skater

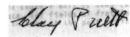

Clay Puett
Horse Racing

Don Quarrie
Track

Bobby Rahal
Auto Racing

Mary Rand
Track and Field
(Long Jump)

Jim Rathmann
Auto Racing

Mary Lou Retton
Gymnast

Peter Revson
Auto Racing

Henri Richard
Hockey

Maurice Richard
Hockey

Gordan Richards
Jockey

Rev. Bob Richards
Track

Steve Riddick

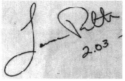

Cathy Rigby
(McCoy)
Gymnast

Louise Ritter
Olympics

Bill Rodgers
Track
(Variants)

Gaston Roelants
Track

Murray Rose
Swimming

Lloyd Ruby
Auto Racing

Ricky Rudd
Auto Racing

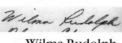

Wilma Rudolph
Track

Johnny
Rutherford
Auto Racing

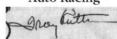

Troy Ruttman
Auto Racing

Jim Ryun
Track

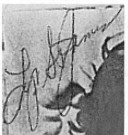

Lyn St. James
Auto Racing

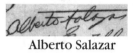

Alberto Salazar
Track

Juan Antonio
Samaranch
Olympic President

Earl Sande
Jockey

Wes Santee
Track

Don Schollander
Swimming

Kari Schranz
Skiing

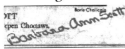

Barbara Ann
Scott
Ice Skating

Ray Scott
Broad Jump

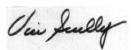

Vince Scully
Broadcaster

Bob Seagren
Track

Wilbur Shaw
Auto Racing

John Shea
Speed Skating

Roy Shipstad
Ice Skating

Willie Shoemaker
Jockey

Eddie Shore
Hockey

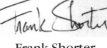

Frank Shorter
Track

Jim Shoulders
Rodeo

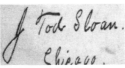

J. Tod Sloan
Jockey

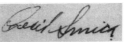

Cecil Smith
Polo

Tommie Smith
Track

Peter Snell
Track

Tom Sneva
Auto Racing

George Snyder
Auto Racing

Jimmy the Greek
(Snyder)

George Souders
Auto Racing

J.G. Taylor Spink
Newspaper
Publisher

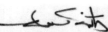

Mark Spitz
Swimming

Pepi Steigler
Skiing

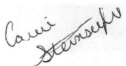

Carrie Steinseifer
Swimming

Jill Sterkel
Olympics

Kelly Garrison
Steves
Gymnast

Jackie Stewart
Auto Racing

Dwight Stones
Track

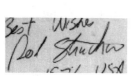

Rod Strachen
Olympics

Danny Sullivan
Auto Racing

Tracee Talavera
Olympics

Richard Tayler
Track

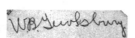

W.B. Tewksbury
Track

Debi Thomas
Ice Skating

John Thomas
Track-Field

Kurt Thomas
Gymnast

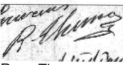

Rene Thomas
Auto Racing

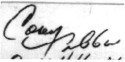

Casey Tibbs
Rodeo

"Tiny" Thompson
Hockey

Karen Mae
Thornton

Kenny Peton
Timmermann

Daley Thompson
Decathlon

Harry Tompkins
Rodeo

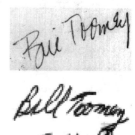

Bill Toomey
Decathlon
(Variants)

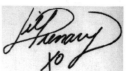

Jill Trenary
Ice Skating

Ron Turcotte
Jockey

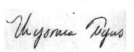

Wyomia Tyus
Track

Al Unser
Auto Racing

Al Unser, Jr.
Auto Racing

Bobby Unser
Auto Racing

Nelson Vails
Cycling

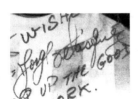

Harold S. Vanderbilt
Yachting

Jorge Valasquez
Jockey

Gene Venzke
Track

Jesse "the Body"
Ventura
Wrestling

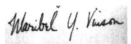

Peter Vidmar
Gymnast

Maribel Vinson
Ice Skating

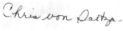

Matt Vogel
Swim Coach

Chris Von Saltza
Swimming

Bill Vukovich
Auto Racing

Greta Waitz
Marathon

Rusty Wallace
Auto Racing

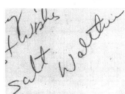

Salt Walther
Auto Racing

Darrell Waltrip
Auto Racing

Rodger Ward
Auto Racing

Cornelius
Warmerdam
Pole Vaulting

Robert Webber
Diving

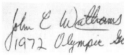

Dick Weber
Bowling
(Variants)

Johnny
Weissmuller
Olympic Swimming

John C. Williams
Olympic Archery

Tom Williams
Hockey

Deborah Keplar
Wilson
Diving

Desiré Wilson
Auto Racing

Hans Winkler
Equestrian

Katerina Witt
Ice Skating

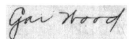

Gar Wood
Power Boat

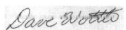

Dave Wottle
Track

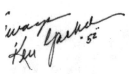

Bernie Wrightson
Diving

Ken Yackel
Hockey

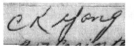

C.K. Yang
Decathalon

Cale Yarborough
Auto Racing

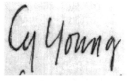

Cy Young
Javelin

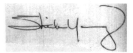

Sheila Young
Speed Skating

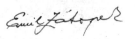

Emil Zatopek
Track

Louis Zamperini
Track

Ice Capade skaters Mr. Frick (Werner Groebli, half of the immortal team of Frick and Frack), Karen Kresge, author George Sanders, and Jill Shipstad, daughter of the Ice Capade's cofounder and herself a champion figure skater.

TENNIS

Andre Agassi

Wilmer Allison

Arthur Ashe

Tracy Austin

Bjorn Borg

Boris Becker

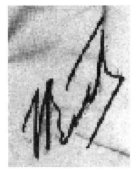

Jean Borotra

Maureen
Connally Brinker

John Edward
Bromwich

Don Budge

Jennifer Capriati

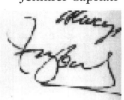

Rosemary Casals

Michael Chang

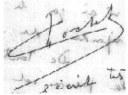

Henri Chochet

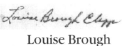

Louise Brough
Clapp

Jimmy Connors

Jim Courier

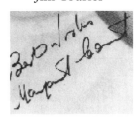

Margaret Court

Sarah (Palfrey)
Cooke

Dwight F. Davis

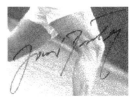

Jaraslav Drobny

Cliff Drysdale

Margaret Dupont

Stefan Edberg

Roy Emerson

Chris Evert

Neale Fraser

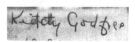
Zina Garrison

Vitas Gerulaitis

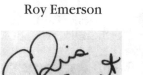
Althea Gibson

Kitty Godfree

Pancho Gonzalez

Evonne Goolagong

Steffi Graf

Helen Hull Jacobs

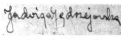
J. Jedrejowska

Ann Jones

Billie Jean King

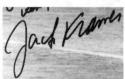
Jack Kramer

Rod Laver

Alice Marble

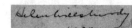
Helen Wills Moody

Ivan Lendl

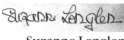
Suzanne Lenglen

Bob Lutz

Gardner Mulloy

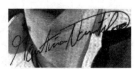
Martina Navratilova

John Newcombe

Yannick Noah

Fred Perry

Vincent Richards

Ham Richardson

Bobby Riggs

I. Nastase

Gabriela Sabatini

Ken Rosewall

Pete Sampras

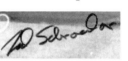

Ted Schroeder

Pancho Segura

Vic Seixas

Monica Seles

Pam Shriver

Stan Smith

Harold Solomon

Charley Steed

Fred Stale

Michael Steich

Bill Talbert

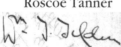

Roscoe Tanner

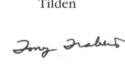

William "Big Bill" Tilden

Tony Trabert

John Van Ryn

Ellsworth Vines

Virginia Wade

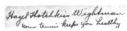

Hazel Hotchkiss Wightman

Mats Wilander

Wightman Cup

George Sanders, during his years as a journalist and TV personality, interviewed many legends of the sports world and never neglected to ask for their autographs. This started the world-famous collection he put together over the years. Here George is shown with pro football's Hall of Fame receiver, Elroy "Crazy Legs" Hirsch. Hirsch and Sanders appeared together in a Hollywood movie in the 1950s and played football on opposing teams in the 1940s.

The
SANDERS
Price Guide to
SPORTS
AUTOGRAPHS

Section 4:
DEALERS

AUTOGRAPH DEALERS

This section contains a Buyer's Guide representing a few of the major dealers in the autograph world. While inclusion here does not mean we endorse a particular dealer over one not participating in this guide, it does mean we believe the dealers here to be reputable experts in their various areas of expertise. And– on the other hand–just because a dealer elected not to participate does not necessarily mean that he or she should be avoided. While we did refuse ads to a few unscrupulous rascals best avoided by the honest, we certainly make no blanket statement about those not advertising in this book.

However, we hasten to point out that the kind folks who *are* in this book deserve a great vote of thanks (and even a little business, perhaps) from all of us, authors and readers alike. They made this huge book practical and allowed us to both add much more than otherwise would have been possible, and to keep the retail price down to a most reasonable $24.95. Believe us, the printing bill on this tome is immense: please at least say "thank you" to our wonderful advertisers.

Index to Advertisers

AUTOGRAPHS - BOXING LEGENDS
8x10 PHOTOS SIGNED IN PERSON

The Largest Selection of Signed Boxing Photos in The World!!!!!
All autographs listed below were obtained at my "Boxing Legends" private autograph signing sessions between 1990 and 1998. All were individually hand-signed by the boxer listed. Many of the names listed below represent some of the toughest autographs to find of any athlete in any sport. *Supplies are limited so take advantage and start building your boxing collection today!!*

LOU AMBERS Two-time world lightweight champion. Member Boxing Hall of Fame..**$35.00**
ALEXIS ARGUELLO One of the greatest ever!! Boxing Hall of Famer** (C) **$18.00**
PAUL BANKE Super bantamweight champ 1990-1992. First champ diagnosed with AIDS (C)..**$15.00**
CARMEN BASILIO Welterweight & Middleweight champion*** **$15.00**
WILFRED BENITEZ Youngest ever to win a world title. A tough autograph*** **$35.00**
NINO BENVENUTI World middleweight and super middleweight champ*** **$35.00**
TREVOR BERBICK WBC heavyweight champ 1986. Last man to fight Ali** **$20.00**
JOE BROWN "Old Bones", one of the greatest lightweight champs EVER! Died 1997** .**$18.00**
KEN BUCHANAN Former lightweight champ. Lives in England** **$20.00**
HECTOR CAMMACHO "The Macho Man". Three-time world champ** **$20.00**
RUBIN "HURRICANE" CARTER Terror of the middleweights in the 50's & 60's.**$15.00**
BOBBY CHACON One of the most exciting fighters ever!! A two-time world champ*** .**$15.00**
SOT CHITALADA - The Muhammad Ali of Thailand. Flyweight champ 1984-1991 (C) ...**$15.00**
GEORGE CHUVALO Top heavyweight, fought Ali. Canadian champ **$15.00**
GERRIE COETZEE WBA Heavyweight Champ 1983-84** **$15.00**
JEFF CHANDLER Bantamweight champ 1980-1984 ....**$15.00**
PIPINO CUEVAS Defended welterweight title ELEVEN times!!!** **$20.00**
BOBBY CZYZ Two-time world champion**. **$15.00**
PADDY DEMARCO Former world lightweight champ. Died 1997 (C) **$18.00**
MICHAEL DOKES Heavyweight champ (WBA) 1982-1983** (C) **$18.00**
BUSTER DOUGLAS Undisputed heavyweight champ 1990** (C) **$25.00**
ROBERTO DURAN "The hands of stone". One of the Greatest ever. Very tough!!!****(C).**$35.00**
JIMMY ELLIS Former heavyweight champ 1967-1970*** **$20.00**
ALFREDO ESCALERA Super featherweight champ 1975-78. Tough autograph **$25.00**
JOHNNY FAMECHON Featherweight champion 1969-70. Lives in Australia** (C)..**$15.00**
JEFF FENECH Three-time world champion in three different divisions** (C) **$18.00**
BOB FOSTER One of the greatest light heavyweights EVER!!** **$15.00**
DON FULLMER Top middleweight contender of the 60's** **$8.00**
GENE FULLMER Two-time middleweight champ. Boxing Hall of Famer*** **$15.00**
KHAOSAI GALAXY - Greatest Jr.-Bantaweight in history. Defended title 19 times ..**$15.00**
KID GAVILAN One of the most televised boxers during TV's "Golden Age"*** **$25.00**
JOEY GIARDELLO Middleweight champ 1963-65. Recent Boxing Hall of Fame inductee.**$15.00**
WILFREDO GOMEZ Three-time world champion. Member Hall of Fame** (C) **$25.00**
EMILE GRIFFITH Six-time world champion!!!!* **$15.00**
MARVELOUS MARVIN HAGLER The most dominant fighter of the 80's** (C) **$45.00**
JEFF HARDING WBC light heavyweight champion. Lives in Australia (C) **$15.00**
LARRY HOLMES Heavyweight champ 1978-85** C) **$25.00**
AL HOSTAK Middleweight champ 1938-40**. **$15.00**
BEAU JACK Headlined Madison Square Garden a record 21 times!!!! **$25.00**
EDER JOFRE Two-time champ 1961-65, 1973-74. Boxing Hall of Famer. **$25.00**
INGEMAR JOHANSSON Former world heavyweight champion 1959-1960*** **$25.00**
HAROLD JOHNSON Light heavyweight champ 1962-63. Member of Hall of Fame ..**$15.00**
MARVIN JOHNSON Three-time light-heavyweight world champ **$15.00**
JAKE LAMOTTA "The Raging Bull", middleweight champ 1949-1951**** **$25.00**
VICKIE LAMOTTA Former wife of "The Ragin Bull". Appeared in *Playboy*** (C)..**$8.00**
ROLAND LASTARZA Top heavyweight contender. Fought Marciano twice!** **$18.00**
DANNY "LITTLE RED" LOPEZ Featherweight champ 1976-80*** (C) **$25.00**
RAY "BOOM BOOM" MANCINI Crowd pleasing lightweight champ** (C) **$15.00**
JOEY MAXIM Light heavyweight champ 1950-52** **$15.00**
JIMMY McLARNIN One of the oldest living former champs **$25.00**
JOE MICELI Famous lefthooking top contender of the 50's*** **$8.00**
ARCHIE MOORE "The ol Mongoose". Holds record for career KO's (145)** (C..**$25.00**
BOB MONTGOMERY "The Bobcat". Two-time lightweight champ (C) **$15.00**
CARLOS MONZON Defended middleweight title an amazing 14 times. A super tough autograph!!!
Died in car crash 1995** (C) **$95.00**
EDDIE MUSTAFA MUHAMMAD Hard-hitting former light heavyweight champ**.**$15.00**
MATTHEW SAAD MUHAMMAD Exciting light heavyweight champ 1977-81** (C).**$15.00**
JOSE NAPOLES "Ring" fighter of the year in 1969. Hall of Famer*** **$25.00**
KEN NORTON Heavyweight champ 1978, fought legendary battles with Ali** (C) ..**$25.00**
RUBEN OLIVARES Three-time world champion. One of the all-time greats!** (C)...**$18.00**
BOBO OLSON A gutsy champion during TV's Golden Era** (C) **$18.00**
CARLOS PALOMINO Welter champ 1976-79. A vicious body puncher*** **$15.00**

WILLIE PASTRANO Light heavyweight champ 1963-65. A clever boxer. Died 1997 ....**$25.00**
FLOYD PATTERSON - World heavyweight champ 1956-1962. Boxing Hall of Famer** (C) **$25.00**
EUSEBIO PEDROZA Defended featherweight title a record 20 times!!!!! (C) **$18.00**
WILLIE PEP Fought 242 bouts and lost only eleven. A legend! **$15.00**
AARON PRYOR - Greatest Jr.-Welterweight champ ever. Legendary battles w/Arguello (C)..**$15.00**
DWIGHT MUHAMMAD QAWI aka Dwight Braxton "The Camden buzzsaw" (C)..**$15.00**
JERRY QUARRY Fought legendary bouts with Muhammad Ali and Joe Frazier** (C)..**$25.00**
SUGAR RAMOS Featherweight champ 1964-64. A tough autograph. Lives in Mexico ..**$18.00**
LUIS RODRIGUEZ Welterweight champ 1963. Died 1996 ....**$35.00**
EDWIN "CHAPO" ROSARIO Three-time world champ. Died 1997 Heroin overdose. (C) ..**$65.00**
LIONEL ROSE The first aboriginal world champion. Lives in Australia** **$15.00**
MIKE ROSSMAN "The Jewish bomber". Light heavyweight champ 1978-79 ....**$18.00**
JOHNNY SAXTON Two-time welterweight champ. Popular 50's Tv fighter **$15.00**
EARNIE SHAVERS One of the hardest hitting heavyweights in history**** **$15.00**
LEON SPINKS 1976 Olympic gold medalist. Heavyweight champ**** **$18.00**
TEOFILIO STEVENSON Cuban legend won Olympic gold medals Heavyweight Division 1972, 1976
and 1980. Extremely tough autograph. Now lives in Cuba. **$35.00**
"BIG JOHN" TATE Heavyweight champ 1979-80. Died 1998** (C) **$45.00**
ERNIE TERRELL Tallest heavyweight champ ever 6'6"**** **$15.00**
PINKLON THOMAS Heavyweight champ 1984-86** (C) **$15.00**
JAMES "LIGHTS OUT" TONEY 1991 Fighter of the Year. Two-time world champion**(C).**$25.00**
VIC TOWELL Bantamweight World Champ 1950-52** (C) **$15.00**
GIL TURNER Top welterweight contender from the 50's. Died1996 ....**$15.00**
JERSEY JOE WALCOTT Heavyweight champion 1951-52. Fought Louis & Marciano**.**$95.00**
MIKE WEAVER Nicknamed "Hercules". Heavyweight champ (WBA) 1980-82....**$15.00**
CLEVELAND WILLIAMS Hard-hitting heavy. Fought Liston & Ali **$15.00**
IKE WILLIAMS Lightweight champ 1947-51. "Ring" fighter of the year 1948**.**$35.00**
ALFONZO ZAMORA Bantamweight champ 1975-77. Won first 29 bouts by KO..**$18.00**

A certificate of authenticity, fighters bio and a photo taken at the signing will be included with all orders at no charge. (*) Asterisks indicate the number of different poses available of each. No asterick means that only on pose is available. (C) indicates photo is in color. Otherwise all photos are black and white. *Please add $5.00 P/H to all orders.*

JIM STINSON
SPORTS COLLECTIBLES
P.O. Box 756 • St. George, Utah 84771 • Phone/Fax (435) 656-1777

Michael J. Masters, M.D.

P.O. Box 432
Clyde, NC 28721

828-627-2642

Buying Autographs, Letters, Signed
Documents, and Signed Photographs
for Personal Collection

- ◆ Baseball Hall of Fame
- ◆ Vintage Sports
- ◆ War Between the States
- ◆ Checks / Financial Documents
- ◆ C.S. Lewis — Clergy — Science
- ◆ Literature — The Arts
- ◆ Historical Americana

UNIVERSAL AUTOGRAPH COLLECTORS CLUB

an invitation to join the U.A.C.C.

The Universal Autograph Collectors Club, Inc. is a federally approved nonprofit organization dedicated to the **education** of the autograph collector. Founded in 1965, the **UACC** is known as "**The Collectors Advocate.**" The organization sponsors shows worldwide and publishes its journal the ***Pen and Quill*** bi-monthly. The UACC is an organization for collectors, run by collectors.

For membership information, please write:

UACC
Dept. PG
P.O. Box 6181
Washington, DC 20044-6181

Check out our new website at: **http://www.uacc.org**

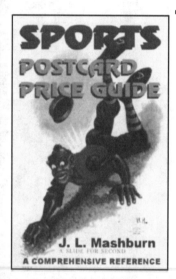

CHUCK McKEEN AUTOGRAPHS

Specializing in Current Entertainment and All Sports

Hit a homerun with Chuck! Call today for your sports needs.

Bowling Hall of Famer Earl Anthony (left) shares a smile with Chuck McKeen.

Want Lists Encouraged

P.O. Box 1599
Hillsborough, OR 97123-1599
503-645-5984

Alexander Books
6x9, paper, 192 pages,
ISBN 1-57090-009-4, **$12.95**.

Order via secure credit card at
www.abooks.com/genealogy
or call 1-800-472-0438.

Ralph Roberts'

GENEALOGY
via the Internet

Use your personal computer to find your family's roots. It's all explained in fun, concise plain English by an expert. Sail the Internet without fear, and search the World Wide Web for the birthplace of your ancestors.

Ralph Roberts is the author of over 70 books for major publishers around the world. His knack of explaining technical subjects both humorously and in plain English make his many books useful and popular. His years of experience in both computers and genealogy are ideally combined in this enjoyable book.

Ralph Roberts

**ALEXANDER
BOOKS**
65 Macedonia Rd.
Alexander, NC
28701USA
800-472-0438
828-255-8719
(voice & fax)
sales@abooks.com